THE CAMBRIDGE ECONOMIC HISTORY OF

THE MODERN WORLD

The second volume of *The Cambridge Economic History of the Modern World* explores the development of modern economic growth from 1870 to the present. Leading experts in economic history offer a series of regional studies from around the world, as well as thematic analyses of key factors governing the differential outcomes in different parts of the global economy. Topics covered include human capital, capital and technology, geography and institutions, living standards and inequality, trade and immigration, international finance, and warfare and empire.

Stephen Broadberry is Professor of Economic History at the University of Oxford and a Fellow of the British Academy. He has been Managing Editor of the *Economic History Review* and also the *European Review of Economic History*, and President of the Economic History Society and the European Historical Economics Society.

Kyoji Fukao is President of the Institute of Developing Economies, Japan External Trade Organization (IDE-JETRO) and Specially Appointed Professor at the Institute of Economic Research, Hitotsubashi University. He has been President of the Asian Historical Economics Society and has published widely on Japanese and global economic history.

THE CAMBRIDGE ECONOMIC HISTORY OF

THE MODERN WORLD

The Cambridge Economic History of the Modern World offers an unprecedented global account of the emergence of modern economic growth and its spread across the world since 1700. Each volume provides a series of regional studies from across the globe, as well as thematic analyses of key factors governing differential outcomes in different parts of the global economy. Written by leading experts in economic history and covering topics such as demography and human development, capital and technology, living standards and inequality, geography and institutions, trade and migration, international finance, and warfare and empire, these volumes offer the most authoritative account to date of modern economic growth.

VOLUME I

1700 to 1870

EDITED BY STEPHEN BROADBERRY AND KYOJI FUKAO

VOLUME II

1870 to the Present

EDITED BY STEPHEN BROADBERRY AND KYOJI FUKAO

THE CAMBRIDGE ECONOMIC HISTORY OF THE MODERN WORLD

*

VOLUME II

1870 to the Present

*

Edited by

STEPHEN BROADBERRY
University of Oxford

KYOJI FUKAO
Hitotsubashi University, Tokyo

CAMBRIDGE
UNIVERSITY PRESS

CAMBRIDGE
UNIVERSITY PRESS

Shaftesbury Road, Cambridge CB2 8EA, United Kingdom

One Liberty Plaza, 20th Floor, New York, NY 10006, USA

477 Williamstown Road, Port Melbourne, VIC 3207, Australia

314–321, 3rd Floor, Plot 3, Splendor Forum, Jasola District Centre, New Delhi – 110025, India

103 Penang Road, #05–06/07, Visioncrest Commercial, Singapore 238467

Cambridge University Press is part of Cambridge University Press & Assessment, a department of the University of Cambridge.

We share the University's mission to contribute to society through the pursuit of education, learning and research at the highest international levels of excellence.

www.cambridge.org
Information on this title: www.cambridge.org/9781316612279

DOI: 10.1017/9781316671603

First published 2021
First paperback edition 2025

A catalogue record for this publication is available from the British Library

Two-Volume Set ISBN 978-1-108-95377-1 Hardback
Volume I ISBN 978-1-107-15945-7 Hardback
Volume II ISBN 978-1-107-15948-8 Hardback
ISBN 978-1-316-61227-9 Paperback

Contents

Figures

Tables

Contributors to Volume II

PABLO ASTORGA, Institut Barcelona d'Estudis Internacionals

RAJABRATA BANERJEE, UniSA Business, University of South Australia

STEPHEN BROADBERRY, Department of Economics, University of Oxford

PAUL CARUANA-GALIZIA, Department of Economic History, London School of Economics

MYUNG SOO CHA, School of Economics and Finance, Yeungnam University

LATIKA CHAUDHARY, Graduate School of Business and Public Policy, Naval Postgraduate School

TRACY DENNISON, Division of Humanities and Social Sciences, California Institute of Technology

BARRY EICHENGREEN, Department of Economics, University of California, Berkeley

JARI ELORANTA, Faculty of Social Sciences, University of Helsinki

RUI PEDRO ESTEVES, Departments of International Economics and International History, The Graduate Institute, Geneva

JAMES FOREMAN-PECK, Cardiff Business School, Cardiff University

EWOUT FRANKEMA, Rural and Environmental History Group, Wageningen University

KYOJI FUKAO, Institute of Economic Research, Hitotsubashi University

LEIGH GARDNER, Department of Economic History, London School of Economics

BISHNUPRIYA GUPTA, Department of Economics, University of Warwick

LESLIE HANNAH, Department of Economic History, London School of Economics

ALFONSO HERRANZ-LONCÁN, Department of Economic History, Institutions, Politics and World Economy, University of Barcelona

GREGG HUFF, Pembroke College, University of Oxford

ROBERT INKLAAR, Faculty of Economics and Business, University of Groningen

DAVID S. JACKS, Department of Economics, Simon Fraser University

HERMAN DE JONG, Faculty of Economics and Business, University of Groningen

ALEXANDER KLEIN, School of Economics, University of Kent

PETER LINDERT, Department of Economics, University of California, Davis

DEBIN MA, Institute of Economic Research, Hitotsubashi University

GARY B. MAGEE, Monash Business School, Monash University

TOSHIHIRO OKUBO, Faculty of Economics, Keio University

LEANDRO PRADOS DE LA ESCOSURA, Department of Social Sciences, Universidad Carlos III, Madrid

PAUL W. RHODE, Department of Economics, University of Michigan

MOHAMED SALEH, Toulouse School of Economics

TOKIHIKO SETTSU, Department of Economics, Musashi University

PAUL SHARP, Department of Business and Economics, University of Southern Denmark

JOHN P. TANG, Department of Economics, University of Melbourne

NIKOLAUS WOLF, Department of Economics, Humboldt University Berlin

Introduction to Volume II

STEPHEN BROADBERRY AND KYOJI FUKAO

This book seeks to provide an overview of the modern world economy since 1870, dealing with the material in such a way as to give due weight to chronology, regional balance, and coverage of the main topics. It forms part of a two-volume publication, with the first volume taking the story from 1700 to 1870. Volume II begins in 1870 because by then modern economic growth had emerged in Britain and already spread to much of the rest of western Europe and the British offshoots in the New World (the United States, Canada, Australia, and New Zealand), and was poised to begin in Asia, following the institutional reforms in Japan associated with the Meiji Restoration of 1868. There was thus a great potential during the period after 1870 for closing the gap in living standards that had opened up between the West and the rest of the world. Although many more countries embarked on the process of sustained modern economic growth between 1870 and 2001, the gap nevertheless continued to grow during the long twentieth century, as catching up proved elusive (Maddison 2005: 11). By 2001, the world was nearly seven times richer than it had been in 1870, but the gains were unevenly distributed, with the West growing by a factor of nearly 12, while the rest of the world grew by a factor of less than 6. As a result, the spread between the West and the rest of the world increased from roughly 3:1 in 1870 to nearly 7:1 in 2001, while the spread between the richest and poorest regions increased from roughly 5:1 to 18:1 over the same period (Maddison 2005: 11).

The volume is divided into two parts, with Part I covering regional developments and Part II focusing on the key factors governing differential outcomes in different parts of the global economy. It draws on the upsurge of literature on the economic history of most regions of the world that has been produced in recent years, much of it available in the English language, but also firmly grounded in national literatures written in other languages. Much of this literature has also been based on quantitative data and makes explicit use of economic analysis in an accessible way. The book is aimed at a wide audience of historians and social scientists.

The central story of this book is of a dramatic increase in living standards between 1870 and 2010 in most parts of the world, but unequally distributed. The biggest gains were in western Europe and the New World, which increased their lead over other regions until after World War II, since when there has been some closing of the gap. The standard summary indicator of these trends is gross domestic product per head of the population (or GDP per capita), which will feature heavily in our story. However, it will also be supplemented by other indicators, such as the Human Development Index (HDI), which attempt to take a broader view of living standards.

Part I: Regional Developments

Volume I charts the beginning of modern economic growth in Britain during the eighteenth century and its spread to other parts of western Europe and the British offshoots in the New World. However, it also draws on recent research to capture the considerable variation in outcomes within regions as well as between the main regions of the world. This included reversals of fortune between north-west Europe and the Mediterranean economies of southern Europe, between China and Japan in Asia, and between the British offshoots and Latin America in the New World, as well as a range of outcomes within Africa.

Volume II encompasses a wide range of outcomes within regions as well as between the main regions, with Table i.1 providing a convenient overview. As in Volume I, the data are taken largely from the Maddison Project Database, version 2013. Following Maddison (2001), GDP per capita estimates for each country are presented in terms of a common currency unit, 1990 international \$, so that they can be compared across both space and time. Although this clearly creates index number problems, it is likely that these are dwarfed by measurement errors, and the exercise should be treated as indicating broad trends rather than being correct to the second decimal point. To fix orders of magnitude, it is worth bearing in mind that in 1990 the World Bank regarded anyone existing on less than \$1 per day as living in poverty. This means that the minimum GDP per capita consistent with a society being able to support itself and reproduce should be around \$400, with most people living on \$1 per day and a small elite who may have been much richer, but had only a small impact on the average income.

The transition to modern economic growth in north-west Europe, documented in Volume I, opened up the possibility of catch-up growth in other

Table i.1 GDP per capita by region, 1870–2010 (1990 international $)

	1870	1913	1929	1950	1973	2010
France	1,876	3,485	4,710	5,186	12,824	21,477
Germany	1,839	3,648	4,051	3,881	11,966	20,661
Italy	1,542	2,305	2,778	3,172	10,414	18,520
Spain	1,207	2,056	2,739	2,189	7,661	16,797
Sweden	1,345	2,874	4,063	6,739	13,494	25,306
United Kingdom	3,190	4,921	5,503	6,939	12,025	23,777
WESTERN EUROPE	2,006	3,488	4,167	4,517	11,346	20,889
Czechoslovakia	1,164	2,096	3,042	3,501	7,041	13,020
Poland	946	1,739	2,117	2,447	5,340	10,762
USSR	–	1,414	1,386	2,841	6,059	7,733
Yugoslavia	551	973	1,256	1,428	4,533	6,693
EASTERN EUROPE	953	1,726	1,982	2,088	5,020	8,678
United States	2,445	5,301	6,899	9,561	16,689	30,491
Australia	3,273	5,157	5,263	7,412	12,878	25,824
BRITISH OFFSHOOTS	2,419	5,233	6,673	9,268	16,179	29,564
Argentina	1,468	3,797	4,367	4,987	7,962	10,256
Brazil	713	811	1,137	1,672	3,880	6,879
Chile	1,290	2,988	3,455	3,670	5,034	13,881
LATIN AMERICA	794	1,586	2,053	2,696	4,874	7,770
China	530	552	562	448	838	8,032
Japan	1,011	1,567	2,302	1,921	11,434	21,935
India	533	673	728	619	853	3,372
Indonesia	517	869	1,087	667	1,566	4,722
ASIA	540	673	–	667	1,566	6,375
Israel	–	–	–	2,817	9,645	19,171
Saudi Arabia	–	–	–	2,231	11,040	10,201
Turkey	825	1,213	1,213	1,623	3,477	8,225
MIDDLE EAST	781	1,133	–	1,776	4,855	7,231
Ghana	439	781	–	1,122	1,397	1,922
Kenya	–	–	–	651	970	1,141
South Africa	807	1,151	1,497	2,535	4,175	5,080
AFRICA	613	758	779	887	1,387	2,034
WORLD	884	1,543	–	2,104	4,081	7,814

Sources: Adapted from Maddison 2001: 264; Maddison Project Database, version 2013; Maddison 2010, incorporating new long-run series as follows: Japan: Fukao et al. 2015; Africa: Prados de la Escosura 2012.

parts of the world, and the extent to which that possibility was realized is most conveniently summarized in Tables i.1 and i.2. Although in 1870 GDP per capita was still higher in the United Kingdom than in the United States, by 1913 the United States had not only caught up, but had gone on to forge ahead

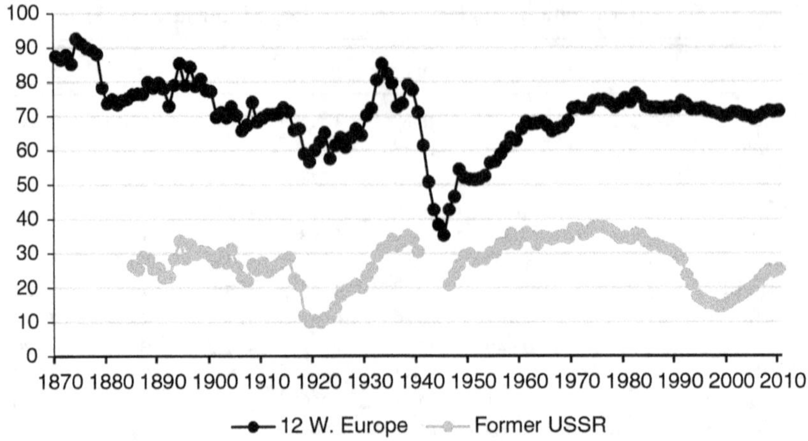

Figure i.1 Regional GDP per capita: western Europe and former USSR

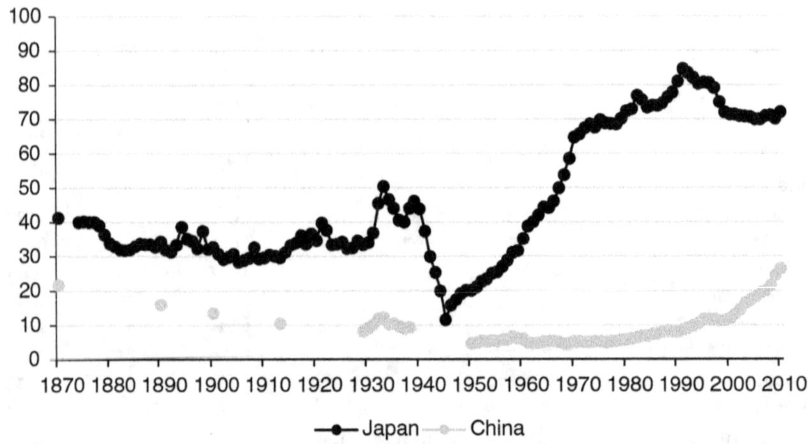

Figure i.2 Regional GDP per capita: East Asia

decisively, remaining the world's most productive large economy throughout the twentieth century.[1] It is therefore instructive to plot regional GDP per capita as a percentage of the US level in Figures i.1 to i.5, to identify episodes of catching up and falling behind.

1 Some small economies have achieved higher per capita incomes for short periods as a result of favourable movements in the terms of trade, particularly associated with the price of natural resources.

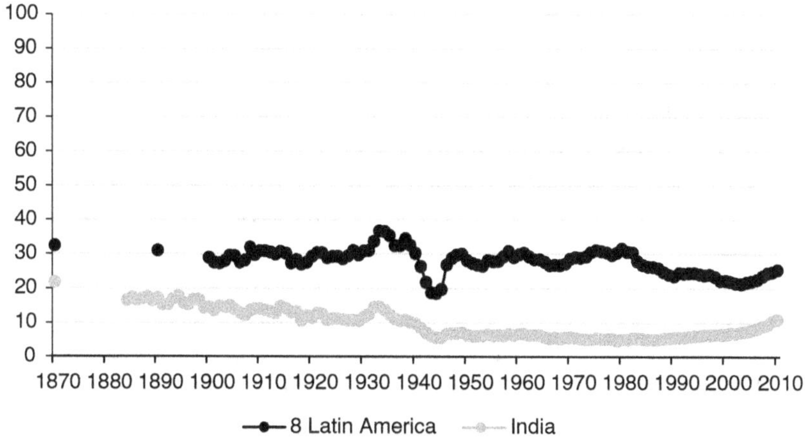

Figure i.3 Regional GDP per capita: Latin America and South Asia

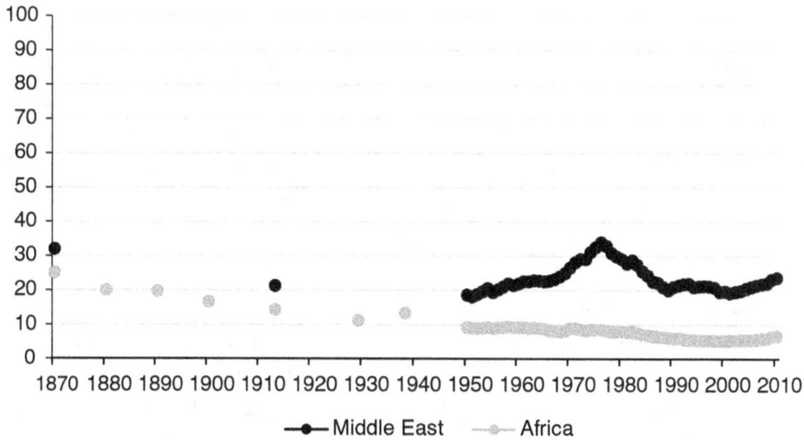

Figure i.4 Regional GDP per capita: Middle East and Africa

The idea that a lagging economy may be expected to grow faster than a leading economy has had a major influence on economic history since the work of Abramovitz (1979; 1986), who saw the period since 1945 as an important phase of catch-up growth. In fact, the idea that economic backwardness may lead to a spurt of catch-up growth was not new in economic history, going back at least to Veblen's (1915) study of Imperial Germany and Gerschenkron's (1962) analysis of European and especially Russian

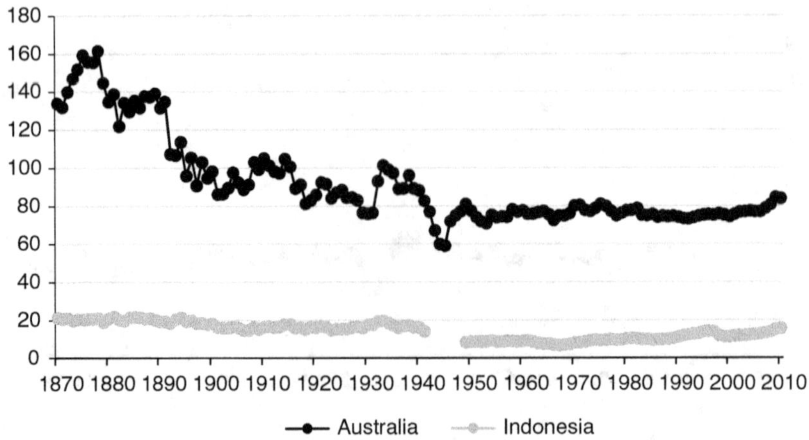

Figure i.5 Regional GDP per capita: Australia and Indonesia

industrialization. However, Abramovitz's (1986) paper appeared in the same year as Baumol's (1986) influential paper which highlighted the negative relationship between the productivity growth rate and the initial level of productivity in a sample of sixteen economies covering the period 1870–1979. The negative relationship, which indicates convergence of living standards between countries, could be expected from a simple neoclassical growth model, either because of diminishing returns to capital or the assumption of exogenous technology. With diminishing returns to capital, an economy that falls behind because of insufficient capital may be expected to have a high rate of return to capital and therefore greater incentive to invest and catch up. Alternatively, a country which falls behind technologically may be expected to catch up by simply adopting the more advanced technology from abroad. In practice, of course, the potential for catching up has not always been realized, and economic historians have often stressed the barriers to catching up. Indeed, Abramovitz (1986) himself noted that only economies with the right 'social capabilities' could be expected to take advantage of the possibilities of catching up. This is borne out by Figures i.1 to i.5, which are characterized as much by falling behind as by catching up, or by divergence as much as by convergence of living standards.

The rise to economic leadership by the United States is the focus of Chapter 1. The United States surpassed the United Kingdom in terms of GDP per capita between 1870 and 1913, then forged further ahead between 1913 and 1950 (Table i.1). Although many countries narrowed the gap after

1950, the United States has remained the richest large economy. It is tempting to link the rise of US economic leadership to modern business enterprise and technological innovation from the time of the Second Industrial Revolution, focused on the electrical, chemical, and automotive industries (Chandler 1990). However, the situation was more complex, since the United States already had higher labour productivity than the United Kingdom in manufacturing by the mid-nineteenth century, and benefited from a later structural shift of labour from low-productivity agriculture, while comparative labour productivity in the whole economy most closely mirrored comparative labour productivity in services (Broadberry 1998).

Turning to the performance of other countries and regions, we begin in Figure i.1 with the situation in western Europe and the former USSR. The series for western Europe is derived from twelve economies for which high quality data are available: Austria, Belgium, Denmark, Finland, France, Germany, Italy, Netherlands, Norway, Sweden, Switzerland, and the United Kingdom. Chapter 2 examines convergence and divergence within western Europe, finding that the region as a whole fell behind the United States between 1870 and 1913, before recovering some ground between the wars. However, World War II saw western Europe falling further behind, with the US continuing to forge ahead technologically, and Europe suffering extensive physical destruction and economic disruption as the main theatre of war. Between 1950 and 1980, western Europe experienced a 'Golden Age' of rapid catch-up growth, but this tailed off at around 70 per cent of the US GDP per capita level rather than closing the gap completely.

Figure i.1 also includes data on the territory of the former USSR, which dominates the path of GDP per capita in eastern Europe. The pattern of catching up and falling behind in the former USSR largely reflects the socialist experiment arising from the Bolshevik revolution of 1917, which forms the focus of Chapter 3. Although imperial Russia did not experience any trend decline relative to the United States before World War I, it was a long way behind, at around 30 per cent of the US level of GDP per capita. War and revolution dealt a devastating blow, but this was followed by rapid Soviet catch-up growth during the 1920s and 1930s, which has sometimes been seen as casting a favourable light on the socialist experiment. After another setback across World War II, Soviet catching up resumed, but after a promising start during the late 1940s, catching up proceeded at best very slowly. The contrast with western Europe during its Golden Age of the 1950s and 1960s in Figure i.1 is particularly striking because the Soviet Union was starting from a much lower level and therefore had much greater potential for catching up. As catching up levelled off in western Europe during the 1970s, the Soviet Union and its east European satellites began to fall further behind. The socialist bloc increasingly became associated with economic stagnation and loss of political freedom, leading to a growing loss of appeal and eventual implosion of the system. The collapse at the end of the 1980s was followed by a spectacular decline in per capita GDP, with the former USSR reaching a low point of just 14.5 per cent of the US level in 1998. By 2010, this had still only recovered to 25.4 per cent.

Since World War II, there have been a series of East Asian miracles and Figure i.2 helps to put these in context by charting the contrasting paths of GDP per capita in Japan and China compared with the United States. Chapter 4 sets out the performance of Japan, which was the first Asian economy to achieve modern economic growth following the Meiji Restoration of 1868. During the pre-World War I period Japan grew at about the same pace as the United States, which was in the process of overtaking the United Kingdom to become world productivity leader. It should be noted that the Japanese data constructed by Fukao et al. (2015) substantially revise upwards the level of GDP per capita before World War II compared with earlier estimates, thus painting a picture of a more advanced Japan before World War I and during the interwar period than that suggested by Maddison (2001). The catastrophic collapse across World War II was followed by a dramatic return to GDP per capita growth of around 8 per cent per annum during the 1950s and 1960s, but this was followed by a return to 3 per cent growth during the 1970s and 1980s, and less than 1 per cent growth after 1990. Although Japan eliminated the productivity gap with western Europe, it stalled before catching up with the United States. A second wave of East Asian countries to develop after Japan, consisting of South Korea, Taiwan, Hong Kong, and Singapore, known collectively as the newly industrializing countries (NICs), began to grow rapidly from the 1960s. By the early 1990s, there was talk of an economic miracle, based on 'Asian values' and activist industrial policies, which attracted some sceptical comment from economists (Krugman 1994; Young 1995). Although all four NICs suffered serious setbacks during the East Asian financial crisis of 1997–98, they resumed catching up in the 2000s, and by 2010 South Korea and Taiwan were on a par with Japan, while the city states of Hong Kong and Singapore had caught up with the United States.

Chapter 5 offers an overview of developments in China, which followed a very different path from Japan, falling further behind the United States during the late nineteenth century and the first half of the twentieth. Chinese GDP per capita reached a nadir of around 5 per cent of the US level during the first thirty years of communist rule. From the late 1970s, however, following institutional reforms to liberalize the economy whilst maintaining the leading role of the Communist Party, China entered a dramatic catching-up phase. Although China did not manage to match the pace of catching up achieved by Japan between the 1950s and the 1970s, it had raised China's comparative GDP per capita position to more than 25 per cent of the US level by 2010. Together with its huge population, this made China the world's second largest economy measured by GDP at purchasing power parity, challenging the economic dominance of the West.

Turning to South Asia in Figure i.3, India has followed a similar trajectory to China, falling further behind the United States between 1870 and 1950 and remaining at around 5 per cent of the US level for the first three decades of independence from Britain. Liberalizing reforms during the 1980s then unleashed a dramatic period of catching up, again echoing the Chinese trajectory. By 2010, Indian GDP per capita had reached more than 10 per cent of the US level. Developments in India are discussed in Chapter 6.

Figure i.3 also shows the performance of Latin America, which is discussed in Chapter 9. The eight Latin American economies covered here are: Argentina, Brazil, Chile, Colombia, Mexico, Peru, Uruguay, and Venezuela. The overall picture is a lack of catching up with the United States over the long run, although this hides important variation in individual country performance. Argentina and also Uruguay, to a lesser extent, were on a par with many west European countries in 1913, as major exporters of primary produce. However, they failed to fulfil their early promise and began a rapid relative decline from the 1930s. Venezuela, by contrast, was relatively poor until the mid-1920s, but then caught up rapidly on the back of oil resources. The whole region suffered a major setback with the debt crisis of the 1980s, leading to a 'lost decade'.

The Middle East, which is plotted together with Africa in Figure i.4, is discussed in Chapter 8.[2] Reliable estimates of GDP per capita in the Middle East before 1950 are confined to Turkey for the interwar period and the Ottoman Empire before World War I, and suggest continued falling behind the United States until 1950. There then followed a period of catching up during the 1950s and 1960s, based on oil. The rate of catching up accelerated during the 1970s as the result of a massive swing in the terms of trade brought about by the Organization of Petroleum Exporting Countries (OPEC), led by

2 Strictly speaking, Chapter 8 covers the Middle East and North Africa (MENA), while Chapter 10 focuses on sub-Saharan Africa.

Saudi Arabia. However, a reversal of the terms of trade during the 1990s brought about an equally dramatic period of falling behind, leaving Middle Eastern GDP per capita at less than 25 per cent of the US level by 2010.

African economic performance is discussed in Chapter 10. GDP per capita grew more slowly in Africa than in the United States between 1870 and 1950 so that Africa fell further behind during this period of colonization by European powers (Figure i.4). African performance during this period is more or less in line with the performance of colonial India, while independent Latin America held its own against the United States. Decolonization did not improve the relative performance of Africa, which continued to fall further behind after World War II, reaching a low point of just 5.3 per cent of the US level at the end of the 1990s. Africa then entered a period of catching-up growth, with GDP per capita recovering to 6.7 per cent of the US level by 2010.

The case of Australia, plotted in Figure i.5 and analysed in Chapter 11, reminds us that the world per capita income leader in the late nineteenth century was neither the United States nor the United Kingdom. The high per capita incomes in Australia were the result of a combination of a small settler population and natural resource abundance in an economy with good institutions. In the late nineteenth century, however, the resource boom faltered and Australian per capita income leadership disappeared. Across World War II, Australian per capita incomes declined further to around 80 per cent of the US level. South East Asia is discussed in Chapter 7, with the GDP per capita of Indonesia, the largest economy in the region, plotted on a comparative basis in Figure i.5. Indonesia fell further behind the United States between 1870 and the mid-1960s, before entering a catch-up phase after the coup to remove President Sukarno, who had presided over a period of slow growth and rapid inflation during the early 1960s. The setback following the East Asian financial crisis of 1998 is also clearly visible in Figure i.5.

The data from Table i.1 can be used to calculate annual growth rates of per capita GDP in Table i.2. The first point to note is that compared with earlier epochs, the period since 1870 has seen a remarkable increase in per capita GDP growth rates. At the world level, GDP per capita grew at just 0.31 per cent between 1800 and 1870, so the increase to 1.3 per cent between 1870 and 1913 was a dramatic improvement. Even with the disruption of the two World Wars and the Great Depression, GDP per capita grew at 0.84 per cent per annum between 1913 and 1950, nearly three times as rapidly as during 1800–1870. Furthermore, the slowdown was dramatically reversed during the period 1950–73, when GDP per capita grew by 2.88 per cent per annum, before falling back to 1.76 per cent between 1973 and 2010. This general pattern of

Table i.2 Growth rates of GDP per capita by region (% per annum)

	1870–1913	1913–50	1950–73	1973–2010
Western Europe	1.29	0.70	4.00	1.65
Eastern Europe	1.38	0.51	3.81	1.48
British offshoots	1.79	1.54	2.42	1.63
Latin America	1.61	1.43	2.57	1.26
Asia	0.51	−0.02	3.71	3.79
Middle East	0.87	1.21	4.37	1.08
Africa	0.49	0.42	1.94	1.03
World	1.30	0.84	2.88	1.76

Source: Table i.1.

a setback between 1913 and 1950, followed by a Golden Age between 1950 and 1973, can be found in most regions, although it should be noted that Asia is the one region to achieve even higher growth during the period 1973–2010.

Although GDP per capita is widely used as a measure of living standards, it is at best an incomplete measure, and needs to be supplemented by additional information. Two important variables widely monitored are life expectancy and education, which tend to show smaller differences between nations than GDP per capita. The Human Development Index (HDI), which combines GDP per capita with measures of life expectancy and education is sometimes used as a composite measure of the standard of living (UNDP 1990). Chapter 16 makes use of a modification of this, known as the Historical Index of Human Development (HIHD), introduced by Prados de la Escosura (2015).[3] Mean values, however, do not tell us anything about the distribution of welfare across individuals. To take account of distributional issues, it is also necessary in Chapter 16 to examine measures of inequality, such as the Gini coefficient and top income shares.

Part II: Factors Governing Differential Outcomes in the Global Economy

Part II explores the factors governing differential outcomes in the various regions that are examined in Part I. An important distinction is made between

3 In the HIHD, non-income variables are transformed non-linearly to allow for the fact that increases in life expectancy and literacy are harder to achieve at higher levels, and quality improvements tend to be associated with an increase in quantity.

the proximate and fundamental sources of growth, while a final section analyses the world economy as a system.

1. *The Proximate Sources of Growth*

Growth accounting helps us to assess whether economic growth came from the use of more factor inputs or from the more effective use of existing inputs (Solow 1957). In the simplest formulation, aggregate output is produced using factor inputs of capital and labour. The growth rate of output can then be related to the growth rates of the inputs of capital and labour and a residual factor representing any change in the efficiency with which the factors are used. Each factor is weighted by its relative importance in the production process, measured by its share in the costs of production. For labour this is the share of wages in the value of output, while for capital it is the share of profits. The residual factor, known as total factor productivity (TFP), is often associated with technological progress, but it can also reflect changes in organization.

Whereas the discussion of the labour input in Volume I focused on the increase in the number of workers as population increased, after 1870 the focus shifts to improvements in the quality of workers, as a growing number of economies completed the demographic transition from a poor economy with high rates of fertility and mortality to a rich economy with low rates of fertility and mortality. Chapter 12 thus focuses on human capital and the investments needed to make the labour force 'healthy, literate, and smart'. Chapter 13 considers the roles of capital and technology. Countries that were catching up often did so with high rates of investment in physical as well as human capital, financed more through high rates of saving than through borrowing from abroad (Feldstein and Horioka 1980). These high rates of investment facilitated the transfer of advanced technology from abroad, which required both hi-tech machinery and the skills needed to operate it effectively.

2. *The Ultimate Sources of Growth*

Even if we had perfect information on the proximate sources of growth, however, this would only tell us *how* the transition to modern economic growth occurred, rather than *why* it occurred. If some economies grew faster than others because of more investment or faster technological progress, we would want to know why investment and technological progress were faster in those economies. Economists divide the more fundamental underlying sources of growth into two categories, geography and institutions.

The role of geography is analysed in Chapter 14 using the distinction between first and second nature geography. First nature geography covers natural endowments such as mineral deposits or climate, while second nature geography covers man-made factors such as access to markets and agglomeration economies. The effects of first nature geography can certainly be seen in the twentieth-century path of GDP per capita in countries with large endowments of oil. This is most obviously the case for the Middle East region, which benefited from rising per capita incomes as oil replaced coal as the chief source of energy. However, dependence on natural resources could also lead to volatility, again illustrated by the case of the Middle East, which formed a cartel to raise dramatically the price of oil during the 1970s, only to see it fall back when the cartel was undermined during the 1980s. The possibility of other negative consequences of resource discovery, such as the crowding out of local industry as a result of exchange rate appreciation in response to a balance of payments surplus, led some economists to coin the term 'resource curse' (Sachs and Warner 2001).

Chapter 14 places more emphasis on the role of second nature geography (Krugman and Venables 1995). The basic idea here is that exogenously given first nature geography advantages or disadvantages become amplified rather than reduced by forces of economic integration. Favourable locations with high productivity are seen as attracting people and investment, which further raises productivity, while unfavourable locations with low productivity attract fewer people and investment, thus falling further behind. In such a world of increasing returns, reductions in the cost of trade may thus have asymmetric effects on different regions, with industry clustering in a few favourable locations rather than being dispersed evenly around the world. A useful summary measure to capture second nature geography of a country or region is market potential, measured by the sum of distance-weighted GDP of all regions in the neighbourhood. Building on the approach of Crafts and Venables (2003), Chapter 14 assesses to what extent the differential outcomes in the global economy over the period 1870–2010 can be explained using this new approach.

The role of institutions is explored in Chapter 15 using the 'new institutional economics' approach of North et al. (2009), who emphasize the need for a society to make the transition from a 'natural state' to an open-access social order so as to achieve sustained economic growth. In the natural state, a coalition of elites controls access to economic rents or profit opportunities, supported by concentration of political power. Economic growth can take place in such societies but is eventually choked off as elite power comes under threat. The transition to sustained economic growth requires the transformation of both political and economic institutions, widening access to economic rents, underpinned by a move towards representative political institutions.

3. *The Global Economy*

The world economy can clearly be broken down into its regional components, as in Part I of this volume. However, it is also helpful to think of the world economy as a global system, governing international transactions, such as international trade and migration and international finance. It is also important to stand back and assess the roles of warfare and empire. This can be useful in guarding against a tendency of earlier generations of economic historians to focus only on the effects of European developments on the rest of the world, without paying much attention to the impact of developments flowing in the opposite direction. Whilst the two-way nature of these reciprocal flows became too obvious to ignore in the second half of the twentieth century, they also need to be borne in mind when considering earlier eras.

The real flows of goods (via international trade) and labour (via migration) between 1700 and 1870 tell the story in Chapter 17 of the integration of product and factor markets in different parts of the world. The global economy became highly integrated between 1870 and 1913 as transport costs fell, trade liberalization led to a reduction in tariffs and other barriers, and there were few restrictions on international migration. Although there were already signs of a backlash against globalization before 1914, World War I led to a decisive reversal of market integration, ushering in a long period of deglobalization across and between the two world wars (O'Rourke and Williamson 1999). There then followed a period of reglobalization after World War II, which proceeded quite slowly at first before gathering pace during the 1980s. Although world exports now account for a higher share of GDP than on the eve of World War I, the peak ratio of migration flows to population occurred during the early 1900s, indicating that while goods market integration has continued to flourish, labour market integration has stalled at the global level.

International finance is considered in Chapter 18, which offers three perspectives. The first perspective follows on naturally from Chapter 17, showing that international mobility of capital has followed a U-shaped pattern, high before World War I and again since the late 1970s, but with an interlude of deglobalization during the interwar period and only a slow reglobalization during the Bretton Woods period after World War II. The second perspective connects the scale of capital flows with exchange rates and monetary policies using the idea of the 'trilemma', which states that economic policy can at best achieve two out of the three policy objectives of free mobility of capital, exchange rate stability, and monetary autonomy (Obstfeld et al. 2005). This trilemma is seen as helpful for understanding the choice of policy regimes adopted at different times in different places. The third perspective looks at the connections between international finance and economic and financial stability, asking whether pegged exchange rates and free mobility of capital are necessarily engines of instability, as has sometimes been argued.

Economic historians often focus on pre-war, post-war, and interwar periods, as if warfare was some kind of anomaly and minor disruption to normal events rather than a common occurrence that could sometimes lead to major turning points in history. And yet, by the late nineteenth century, a combination of military and economic advantages had enabled imperial powers to expand the territories and populations that they controlled to an unprecedented extent. Chapter 19 discusses the ways in which this expansion of imperialism facilitated the global movement of people, goods, and capital, but at the same time set up imperial rivalries that shaped the major conflicts of the twentieth century. World War I ushered in a period of deglobalization that lasted until after World War II, as the liberal world order gave way to increased controls over the international movement of commodities, labour, and capital. Although there were growing pressures for reform and greater autonomy for the colonized peoples, there was also a move towards greater integration within each empire to counter the growing trend towards protectionism and autarkic commercial policies. After World War II, by contrast, the return to globalization, combined with the weaker economic and financial position of even the victorious imperial powers, led to a period of decolonization, effectively ending the global hegemony of western Europe. However, the world then reoriented itself around two rival blocs led by the United States and the Soviet Union, based on an ideological divide between capitalism and communism. Although the end of the Cold War after the fall of the Berlin Wall in 1989 and the break-up of the Soviet Union initially reduced global tensions and led to reductions in defence spending, in the twenty-first century tensions have resurfaced between the United States and Russia, while China has emerged as a new superpower.

Concluding Comments

The economic history of the twentieth century is essentially an optimistic story of rising living standards everywhere. And yet the gains have not been equally distributed. Part I of this volume sets out the main trends in the different regions of the world. This is essentially a story of divergence between 1870 and 1950, as western countries pulled further ahead, while the period since 1950 has seen more convergence. Nevertheless there is a long way to go before the poorer countries catch up with the developed world. Part II seeks to shed light on the factors governing the differential outcomes outlined in Part I. It is clear that investment in proximate factors such as physical capital and human capital have played their part in the adoption of advanced technology, but that merely raises a further question of why some societies were better able to make those investments than others. More fundamental factors, such as geography and institutions, must also have played a role. The role of geography can be seen as operating through both first nature factors such as endowments of natural resources, and through second nature factors such as location near to buoyant markets. Institutions can be seen as playing an important role through setting incentives for socially productive activities such as investment and innovation. Finally, the pace of world economic growth was influenced by the institutions affecting the international flows of goods, labour, and capital, and there were striking contrasts between the extent of globalization in the pre-1914, interwar, and post-war worlds. The two world wars and the imperial struggles with which they were inextricably linked, also inevitably had their impact on economic performance.

References

Abramovitz, M. (1979). 'Rapid Growth Potential and its Realisation: The Experience of the Capitalist Economies in the Postwar Period', in Malinvaud, E. (ed.), *Economic Growth and Resources: Proceedings of the Fifth World Congress of the International Economic Association, Vol. I*, London: Macmillan, 1–51.

(1986). 'Catching-Up, Forging Ahead and Falling Behind', *Journal of Economic History*, 46, 385–406.

Baumol, W. J. (1986). 'Productivity Growth, Convergence and Welfare: What the Long Run Data Show', *American Economic Review*, 76, 1072–1159.

Broadberry, S. (1998). 'How Did the United States and Germany Overtake Britain? A Sectoral Analysis of Comparative Productivity Levels, 1870–1990', *Journal of Economic History*, 58, 375–407.

Chandler, A. D. Jr. (1990). *Scale and Scope: The Dynamics of Industrial Capitalism*, Cambridge, MA: Harvard University Press.

Crafts, N. F. R. and Venables, A. J. (2003). 'Globalization in History: A Geographical Perspective', in Bordo, M., Taylor, A. M. and Williamson, J. G. (eds.), *Globalization in Historical Perspective*, Chicago University Press, 323–364.

Feldstein, M. and Horioka, C. (1980). 'Domestic Saving and International Capital Flows', *Economic Journal*, 90, 314–329.

Fukao, K., Bassino, J.-P., Makino, T., Paprzycki, R., Settsu, T., Takashima, M., and Tokui, J. (2015). *Regional Inequality and Industrial Structure in Japan: 1874–2008*, Tokyo: Maruzen Publishing.

Gerschenkron, A. (1962). *Economic Backwardness in Historical Perspective*, Cambridge, MA: Harvard University Press.

Krugman, P. (1994). 'The Myth of Asia's Miracle', *Foreign Affairs*, 73(6), 62–78.

Krugman, P. and Venables, A. (1995). 'Globalization and the Inequality of Nations', *Quarterly Journal of Economics*, 110, 857–880.

Maddison, A. (2001). *The World Economy: A Millennial Perspective*, Paris: Organisation for Economic Co-operation and Development.

(2005). 'Measuring and Interpreting World Economic Performance 1500–2001', *Review of Income and Wealth*, 51, 1–35.

(2010). 'Statistics on World Population, GDP and Per Capita GDP, 1–2008 AD', Groningen Growth and Development Centre, www.ggdc.net/MADDISON/oriindex.htm (accessed 29 September 2020).

Maddison Project Database, version 2013. Bolt, J. and van Zanden, J. L. (2014). 'The Maddison Project: Collaborative Research on Historical National Accounts', *Economic History Review*, 67, 627–651.

North, D. C., Wallis, J. J., and Weingast, B. R. (2009). *Violence and Social Orders: A Conceptual Framework for Interpreting Recorded Human History*, Cambridge University Press.

Obstfeld, M., Shambaugh, J. C., and Taylor, A. M. (2005). 'The Trilemma in History: Tradeoffs Among Exchange Rates, Monetary Policies, and Capital Mobility', *Review of Economics and Statistics*, 87, 423–438.

O'Rourke, K. H. and Williamson, J. G. (1999). *Globalization and History: The Evolution of a Nineteenth-Century Atlantic Economy*, Cambridge, MA: MIT Press.

Prados de la Escosura, L. (2012). 'Output per Head in Pre-Independence Africa: Quantitative Conjectures', *Economic History of Developing Regions*, 27(2), 1–36.

(2015). 'World Human Development: 1870–2007', *Review of Income and Wealth*, 61, 220–247.

Sachs, J. D. and Warner, A. (2001). 'The Curse of Natural Resources', *European Economic Review*, 45, 827–838.

Solow, R. (1957). 'Technical Change and the Aggregate Production Function', *Review of Economics and Statistics*, 39, 312–320.

UNDP (United Nations Development Programme) (1990). World Development Report, New York: Oxford University Press.

Veblen, T. (1915). *Imperial Germany and the Industrial Revolution*, New York: Macmillan.

Young, A. (1995). 'The Tyranny of Numbers: Confronting the Statistical Realities of the East Asian Growth Experience', *Quarterly Journal of Economics*, 110, 641–680.

PART I

★

REGIONAL DEVELOPMENTS

1

North America

The Rise of US Technological and Economic Leadership

PAUL W. RHODE

Introduction

The American economy, according to the standard view in macroeconomics, has been growing on a balanced path over the past two centuries. Some macro-growth economists point to the near constancy of total income growth since 1790; others highlight the near constancy of per capita income growth after the 1870s. The underlying data are displayed in Figure 1.1, which graphs the level of total income, per capita income, and population. What pops out in Figure 1.1 is that the growth of total and per capita income series return to trend after the disruptions of the Great Depression and World War II. The standard macroeconomic view adheres to Kaldor's 'stylized facts' (1957; 1961), asserting that many key economic variables are constants.

But the assertions about balanced growth of total income and per capita income are inconsistent because they are linked together by demographic growth which experienced profound change. Population expansion has transitioned from a very high rate of growth in the first half of the nineteenth century to a far lower rate in the second half of the twentieth century. As Nobel laureate Simon Kuznets (1964) asserted long ago, one of the 'distinctive' features of American economic growth is that population growth was slowing throughout the whole period when per capita income growth began accelerating.

Most economic historians see the development of the American economy differently from the balanced growth vision commonly held by macroeconomists. In its development process, the US economy passed through a series of important transitions (Abramovitz and David 1973). One transition, occurring in the early nineteenth century, involved a shift from a process of extensive growth to intensive growth. The economy had been growing in size by adding people (through rapid rates of natural increase and later

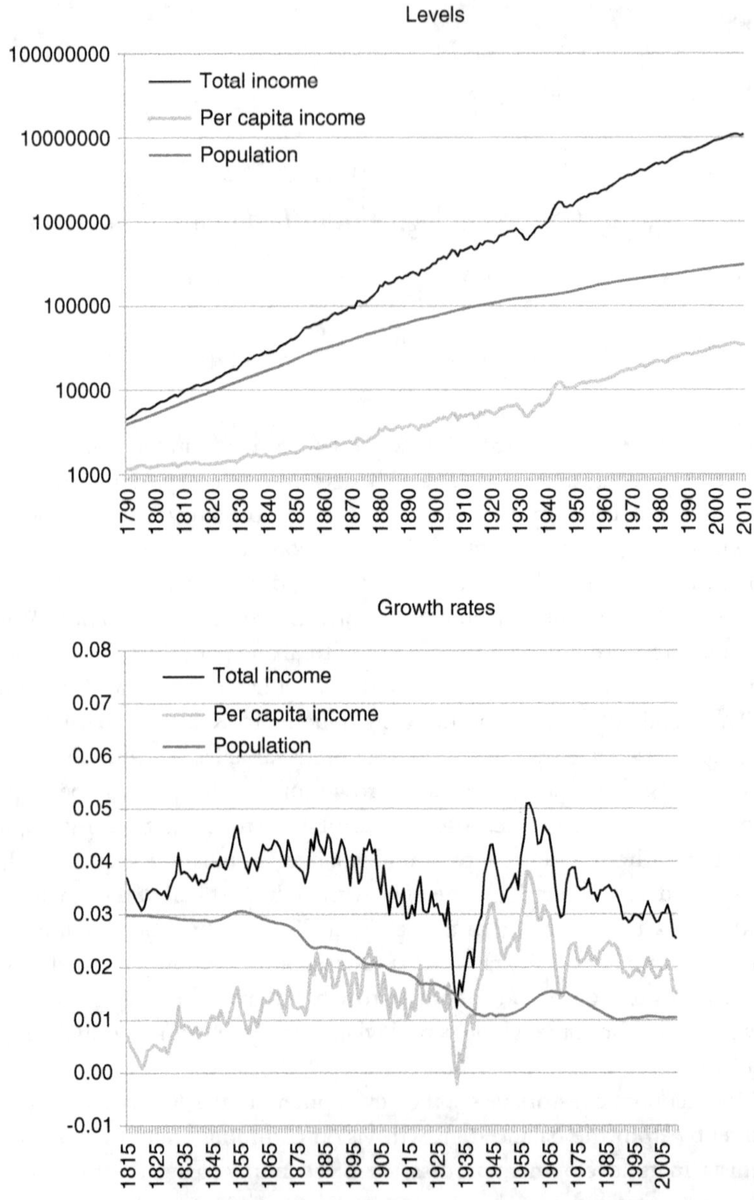

Figure 1.1 Growth of total income, per capita income, and population, 1790–2010
Sources: Carter et al. 2006, Ca 9, 11, Income in 1996 $; spliced to data from FRED, https://fred.stlouisfed.org (accessed 29 September 2020).

through immigration) and by offsetting the pressure of resources by settling new land. It began to grow by increasing per capita income – by saving more to increase capital per worker, by working more hours per year, and by generating innovative technologies suited to the American setting. This transition witnessed the emergence of 'modern economic growth', of a high sustained rate of per capita income increase.

A second transition noted by economic historians, occurring around the turn of the twentieth century, saw the emergence of a knowledge-based economy. Per capita income continued to expand at a high pace, but now it was driven by increases in the productivity of the factors, by technological and organizational advances, and by investments in human capital. In the words of Claudia Goldin (2001), the twentieth century in the United States was the 'human capital century'. A third transition is occurring in the present period, as we move to becoming a globalized information economy. This transition is ongoing, and economic historians, who study completed historical processes, have little to say about it, beyond pointing to the disruptive nature of the prior transitions. The view of economic historians has several virtues. It is closer to the facts than is the standard macro view. And it is also far more interesting and yields more insights into the effects of major structural transformations.

Capital Is Back

The view of economic historians allows for change over time. Constancies are not assumed when, in fact, variables show dramatic changes. Thomas Piketty's (2014) path-breaking *Capital in the Twenty-First Century* has brought renewed attention to the role of capital–income dynamics and the changing share of property in the income distribution. Attention had shifted away from the process of capital accumulation, largely because modern macroeconomic thinking constrained its role to be passive. According to Kaldor's 'stylized facts' (1957; 1961), the following key variables were all constant:

1. the rate of capital formation
2. the capital–output ratio
3. capital's share of income
4. the rate of return on capital
5. the growth of per capita output (driven by technological progress).

These widely espoused claims bear little resemblance to the actual historical record.

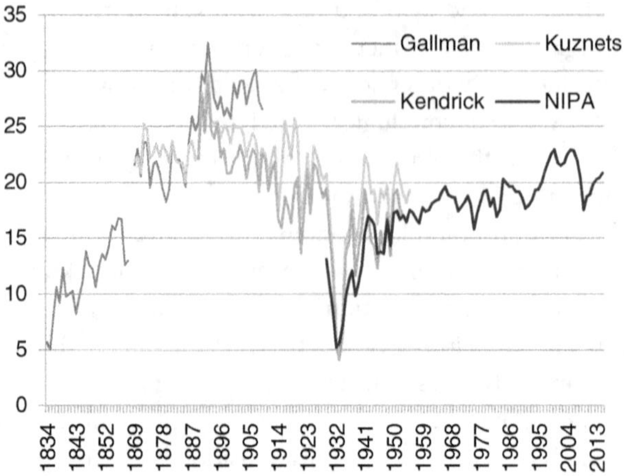

Figure 1.2 US capital formation rate, 1834–2015
Sources: Constant price series from Gallman and Rhode 2019; Kuznets 1961; Kendrick 1961; www.bea.gov/iTable/index_nipa.cfm (accessed 29 September 2020).

In US economic history, the constancy of the rate of physical capital formation – that is, the share of national product invested to sustain and increase the capital stock – is a twentieth-century phenomenon. Over the long nineteenth century, as the seminal work of Robert Gallman demonstrated, the rate of capital formation increased dramatically. Figure 1.2 plots four series on the US capital formation rate – the share of income withdrawn from current consumption to increase future output – from 1834 to 2015. Gallman showed that the share of real gross capital formation in gross national product (GNP) increased two- to threefold between the 1830s and the end of the twentieth century. Simon Kuznets' (1961) constant price series showed a rise in the late nineteenth century and then a gradually declining trend. John Kendrick (1961) found a similar pattern of rise and fall. The official national income and product account (NIPA) numbers show a rise over the second half of the twentieth century and the early years of the twenty-first century.

The sharp rise of the capital formation rate over the nineteenth century led to higher capital–output ratios. Figure 1.3 shows indices on the capital–output ratio from 1774 to 1900. The capital stock and GNP figures are from Gallman and Rhode (2019). Gallman found that the capital–output ratio almost tripled between 1800 and 1900. The ratio grew between 1850 and 1860, and then retreated in the 1860s and 1870s, during the Civil War and reconstruction. The ratio jumped in the 1880s and continued its upward track in the 1890s. In the

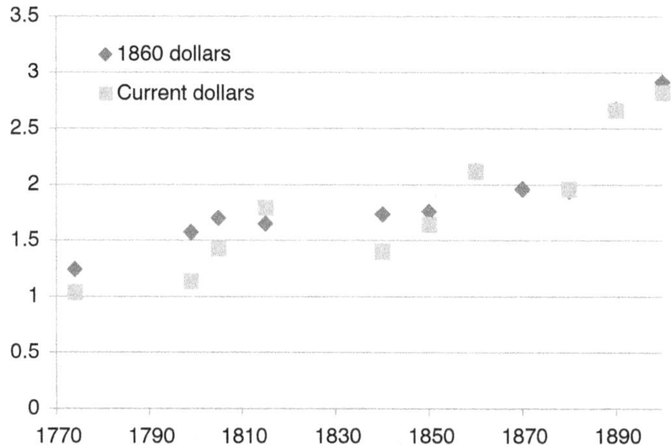

Figure 1.3 National capital–GNP ratio, 1774–1900
Source: Gallman 1992.

twentieth century, the ratio stabilized in a way consistent with Kaldor's 'stylized facts'. But it was hardly a constant before 1900. The rise fits the story of Thomas Piketty and Gabriel Zucman (2014) and reflects the war-related interruptions. Gallman's account of late nineteenth-century growth differs from Piketty's in several key details. Gallman found that as capital accumulated, real interest rates fell markedly (perhaps even below the rate of income growth). Gallman also conceived of capital formation, at least in nineteenth-century America, as a broadly based process, not restricted to the saving behaviour of the top of the earnings distribution.

It is tempting to think that the process of industrialization drove the rise in the economy-wide capital–output ratio in the United States over the late nineteenth century. But as Gallman showed, manufacturing was less capital intensive than agriculture. So industrialization, narrowly defined as the shift of economic activity from agriculture to manufacturing, worked to reduce the aggregate capital–output ratio. Gallman (1986, table 4.8) reported the results of a shift-share analysis, which highlights the role of increasing capital–output ratios within every sector and casts shade on the role of sectoral shifts. If one held the sectoral shares constant at 1860 levels and allowed the sectoral capital–output ratio to change as they did, the aggregate capital–output ratio would have almost doubled between 1840 and 1900 (table 4.8, line 7b). If one held the sectoral capital–output ratios constant at their 1860 ratios and allowed the sectoral distributions to change as they did (including increasing the manufacturing share of value added from 17 per cent in 1840 to 31 per cent in 1900), the overall capital–output ratio would have declined (table 4.8, line 7c). The forces driving up the capital–output ratio were broadly felt; rather than being limited to a few sectors, the ratio rose substantially in every sector. Sectoral shifts, in fact, tended to counteract the rise.

Gallman's analysis of the rise of the capital–output ratio can be translated into the yeast versus mushroom growth process dichotomy of Arnold Harberger (1998). A yeast-like process yields a general, global, even, and predictable expansion, where mushroom growth is specific, local, uneven, and yielding an unpredictable expansion (popping up here but not there). Gallman viewed the rise of the physical capital–output ratio as a broadly diffused rather than a localized phenomenon. Following his teacher Simon Kuznets (1961), Gallman took this pattern as a sign that increasing capital supplies rather than idiosyncratic technology-driven demand shocks drove the increase.[1]

Table 1.1 uses Gallman's capital stock data to analyse the sources of economic growth in the United States across four long eras. The growth accounting exercise explains GNP and GNP per capita. The numbers in the left columns relate to total income. Those on the right relate to income per capita; they are formed by subtracting the population growth rates from the growth rates of income and the factor supplies.[2] Over the 1840–1900 period, the capital stock (growing at 4.84 per cent per annum) rose far more rapidly than GNP (3.98 per cent) or labour supply (2.73 per cent) or population (2.49 per cent). The rapid growth in capital per capita (2.36 per cent per annum) stands out in the top right panel. Physical capital formation contributed a large share of income growth over the 1840–1900 period – it accounted for 35 per cent of total income growth. It contributed to an even larger share – 46 per cent – of per capita income growth. The measured rate of productivity growth climbed slightly between the 1800–1840 period and

1 Economic historians have actively debated why the saving/investment rate rose over the late nineteenth century. Abramovitz and David (1973; 2001) attribute the change to capital-using technological change. Davis and Gallman (1978) reject this argument, noting that the capital–output ratio rose in too many sectors to be easily explained by technological forces. Instead, they advanced an argument based on increased supplies of capital, specifically through improved financial intermediation. These changes would reduce the gap between the interest rates investors paid and savers received, increasing both investment and saving rates. Other scholars point to demographic forces, most notably the decline in the birth rate and associated child-rearing costs, and the extension of life expectancy and the increased demand for retirement savings, to explain the increase in available loanable funds. Shifts in the distribution of income and wealth have also received attention.

2 The calculations combine the factors in the same way over the entire span, assigning a 0.68 weight to labour, 0.29 to capital, and 0.03 to raw land. See Gallman 1992.

Table 1.1 Accounting for growth over four epochs

	Total				Per capita			
	1800–1840	1840–1900	1900–1970	1970–2014	1800–1840	1840–1900	1900–1970	1970–2014
Annual growth rate								
Real GNP: $\dot{Y}/Y$	3.89	3.98	3.24	2.77	0.91	1.49	1.82	1.81
Labour: Workers $\dot{L}/L$	3.04	2.73	1.56	1.28	0.06	0.24	0.18	0.32
Capital: $\dot{K}/K$	3.90	4.84	2.83	2.64	0.91	2.36	1.41	1.69
Land: $\dot{T}/T$	2.76	2.38	2.64	0.00	−0.22	−0.11	1.22	−0.96
Population: $\dot{N}/N$	2.98	2.49	1.42	0.96				
Contribution to GNP growth								
Labour: $\theta_L\ \dot{L}/L$	2.07	1.86	1.08	0.87	0.04	0.16	0.11	0.20
Capital: $\theta_K\ \dot{K}/K$	1.13	1.40	0.82	0.77	0.27	0.68	0.41	0.49
Land: $\theta_T\ \dot{T}/T$	0.08	0.07	0.01	0.00	−0.01	0.00	0.04	−0.03
Productivity: $\mathring{A}/A$	0.61	0.65	1.26	1.14	0.61	0.65	1.26	1.14
Shares of GNP growth								
Labour: $(\theta_L\ \dot{L}/L)/(\dot{Y}/Y)$	0.53	0.47	0.33	0.31	0.04	0.11	0.07	0.12
Capital: $(\theta_K\ \dot{K}/K)/(\dot{Y}/Y)$	0.29	0.35	0.25	0.28	0.29	0.46	0.22	0.27
Land: $(\theta_T\ \dot{T}/T)/(\dot{Y}/Y)$	0.02	0.02	0.02	0.00	−0.01	0.00	0.02	−0.02
Productivity: $(\mathring{A}/A)/(\dot{Y}/Y)$	0.16	0.16	0.39	0.41	0.67	0.43	0.69	0.63

Notes: Capital is conventional; Y = income; L = labour; K = capital; T = land; A = productivity; θ_I is the contribution of factor i to income; dots over symbols indicate changes over time; productivity growth is $\mathring{A}/A = \dot{Y}/Y - \theta_L\ \dot{L}/L - :\theta_K\ \dot{K}/K - \theta_T\ \dot{T}/T$.

Sources: Gallman and Rhode 2019; data for post-1960 period: FRED, https://fred.stlouisfed.org (accessed 29 September 2020).

the 1840–1900 period, then jumped substantially in the 1900–1960 period. According to this exercise, capital formation was the *most important source* of per capita income growth in the 1840–1900 period.[3]

In the 1900 to 1970 period, productivity growth assumes the starring role. It rose both in magnitude – leading to an estimated increase in per capita income of 1.26 per cent per annum – and accounting for nearly a 70 per cent share. The share of physical capital formation in per capita income growth is one-half as large over the 1900–1970 period as it was over the 1840–1900 period. Productivity growth diminished after 1970, although by these admittedly crude calculations the effects are not dramatic.

A first obvious caveat related to these calculations is that the labour input is treated as a stock, without adjustment for hours of work or for worker quality. We know that hours of work per week rose over the nineteenth century and declined over the twentieth. The latter decline means labour inputs would rise even less than the numbers in the calculations suggest. Offsetting this force was an increase in the effectiveness of labour associated with investments in human capital. The average years of schooling of the US population increased from about seven years for the cohort born in the mid-1870s, to about ten years for those born *c.*1900, to about fourteen years in 1950, and since has remained near this level (Goldin and Katz 2008: 20). Educational investments coincide closely with the patterns of productivity advance, a point that has not escaped the attention of economic historians.[4]

A second, presumably less important caveat relates to the measure of land in the growth accounting calculations. The numbers reflect the total land mass and do not adjust for quality. This does not fully account for the availability of natural resources such as mineral deposits or forests. In combination with the low weight in output, this inherently de-emphasizes the role of geography in US growth.[5] American economic historians generally view territorial expansion as a determent to per capita income growth.

3 One can take the analysis a step further by investigating the causes of the acceleration of per capita income growth between the 1800–1840 period and the 1840–1900 period. Per capita income growth increased by 0.58 (= 1.49−0.91) percentage points. The contribution of capital formation increased by 0.41 (= 0.68−0.27) percentage points, explaining over 70 per cent of the acceleration of per capita income.

4 For excellent entries into the literature on the roles of education and human capital in the US, see Goldin and Katz 2008 and the chapters in Boustan et al. 2014. The rise of educational investments is obviously related to the reductions in the birth rate and the changes in the capital formation rate discussed above.

5 Wright 2018 provides an insightful commentary on the role of natural resources in US growth, with key emphasis on the importance of scientific knowledge and property right regimes in the discovery and exploitation process.

Structural Change

The acceleration of per capita income growth in the United States was associated with fundamental structural changes. Population shifted from rural areas to urban centres and their suburbs. In 1790, one out of twenty Americans lived in urban areas (in places with 2,500 or more people). And as late as 1840, the figure was one out of ten. Urbanization accelerated between 1870 and 1920. By the latter date, the rural and urban populations were evenly split.

The economy has also experienced fundamental changes. Employment and economic activity has shifted from the primary sector (agriculture, forestry, and fisheries) to the secondary sector (manufacturing, mining, and construction), and then to the tertiary sector (services). Figure 1.4 reports the share of the labour force and income in each of these major sectors at Census years.

The panels to Figure 1.4 tell, with some nuance, the same story: the decline of the primary sector, the rise and then fall of the secondary sector, and the rise of the tertiary sector. The nuance matters – that is, the differences between the labour force and income panels help to tell the story. And the story is not as simple as one, two, three. Throughout the period, the tertiary sector rivalled and generally exceeded the secondary sector in importance.

The process of structural change was driven by forces operating on both the demand and supply sides. The demand for food, according to Engel's law, increases with rising per capita incomes, but at a slower rate; the income elasticity of food demand is less than one. This implies that the agricultural sector will grow more slowly than the economy as a whole. The service sector, by way of contrast, produces 'superior' goods; their income elasticity of demand exceeds one. As income per capita rises, the service sector will grow faster than the economy as a whole.

On the supply side, differential productivity growth drives structural change. Goods and services experiencing more rapid productivity growth generally become cheaper. How differential productivity growth affects sectoral size depends on the interaction of demand and supply. If demand is highly responsive to price, then the sector will grow with technological progress. If demand is relatively unresponsive to price (and again, agriculture is a leading example), then the quantity demanded will not experience much growth, even as technology progresses. The sector will release labour and other resources.

The differences between the labour force shares and the income shares in the panels of Figure 1.4 help to tell the story of the sectoral shift. The

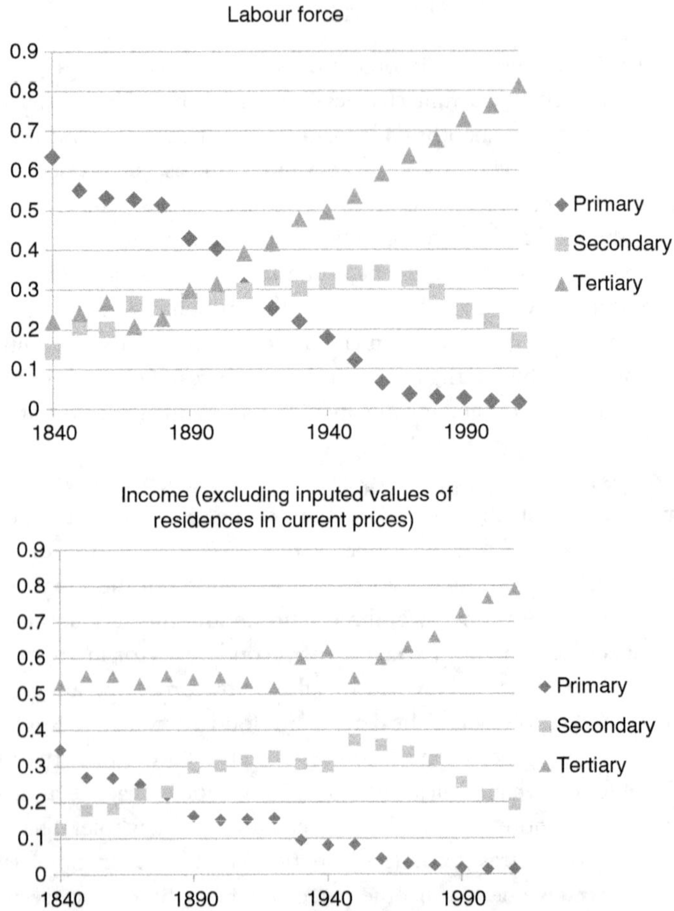

Figure 1.4 Sectoral composition of the US labour force and income
Sources: Income, 1840–1900: Gallman 1986; 1910 interpolated; 1920: Kuznets 1937, table 1.3; 1930–2000: Carter et al. 2006, series Ca38–Ca53; 2010: US Department of Commerce, Bureau of Economic Analysis, National Income and Product Accounts, value added by industry.
Labour force, 1840–1900 (1930): Carter et al. 2006, series Ba 814–30; 1910–90 (with 1930 interpolated): Carter et al. 2006, series Ba 652–59; 2000 and 2010: US Bureau of Labor Statistics, 'Employment and Earnings Online', January 2011 issue, published March 2011, www.bls.gov/opub/ee/home.htm and www.bls.gov/cps/home.htm (both accessed 29 September 2020), table 619.

differences reflect differences in sectoral income per worker. In 1840, the primary sector (that is, principally the agricultural sector) made up almost two-thirds of the labour force but accounted for only a little more than one-third of income. This implies that income in the primary sector was only about one-half as large as income outside the primary sector, while the labour force was nearly twice as large. So income per worker in the primary sector was much smaller than income per worker outside of the primary sector. The classic name for the associated income disparity is the 'development gap'. The gap was substantial in 1840, with income per worker in the primary sector about 34 per cent of income per worker outside of it. And the development gap grew over the nineteenth century, with the ratio reaching about 28 per cent in 1890 and 1900. Given this large disparity, it is not surprising that the labour force share in the primary sector was declining. As the primary sector grew smaller, the development gap closed. By 2010, income per worker in the primary sector was essentially equal to income per worker outside of it. In other words, its income and labour force shares were essentially the same.[6]

In Figure 1.4, the drama is the rise and then fall in the importance of the secondary sector, following an inverted-U pattern. This is a story of industrialization and then deindustrialization.

Manufacturing

Expansion of the manufacturing sector is typically considered the main driver of modern economic growth. Between 1800 and 1970, industrial activity generally expanded faster than the economy as a whole. As a result, this sector grew to account for sizeable shares of output, employment, and trade. Manufacturing activities generally experienced faster rates of productivity growth than the economy as a whole, and its labourers were often paid higher incomes. Manufacturing also contributed materiel and technology for military purposes. For these reasons, policymakers and the public have long viewed manufacturing as having greater importance than other activities.

Manufacturing attracts attention for another reason as well. Manufacturing outputs are tangible goods that are relatively easy to measure. Production takes place in commercial firms using reproducible capital (structures, equipment, and goods in process), which, again, is relatively easy to measure. Production requires labour, often hired on an hourly (or daily) basis. Again, this input is relatively easy to measure and its compensation can be readily distinguished from that of property income. Manufacturing activity fits well

6 Jones (2016) offers a current macro-growth perspective linking structural change to misallocation.

with how economists model the production function and measure inputs and outputs. It is hardly surprising that national income accounting arose in a period when manufacturing was a core economic activity.

It is common to use the term 'Industrial Revolution' for three major periods. The first (1810–60) witnessed the development of many machines, new modes of power, and the rise of the factory. The second (1870–1920) was focused on the electrical, chemical, and automotive industries; the third (1970–present) is centred on information technology (IT). Table 1.2 highlights the timing and key differences between the First, Second, and Third Industrial Revolutions.

The First Industrial Revolution took place in the United States roughly between 1810 and 1860, one generation after it occurred in Great Britain. This epochal period saw the mechanization of textile production, the application of fossil fuels to the metal industries, and the advent of the factory system (Freeman 2018). Early manufacturing growth in the United States largely involved imitating the techniques and practices from Great Britain. American manufacturers copied the British in (a) their substitution of machinery for handicraft skills, in activities such as textiles; (b) the widespread application of inanimate power sources (waterwheels and steam engines); and (c) the mass utilization of cheap materials, especially iron made using coked coal. In these activities, Americans generally followed the British with a lag of one or more generations. In many cases, Americans copied selectively, adopting specific techniques better suited to the nation's distinctive resource endowment and product markets. In a handful of cases, Americans created technologies in place of the British or made important advances on top of what the British had accomplished (Lee and Rhode 2018).

The Second Industrial Revolution occurred between 1870 and 1920 simultaneously in the United States, Britain, and other countries on the European continent (Mokyr 1990). It saw the creation of entirely new sectors, such as electricity, and the rapid expansion of previously insignificant sectors, such as chemicals. These sectors' growth accelerated as movement towards a higher capital–labour ratio and greater scale accelerated. It is tempting to think that the rise in the economy-wide capital–output ratio in the United States over the late nineteenth century was solely the product of the Second Industrial Revolution. But as noted above, the reality was somewhat more complicated. (The rise of the capital–output ratio means, obviously, but not in a way that leaps to one's mind, that the average productivity of capital is falling.)

The Second Industrial Revolution also witnessed important changes in business organization, as the pursuit of the economies of scale and scope gave

Table 1.2 The three Industrial Revolutions

	First	Second	Third
Timing	UK 1780–1830; US 1810–60	1870–1920	1970–
Technological base	Tinkering	Engineering	Formal science
Products	Iron	Steel, electrical machinery	Integrated circuits
	Textiles	Chemicals, automobiles	Computers, mobile phones
Power	Steam engine	Electric dynamo Internal combustion engine	Lithium battery
Newly cheap inputs	Cotton	Steel, coal	Information
	Coal, iron	Petroleum	Silicon chips
Organization	Factory	Modern business enterprise	Global supply chain
	Family firm	Clerical sector	
Finance	Kinship networks Retained earnings	Investment banks Equity markets	Venture capital IPOs

Table 1.3 Agricultural changes in the nineteenth and twentieth centuries

	First-wave evolution	Second-wave 'Green Revolution'
Timing	US 1870–1914	1935–
Growth regime	Extensive settlement	Labour release
Mechanization	Grain harvest	Previously hand-picked crops
Power	Draft animals	IC engine, electricity
Biological innovation	Adapt crops to new lands; resist pests	Scientific crop improvement
	Breed specialized animals	Intensified animal breeding
Inputs	Farm-raised, including labour	Purchased seed, chemicals, fuel
Role of government	Territorial expansion; research system	Farm programmes; IP protection

rise to the modern business enterprise (MBE). Chandler (1977; 1990) narrates the long evolution in this new business form. As transportation and communication costs fell, a large national market emerged in North America. Over the same time, technologies allowing high-volume production, either in large batch or continuous process, appeared. These two forces created a new competitive environment that hastened the marriage of mass production and mass distribution. Distributers retained power in the traditional industries, while mass producers discovered reasons to coordinate the whole flow from production to distribution themselves in new, more capital-intensive industries. Producers of perishable goods (dressed meat), sophisticated goods that required after-sale contact (the sewing machine), and high-volume goods (tobacco, soap, canning) all found advantages in setting up the distribution networks suitable to their own products. The pursuit of higher 'throughput' (fuller capacity utilization) drove greater integration of production. Vertical integration assured input supplies and output markets, cut transactions costs, and reduced hold-ups in cases of asset specificity. Greater optimal size of production facilitated horizontal integration to realize the economies of scale. The twentieth century witnessed the rise of the multidivisional form of business organization.[7] See Figure 1.5 for the growth of shares of employment and value added of Chandler's industries.[8]

An epochal technological development at the end of the Second Industrial Revolution was the birth of the moving assembly line. David Nye (2013) observes that a manufacturing process that 'looks like an assembly line' can be found as early as in the 1880s in meat slaughtering. However, Henry Ford's assembly line of 1913 was special because of its accomplishments: the subdivision of labour, interchangeable parts, and single-purpose machines, the sequential ordering of machines, and the movement of work to worker by

7 In the early twentieth century, large US corporations began to adopt the multidivisional form (M-form), creating semi-autonomous divisions within the larger organization (Chandler 1962). Du Pont, General Motors, and Standard Oil were pioneers in developing the more decentralized system of management in place of the prior centralized unitary form (U-form). The M-form allowed operating units to focus on short-term decisions about the making and marketing of diverse products, while the headquarters pursued a unified long-term investment strategy and exercised common financial controls. By the 1960s, the M-form came to dominate large complex corporations in the US.

8 Chandler (1990) expands his analytical frame to investigate the rise of giant corporations in Britain and Germany, as well as the US. In Britain, the owner family continued to manage operations personally, maintaining traditional practices, reinvesting through retained earnings, and as a result, growing more slowly than their American counterparts. In Germany, investment bankers played a larger role in management, especially in the machinery, steel, chemical, and electrical sectors. The legal structure, most notably the absence of anti-trust laws, allowed cartelization. MBE spread more slowly in Britain than in Germany, and even more slowly than in the US. Critics of Chandler point to other differences, including the European expertise in craft labour, to explain the divergent paths and, indeed, to question Chandler's privileging MBE as the single best way to manage industrial production.

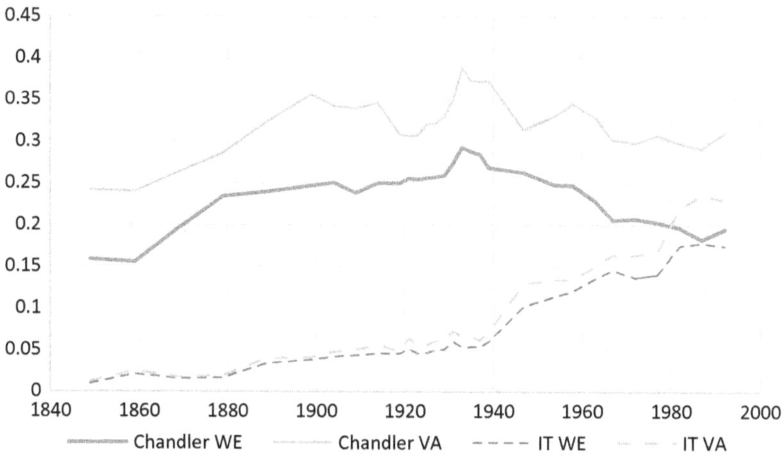

Figure 1.5 Employment (WE) and production shares (VA) of the 'Chandler' and IT industries
Source: Lee and Rhode 2018: 204.

belts and slides. Most of all, Ford's assembly line successfully combined all these in a systematic way. The introduction of the moving assembly line was the culmination of a century-long process leading to the adoption of mass production.

Electric power became the most important power source, letting businesses more easily locate production closer to markets for workers or consumers, rather than close to access to cheap coal. Electrification also improved productivity of plants, by providing illumination and allowing greater flexibility in redesigning factory floors to take advantage of straight-line production principles. Electricity is a leading example of a general-purpose technology (GPT) à la Bresnahan and Trajtenberg (1995). It was pervasive, affecting most sectors in the economy; it had scope for improvement, and spawned numerous complementary innovations. But it required time for its impact to be fully realized. Paul David (1990) pointed out that the faster growth of total factor productivity in the 1920s had not 'exhausted the full productivity ramifications of the dynamo revolution'. It took time for more plants to adjust the production designs to fully realize the potential of electric power in the 1930s.

There has been an active debate about the timing and sources of productivity growth in US manufacturing over the late nineteenth and early twentieth centuries, and whether the growth was driven by general/global forces or by localized/specific forces, whether it fits Harberger's yeast-like growth or mushroom-like growth. Paul David and Gavin Wright (2003) argue that the immediate post-World War I period witnessed rapid, broadly based productivity advances associated with the adoption of electricity as a GPT and of high-wage labour practices. Alexander Field (2011) finds the 'most technologically progressive' decade was the 1930s, not the 1920s. He argues that productivity advances in the 1930s were exceptionally rapid and extended more broadly than the David-Wright analysis of manufacturing suggests. Vaclav Smil (2005; 2006) views the interwar period as reaping the benefits of key innovations made a generation before, between 1870 and 1914. Robert Gordon (2016) sees a never-to-be-repeated 'golden age' arising from the combination of these innovations in transportation, electricity, communications, sanitation, and medicine.

The years between 1920 and 1970 – although punctuated by the Great Depression and World War II – are often considered the period of 'normalcy'. This was the period when the concept of GDP was defined, when manufacturing 'dominated' the US economy, and when hired employment was the standard labour system. This is the period when Kaldor's great macro constants – the saving rate, capital–output ratio, capital's share of income, and real interest rate – can legitimately be treated as constants. It also contains the high points in American economic leadership, as the nation was transformed from an isolationist, almost autarkic, and militarily weak country into a global superpower. The change involved not merely the expansion of US manufacturing capability, but also the rise of its financial, scientific, and military strength.

The period after 1970 witnessed a slowing of total factor productivity growth (see Table 1.1 above), real wage stagnation, deindustrialization, increasing globalization in both input and output markets, and, with some lags, rising income inequality. The period saw US economic leadership challenged by a series of rivals, who rose and then faded (the European Union, then Japan, and then China). Within North America, the geographic location of economic activity has also shifted from the industrial core of the Northeast and Midwest to the Pacific Coast and other parts of the Sun Belt. A subsidiary theme is the opening of economic opportunities for women and minorities, and the closing of opportunities for economic mobility.

The Third Industrial Revolution, tied to IT, began in the 1970s and continues today. Since 1970, the cost of automated information processing has fallen by a factor of over 1,000 (Nordhaus 2007). The driving force is captured by Moore's law, which asserts that the computing performance (available at a given cost) doubles every eighteen to twenty-four months. The

Third Industrial Revolution is linked to the globalization of production and deindustrialization in the traditional manufacturing heartland. The IT sector commonly refers to computers and telecommunication devices that are used to collect, analyse, and disseminate information (Porat 1977). See Figure 1.5 for the growth of the share of employment and value added of the IT industries. The fall in costs has been so rapid that whether one uses current or constant prices affects how one views the 'deindustrialization' process. The share of the secondary sector has fallen since 1970 if viewed in current prices, as in Figure 1.4, Income panel. The share has remained relatively stable if constant (pre-IT revolution) prices are used. The recent epoch has been associated with rising income inequality, as demonstrated by Figure 1.6, which graphs the share of total income accruing to the top 1 per cent of US income earners. By the beginning of the twenty-first century, the share was nearly twice the level of the middle of the previous century. It was nearly equal to the level at the beginning of the twentieth century, at the height of the Second Industrial Revolution. IT's revolutionary effects are ongoing, however; their analysis is best left to future economic historians.

Agriculture

In the pursuit of 'modern economic growth', agriculture is often considered a problematic sector. As noted above, Engel's law, operating within a closed economy, implies that demand for the sector's products will grow more slowly than per capita income. Opening up the economy to foreign trade can help provide a 'vent for surplus' and create greater growth opportunities than is suggested in the discussion above. But trade also has its problems. The domestic agricultural sector becomes subject to the vagaries of foreign markets – adverse net demand shocks due to wars, trade conflicts, and bumper crops in distant lands. (In a closed market, a poor crop year might yield higher domestic prices, providing some income insurance to farmers. In an open global market, the offsetting price response is dissipated and the insurance function is lost.) In addition, over the long run, Engel's law applies to world demand as well, leading to adverse movements in the terms of trade for primary products.

One notable feature of American economic development over the nineteenth and early twentieth centuries is that the agricultural sector continued to expand even as the country industrialized. Although the agricultural sector experienced a relative decline, the number of farms, agricultural labour force, and farm population continued to grow in absolute terms into the early twentieth century

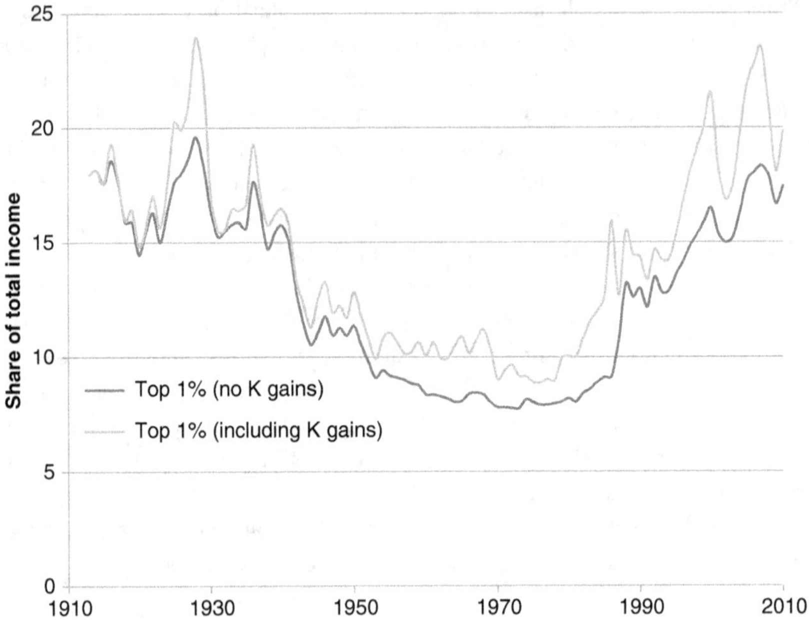

Figure 1.6 Share of total income accruing to top 1 per cent of US income earners, 1913–2010
Source: Piketty and Saez 2003, as updated.

(see Figure 1.7). The agricultural labour force increased from 4.5 million in 1850 to 11.8 million in 1910 (Lebergott 1966: 118). Much of the build-up of the capital stock that Gallman chronicled was devoted to bringing new land into cultivation. (The stock of farm land rose even faster than the agricultural labour force; increasing from 294 million acres in 1850 to 881 million in 1910.) The combination of agricultural expansion and rapid industrialization was a rarity in countries experiencing modern economic growth.

In countries where a peasantry dominates the agricultural sector, technological conservatism can slow the adoption of new production methods. Indeed, the expectation of weak adoption can diminish investment in the innovation activity directed to developing new seeds, animal breeds, and agricultural implements. Such concerns have been much less pressing in North America, where commercialized (though family-based) farms have dominated the landscape. Rapid technological changes, including biological innovation and mechanization, have allowed a smaller number of farmers to feed a growing population, in North America and around the world. See Table 1.3 on major changes in American agriculture over the period 1870 to 2010.

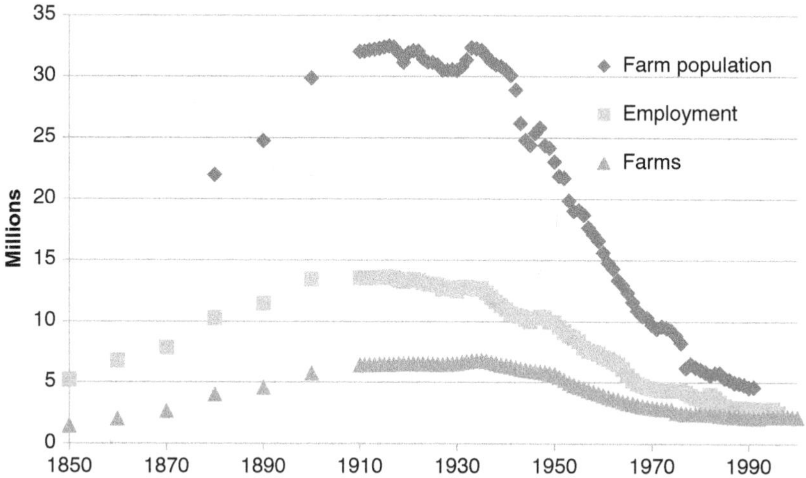

Figure 1.7 Farm population, employment, and number of operating units
Sources: Carter et al. 2006: Da 1, Da 4, Da 14, Da 16, Da 612; with employment linked to Lebergott 1966: 118.

Mechanization in American agriculture has classically been viewed as the application of machinery and non-human power sources to allow one worker to cultivate more land. Biological innovation has been viewed as the application of improved seeds and fertilizer to increase land yields. The two processes are typically viewed as separate and independent. Mechanization is often given priority as a driver of productivity growth, at least until the so-called 'Green Revolution' of the 1930s and 1940s, when US farmers began to adopt hybrid maize seeds, nitrogen-based fertilizers, and pesticides/herbicides.

This traditional view misses the crucial role of earlier biological innovations in adapting plants and animals to the new-settled lands on the American frontier, and in combating emergent productivity-sapping pests and diseases. This said, it is clear that the direction of change shifted in the mid-twentieth century – expansion onto new lands slowed dramatically; the US farm sector began to release labour more quickly; and those remaining in the sector became increasingly reliant on purchased inputs, produced by the machinery and chemical industries. These technological innovations and associated structural changes, especially when exported to developing countries around the world, were given the name 'Green Revolution' (see Olmstead and Rhode 2008). Within North America, the agricultural sector became among the most technologically advanced sectors of the economy.

Services

Much as the first phase of the Industrial Revolution was, in reality, the decline of the relative importance of the agricultural sector, much of the process of 'deindustrialization' in the late twentieth century was, in reality, the rise of the service sector (see Broadberry 2006). The service sector combines a wide array of activities, from the very traditional – haircuts and domestic services – to the very modern – software programming and genetic sequencing. The sector is often defined by what it is not – that is, not the production of physical commodities. Historical treatments of the service sector have to take account of its great heterogeneity. Some parts, such as the provision of medical services, have expanded greatly, while others, such as the provision of domestic services, have contracted.

Circa 1870, there were roughly a million domestic servants, 7.7 per cent of the labour force, in the United States. It was the leading source of paid employment for women. There were about six times as many domestic servants as school teachers (Lebergott 1966: 118–119). Employment of domestic servants continued to climb in absolute terms, with some oscillations, over the next ninety years. The number reached about 2.5 million in 1960. But the sector share of the labour force dropped by half, to about 3.4 per cent in that year. The adoption of household appliances cut into demand. Even with the reopening of immigration – a key source of supply for domestic workers – and an increase in income inequality, the domestic service sector in the United States continues to decline in relative terms. Circa 2010, there were about 600,000–700,000 domestic servants in America.

Productivity is often thought to grow more slowly in the service sector than in the commodity-producing sectors. This phenomenon is known as Baumol's cost disease. Cutting hair takes about the same time today as it did a century ago; technology has advanced, but not nearly as rapidly as in harvesting grain, printing books, or other forms of commodity production. This said, part of Baumol's cost disease is real and part is not; that part reflects the difficulties in measuring the quantity and quality of services provided. For many services, such as governmental activities, output is measured by the inputs used in production, which inherently limits measured productivity change. Prices in the service sector have tended to rise relative to prices in the commodity-producing sector. This means the service sector's share of output in current-price terms (as in Figure 1.4) rises faster than its share in constant-price terms.

One key long-run process in the US context is what Stephen Broadberry calls the 'industrialization' of services. This process involved: 'the transition from customized, low-volume, high-margin business organized on the basis of networks to a standardized, high-volume, low-margin business with hierarchical management' (Broadberry 2006: 2). The 'industrialization' of services was associated with the birth of the 'modern office' and the rise of the clerical sector.[9] Table 1.4 charts the rise of the clerical labour force in the United States, from fewer than 1 million workers in 1900, or about 4 per cent of the civilian labour force, to over 14 million by 1970, about 18 per cent. As Claudia Goldin (1990) has noted, this sector's growth was associated disproportionally with an expansion of the employment of women.

In many ways, the 'industrialization' of services was a continuation of Chandler's narrative about the rise of modern business enterprise. Chandler (1965) treated railroads, which are part of the service sector, as 'America's first big business'. The rise of hierarchical professional management and the corporate form in this segment of the transportation sector preceded and provided a model and, in some cases, the personnel for the changes in manufacturing associated with the Second Industrial Revolution. Labour productivity in US railroads more than doubled between 1870 and 1910, growing over 2 per cent per annum. Capital productivity increased, at the slightly slower rate of 1.5 per cent per annum, as railroad traffic managers learned to achieve higher rates of capacity utilization in this high-fixed-cost sector (Fishlow 1966: 626; Broadberry 2006: 167). Chandler (1977) also viewed vertical integration as the marriage of mass production and mass distribution. Mass retailers such as Sears, Roebuck and Co. integrated backwards into the production chain to secure the quality and quantities of consumer goods required (see also Field 1996).

Structural changes are often disruptive and challenge previously held beliefs about the normal order of things. The shift away from agriculture in the late nineteenth century led to the populist response. Apart from episodic negative shocks, American farmers (outside the South, at least) did not experience economic distress in absolute terms. They did fare poorly relative to their previous expectations and relative to other participants in the economy. They suffered from status anxiety, engaged in conspiratorial thinking, and lashed out at the representatives of the globalizing forces

9 The rise of the clerical sector was associated with increased efforts to monitor and manage transactions costs. In their pioneering effort to measure the 'transaction sector', John Wallis and Donald North (1986) found that the share of the US labour force devoted to managing such costs rose from around 25 per cent in 1870 to 40 per cent in 1970. The private and public sectors contributed roughly equally to the change.

Table 1.4 The rise of the clerical sector

	Number of clerical workers (millions)		Share of civilian labour force (%)		Female share of labour force (%)		Female clerical
	Total	Female	Total	Female	Total	Clerical	Ratio
1900	1.1	0.2	3.8	4.3	18.7	21.0	1.13
1910	1.9	0.7	7.4	8.8	28.8	34.4	1.21
1920	3.3	1.6	8.1	19.4	20.4	48.7	2.72
1940	4.9	2.5	10.3	21.6	24.6	51.2	2.38
1950	7.1	4.4	12.5	28.0	27.9	62.2	2.71
1960	9.2	6.2	14.4	29.8	32.8	67.8	2.52
1970	13.9	10.1	17.9	35.0	38.0	74.1	2.46
1980	18.7	14.6	19.2	35.0	42.3	78.0	2.27

Note: The female clerical ratio is the share of females in the clerical sector divided by the share of females in the non-clerical sector (Total minus Clerical).
Source: Carter et al. 2006: Ba 1033, Ba 1038, Ba 1061, Ba 1066.

they were facing. The shift away from manufacturing towards services in recent times has produced similar responses.

American Leadership

It was during the late nineteenth and early twentieth centuries, in the period of the Second Industrial Revolution, when the United States accelerated past the United Kingdom into a position of global economic and technological leadership. The standard measure of economic performance is income per person. Figure 1.8 graphs GDP per capita in real 1990 purchasing power for the United States, the United Kingdom, and twelve western European countries (including the UK) from 1870 to the present. The figure uses data from the pioneering cross-country comparisons of Angus Maddison (focusing on times and places where the data are solid rather than speculative). Figure 1.8 shows the United States departing from the western European pack in the 1870s and passing the United Kingdom in 1905. The United States continued to grow between 1913 and 1947, during a period when western Europe was mired in repeated wars and economic conflict. The post-war (1947–73) miracle allowed western Europe to resume per capita income growth and to catch up in relative terms. Nonetheless, there remains an absolute income gap of about $8,000–$9,000 per person.

It is tempting to attribute US leadership to the effects of the Second Industrial Revolution on the relative performance of the American

Table 1.5 Relative productivity performance and leadership

	UK/US labour productivity			US = 100
	Agriculture	Industry	Services	Total
1870	115.1	65.1	116.4	111.4
1890	97.9	60.9	118.8	106.3
1910	96.9	51.8	93.1	85.0
1920	78.1	50.5	84.1	75.0
1929	91.2	43.9	82.6	71.7
1937	96.8	52.5	83.3	75.4
1950	79.4	41.1	71.0	59.9
1963	76.2	46.6	72.8	65.7
1990	66.2	61.3	77.2	75.2

Source: Broadberry 2006: 20.

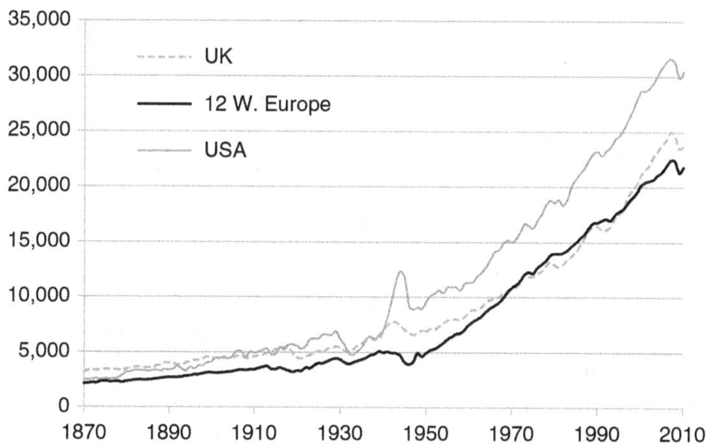

Figure 1.8 GDP per capita, 1870–2010, US, UK, and western Europe
Sources: Maddison Project Database, version 2013.

manufacturing sector. But as Broadberry (1997) has convincingly argued, the picture is more complex. Table 1.5 displays his main data, converted onto an American standard. In the manufacturing sector, workers in the United States had long been about twice as productive as their British and German counterparts. The gap predated the Second Industrial Revolution, though it widened somewhat over this period.

The emergence of the United States as the income leader was due to: (a) the transition of labour out of agriculture where the productivity of US workers typically just matched that of their UK counterparts;[10] and (b) more importantly, the relatively more rapid growth of productivity of workers in the US service sector. Changes in the relative productivity of US workers in the service sector mirrored the changes overall. As we have seen, the forces associated with the rise of the modern business enterprise helped to drive these changes. But clearly, more research to understand the evolution of the US service sector is desirable.

Conclusion

This chapter has traced several grand transformations of the North American economy. The first process – the shift from a rural agricultural economy to an urban industrial economy and the emergence of 'modern economic growth' – began before 1870. The second process – the shift from growth based on increasing factors of production (physical capital, land, hours of work) per person to growth based on enhancing the productivity of the factors – began in the decades immediately before and after 1900. It was tied to the assumption of the United States as a global economic leader. The third process – the shift from an internally focused industrial economy to a globally integrated, information-based economy began after 1970 and is ongoing. Focusing on these transformations complicates the story of balanced growth common in macro-growth accounts, but is crucial for enriching our understanding of the evolution of the US economy.

The chapter defines the Second Industrial Revolution, contrasting it with the First Industrial Revolution and the Third Industrial Revolution. The First Industrial Revolution took place in North America roughly between 1810 and 1860, one generation after it occurred in Great Britain. The Second Industrial Revolution occurred between 1870 and 1920, simultaneously in the United States, Britain, and other countries on the European continent. It saw advances associated with chemicals, electrical equipment, and the internal combustion engine. It also witnessed important changes in business organization, as the pursuit of economies of scale and scope gave rise to the modern business enterprise. This chapter has investigated how these changes helped to propel the United States to become the global economic leader.

10 In the 'Green Revolution' period, and especially after 1960, agricultural labour productivity in the US climbed past that in the UK. But the shares of the labour force in the sector were too small for the emerging differential to have much effect on the aggregates.

This chapter has focused on the proximate causes of the US rise to economic and technological leadership. Examining the fundamental causes is a deeper issue, one that other chapters in this volume help to address. It is also crucial to attend to all of the destructive forces – wars, colonialism, and oppression – that inhibited economic growth in many parts of the world.

References

Abramovitz, M. and David, P. A. (1973). 'Reinterpreting Economic Growth: Parables and Realities', *American Economic Review, Papers and Proceedings* 63, 428–439.

(2001). 'Two Centuries of American Macroeconomic Growth from Exploitation of Resource Abundance to Knowledge-Driven Development', Stanford Institute of Economic Research working paper 01–005.

Boustan, L. P., Frydman, C., and Margo, R. A. (eds.) (2014). *Human Capital in History: The American Record*, University of Chicago Press.

Bresnahan, T. F. and Trajtenberg, M. (1995). 'General Purpose Technologies "Engines of Growth"?', *Journal of Econometrics* 65(1), 83–108.

Broadberry, S. N. (1997). *The Productivity Race: British Manufacturing in International Perspective, 1850–1990*, Cambridge University Press.

(2006). *Market Services and the Productivity Race, 1850–2000*, Cambridge University Press.

Carter, S. et al. (2006). *Historical Statistics of the United States, Millennial Edition*, New York: Cambridge University Press.

Chandler, A. D., Jr. (1962). *Strategy and Structure: Chapters in the History of American Industrial Enterprise*, Cambridge, MA: MIT Press.

(1965). *The Railroads: The Nation's First Big Business*, New York: Harcourt, Brace & World.

(1977). *The Visible Hand: The Managerial Revolution in American Business*, Cambridge, MA: Belknap Press.

(1990). *Scale and Scope: The Dynamics of Industrial Capitalism*, Cambridge, MA: Harvard University Press.

David, P. A. (1990). 'The Dynamo and the Computer: An Historical Perspective on the Modern Productivity Paradox', *American Economic Review, Papers and Proceedings*, 80, 355–361.

David, P. A. and Wright, G. (2003). 'General Purpose Technologies and Surges in Productivity: Historical Reflections on the Future of the ICT Revolution', in David, P. and Thomas, M. (eds.), *The Economic Future in Historical Perspective*, New York: Oxford University Press, 135–166.

Davis, L. E. and Gallman, R. E. (1978). 'Capital Formation in the United States during the Nineteenth Century', in Mathias, P. and Postan, M. M. (eds.), *Cambridge Economic History of Europe, Vol. 7: The Industrial Economies: Capital, Labour and Enterprise, Pt 2: The United States, Japan and Russia*, New York: Cambridge University Press, 1–69.

Field, A. J. (1996). 'The Relative Productivity of American Distribution, 1869–1992', *Research in Economic History*, 16, 1–37.

(2011). *A Great Leap Forward: 1930s Depression and US Economic Growth*, New Haven: Yale University Press.

Fishlow, A. (1966). 'Productivity and Technological Change in the Railroad Sector, 1840–1910', in Brady, D. S. (ed.), *Output, Employment, and Productivity in the United States after 1800*, Studies in Income and Wealth, Vol. 30, New York: Columbia University Press, 583–647.

Freeman, J. B. (2018). *Behemoth: A History of the Factory and the Making of the Modern World*, New York: W. W. Norton.

Gallman, R. E. (1986). 'The United States Capital Stock in the Nineteenth Century', in Engerman, S. and Gallman, R. E. (eds.), *Long-Term Factors in American Economic Growth*, University of Chicago Press, 185–206.

(1992). 'American Economic Growth before the Civil War: The Testimony of the Capital Stock Estimates', in Gallman, R. E. and Wallis, J. J. (eds.), *American Economic Growth and Standard of Living before the Civil War*, University of Chicago Press, 79–90.

Gallman, R. E. and Rhode, P. W. (2019). *Capital in the Nineteenth Century*, University of Chicago Press.

Goldin, C. (1990). *Understanding the Gender Gap: An Economic History of American Women*, University of Chicago Press.

(2001). 'The Human-Capital Century and American Leadership: Virtues of the Past,' *Journal of Economic History*, 61(2), 263–293.

Goldin, C. and Katz, L. F. (2008). *The Race between Education and Technology*, Cambridge, MA: Harvard University Press.

Gordon, R. J. (2016). *The Rise and Fall of American Growth: The US Standard of Living since the Civil War*, Princeton University Press.

Harberger, A. (1998). 'A Vision of the Growth Process', *American Economic Review*, 88 (1), 1–32.

Jones, C. I. (2016). 'The Facts of Economic Growth', *Handbook of Macroeconomics*, 2A, 3–69.

Kaldor, N. (1957). 'A Model of Economic Growth', *Economic Journal*, 67(268), 591–624.

(1961). 'Capital Accumulation and Economic Growth', in Lutz, L. A. and Hague, D. C. (eds.), *The Theory of Capital*, New York: St Martin's Press, 177–222.

Kendrick, J. W. (assisted by M. R. Pech) (1961). *Productivity Trends in the United States*, Princeton University Press for the NBER.

Kuznets, S. (1937). *National Income and Capital Formation, 1919–1935*, New York: NBER.

(assisted by E. Jenks) (1961). *Capital in the American Economy: Its Formation and Financing*, Princeton University Press for the NBER.

(1964). 'Notes on the Patterns of US Economic Growth', in Edwards, E. O. (ed.), *The Nation's Economic Objectives*, University of Chicago Press.

Lebergott, S. (1966). 'Labor Force and Employment, 1800–1960', in Brady, D. S. (ed.), *Output, Employment, and Productivity in the United States after 1800*, Studies in Income and Wealth, Vol. 30, New York: Columbia University Press, 117–204.

Lee, C. and Rhode, P. W. (2018). 'Manufacturing Growth and Structural Change in American Economic History', in Cain, L. P., Fishback, P. V., and Rhode, P. W. (eds.), *Oxford Handbook of American Economic History*, New York: Oxford University Press, 183–212.

Maddison Project Database, version 2013. Bolt, J. and van Zanden, J. L. (2014). 'The Maddison Project: Collaborative Research on Historical National Accounts', *Economic History Review* 67(3), 627–651.

Mokyr, J. (1990). *The Lever of Riches: Technological Creativity and Economic Progress*, New York: Oxford University Press.

Nordhaus, W. D. (2007). 'Two Centuries of Productivity Growth in Computing', *Journal of Economic History*, 67(1), 128–159.

Nye, D. E. (2013). *America's Assembly Line*, Cambridge, MA: MIT Press.

Olmstead, A. L. and Rhode, P. W. (2008). *Creating Abundance: Biological Innovation and American Agricultural Development*, New York: Cambridge University Press.

Piketty, T. (2014). *Capital in the Twenty-First Century* (trans. Arthur Goldhammer), Cambridge, MA: Harvard University Press.

Piketty, T. and Saez, E. (2003). 'Income Inequality in the United States, 1913–1998', *Quarterly Journal of Economics*, 118, 1–39.

Piketty, T. and Zucman, G. (2014). 'Capital Is Back: Wealth–Income Ratios in Rich Countries, 1700–2010', *Quarterly Journal of Economics*, 129, 1255–1310.

Porat, M. U. (1977). *The Information Economy: Sources and Methods for Measuring the Primary Information Sector*, OT Special Publication, 77-12(1), US Department of Commerce, Office of Telecommunications.

Smil, V. (2005). *Creating the Twentieth Century: Technical Innovations of 1867–1914 and their Lasting Impact*, New York: Oxford University Press.

(2006). *Transforming the Twentieth Century: Technical Innovations and their Consequences*, New York: Oxford University Press.

US Department of Commerce, Bureau of Economic Analysis. Gross Domestic Product and Fixed Assets Accounts, www.bea.gov/ (accessed 29 September 2020).

Wallis, J. J. and North, D. (1986). 'Measuring the Transaction Sector in the American Economy, 1870–1970', in Engerman, S. and Gallman, R. E. (eds.), *Long-Term Factors in American Economic Growth*, University of Chicago Press, 95–162.

Wright, G. (2018). 'Natural Resources in American Economic History', in Cain, L. P., Fishback, P. V., and Rhode, P. W. (eds.), *Oxford Handbook of American Economic History*, New York: Oxford University Press, 425–442.

2

Western Europe

Convergence and Divergence

PAUL SHARP

Introduction

The economic history of western Europe from 1870 is of course connected to the economic history of the rest of the world, as described in the other chapters of this volume. This is partly through formal political control, but also in terms of other forms of economic contact. The extent of this integration has fluctuated over time, however. These periods of greater or lesser integration have also been related to periods when western Europe has either diverged from or converged with other world regions. At the same time, western Europe has also seen divergence and convergence among its constituent countries, and the extent of this is explored in this chapter, with some reference to the substantial literature which explains both individual country experiences and comparative studies.

The above, as well as the theoretical connection between economic convergence and openness that we will explore below, motivates the division of the economic history of Europe after 1870 into three periods. The first is before World War I, a period of exceptional economic integration known as the first era of globalization, as well as one in which Europe enjoyed a position as the leading centre of economic and political power and influence. Economies grew, late industrializers caught up with early industrializers, and many Europeans became both healthier and better educated. This period also marked the high point of monetary and capital market integration, as most western European countries (and of course others outside Europe) maintained a peg to the Gold Standard. The second period begins and ends with the tragedies of World Wars I and II, and also witnesses the beginning of the gradual eclipse of Europe by the emerging superpower of the United States. A combination of war, politics, and economic policy, particularly protectionism, conspired to erase much of the economic integration of the previous decades, and the Gold Standard became more and more unsustainable. Even before the Great Depression of the 1930s brought mass unemployment and the rise of fascism, growth became more volatile and hyperinflation and banking instability impacted on much of the continent. Millions died, although for those who survived there were some economic advances in terms of technological and structural change, as well as education and health. Finally, the period after World War II saw a recognition by policymakers of the failures of the interwar period. Although attempts to maintain a pseudo-Gold Standard, the Bretton Woods dollar-exchange standard, ultimately failed, other international institutions played a role in leading to falling barriers to trade and political cooperation, with the ultimate realization of this being the creation of the European Union, with its single market, common currency, and free mobility of labour. The 1950s to the beginning of the 1970s marked Europe's Golden Age of rapid economic growth and convergence, although the oil crises of the 1970s led to considerable slowdown, and the 2007/8 financial crisis, although considerably less severe than the Great Depression, hit some countries much harder than others, and seems at the time of writing to have ushered in a new period of anti-globalization, although not only for those countries which suffered most. Indeed, it seems to be a truly international phenomenon – not confined only to western Europe.

For each of these periods, this chapter considers the extent of economic convergence or divergence, providing some pointers as to what economic historians have considered to be the reasons for the successes and failures of the western European region as a whole, as well as individual country experiences. However, before we turn to exactly how we are to understand convergence, as well as its connection to openness, it is necessary to consider how we measure it. The convergence considered in this chapter is that between the living standards of individual countries, and in particular between levels of GDP per capita. Broader measures of welfare, such as the United Nations' Human Development Index (a weighted average of measures of health and education, as well as income), are therefore not considered. Neither does this chapter speak to the growing literature on regional convergence, notwithstanding the important recent work on this (see Rosés and Wolf 2018). The data used are those provided by the recent updates of the Maddison Project Database, version 2013 (Bolt et al. 2018), which give a unit of analysis based on modern country borders and define western Europe as the following sixteen countries: Austria, Belgium, Denmark, Finland, France, Germany, Italy, the Netherlands, Norway, Sweden, Switzerland, the UK, Ireland, Greece, Portugal, and Spain. Note that this implies some differences in the conclusions regarding convergence compared to other related studies which consider Europe as a whole (i.e. including eastern Europe), and which are based on the original Maddison data set (Maddison 2003); see, for example, Carreras and Josephson 2010; Crafts and Toniolo 2010; Rosés and Wolf 2010; and Persson and Sharp 2015.

The remainder of this chapter is structured as follows. The next section explains why convergence is predicted by economic theory, and provides some empirical evidence for the whole period 1870–2016. This is followed by three sections presenting the periods from 1870 until World War I, the interwar period, and the post-World War II period, before a final section offers some conclusions.

What Is Economic Convergence, and How Do We Measure It?

Economic convergence implies that initially poor countries should grow faster than richer countries. Thus, the early industrializers such as the United Kingdom should grow slower than late industrializers in southern Europe, for example. If this is the case, so-called 'unconditional convergence' would imply that all countries should eventually enjoy the same GDP per capita. We start by examining this by looking at the entire 1870–2016 period. Table 2.1 ranks countries by their income per capita in 1870, and presents a simple way of looking at whether there has been convergence in western Europe over the whole period. GDP per capita for the sixteen countries in our sample is presented for the beginning of the period in 1870, as well as for the end of the period in 2016; 2006 is also illustrated since the 2007/8 financial crisis impacted some countries far more than others, for reasons we will return to briefly below.

Clearly, the economies of all countries expanded massively. Convergence implies that the ranking of countries should not change, however, which is clearly not the case. It also predicts that there should be a compression of the variance in incomes over time, which is indeed the case, although this is not particularly impressive. For example, the poorest country in 1870, Portugal, had an income per head which was just 31 per cent of that of the richest, the UK. By 2006 Portugal was still the poorest country, with an income per head at 51 per cent of the richest, which by this time was Norway. This leads to another interesting point: convergence does not imply that early leaders should be overtaken, but by 2006 the UK was only the fifth richest country, with an income of 87 per cent that of Norway (or 90 per cent of the income in 2016). The southern European countries – Greece, Italy, Portugal, and Spain –

Table 2.1 GDP per capita, GDP per capita as percentage of the richest European country, and GDP per capita ranking for 1870, 2006, and 2016

	1870			2006			2016		
	GDP/ cap	% richest	Rank	GDP/ cap	% richest	Rank	GDP/ cap	% richest	Rank
GBR	3,190	100	1	24,285	87	5	26,517	90	6
CHE	2,876	90	2	24,262	87	6	28,471	97	2
NLD	2,755	86	3	23,867	85	7	26,963	92	3
BEL	2,692	84	4	22,867	82	10	24,253	82	9
DNK	2,003	63	5	24,749	89	3	24,989	85	8
FRA	1,876	59	6	21,842	78	11	23,206	79	12
AUT	1,863	58	7	23,388	84	9	26,779	91	4
DEU	1,839	58	8	20,041	72	12	23,482	80	10
IRL	1,775	56	9	24,989	89	2	25,048	85	7
ITA	1,542	48	10	19,630	70	13	18,759	64	13
NOR	1,360	43	11	27,921	100	1	29,460	100	1
SWE	1,345	42	12	24,602	88	4	26,708	91	5
GRC	1,216	38	13	15,392	55	15	13,350	45	16
ESP	1,207	38	14	17,552	63	14	16,482	56	14
FIN	1,140	36	15	23,434	84	8	23,450	80	11
PRT	9,75	31	16	14,343	51	16	15,472	53	15
USA	2,445	77	(5)	31,358	112	(1)	32,811	111	(1)

Note: All data are in 1990 international $.
Sources: Maddison Project Database, version 2013 for the period up to 2010, updated to 2016 using the Maddison Project Database, version 2018.

were among the poorest countries in 1870, and remained so in 2006 and 2016, with even the richest of them in 1870, Italy, falling from tenth to thirteenth place. The Nordic countries (Finland, Norway, and Sweden), with the exception of Denmark, were also among the poorest in 1870, but had all overtaken the UK by 2006, with the exception of Finland, which had very similar GDP per capita. Germany fell from eighth to twelfth place, France fell from sixth to eleventh place, and the UK fell from first to fifth place. Finland – the second poorest country in 1870 – rose to eighth place. Ireland rose from ninth to second place. Clearly, a general narrowing of incomes took place, but convergence favoured some countries more than others. For comparison, the United States is included in the last line of the table, maintaining its rank as one of the richest countries throughout the period. This implies that convergence within western Europe also implies convergence with the

United States, but there was more impressive convergence between lower income countries, such as China and India, with both western Europe and the United States in recent decades, as will be explored elsewhere in this volume.

At this point, we choose to sidestep the abundant literature which attempts to test formally the hypothesis of convergence (both unconditional and conditional), which is inconclusive at best. Instead, we rely on the simple concepts of beta and sigma convergence described by Barro and Sala-i-Martin (2003). Beta convergence is a negative relationship between per capita income growth and the initial level of per capita income, with the beta coefficient measuring the speed of convergence. It should be noted that the literature on regional convergence has found that giving more weight to large regions than to smaller ones in the beta convergence analysis can result in substantially different conclusions regarding convergence and divergence: see, for example, Petrakos and Artelaris (2009), who suggest a weighted least squares approach. Although the number of observations at the country level is too small to be able to perform such an analysis here, it should be noted that since the outliers in our analysis constitute a small proportion of the total population, such an analysis, if possible, would not change the qualitative results we present.

Thus, as Figure 2.1 illustrates, for the whole period 1870–2016 there is striking evidence of beta convergence for our sample of countries, although the coefficient (the slope of the trend line) is very small at just −0.000002 (or just −0.78 per cent if we express GDP per capita in logarithms, allowing us to interpret beta as an elasticity), so the speed of convergence was negligible over this period, as Table 2.1 has already suggested. Nevertheless, it can be seen that those countries that were already rich in 1870, such as the UK, Switzerland, and the Low Countries, had average annual rates of growth of around 1.5 per cent per year, whereas the poorest countries, mostly those in southern Europe and the Nordic countries, with the exception of Denmark, experienced growth of around 2 per cent. It is already clear, however, that the Nordic countries generally 'overperformed' – that is, they lie above the trend line, whereas the southern European countries 'underperformed'. The reasons for this will be discussed in the following sections, where beta convergence is also considered for subsamples. To a certain extent, we can take the outliers as the interesting cases requiring explanation.

Turning to sigma convergence, this implies that the dispersion of per capita income, measured, for example, by the coefficient of variation, is falling over time. Figure 2.2 reveals that there is a lack of convergence before World War I, contrasting with strong convergence after World War II, and

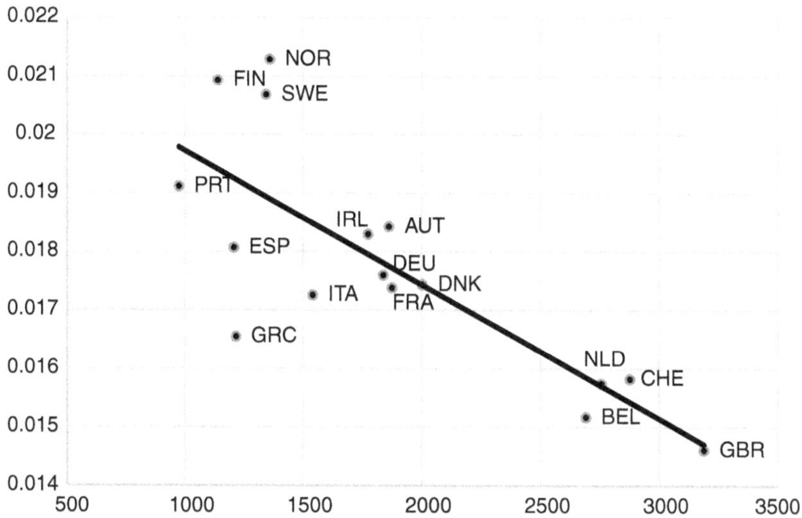

Figure 2.1 Annual rate of growth of GDP per capita, 1870–2016, and GDP per capita in 1870
Source: See Table 2.1.

an uptick of divergence from around 2000. Although beta and sigma convergence do not necessarily mirror each other (countries can be converging in income overall, even as the dispersion is increasing), this provides one motivation for our division of the whole period into sub-periods, as described above.

Another motivation is the theoretical relationship between convergence and openness. Thus, the Russian-American economic historian Alexander Gerschenkron (1962) suggested the possibility of an 'advantage of backwardness', whereby poor countries might be expected to grow faster than rich countries due to their ability to import knowledge and technology from the more advanced economies. Likewise, Abramovitz (1986) argued that catch-up was mostly fuelled by importing technology from producers at the productivity frontier, which will often be those with the highest income per capita. As a non-rival good, useful knowledge is something that can be consumed free of charge when access costs are low – something that openness might be expected to facilitate. Patents delay this process, but by patenting an invention, the science behind it is put into the public domain, where it can be learned from later. The larger the gap in knowledge between two countries, the more scope there is for catch-up. How efficiently a country

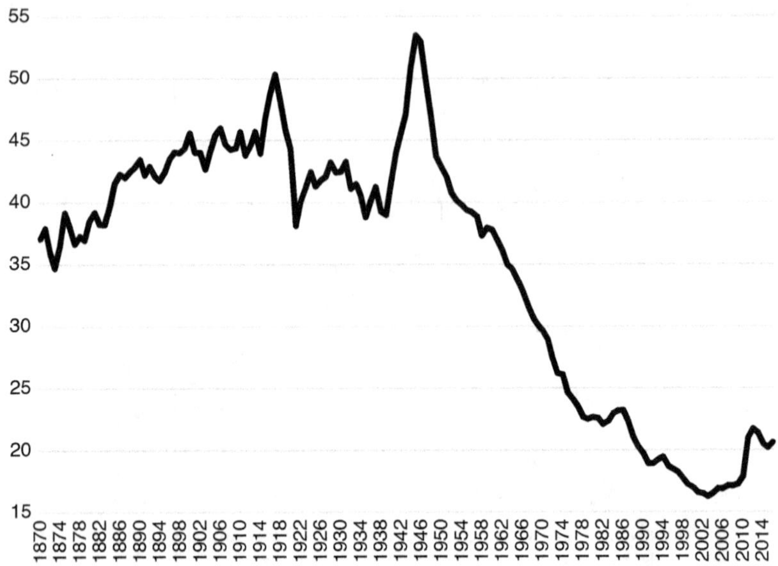

Figure 2.2 Coefficient of variation of GDP per capita, 1870–2016
Note: Missing values for Ireland from 1871–1912 and 1914–20 are linearly interpolated.
Source: Table 2.1.

is able to do this depends on 'social capability' – that is, a large enough section of the public capable of understanding the science and technology, thus implying again that education might contribute to catch-up – and 'technological congruence'. In other words, national policies and institutions, as well as the size of the market, matter (North 1990; Mauro 1995; Engerman and Sokoloff 1997; Hall and Jones 1999; Acemoglu et al. 2002; Easterly and Levine 2003).

Thus, much of the ability for countries to catch up is dependent on openness, which might stimulate the competition to drive out inefficient industries, and allow for the transfer of knowledge across borders (for example, through migration or embodied in international trade). However, the evidence on the association between globalization and openness more generally and economic growth is mixed (see, for example, the survey in Lampe and Sharp 2016). Generally, as we will see, European economies converged more during the periods of globalization than during the interwar period, although there are exceptions. Moreover, it should be noted that neither does this general picture hold for the world as a whole.

Convergence outside Europe and the areas of European settlement was weak during the pre-World War I period, while the interwar period witnessed the convergence of parts of coastal Africa, much of Latin America, and the Soviet Union. Finally, the post-World War II world saw the convergence of much of Asia, but the divergence of much of the rest of the developing world, including most of eastern Europe (Dowrick and Bradford DeLong 2003).

The prediction of convergence in levels of GDP per capita has its simplest theoretical exposition in the neoclassical Solow growth model, with labour-augmenting technological progress (see Solow 1956; Swan 1956), where growth of GDP per capita is caused by capital accumulation (subject to diminishing returns) and technological change, and is typically summarized in the following Cobb-Douglas production function:

$$Y = K^{\alpha}(AL)^{1-\alpha} \tag{1}$$

where Y is GDP, K is capital, L is labour, and A is the level of technology. One of the main predictions of this model is convergence: everything else being equal (including technology), poor countries will grow faster than rich countries due to diminishing returns to capital accumulation. However, growth theory has since suggested that by supporting R&D, governments can generate different growth paths, and the assumption of diminishing returns has been questioned.

Nevertheless, the Solow model provides a useful framework for understanding both convergence and the lack thereof between western European countries. This is partly because it assumes that the markets for labour, capital, and technology transfer are efficient, an assumption which might be appropriate for the two eras of globalization before World War I and from the 1970s until today. It is, however, unlikely to be true for the interwar period, for instance, or it might be more or less true for certain countries at different points in time, due to differences in domestic policy, for example. Such imperfections will cause lower speeds of convergence. Besides this, the model predicts that if there are differences in the savings rate (the proportion of output used to create more capital instead of being consumed) and/or the rate of capital depreciation, then convergence will be conditional on these differences. Moreover, empirical applications of the model have needed to take account of other factors, such as the importance of human capital (Mankiw et al. 1992), endogenous innovation (Romer 1990), benefits from proximity (Krugman and Venables 1995), and structural change (Broadberry 1998). Relatively poor countries will usually have relatively large parts of the economy dedicated to traditional and less efficient sectors, often initially agriculture, although the potential gains from this might be expected to decline over time. Some of these factors are touched on below.

Nevertheless, the Solow model lies at the heart of one of the popular ways in which economic historians have attempted to explain convergence: growth accounting (see, for example, Crafts 2009). Thus, equation (1) above can be rewritten as:

$$\Delta ln(Y/L) = \alpha \Delta ln(K/L) + \Delta lnA \tag{2}$$

which is the basic growth accounting formula, later extended to include a measure of human capital (Denison 1962). Crafts (2009) applied this idea to a variety of European countries, and some of his results are illustrated in panel A of Table 2.2. Panels B and C extend his analysis forward for the period after World War I, and are taken from Rosés and Wolf (2010) and Crafts and Toniolo (2010). Crafts finds that as modern economic growth spread through nineteenth-century Europe, the contribution from TFP growth was quite modest, and only came to dominate capital deepening around the turn of the nineteenth and twentieth centuries. This is confirmed by the more recent estimates, although there are exceptions, and more so from the 1970s.

As regards structural change, Table 2.3 compares GDP per capita and its ranking with the percentage of the labour force in agriculture for 1870 and 1913. There is a striking negative correlation between GDP per capita and the size of the agricultural sector, reflecting the productivity improvements that might be experienced by diversifying out of traditional sectors. There are exceptions, however. Denmark, for example, one of the richest countries in both periods, maintained a large agricultural sector throughout this period (and indeed until after World War II), reflecting the fact that agriculture need not hamper economic performance if it is able to match the productivity improvements in other sectors (Lampe and Sharp 2018).

Integration and Convergence before World War I

The period from 1870 until World War II was one where Europe and its empires dominated the world both economically and politically. This was

Table 2.2 Contributions of various factors to economic growth

A. Pre-World War I

	Labour productivity	Capital deepening	TFP
Austria			
1870–90	0.90	0.64	0.26
1890–1910	1.69	0.66	1.03
Germany			
1871–91	1.10	0.39	0.71
1891–1911	1.76	0.58	1.18
Great Britain			
1873–1913	0.90	0.38	0.52
Netherlands			
1870–90	0.94	0.61	0.33
1890–1913	1.35	0.46	0.89
Spain			
1884–1920	1.00	0.80	0.20
Sweden			
1890–1913	2.77	0.94	1.83

B. 1922–38

	Total hours worked	Capital deepening	TFP
Belgium	−0.50	0.56	1.61
Denmark	1.10	1.03	1.10
Finland	0.89	1.18	2.56
France	−0.99	0.92	2.66
Germany	−0.52	0.48	3.52
Italy	−0.23	1.72	0.94
Netherlands	0.60	0.65	1.09
Norway	0.11	1.32	2.41
Spain	−0.03	1.36	−1.60
Sweden	0.87	1.28	1.55
Switzerland	−0.17	0.55	2.54
UK	0.80	1.44	0.23

C. Post-World War II

	Labour productivity	Capital deepening	TFP	Human capital deepening
Austria				
1960–70	5.47	2.39	2.90	0.18
1970–90	2.54	1.32	1.00	0.22
1990–2003	1.50	0.86	0.37	0.27
Belgium				
1960–70	4.11	1.36	2.33	0.42
1970–90	2.52	0.96	1.38	0.18
1990–2003	1.27	0.76	0.26	0.25
Denmark				
1960–70	3.53	2.15	1.25	0.13
1970–90	1.08	0.82	0.02	0.24
1990–2003	1.86	0.72	0.95	0.19
Finland				
1960–70	4.67	1.66	2.64	0.37
1970–90	2.50	0.98	0.90	0.62
1990–2003	2.29	0.49	1.49	0.31
France				
1960–70	4.93	2.02	2.62	0.29
1970–90	2.48	1.28	0.84	0.36
1990–2003	0.98	0.58	0.13	0.27
(West) Germany				
1960–70	4.36	2.10	2.03	0.23
1970–90	1.88	0.79	0.69	0.40
1990–2003	1.53	0.76	0.60	0.17
Greece				
1960–70	8.34	3.63	4.45	0.26
1970–90	1.80	1.24	0.06	0.50
1990–2003	2.21	0.61	1.25	0.35
Ireland				
1960–70	4.21	1.78	2.21	0.22
1970–90	3.03	1.47	1.18	0.38
1990–2003	2.99	0.49	2.24	0.26
Italy				
1960–70	6.25	2.39	3.50	0.36
1970–90	2.52	0.98	1.22	0.32
1990–2003	1.12	0.60	0.14	0.38
Netherlands				
1960–70	3.06	1.43	0.89	0.74
1970–90	1.62	0.72	0.65	0.25
1990–2003	0.61	0.26	0.07	0.28

C. (cont.)

	Labour productivity	Capital deepening	TFP	Human capital deepening
Norway				
1960–70	3.46	1.18	1.80	0.48
1970–90	2.44	0.90	0.84	0.70
1990–2003	2.33	0.31	1.81	0.21
Portugal				
1960–70	6.39	2.05	3.99	0.35
1970–90	2.35	0.90	1.01	0.44
1990–2003	1.29	1.13	−0.31	0.47
Spain				
1960–70	6.56	2.45	3.73	0.38
1970–90	3.04	1.54	1.13	0.37
1990–2003	0.63	0.63	−0.37	0.37
Sweden				
1960–70	3.93	1.34	2.40	0.19
1970–90	1.30	0.67	0.27	0.36
1990–2003	2.33	0.73	1.16	0.44
Switzerland				
1960–70	3.17	1.40	1.37	0.40
1970–90	0.64	0.72	−0.38	0.30
1990–2003	0.45	0.60	−0.23	0.08
UK				
1960–70	2.86	1.45	1.24	0.17
1970–90	1.89	0.83	0.74	0.32
1990–2003	2.06	0.91	0.74	0.41

Sources: Pre-World War I: Crafts 2009: 212; 1922–38: Rosés and Wolf 2010: table 8.5; post-World War II: Crafts and Toniolo 2010: table 12.7.

Table 2.3 GDP per capita and the percentage of the labour force in agriculture, 1870 and 1913

	1870				1913			
	GDP/ cap	Rank	% agriculture	Rank	GDP/ cap	Rank	% agriculture	Rank
CHE	2875.65	2	42.3	12	7092.61	1	26.8	13
GBR	3190.43	1	22.2	14	4920.55	2	11.8	15
BEL	2691.52	4	44.4	11	4219.54	3	23.2	14

Table 2.3 (cont.)

	1870				1913			
	GDP/ cap	Rank	% agriculture	Rank	GDP/ cap	Rank	% agriculture	Rank
NLD	2755.23	3	39.4	13	4048.51	4	28.3	12
DNK	2003.18	5	47.8	10	3912.17	5	41.7	8
DEU	1839.08	8	49.5	9	3648.01	6	34.5	11
FRA	1875.65	6	49.8	7	3484.77	7	41.0	9
AUT	1862.59	7	67.0	3	3465.49	8	59.5	2
SWE	1345.06	11	67.4	2	2874.08	9	45.0	7
NOR	1360.14	10	49.6	8	2447.06	10	39.6	10
ITA	1541.75	9	61.0	6	2304.79	11	55.4	5
FIN	1139.68	14	75.5	1	2110.67	12	69.3	1
ESP	1207.09	13	66.3	4	2055.62	13	56.3	4
PRT	975.04	15	65.0	5	1250.33	14	57.4	3
GRC	1215.71	12	–	–	1177.07	15	49.6	6

Notes: The Austrian % agriculture is for Austria-Hungary. All data are in 1990 international $.
Sources: Maddison Project Database, version 2013; Broadberry et al. 2010: 61.

a result of the earlier Industrial Revolution, which gradually spread around western Europe, leading to the Great Divergence with the rest of the world. During this first era of globalization, characterized by free trade and capital mobility under the Gold Standard, integration intensified within Europe. However, although Europeans became richer and lived longer and healthier lives, this was also a time when external balance (fixed exchange rates and balanced trade) was the primary policy objective at the cost of internal balance, leading to certain groups in society benefiting at the expense of others. This led, in part, to a globalization backlash before World War I, with countries returning to the protection of certain sectors.

Since this period marked, to some extent, unprecedented globalization and openness, even regarding international mobility of labour, we would expect it to be associated with more scope for catch-up (see the discussion above). Moreover, largely free trade allowed ideas to flow with goods, and capital mobility under the Gold Standard allowed for the import of capital goods such as machinery and transport equipment. Indeed, this period also saw a first wave of industrialization in many western European countries. Figure 2.3

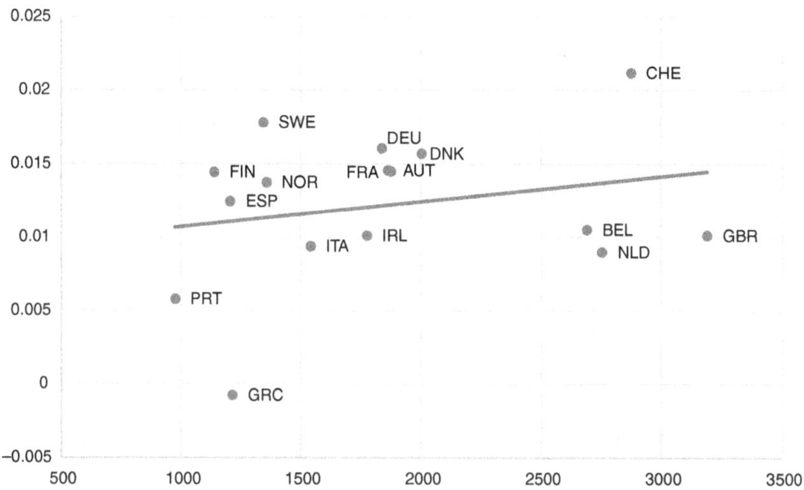

Figure 2.3 Annual rate of growth of GDP per capita, 1870–1913, and GDP per capita in 1870
Source: See Table 2.1.

illustrates this period, which at first glance appears to show a striking contrast with Figure 2.1. Closer inspection reveals, however, that if we were to remove the 'outliers' – in particular, the underperforming Greek and, to a lesser extent, Portuguese economies, as well as the overperforming Swiss economy – then we would also see some evidence of convergence, although all bar those three were growing at roughly comparable rates of around 1.0–1.5 per cent per annum.

It is noticeable that initially poor countries can be divided into roughly two camps: southern Europe plus, to a certain extent, Ireland, and the Nordic countries, except Denmark. Why did Greece, Spain, and Portugal perform so poorly in this period, whereas Scandinavia performed relatively strongly? If we believe that proximity to dynamic markets was important, this might have had a negative impact on Greece, which also experienced war and sovereign debt defaults in this period. Portugal was close to another slow-growing country, Spain. By contrast, the Scandinavian countries were close to dynamic Germany and traded a lot with each other. Denmark benefited greatly from trade with the UK, particularly in agricultural products, which means it is often contrasted with Ireland, which presumably should have been able to develop similarly. Explanations for this often centre on Ireland's relative failure to implement the cooperative form of organization in agriculture (O'Rourke 2006; Henriksen et al. 2015; McLaughlin and Sharp 2019). Elsewhere in the

Nordic countries, the impressively rapid Swedish catch-up motivated the famous work of Heckscher and Ohlin, who suggested that it might be explained by commodity price convergence and trade creation. Williamson (1996) finds, however, that these gains were modest. Another factor might have been Swedish mass emigration to the United States in particular, increasing real wages for those left behind. Finally, it has been suggested that Sweden was an 'impoverished sophisticate' (for the classic account regarding Sweden, see Sandberg 1979): they had a high level of educational attainment relative to their income levels, and had in fact some of the highest levels of patenting per capita. The proportion of children aged between five and fourteen was almost 60 per cent in Sweden, compared to just half that in Italy and Ireland (see O'Rourke and Williamson 1997 for more on the role of education). Finally, Ireland may also have been hampered by her proximity to the UK: many of the most talented Irish went there or to the US.

Natural resources, and particularly proximity to coal, are also often given a central role when explaining the relative success of countries during this period (see, for example, Pounds 1957; Pollard 1981; Cameron 1985). Thus, countries like Germany and France were able to industrialize and catch up with the UK relatively rapidly. Certainly, southern Europe was hampered in this regard, but this does not explain the success of Denmark, which lacked almost all forms of natural resources, although this exception might be due to a unique geography that made it relatively cheap to import coal from the UK (Henriques and Sharp 2015).

Disintegration and Divergence, 1914–50

World War I led to social and political instability and seriously disrupted the economies of western Europe. Massive loss of life on the battlefield was followed by the Spanish flu, which by all accounts was even more devastating (see, for example, Karlsson et al. 2014). Transport networks, factories, farms, and mines were destroyed, and industries such as shipbuilding, which had enjoyed investment during the war, subsequently suffered issues with overcapacity. European producers also faced renewed competition from countries such as the US and Japan, which had been less affected by the war. Moreover, the Treaty of Versailles brought reparations, which imposed serious burdens on already fragile economies. On top of all this, the interwar period saw the globalization backlash before World War I being taken to extremes. The Great Depression, which started in the United States, led to the total collapse of the pre-World War I liberal order. The Gold Standard proved impossible to maintain, and countries resorted to protectionism and, in some cases, fascism, ultimately resulting in World War II. Besides the obvious impact on international cooperation, the rise of fascism was associated with a belief in autarky, which was mirrored to a certain extent by other countries.

The two world wars meant that borders were effectively closed. Although the interwar period started with a brief return to international cooperation and openness to trade, this soon collapsed after the Great Depression from 1929. Trade barriers were raised, and nationalism meant that foreign ideas were often viewed with suspicion. Generally, this is considered to be a time of political chaos and poor macroeconomic policy (Feinstein et al. 1997). Nevertheless, it was also a time of significant technological progress – for example, in the transportation, chemical, and electrical industries. American-style mass production was also introduced to Europe, while agriculture shrank further and school enrolment continued to increase. Indeed, Figure 2.4 reveals that the period 1921–39 (we have removed the war years to avoid any issues with unreliable data) witnessed a pattern rather similar to that for before World War I, with the Nordic countries performing strongly, and the southern European countries performing less strongly – and in the case of Spain, disastrously.

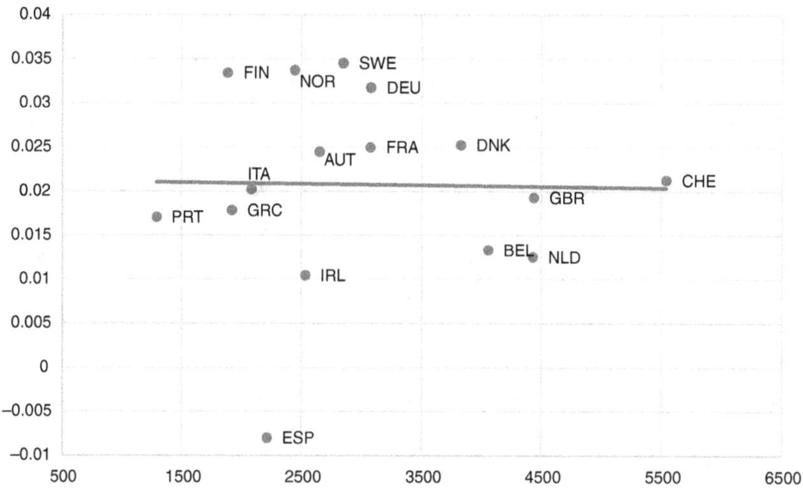

Figure 2.4 Annual rate of growth of GDP per capita, 1921–39, and GDP per capita in 1921
Source: See Table 2.1.

It is difficult to attribute much growth in this period to reconstruction after World War I. For example, the fastest-growing economies were in the Nordic area, which had been neutral. Otherwise, some outliers are easy to explain: Spain performed poorly due to the civil war. Elsewhere, the pattern is not too different from that of the pre-World War I period. However, this masks the fact that, although all economies were badly hit by the Great Depression, there were significant differences in the timing of recovery. This has famously been linked to the decision to leave the Gold Standard, and in this respect the UK is often compared to France. The UK rejoined the Gold Standard after World War I at the original mint parity, whereas France allowed her currency to devalue and grew more strongly as a consequence. By contrast, the UK left the Gold Standard shortly after the Great Depression, whereas France held on for longer. Thus, the UK recovered faster (Strakosch 1935; Eichengreen 1992). The impressive performance of the Nordic countries in this period has been attributed, in part, to their decision to devalue their currencies early on (Klovland 1998). Ireland left the Gold Standard with the UK, but continued to peg its currency to the British pound, which might be part of the explanation for her poor economic performance, although the beginning of this period was also one of civil war.

Integration and Convergence after 1950

World War II, like World War I, led to large losses of capital and human life. However, only a few years after hostilities ceased, even the worst affected countries had already recovered to their highest pre-war levels of GDP per capita. Nevertheless, it was clear that western Europe had lost its economic predominance to the new superpowers of the United States and the Soviet Union. A new world order based around Washington came to dominate western Europe, exemplified by the Bretton Woods system. A couple of decades of rapid growth in some parts of western Europe (the so-called Golden Age), however, was followed by the oil shocks and stagnation of the 1970s. Nevertheless, Europe continued to integrate more and more closely through the European Economic Community and the European Union; trade and other barriers fell; and Europe participated fully in the new globalization ushered in by the collapse of the Soviet Union, which saw eastern Europe reintegrating with the West. Although southern and eastern Europe began converging with north-western Europe, the 2007/08 global financial crisis proved a major challenge, and in particular the European Union's experiment with a common currency led to difficult strains, and ultimately a new divergence of the European economies, as can be seen in Figure 2.2. Although a protectionist backlash seems to have been avoided, politics increasingly focused on immigration, and populist movements have been on the rise in the continent, as well as abroad.

Starting with the period 1950–75, this saw a reduction in the barriers to trade introduced during the interwar period, and marked a Golden Age of economic growth as American investment flowed into Europe and countries rebuilt after the war years. From the 1970s, capital movements also became freer after limitations imposed under the Bretton Woods system. Figure 2.5 illustrates the period 1950–2016. The countries show a clear pattern of convergence, with the main exception of Norway, which grew to become the richest economy in western Europe after the discovery of oil in the North Sea. However, this actually masks considerable diversity of performance within this period, which we separate into two: before and after 1972.

For the period 1950–72, illustrated by Figure 2.6, the pattern of convergence is even more striking, although Britain and Ireland were notable underperformers. There has been much scholarly debate about convergence and economic growth during the Golden Age (see, for example, Crafts and Toniolo 1996; Temin 2002; Vonyó 2008). Part of the overperformance of Germany, the *Wirtschaftswunder*, in the 1950–72 period was simply the result of reconstruction. Nevertheless, Germany not only caught up with the UK,

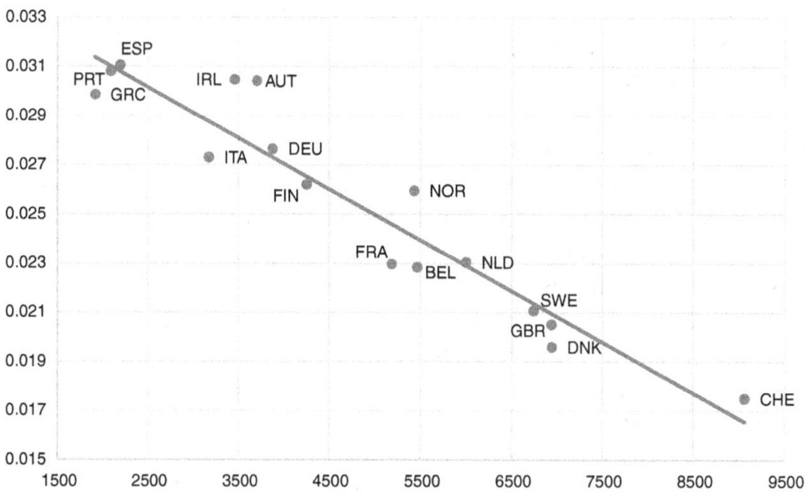

Figure 2.5 Annual rate of growth of GDP per capita, 1950–2016, and GDP per capita in 1950
Source: See Table 2.1.

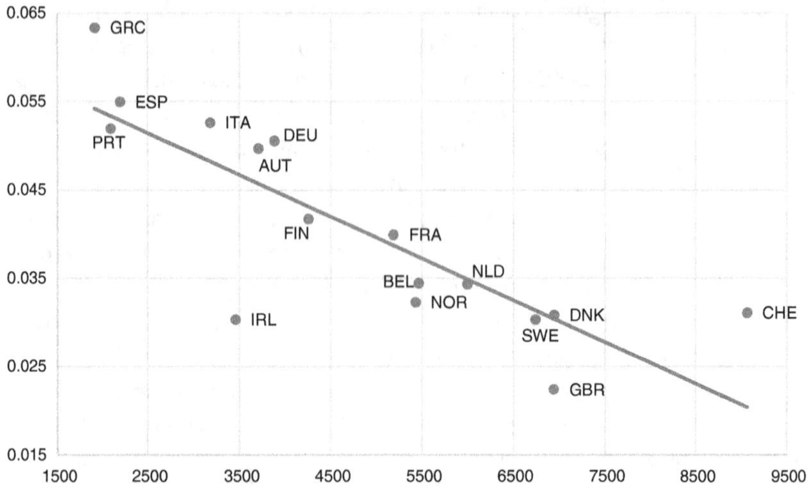

Figure 2.6 Annual rate of growth of GDP per capita, 1950–72, and GDP per capita in 1950
Source: See Table 2.1.

but had overtaken it by 1970, something which convergence would not predict. This has led many scholars to speculate about why this might have been the case, although in fact the UK enjoyed higher per capita incomes from the 1990s after sweeping institutional reforms. Britain's 'relative decline' has been put down to insufficient investment in human and physical capital and poor industrial relations. The elite universities of Oxford and Cambridge neglected for a long time the hard sciences, whereas Germany had a well-developed apprenticeship system for training skilled labour. Probably more important than this was the fact that the UK had exceptionally low levels of domestic investment – far from having a 'home bias', it seems British investors preferred to channel their capital abroad. German universal banks, on the other hand, channelled investment towards German industry (Carlin 1996). British investment converged to the European average after World War II, however. As far as industrial relations are concerned, Britain seems to have suffered from trade unions based for a long time around skills, meaning that individual industries were represented by a large number of unions, thus giving 'hold-up' power in wage negotiations and the introduction of new technologies, and there was little cooperation with employers, unlike in Germany (Bean and Crafts 1996). Moreover, Britain had rather large, nationalized steel and coal sectors, with extremely low TFP growth, which contributed to TFP growth being just one-third of that in Germany from 1950 until the 1970s. Finally, Britain already had a small agricultural sector, whereas other European countries had plenty of agricultural labour that could be reallocated to other sectors. Indeed, Temin (2002) attributes much of the growth during the Golden Age to the reallocation of labour from agriculture.

Other countries, such as Italy and France, also participated in the Golden Age, partly due to reconstruction and technological catch-up. Spain and Portugal suffered under authoritarian dictatorships until the 1970s, but caught up once their economies started to open again. Others, however, such as Denmark, which was initially still very dependent on the slow-growing UK economy, did not. Ireland remained protectionist until the late 1950s and this, combined with dependency on the British market, probably led to her being the poorest country in western Europe in 1973 (Ó Gráda and O'Rourke 1996).

As illustrated in Figure 2.7, this was reversed for the period 1973–2016, where Ireland massively overperformed, with growth rates of over 3 per cent per annum – although this was starting from a low level, since by 1973 Ireland was the poorest country in the sample, having been in the middle of the income distribution in the nineteenth century. This second period also marks a return to 'normality' in the sense that the southern European countries underperformed. Another significant overperformer was Norway, which, despite being in the middle of the income distribution in 1973, grew at over

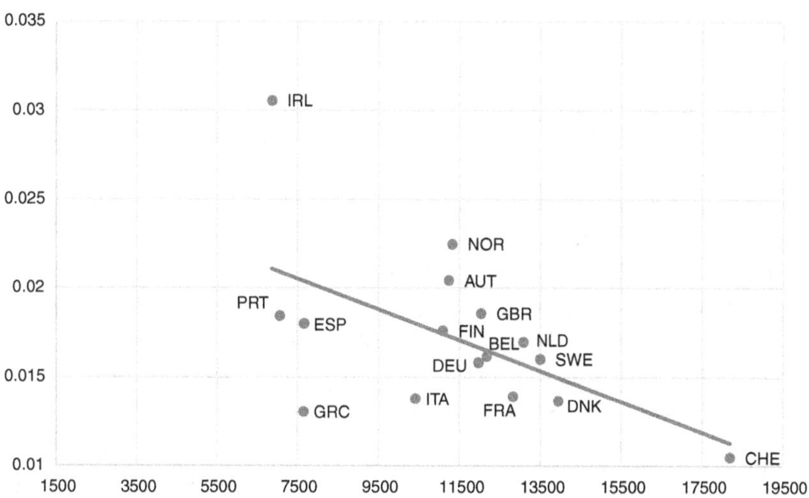

Figure 2.7 Annual rate of growth of GDP per capita, 1973–2016, and GDP per capita in 1973
Source: See Table 2.2.

2.2 per cent per annum – the second highest after Ireland – and became the second richest country in the sample by 2010.

Although the Norwegian experience is relatively easy to explain, the performance of Ireland deserves more attention. When Ireland opened up her economy, she became known as the 'Celtic Tiger', enjoying extremely fast rates of growth (Barry 2002). Although Ireland had in fact already opened up its economy in the 1950s, it pursued a policy of fiscal expansion following the oil crises of the 1970s, which resulted in near bankruptcy by the 1980s. Although the end of the 1980s saw the birth of the Celtic Tiger and rapid economic growth, Ó Gráda does not believe this was due to catch-up alone, although a large part was certainly compensation for earlier underperformance. Thus, productivity growth in the 1990s was not spectacular; and once spare capacity, accumulated since the early 1980s, was used up, the rate of economic growth slowed down, although it was still very high. Ó Gráda (2007) suggests that an interesting comparison is with Italy, since both countries were relatively backward in the middle of the twentieth century, with levels of GDP per capita just half those of the United Kingdom, for example. Italy (briefly) celebrated its *il sorpasso* of the UK economy in the 1980s, but by 2002 Ireland had overtaken both. However, this came at a price. While Italy, like many other countries, was enjoying its 'economic miracle' in the 1950s, Ireland experienced its 'lost decade'. And when Italy experienced its 'splendid eighties', Ireland was only recovering from a long period of crisis. All this leads Ó Gráda to conclude that an average citizen in 1950, asked to choose between the Irish or the Italian route to affluence, would certainly choose the latter option. He calculates that the lost decade of Irish growth corresponds to a cumulative difference in consumption of thirty-three times the Irish 1950 consumption per capita, or six times that of 1998. If Ireland had followed the Italian path, it would have had a consumption one-third greater, with obvious implications for economic well-being.

Elsewhere, the period since 1973 witnessed another important change, with the expansion of the European Union. Founded in the 1950s by Belgium, France, Italy, Luxembourg, the Netherlands, and West Germany, 1973 saw the entry of Denmark, Ireland, and the United Kingdom, with Greece, Portugal, and Spain joining in the 1980s; 1995 saw the entry of Austria, Finland, and Sweden, who were soon joined by many eastern European countries, taking the total number of members to twenty-eight at the time of writing. The European Union, by introducing the Single European Act in 1987 (forming a single internal market), the Schengen Treaty in 1995 (removing internal border controls), and the Maastricht

Treaty in 1993 (introducing, among other things, the single European currency, the euro), has led to unprecedented levels of integration between its members, both at the economic and political level, although it maintains high barriers to trade to the outside world in terms of agricultural goods, in particular through the Common Agricultural Policy.

Evidence for the impact of the EU on European performance is somewhat mixed, however. Crafts (2016) provides a review of the literature, finding that membership of the EU raised UK income levels due to its impact on increasing trade, and as a result of increased competition increasing productivity. In recent work, however, Andersen et al. (2019), using a variety of causal identification strategies, different time periods, different country samples, and different data sets, find no significant effects of EU membership on economic growth. Indeed, one of the EU's flagship policies, the common currency, is seen by many to have had a disastrous impact on some European countries following the 2007/08 financial crisis, which has led some to see a parallel with the impact of the Gold Standard in the interwar years. The poor performance of the Danish economy in recent years seems to add some support to this idea, since despite having voted in a referendum to remain outside the euro, it maintains a currency peg. In a comparison with eighteen non-eurozone OECD countries, all of which have flexible exchange rates, Andersen and Malchow-Møller (2017) find that Denmark has the worst growth performance of all, and that a lack of monetary policy independence is central to understanding this. The southern European countries and Ireland were hit particularly hard, and experienced subsequent sovereign debt crises, which, for a time, seemed to threaten the euro itself. Nevertheless, it might be noted that the divergence which can be seen in the final years of Figure 2.2 predates the euro. One suggestion for this is that the 'new economy' and the emergence of ICT since the mid-1990s led to large productivity growth in countries with more flexible markets, such as Sweden, the Netherlands, and the UK, but was not as keenly felt elsewhere.

Conclusion

There has certainly been some convergence over time, but this has been more marked in periods of openness than others. All countries are significantly richer today than they were in the nineteenth century, but some countries have become much richer than others, particularly the Nordic countries, which overperformed in every period of analysis. The Golden

Age seemed to mark the catch-up of southern Europe, but this region lost ground from the 1970s. The richest countries in western Europe today are still located in the north-west of the continent, although they have been joined by the Nordic countries. A note of caution is necessary here, however. Nation states are not always a useful unit of analysis, so future work should look (and is doing so) more into regional convergence rather than relying on national borders. For example, Catalonia in Spain and the northern part of Italy developed much more similarly to other parts of western Europe, something which is not at all visible from the above analysis.

References

Abramovitz, M. (1986). 'Catching Up, Forging Ahead, and Falling Behind', *Journal of Economic History*, 46, 385–406.

Acemoglu, D., Johnson, S., and Robinson, J. A. (2002). 'Reversal of Fortunes: Geography and Institutions in the Making of the Modern World Income Distribution', *Quarterly Journal of Economics*, 117, 1231–1294.

Andersen, T. B. and Malchow-Møller, N. (2017). 'The Macroeconomics of a Delayed Recovery from the Global Financial Crisis: A Comparative Approach', *Singapore Economic Review*, 62(5), 1179–1194.

Andersen, T. B., Barslund, M., and Vanhuysse, P. (2019). 'Join to Prosper? An Empirical Analysis of EU Membership and Economic Growth', *Kyklos*, 72(2), 211–238.

Barro, R. J. and Sala-i-Martin, X. (2003). *Economic Growth*, 2nd ed., New York: McGraw-Hill.

Barry, F. (2002). 'The Celtic Tiger Era: Delayed Convergence or Regional Boom?' *ESRI Quarterly Economic Commentary*, summer, 84–91.

Bean, C. and Crafts, N. (1996). 'British Economic Growth since 1945: Relative Economic Decline . . . and Renaissance?', in Crafts, N. and Toniolo, G. (eds.), *Economic Growth in Europe since 1945*, Cambridge University Press, 131–172.

Bolt, J., Inklaar, R., de Jong, H., and van Zanden, J. L. (2018). 'Rebasing "Maddison": New Income Comparisons and the Shape of Long-Run Economic Development', Maddison Project working paper 10.

Broadberry, S. N. (1998). 'How Did the United States and Germany Overtake Britain? A Sectoral Analysis of Comparative Productivity Levels, 1870–1990', *Journal of Economic History*, 58, 375–407.

Broadberry, S. N., Federico, G., and Klein, A. (2010). 'Sectoral Developments, 1870–1914', in Broadberry, S. N. and O'Rourke, K. (eds.), *The Cambridge Economic History of Modern Europe, Vol. 2: 1870 to the Present*, Cambridge University Press, 59–83.

Cameron, R. (1985). 'A New View of European Industrialization', *Economic History Review*, 38, 1–23.

Carlin, W. (1996). 'West German Growth and Institutions, 1945–90', in Crafts, N. and Toniolo, G. (eds.), *Economic Growth in Europe since 1945*, Cambridge University Press, 455–497.

Carreras, A. and Josephson, C. (2010). 'Aggregate Growth, 1870–1914: Growing at the Production Frontier', in Broadberry, S. N. and O'Rourke, K. (eds.), *The Cambridge Economic History of Modern Europe, Vol. 2: 1870 to the Present*, Cambridge University Press, 30–58.

Crafts, N. (2009). 'Solow and Growth Accounting: A Perspective from Quantitative Economic History', *History of Political Economy*, 41, 200–220.

(2016). 'The Growth Effects of EU Membership for the UK: Review of the Evidence', *Social Market Foundation/CAGE Global Perspectives Series*, paper 7.

Crafts, N. and Toniolo, G. (1996). 'Postwar Growth: An Overview', in Crafts, N. and Toniolo, G. (eds.), *Economic Growth in Europe since 1945*, Cambridge University Press, 1–37.

(2010). 'Aggregate Growth, 1950–2005', in Broadberry, S. and O'Rourke, K. (2010). *The Cambridge Economic History of Modern Europe, Vol. 2: 1870 to the Present*, Cambridge University Press, 296–332.

Denison, E. (1962). *The Sources of Economic Growth in the United States and the Alternatives before Us*, New York: Committee for Economic Development.

Dowrick, S. and Bradford DeLong, J. (2003). 'Globalization and Convergence', in Bordo, M. D., Taylor, A. M., and Williamson, J. G. (eds.), *Globalization in Historical Perspective*, University of Chicago Press, 191–226.

Easterly, W. and Levine, R. (2003). 'Tropics, Germs, and Crops: How Endowments Influence Economic Development', *Journal of Monetary Economics*, 50, 3–39.

Eichengreen, B. (1992). *Golden Fetters: The Gold Standard and the Great Depression 1919–1939*. Oxford University Press.

Engerman, S. L. and Sokoloff, K. L. (1997). 'Factor Endowments, Institutions, and Differential Paths of Growth Among New World Economies: A View from Economic Historians of the United States', in Haber, S. (ed.), *How Latin America Fell Behind*, Stanford University Press, 260–304.

Feinstein, C. H., Temin, P., and Toniolo, G. (1997). *The European Economy between the Wars*. Oxford University Press.

Gerschenkron, A. (1962). *Economic Backwardness in Historical Perspective*, Cambridge, MA: Harvard University Press.

Hall, R. E. and Jones, C. I. (1999). 'Why Do Some Countries Produce So Much More Output Per Worker than Others?', *Quarterly Journal of Economics*, 114, 83–116.

Henriksen, I., McLaughlin, E., and Sharp, P. (2015). 'Contracts and Cooperation: The Relative Failure of the Irish Dairy Industry in the Late Nineteenth Century Reconsidered', *European Review of Economic History*, 19, 412–431.

Henriques, S. T. and Sharp, P. (2016). 'The Danish Agricultural Revolution in an Energy Perspective: A Case of Development with Few Domestic Energy Sources', *Economic History Review*, 69(3), 844–869.

Karlsson, M., Nilsson, T., and Pichler, S. (2014). 'The Impact of the 1918 Spanish Flu Epidemic on Economic Performance in Sweden: An Investigation into the Consequences of an Extraordinary Mortality Shock', *Journal of Health Economics*, 36, 1–19.

Klovland, J. T. (1998). 'Monetary Policy and Business Cycles in the Interwar Years: The Scandinavian Experience', *European Review of Economic History*, 2(3), 309–344.

Krugman, P. R. and Venables, A. J. (1995). 'Globalization and the Inequality of Nations', *Quarterly Journal of Economics*, 110, 857–880.

Lampe, M. and Sharp, P. (2016). 'Cliometric Approaches to International Trade', in Diebolt, C. and Haupert, M. (eds.), *Handbook of Cliometrics*, Heidelberg: Springer, 295–330.

(2018). *A Land of Milk and Butter: How Elites Created the Modern Danish Dairy Industry*, University of Chicago Press.

McLaughlin, E. and Sharp, P. (2019). 'Competition between Organisational Forms in Danish and Irish Dairying around the Turn of the Twentieth Century', *Business History*, April (published online).

Maddison, A. (2003). *The World Economy: Historical Statistics*, Paris: OECD.

Maddison Project Database, version 2013. Bolt, J. and van Zanden, J. L. (2014). 'The Maddison Project: Collaborative Research on Historical National Accounts', *Economic History Review*, 67(3), 627–651.

Mankiw, N., Romer, D., and Weil, D. N. (1992). 'A Contribution to the Empirics of Economic Growth', *Quarterly Journal of Economics*, 107, 407–437.

Mauro, P. (1995). 'Corruption and Growth', *Quarterly Journal of Economics*, 110, 681–712.

North, D. C. (1990). *Institutions, Institutional Change and Economic Performance*, Cambridge University Press.

Ó Gráda, C. (2007). 'You Take the High Road and I'll Take the Low Road: Economic Success and Well-Being in the Longer Run', in Hatton, T. J., O'Rourke, K. H., and Taylor, A. M. (eds.), *The New Comparative Economic History: Essays in Honor of Jeffrey G. Williamson*, Cambridge, MA: MIT Press, 343–364.

Ó Gráda, C. and O'Rourke, K. H. (1996). 'Irish Economic Growth, 1945–88', in Crafts, N. and Toniolo, G. (eds.), *Economic Growth in Europe since 1945*, Cambridge University Press, 388–426.

O'Rourke, K. H. (2006). 'Late Nineteenth-Century Denmark in an Irish Mirror: Land Tenure, Homogeneity and the Roots of Danish Success', in Campbell, J. L., Hall, J. A., and Pedersen, O. K. (eds.), *National Identity and the Varieties of Capitalism: The Danish Experience*, Montreal: McGill–Queen's University Press, 159–96.

O'Rourke, K. H. and Williamson, J. G. (1997). 'Around the European Periphery, 1870–1913: Globalization, Schooling and Growth', *European Review of Economic History*, 1, 153–190.

Persson, K. G. and Sharp, P. (2015). *An Economic History of Europe: Knowledge, Institutions and Growth, 600 to the Present*, Cambridge University Press.

Petrakos, G. and Artelaris, P. (2009). 'European Regional Convergence Revisited: A Weighted Least Squares Approach', *Growth and Change*, 40(2), 314–331.

Pollard, S. (1981). *Peaceful Conquest: The Industrialization of Europe 1760–1970*, Oxford University Press.

Pounds, N. J. G. (1957). *Coal and Steel in Western Europe: The Influence of Resources and Technique on Production*, Bloomington: Indiana University Press.

Projer, E. (1990). 'III Schätzung der Bruttowertschöpfung im 2. Sektor NF-Projekt: Geldmenge und Wirtschaftswachstum in der Schweiz, 1851 bis 1913 1. *Aufl*', Socioeconomic Seminar, Department of Economic History, University of Zurich.

Romer, P. M. (1990). 'Endogenous Technological Change', *Journal of Political Economy*, 98, 71–102.

Rosés, J. R. and Wolf, N. (2010). 'Aggregate Growth, 1913–1950', in Broadberry, S. and O'Rourke, K. (2010). *The Cambridge Economic History of Modern Europe, Vol. 2: 1870 to the Present*, Cambridge University Press, 181–207.

(eds.) (2018). *The Economic Development of Europe's Regions: A Quantitative History Since 1900*, Abingdon: Routledge.

Sandberg, L. G. (1979). 'The Case of the Impoverished Sophisticate: Human Capital and Swedish Economic Growth before World War I', *Journal of Economic History*, 39(1), 225–241.

Solow, R. M. (1956). 'A Contribution to the Theory of Economic Growth', *Quarterly Journal of Economics*, 70, 65–94.

Strakosch, H. (1935). 'The Road to Recovery', *Economist*, 5 January, 1–12.

Swan, T. W. (1956). 'Economic Growth and Capital Accumulation', *Economic Record*, 32, 334–361.

Temin, P. (2002). 'The Golden Age of European Growth Reconsidered', *European Review of Economic History*, 6, 3–22.

Vonyó, T. (2008). 'Post-War Reconstruction and the Golden Age of Economic Growth', *European Review of Economic History*, 12(1), 221–241.

Williamson, J. G. (1996). 'Globalization, Convergence, and History', *Journal of Economic History*, 56:2, 277–306.

3

The Socialist Experiment and Beyond

The Economic Development of Eastern Europe

TRACY DENNISON AND ALEXANDER KLEIN

Introduction

The path of eastern Europe since the late nineteenth century has been one marked by a series of significant shocks and disruptions. However, as this chapter makes clear, there were also significant continuities in eastern Europe's economic position relative to other parts of Europe. We try here to assess the trajectory of eastern European economic development between 1870 and the present in light of recent economic history scholarship, and offer some explanations for the patterns that emerge from the quantitative evidence. This task is beset with challenges, ranging from changes in political boundaries to abrupt changes in political and economic systems, all against the backdrop of two devastating world wars. The political map of the region was altered three times in the period under examination: through the dissolution of the old empires at the time of World War I, followed by changes to national borders after 1945, and then the more recent changes to borders following the collapse of the communist regimes. For many of these countries, all of this coincided with the imposition of new political and economic systems, beginning in Russia in 1917, and spreading outwards after World War II. This was further complicated by the human and physical capital losses of the world wars, which took an enormous toll on economies that were only in the nascent stages of industrialization on the eve of war. Disentangling causes and effects is thus a considerable challenge; all of these factors must be taken into account when assessing the economic performance of these countries over the past 130 years.

This chapter relies on existing quantitative research, but will try to situate the findings in a larger political economic context and attempt to qualify them, where appropriate, using additional evidence. The quantitative dimension derives from a long-running research project on historical national accounts, which currently offer the best approximation of long-run trends in the economic development of eastern European economies. It also employs the work of Angus Maddison (e.g. Maddison 1995), who generated internationally comparable figures of GDP per capita in 1990 international $. Notwithstanding the fact that the project is still far from finished, with new and improved estimates of historical GDP constantly being incorporated, the existing estimates offer a reasonable starting point for measuring long-run economic trends. Our use of these data does not imply, however, that these estimates are unanimously agreed upon by economic historians. Concerns have been raised about the reliability of the data, the extent to which GDP is an adequate measure of pre-modern economic performance, and the ways the findings have been interpreted. We do our best to contextualize the estimates and qualify conclusions we draw. We see these figures as a useful starting point; they are the best sources we have at the moment for the kind of broad comparisons this volume undertakes.

Fortunately, some of the issues raised by the national accounts project can be addressed more straightforwardly, and where that is the case, we do so. For instance, the GDP figures offered by the Maddison Project were constructed using constant borders. This is one way of approaching the calculations, but it does distort historical realities in the process. We therefore prefer to take into account border changes to the extent that we can, despite the challenges that imposes. To do so, we use the border-adjusted GDP figures calculated by Broadberry and Klein (2012). So we refer to Czechoslovakia 1918–92 rather than Czechoslovakia 1870–2010. We use two GDP per capita figures instead of one: one for the pre-World War I borders and one for the post-World War I borders. We are aware that other questions about defining the region are more difficult to address. What counts as 'eastern Europe' changes considerably over this period. What are the implications for such changes over time? The inclusion of Austria in the earlier period could make growth appear stronger than it actually was in the areas that subsequently became the 'Eastern bloc'. The same is true for the inclusion of the Baltic region in the later period, as it was historically more economically advanced than the other Soviet republics. We acknowledge that these are significant issues, but maintain that they are unlikely to distort our attempt to *compare* rates of growth in the region with those in other parts of Europe.

An initial picture of Europe in GDP and population figures is presented below. Table 3.1 shows regional shares of GDP and population between 1870

Table 3.1 Regional shares of GDP and population, 1870–2010

	Eastern Europe	North-western Europe	Southern Europe
Regional share of GDP (% from total)			
1870	29.7	54.7	15.6
1913 pre-WWI borders	30.9	56.1	13.0
1913 interwar borders	27.5	58.4	14.1
1950	31.4	54.4	14.3
1950 post-WWII borders	32.8	53.0	14.2
1990	30.6	48.0	21.4
1990 post-1990 borders	27.7	50.2	22.2
2010	24.1	41.1	34.8
Regional share of population (% from total)			
1870	40.2	41.3	18.5
1913 pre-WWI borders	47.2	37.2	15.6
1913 interwar borders	45.1	38.2	16.7
1950	43.7	37.4	18.9
1950 post-WWII borders	45.1	36.0	18.9
1990	50.7	28.8	20.5
1990 post-1990 borders	45.6	32.6	21.8
2010	41.7	34.1	24.2

Source: Broadberry and Klein (2012).

and 2010, to put the east into comparative perspective. We can see that eastern Europe, measured in population, was the largest region in 1913. When measured by total GDP, however, eastern Europe falls well behind north-western Europe, though it still exceeds southern Europe. What are the implications for standards of living measured by GDP per capita? Table 3.2 reveals a pattern: eastern Europe has consistently exhibited the lowest GDP per capita relative to north-western and southern regions from the late nineteenth century to the present day. This is even more pronounced when measured relative to Europe as a whole: GDP per capita in east European countries comprised between 60 and 74 per cent of the GDP per capita of Europe throughout the entire period, suggesting a remarkable persistence in aggregate standards of living. Table 3.3 presents average annual growth rates for the European regions in four time periods: 1870–1913, 1913–50, 1950–90, and 1990–2010. These appear to have been rather unimpressive, except for the decades between 1950 and 1990. Given the low levels of GDP per capita in all regions, one might have expected a catching-up process

Table 3.2 GDP per capita, and relative per capita GDP, 1870–2010

	Eastern Europe	North-western Europe	Southern Europe	Europe
GDP per capita (1990 international $)				
1870	1,240	2,227	1,418	1,680
1913 pre-WWI borders	1,756	4,037	2,224	2,678
1913 interwar borders	1,597	4,004	2,207	2,619
1950	2,573	5,213	2,712	3,586
1950 post-WWII borders	2,603	5,273	2,697	3,582
1990	6,407	17,700	11,051	10,610
1990 post-1990 borders	6,618	16,954	11,051	10,939
2010	8,390	22,505	13,964	14,549
GDP per capita relative to Europe (%)				
1870	73.81	132.53	84.39	100.00
1913 pre-WWI borders	65.59	150.75	83.03	100.00
1913 interwar borders	60.99	152.87	84.26	100.00
1950	71.73	145.36	75.61	100.00
1950 post-WWII borders	72.67	147.20	75.27	100.00
1990	60.39	166.83	104.16	100.00
1990 post-1990 borders	60.50	154.99	101.02	100.00
2010	57.67	154.69	95.98	100.00

Sources: Broadberry and Klein 2012; Maddison Project Database, version 2013.

Table 3.3 GDP per capita average annual growth rates (%), 1870–2010

	Eastern Europe	North-western Europe	Southern Europe	Europe
1870–1913	0.81	1.38	1.05	1.08
1913–50	1.29	0.71	0.56	0.85
1950–90	2.25	3.03	3.53	2.71
1990–2010	1.17	1.45	1.14	1.43

Sources: Broadberry and Klein 2012; Maddison Project 2014.

in the east, but no discernible trend is apparent. Of course, regional grouping conceals inter-country differences. This is highlighted in Table 3.4, which shows average annual GDP per capita growth rates along with GDP per capita levels for individual countries in eastern Europe. Here the point of comparison is north-west Europe, the most economically advanced region at

Table 3.4 GDP per capita average annual growth rates and GDP per capita levels in 1990 international $, individual countries, 1870–1990

					1870–1913					
	Austria-Hungary	Bulgaria	Romania	Russia	Serbia					NW Europe
GDP pc in 1870	1,584	809	1,143	1,129	599					2,227
% annual growth	1.13	1.36	0.93	0.74	1.32					1.38
					1913–50					
	Bulgaria	Czechoslovakia	Hungary	Poland	Romania	USSR	Yugoslavia			NW Europe
GDP pc in 1913 inter-war borders	1,450	2,112	2,442	1,941	1,705	1,020	1,482			4,004
% annual growth	0.23	1.31	0.04	0.63	0.19	1.76	1.02			0.71
					1950–90					
	Albania	Bulgaria	Czechoslovakia	East Germany	Hungary	Poland	Romania	USSR	Yugoslavia	NW Europe
GDP pc in 1950 post-WWII borders	1,001	1,577	3,429	3,127	2,481	2,447	1,176	2,827	1,546	5,273
% annual growth	2.29	3.14	2.26	1.50	2.39	1.84	2.70	2.23	3.16	3.03

Note: NW stands for North-western.
Source: Broadberry and Klein (2012).

this time. The figures are suggestive of unconditional convergence among eastern European countries, most notably in the periods 1950–90, and 1990–2010. However, it would be misleading to conclude that east European economies converged with the north-west European economies for two important reasons. First, the convergence in the period 1913–50 was driven by Hungary and the USSR – two clear outliers – making it difficult to generalize across the region for these decades. Second, when we compare growth rates and levels of GDP per capita in the east with those of north-western Europe, the growth rates were, in almost all cases, lower in the east (with the exception of the USSR and Czechoslovakia in 1913–50 and Bulgaria in 1950–90). This indicates that eastern Europe had *not* joined the convergence club of north-west Europe, as was already pointed out by Vonyó (2017) for the period 1950–89.

The Late Nineteenth Century

Economic development in eastern Europe was slow to gain momentum, even before the massive upheavals of the twentieth century. At the end of the nineteenth century, the region was still largely agrarian, characterized by weak central states beholden to strong corporative interests. In many areas, serfdom was only recently abolished; local factor markets were still impacted by mobility restrictions and weak property rights. Institutional constraints in various forms – including town and guild privileges, noble privileges (including the residual effects of serfdom), and communal regulations – kept agricultural productivity low (Janoušek 1967). The decades just before the outbreak of World War I witnessed some signs of economic life in distinct parts of the region (Klein 2011), but development was fairly lacklustre, and failed to bring about any substantial convergence with north-west Europe, as the growth rates in Table 3.4 indicate. A closer look at the trends in specific countries can shed some light on the underperformance of the region as a whole.

The economic development of the Habsburg Empire was a history of simultaneous successes and failures. While the empire was economically on a par with other parts of German-speaking central Europe at the beginning of the nineteenth century, this was no longer the case as the century came to a close. The monarchy comprised regions varying widely in their economic performance – lower Austria and the Czech lands were among the most advanced and reached levels of development comparable (though not equal) to parts of Germany, while the territories of the future

Yugoslavia were among the poorest (especially Dalmatia). Industrialization in the more precocious regions was well under way, and its origins can be traced back to the eighteenth century. The observed gradient confirms that proximity to western Europe played a role, with the Czech and Alpine territories leading the way. By the second half of the nineteenth century, large differences had developed, with Hungary growing significantly more rapidly than Austria. This occurred against the backdrop of the 1867 constitutional settlement, which established the dual monarchy with a customs and monetary union. Looking at sectoral composition, Hungary was dominated by agriculture, with over 70 per cent of the labour force in this sector in 1910, while in Austria, agriculture comprised only about 50 per cent of the labour force in 1910, with manufacturing and distribution coming in second, followed by finance and transport (Schulze 2007). The large agricultural sector in relatively more advanced Austria was in stark contrast to Germany, where the agricultural sector had been steadily shrinking over forty years. Growth rates in different sectors were uneven in the decades before World War I (Schulze 2000), though it is clear that growth in Austria was driven primarily by the expansion of manufacturing, whereas in Hungary it was driven by growth in agriculture. The relatively modest growth rates for the Habsburg monarchy might be explained by the low rate of productivity growth in Austrian agriculture, and the very modest increase in manufacturing. The same rates were significantly higher in the German lands (Schulze 2007).

The proximate sources of economic growth, such as physical capital and human capital, as well as the extent of structural change, can provide some clues as to why the Habsburg lands underperformed relative to north-west Europe. It is possible for an economy to exhibit growth through the reallocation of labour from agriculture to the manufacturing sector. But the story of structural transformation in the Habsburg lands turns out to be complex. The structural change that occurred was growth-promoting; however, its effects were more pronounced in economically less developed parts of the empire. Standard growth accounting exercises suggest that aggregate productivity growth in Austria was hampered by a large rural sector with low rates of capital formation, in stark contrast with Hungarian agriculture, which exhibited rapid capital stock growth (Schulze 2007). Interestingly, industrial capital stock growth did not translate into respectable productivity growth – an observation that economic historians struggle to explain.

Table 3.5 Sectoral employment (%), 1870–1913

	Agriculture		Industry		Services	
	c.1870	c.1913	c.1870	c.1913	c.1870	c.1913
Austria-Hungary	67.0	59.5	15.5	21.8	17.5	18.7
Bulgaria		81.9		8.1		10.0
Romania		79.6		8.0		12.4
Russia		58.6		16.1		25.3
Serbia		82.2		11.1		6.7
North-west Europe	31.7	20.9	35.0	39.5	33.3	39.6
Southern Europe	58.6	49.3	23.2	26.8	18.2	23.9

Source: Broadberry et al. 2010: table 3.1.

The growth patterns in south-eastern Europe were not much better than those in the Habsburg lands. Growth rates were higher in Bulgaria and Serbia, but they started at considerably lower levels of GDP per capita. The economies of Bulgaria, Romania, and the Kingdom of Serbia were largely agrarian, with around 80 per cent of the population employed in agriculture as late as 1913 (see Table 3.5). Interestingly, it was not the industrial sector but the service sector which employed the second largest number of workers (except in Serbia). Industrial dynamics were concentrated in large private industries, and in mineral and oil extraction. Existing light industries were not capital-intensive; they produced goods with cheap labour. Growth in these areas initially surpassed that of agriculture, but it was short-lived and failed to create conditions for sustainable industrialization (Kopsidis 2012a; 2012b). Profound structural change did not occur.

The Russian Empire faced similar challenges. Like most of its neighbours to the west, its largest sector was agriculture, and grain was its main commodity by far. However, despite employing some 75 per cent of the population, agricultural productivity remained low, with per capita output figures similar to those in the more sluggish regions of the Habsburg Empire, and well behind western Europe (Gregory 1994). Industrial productivity was even lower, and remained so in heavy industry. The growth observed in this period was primarily in textiles and railroads. While the Russian economy did show signs of increased dynamism in the late nineteenth century, sustained long-term growth was inhibited by chronic political instability (manifestations of which included the assassination of Alexander II, continued rural uprisings, and the 1905 and 1917 revolutions) and growth-inhibiting institutional features, such as communal land tenure and communal tax responsibility.

The causes of agrarian stagnation in eastern Europe have been debated among scholars, who note that low levels of urbanization and an underdeveloped industrial sector generated a low-productivity equilibrium (Kopsidis 2012a; 2012b). This is reflected in occupational structure, as shown in Table 3.5. But this is not so much an explanation as a restatement of the problem; these are two sides of the same coin. While lack of urban (or industrial) demand probably did contribute to stagnation, a poor agrarian sector could hardly release the labour required for urbanization and industrialization. The equilibrium remained entrenched; structural change in these conditions posed significant challenges. Policies aiming to promote industrialization were characterized by inefficiencies inherent in bureaucratic government, amplified by a policy of import tariffs which protected inefficient domestic industries. While there has been little work to date on the institutional barriers to growth in this region, the existing historical literature paints a picture of weak states beholden to powerful interests, struggling to build the infrastructure required for efficient tax collection, the assignment and enforcement of property rights, and the implementation of economic and social reform – all of which affected incentives for and perceived risks to innovation and improvements in productivity.

1913–50

The institutional equilibrium that characterized eastern Europe became increasingly precarious in the decades before World War I. Various attempts at top-down industrialization did little to significantly raise standards of living for the majority of inhabitants, or to expand the range of economic opportunities available to those who, as we have seen, still laboured predominantly in agriculture (Radice 1985). The weak development of property rights and those civil institutions required to enforce them, as well as the enduring strength of corporative interests, limited the availability of capital, and undermined incentives to invest in projects that required longer time horizons. Frustration and dissatisfaction with the existing equilibrium, already apparent in the nineteenth century and bolstered by the new ideologies of nationalism and socialism, began to spread, and eventually erupted in a devastating series of conflicts. The inauspicious conditions created by the violent disruptions that characterized the first half of the twentieth century – World War I, the Russian Revolution, the Great Depression, World War II –

further undermined all earlier attempts of east European countries to generate growth and catch up to their more dynamic western neighbours.

The aftermath of World War I brought significant political changes to the region. Borders were redrawn and new national states emerged from the ruins of the Habsburg and Ottoman Empires, including Czechoslovakia, Hungary, Poland, Yugoslavia, Albania, Bulgaria, and Romania. The shock of these geopolitical changes affected economic development profoundly: access to foreign markets, transportation networks, and internal factor and commodity market flows all had to be reconfigured; new economic policies were required. A different international economic environment emerged: the Gold Standard of the 'first globalization' era ended, international factor flows were disrupted, and domestic issues dominated the agendas of policymakers everywhere. Furthermore, the former subject states of the old empires had to reorganize themselves politically along democratic lines for the first time in history. At the same time, on the eastern frontier of Europe, the Russian Empire was busy reorganizing itself politically, but along 'Marxist-Leninist', rather than democratic, lines. The USSR emerged in the 1920s as the first socialist state in history – a vast territory comprised of fifteen republics, with a planned economy managed by officials in Moscow. The political and economic challenges faced by the region were enormous.

The initial economic conditions of east European countries in this period differed significantly: at one end of the spectrum was the relatively advanced economy of the newly formed Czechoslovakia, while at the other end were the mainly agricultural economies of the Balkans and the Soviet Union. The aggregate growth performance of the region was not impressive, and even though GDP per capita growth rates were higher for several of these countries than the north-west European average (in contrast to the findings for the period before 1913), we must bear in mind that they started at much lower initial levels. The occupational data presented in Table 3.6 suggest very little, if any, structural change.

The sudden creation of so many newly independent states, all trying to protect their emerging industries with high tariff walls, very likely had a negative effect on their longer-run economic performances. Policies aimed at the protection of fledgling domestic firms likely resulted in the inefficient utilization of resources, thus suppressing growth and complicating these countries' attempts to adapt to the new external economic environment. The existing evidence is not entirely clear on this question. Some have argued that, on the contrary, the dissolution of the Habsburg monarchy had little impact on trade, since the political borders erected after World War

Table 3.6 Sectoral employment (%), 1920–50

	Agriculture			Industry			Services		
	*c.*1920	*c.*1930	*c.*1950	*c.*1920	*c.*1930	*c.*1950	*c.*1920	*c.*1930	*c.*1950
Bulgaria*	82.4	81.9	77.4	8.1	8.2	10.5	9.4	9.9	12.1
Czechoslovakia	40.9	37.5	37.8	37.4	37.7	37.5	21.7	24.8	24.7
Hungary	59.7	54.8	47.8	20.2	24.9	29.8	20.1	20.3	22.4
Poland	77.5	67.3	57.6	9.6	17.5	23.1	13.0	15.2	19.3
Romania*	80.0	80.7	70.1	8.1	9.3	16.8	12.0	10.0	13.1
Yugoslavia	82.2	79.7	66.9	11.0	11.2	18.2	6.7	9.0	14.9
Greece	57.1	61.1	51.3	18.7	18.0	20.7	24.2	20.9	28.0
North-west Europe*	22.5	17.7	13.4	39.3	40.6	44.2	38.2	41.7	42.4
Southern Europe*	50.8	43.1	40.7	27.6	29.8	30.2	21.5	27.2	29.1

* *c.*1913.
Source: Buyst and Franaszek 2010: table 9.1.

I still reflected pre-1914 economic reality (Wolf et al. 2011). Tariffs appear to have been a mixed bag; on some commodities (e.g. rye) they were indeed low, while on others, such as iron and steel, they were set as high as 109 per cent (Wolf et al. 2011).

Generally, the region's performance in agriculture was disappointing; relatively little technological innovation occurred in this period. This was largely due to piecemeal reforms, low levels of investment, and land reforms that often maintained antiquated practices on small holdings (Aldcroft and Morewood 1995). This sector was still employing over 60 per cent of the labour force as late as 1930 in countries like Bulgaria, Poland, Romania, and Yugoslavia (Table 3.6). The industrial sector in these countries fared better, as the figures for industrial output indicate (Table 3.7). We hesitate, however, to conclude that the expansion of industrial output implied an increase in labour productivity and the efficient allocation of resources. The industrial sector in eastern Europe continued to suffer from low levels of capital investment, low agricultural productivity, skill-mismatch, and disorientation from the shocks of World War I and the Great Depression (see e.g. Eckstein 1955; Teichová 1988). The protectionist policies of national governments did little to incentivize productivity growth. The industrial sector was dominated by consumer goods industries; the development of heavy industries was very uneven. For instance, metal, chemical, and engineering production increased in Czechoslovakia (Teichová 1988), and Hungary's electrical engineering and railway industry raised global market shares (Klein et al. 2017), while heavy

Table 3.7 Manufacturing production, 1913–38 (index number 1925–29 = 100)

	Czechoslovakia	Hungary	Poland	Romania	UK
1913	65.9	104.1	135.1	85.7	101.6
1920	46.0	50.0	47.4	30.0	97.6
1921	65.9	66.6	63.2	40.4	58.2
1922	60.5	83.2	99.9	62.7	78.3
1923	63.7	58.9	96.2	62.7	84.6
1924	85.0	69.3	76.8	76.3	94.4
1925	89.9	79.8	85.3	79.0	93.3
1926	86.0	86.8	79.6	88.9	85.7
1927	101.4	102.7	102.8	101.8	105.1
1928	109.4	112.4	116.4	112.9	104.8
1929	113.2	118.5	116.1	117.3	111.1
1930	102.5	112.5	102.4	113.5	101.8
1931	91.3	102.6	87.0	120.5	92.3
1932	70.9	95.0	71.2	95.9	93.0
1933	66.8	105.2	80.3	116.7	100.2
1934	74.8	119.0	92.2	143.8	114.2
1935	79.2	128.9	100.3	141.6	123.9
1936	91.2	142.1	112.6	150.0	136.9
1937	108.6	156.1	131.9	156.7	146.9
1938	95.9	149.1	142.2	152.4	135.1

Source: Teichová 1985: 230.

industry failed to develop as a separate sector in countries like Yugoslavia and Bulgaria.

One key factor in aggregate performance during the 1920s was the financing of the industrialization process. Given the low level of per capita income, domestic surpluses were limited. The revenue potential of exports was constrained by the foreign-trade policies of other countries, as well as by the dislocation of foreign trade once borders had been redrawn. That said, the export potential of most countries here was concentrated in agriculture and primary production goods, which were seeing few productivity gains and declining prices. Thus the optimal solution for these states was to borrow on foreign capital markets (Feinstein et al. 2008). However, foreign capital flows appear to have had limited effects on industrialization in these countries. This conjecture is supported by import data, which show that the share of imported consumer goods in Bulgaria, Romania, Yugoslavia, and Hungary stood at about 50 per cent of total imports by the 1920s. Only in Czechoslovakia and Poland was it lower – just over 20 per cent (Drabek 1985). While machinery imports increased in the second half of the 1920s, that share was still small compared to consumer goods.

The Great Depression years affected east European economies significantly (complicated in the USSR by shocks related to central planning and collectivization), as the primary goods they produced were highly exposed to price fluctuations. High levels of foreign debt, the collapse of agricultural prices, and the reversal of flows of foreign capital in the late 1920s (Eichengreen 1992) left these countries with difficult choices. Deflation made them increasingly dependent on foreign capital, which they used mainly to finance the import of consumer goods. Restrictive monetary policies implemented in compliance with the interwar Gold Exchange Standard exacerbated the lack of capital, and ultimately pushed these countries into depression (Aldcroft and Morewood 1995). Vulnerability varied: agrarian countries were more vulnerable to changes in the terms of trade and flows of foreign capital which financed their imports, while more industrialized countries were vulnerable to changes in the demand for their exports. By the early 1930s, however, all the countries of eastern Europe were experiencing the Great Depression. The recovery process was uneven and depended, among other things, on monetary policies and adherence to the Gold Exchange Standard. Indeed, countries which adhered to the Gold Standard, such as Poland, did not manage to return to pre-depression per capita GDP levels before the outbreak of World War II.

The newly formed Soviet Union faced many of the same challenges as its neighbours immediately to the west: the breakdown of old imperial institutions, border adjustments, and war-related devastation set back economic reform efforts considerably. There were both economic and ideological pressures to industrialize as quickly as possible, as the communist society the Bolsheviks intended to build required an urban, industrial economy with a proletarian citizenry. In their attempt to achieve this goal, the Bolsheviks lurched, in the space of a decade, from a system of total central command of the economy (war communism), back to one of limited market freedoms (the New Economic Policy), before moving, finally, to an even more centralized command system, which would persist until the USSR's collapse in 1991.

Under the New Economic Policy (NEP), in the years *c.*1921–28, industrial production figures recovered to their pre-World War I levels (Markevich and Harrison 2011). This recovery was uneven though, and concentrated mostly in capital goods industries (such as chemical or electrical goods), with consumer goods industries considerably behind (Davies 1994). The NEP plan to use market incentives to increase grain production and finance industrialization had limited success overall. The market incentives were effective, but peasants proved reluctant to sell their grain to the state at set prices and the state-subsidized industrialization project soon foundered. After Stalin's rise to power in 1928, the NEP was aborted, and the entire Soviet economy was brought under the control of the central state. Peasants were expropriated in the process of 'collectivization', after which agriculture was run as a state enterprise, with output goals set centrally. Agricultural productivity plummeted in the process and famine devastated the western grain belt in the early 1930s. At the same time, transport, industry, and all services were nationalized and brought under central command. A central committee decided which goods would be produced, set all prices and production quotas, and organized distribution – all within the framework of 'Five-Year Plans'. The flaws inherent in this system and the outcomes it generated, as well as the rationale for its existence, have been discussed extensively in the literature (see, for instance, Gregory 2003). The early years of command and Five-Year Plans saw significant acceleration in the industrialization process. However, while existing figures may demonstrate growth and increased industrial output, they tell us little about chronic shortages, the poor quality of goods produced, the dearth of consumer goods, or the role of forced labour in the economy – all of which have been well established in the literature.

1950–90

The years after World War II saw watershed changes in the economic systems of eastern Europe. Following the rise of communist parties in east European countries (with support from the Soviet Union), central planning replaced market economies throughout the region. While state interventions in the economy were undertaken in most of Europe during the post-war period, these were trivial compared to the changes brought to eastern Europe. Private ownership of enterprises was abolished and the collectivization of agriculture was undertaken everywhere (with the exceptions of Poland and Yugoslavia). Soviet-style Five-Year Plans were launched in Yugoslavia in 1947, Czechoslovakia and Bulgaria in 1949, Poland and Hungary in 1950, and Romania and Albania in 1951 (Eichengreen 2007; Berend 2016). Centralized command economies, modelled on that of the USSR, were established throughout the region. Central planning commissions set targets that could be met by existing levels of production, using input–output models. Central planners not only set targets for production, they also set prices, distributed wages, managed labour, investment, technological innovation, and foreign trade. (On the structural details, see Gregory 2003; Eichengreen 2007; Berend 2016.) The Eastern bloc of centrally planned economies was united under an umbrella organization known as CMEA or Comecon – the Council for Mutual Economic Assistance – which operationalized bilateral trade agreements among affiliated countries. The effect was to consolidate trade within the bloc itself, such that, from the early 1950s, 60–75 per cent of the overall foreign trade of east European countries was with other command economies.

After the death of Stalin, protests against communist regimes spread across eastern Europe, and while the most pronounced forms of resistance were crushed in Hungary and Czechoslovakia by the Soviet Army and the armies of the Warsaw Pact in 1956 and 1968 respectively, they marked significant points of divergence from the Soviet model. This became more and more apparent in the 1970s and 1980s, when partial reforms to relax central planning and introduce market mechanisms at the margins appeared in some countries, most notably Hungary. Yugoslavia followed a distinct path from the beginning, sometimes called the 'Yugoslav alternative' (Jeffries 1993; Berend 2016). There prices were partially liberalized already in the 1950s, collectivization was halted, and firms were managed by elected workers' councils, somewhat independent of central authorities. Still, neither Yugoslavia nor Hungary could have been called a market-oriented economy. That shift only happened with the collapse of the Soviet system after 1989.

The economic performance of these centrally planned economies in eastern Europe, to judge by their growth rates alone, was respectable. As shown in Table 3.4, GDP per capita growth rates were higher than in the period before World War II. However, their magnitudes relative to north-western Europe again reveal that the east European countries were under-performing, and that, together with lower initial GDP per capita, suggests that they did not catch up to western economies. The growth rates over the entire existence of the centrally planned economies conceal two phases in their development, as seen in Table 3.8. The first one, from 1950 to 1973, often called the Golden Age, is a phase in which these countries showed high GDP per capita growth rates, comparable to and even higher than the average of north-west Europe. The second phase is from 1973 to 1989, and it shows a substantial decline in growth rates, now lower than the north-west average. The upward economic trajectory of the centrally planned economies in the early phase reflected their largely low level of economic development, with

Table 3.8 GDP per capita average annual growth rates (1990 international $)

	GDP per capita levels			GDP per capita growth rates	
	1950	1973	1990	1950–73	1973–90
Albania	1,001	2,273	2,499	3.57	0.56
Bulgaria	1,577	5,296	5,537	5.27	0.26
Czechoslovakia	3,429	7,000	8,464	3.10	1.12
East Germany	3,127	8,559	–	4.38	–
Hungary	2,481	5,596	6,454	3.54	0.84
Poland	2,447	5,334	5,113	3.39	−0.25
Romania	1,176	3,457	3,460	4.69	0.01
USSR	2,827	6,101	6,888	3.34	0.71
Yugoslavia	1,546	4,237	5,470	4.38	1.50
North-western Europe	5,273	12,745	17,700	3.84	1.93

Source: Broadberry and Klein 2012.

agriculture being the dominant sector, in some countries employing more than 70 per cent of the labour force (Vonyó 2017). That changed over time as the policies of industrialization were implemented. Table 3.9 shows the sectoral composition of Czechoslovakia, Poland, and Hungary from 1950 to 1989, indicating a decline in agriculture and an increase in industry. These figures also suggest stagnation across all sectors in the 1980s and signs of significant economic decline in Poland.

The policies implemented for rapid industrialization skewed towards heavy industries such as metal, mining, and chemical industries. They relied on extensive growth: large investments in capital goods and use of abundant labour from the agricultural sector. It is obvious from Table 3.10 that capital accumulation played an important role in most countries throughout the period of central planning. It is important to compare growth accounts with GDP per capita growth rates: the stagnation in growth accounts in the two decades before the collapse of the socialist system is consistent with stagnation in total factor productivity and the decline of capital accumulation. Focusing on industrialization had a positive effect on aggregate growth in the 1950s and 1960s, when many poor regions saw considerable improvement. However, diminishing returns soon set in. The lack of investment in light, consumer-oriented industries and agriculture, as well as shortcomings in infrastructure, housing, and basic utilities meant that the standard of living was significantly lower than what was implied by the impressive GDP per

Table 3.9 GDP by sector of origin (% share)

	1950	1960	1970	1980	1989
Czechoslovakia					
Agriculture	32.4	23.6	17.7	16.3	17.0
Industry	25.5	32.2	37.5	39.8	40.0
Construction	6.6	9.4	8.7	8.6	7.6
Transport and communications	4.0	7.2	7.7	8.2	8.3
Trade	5.5	6.3	7.9	8.5	8.7
Non-material services	25	21.3	20.5	18.4	18.4
Hungary					
Agriculture	36.6	30.0	23.2	23.4	24.3
Industry	22.5	28.1	33.4	32.7	32.4
Construction	4.5	5.8	7.5	7.0	5.3
Transport and communications	5.1	7.8	8.3	9.0	8.2
Trade	3.4	4.3	6.1	7.0	7.0
Non-material services	27.8	23.9	21.7	20.9	22.8
Poland					
Agriculture	49.5	42.4	32.3	24.1	28.9
Industry	15.5	23.1	30.7	33.7	29.1
Construction	2.5	4.5	5.5	6.6	5.0
Transport and communications	3.2	4.3	5.7	9.2	8.3
Trade	3.7	4.3	5.2	6.5	6.5
Non-material services	24.5	21.3	20.6	19.9	22.3

Notes: Agriculture includes farming, fishing, and forestry. Industry includes mining, manufacturing, and electrical power. Trade includes both wholesale and retail. Non-material services include finance, housing, water and gas utilities, government services, catering, and personal services.
Source: Vonyó and Klein 2019.

capita growth rates. As noted above, one of the most salient features of central planning was chronic shortages (Kornai 1980). Long waiting lists for consumer durables such as cars, televisions, and especially housing were the norm; long queues for basic foodstuffs such as meat and fruit were not uncommon; and the black market flourished, alongside rent-seeking by shop managers and clerks (Berend 1996; Gregory 2003).

The 1970s and early 1980s were the era of stagnation in the Eastern bloc. The communist regimes attempted to reinvigorate their economies by replicating earlier investment-driven policies (as we see in Table 3.9; Berend 1996), only to slow them down again in the 1980s. Partial reforms were introduced in various

Table 3.10 Growth accounting for Czechoslovakia, Hungary, and Poland, 1950–90

	1950s	1960s	1970s	1980s
Czechoslovakia				
GDP per worker hour	4.1	2.6	2.1	1.1
Capital intensity	3.2	3.3	2.8	1.7
Capital deepening	1.3	1.3	1.1	0.6
TFP I	2.8	1.3	1.0	0.5
Education	0.3	0.3	0.3	0.3
TFP II	2.5	1.0	0.7	0.2
Hungary				
GDP per worker hour	3.1	4.0	2.6	2.5
Capital intensity	1.8	3.9	3.6	2.9
Capital deepening	0.7	1.6	1.4	1.2
TFP I	2.4	2.4	1.2	1.3
Education	0.2	0.4	0.5	0.0
TFP II	2.2	2.0	0.7	1.3
Poland				
GDP per worker hour	2.6	2.1	2.6	2.3
Capital intensity	−1.0	0.4	3.5	2.7
Capital deepening	−0.4	0.2	1.4	1.1
TFP I	3.0	1.9	1.2	1.2
Education	0.4	0.8	0.4	0.4
TFP II	2.6	1.1	0.8	0.8

Notes: TFP I and TFP II are the residuals of growth accounts, not accounting and accounting for educational attainment, respectively. 'Education' refers to human-capital deepening and is the weighted contribution of average improvement in educational attainment to aggregate labour productivity growth.
Source: Vonyó and Klein 2019.

countries in the 1980s. For example, price reforms in Hungary from 1968 had created a system in which 78 per cent of industrial prices became free market prices, while 70 per cent of raw materials and energy sources were fixed. This was replaced with a reform in 1979–80 which gradually linked domestic prices to world market prices.[1] Other countries tried to break out of stagnation through import-oriented growth and consumption (Aldcroft and Morewood 1995; Berend 2016). The availability of cheap credit in the 1970s allowed some countries, including Hungary, Poland, Romania, and Yugoslavia, to borrow

1 For more on reforms in the 1970s and 1980s, see Jeffries 1993.

heavily. However, once the cheap credit dried up in the early 1980s and interest rates increased, countries quickly depleted their foreign reserves servicing their debts (Berend 1996). The import-oriented strategy included not only consumer goods, but also technology, in an attempt to bridge the growing gap with the West. The results were not encouraging and many joint projects with Western counterparts either failed to materialize or turned out to be inefficient (Aldcroft and Morewood 1995). In the end, neither marginal reforms nor import-led growth bolstered these stagnating economies and, by end of the 1980s, GDP per capita in eastern Europe was only about 60 per cent of the European level, down from about 73 per cent in 1950.

One ambition of the early communist parties was greater equality. Did they deliver on a more egalitarian society? This has been debated by scholars (see Atkinson and Micklewright 1992) and the consensus seems to be that, on average, money incomes in socialist economies were more equally distributed than in market economies. That said, there were subtle differences among socialist economies: some countries had more egalitarian income distribution than others, and some experienced even higher income inequality than market economies. Figures 3.1A and 3.1B present the evolution of the Gini coefficients and decile ratios (the latter defined as the ratio of earnings in the top decile to the earnings in the bottom decile) for Czechoslovakia, Hungary, Poland, and the USSR from 1970 to 1989. Great Britain is used as the comparison country. Both figures show qualitatively similar patterns: the socialist economies had indeed, on average, lower income inequality than the market economy of Great Britain, with Czechoslovakia being the most egalitarian in that group. However, these figures must be treated with caution. First, income inequality in these countries was not static. Poland and the USSR experienced a significant increase in inequality in the mid-1970s and then again in the mid-1980s, while Hungary witnessed quite a dramatic rise in inequality in the 1980s. The reasons behind those patterns relate largely to changes in policies, such as minimum wage reforms and Gorbachev's perestroika (Atkinson and Micklewright 1992). Second, it is important to bear in mind that inhabitants of these countries did not view income as the main determinant of equality, since everyone was poor. Those who enjoyed some kind of privileged status (party members, for instance) were granted greater access to goods and services, education, jobs, travel, and other perks, which distinguished them from the majority. This kind of inequality pervaded all these societies; it is more difficult to capture, however, with Gini coefficients and similar metrics.

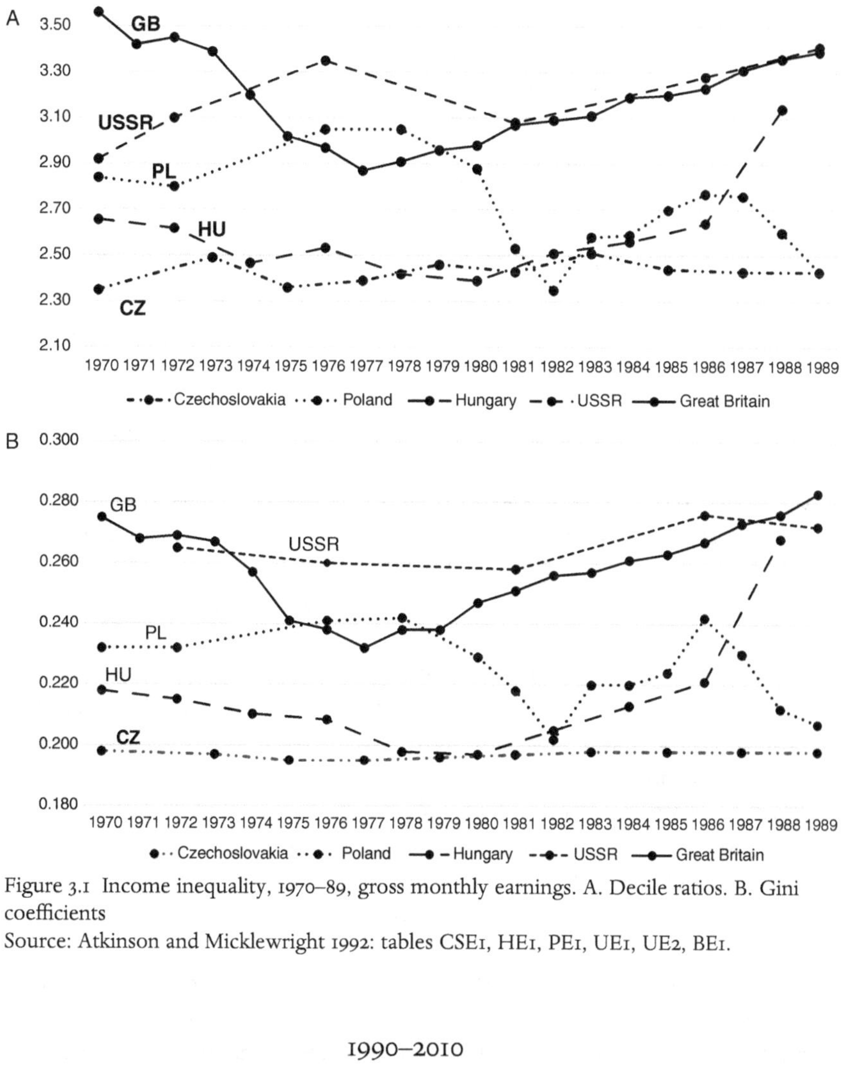

Figure 3.1 Income inequality, 1970–89, gross monthly earnings. A. Decile ratios. B. Gini coefficients

Source: Atkinson and Micklewright 1992: tables CSE1, HE1, PE1, UE1, UE2, BE1.

1990–2010

When the Berlin Wall fell in 1989, followed by the collapse of the Soviet Union in 1991, there was the widespread expectation – in both East and West – that the economic convergence which had so long eluded the East would finally be realized. The immediate dismantling of the command system, accompanied by moves to implement market reforms, bolstered this expectation. New political parties were formed, elections were held, new constitutions were drafted. Foreign investment flowed into these so-called 'transition' economies. People and goods began to move between eastern and western Europe in ways that had not occurred since World War II. After a decade of reform, the cracks began to show, however, and optimism gradually began to fade. In many of the former Eastern bloc countries, the old system proved more difficult to dislodge than expected. At one end of the spectrum, the German Democratic Republic was peacefully reintegrated into Germany, while at the other end, the former Yugoslavia was plunged into a long and bloody civil war, resulting in a new constellation of nation states. In between, there were protracted struggles to redefine political systems, establish new institutions, and privatize key industries. Success was largely uneven, from the earliest days of transition.

The problematic nature of the transition from central planning to markets is visible in Table 3.11, which shows five measures of economic growth between 1990 and 2010: initial GDP per capita, average annual growth rate, the year when a country reached the lowest GDP per capita after the fall of central planning, and the percentage of that lowest GDP per capita from the initial one in 1990. We see that the transition period witnessed a dramatic drop in living standards in *all* countries, but especially among the countries of the former Soviet Union and Yugoslavia. Indeed, some, such as Georgia and Ukraine, still had not reached their GDP per capita levels of 1990 some twenty years later. Central European countries were more successful, but even they experienced an initial drop in the early 1990s and recovered only later in that decade. The profound drop in GDP was unexpected and thus attracted a lot of scholarly attention. Two main explanations emerged: credit market imperfections and low liquidity due to restrictive macroeconomic policies (Calvo and Frenkel 1991; Calvo and Coricelli 1993), and the disruption of supply chains due to the breakdown of old regimes (Blanchard and Kremer 1997; Roland and Verdier 1999).

Altogether, the transition process was characterized not only by output decline, but also by declines in capital stock and difficulties related to labour reallocation, trade reorientation, structural change, and institutional collapse (Campos and Coricelli 2002). The shrinking of capital stock was contrary to expectations, as it was assumed that the introduction of market forces would improve investment efficiency, and that foreign direct investment would provide the necessary capital for restructuring. The evidence indicates, however, that investment fell more than GDP (Campos and Coricelli 2002) and that the flow of foreign direct investment, though a significant source of technological transfers, was highly uneven among the transition economies. Labour reallocation was probably the most visible challenge of the transition

Table 3.11 Economic growth in eastern Europe, 1990–2010 (1990 international $)

	GDP pc in 1990: post-1990 borders	% annual growth	Year of lowest GDP pc	Year when surpasses 1990 GDP pc levels	% of lowest GDP pc from 1990 GDP pc
Albania	2,499	3.83	1992	1999	70.6
Romania	3,511	1.41	1992	2003	79.8
Bosnia	3,697	1.74	1994	2002	24.8
Serb./Mont.	4,144	2.85	1993	1996	69.3
Azerbaijan	4,639	3.22	1996	2006	39.0
Poland	5,113	3.72	1991	1994	92.7
Bulgaria	5,597	2.34	1996	2001	82.7
Macedonia	5,755	0.32	1995	2007	76.6
Armenia	6,066	2.61	1993	2003	49.0
Moldova	6,170	−1.99	1999	–	35.3
Hungary	6,459	1.29	1993	1999	85.3
Belarus	7,194	3.21	1996	2003	65.1
Georgia	7,616	−1.05	1994	–	29.2
Slovakia	7,763	2.53	1992	1998	79.3
Russia	7,779	0.54	1998	2006	57.4
Croatia	8,123	0.96	1993	2002	66.0
Lithuania	8,663	1.20	1994	2003	56.4
Czech Rep.	8,895	1.93	1993	1999	87.8
Latvia	9,916	0.91	1993	2004	54.6
Estonia	10,820	2.82	1994	1998	74.4
Slovenia	11,351	2.17	1992	1996	86.2
Ukraine	6,027	−0.01	1998	–	42.2

Source: Maddison Project 2014.

process. Moving from zero unemployment in the command system, transition economies suddenly experienced unemployment in double digits, which, in many places, failed to decline in later stages of development (Jurajda and Terrell 2009). High levels of unemployment were accompanied by low levels of geographical labour mobility, suggesting that significant barriers to mobility hindered the successful reallocation of labour under market conditions. The reorientation of trade relationships came as a response to the collapse of Comecon, leading to a decline in foreign trade in the early years of transition. Most countries increased their trade with Western economies, and their openness increased relative to that under command conditions. The reorientation of external trade went hand-in-hand with restructuring the internal economy, as countries moved away from manufacturing and towards services. Overall, the performance of the transition economies in this region has fallen well short of expectations. There are many reasons for this, but underestimation of the challenge of transition, together with questionable policy decisions, were among the most critical (Švejnar 2002).

Radical economic reforms were undertaken to transition centrally planned economies to the market. Debates raged over the nature, timing, and scope of reforms, with the majority of countries opting for the fastest option, often referred to as a 'big bang' reform strategy. The strategy involved macroeconomic stabilization, as well as microeconomic restructuring. The former included price liberalization, restrictive fiscal and monetary policies, wage controls, and, in many cases, fixed exchange rate regimes. Microeconomic restructuring included the privatization of state-owned enterprises, the creation of a competitive banking system, and the introduction of a welfare safety net. These reforms simultaneously required the creation of a market-oriented legal framework, including labour regulations, banking regulations, and antitrust regulations. Privatization was one of the most contentious parts of the transition process and countries employed a range of approaches. Mass-scale and equal-access 'voucher' privatization was used in the Czech Republic, Lithuania, and, to a certain extent, in Slovakia; Poland and Slovenia transitioned more slowly, having state-owned firms run by independent supervisory boards rather than directly by the state; Ukraine and Russia relied on subsidized management-employee buyouts; and Estonia and Hungary began to sell off state firms one by one to outside buyers. The success of privatization has been mixed, not only with regard to the macroeconomic performance, but also in terms of firm-level productivity (Estrin et al. 2009). Furthermore, it has varied enormously between the countries of central and eastern Europe and the former Soviet Union, respectively. Overall, privatization has had a positive effect on total factor productivity, though the effect was larger when foreign owners took over than when domestic ones did so. For the countries of the former Soviet Union, the effect is outright negative. The effect on labour productivity is visible among firms privatized by foreigners, while privatization by employees or management demonstrated no effect. Despite these mixed results, all transition countries managed to substantially increase the share of their private sectors irrespective of privatization methods, in a relatively short period of time; and by the year 2000, more than half of GDP in most of these countries was generated in the private sector (Švejnar 2002).

Conclusion

The persistence of low-growth equilibria in east European countries is generally viewed as the legacy of the socialist 'experiment'. But as we have shown, the divergence between north-west Europe and the eastern countries was already evident in the nineteenth century; the countries of eastern Europe were struggling to industrialize on the eve of World War I. The institutional weaknesses associated with the communist era – insecure property rights and mechanisms for enforcement, imperfect factor markets, large-scale inefficiencies, and endemic corruption – were all present before the Russian Revolution of 1917, and in most countries of the Eastern bloc before Potsdam. The challenges of transition since 1990 are thus, in many ways, the same ones these countries faced in their late nineteenth-century attempts to grow their economies and 'catch up' to their neighbours in the West. It seems the socialist 'experiment' did not result in the significant break with the past that its architects had envisaged.

References

Aldcroft, D. H. and Morewood, S. (1995). *Economic Change in Eastern Europe since 1918*, Aldershot and Brookfield, VT: Edward Elgar Publishing.

Atkinson, A. B. and Micklewright, J. (1992). *Economic Transformation in Eastern Europe and the Distribution of Income*, Cambridge University Press.

Berend, I. T. (1996). *Central and Eastern Europe 1944–1993: Detour from the Periphery to the Periphery*, Cambridge University Press.

(2016). *An Economic History of Twentieth-Century Europe: Economic Regimes from Laissez-Faire to Globalization*, Cambridge University Press.

Blanchard, O. and Kremer, M. (1997). 'Disorganization', *Quarterly Journal of Economics*, 112, 1091–1126.

Broadberry, S. and Klein, A. (2012). 'Aggregate and Per Capita GDP in Europe, 1870–2000: Continental, Regional and National Data with Changing Boundaries', *Scandinavian Economic History Review*, 60(1), 79–107.

Broadberry, S., Federico, G., and Klein, A. (2010). 'Sectoral Developments, 1870–1914', in Broadberry, S. and O'Rourke, K. H. (eds.), *Cambridge Economic History of Modern Europe, Vol. 2: 1870 to the Present*, 2nd ed., Cambridge University Press, 59–83.

Buyst, E. and Franaszek, P. (2010). 'Sectoral Developments, 1914–1945', in Broadberry, S. and O'Rourke, K. H. (eds.), *Cambridge Economic History of Modern Europe, Vol. 2: 1870 to the Present*, 2nd ed., Cambridge University Press, 208–31.

Calvo, G. A. and Frenkel, J. A. (1991). 'Credit Markets, Credibility, and Economic Transformation', *Journal of Economic Perspectives*, 5, 139–148.

Calvo, G. A. and Coricelli, F. (1993). 'Output Collapse in Eastern Europe: The Role of Credit', *IMF Staff Papers*, 40, 32–52.

Campos, N. F. and Coricelli, A. (2002). 'Growth in Transition: What We Know, What We Don't, and What We Should', *Journal of Economic Literature* 40, 793–836.

Davies, R. W. (1994). 'Industry', in Davies, R. W., Harrison, M., and Wheatcroft, S. G. (eds.), *The Economic Transformation of the Soviet Union, 1913–1945*, Cambridge University Press, 131–157.

Drábek, Z. (1985). 'Foreign Trade Performance and Policy', in Käser, M. C. and Radice, E. A. (eds.), *The Economic History of Eastern Europe 1919–1975, Vol. I: Economic Structure and Performance between the Two Wars*, Oxford: Clarendon Press, 23–66.

Eckstein, A. (1955). 'National Income and Capital Formation in Hungary, 1900–1950', *Review of Income and Wealth*, 5, 152–223.

Eichengreen, B. J. (1992). *Golden Fetters: The Gold Standard and the Great Depression, 1919–1939*, Oxford University Press.

(2007). *The European Economy since 1945: Coordinated Capitalism and Beyond*, Princeton University Press.

Estrin, S., Hanousek, J., Kočenda, E., and Švejnar, J. (2009). 'The Effects of Privatization and Ownership in Transition Economies', *Journal of Economic Literature*, 47, 699–728.

Feinstein, C. H., Temin, P., and Toniolo, G. (2008). *The European Economy between the Wars*, Oxford University Press.

Gregory, P. R. (1994). *Before Command: An Economic History of Russia from Emancipation to the First Five-Year Plan*, Princeton University Press.

(2003). *The Political Economy of Stalinism*, Cambridge University Press.

Janoušek, E. (1967). *Historický Vývoj Produktivity Práce v Zemědělství v Období Pobělohorském*, Prague: Czechoslovak Agricultural Museum.

Jeffries, I. (1993). *Socialist Economies and the Transition to the Market: A Guide*, London: Routledge.

Jurajda, Š. and Terrell, K. (2009). 'Regional Unemployment and Human Capital in Transition Economies 1', *Economics of Transition*, 17, 241–274.

Klein, A. (2011). 'Did Children's Education Matter? Family Migration as a Mechanism of Human Capital Investment: Evidence from Nineteenth-Century Bohemia', *Economic History Review*, 64, 730–764.

Klein, A., Schulze, M. S., and Vonyó, T. (2017). 'How Peripheral Was the Periphery? Industrialization in East Central Europe since 1870', in O'Rourke, K. H. and Williamson, J. G. (eds.), *The Spread of Modern Industry to the Periphery since 1871*, Oxford University Press, 63–91.

Kopsidis, M. (2012a). 'Missed Opportunity or Inevitable Failure? The Search for Industrialization in Southeast Europe 1870–1940', European Historical Economics Society, working paper 0019.

(2012b). 'Peasant Agriculture and Economic Growth: The Case of Southeast Europe c.1870–1940 reinterpreted', European Historical Economics Society, working paper 0028.

Kornai, J. (1980). *Economics of Shortage*, Amsterdam: North-Holland.

Maddison, A. (1995). *Monitoring the World Economy, 1820–1992*, Paris: Development Centre of the Organisation for Economic Co-operation and Development.

Maddison Project Database, version 2013. Bolt, J. and van Zanden, J. L. (2014). 'The Maddison Project: Collaborative Research on Historical National Accounts', *Economic History Review*, 67, 627–651.

Markevich, A. and Harrison, M. (2011). 'Great War, Civil War, and Recovery: Russia's National Income, 1913 to 1928', *Journal of Economic History*, 71, 672–703.

Radice, E. A. (1985). 'General Characteristics of the Region between the Wars', in Käser, M. C. and Radice, E. A. (eds.), *The Economic History of Eastern Europe 1919–1975, Vol. I: Economic Structure and Performance between the Two Wars*, Oxford: Clarendon Press, 23–66.

Roland, G. and Verdier, T. (1999). 'Transition and the Output Fall', *Economics of Transition*, 7, 1–28.

Schulze, M. S. (2000). 'Patterns of Growth and Stagnation in the Late Nineteenth Century Habsburg Economy', *European Review of Economic History*, 4, 311–340.

(2007). 'Origins of Catch-Up Failure: Comparative Productivity Growth in the Habsburg Empire, 1870–1910', *European Review of Economic History*, 11, 189–218.

Švejnar, J. (2002). 'Transition Economies: Performance and Challenges', *Journal of Economic Perspectives*, 16, 3–28.

Teichová, A. (1985). 'Industry', in Käser, M. C. and Radice, E. A. (eds.), *The Economic History of Eastern Europe 1919–1975, Vol. I: Economic Structure and Performance between the Two Wars*, Oxford: Clarendon Press, 222–323.

(1988). *The Czechoslovak Economy 1918–1980*, London: Routledge.

Vonyó, T. (2017). 'War and Socialism: Why Eastern Europe Fell Behind between 1950 and 1989', *Economic History Review*, 70, 248–274.

Vonyó, T. and Klein, A. (2019). 'Why Did Socialist Economies Fail? The Role of Factor Inputs Reconsidered', *Economic History Review*, 72, 317–345.

Wolf, N., Schulze, M. S., and Heinemeyer, H. C. (2011). 'On the Economic Consequences of the Peace: Trade and Borders after Versailles', *Journal of Economic History*, 71, 915–949.

4

Japan

Modern Economic Growth in Asia

KYOJI FUKAO AND TOKIHIKO SETTSU

Introduction

After the Meiji Restoration of 1868, Japan introduced Western institutions and new technologies. As the first Asian economy to make the transformation to 'modern economic growth', Japan's development process was not smooth and economic growth accelerated only gradually. Following the devastating defeat of World War II, Japan experienced an era of unprecedented high-speed growth (HSG; 1955–70). Although economic growth slowed down substantially in the early 1970s, Japan continued to maintain steady growth, and by the mid-1980s, Japan's per capita GDP had reached the level of most other developed countries. However, following the burst of the bubble economy in 1990–91, Japan became trapped in secular stagnation, and labour productivity growth fell behind that of other major developed countries. This chapter examines these changes in Japan's economic performance from the 1870s to the present.

In this chapter, we divide the period overall into four sub-periods, 1870–1913, 1913–40, 1940–70, and after 1970, and then discuss each of these in separate sections. We focus mainly on two issues. The first is a comparison of pre-World War II industrialization with industrialization after the war. Japan's heavy chemical and machinery industries started to expand rapidly during the interwar period and GDP growth accelerated. Nevertheless, Japan's economic growth during this period was much slower than during the HSG era. We compare Japan's economic growth before World War II and during the HSG era both from a supply-side perspective (growth accounting) and a demand-side perspective. The second issue we focus on is the characteristics of Japan's economy created in the process of economic development, mainly from the viewpoint of Japan's present economic stagnation. Some characteristics, such as the lifetime employment system and the dual economy (i.e., the large gap in productivity and wages between large firms on the one hand and small and medium-sized firms on the other) emerged during the interwar period or even earlier. Moreover, these features have been regarded as important foundations for Japan's rapid growth after World War II (Okazaki and Okuno-Fujiwara 1999). However, since the 1990s, these characteristics, plus Japan's high saving rate, which also contributed to the country's HSG in the decades following World War II, seem to have become obstacles to productivity growth in an environment shaped by globalization and slow/negative growth in the working-age population.

Balanced Growth and Trend Acceleration, 1870–1913

During the Tokugawa period, Japan experienced a slow but steady increase of per capita GDP through proto-industrialization,[1] so that by 1874[2] Japan's GDP per capita had reached 1990 international $1,013 (Fukao et al. 2015; Bassino et al. 2016),[3] which is about 40–50 per cent higher than most other Asian countries (Maddison Project Database, version 2013). Moreover, the level was almost equivalent to the per capita GDP of poorer countries on the European periphery.

Japan opened its ports to the major international powers in 1859. However, it is not plausible to assume that the per capita GDP gap vis-à-vis other Asian countries in 1874 arose as a result of rapid economic growth in the years following the opening of Japan's ports. In fact, Japan's per capita GDP already stood at 1990 international $905 in 1846. It is true that exports of raw silk doubled in the years following the opening to trade, and tea exports also increased rapidly (Okazaki et al. 2005). Yet given that total nominal exports in 1874 were 19.7 million yen (Yamazawa and Yamamoto 1979), equivalent to

1 Saito and Takashima (2016) have shown that not only proto-industrialization, but also expansion of the service sector made a substantial contribution to economic growth in the Tokugawa period.

2 In 1874, Japan's first nationwide and detailed modern survey on the output of the primary, mining, and manufacturing sectors (Meiji 7-nen Fuken Bussan-hyo) was conducted. Therefore, from this year onwards, it is possible to construct relatively reliable GDP estimates.

3 Their new estimates of Japanese GDP per capita are about one-third higher than Maddison's (2003) estimates for the beginning of the Meiji period. The main reasons for this upward revision are as follows: (1) They revised estimates of value added in agriculture, taking into account the underreporting of non-rice staple output (barley, buckwheat, millet, etc.); (2) estimates of the gross value-added ratio in the manufacturing sector were re-examined and revised; and (3) instead of Maddison's (2003) estimates, Mizoguchi and Nojima's (1993) estimates are used to link real GDP in 1940 and 1955. See the appendices in Bassino et al. 2016 for details.

only 2.7 per cent of Japan's nominal GDP, which stood at 716.8 million yen (Bassino et al. 2016), and that international trade created not only winners but also losers, such as cotton-producing farmers, it seems that the boost to GDP growth provided by international trade in the short run was likely not very large.[4] On the other hand, international trade likely boosted economic growth through long-term effects such as the introduction of advanced technologies embodied in imported capital goods, the substitution of imported intermediate and final goods through domestic production, and learning through improvements, as well as quality control of export goods. These developments imply that during the Tokugawa period Asia experienced a 'little divergence' (Bassino et al. 2019). From the Tokugawa period, Japan also inherited relatively high labour quality in terms of numeracy, education, and life expectancy compared to other East Asian and South East Asian countries (Bassino et al. 2016).

After the Meiji Restoration of 1868, Japan swiftly introduced many reforms to westernize the economy and society, such as the creation of a national army based on a conscription system in 1870, the transformation from the feudal system to a centralized government system (abolition of feudal domains) in 1871, the establishment of the Department of Justice in 1871, and the introduction of a compulsory education system at the primary level (started in 1872 and gradually expanded). The Meiji government was also keen to implement policies to facilitate factor movements across regions and sectors at a very early stage of development. Barrier stations were abolished in 1868; the caste system, which divided the population into four separate hereditary status groups – *samurai*, farmers, merchants, and craftsmen – was also abolished in 1868, and the requirement for farmers to obtain official permission for commercial activities was abolished in 1872 (although the effects of the latter may have been limited, since many farmers were already engaged in local trade even without official permission). Although public expenditure for the promotion of new industries was not large relative to GDP, it nevertheless played a crucial role in key areas, such as the creation of the railroad network, the modernization of maritime transportation, and the introduction of postal and telegraph systems, as well as a national banking system (Nakamura 1983). Table 4.1 shows the average annual composition of

4 Japan did not have tariff autonomy until 1899, and before that tariff rates were kept at around 5 per cent for most imports (Yamazawa and Yamamoto 1979). As a result of both international and domestic competition after the abolition of regulations on international and domestic trade, many districts with traditional industries experienced an economic decline.

Table 4.1 Composition of Japan's gross domestic expenditure: average annual values for each period (%)

	Private consumption	Military expenditure	Government consumption (excl. military expenditure)	Private investment	Public investment	Net exports	Exports	Imports
1875–1913	78.2	4.5	4.9	11.3	2.5	−1.4	9.2	10.6
1914–18	68.6	3.7	4.1	14.0	3.1	6.7	22.3	15.6
1919–30	75.4	3.4	6.3	11.1	5.4	−1.5	16.9	18.4
1931–40	66.7	9.3	8.4	11.9	4.5	−0.7	19.3	20.0
1941–44	41.8	30.0	3.8	23.6	2.9	−2.1	8.3	10.4
1946–54	63.7	1.3	9.1	19.5	7.0	−0.6	9.1	9.7
1955–70	58.8	1.1	7.2	24.8	7.9	0.4	10.4	10.1
1971–90	55.0	0.9	10.9	23.4	8.3	1.4	12.3	10.9
1991–2016	55.6	0.9	16.6	19.5	6.5	0.8	12.8	12.0

Source: Fukao et al. 2017–18.

Japan's gross domestic expenditure (GDE) from 1875 to 2016. The table shows that during the period 1875–1913, most of Japan's GDE was used for private consumption, while only 2.5 per cent was used for public investment.

Despite these structural reforms, Japan's economic growth did not start with a big spurt, as assumed by Gerschenkron. As shown in Table 4.2, per capita real GDP growth gradually accelerated from 0.41 per cent (average annual rate) in 1846–74 to 0.64 per cent in 1874–85, and to 1.22 per cent in 1885–1913. The slow per capita GDP growth in the early Meiji era was probably partly caused by the stormy macroeconomic conditions during this period. After the opening of its ports, Japan experienced rapid inflation until the Boshin War (a civil war between imperial and Tokugawa forces, 1868–69). Following this war, Japan experienced severe deflation, followed by another bout of inflation from 1877, caused by the Satsuma Rebellion and industry promotion policies based on money printing after that. Japan then experienced another bout of severe deflation from 1881 as a result of a tightening of fiscal policy and a reduction of the money supply ('Matsukata deflation').

After 1885, price levels increased gradually until 1913. This was a period of relatively stable macroeconomic conditions, with mild inflation. The economic boom Japan experienced during this period was owing to several factors, such as an improvement in Japan's international competitiveness through a slow and steady depreciation of the yen against the US dollar, increases in government expenditure for two wars (the First Sino-Japanese

Table 4.2 Japan's GDP and population growth

	Per capita GDP in the final year of each period (1990 international $)	Total population at the end of each period (1,000 persons)	Growth rate of GDP per capita (%)	Growth rate of total population (%)
1846–74	1,013	34,840	0.41	0.28
1874–85	1,087	38,230	0.64	0.84
1885–1913	1,529	51,727	1.22	1.08
1913–40	3,071	71,869	2.58	1.22
1940–55	2,771	89,276	−0.69	1.45
1955–70	9,714	104,665	8.36	1.06
1970–90	18,789	123,611	3.30	0.83
1990–2010	21,935	128,057	0.77	0.18

Sources: Saito and Takashima 2016; Bassino et al. 2016.

Table 4.3 Total number of gainfully occupied persons and sectoral shares

	Total number of persons	Primary sector (%)	Secondary sector (%)	Tertiary sector (%)
1874	21,745,206	70.5	12.9	16.6
1890	23,263,244	62.0	19.0	19.1
1913	26,097,452	58.0	19.5	22.5
1930	29,619,600	48.1	22.6	29.4
1940	32,941,600	43.0	26.5	30.5
1955	40,763,353	41.4	24.5	34.2
1970	54,259,458	19.9	34.4	45.8
1990	64,262,899	8.8	32.9	58.3
2008	64,202,212	5.0	25.5	69.5

Note: By-employment is taken into account.
Sources: Fukao et al. 2015; Fukao and Settsu 2017.

War in 1894–95 and the Russo-Japanese War in 1904–05), industry promotion policies based on reparations from the First Sino-Japanese War, the establishment of many foreign affiliates in Japan after the deregulation of inward foreign direct investment (FDI) in 1899, and increases in fixed capital formation stimulated by inflation expectations.

Although economic growth accelerated only gradually, the transformation of Japan's industrial structure proceeded swiftly, especially during the first half of this period, 1870–1913. The GDP share of the primary sector (agriculture, forestry, and fishery) declined from 60 per cent in 1874 to 44 per cent in 1890, and 36 per cent in 1913. On the other hand, the GDP share of the mining and manufacturing sector increased from 9 per cent to 15 per cent to 21 per cent during the same period. The sectoral composition of the labour force also changed dramatically, especially in the first half of the period. Table 4.3 shows the total number of gainfully occupied persons (taking by-employment into account) and sectoral shares. The share of the primary sector declined from 71 per cent in 1874 to 62 per cent in 1890 and 58 per cent in 1913.[5] On the other

5 Although the labour input share of the primary sector declined rapidly (Table 4.3), the total number of workers in the primary sector did not decline substantially before World War II. The number of workers in the primary sector was 15.3 million in 1874 and 14.2 million in 1940. The rapid expansion of labour input in the secondary sector during the period 1874–90 mainly corresponds to the increase in the labour force caused by accelerating population growth (Table 4.2). Masui (1969) argues that it was only during the post-World War II period that factory workers' wages came to clearly exceed the cost of leaving agriculture for the household head and the heir (eldest son), and that

Table 4.4 Sectoral labour productivity: output per gainfully occupied person in constant prices

	Primary sector	Secondary sector	Tertiary sector
1874	114	115	548
1890	133	148	624
1913	177	375	764
1940	242	981	1,146
1955	477	1,467	2,240
1970	783	4,317	4,134
1990	1,643	7,364	6,676
2008	2,531	11,035	7,507

Notes: Figures are in yen (average in 1934–36 prices) for 1874–1940 and in 1,000 yen (2000 prices) for 1955–2008.
Sources: Fukao et al. 2015; Fukao and Settsu 2017.

hand, the share of the secondary sector (mining, manufacturing, and construction) increased from 13 per cent in 1874, to 19 per cent in 1890, and to 20 per cent in 1913.[6]

Table 4.4 shows how sectoral labour productivity measured in constant prices changed over time. Probably reflecting the fact that most Japanese manufacturing activities in the early Meiji period have their origins in the proto-industrialization during the Tokugawa period, labour productivity in the secondary sector in 1874 was not very high, almost at the same level as in the primary sector. Both the primary and the secondary sectors experienced mild labour productivity growth from 1874 to 1890, and the gap in labour productivity between the two sectors remained relatively small. After 1890, however, even though labour productivity in the primary sector continued to grow, this was far surpassed by labour productivity growth in the secondary sector, so that the labour productivity gap between the two sectors widened. Moreover, this trend continued after 1913. Meanwhile, the tertiary sector registered the highest level of labour productivity among the three sectors in the pre-World War II period, but the growth of labour productivity was much slower than in the other sectors.

when it did, farmers did leave agriculture and the transition out of agriculture proceeded rapidly. On this issue, see also Hayashi and Prescott 2008 and Fukao et al. 2015.

6 The data on industrial structure are taken from Fukao et al. (2015) and Fukao and Settsu (2017).

As the description of trends in the secondary sector shows, there was a clear difference in development patterns between the 1874–90 period and the 1890–1913 period. The 1874–90 period was characterized by socio-economic disorder, slow economic growth, and the expansion of labour-intensive and traditional manufacturing activities, which newly absorbed large numbers of workers (Nakamura 1983). During this period, not only advanced prefectures (regions with higher labour productivity), but also backward prefectures experienced an increase in the secondary sector labour input share.[7] In contrast, the 1890–1913 period was characterized by relatively stable macroeconomic conditions after the Matsukata deflation, as well as higher economic growth, the expansion of internationally competitive modernized light industries, such as textiles (Tanimoto 2006), and the establishment of capital-intensive heavy and chemical industries, which depended on imported technologies,[8] in advanced regions such as Osaka and Tokyo.[9]

Unbalanced Growth, 1914–40

The next sub-period, from 1914 to 1940, was characterized by unstable macroeconomic conditions reflecting upheaval in the international political and economic order, as well as inappropriate macroeconomic policies. Nevertheless, avoiding devastation during World War I and suffering less from the Great Depression than other countries, Japan managed to increase its per capita GDP by more than 100 per cent during this period (Table 4.2). Growth was particularly rapid during World War I and in the 1930s.

7 The structural change in these backward prefectures provides support for the labour-intensive industrialization hypothesis proposed by Sugihara (2013). However, while the hypothesis also suggests that human capital development played a key role in improving labour productivity during the early stages of Japan's modern economic growth, the growth accounting analysis of Ohkawa and Rosovsky (1972) indicates that, before World War II, the contribution of labour quality improvements to labour productivity growth was not very large.

8 The government pursued a number of initiatives for the development of the heavy and chemical industries. On the other hand, development of light industries was mainly led by the private sector. In 1899, the Japanese government deregulated inward FDI, which subsequently made an important contribution to the introduction of new technologies to Japan. In the case of electrical machinery, many Japanese firms were established as joint ventures of Japanese and Western firms. For example, NEC was established in 1899 as a joint venture with Western Electric, while Toshiba was established in 1905 as a joint venture with General Electric (Paprzycki and Fukao 2008).

9 For example, Japanese army arsenals and plants were located in Osaka and Tokyo in the early 1870s, which markedly contributed to the expansion of the machinery sector around 1890.

When World War I started, Japan suffered from the sudden disarray in international financial and trade markets. However, from 1915, Japan experienced an unprecedented export boom, not only by providing goods for military use, such as military equipment and food, but also by providing machines, metals, chemicals, and so on, to Asia as substitutes for Asian imports from Europe and the United States. Exports of marine transportation services also increased substantially. From 1914 to 1918, real value added in the mining and manufacturing sectors increased by 49 per cent (Ohkawa and Shinohara 1979). Because of the export boom and constraints on the import of key materials and investment goods, the corporate goods price index increased by 102 per cent. After the war, as many countries, including Japan, pursued deflationary policies in an attempt to return to the Gold Standard at old parities (Japan returned to the Gold Standard in 1930), Japan suffered from prolonged stagnation and deflation. However, after 1931, Japan was able to overcome the economic slump through a sharp depreciation of the yen (the yen depreciated against most currencies of other developed countries; see Hatase 2002) in the wake of abandoning the Gold Standard and through the adoption of expansionary fiscal policies (Cha 2003). Japan's military expansion in Asia (Japan invaded Manchuria in 1931; the Second Sino-Japanese War started in 1937) further intensified the economic boom (Table 4.1).

Japan's economic growth from 1914 to 1940 was characterized by very rapid industrialization. Real value added in the mining and manufacturing sectors increased more than fivefold. Further, after 1925, manufacturing activities shifted from light industry to the heavy, chemical, and machinery industries: the value-added share of the textile industry continued to increase substantially until 1925, but then started to fall, while the combined value-added share of the chemical, metal and metal products, and machinery industries increased from 27.5 per cent to 60.1 per cent (Fukao and Settsu 2017).

In the 1920s, the government invested actively in infrastructure in large cities (roads, sea ports, water supply, etc.). This investment in infrastructure, scale economies in the heavy and chemical industries, improvements in the electric power supply system, the growing role of processing trade, and so on, further reinforced the agglomeration of manufacturing activities around large, mainly coastal cities such as Tokyo, Yokohama, Nagoya, Osaka, and Fukuoka (Nakamura 1983; Fukao et al. 2015). Since labour productivity in these industries is high, this concentration raised the labour productivity gap between metropolitan and rural areas. On the other hand, regional differences in labour productivity within each manufacturing subsector, as in the

1890–1913 period, declined substantially. This convergence in labour productivity within manufacturing subsectors was likely the result of the diffusion of technology and management skills, such as the spread of electric motors even to small rural factories (Minami 1976) and improvements in management through mergers and acquisitions (Braguinsky et al. 2015).

The pattern of structural transformation during this period is closely related to changes in the composition of final demand. As shown in Table 4.1, during World War I, the average annual value of Japan's net exports to GDP ratio was very large, at 6.7 per cent. There was also a boom in private investment. These factors must have contributed to the rapid expansion of the manufacturing sector, as a result of which the value-added share of the sector in nominal GDP increased from 21 per cent in 1913 to 30 per cent in 1918 (Fukao and Settsu 2017).

Turning to the period 1919–30, Table 4.1 shows that public investment and household consumption accounted for a large share of GDE. The large public investment share reflects active government investment in response to urbanization and industrialization in large cities. On the other hand, net exports were negative and military expenditure was relatively small (Table 4.1). Reflecting stagnating final demand, the value-added share of the mining and manufacturing sectors in nominal GDP declined from 30 per cent in 1918 to 25 per cent in 1930. Changes in Japan's comparative advantage (an increase in rice imports and decline in silk exports), the decline in primary goods prices in world markets, especially after the Great Depression, changes in consumer preferences (new city dwellers had a stronger preference for Western products), among other factors, led to a crisis in the primary sector (Nakamura 1983), so that the value-added share of the primary sector in nominal GDP declined from 31 per cent in 1918 to 16 per cent in 1930.

During the period 1931–40, military expenditure increased substantially and exports recovered with the depreciation of the yen (Table 4.1). These changes created another boom in the manufacturing sector, and the value-added share of the mining and manufacturing sectors in nominal GDP jumped from 25 per cent in 1930 to 37 per cent in 1940. On the other hand, the critical situation in the primary sector continued during this period.

Although labour productivity in the secondary sector increased substantially (rising 2.6-fold between 1913 and 1940; Table 4.4), job creation in this sector was limited until the mid-1930s. As a result, with the labour force growing (Table 4.3), additional workers were absorbed mainly in low-wage services or the primary sector (Nakamura 1983; Bassino et al. 2016). The relatively sluggish growth in real wages, the high rate of return on capital, low taxes on capital income, the crisis in the primary sector, and so on, in this period resulted in a highly unequal income distribution (Moriguchi and Saez 2008).

It is important to note that some of the key characteristics of Japan's present-day economic system have their origin in this period, especially in the 1930s (Okazaki and Okuno-Fujiwara 1999). The first such characteristic is the lifetime employment system, which means that jobs of full-time workers at large firms are secure. Job security, the seniority wage system, and large retirement payments helped to raise the retention ratio and workers' loyalty to firms. These factors, in turn, contributed to the accumulation of firm-specific and non-firm-specific skills, mainly through on-the-job training. Moreover, as the number of skilled workers employed under the lifetime employment system increased, the importance of the labour market for new graduates increased, while the secondary labour market became thinner. This change further enhanced workers' loyalty. The lifetime employment system was initially introduced in the 1930s by large machinery firms in order to retain skilled workers and train them effectively, but it subsequently spread to other sectors, especially during World War II.

The second characteristic is long-term supplier relationships. In the machinery industry, large and technology-intensive assemblers and their small and low-wage parts suppliers maintained long-term relationships and frequently shared technology and information. It is likely that this relationship enhanced technology spillovers from large firms.

Third, in the 1930s, shareholders' influence on firms was weakened as part of an authoritarian allocation system to support the war effort. Subsequently, funds to finance industry were mainly supplied by banks.

Fourth, a new relationship between government and business was established in the 1930s. Each industry came to be supervised independently from above by a single administrative authority, and industry associations were created in most sectors for monitoring by the government and for collaboration and information sharing within each sector.

World War II and the High-Speed Growth Era, 1940–73

When World War II came to an end, about 3 million Japanese had died and Japan had lost about one-third of its industrial machinery and a quarter of all buildings (Nakamura and Miyazaki 1995). In addition, the transportation sector was in serious disarray due to the lack of ships, trains, and trucks. International trade also came to an almost complete standstill and Japan faced a severe lack of food, fuel, and raw materials. Japan's real GDP in 1946 was 37 per cent smaller than in 1940 (Fukao et al. 2019).

After World War II, it took nine years for Japan's GDP to recover to the level of 1940. Moreover, because of the rapid population growth due to the baby boom and the return of demobilized soldiers and residents from abroad (between 1945 and 1950, 6.25 million persons returned to Japan), Japan's per capita GDP in 1955 was still 10 per cent less than that in 1940 (Table 4.1).

From 1955, Japan's GDP growth accelerated and during the HSG era from 1955 to 1970, Japan's per capita GDP grew at an average annual rate of 9.4 per cent and per capita GDP increased 3.5-fold (Table 4.2). As a result, as shown in Figure 4.1, by the early 1970s, Japan had caught up with the UK. Such rapid and sustained growth was unprecedented in the world (Komiya 1975: ch. 1).

Figure 4.1 also shows that other East Asian economies, such as Singapore, Taiwan, South Korea, and China, have subsequently experienced similar 'growth miracles'. However, the patterns of HSG differ somewhat across countries. For example, in the case of Taiwan, South Korea, and China, HSG started from a much lower level of per capita income and was sustained longer than in Japan. Moreover, in the case of China, inward FDI played a much more important role than in Japan. However, there are also noteworthy similarities. For instance, an important source of HSG in all cases was very rapid capital accumulation based on a high domestic saving rate. In addition, all these economies enjoyed relatively open markets in Western countries for their exports. Furthermore, the HSG era (except in the case of city states such as Singapore) saw rapid labour movement from the primary to the non-primary sector.

As mentioned earlier, Japan had already experienced an acceleration of economic growth in the 1930s, driven mainly by the heavy, chemical, and machinery industries. The rapid increase in the value-added shares of these industries in the manufacturing sector overall during the HSG era simply looks like a repetition or continuation of the structural transformation observed in the pre-World War II period. Can the HSG era simply be regarded as an (upscaled) continuation of pre-war industrialization? Or are there stark qualitative differences between the two industrialization periods? To answer these questions, we compare the two

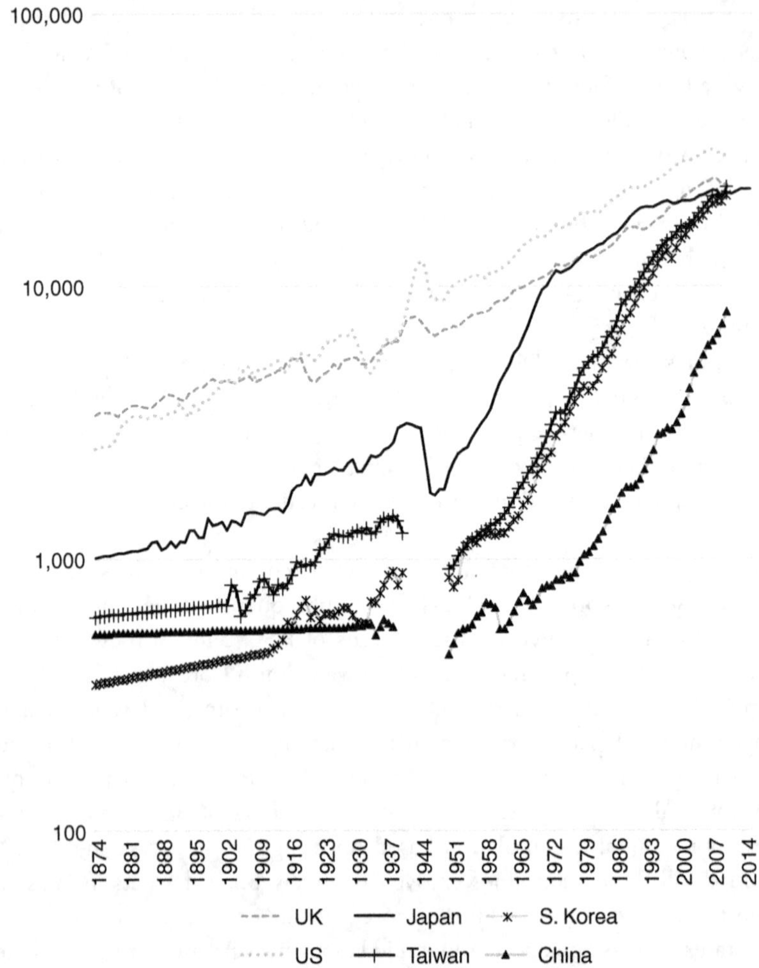

Figure 4.1 Trends in per capita GDP: comparison of Japan, US, UK, and the Asian Tigers, 1874–2010

Note: Except for the years around World War II, missing data were filled in through log-linear interpolation.

Sources: Japan: Fukao et al. 2019; other countries: Maddison Project Database, version 2013.

industrialization periods both from the supply side and the demand side of the economy.

Starting with the supply side, we conduct a growth accounting analysis. The primary sector and structural transformation played an important role in

Japan's growth during the pre-World War II period and the HSG era. We therefore conduct our growth accounting analysis based on a two-sector model consisting of a primary sector and a non-primary sector. As factors of production, we incorporate labour (number of workers), capital stock, and land in the case of the primary sector, and labour and capital stock in the case of the non-primary sector. The result of the growth accounting exercise is presented in Table 4.5.

When we estimate the contribution of the increase in capital intensity (column *c*), we assume that one of the following two conditions holds: either there is no gap in the marginal product of capital (which is measured by the rate of return on capital) between the two sectors, or the growth rate of capital is identical in the two sectors. If neither of the two conditions hold, the contribution of the increase in capital intensity on the macroeconomy will take different values to those shown in column *c*. For example, if the marginal product of capital is higher in the non-primary sector than in the primary sector and the growth rate of capital in the non-primary sector is greater than that in the primary sector, the contribution of an increase in capital intensity to labour productivity growth in the economy overall will be larger than the values shown in column *c*. This additional effect is included in column *f* (TFP growth caused by resource allocation). Similarly, if labour input growth in the sector with higher wages is greater than that in the sector with lower wages, the positive impact of this resource allocation will be included in column *f*.

Table 4.5 shows that labour productivity growth during the 1955–70 period, at an average annual rate of 6.80 per cent, was much higher than during the period 1930–40, when it was 3.89 per cent. In addition, the drivers of this growth in labour productivity also differed. During 1930–40, 65 per cent of the labour productivity growth was due to within-sector TFP growth, all of which occurred in the non-primary sector. The contributions of the increase in capital intensity and resource reallocation were not very large: 25 per cent and 11 per cent of the total labour productivity growth, respectively. During the HSG era, the contributions of the increase in capital intensity and resource reallocation were much larger: 40 per cent and 15 per cent of the total labour productivity growth, respectively. On the other hand, during this period, 46 per cent of labour productivity growth was due to within-sector TFP growth (TFP grew not only in the non-primary sector, but also in the primary sector), and 15 per cent was due to resource reallocation, most of which was caused by labour movement from the primary to the non-primary sector.

Table 4.5 Growth accounting results, 1885–1970 (%)

	Growth rate of labour productivity (real value added/ number of workers)	Contribution of the increase in capital intensity	Contribution of the increase in arable land per worker	TFP growth	Contribution of TFP growth within each sector	TFP growth caused by resource reallocation	TFP growth in the primary sector	TFP growth in the non-primary sector
	$a = b + c + d$	b	c	$d = e + f$	e	f	g	h
1885–1913	1.77	0.45	0.01	1.31	1.11	0.20	0.95	1.13
1913–30	2.38	0.75	−0.03	1.66	1.25	0.42	1.05	1.31
1930–40	3.82	0.95	−0.04	2.91	2.49	0.42	−0.38	3.05
1940–55	1.16	−0.08	−0.03	1.26	1.06	0.20	−0.23	−1.30
1955–70	6.80	2.69	−0.05	4.15	3.13	1.03	1.97	3.17

Source: Fukao et al. 2019.

To sum up the comparison of the two periods based on growth accounting, the main engine of labour productivity growth during the 1930–40 period was TFP growth in the non-primary sector.[10] TFP growth in the non-primary sector during the HSG era was not much faster than in the 1930s. What caused labour productivity growth in the HSG era to be much faster than in the 1930s was – first and foremost – rapid capital deepening, as well as other factors such as labour reallocation from the primary to the non-primary sector and TFP growth in the primary sector. Moreover, as shown in Table 4.3, the number of workers increased at a much more rapid pace in the HSG era (at an average annual rate of 1.9 per cent) than in the 1930–40 period (1.1 per cent). This means that capital accumulation in the HSG era proceeded at an incredibly high pace. During this period, the real capital stock increased at an annual rate of 11.5 per cent compared to 3.7 per cent during the 1930s.

What made the rapid capital accumulation in the HSG era possible? To answer this question, let us examine how private investment was financed. Figure 4.2 shows Japan's saving–investment balance during the periods 1885–1944 and 1946–2014. Japan never depended heavily on inflows of foreign capital to finance investment, so that domestic private saving was the main source of private investment. During both periods, the private gross saving to GDP ratio increased gradually over time. In the case of the pre-war period, private saving skyrocketed after 1938, probably as a result of regulations on private consumption due to the total war with China and the United States. The average private gross saving to GDP ratio during the 1930–40 period was 19.3 per cent, out of which 11.7 percentage points were used for financing private gross investment, while 7.8 percentage points financed the government deficit caused mainly by exploding military expenditure.[11] On the other hand, the average gross private saving to GDP ratio during the 1955–70 period was 23.8 per cent,[12] while the average private gross investment to GDP ratio

10 Since we measure labour input by the number of workers, the contribution of labour quality improvements (human capital accumulation) and increases in working hours per worker to economic growth are included in our TFP growth. However, as already mentioned in footnote 7, it appears that before World War II, the contribution of labour quality improvements to labour productivity growth were not very large.

11 The explosion in military expenditure can be seen in Table 4.1, which shows that such expenditure jumped from 3.4 per cent of GDP in 1919–30 to 9.3 per cent in 1931–40.

12 According to the permanent income hypothesis, when the actual growth rate of income is greater than the expected growth rate of income, the household saving rate will increase. Komiya (1975: 44–45) argues that this mechanism is the main reason for Japan's high private saving rate during the HSG era. After the HSG era, the household saving rate declined gradually, but this decline was offset by the increase in the corporate saving rate, which means that the saving rate in the macroeconomy overall has remained high (Fukao 2012: figs. 4.1–4.3).

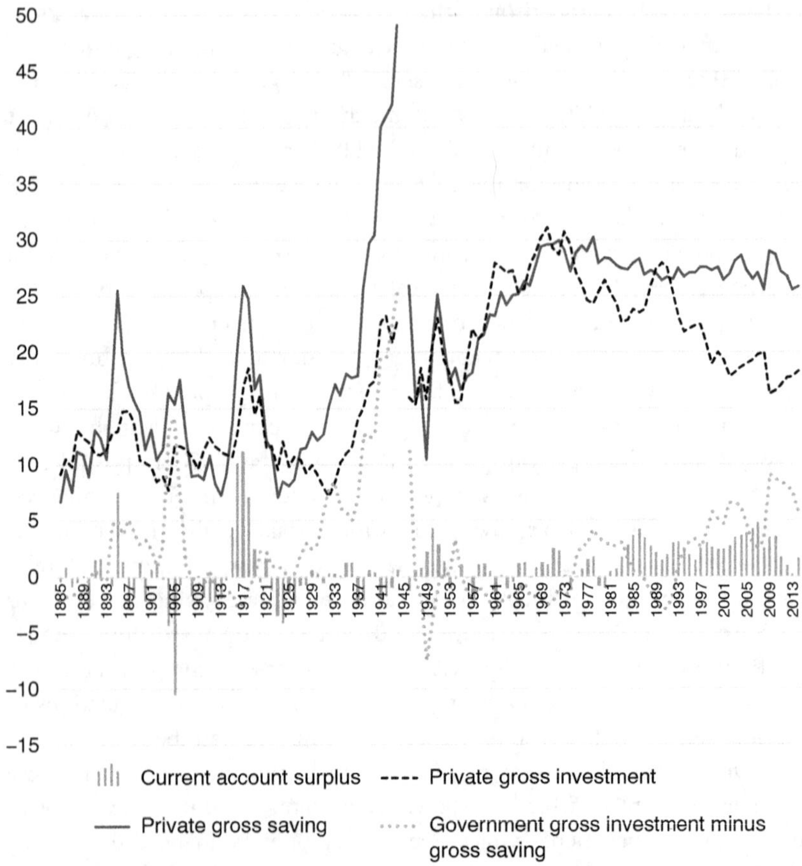

Figure 4.2 Japan's saving–investment balance, 1885–1944 and 1946–2014
Sources: Ohkawa and Shinohara 1979 and Japan's GDP statistics.

was 25.2 per cent. The private saving gap was filled by a government surplus. The government surplus to GDP ratio was 1.7 per cent, 0.3 percentage points of which was used for financing the accumulation of foreign assets (current account surplus).

From the viewpoint of the financing of private investment, the most important difference between the two periods is the government deficit. In the pre-war period, a large part of private saving was used not for private investment, but for military expenditures. After World War II, Japan's military expenditure became almost zero because of

Allied restrictions. As the Cold War intensified from the 1950s, the United States asked Japan to increase its military expenditure, but the Japanese government tried to keep military expenditure small to avoid the economic burden. The average military expenditure to GDP ratio during 1955–60 was 1.6 per cent and remained below 1.0 per cent after 1960 (Komiya 1975: tables 1–12). During the post-World War II era, Japan's ratio tended to be lower than that of the United States and major western European countries, including West Germany and Italy. Japan's very rapid capital accumulation during the HSG era was partly supported by this peace dividend created by the Pax Americana, in addition to its high private saving rate.

Next, let us compare the two industrialization periods from a demand-side perspective. What demand factors supported the rapid expansion of output in the heavy, chemical, and machinery sectors during the two industrialization periods? To examine this issue, Fukao and Saumik (2019) conducted an input-output analysis for the period 1885–1985. They found that the main difference between the increase in demand for the mining and manufacturing sectors' output (excluding food and textiles) during the pre- and post-World War II periods is that during 1925–35 the expansion was driven by military expenditure, while during the 1955–70 period it was driven by private investment.

To sum up our analysis, the HSG era was characterized by rapid capital accumulation, which contributed to labour productivity growth in the economy as a whole and also generated rapid growth in demand for heavy, chemical, and machinery industry output. Moreover, most of the capital accumulation during this period was financed by private saving. In contrast, in the 1930–40 period, a large part of private saving was used to finance military expenditure, and both capital accumulation and the labour productivity growth resulting from capital deepening were much slower than during the HSG era. Moreover, although the heavy, chemical, and machinery sectors expanded rapidly, demand for the output of these sectors was driven mainly by military expenditure.

During the HSG era, labour productivity growth due to capital accumulation led to rising wages and household incomes. This income rise created new consumption demand, while the new consumption demand in turn stimulated further capital accumulation. This kind of virtuous cycle did not operate in the pre-war period.

Another important difference from the pre-war period was the relatively equal income distribution. The devastation of World War II, hyperinflation, the dissolution of corporate groups (*zaibatsu*), and land reforms after World War II made the income and wealth distribution in Japan much more equal (Moriguchi and Saez 2008). A progressive tax system, rapid wage increases, and protection of the agricultural sector during and after the HSG era further helped to maintain a relatively equal income and wealth distribution. In addition, from a nationwide perspective, rapid structural transformation in the less advanced regions of Japan also helped to reduce income inequality across regions (Fukao et al. 2015).

Japan's Emergence as a Giant Exporter and Slowdown of Economic Growth after 1990

Beginning in the early 1970s, Japan experienced a series of major economic shocks, such as the sharp appreciation of the yen after the Nixon Shock of 1971, a real estate bubble in 1973, the first oil crisis in 1973 and serious inflation after that, and the second oil crisis in 1978.

In response to the first oil crisis, Japan improved its energy efficiency substantially through the scaling down of energy-intensive sectors and the introduction of energy-saving technologies. As a result, between 1974 and 1990, Japan's energy consumption to real GDP ratio declined by one-third (Fukao 2018). In contrast, in the United States, oil price controls impeded the introduction of energy-saving measures. After the second oil crisis, most industrialized countries suffered from macroeconomic problems such as inflation, trade deficits, high unemployment rates, and stagnating manufacturing output. Compared with other developed economies, Japan achieved a much better macroeconomic performance and managed to maintain relatively high growth. By the late 1980s, Japan's per capita GDP exceeded that of major European countries such as the UK by about 10 per cent (Figure 4.1). From the second half of the 1970s, labour unions in Japan started to give priority to employment rather than to higher wages. Moreover, appropriate monetary policies were pursued, while energy consumption was kept in check. These factors also seem to have contributed to Japan's good macroeconomic performance.

As capital investment declined from the 1970s, the dependence of Japan's machinery sector on exports increased. The share of machinery exports in Japan's total manufacturing exports increased from 48 per cent in 1970 to 63 per cent in 1980, and 76 per cent in 1990. After the start of 'Reaganomics' in 1981, the appreciation of the US dollar, the increase in US domestic absorption, and the declining trend of capital investment in Japan made Japan the country with the largest current account surplus, and the United States the country with the largest current deficit in the world. This imbalance created serious trade friction between the United States and Japan.

However, trade friction with other developed economies had started even earlier, in the early 1950s, although this tended to be confined to specific sectors, such as textiles from the 1950s to the early 1970s, steel in trade with the United States from the 1960s, and TV receivers and video recorders in trade with the United States and European countries from the late 1960s. In the 1980s, Japan started to threaten the United States in the production of machinery embodying advanced technologies, such as automobiles and semiconductors. The share of Japanese automobiles in total US new automobile sales increased from 8.6 per cent in 1975 to 20.8 per cent in 1980 (Nelson 1996). In fact, in 1980, Japan became the largest producer of automobiles (in terms of the number of vehicles produced) in the world. Moreover, the share of Japanese firms in the sales of the world's top forty semiconductor firms surpassed that of US firms in 1986 (Linden et al. 2003).

Several factors that contributed to making Japan a giant exporter of advanced technological machinery can be pointed out. First, Japan strictly protected its market for such machinery (through restrictions on both imports and inward direct investment) until the early 1970s, by which time Japanese machinery firms had managed to catch up with Western firms (Ito and Kiyono 1984; Jorgenson et al. 2016). Second, large assemblers of automobiles and electronic devices conducted active research and development (R&D), especially applied R&D. The Japanese government promoted such R&D activities by subsidizing research consortiums and providing tax incentives. Third, Japan's lifetime employment system instilled loyalty of the workforce to their employer and enhanced the accumulation of both firm-specific and non-firm-specific human capital, especially at the factory shop level (Okazaki and Okuno-Fujiwara 1999). Fourth, Japan's tight supply-chain system contributed to the rapid development of new products (Clark et al. 1987). Both the lifetime employment system and the tight supply-chain system were created during the late 1930s and early 1940s.

Through negotiations with the United States and European countries to reduce trade frictions, Japan introduced 'voluntary' restraints on exports of automobiles and some electronic devices. To respond to these restraints and the appreciation of the yen after the Plaza Accord of 1985, large assemblers and their key suppliers relocated production abroad in the late 1980s and the 1990s. Although trade friction with the United States and Europe had waned by the mid-1990s, Japanese manufacturing firms continued to relocate machinery production abroad, especially to China. In the case of the electronics industry, firms in other East Asian countries, such as Taiwan, South Korea, and China, which were endowed with cheap and relatively high-quality labour, like Japan in the HSG era, quickly caught up with Japanese firms. In addition, in information technology, the importance of basic research and computer software, areas in which Japanese firms do not have an advantage, increased (Branstetter et al. 2015). Through these changes, many of the products of Japanese firms were commoditized (Kushida 2015).

In order to reverse the yen appreciation after the Plaza Accord and to satisfy US demands to boost domestic absorption, Japan's monetary authorities continued with expansionary monetary policies even after the first symptoms of a bubble, such as rapid increases of asset prices and an investment boom in the real estate sector, became visible. When the authorities finally tightened monetary policy in 1989, the bubble economy burst.

Following the burst of the bubble economy in 1990–91, Japan became trapped in secular stagnation and labour productivity growth fell behind that in other major developed economies, even after Japan had resolved the non-performing loan problem in its banking sector and the damaged balance sheets of many firms after the financial crisis of 1998. The underlying reason for the secular stagnation since the 1990s is that Japan suffers from two structural problems: insufficient demand (which below we refer to as the 'excess saving problem') and the gradual slowdown of TFP growth. These two structural problems started to emerge during the 1970s and 1980s and subsequently became increasingly serious. The remainder of this section looks at Japan's economic development since 1970 from the perspective of these two structural problems.

Let us start by examining Japan's excess saving problem, which started to rear its head during this period (Krugman 1998; Fukao 2012). Despite Japan's exceptionally high private gross saving rate when compared with other advanced economies, it did not experience any excess saving until the 1970s, due to extremely high investment during the HSG era. However, as can be seen in Figure 4.2, from the beginning of the 1970s, Japan's economy started to experience chronic excess savings. This is due to the large decline in private investment, for which there are the following reasons.

First, after the 1960s, when the first baby-boomer generation reached adulthood, the growth rate of the working-age population slowed considerably. Looking at the average growth rate of the working-age population (those aged 15–64) by decade, we find a steady decline in the growth rate, from 1.9 per cent in the 1950s to 1.8 per cent in the 1960s, 1.0 per cent in the

1970s, 0.9 per cent in the 1980s, 0.0 per cent in the 1990s, and −0.6 per cent in the 2000s (Statistics Bureau, Ministry of Internal Affairs and Communications 2014). The decline in the growth rate of the working-age population reduced the need to invest in capital equipment for new workers, thus exerting a negative impact on capital investment.

Second, the process of catching up with manufacturing technologies in the United States and Europe and increases in TFP driven by this process had more or less run their course by the early 1970s, and probably as a result of this, TFP growth started to slow down from the 1970s onwards.

Table 4.6 shows growth accounting results for Japan and weighted average data for the four other major developed countries: the United States, Germany, the United Kingdom, and France. Since the importance of the primary sector declined substantially in the 1960s, the growth accounting analysis here is based on a one-sector macro model, with two production factors, capital and labour. In addition, since data on changes in the quality of labour and capital are available for this period, such changes are taken into account in the analysis. Because of these differences, the results on Japan for the period 1955–70 in Table 4.6 differ from the corresponding results reported in Table 4.5.

As Table 4.6 shows, the decline in labour input growth (from 2.0 per cent in 1955–70 to 1.6 per cent in 1970–90) was much milder than the decline in the growth of the working-age population. The reason is improvements in labour quality (the spread of higher education and the accumulation of skills by older workers), as well as increases in the labour force participation rate.

Meanwhile, TFP growth declined by 1.4 percentage points between 1955–70 and 1970–90. This decline in TFP growth, by lowering the rate of return on capital, likely reduced private investment. These two structural factors explain the largest part of the decline in private investment. For example, assuming balanced growth and Harrod-neutral (labour-saving) technical change in a Solow-type neoclassical growth model, and further assuming a capital–GDP ratio of 3, a 0.4 percentage point decline in the growth rate of labour input and a 1.4 percentage point decline in TFP growth reduce Japan's economic growth rate by 0.4 and 2.5 percentage points respectively (for a total of 2.9 percentage points) and lower the investment–GDP ratio by 1.2 and 7.5 percentage points (for a total of 8.7 percentage points), respectively. In addition to these two factors, while in the immediate post-war period Japan was able to achieve high-speed growth by raising the capital stock per worker, the increase in the capital ratio lowered the rate of

Table 4.6 Growth accounting results for Japan, 1955–2012, and four other major developed countries, 1990–2011

		Japan			Weighted average of US, Germany, UK, and France
		1955–70	1970–90	1990–2012	1990–2011
Real GDP growth	$c + d + e$	8.4	4.4	0.9	2.2
Growth rate of labour input	a	2.0	1.6	0.0	0.8
Growth rate of capital service input	b	11.0	6.2	1.9	3.1
Contribution of labour input growth	c	1.3	1.1	0.0	
Contribution of man-hour growth		1.0	0.4	−0.5	
Contribution of labour quality improvement		0.3	0.7	0.5	
Contribution of capital service input growth	d	4.3	1.9	0.6	
TFP growth	e	2.8	1.4	0.3	0.5
Growth rate of labour efficiency (Harrod-neutral technical progress)	f	4.6	2.1	0.4	0.8
Rate of natural growth	$a + f$	6.6	3.7	0.4	1.7

Source: Fukao and Yuan 2016.

return on capital through the accumulation of excess capital, likely making the reduction in investment more severe than otherwise would have been the case.

The saving–investment balance of the private sector (private saving surplus) will be either invested abroad (current account surplus) or borrowed by the government (general government deficit). Moreover, according to Keynesian economics, if intended private saving is greater than the intended current account surplus plus the intended government deficit, there arises an excess supply of goods. In this case, a reduction in GDP, through a reduction in excess private saving, restores balance in the goods market.

Figure 4.2 shows how much of the private saving surplus was used for investment abroad (current account surplus) or for financing of the government (government gross investment minus gross saving). The figure shows that during most of the period, the largest part of excess saving – that is, the difference between private gross saving and private gross investment – went towards financing the government deficit. However, there are some exceptions. During the mid-1980s, Japan recorded large current account surpluses as a result of 'Reaganomics'. There was also another export-driven boom during 2006–08. Nevertheless, due to trade friction and yen appreciation, Japan was never able to maintain a substantial current account surplus for a prolonged period of time. In the second half of the 1980s, loose monetary policy – introduced by Japan's monetary authorities to rein in yen appreciation and stimulate private investment – was maintained too long, giving rise to the bubble economy. Since the early 1990s, aggregate demand has relied heavily on huge government deficits, which is not sustainable.

Next, let us examine the slowdown in TFP growth in more detail. During the HSG era, Japan actively conducted R&D and licensed technology from abroad. As a result, by around 1970, Japan had caught up with the United States in many manufacturing subsectors, such as motor vehicles and computer and electronic products. With room for technological catch-up in these areas exhausted, TFP growth in Japan slowed down substantially. Additional factors for the slowdown in TFP growth include the fact that from the mid-1980s, Japanese firms in the automobile and electronics industries – two industries with high productivity growth – increasingly relocated production abroad, and it was typically the most productive firms that relocated production abroad.

It is also important to note that since the 1990s, some core characteristics of Japanese firms, such as tight customer–supplier relationships and the lifetime employment system, have become obstacles to their TFP growth in an environment shaped by globalization and slow/negative growth in the working-age population. The reasons are as follows.

First, from the 1990s, firms have increased the number of part-time workers in order to maintain the flexibility of employment levels. Given the decline of the working-age population and economic stagnation, most firms cannot expect their need for employees to increase steadily, as was the case during the HSG era. At the same time, areas in which individual firms have a competitive advantage over their rivals are changing quickly, and Japan's comparative advantage as a whole is also changing over time. Given the high job security provided under traditional employment practices, increasing the reliance on part-time workers is almost the only way for firms to keep both the level and the mix of employment flexible. The structural causes of Japan's lacklustre economic growth, such as the slow operation of the market selection mechanism (entry of productive firms and exit of unproductive firms), sluggish investment in information and communication technology (ICT) and the ineffective use of ICT, as well as insufficient investment in intangibles (training, new methods, brands) are closely related with labour issues. An example of the ineffective use of ICT is that firms often choose to purchase custom software rather than packaged software in order to avoid changes in corporate structure, employment adjustment, and training of workers. Another is that the high cost of closing a firm decreases the incentive for starting up new businesses in the first place. Meanwhile, many firms do not or cannot expand their reliance on outsourcing because they are reluctant to adjust their employment levels (for example, through layoffs).

Second, Japan's leading export industries, such as the automotive industry, to a substantial extent have relocated production abroad. Partly linked to this, as well as other factors such as restructuring at large assemblers, buyer–supplier relationships in the automobile and electronics industries in Japan have become more open (Paprzycki and Fukao 2008). It seems that the exit of geographically proximate plants operated by R&D-intensive large firms reduced technology spillovers from large firms to small and medium-sized firms (SMEs) (Belderbos et al. 2016). During the two lost decades, TFP growth of large firms in the manufacturing sector actually accelerated. On the other hand, SMEs have been left behind (Fukao 2012), showing much lower TFP growth that reflects lacklustre R&D and a low degree of internationalization. For example, in Japan, the R&D intensity of SMEs is much lower than that of large firms.

Conclusion

Following the Meiji Restoration in 1868, the Japanese government set the goal of catching up with Western economies through the promotion of industrialization (*Shokusan-kogyo*). In practice, it took until the 1970s, that is, a hundred years, to achieve this goal. As this chapter has shown, from a supply-side perspective, the main drivers of economic growth in Japan from the 1870s to the 1970s were capital accumulation and TFP growth. From a demand-side perspective, in line with this emphasis on capital accumulation, private and government investment played a more significant role than private consumption. In this sense, Japan's economic growth in the long run is attributable to capital accumulation and technological progress.

After the HSG era, investment and TFP growth slowed down and exports took centre stage in propelling the economy forward. Further, especially since the 1990s, some of the features of Japan's economy that played a key role in Japan's remarkable economic performances, such as the lifetime employment system, the dual economy, and the high saving rate, turned into shackles. In addition, globalization and slow/negative growth in the working-age population have posed new challenges to the economy. Because of these factors, Japan's labour productivity growth fell behind that of other major developed countries. It seems that Japan needs fundamental structural reforms to overcome the current situation of sluggish growth.

References

Bassino, J.-P., Fukao, K., and Settsu, T. (2016). 'Revisiting Meiji Japan's Economic Miracle: Changes in Regional Industrial Structure and Productivity (1874–1909)', paper presented at the Asian Historical Economics Conference, Seoul National University, 2–3 September 2016.

Bassino, J.-P., Broadberry, S., Fukao, K., Gupta, B., and Takashima, M. (2019). 'Japan and the Great Divergence, 730–1874', *Explorations in Economic History*, 72, 1–22.

Belderbos, R., Ikeuchi, K., Fukao, K., Kim, Y. G., and Kwon, H. U. (2016). 'Public and Private R&D Spillovers and Productivity at the Plant Level: Technological and Geographic Proximity', paper presented at the 34th IARIW General Conference, Dresden, Germany, 21–27 August 2016.

Braguinsky, S., Ohyama, A., Okazaki, T., and Syverson, C. (2015). 'Acquisitions, Productivity, and Profitability: Evidence from the Japanese Cotton Spinning Industry', *American Economic Review*, 105(7), 2089–2119.

Branstetter, L. G., Drev, M., and Kwon, N. (2015). 'Get with the Program: Software-Driven Innovation in Traditional Manufacturing', NBER working paper 21752, National Bureau of Economic Research.

Cha, M. S. (2003). 'Did Takahashi Korekiyo Rescue Japan from the Great Depression?', *Journal of Economic History*, 63(1), 127–144.

Clark, K. B., Chew, W. B., and Fujimoto, T. (1987). 'Product Development in the World Auto Industry', *Brookings Papers on Economic Activity*, 3, 729–771.

Fukao, K. (2012). *'Ushinawareta 20nen' to Nihonkeizai: Kouzoutekigenin to Saisei no Gendouryoku* [The Structural Causes of Japan's 'Two Lost Decades': Forging a New Growth Strategy], Tokyo: Nikkei Publishing Inc.

(2018). 'Seicho to Makuro Keizai' [Growth and the Macroeconomy], in Fukao, K., Nakamura, N., and Nakabayashi, M. (eds.), *Nihon Keizai no Rekishi, Iwanami Koza, Vol. 6, Gendai 2* [History of the Japanese Economy, Iwanami Lecture Series, Vol. 6, The Contemporary Period 2], Tokyo: Iwanami Shoten, 2–28.

Fukao, K. and Saumik, P. (2019). 'Baumol versus Engel: Accounting for 100 Years (1885–1985) of Structural Transformation in Japan', IER Discussion Paper Series A, No. 694, Institute of Economic Research, Hitotsubashi University.

Fukao, K. and Settsu, T. (2017). 'Seicho to Makuro Keizai' [Growth and the Macroeconomy], in Fukao, K., Nakamura, N., and Nakabayashi, M. (eds.), *Nihon Keizai no Rekishi, Iwanami Koza, Vol. 4, Kindai 2* [History of the Japanese Economy, Iwanami Lecture Series, Vol. 4, The Modern Period 2], Tokyo: Iwanami Shoten.

Fukao, K. and Yuan, T. (2016). 'China's Growth Slowdown: Lessons from Japan's Experience and the Expected Impact on Japan, the USA and Germany', *China and the World Economy*, 24(5), 122–146.

Fukao, K., Bassino, J.-P., Makino, T., Paprzycki, R., Settsu, T., Takashima, M., and Tokui, J. (2015). *Regional Inequality and Industrial Structure in Japan: 1874–2008*, Tokyo: Maruzen Publishing Co.

Fukao, K., Nakamura, N., and Nakabayashi, M. (eds.) (2017–18). *Nihon Keizai no Rekishi, Iwanami Koza, Vols. 3–6* [History of the Japanese Economy, Iwanami Lecture Series, Vols. 3–6], Tokyo: Iwanami Shoten.

Fukao, K., Makino, T., and Settsu, T. (2019). 'Structural Change, Capital Deepening, and TFP Growth in Japan: 1885–1970', IER Discussion Paper Series A, No. 693, Institute of Economic Research, Hitotsubashi University.

Hatase, M. (2002). 'Devaluation and Exports in Interwar Japan: The Effects of Sharp Depreciation of the Yen in the Early 1930s', *Bank of Japan Monetary and Economic Studies*, 20(3), 143–180.

Hayashi, F. and Prescott, E. C. (2008). 'The Depressing Effect of Agricultural Institutions on the Prewar Japanese Economy', *Journal of Political Economy*, 116 (4), 573–632.

Ito, M. and Kiyono, I. (1984). 'Dai 5-sho, Boeki to Chokusetsu Toshi' [Trade and Direct Investment], in Komiya, R., Okuno, M., and Suzumura, K. (eds.), *Nihon no Sangyo Seisaku* [Japan's Industrial Policy], University of Tokyo Press, ch. 5.

Jorgenson, D. W., Nomura, K., and Samuels, J. D. (2016). 'A Half Century of Trans-Pacific Competition: Price Level Indices and Productivity Gaps for Japanese and US Industries, 1955–2012', in Jorgenson, D. W., Fukao, K., and Timmer, M. P. (eds.), *The World Economy: Growth or Stagnation?*, Cambridge University Press, 469–507.

Komiya, R. (1975). *Gendai Nihon Keizai Kenkyu* [A Study of the Contemporary Japanese Economy], Tokyo University Press.

Krugman, P. (1998). 'It's BAAACK! Japan's Slump and the Return of the Liquidity Trap', *Brookings Papers on Economic Activity*, 2, 137–205.

Kushida, K. E. (2015). 'The Politics of Commoditization in Global ICT Industries: A Political Economy Explanation of the Rise of Apple, Google, and Industry Disruptors', *Journal of Industry, Competition and Trade*, 15(1), 49–67.

Linden, G., Brown, C., and Appleyard, M. M. (2003). 'The Semiconductor Industry's Role in the Net World Order', Institute for Research on Labor and Employment (IRLE) working paper 94-03, University of California Berkeley.

Maddison, A. (2003). *The World Economy: Historical Statistics*, Paris: Organisation for Economic Co-operation and Development.

Masui, Y. (1969). 'The Supply Price of Labor: Farm Family Workers', in Ohkawa, K., Johnston, B. F., and Kaneda, H. (eds.), *Agriculture and Economic Growth: Japan's Experience*, University of Tokyo Press, 222–249.

Minami, R. (1976) *Doryoku Kakumei to Gijustu Shinpo: Senzen-ki Senzogyo no Bunseki* [The Power Revolution and Technological Progress: Analysis of the Pre-War Manufacturing Sector], Tokyo: Toyo Keizai Shinpo-sha.

Mizoguchi, T. and Nojima, N. (1993). '1940–1945-nen ni okeru Kokumin Keizai Keisan no Ginmi' [Nominal and Real GDP of Japan: 1940–45], in Mizoguchi, T. (ed.), *Dainiji Taisen-ka no Nihon Keizai no Tokei-teki Bunseki* [A Statistical Analysis of the Japanese Economy during World War II], report on the research results of a 1990–92 grant in aid for scientific research, scientific research (A), Tokyo: Institute of Economic Research, Hitotsubashi University, 5–30.

Moriguchi, C. and Saez, E. (2008). 'The Evolution of Income Concentration in Japan, 1886–2005: Evidence from Income Tax Statistics', *Review of Economics and Statistics*, 90 (4), 713–734.

Nakamura, T. (1983). *Economic Growth in Prewar Japan*, New Haven: Yale University Press, originally published in 1971 in Japanese as *Senzenki Nihon Keizai Seicho no Bunseki*, Tokyo: Iwanami Shoten.

Nakamura, T. and Miyazaki, M. (1995). *Shiryo: Taiheiyo Senso Higai Chosa Hokoku* [Damage Survey Report of the Second World War], University of Tokyo Press.

Nelson, D. R. (1996). 'Making Sense of the 1981 Automobile VER: Economics, Politics, and the Political Economy of Protection', in Krueger, A. O. (ed.), *The Political Economy of Trade Protection*, University of Chicago Press, 35–42.

Ohkawa, K. and Rosovsky, H. (1972). *Japanese Economic Growth: Trend Acceleration in the Twentieth Century*, Stanford University Press.

Ohkawa, K. and Shinohara, M. (eds.) (1979). *Patterns of Japanese Economic Development: A Quantitative Appraisal*, New Haven: Yale University Press.

Okazaki, T. and Okuno-Fujiwara, M. (eds.) (1999). *The Japanese Economic System and its Historical Origins*, Oxford University Press.

Okazaki, T., Taniyama, E. and Nakabayashi, M. (2005). 'Role of Local Communities in Economic Development: A Survey Focusing on the Export Industries in Nineteenth-Century Japan', CIRJE J-Series 133, Faculty of Economics, University of Tokyo.

Paprzycki, R. and Fukao, K. (2008). *Foreign Direct Investment in Japan: Multinationals' Role in Growth and Globalization*, Cambridge University Press.

Saito, O. and Takashima, M. (2016). 'Estimating the Shares of Secondary- and Tertiary-Sector Output in the Age of Early Modern Growth: The Case of Japan, 1600–1874', *European Review of Economic History*, 20(3), 368–386.

Sugihara, K. (2013). 'Labour-Intensive Industrialization in Global History: An Interpretation of East Asian Experiences', in Austin, G. and Sugihara, K. (eds.), *Labour-Intensive Industrialization in Global History*, London: Routledge.

Tanimoto, M. (ed.) (2006). *The Role of Tradition in Japan's Industrialization: Another Path to Industrialization*, New York: Oxford University Press.

Yamazawa, I. and Yamamoto, Y. (1979). *Boeki to Kokusai Shushi* [Foreign Trade and Balance of Payments, Vol. 14 of Estimates of Long-Term Economic Statistics of Japan since 1868, ed. Okawa, K., Hinohara, M., and Umemura, M.], Tokyo: Toyo Keizai Shinposha.

5
Economic Changes in China
The Role of Institutions and Ideology

DEBIN MA

Institutions and Ideology: An Introduction

China's enormous economic boom, now well into its fourth decade, invites re-examination of the historical antecedents of this unprecedented surge of productivity and prosperity that has lifted hundreds of millions from dire poverty, pushed the People's Republic to the forefront of global manufacturing and trade, and unleashed sweeping transformations of economic life in the world's most populous nation. Writing before the onset of China's current boom, earlier generations of scholars attributed China's reversal of fortune to the prevalence of nepotism, corruption, and other elements of Chinese social structure and behaviour that prevented a dynamic response of the sort attained during Japan's Meiji era (1868–1912). Subsequent events have overtaken these views; indeed, some observers now advance the opposite view, attributing recent Asian prosperity to the same 'Confucian values' formerly thought to have obstructed economic dynamism. More recently, new work, often identified as the 'California school', has reshaped perspectives on the dynamism and development of the mid-Qing (1644–1911) economy. Their key argument, most clearly articulated in Pomeranz' influential book on *The Great Divergence* (2000), is that there was little difference in economic structure or per capita income between the most commercialized regions of China and Europe prior to the British Industrial Revolution, and there were no fundamental shortfalls in China's political, legal, or other institutional traditions.

These bold claims have kindled intense controversy and indeed raised more questions than answers. More specifically, were the Chinese initial conditions as advanced as claimed, and if so, how did China fall behind? More importantly, why did it take so long for China to industrialize after the Industrial Revolution had been well under way elsewhere. This chapter provides an overview of the Chinese economy during 1850–2000 and attempts to answer the second question posed. To this end, I highlight the importance of institutions and ideology, and their interaction in a feedback loop as critical elements accounting for the remarkable transformations as well as great inertia during this 150 years of Chinese response to Western or modernization challenges. To understand changes or lack thereof in the Chinese economy during this period, we need to bring in ideology and ideological change as a relatively autonomous causal factor. As ideas or ideology were used to justify and legitimatize existing institutions and regimes, their transformations were also necessary in order for institutional change or political reform to take place. Changes, however, had to start with the recognition of cognitive dissonance, or an intellectual challenge to the existing ideological framework which had been reinforced by the repeated regularity and predictability of past events. So the critical element is not so much the existence of such a challenge, but rather how this challenge is perceived and accepted by public opinion or by elites who can effect changes. So events are important, but perceptions or the formation or build-up of public opinion around the events may be even more important.

The emphasis on perceptions and interpretation rather than the 'realities' themselves are of particular relevance with regard to the absolutist nature of the Chinese regime, which relies on the systematic control of information and public opinion. For example, catalytic events, such as the 1842 Sino-British Opium War or the tragic death of 30 million lives in the Great Leap Famine during 1959–61, did not propel immediate institutional or political changes, but had to wait for decades for their full impact to be revealed. Often, ideas or a change of ideas can lag behind events, as changes upset the traditional ideological equilibrium and often require the establishment of a new equilibrium which could be riskier. Although they could be triggered by historical accidents, major institutional changes are driven by purposeful and intentional human actions. But to act on cognitive dissonance that will lead to real change, there is often the need for a feedback loop between ideas, outcomes, and public opinion, as well as shifts in public opinion. In other words, for changes to take place or for reform to take shape, not only should challenges be properly perceived among policymakers or public opinion, but also there needs be some perception of plausible solutions. So, in this sense, institutional change requires time, experiments (and accidents), and a feedback loop between events, experiments, and ideas.

All these imply that fundamental institutional transformation may not take place unless new ideas or paradigms have grown to replace the old ways and provide a new and consistent framework to explain the cognitive dissonance. Changes are also more likely to take place when there seem to be practical ways forward or a road map for change. This is one reason that institutional and ideological transformations were more likely to take place in the late nineteenth century than before, as China had by then witnessed the success of Meiji Japan, which succeeded in experimentation with Western models. Similarly, in the 1980s, the successful examples of capitalist Hong Kong, Taiwan, and other East Asian tigers also became a driving force for change towards market-oriented reform in China. Not surprisingly for the 1940s, the Soviet Union supplied both model and ideology, as well as direct assistance for the establishment of communism in China in 1949. With this framework, we now turn to our narrative of economic change, or lack thereof, and occasional backtracking during China's remarkable last century and a half.

China's Pre-Modern Institutions and Economy: An Overview

In the two millennia dynastic history of China, the three imperial or political regimes covered in this chapter – Qing (1644–1911), Republican (1911–49) and communism (since 1949) – displayed both unprecedented transformations and dramatic reversals, as well as historical resilience. Although an ethnic minority from China's semi-nomadic north-eastern frontier, the ascendancy of Manchu rule under the Qing actually marked the culmination of a millennia-long evolution and the maturing of a highly centralized, unitary Chinese political regime, governed by an absolutist emperor at the top of the power pyramid. Aided by a formal bureaucracy recruited through a highly structured nationwide (national-metropolitan-provincial) civil service examination rooted in Confucian classics, imperial China could implement a system of direct administrative rule (郡县), with mostly educated officials assigned to govern directly over one thousand counties nationwide over her vast territories, on a two- to five-year rotating basis. Hence the combination of direct administrative rule and the legitimacy of imperial personnel appointment became a potent instrument of political control and rule that no, or few, other traditional regimes had mastered. In this regard, Chinese rulers managed to break free from the constraints of feudal and local autonomous institutions that had characterized Europe, and much of the rest of the world for that matter (Fukuyama 2011; Ma 2012). Beyond the borders of empire, where they could not implement direct rule, the Qing, like previous dynasties, constructed a China-centred international order through the so-called tributary states trade system. This system engulfed neighbouring small states or territories in East and South East Asia as near protectorates, which would pose no major military or political threat. Hence, absolutism Chinese-style curtailed inter-state competition and weakened independent vested interests, civil society, or autonomous political and social groups, all to serve the purpose of minimizing any potential threat to the throne from below (Ma 2012; Ma and Rubin 2019).

In this system, imperial or political legitimacy hinged on the state's capacity to suppress internal dissent and external challenge. Although military superiority or repressive capacity remained paramount to political legitimacy, they were insufficient by themselves and were only resorted to under extreme cases of threat. Hence, crucial to this legitimacy is the development of a consistent ruling ideology or belief system, which – in our case – would be Confucianism or neo-Confucianism. To establish the monopoly of this ideology over the interpretation of political and social events, systematic control and manipulation of information or alternative ideologies was an essential part of the system, as characterized by the widespread incidence of literary inquisitions and intellectual persecutions (Jin and Liu 2011). Although this system was effective in perpetuating imperial rule and the status quo and helps to explain the super-stability of the Chinese empire before the mid-nineteenth century, it also led to the stagnation of ideology (Jin and Liu 2011). The lack of intellectual development in major paradigms of political and institutional ideologies meant that violent revolution or dynastic overthrow (as happened very often in Chinese history) only resulted in the replacement of the previous regime with the same political system or ideology. So what we witness before the mid-nineteenth century is dynastic cycles rather than fundamental institutional revolution.[1]

How did this regime fare economically in the years leading up to our study? Recent attempts at constructing new long-term GDP series, most notably by Stephen Broadberry, Hanhui Guan, and David Daokui Li (2019), as summarized in Figure 5.1A, suggest that Chinese GDP per capita fluctuated around a level of $1,000 in 1990 international prices during the Northern Song and Ming dynasties, before declining to around $600 by the early nineteenth century, about one-third of the level of the world's leading, but much

1 Two caveats were important to this system. First, however much impersonality and neutrality characterized China's imperial regime, they were frequently compromised by the emperor's personal rule, his personal entourage of eunuchs, consort, and other inner court staff. Second, the highly centralized personnel appointment coexisted with a very decentralized delegation of economic resources at the local level (Ma 2012).

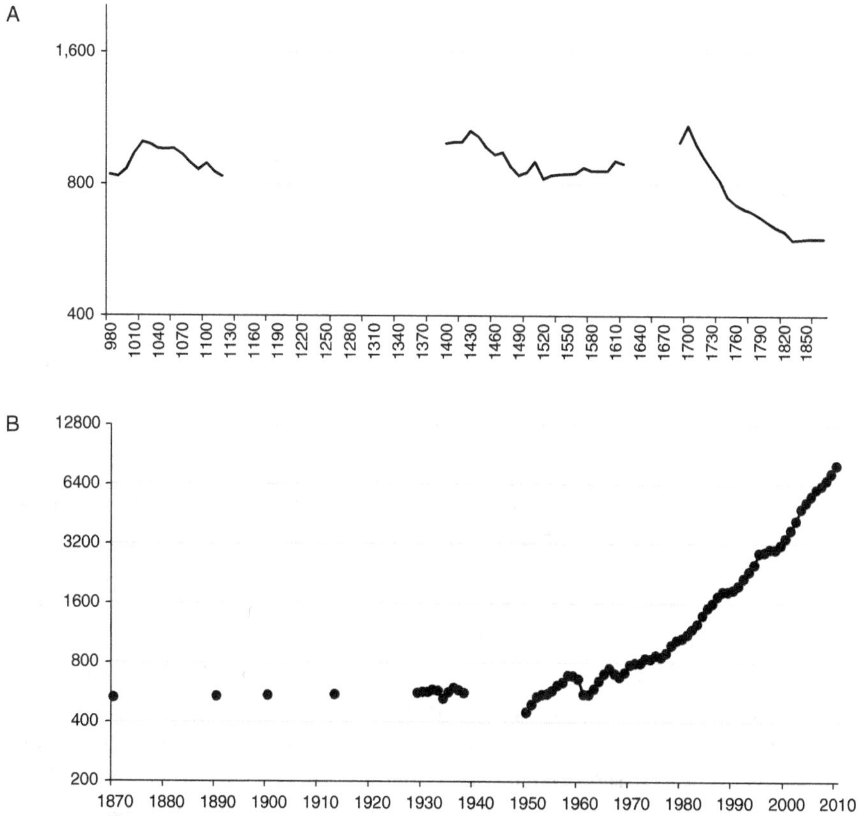

Figure 5.1 Chinese GDP per capita, 980–2010 (1990 international $)
Source: A: Broadberry et al. 2018; B: Maddison Project Database, version 2013.

smaller, economies.[2] Real-wage data from Allen et al. (2011) also reveal that Chinese living standards were probably closer to those of the relatively backward parts of Europe, but lower than north-western Europe in the eighteenth and nineteenth centuries. The structure of Chinese GDP even in the 1910s reveals a typical agrarian economy, with a 70 per cent share of the economy in the agriculture sector (Maddison 2007; Ma 2008). These reviews confirm that the divergence in living standards and per capita incomes

2 For other works estimating Chinese GDP, see Ma and de Jong 2019.

between Europe and China already existed before the Industrial Revolution, and only widened from the nineteenth century onwards.

Turning to the period since 1870, the GDP per capita estimates for China in Figure 5.1B are taken from the Maddison Project Database, version 2013, an updated version of the estimates set out in Maddison 2007, which incorporate adjustments to the official Chinese series to make them consistent with standard international measurement procedure. GDP per capita exhibited no trend growth before World War II, and indeed reached a low point at the time of the 1949 Revolution. Although there was rapid growth during the early years of communist rule, there were also major setbacks, such as the Great Leap Famine of 1959–61 and the Cultural Revolution of the mid-1960s, which limited trend progress until the death of Mao Zedong in 1976. The reform initiatives of the late 1970s under Deng Xiaoping then set China on a path of rapid sustained growth, which has lasted until the time of writing.

Other indicators of the evolution of Chinese living standards and human capital in the nineteenth and twentieth centuries are based on integrated estimates of real wages and anthropometric evidence (see Baten et al. 2010). These estimates confirm the picture of generally static living conditions in China before the 1950s, and also add a comparative dimension. Although Chinese heights fell back relative to Taiwan during the late nineteenth century, for example, Japanese stature was still much lower.[3] The Japanese reached the Chinese height level only during the 1980s. However, in contrast to the findings based on real wages and heights, the basic numeracy index – a measure of tendencies to report a rounded rather than an exact age – reveals a relatively high level of Chinese human capital, which was closer to that of north-western Europe for the eighteenth and nineteenth centuries than to that of countries with a comparable low level of living standards, such as India or Turkey. However, in comparison to Japan, Chinese numeracy displayed greater volatility during the nineteenth century. The importance of Confucian cultural heritage was highlighted in a recent study by Chen et al. (2018).

Any claim that China was the world's leading economy in the eighteenth to nineteenth centuries is a misleading conflation of GDP in aggregate and per capita terms. China in the eighteenth century was a large economy thanks mainly to the sheer size of its population, and the fact that per capita income differences in the pre-industrial world still remained relatively minor

3 This was caused by the absence of animal protein in the Japanese diet of this period; see Baten et al. (2010).

before the onset and spread of the Industrial Revolution. But in per-capita terms, the Chinese economy was just as poor as most pre-modern agrarian economies, with little impact on the global economy, which was falling increasingly under the orbit of Western colonial expansion. It is true that not everything remained stagnant. The export of Chinese silks and tea fuelled the fetish of chinoiserie in western Europe, which formed the basis for import substitution within western Europe. On the other side of the trade equation, inflow of Latin American silver ingots and coins greased the engine of Chinese commerce and supported the monetization of public finance from the sixteenth century. There was a tripling of population and a doubling of territory under the Qing between the fifteenth and eighteenth centuries. No single political entity at the time achieved such size in both geography and population under such stability and durability. But it is a far cry to claim that China in the eighteenth century was the world's leading economy, as it may have been under the Song (960–1279), when Europe was still in its dark age. Indeed, by the mid-nineteenth century, centuries of waves of commercial, financial, political, technological, and scientific revolutions powered a fragmented, contentious Europe to largely eclipse the Qing and begin to haunt her with the spectre of Western imperialism.

The Nineteenth Century: An Ominous Beginning

The beginning of the nineteenth century may have seen the turn of the tide that had once favoured the fortunes of the Qing. Population growth, sustained by rising agricultural land productivity and the introduction of new crops, may have finally stretched the limits of the resource constraint. Beginning with the White Lotus (1796–1804), a series of domestic rebellions, culminating in the vast Taiping Rebellion (1851–64), both reflected and contributed to the erosion of the Qing regime. Externally, following the collapse of the East India monopoly in 1833, private commercial interests driving British imperialism intensified their interest in the Chinese trade. The rise of a triangular trade, with the export of Indian opium to China, reversed China's long-standing trade surplus, draining silver species out of China. This occurred against a background, during the sixteenth and seventeenth centuries, when mid-Ming fiscal reform led to the silverization of fiscal revenue, and the increasing penetration of silver used as a medium of exchange in the next two to three centuries. The increasing scarcity of silver species, as reflected in the rising copper cash–silver ratio, was wreaking havoc on people's livelihoods, governmental tax collection, and the morale of the military (Lin 2006).

Prompted by an urge to act, but armed with little knowledge of the potency of the newly rising Western imperialism, the Qing's military confrontation with Britain in the now famous Opium War of 1842 turned out to be a humiliating defeat, and also marked the beginning of the world's largest and most remote empire now in the orbit of Western imperialism. The British forced the Qing to accept the Treaty of Nanking (1842), which ceded Hong Kong to Britain, imposed a regime of virtual free trade, and initiated the 'treaty port' system by opening five Chinese ports to British merchants. This agreement, which set the tone of China's international economic relations during the century prior to the Pacific War, subsequently expanded to include dozens of treaty ports where foreign residents were protected by extraterritoriality at the expense of Chinese sovereignty.

The challenge of Western imperialism represented an external threat drastically different from China's traditional nemesis on her northern frontier. It triggered not only a series of economic shocks to trade, production, and finance, but also a series of ideological and intellectual shocks that took time to absorb in the Chinese imperial context. Military defeat by external enemies, or challenges that were difficult to conceal or manipulate even under internal control of information, represented a cognitive dissonance that would pose a particular threat to the Qing's political legitimacy. Dissonance from the Opium War and other military defeats did not necessarily lead to immediate ideological change, as it was not the events or challenges themselves, but the internal perceptions and interpretation of these challenges that often mattered more for real changes.[4]

This evolving pattern of Western challenges and Chinese responses in China's modern era was succinctly summarized by Liang Qichao, China's foremost intellectual and reformer of the era. Liang characterized Chinese reform as occurring in three stages. The first stage of reform was an attempt to introduce Western technology (particularly military technology), followed by the second stage of institutional reform. These institutional reforms included the introduction of Western-style government, law, and modern enterprise, such as banks and corporations. It seems that when all failed, there came the third stage of cultural reform or revolution, which eventually led to the radical abrogation of Confucian ideology (Yang 1997: 1–3). Liang's

4 For the controversies among Qing officials' interpretation of the Opium War defeat, see Mao 1995.

observations reflected the very gradual nature of the ideological incorporation of the Western challenge and the complicated process of a feedback loop leading to institutional change. We turn now to a narrative of these three stages of change.

Political Accommodation and Institutional Adjustment to 1895

The new era marked by China's forced opening under Western imperialism started off disastrously for the Qing dynasty, which was brought to the brink of collapse by the devastating Taiping Rebellion. The Qing under the so-called Tongzhi Restoration (1861–75) also engineered a remarkable economic recovery through the revitalization of traditional institutions: the reinstatement of Confucian orthodoxy, the restoration of the national civil service examination (largely interrupted during the Taiping Rebellion), and the initial exemption from land taxes to lure cultivators back to war-torn agricultural regions.

Neither did the Qing remain entirely passive to Western incursions. As a natural extension to the Tongzhi Restoration, powerful regional bureaucrats, such as Li Hongzhang and Zhang Zhidong, sponsored the Self-Strengthening Movement (1860–94), a programme that aimed to expand Chinese military strength by developing a small number of Western-style, capital-intensive enterprises, financed by the state and directed by prestigious officials who possessed the highest credentials awarded under the Confucian academic system. Although these enterprises, which included arsenals, factories, and shipyards, were fraught with inefficiency and corruption, they did manage to record modest achievements. Nonetheless, the overall ideological orientation during this period remained conservative. In contrast to the concurrent Meiji reform in Japan, there was no introduction of any reforms that touched the fundamentals of the traditional regime: no introduction of a modern constitution or commercial law; no reform in the currency system; modern banks or modern infrastructures such as railroads were expressly prohibited; steamships were limited to major river ways such as the Yangzi.

The direct impact of the treaty port system, where Chinese trade tariffs were restricted to a modest 3 or 5 per cent, was the expansion of China's international trade. China's Maritime Customs data show real imports more than doubling in the two and a half decades prior to 1895, and exports increasing by half this amount. Trade statistics suggest slower growth of real trade in the range of 2–3 per cent per annum after 1895. Despite its modest scale, trade gradually pulled major domestic commodity markets into close alignment with their counterparts throughout the Pacific Basin.

The treaty system accelerated the arrival of new technologies, initially to the treaty ports themselves, which in the nineteenth- and twentieth-century versions of global entry became staging points for the spread of technologies into the domestic economy. However, it was in this area where we see industrialization lagging far behind the opportunities opened up by the inflow of trade and technology during this era. Attempts by Chinese and European entrepreneurs to take advantage of new opportunities linked to new technologies and new trade arrangements reveal the presence of powerful obstacles to innovation within China's late-Qing economy. These barriers, which affected the expansion of key public infrastructure, such as modern railroads and inland steamshipping, are most clearly visible in the history of private efforts to introduce new technologies and new business arrangements in the processing of agricultural commodities like soybeans and silk larvae (see Brandt et al. 2014). Despite these, new information and knowledge transmitted through the treaty ports and other channels were eroding the monopoly of traditional ideology and softening its rigidities.

China's Turning Point at the Turn of the Century

China's defeat in the Sino-Japanese War of 1894–95, by a nation long regarded as a student rather than an equal, marked the end of the Self-Strengthening Movement, which events revealed to be feeble and ineffective. This ignominious military failure inflicted a profound mental shock on Chinese elites and the public at large. The immediate economic impact followed the 1896 signing of the Treaty of Shimonoseki, which granted foreigners the right to establish factories in the treaty ports. Eliminating the prohibition against foreign factories in the treaty ports sparked a rapid expansion of foreign direct investment. This new arrangement indirectly legitimized Chinese modern enterprises. Despite some setbacks from the repression of the Hundred Days of Reform, centred in the southern province of Hunan in 1898, followed by the subsequent debacle surrounding the Boxer Rebellion in 1900, the Qing constitutional movement of 1903–11 was far more comprehensive and ambitious. It aimed at steering China towards a constitutional monarchy by drafting a formal modern constitution, with national, provincial, and local parliaments. Military modernization was high on the reform agenda. Administrative reforms sought to modernize public finance and adopt a national budget. The reform initiative gave birth to new Ministries of

Education, Trade, and Agriculture, and encouraged the founding of local chambers of commerce. There were policy initiatives aimed at currency reform, efforts to establish modern banks, and to expand railroads and other public infrastructure.

The late-Qing constitutional reform (1905–11), which led to political decentralization, may have inadvertently accounted for the collapse of the Qing. But the fall of the Qing and the rise of the Republic opened the door to a massive introduction of new ideology and new institutions from the West, and Chinese experimentation with them, much of which was intermediated through Meiji Japan. The abolition of the millennia-old civil service examination in 1905 opened the door to a modern school system and the rise of China's most well-known universities, and, more importantly, a new avenue to social mobility. This indeed began China's age of modernity, a genuine experiment with constitutionalism, the rise of regional cosmopolitanism, and the introduction of modern legal codes, such as company law and double-entry bookkeeping (Dikotter 2010). It also saw the rise of modern industry, banking, public finance, and monetary regime. Further, local autonomy under a decentralized system strengthened the growth and maturing of civil society and, more importantly, boosted political and ideological competition across different provinces and towns as well as treaty ports (Ma 2019).

But these wrenching changes carried large side-effects as well. Today, the Republican era of the 1910s and 1920s is often more remembered for the rise of warlordism, regional division, military and civil strife, governmental fiscal bankruptcy and predation, and, more importantly, the widespread sense of China's national decline on the international stage. Despite that, the ideological, political, and economic foundation was set for an economic take-off of some sort.

The Onset of China's Industrial Revolution, 1895–1949

Beginning at the very end of the nineteenth century, activity in mining and manufacturing accelerated sharply from its small initial base. Overall industrial output showed double-digit real annual growth during 1912–36, a phenomenal result for that period, especially in view of China's turbulent political scene and the impact of the Great Depression (Chang 1969). Factory production, initially focused on textiles, food processing, and other consumer products, was concentrated in two regions: the lower Yangzi area, where both foreign and Chinese entrepreneurs pursued factory expansion in and around Shanghai; and China's north-east or Manchurian region, where Japanese initiatives predominated. By 1935, Chinese factories, including some owned by British or Japanese firms, produced 8.0 per cent of the world's cotton yarn (more than Germany, France, or Italy) and 2.8 per cent of global cotton piece goods production. Despite the importance of foreign investment in Shanghai, and especially in Manchuria, Chinese-owned companies produced 73 per cent of China's 1933 factory output. Growing production of light consumer and industrial goods, combined with the accumulation of experience in operating and repairing modern machinery, generated backward linkages that spurred new private initiatives in machinery, chemicals, cement, mining, electricity, and metallurgy. Official efforts (including semi-official Japanese activity in Manchuria) also promoted the growth of mining, metallurgy, and arms manufacture (Rawski 1989: ch. 2).

China's economic prospects acted as a magnet for trade and investment during the pre-war decades. China's foreign trade rose to a peak of more than 2 per cent of global trade flows in the late 1920s, a ratio that was not regained until the 1990s. Between 1902 and 1931, inflows of foreign direct investment grew at annual rates of 8.3 per cent, 5 per cent, and 4.3 per cent for Shanghai, Manchuria, and the rest of China, respectively. By 1938, China's stock of inward foreign investment amounted to US$2.6 billion – more than any other underdeveloped region except for the Indian subcontinent and Argentina. Although estimates of pre-war capital flows often blur the distinction between direct and portfolio holdings, it is evident that China played a substantial role in global capital flows. The 1938 figure of US$2.6 billion for China's stock of foreign investments amounts to 8.4 per cent of worldwide stocks of outward foreign investment and 17.5 per cent of outward foreign direct investment in that year. By contrast, China's 2001 share of worldwide inward foreign direct investment was only 2.1 per cent. Domestic investment also showed substantial growth. 'Modern-oriented' fixed investment (calculated from consumption of cement, steel, and machinery) grew at an average annual rate of 8.1 per cent between 1903 and 1936, outpacing Japanese gross domestic fixed capital formation in mining, manufacturing, construction, and facilitating industries, which advanced at an annual rate of 5.0 per cent. Despite the effects of the Great Depression and political turmoil, economy-wide gross fixed investment exceeded 10 per cent of aggregate output during 1931–36 (see Brandt et al. 2014 for details).

Transport development contributed substantially to economic expansion. China's railway track length grew from 364 kilometres in 1894 to over 21,000 by 1937, and newly constructed north–south lines slashed economic distances across a landscape dominated by rivers flowing from west to east. Completion of railway and telegraph connections linking Peking (now Beijing) and the central China river port of Wuhan in 1906 reduced the time needed to ship commodities between these cities. In a remarkable triumph of a free banking version of the silver standard, privately held Chinese banks, often cooperating with foreign financial institutions and traditional money shops, transformed the financial face of China by persuading households and businesses to transact with paper banknotes that were convertible into silver on demand. This monetary transformation reduced transaction costs. The expansion of branch networks allowed major domestic banks to attract deposits from all regions and recycle them to the areas of greatest demand, contributing to the emergence of an embryonic national market for funds (Rawski 1989).

These forces resulted in increased per capita output and structural changes of the sort associated with Simon Kuznets' concept of modern economic growth in two major regions: the Lower Yangzi, where private domestic and foreign investment in and around Shanghai served as the key driver (Ma 2008), and the north-east (Manchuria), where Japanese investment and eventual takeover provided the key momentum. However, these regional developments did not have a very significant effect on GDP per capita at the aggregate level (Figure 5.1B). At this stage, the national economy continued to be dominated by its large agricultural sector, where productivity remained low.

Beginning in 1929, China's economy faced a succession of shocks, arising from the Great Depression and falling export demand, the severance of Manchuria in 1932 by the Japanese, and rapidly rising silver prices triggered by Britain's decision to go off gold and the United States' Silver Purchase Act of 1934. Considerable debate persists over how well the Chinese economy weathered the storm, and the severity of the combined impact of these events on aggregate economic activity. There is little controversy about what followed. Twelve years of war, with large-scale civil strife following the defeat of Japan's invading armies, battered China's economy and rolled back much of the progress achieved during the preceding decades. Roaring inflation crippled China's financial sector, and corruption hobbled the public sector and embittered the populace.

People's Republic of China, 1950–2000

The ascendancy of communist rule and ideology followed decades of gradual but increasing radicalization of modernization ideology. By the late 1920s, even the new nationalist government established in Nanjing in 1928 had largely abandoned the Constitutionalist experiment and aimed for the recentralization of political power. The full-scale Japanese invasion in 1937, and China's drive for resource mobilization, pushed towards the rise of a wartime command economy. When the communists took power, they were armed with another borrowed ideology from the Soviet Union.

The broad contours of economic change following the establishment in 1949 of the People's Republic of China (PRC) are well understood. The new communist government quickly implemented an orthodox mix of fiscal and monetary policies to restore fiscal balance and quell hyperinflation in an economy wrecked by twelve years of war and civil strife. But these measures towards the implementation of socialist planning were accompanied by violent campaigns that expropriated the assets of urban and rural elites, and by massive brainwashing propaganda around the cult of Mao's personal rule. By establishing near total control, the new government vastly expanded state control over resources, rapidly eliminating the long-standing shortage of fiscal revenue that had prevented earlier governments from financing aggressive development initiatives.

China's planning system, introduced with Soviet advice during the early 1950s, bore strong resemblances to its Soviet counterpart. But starting in 1958, China distanced itself both from Moscow's political leadership and from Soviet economic strategy, as Mao Zedong embarked on a daring campaign to accelerate the pace of development by amalgamating rural households into large-scale collective units, or people's communes, and by promoting rural industrialization. The communes proved to be a costly failure: poor incentives, false reports of rising crop output, excessive grain procurement, and a massive reallocation of labour from agriculture to industry inflicted an immense famine on China's peasantry that cost tens of millions of lives in the so-called Great Leap Famine of 1959–61 (Kung and Chen 2011). The Great Leap Forward saw the frenzy of the rise of Mao's cult of personality. Efforts to revive forward momentum in the early 1960s met with some success, but the economy suffered further setbacks in the mid-1960s, when a new political campaign known as the 'Cultural Revolution', sparked a new reversal in economic policies and incentive mechanisms (see Figure 5.1B).

Mixed economic outcomes characterize China's quarter-century of socialist planning under Mao and his colleagues. The plan era brought notable expansion of industrial and technological capabilities, as well as major improvements in literacy, school attendance, maternal and infant survival rates, public health, and life expectancy. Real annual GDP growth of roughly

6 per cent in aggregate and 4 per cent in per capita terms surpassed gains in India, Pakistan, Indonesia, Egypt, Brazil, and other large, low-income nations, often by large margins. However, these successes paled in comparison with the other East Asian miracle economies within the same cultural zone, and, moreover, were accompanied by large shortcomings and setbacks, which occurred in part because the PRC government, while eliminating institutional barriers inherited from the past, used its unprecedented administrative capacity to implement a succession of perverse economic policies. These included an assault on individual and firm-level incentives, the persecution of intellectuals and educators, forced collectivization of farming, a destructive regimen of local self-reliance, the diffusion of unsuitable technological innovations in both agriculture and industry, and policies severely constricting cross-border flows of trade, investment, people, and information. A substantial gap emerged between the living standards of urban and rural households. Overall, per capita food supply scarcely increased between 1958 and 1978 (see Brandt et al. 2014).

The death of Mao Zedong (1893–1976) marked the beginning of the Deng Xiaoping era, the full significance of which China and the rest of the world were slowly beginning to grasp. Nudging the immense country away from the grip of Mao's cult of personality and rigid ideological control, Deng's reform started a careful and often risky ideological liberalization. China's reform initiatives of the late 1970s focused on four areas: rural liberalization, expansion of foreign trade and investment, policies aimed at 'enlivening' state-owned enterprises, and fiscal decentralization. Despite obvious limitations, we can see in retrospect that these initial reforms represent a watershed in Chinese economic history. For the first time, China's economy avoided most of the Qing-era institutional constraints, as well as the most restrictive of the fresh obstacles imposed by the PRC. The greatest success occurred in the rural economy, where the explosive response to the implementation of the household responsibility system banished the spectre of food shortages and sparked the largest episode of poverty alleviation in human history. Rural economic revival, however, went far beyond an intensification of effort in response to the restoration of individual incentives. The reform unleashed a torrent of entrepreneurship in the rural areas, and later in the cities. Rapid expansion of international trade and investment eliminated long-standing shortages of foreign exchange, began to tap the wealth and expertise of Overseas Chinese and of multinational corporations, and introduced a long-absent element of economic rationality into investment policies by channelling resources into labour-intensive export production that matched China's resource endowment. Efforts to upgrade state enterprises were far less successful, and losses mounted, despite massive direct and indirect subsidies. China's economy throughout much of the 1980s was a halfway house, combining elements of old and new. Although the reform process spawned episodes of social unrest – partly due to the relaxation of political control, as seen in the outbursts of the 1989 Tiananmen demonstration – overall, the first fifteen years of reform produced no substantial group of losers – a rare outcome in episodes of substantial socio-economic change (Naughton 2007; Xu 2011).

Despite fifteen years of GDP growth averaging 8 per cent per annum, China was at a critical crossroads during the early 1990s. Growth had become highly cyclical, with successive periods of liberalization and reform accompanied by high growth, but also higher rates of inflation. Reform stalled or became very timid in the aftermath of the 1989 Tiananmen Square crackdown. In a surprising twist, however, an ailing Deng Xiaoping came out and made his last, perhaps most famous, tour of southern China, with his boldest call for economic reform yet. By the mid-1990s, China's policymakers began to attack these difficulties with a remarkable sequence of policy changes. These included a sweeping overhaul of the fiscal system, a reorganization of the financial system, a comprehensive restructuring of the enterprise sector, including the furloughing and eventual dismissal of over 50 million redundant employees, mostly in the state sector, substantial privatization of both state and collective enterprises, along with further reforms. These included the virtual elimination of the planned allocation of materials, and a broad embrace of globalization that reduced tariffs and other trade barriers in advance of China's 2001 entry into the World Trade Organization. These reform efforts were far more systematic and aggressive than during the early years of reform. They contributed to China's enormous growth spurt from the 1990s, setting China on course to surpass the Japanese economy and possibly to become the world's largest economy in due course.[5]

Economic Change and Continuity in China: A Long-Term Perspective

The Chinese economic miracle has stimulated efforts to define a 'Chinese model' of growth or to establish a 'Beijing consensus' of development-

5 In per capita terms, however, China remained a long way behind Japan and other OECD economies.

enhancing policies. However, China's recent economic success should also be seen in the context of the deep historical roots of the current institutional structure and the central role of China's unusual legacy of human capital. While the historic accumulation of resources and capabilities deserves recognition as an important contributor to China's recent growth, the historical legacy may well become a burden to China's economic future, as it has served to impede China's response to challenges in the past. We argue that despite remarkable transformations, Chinese institutions and culture have displayed remarkable continuities, summarized as follows:

Authoritarian System

Major elements of institutional continuity begin with China's authoritarian political system. In the People's Republic, as under Qing rule, self-perpetuating elites exercise supreme authority, with no formal checks and balances. Although the Qing memorial system and the Communist Party's practice of democratic centralism provide avenues for lower-ranking individuals to influence policy outcomes, decisions emanating from the throne or politburo are final. Despite the nominal introduction of a Western legal system and codes, the Chinese legal system, as before, has remained under the control of the administrative hierarchy.

Personnel

To implement central policies, both the Qing and the People's Republic rely on centrally managed, merit-based personnel systems. The Confucian approach emphasizing 'rule of (properly trained, selected and motivated) men', rather than 'rule of law' prevails. Both systems rely on a combination of ideology and oversight to limit the inevitable agency costs associated with granting substantial autonomy to lower-level officials, whose career prospects depend more on outcomes than on adherence to carefully prescribed procedures.

Education, Human Capital, and Entrepreneurship

The historical legacy of a national civil service examination, formulated as the administrative tool of imperial rule, has also helped to produce remarkable cultural and ethnic homogeneity for a nation of China's size. Pursuit of education has been a hallmark of Chinese society throughout the past millennium. While the PRC emphasis on mass education has delivered notable improvements in school attendance and other dimensions of human development, stocks of human capital accumulated long before

1949 have contributed massively to China's recent economic gains. Reflecting long-standing cultural values, three decades of negative financial returns for graduates, school closures and suspension of merit-based admissions during the Cultural Revolution (*c*.1966–75), and persecution of intellectuals did not deter millions of Chinese families from emphasizing learning and study. Restoration of university entrance examinations in 1977 attracted swarms of self-taught candidates.

The long tradition of de facto private property rights created a massive class of smallholder farmers, peasants, craftsmen and merchants in charge of their production, distribution, and consumption. Rapid expansion of production, employment, and exports in millions of 'township and village enterprises' relied on China's deep reserves of rural management capability, highlighting China's historic 'abundance of small-time entrepreneurs'.

Economic Decentralization

Both the Qing and the People's Republic combine centralization of political authority with relatively decentralized economies. The Qing economy was essentially a market system with private ownership. During the pre-reform decades under the People's Republic, China's planned economy, though patterned after the Soviet example, was far less centralized than the USSR's, with provincial and local governments controlling a substantial portion of state-owned enterprises and managing considerable resource flows. This led provinces to build 'complete sets' of industries, creating a potential for competition that was activated once reform created new opportunities for cross-provincial trade.

Alignment of Incentives

The Qing achieved considerable success in aligning incentives among the throne, the bureaucracy, the gentry, and the common people – all of whom sought prosperity and stability. The plan era, during which the state called on ordinary Chinese to suppress their desire for better living standards for the sake of 'building socialism', emerges as a historical outlier. Following the death of Mao Zedong, reform policies restored the traditional unity of objectives, with leaders, officials, and populace all pursuing economic growth. Under both the Qing and the PRC, fiscal arrangements often left lower-level governments with insufficient revenue to fulfil their responsibilities, including compensation of local officials. Both regimes took vigorous measures to curb what the centre viewed as corrupt diversion of tax payments intended for the central treasury. But corruption is endemic and part and parcel of the system (Ma and Rubin 2019).

But Chinese success in the reform era cannot be explained by historical legacy alone. It was a major discontinuity, in both legacy and external environment, that allowed the spurt of Chinese growth from the 1980s. We summarize these discontinuities as follows:

Vision/Objectives

Qing emperors focused on stability rather than growth. Reform leader Deng Xiaoping's famous observations that 'to get rich is glorious' and 'it does not matter if a cat is black or white as long as it catches mice' mark the completion of a century-long process, which established economic expansion as a key element in the objective function of China's top leaders (Chenggang Xu 2011: 13). The capacity to deliver economic growth and improve living standards constituted a source of political legitimacy of communist rule in the reform era.

Public Administration

China's Qing and Republican governments remained fiscally weak because of severe agency problems in the collection of taxes, and the necessity of maintaining political alliances prevented them from taxing the deepest pools of income and wealth. Following the rapid confiscation of assets held by landlords and the urban bourgeoisie, the PRC quickly expanded its fiscal resources to levels consistent with the requirements of development. Building on experience accumulated in the administration of isolated rural areas during China's protracted civil war and in the civil war itself, the PRC vastly expanded the reach and control of formal administration down to the village level.

Elite Recruitment

During the Ming-Qing era, elite status derived from examination success, which required massive investment. Qing gentry resisted efforts to open the door to newcomers whose non-traditional mobility paths threatened to devalue traditional Confucian education. Following the Mao years, which enforced even stricter ideological limits on its political elites and actively persecuted excluded groups, the reform-era PRC has broadened elite recruitment to include two major channels – education and wealth. The new combination of large, widely shared economic gains and wholesale absorption of potential regime opponents into elite ranks has tilted policymaking in economically beneficial directions, while assisting official efforts to marginalize dissident groups.

Globalization

Foreign military power compelled the partial opening of China's nineteenth-century economy. The Qing government sought to limit the scope of foreign activity; individual foreigners, as well as their products and technologies, faced powerful informal opposition by local gentry. China's initial reform policies resembled those of their Qing predecessors, confining foreign commerce to a few localities. But over time, Chinese reform deepened, leading to the gradual dismantling of the fundamental institutional structure of a planned economy. The prolonged era of peace and order in the last few decades – a sharp contrast to China's Republican era during the first half of the twentieth century, marked by two world wars and Japanese aggression – allowed time and space for gradual reform. The peaceful and prosperous rise of Japan and the East Asian tigers in the post-World War II era offered powerful models of export-oriented economies. China today has moved from extreme isolation to the opposite extreme, achieving trade ratios that dwarf those of other major economies, absorbing large flows of foreign investment, and, most recently, emerging as a substantial originator of outbound foreign direct investment.

Despite three decades of near double-digit economic growth and four decades of reform and opening, the Chinese political system remains highly centralized, authoritarian, lacking in transparency, subject to the rule of law, but rife with corruption, with restrictions on public opinion and freedom of information or expression. In this system, ideology often plays a dominant role, although it has been significantly downplayed to suit the more pragmatic, market-oriented policy. Interestingly, after three decades of unprecedented growth, the last decade saw an unexpected attempt to rebuild or strengthen a Leninist party-state. Indeed, the political power that had once supported market-oriented growth may well be converted to power for political control. How the Chinese economy would fare under this political regime in the face of rising expectation and increasing globalization remains to be seen.

References

Allen, R., Bassino, J.-P., Ma, D., Moll-Murata, C., and van Zanden, J. L. (2011). 'Wages, Prices, and Living Standards in China, Japan, and Europe, 1738–1925', *Economic History Review*, 64(S1), 8–38.

Baten, J., Ma, D., Morgan, S., and Wang, Q. (2010). 'Evolution of Living Standards and Human Capital in China in Eighteenth to Twentieth Centuries', *Explorations in Economic History*, 47(3), 347–359.

Brandt, L., Ma, D., and Rawski, T. (2014). 'From Divergence to Convergence: Re-Evaluating the History Behind China's Economic Boom', *Journal of Economic Literature*, 52(1), 45–123.

Broadberry, S., Guan, H., and Li, D. D. (2018). 'China, Europe, and the Great Divergence: A Study in Historical National Accounting, 980–1850', *Journal of Economic History*, 78, 955–1000.

Chang, J. K. (1969). *Industrial Development in Pre-Communist China*, Chicago: Aldine Publishing.

Chen, T., Kung, J. K.-S., and Ma, C. (2018). 'Long Live Keju! The Persistent Effects of China's Civil Examination System', unpublished working paper.

Dikötter, F. (2010). *The Age of Openness: China before Mao*, Hong Kong University Press.

Fukuyama, F. (2011). *The Origins of Political Order: From Prehuman Times to the French Revolution*, New York: Farrar, Straus and Giroux.

Jin, G. T. and Liu, Q. F. (2011). [The Cycle of Growth and Decline: On the Ultrastable Structure of Chinese Society] (in Chinese), Beijing: Law Press China.

Kung, J. K.-S. and Chen, S. (2011). 'The Tragedy of the Nomenklatura: Career Incentives and Political Radicalism during China's Great Leap Famine', *American Political Science Review*, 105, 27–45.

Lin, M.-h. (2006). *China Upside Down: Currency, Society, and Ideologies, 1808–1856*, Cambridge, MA: Harvard University Asia Center.

Ma, D. (2008). 'Economic Growth in the Lower Yangzi Region of China in 1911–1937: A Quantitative and Historical Perspective', *Journal of Economic History*, 68(2), 385–392.

(2012). 'Political Institution and Long-Run Economic Trajectory: Some Lessons from Two Millennia of Chinese Civilization', in Aoki, M., Kuran, T., and Roland, G. (eds.), *Institutions and Comparative Economic Development*, Basingstoke: Palgrave Macmillan, 78–98.

(2019). 'Financial Revolution in Republican China during 1900–37: A Survey and a New Interpretation', *Australian Economic History Review*, 59(3), 242–262.

Ma, D. and Rubin, J. (2019). 'The Paradox of Power: Principle-Agent Problems and Administrative Capacity in Imperial China (and Other Absolutist Regimes)', *Journal of Comparative Economics*, 47(2), 277–294.

Ma, Y. and de Jong, H. (2019). 'Unfolding the Turbulent Century: A Reconstruction of China's Historical National Accounts, 1840–1912', *Review of Income and Wealth*, 65(1), 75–79.

Maddison, A. (2007). *Chinese Economic Performance in the Long Run*, 2nd ed., rev. and updated, Paris: Development Centre of the Organisation for Economic Co-operation and Development.

Maddison Project Database, version 2013. Bolt, J. and van Zanden, J. L. (2014). 'The Maddison Project: Collaborative Research on Historical National Accounts', *Economic History Review*, 67(3), 627–651.

Mao, H. (1995). [The Collapse of the Celestial Empire: A Re-Examination of the Opium War] (in Chinese), Beijing: Sanlian Publishers.

Naughton, B. (2007). *The Chinese Economy: Transitions and Growth*, Cambridge, MA: MIT Press.

Pomeranz, K. (2000). *The Great Divergence*, Princeton University Press.

Rawski, T. G. (1989). *Economic Growth in Prewar China*, Berkeley: University of California Press.

Xu, C. (2011). 'The Fundamental Institutions of China's Reforms and Development', *Journal of Economic Literature*, 49(4), 1076–1151.

Yang, N. (1997). [The Modern Form of Regional Schools of Confucius] (in Chinese), Beijing: Sanlian Publisher.

6

From Free Trade to Regulation

The Political Economy of India's Development

BISHNUPRIYA GUPTA

India formally came under Crown rule in 1858. A century after the battle of Plassey that established the rule of the East India Company in Bengal, India came under the governance structure of the British Empire. This entailed three main changes: (1) being subjected to the policies of the British government; (2) paying 'home charges', which was equivalent to a tribute to the imperial power; and (3) providing an army that would support the objectives of the Empire both at home and abroad (Tomlinson 1982). The post-Corn Law free trade regime of Britain was transferred to the colonies, which adopted it without much resistance. India was formally integrated into a global economy where trade, capital, and labour flows did not face formal restrictions. Home charges became the basis of the nationalist critique of the Empire. This was seen as a drain of wealth from India to Britain, resources that could have been invested in economic development within the country. A second critique of the Empire was the destruction of the traditional textile industry and turning India into an agricultural exporter. India also played a role in Britain's war effort. Thousands were recruited into the imperial army during the world wars, not only to defend the Eastern Front, but many battalions were also stationed in other parts of the Empire and the battlefields of the world. This chapter will focus mainly on aspects of globalization and the consequences of the policies of the British government in India. The first section discusses the consequences of being part of the British Empire. The second section will discuss the transition from an open economy to a regulated one and look at the consequences of independent India's retreat from the global economy. A third section looks at India's reintegration into the global economy after 1980 and the consequences for economic growth.

India and the British Empire

Trade in the days of the monopoly trading companies from Europe depended on the company getting trading rights from local rulers. The English East India Company competed in the Indian market with other European companies, mainly to buy textiles in India to be sold in world markets. They had few goods from Europe to sell in India. The term 'bullion for goods' (Prakash 1976) aptly describes the pattern of this trade. Indians showed little appetite for European goods before the Industrial Revolution, but absorbed large quantities of silver bullion, which led to monetization of the economy. Gaining territorial rights in India in 1757 changed the nature of this trade. Land revenue could now be used to pay for textiles bought for exports, constituting an unequal exchange. This was short-lived. By the mid-nineteenth century, goods of the British Industrial Revolution had come to dominate the international market, displacing Indian textiles. The transition to Crown rule integrated India into the economic project of the British Empire. India became a supplier of agricultural goods to Britain and imported industrial products. Policies relating to public finance had to fit in with the objectives of the British Empire. Crown rule also opened up Indian policy-making to lobbying by British industrial and commercial interests.

Empire and Revenue

Indian public finance was the main objective of the East India Company as the ruler. This led to the introduction of new systems of land revenue, either through taxing landlords or peasant cultivators. The first land revenue system, introduced in Bengal, conferred property rights to landlords and it was left to them to extract the requisite rent from the cultivators and pay taxes to the government. The landlords failed to invest in land and increase productivity. A different system was introduced in other regions that were conquered later. In the non-landlord system, the cultivators paid taxes directly to the government. The objective was maximization of revenue and marketization of the agricultural sector through clearly defined property rights. Most of the revenue was raised through land tax, with consequences for the cultivators, who were close to subsistence. Opium and salt yielded large revenues. Revenue from other trade taxes was a small share in the nineteenth century. British exports to India incurred tariffs of 5 per cent on cotton piece goods and 3.5 per cent on yarn. J. P. Grant, who was a member of Governor General Canning's Council in 1857, increased tariffs, a policy that was against British textile interests (Harnetty 1972: 7–10). Tariffs were substantially increased in 1859. Harnetty argues: 'For the moment the critical state of the Indian finances overrode the dogmatic free trade argument' (Harnetty 1972: 10).

Crown rule, however, changed the role of trade. Free trade policies of the British Empire applied to India. Harnetty argues that although the increase in import duties did not face much resistance from the British mercantile community in India, who could pass on the increased costs to consumers, they were strongly resisted by the Manchester Chamber of Commerce, whose members feared a decline in market share in India. British textile interests lobbied the colonial government in India and in the British Parliament, and before long the tariffs on cotton textiles went back to a lower level. Tariffs for revenue purposes only, together with a countervailing excise tax on imported competing goods in India was consistent with the overall principle of free trade. Until World War I, whenever import duties were in place, countervailing excise duties followed.

The changes in the composition of revenue and expenditure are shown in Table 6.1. Land tax was the largest share of revenue until the turn of the century, followed by revenue from opium and salt. There was a marked change in the way revenue was collected thereafter. Land revenue began to lose its importance and the share of customs revenue and other indirect taxes increased after World War I (see Table 6.1A).

The newly developed industries of the late nineteenth century, in particular, cotton textiles expanded during the war and established themselves as a well-defined interest group. They lobbied for tariff protection. The war also marked significant changes in attitude of the policymakers towards domestic industry. The rising nationalist movement was forging alliances with industrial interests, and the British government sought to gain support among the industrial groups (Markovits 2002). The first Tariff Commission was set up to consider applications for tariffs by specific industries, and protectionist tariffs were given to many industries in the interwar period leading up to imperial preference in 1933. Direct taxes on income gained ground, reflecting the changing composition of GDP and the rising importance of modern industries.

The pattern of expenditure did not change much. The two major areas of government spending were civil administration and the military. Railways were a significant component, while spending on irrigation and famine prevention was low (see Table 6.1B). This picture fits in with the nationalist critique that benefit to the Empire rather than the economic development of

Table 6.1 Composition of revenue and expenditure

A. Composition of revenue, 1858–59 to 1940–41 (%)

	1858–59	1870–71	1900–1901	1921–22	1930–31	1940–41
Land revenue	50.0	40.0	53.0	27.0	23.0	19.0
Customs	8.0	5.0	9.0	30.0	36.0	–
Excise	4.0	6.0	10.0	14.0	13.0	16.0
Income tax	0.3	4.0	3.0	15.0	12.0	19.0
Salt	7.0	16.0	16.0	5.0	5.0	5.0
Opium	17.0	12.0	–	–	–	–
Others	13.0	18.0	9.0	10.0	11.0	13.0

B. Share of expenditure against revenue, 1884–1935 (%)

	Civil administration	Army	Famine relief	Railways	Irrigation
1884–85	16	24	2	18	3
1894–95	16	25	3	25	3
1904–05	16	30	1	16	4
1918–19	19	37	1	11	3
1924–25*	27	29	1	14	2
1934–35*	30	22	1	16	3

* All spending on civil administration.

Sources: Part A: Kumar 1983: tables 12.4 and 12.7; Part B: India, Commercial Intelligence Department.

India was the objective of the British administration. The next section considers the impact of project Empire in the three dimensions of globalization – trade, capital flows, and migration.

Empire and Trade

The cheap cotton textile products of the Industrial Revolution began to displace Indian textiles in international markets from the turn of the nineteenth century. By 1850, these goods had a dominant market share in India, supplying 60 per cent of the market by 1870. The dynamics of deindustrialization spanned several decades, first through the loss of export markets and then through loss of local markets to British imports, but its impact was less catastrophic than previously thought (Twomey 1983; Broadberry and Gupta 2009; Ray 2009). The fortunes of the East India Company, which had been tied to the textile trade from India, took a new dimension after its conquest of Bengal in 1757 (see Swamy in Volume I, Chapter 5 of this book).

As India integrated into the world of the British Empire, the volume of trade increased and the composition of Indian trade changed drastically. The share of trade in GDP increased from under 5 per cent in 1857 to over 11 per cent in 1913 (see Table 6.2). From an exporter of cotton textiles, India became an agriculture exporter, selling food and raw materials to Britain and the rest of the world (see Table 6.3A). Opium and raw cotton became the main exports of British India in the middle of the nineteenth century. Exports of food grain began to rise. Another product which gradually increased its share in the export basket was tea. This was a product neither produced nor consumed in India before 1840. The plant grew naturally in Assam, and British companies were given land grants to set up tea plantations so that the supply of tea to British consumers could be switched from China to India in the aftermath of the Opium Wars. The rising trade in opium reflects the importance of tea in the triangular trade between Britain, China, and India. China was the main supplier of tea to Britain. This market was expanding. Britain paid for the import of tea by exporting opium to China from India. When tea plantations were set up in India from the mid-nineteenth century, there was a gradual shift in the direction of trade. A new economic relationship developed through large sterling investments in tea companies. Indian tea increasingly gained market share in Britain and by the start of the twentieth century had become the largest supplier.

Table 6.2 Share of trade in income: from colonial times to independent India (%)

	(Trade/GDP)	Annual export growth
1835	1.1–2.4	–
1857	3.6–4.8	4.9 (1835–57)
1900	7.8	–
1910	10.8	5.3 (1858–1913)
1930	8.0	–
1950–60	6.8	1.9
1960–70	5.2	4.5
1970–80	6.0	6.2
1980–90	7.0	6.0
1990–2000	10.0	8.2

Sources: Sivasubramonian 2004: table 5.7; 1835 and 1857: Roy 2006: table 2.1; 1900 and 1930: Roy 2012: table 10.1.

Table 6.3 Changing composition of Indian trade

A. Exports (%)

	Raw cotton	Cotton goods	Indigo	Raw silk	Food grains	Raw jute	Jute goods	Opium	Sugar	Tea
1811	4.9	33.0	18.5	8.3	–	–	–	23.8	1.5	–
1828	15.0	11.0	27.0	10.0	–	–	–	17.0	4.0	–
1850	19.1	3.7	10.9	3.8	4.1	1.1	0.9	30.1	10.0	0.2
1870	33.2	2.5	5.8	–	8.1	4.7	0.6	–	–	2.1
1890	16.5	9.5	3.1	–	19.5	7.6	2.5	–	–	5.3
1910	17.2	6.0	0.2	–	18.4	7.4	8.1	–	–	5.9
1935	21.0	1.3	–	–	13.5	8.5	14.5	–	–	12.3

B. Imports (%)

	Cotton yarn	Cotton goods	Metals	Machinery	Railway material	Mineral oils
1828	7.8	22.0	16.0	–	–	–
1850	9.0	31.5	16.8	–	8.1*	–
1870	10.0	47.0	8.1	–	4.4	–
1890	5.2	37.9	8.4	3.0	4.5	3.3
1910	2.3	31.2	11.2	3.7	4.6	2.5
1933	2.3	13.1	8.2	11.1	–	5.1

* 1860.

Sources: Part A: Chaudhuri 1983: tables 10.10 and 10.11; Part B: Chaudhuri 1983: tables 10.17 and 10.18.

On the import side, cotton yarn and cotton goods became the main items, reflecting the change in Indian domination in the global market for cotton goods. Other important items in the import basket were metals and railway materials. The rise in machinery imports after 1900 reflects the rise of modern industries that relied on imported machinery (see Table 6.3B).

Britain was India's largest trading partner and relied on Britain for importing machinery for the nascent industries and rolling stock for the railways. India's net exports with the United Kingdom turned negative from 1890, while her net exports with the rest of the world remained positive (Gupta and Roy 2018).

Did the rising volume of trade lead to economic development? The Dependency school (Frank 1966; Amin 1976) argued that it created underdevelopment of the colonies through specialization in agriculture and the failure to develop a modern industrial sector. To trade theorists, starting with David

Table 6.4 Long-run growth: annual growth rate in per capita GDP

	GDP per capita (% per year)
1870–85	0.5
1885–1900	0.8
1900–1914	0.8
1914–45	−0.0
1900–1945	0.2
1950–80	1.4
1980–90	3.0
1990–2000	4.1
1950–2000	1.9

Sources: 1870–1900: Heston 1983: table 4.5; 1900–2000: Sivasubramonian 2000: table 6.11.

Ricardo, specialization by comparative advantage increased welfare. India had comparative advantage in agriculture and not in industry. Recent empirical work on trade and growth finds evidence of a positive causal effect of trade on per capita GDP using post-World War II data (Frankel and Romer 1999). Historical data tell a different story. Pascali (2017) shows that in the first phase of globalization, not all countries benefited from trade. Trade share had a positive effect on per capita GDP for countries that had inclusive institutions. For others, the effect of trade on per capita GDP was negative. Many colonies are on this list. Trade in this period was a source of the Great Divergence.

In the Indian context, opinion is divided on the effects of globalization. The nationalists claimed that imperial connections destroyed the textile industry and artisanal jobs and led to reliance on agriculture. Morris (1983), on the other hand, has emphasized the positive effects of globalization. Similarly, Tomlinson (1982) argued that globalization before 1914 brought an increase in trade in cash crops and rising prices. This ended with the Great Depression of 1929. It is difficult to show that trade had a beneficial effect on Indian incomes when there was only a short-lived increase in per capita GDP of less than 1 per cent per year during the late nineteenth century (Table 6.4).

Empire and Capital Flows

Lucas's (1990) well-known paper, 'Why Doesn't Capital Flow from Rich to Poor Countries', used colonial India as an illustration of low capital flows from Britain to a colony, even with a low risk of expropriation. Lucas argued that the imperial power might seek to exploit its monopoly position by restricting capital flows as a way of keeping wages low and the return to capital high. There is no evidence that British India discouraged capital investments. On the contrary, large inflows of capital into railways was encouraged by guaranteeing favourable rates of return. British capital flows abroad consisted of shares and debentures, but also funds borrowed by governments in the London capital market. Colonies received 40 per cent of British capital flows during 1865–1914. India, Australia, Canada, New Zealand, and South Africa accounted for 88 per cent. Investment in industry was mainly located outside the Empire, the USA being the major recipient (Stone 1999: 27–28). At the same time, India was among the top five recipients of British capital flows. But in per capita terms, India looked worse than the others. Table 6.5 shows India's share in total British investment by category in comparison to the rest. Amongst them, two were outside the Empire, and the USA was the largest by all comparisons.

In India, railways and government departments received the bulk of foreign capital inflow. Industry had a very small share. In 1930, India and Ceylon accounted for 14 per cent of British overseas investment, similar to Canada, and slightly lower than Australia. Over half of this investment was in government departments and 25 per cent was in the railways (Kindersley 1933). Mines and industries were still a very small component. The railways were important for the Empire. They connected the agricultural hinterland to the ports, which reduced transportation costs and helped in integrating India into the global market, but as the network expanded, it also integrated markets within India and reduced dispersion in food prices (Hurd 1975; Donaldson 2018).

The sector that developed with British investment was tea, which was sold mainly in the British market. The economic and political influence of tea went far beyond what is reflected in its share in investment. The industry was dominated by British capital and gained concessions from the government with regard to using indentured labour and cartelization. Another export industry also developed with British investment: the jute industry. This industry produced packaging material before the age of plastic. Jute sand bags were used extensively in trenches. The jute plant was grown in hot and humid areas of eastern India, and raw jute was exported for use in the jute industries around Dundee. Bengal attracted British investment even as a competitor to the industry in Dundee. Proximity to the source of raw material and low labour costs made Calcutta an attractive place to set up jute

Table 6.5 Share of British capital exports by recipients, 1865–1914 (%)

	Share of total	Share of capital exports by category					
		Government	Railways	Public utilities	Financial	Mines and plantation	Industry
USA*	21	3	40	30	18	11	31
Canada	10	5	13	9	9	4	14
Argentina*	8	9	16	12	6	0	5
Australia	8	15	0	5	13	11	4
India	8	10	10	4	2	5	2

* Outside the Empire.
Source: Stone 1999: statistical tables.

manufacturing. From the mid-nineteenth century, many jute mills were established with investment from London and British expatriates in India. Two of the main exporting industries were dominated by British capital and developed around the city of Calcutta.

A third sector that attracted British investment was coal. Coal deposits were located in eastern India, and joint stock coal companies were set up in the hub of British mercantile capital: the city of Calcutta. Coal mines sold to the railways and also exported. The interlocking directorships of the tea, jute, and coal companies created a dominant position of British capital in eastern India. The managing agency system, where British agents exercised managerial control across several industries by part-ownership and long-term management contracts was at the heart of the corporate structure of British industrial investment. The nationalist critique emphasized the interlinkages between British industry, banking, and commerce, which made it difficult for the entry of Indian capital (Bagchi 1972).

However, British investment in the import-substituting cotton textile industry was low. Social networks of Indian cotton and opium traders set up the modern cotton textile industry. Production of cotton textiles in the cottage industry had been widespread across India. Many weavers survived the inroad of British goods, while others found niche markets or mechanized. A modern industry in cotton textiles developed around Bombay in western India from the middle of the nineteenth century by importing British equipment. Capital and entrepreneurship was supplied mainly by Indians. Profits of the cotton trade during the American Civil War found their way into the cotton textile industry. Although Indian entrepreneurs lacked the connections of British firms, Parsi, Hindu, and Muslim traders used their community networks to raise capital (Gupta 2014; Gupta et al. 2020). As in the case of Greif's (1993) Maghribi traders, the community network solved the problem of information and trust in an economy that lacked formal contract enforcement mechanisms.

While in western India, the domination and influence of Indian capital could be found in trade, industry, and banking, eastern India remained a bastion of British interests until the entry of the Indian trading group of Marwaris in the jute industry after World War I. As in the case of the raw cotton trade, trade in raw jute was controlled by the Marwaris. Profits made during the war found a new investment opportunity in the jute industry (Goswami 1991). Table 6.6 shows the sectors that attracted sterling and rupee investment in 1914. Sterling companies were incorporated in London.

The Tata Iron and Steel Company was set up before 1914 and expanded during the war. Other industries, such as paper, cement, and chemicals, developed too. The interwar years saw the consolidation and growth of Indian capital and the entry of new types of British firms that did not operate within the structure of the managing agency system. These were the early multinational firms. Hindustan Unilever Limited, established in 1933, was one such company (Tomlinson 1978).

Table 6.6 Sterling and rupee company investment, 1914–15 (£m)

Companies	Sterling	Rupee	Total
Tea	19.7	2.9	22.6
Cotton	0.4	13.0	13.9
Jute	2.7	7.8	10.5
Gold	2.3	0.3	2.4
Cotton & jute press	1.2	1.2	2.4
Total	27.4	29.0	56.9

Notes: Sterling investment was raised in Britain. Rupee investment was funded by both British and Indian investors.
Source: Chapman 1992: 123.

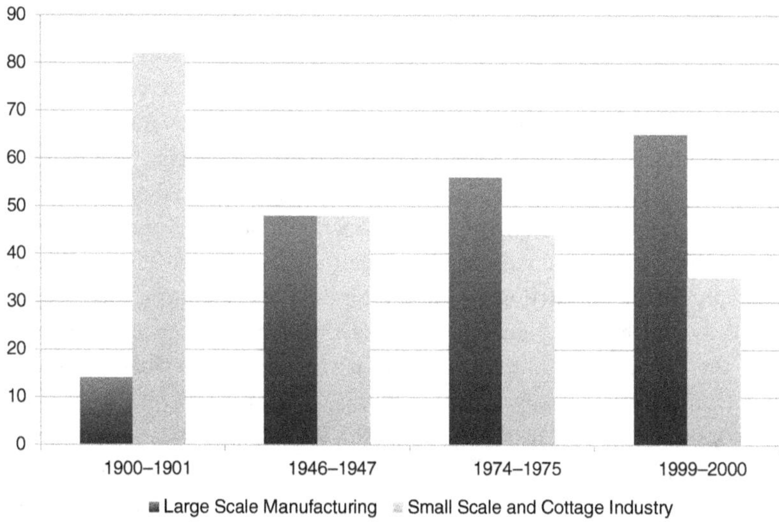

Figure 6.1 Shares of industrial output in large and small industries at 1948/49 prices (%)
Source: Sivasubramonian 2000: table 6.11.

The colonial economy saw little development in machinery production. Most capital goods were imported. The nationalist critique has focused on the failure of colonial policy to build a capital goods industry. The development of the Indian railways, financed by British investment, generated few backward and forward linkages as in Europe and North America. This was partly due to lack of state support, but also to the absence of skills and entrepreneurship in a sector that was more capital- and skill-intensive, and riskier in terms of rates of return. Overall, growth of the large-scale manufacturing industry was fast in the colonial period, from a very small base, and the share of the small-scale sector[1] remained high. In 1946, both sectors had exactly the same share of industrial output (see Figure 6.1).

Empire and Migration

The global economy of the British Empire used labour-abundant regions as a source of labour for regions of labour scarcity. This was especially important for plantations and mines that produced for the British market. One of the most important products of the Empire was sugar. Sugar plantations were set

1 Firms in the small-scale and cottage industry employed fewer than ten workers and remained outside many of the regulations of the large-scale sector.

up by British planters in the Caribbean, Fiji, and Mauritius. Thousands of Indian workers migrated to these regions. Other destinations were Malaya, Ceylon East, and South Africa. The workers were too poor to travel in search of higher wages. At a time when thousands of Europeans migrated to the New World as free workers in search of better living standards, many thousands migrated from India under indentured labour contracts. Although Indian migration was less than 5 per cent of European migration between 1850 and 1880, and even lower in the following years, the numbers were large for a country where free long-distance migration was not economically possible (see Figure 6.2). Contracting companies recruited workers from the villages, establishing migration channels. The workers boarded ships from Madras, Bombay, or Calcutta. The cost of travel was paid and the workers were tied to an employer for a number of years. There were push factors that encouraged migration. Most migrants were agricultural workers. Bad harvests due to weather shocks increased the attraction of the distant countries. Persaud (2019) finds that high volatility in food grain prices encouraged migration under indentured contracts.

There were pull factors too, as wages were higher in the receiving regions. Labour recruiters were not always truthful about the conditions of work and the perils of the journey. Death rates en route were not insignificant. The role of

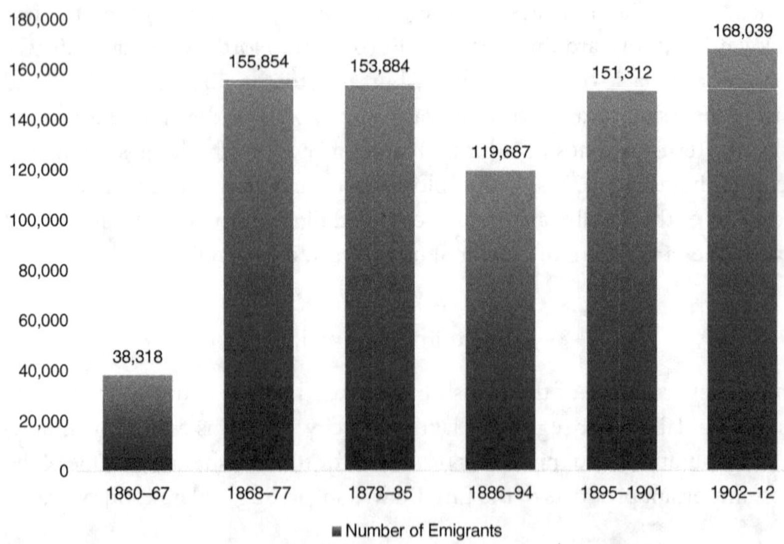

Figure 6.2 Total number of emigrants to different parts of the British Empire, 1860–1912
Source: *Statistical Abstracts of British India*.

the contractors in misinformation and ill treatment became a serious concern for policymakers in India and Britain, and laws were introduced to regulate indentured migration. On expiry of the contract, the workers could choose to return. The majority of the migrants returned, but many stayed on and made a home in an unfamiliar part of the British Empire. By 1920, two-thirds of the population in Mauritius, one-third to half of the population in Trinidad and Fiji, and 10 per cent of the population in Ceylon, East Africa, and South Africa, was of Indian origin (Roy 2012). There was also free migration of traders, defined by caste networks, to various parts of the Empire. These included colonies in South East Asia, as well as East and South Africa, where many of these groups came to have a presence in the commercial sector (Jain 1989).

Stagnation in a Globalized Economy

The Indian economy gained very little from being integrated into the global project of the British Empire. The economy developed better infrastructure, new industries, and new cash crops. But there was little improvement in living standards. Niall Ferguson (2004), in his well-known book, claimed that by the 1880s, Britain had invested one-fifth of its overseas investment in India. Railways and irrigation expanded, as did modern industries. Being part of the Empire prevented further impoverishment of India. Ferguson's counterfactual is difficult to construct. There was expansion of infrastructure and trade. Modern industries developed, but not just with British investment. The second-largest industry, cotton textiles, was under Indian ownership. By the mid-nineteenth century, Indian incomes were close to subsistence levels. The last three decades of the nineteenth century and the first decade of the twentieth saw a small increase in per capita income, but this was not sustained, despite the development of the railways and the rise of modern industry (see Table 6.4). From 1914 until the end of World War II, per capita GDP growth stagnated. This was driven by lack of productivity growth in agriculture, the largest sector of the economy, which employed over 70 per cent of the workforce, but produced less than 50 per cent of GDP. Agricultural output stagnated despite the rise in agricultural exports. The failure of the colonial government to invest in agricultural infrastructure led to declining yields per acre and stagnation in the main sector of the economy.

The Great Depression affected agricultural incomes as the terms of trade shifted against agriculture. But the decline in agricultural productivity had begun well before 1929. Industry did well in the first half of the twentieth century. It grew from a small base. Output per worker rose steadily in

Table 6.7 Output per worker in 1948/49 prices, 1900–2000 (Rs)

	Primary	Secondary	Tertiary	GDP
1900–1901	438	586	874	516
1930–31	479	998	1,311	652
1950–51	376	806	966	515
1980–81	511	1,831	2,230	962
1999–2000	578	3,511	3,268	1,574
% increase 1950–2000	53.7%	335.6%	238.3%	205.6%

Source: Sivasubramonian 2000: tables 7.19 and 9.32.

industry (see Table 6.7). However, this sector was still too small to have an impact on overall growth. Output per worker in services rose, but stagnated in agriculture.

From a Global Economy to Regulation

In 1947, the newly independent state of India moved away from policies of the colonial economy. Global integration and specialization in agriculture were seen as a hindrance to economic development. The first step was to set out an agenda for industrialization. Similar views were expressed in other parts of the underdeveloped world. The Economic Commission of Latin America raised similar concerns. Independent states of South Korea and Taiwan adopted industrialization as a goal and looked towards Japan. Newly independent states in Africa moved in a similar direction a decade later. As independent India adopted inward-looking policies, the share of trade in GDP declined sharply from 1950. The economy moved to a strategy of import-substituting industrialization, to replace the imported industrial goods with domestic production.

The Congress Party that led the nationalist movement in India had discussed industrialization as a strategy in the 1940s. The Bombay Plan, as it was known, saw a joint role for the public and the private sectors. In reality, the public sector took the lead in the project to build an industrial base. Jawaharlal Nehru, the first prime minister, favoured a top-down development based on the experience of Soviet industrialization. The Nehru–Mahalanobis model, as it became known, after the statistician who designed the plan, put development of capital goods production at the heart of this policy, and therefore questioned the role of comparative advantage and the suitability of factor endowments as determinants of economic development. In this framework, economic growth depended on the share of investment in national income, and in a closed economy, the composition of output between capital and consumer goods sectors determined the investment rate. Limited availability of capital goods could explain agricultural stagnation too. The strategy was to have a fast-growing capital goods sector by a disproportionate increase in its share of investment. India 'planned' for development by adopting Soviet-style Five-Year Plans.

The idea of public-private partnership and a mixed economy was at the centre of this policy. Private investment in consumer goods industries had defined industrial development in the colonial period. In 1947, the private sector was less willing to enter into production of capital and intermediate goods. These included heavy plant and machinery, telecommunications and telecom equipment, petroleum, mining, air transport services, and electricity generation and distribution. The second plan regulated the spheres of private investment. Several industries producing machinery and equipment were in the public sector. Private investment required licences to enter into any industry. Consequently, the government could decide on the sector and location of private investment. The Licence Raj, as it came to be known, regulated foreign trade and industrial investment through quantitative controls. The share of the public-sector in investment rose (see Table 6.8).

Domestic production of capital goods required high tariffs, as this sector did not have a comparative advantage. Trade became regulated not only by tariffs, but also by quantitative restrictions, such as import quotas. By the end of the 1960s, the Indian economy was one of the most regulated in the world. Under the protective regime of tariffs and quotas and regulation of industrial activity, Indian industry became inefficient and uncompetitive. Once the initial growth spurt through import substitution had been exhausted, economic growth slowed down. But the policies in independent India had pulled the economy out of stagnation and built an industrial base (see Table 6.4).

While the colonial economy had tried to deal with capital shortage through capital flows from Britain, the independent state of India chose to raise the capital from internal sources. Table 6.8 shows the steady rise in the saving rate and investment rate from 1950. The nationalization of the banking sector in 1969 widened access and raised household savings (Burgess and Pande 2005).

There was a major change in agricultural policy too. The first plan invested in agricultural infrastructure. The Green Revolution from the mid-1960s saw big changes in the agricultural sector. High yielding varieties of seeds were

Table 6.8 Capital formation and the public sector (%)

	Gross domestic capital formation as share of GDP	Share of the public sector	Saving rate
1850–51	5.0*	2.24	–
1880–81	4.8*	25.21	–
1900–1901	7.0*	21.59	–
1930–31	6.3*	31.95	(1930–39) 3.2
1940–41	6.7*	19.81	(1940–46) 3.3
1961–65	17.7	43.20	(1960) 6.1
1981–85	20.8	51.40	(1980) 12.5
1990–95	23.7	38.40	(1990) 21.5
1995–2000	24.8	29.20	(2000) 24.0

* Ratio to gross national income in 1980–81 prices.
Sources: Nagaraj 1990; Roy 1996: tables 7.9, 9.1, 9.4; Kohli 2006. Saving rate up to 1947: Roy 2006: table 3.16; post-1960: World Bank database: https://data.worldbank.org/indicator/NY.GDS.TOTL.ZS?end=2019&locations=IN&start=2019&view=bar (accessed 29 September 2020).

introduced, first in wheat, and then extended to rice cultivation. This raised agricultural productivity and changed the way agriculture was organized. High yielding seeds required greater use of water and fertilizers, leading to an expansion in irrigation, but also the introduction of subsidies to cultivators for water and fertilizers, and differentiation within the peasantry.

The inward-looking policies had consequences for India's external sector. From a share of over 10 per cent of GDP in the colonial period, India's trade share dropped to 5 per cent in 1960 (see Table 6.2). India moved away from dependence on Britain. Britain's share in Indian exports declined from over 25 per cent in 1950 to 11 per cent in 1971, as did the share of imports, from 18 per cent to 8 per cent. India's trade links with the USSR were strengthened. The import share of the USSR rose from 0.1 per cent to 7 per cent, and the export share from 1 per cent to 14 per cent, indicating the uncompetitive nature of Indian trade (Panchamukhi 1978: 30–32). India's share of the world market declined, at a time when countries in East Asia were improving their position.

Another aspect of retreat from the global economy was restrictions on foreign investment. British companies were required to reduce share ownership by foreigners to 40 per cent, except in some specified export sectors, such as tea. New restrictions came in on foreign direct investment. Consequently, India received a small share of foreign direct investment, but was one of the largest recipients of foreign aid between 1960 and 1985. However, even at the peak in

1966, it was 4.5 per cent of GDP, declining to 1.4 per cent in 1984 (Gang and Khan 1990).

On the third front of a global economy, the labour market, regulations came from the receiving countries of Europe and North America. Immigration control in the recipient countries focused on shortages in the labour market. This opened the way to a steady stream of emigration to Europe, North America, and the Gulf countries to fill these shortages. Unlike in the colonial period, this was mainly free migration of both skilled and unskilled workers. The term 'brain drain' refers to the exodus of India's highly skilled professionals to the developed countries from the 1950s (Khadria 1999: 62–64). Thousands of unskilled and semi-skilled workers migrated to the Gulf countries following the oil boom of the 1970s. However, in terms of total population, the number is small: 1.6 per cent of the population of India in 1979, and 2 per cent in 2000 (Khadria 2013). Between 1834 and 1937, 6 million Indians migrated to different parts of the world (Jain 1989). This is net migration and takes into account the large numbers that returned. In comparison, 20 million Indians lived abroad in 2000 (Khadria 2013). Remittances from Indian emigrants account for a significant share of foreign exchange inflows.

Reintegrating into the Global Economy

The slowing down of economic growth and the political crisis of the 1970s turned attention to the need for economic reforms. From the early 1980s, the focus shifted from redistribution to growth. Reforms in industrial and trade policy were implemented. None of this was dramatic in the early stages. Rather than announcing an IMF-style structural adjustment, reforms proceeded by 'stealth' (Kohli 2006). Rodrik and Subramanian (2005) and Kohli (2006) have termed this 'pro-business', in contrast to the 'pro-market' reforms from 1991. The reforms of the 1980s have been described as 'pro-business' as they allowed the private sector more opportunities. Industrial policy saw the greatest change as licensing was dismantled, except in a few environmentally sensitive industries. Eighteen industries had been reserved solely for the public sector. This was reduced to three: defence aircraft and warships, atomic energy generation, and railway transport. Old policies continued towards the small industries, where certain industries were ring-fenced for the small-scale sector. Figure 6.1 shows the rebalancing of the industrial sector. From a large presence of small-scale industries in the colonial period, large-scale industries became dominant.

The second phase of reforms began with the devaluation of the rupee in 1991. The pro-market economic reforms sought to phase out import licensing and import duties. Import licensing was abolished relatively early for capital and intermediate goods, which became freely importable in 1993. Removing quantitative restrictions on imports of capital goods and intermediaries was relatively easy, because the number of domestic producers was small and Indian industry welcomed the move. It was much more difficult in the case of consumer goods because the number of domestic producers affected was very large. Quantitative restrictions on imports of manufactured consumer goods and agricultural products were finally removed on 1 April 2001, almost ten years after the reforms began.

Panagariya (2013) shows that India's share in world exports of goods and services rose from 0.5 per cent in 1982 to 0.9 per cent in 2003; a much slower growth compared to China, where the share rose from 1.1 per cent to 5.2 per cent. However, disentangling trade between goods and services shows a different picture. Export of services from India rose by 7.5 per cent in the 1980s and 9.2 per cent in the 1990s (Kotwal et al. 2011). India's share of the world market in export of services was 20 per cent in 1990, rising to 29 per cent in 2003.

From the late 1980s, Indian policy towards foreign investment began to change. The reforms allowed 100 per cent ownership by foreigners in several industries, and majority shareholding in sectors such as telecommunications and airlines. The regulations for entering the Indian market were simplified. Between 1987 and 1990, FDI inflows accounted for just 0.3 per cent of gross fixed capital formation. India has received a much smaller share of FDI compared to China. The share of FDI in gross capital formation in China was 10 per cent in the 1990s. For India, that figure stands at 1.7 per cent (Kamalakanthan and Laurenceson 2005). Between 2001 and 2004, the share of FDI rose to 3.2 per cent of gross fixed capital formation, but still well below that of China at 14.9 per cent in 2004 (Chakraborty and Nunnenkamp 2006). FDI has not played an important role in the export of manufactured goods, as in China, but has targeted the domestic market.

From Stagnation to Growth

Indian per capita GDP growth has been twice as high in the last two decades compared to the historical average after independence. Estimates of a structural break in GDP pick 1980 for the period 1950–2000 (Wallack 2003; Rodrik and Subramanian 2005; Balakrishnan and Parameswaran 2007). For different sectors of the economy the break-point is staggered: the mid-1960s for agriculture, the mid-1970s for services, and the early 1980s for industry (Wallack 2003). However, taking a long-run view, a structural break is found in 1950–51, as the economy moved from stagnation to growth (Hatekar and Dongre 2005). Although planned industrialization did not put India on a high-growth path, it marked a dramatic change in India's industrial capability. Most importantly, the change in agricultural policy and the Green Revolution moved agriculture from stagnation to growth.

Why does 1980 show up as a major turning point? Rodrik and Subramanian (2005) argue that the Indian economy was at some distance from the production possibilities frontier in the 1970s, and the new environment incentivized the private sector and encouraged a move towards the frontier. The 'pro-business' environment created favourable conditions for existing firms and led to a large productivity increase. DeLong (2003) similarly suggests that Indian growth before 1980 was built on capital accumulation, with little contribution from total factor productivity. The small steps taken in the direction of reducing regulation in the 1980s generated productivity gains and a large effect on GDP. Bosworth et al. (2007) show that for growth in labour productivity and total factor productivity, the 1980s marks a clear break with the past. The deregulation of the 1980s laid the framework for more drastic changes in the 1990s. Others have pointed to the importance of fiscal spending during the 1980s in driving economic growth, which would not have been sustained without the reforms (Srinivasan and Tendulkar 2003).

Bosworth et al. (2007) analyse India's growth in a growth-accounting framework for the period 1978–2004, when Indian GDP grew at 5.4 per cent in comparison to 3.4 per cent in the previous twenty years. Employment growth reflected population growth rather than a rise in labour force participation. The effect on growth from capital deepening was low in India compared to East Asia and China. Improvements in human capital were much less impressive too. Half of labour productivity growth in India can be explained by input growth, the rest by TFP. Recent estimates by Wu et al. (2017) find that although China's output growth is twice as high from 1980, TFP growth in India has been higher during 1981 to 2011, using Domar aggregation methods that weight the component industries.

Services has been the fastest-growing sector in India. This is not only modern business services, but broadly the sector itself (see Table 6.9).

Business services, although the fastest-growing sector, are only a small part of the service sector. They represented only 1 per cent of services in 1980, rising to 6 per cent in 2000 (Bosworth et al. 2007: table 6.6). Business services include telecommunications and software, and have attracted foreign direct investment and skilled labour. Software is one-third of service sector exports. Improvement in communications technology had spillovers into sectors such as trade, banking, education, and health. However, it did not have much effect on manufacturing.

Structural change in India has seen a slow decline in the share of agriculture in employment, and a slow rise in employment in industry, and even in services (see Table 6.10). The sectoral shares in GDP and employment illustrate a rapid shrinking of the share of agriculture in GDP (but not in employment) and the unusual performance of the service sector. Kotwal et al. (2011) argue that most unskilled employment is in the unorganized sector. The fast-growing non-farm sectors use skilled labour, while most of the labour in agriculture is unskilled. Bosworth et al. (2007) show that the relocation effect in India is very low compared to China and other East Asian countries. Wu et al. (2017), based on Domar aggregation, however, find that the effect of relocation of capital and labour on TFP growth is positive in India, but negative in China, suggesting a degree of misallocation of resources in China.

The service sector in India had a historical advantage. Productivity in the service sector was higher than in industry and agriculture in 1900, and that advantage lasted until the closing years of the twentieth century. Only in 2000 had the secondary sector overtaken the tertiary sector in labour productivity (see Table 6.7). Comparing India's sectoral labour productivity with that of an industrialized country such as the UK shows an early advantage of the service sector (Broadberry and Gupta 2010).

Where does India's advantage in services come from? The 2001 census shows that most highly educated workers in India were disproportionately employed in services. Within the service sector, trade and finance and public administration have a high share of workers with secondary and tertiary education. In the early twentieth century too, caste groups in sectors like trade had high literacy compared to the rest of the population. The high share of secondary and tertiary education in education spending in colonial India provided an advantage to upper castes in the service sector, in particular in government services. This bias in the allocation of resources to education has continued in independent India. The emphasis

Table 6.9 Sectoral growth in output and productivity, 1960–2000 (% per year)

	Output	Output per worker	Total factor productivity
Agriculture			
1960–80	1.9	0.1	−0.1
1980–2004	2.8	1.7	1.1
Industry			
1960–80	4.7	1.6	−0.4
1980–2004	6.4	3.0	1.1
Services			
1960–80	4.9	2.0	0.4
1980–2004	7.6	3.8	2.7

Source: Bosworth et al. 2007: table 6.5.

Table 6.10 Sectoral shares of GDP and employment (%)

	Primary		Secondary		Tertiary	
	GDP	Employment	GDP	Employment	GDP	Employment
1900–1901	66.2	75.0	10.8	10.6	23.0	14.4
1930–31	56.2	76.0	14.1	9.0	29.7	15.0
1950–51	53.8	73.6	15.9	10.2	30.3	16.2
1980–81	37.5	70.5	25.3	13.4	37.2	16.1
1999–2000	23.6	64.2	30.9	13.9	45.5	21.9

Source: Sivasubramonian 2000: tables 2.8, 6.11, Appendix, table 6.9(d).

on tertiary education from the 1950s has created a pool of skilled labour that has assisted the growth of skill-intensive service industries (Kochhar et al. 2006).

Conclusion

This chapter has traced the changes in the Indian economy following the transition from colonial rule. The shift from the globalized economy of the British Empire to a regulated one saw changes in trade and investment. Migration patterns changed too, in response to changing international restrictions on labour mobility. The globalized economy before 1947 did not see growth, and Indian incomes stagnated in the first half of the twentieth century. The economy began to grow in independent India. India retreated from global connections and the economy was strapped with myriad regulations. Yet there was growth. Growth in GDP per capita was low compared to the fast-growing economies of East Asia, but higher than the historical average. Economic reforms after 1980 and reintegration with the global economy have seen an increase in growth, turning India into one of the fastest-growing economies at the turn of the twentieth century. This growth was built on the policies of industrialization of the first government of independent India. The sector driving Indian growth after 1980 has been services. This sector enjoyed an advantage historically.

References

Amin, S. (1976). *Unequal Development: An Essay on the Social Formations of Peripheral Capitalism*, Hassocks: Harvester.

Bagchi, A. K. (1972). *Private Investment in India*, Cambridge University Press.

Balakrishnan, P. and Parameswaran, M. (2007). 'Understanding Economic Growth in India: A Prerequisite', *Economic and Political Weekly*, 42(27–28), 2915–2922.

Bosworth, B., Collins, S., and Virmani, A. (2007). 'Sources of Growth in the Indian Economy', in Bosworth, B. and Panagariya, A. (eds.), *India Policy Forum, 2006–07*, Washington, DC: Brookings Institution Press.

Broadberry, S. N. and Gupta, B. (2009). 'Lancashire, India and Shifting Competitive Advantage in Cotton Textiles, 1700–1850: The Neglected Role of Factor Prices', *Economic History Review*, 62, 279–305.

(2010). 'The Historical Roots of India's Service-Led Development: A Sectoral Analysis of Anglo-Indian Productivity Differences, 1870–2000', *Explorations in Economic History*, 47, 264–278.

Burgess, R. and Pande, R. (2005). 'Do Rural Banks Matter? Evidence from the Indian Social Banking Experiment', *American Economic Review*, 95(3), 780–795.

Chakraborty, C. and Nunnenkamp, P. (2006). 'Economic Reforms, Foreign Direct Investment and its Economic Effects in India', Kiel working paper 1272, Kiel Institute for the World Economy.

Chapman, S. (1992). *Merchant Enterprise in Britain: From the Industrial Revolution to World War I*, Cambridge University Press.

Chaudhuri, K. N. (1983). 'Foreign Trade and Balance of Payments (1757–1947)', in Kumar, D. and Desai, M. (eds.), *The Cambridge Economic History of India, Vol. II*, Delhi: Cambridge University Press, 804–877.

DeLong, B. (2003). 'India since Independence: An Analytical Growth Narrative', in Rodrick, D. (ed.), *In Search of Prosperity: Analytical Narratives on Economic Growth*, Princeton University Press, 184–204.

Donaldson, D. (2018). 'Railroads of the Raj: Estimating the Impact of Transportation Infrastructure', *American Economic Review*, 108, 899–934.

Ferguson, N. (2004). *Empire: How Britain Made the Modern World*, London: Allen Lane.

Frankel, J. A. and Romer, D. H. (1999). 'Does Trade Cause Growth?', *American Economic Review*, 89(3), 379–399.

Gang, I. N. and Khan, H. A. (1990). 'Some Determinants of Foreign Aid to India, 1960–1985', *World Development*, 18(3), 431–442.

Goswami, O. (1991). *Industry, Trade and Peasant Society: The Jute Economy of Eastern India, 1900–1947*, Delhi: Oxford University Press.

Greif, A. (1993). 'Contract Enforceability and Economic Institutions in Early Trade: The Maghribi Traders' Coalition', *American Economic Review*, 83(3), 525–548.

Gupta, B. (2014). 'Discrimination or Social Networks: Industrial Investment on Colonial India', *Journal of Economic History*, 74(1), 141–168.

Gupta, B. and Roy, T. (2018). 'South Asia in the World Economy, 1600–1950', in Roy, T. and Riello, G. (eds.), *Global Economic History*, Bloomsbury, 319–336.

Gupta, B., Mookherjee, D., Munshi, K., and Sanclemente, M. (2020). "Community Origins of Industrial Entrepreneurship in Pre-Independence India', CEPR Discussion Paper 14263 (v. 2), Centre for Economic Policy Research.

Harnetty, P. (1972). *Imperialism and Free Trade: Lancashire and India in the Mid-Nineteenth Century*, Manchester University Press.

Hatekar, N. and Dongre, A. (2005). 'Structural Breaks in India's Growth: Revisiting the Debate with a Longer Perspective', *Economic and Political Weekly*, 40, 1432–1435.

Heston, A. (1983). 'National Income', in Kumar, D. and Desai, M. (eds.), *The Cambridge Economic History of India, Vol. II*, Delhi: Cambridge University Press, 463–532.

Hurd, J. (1975). 'Railways and the Expansion of Markets in India, 1861–1921', *Explorations in Economic History*, 12(3), 263–288.

India, Commercial Intelligence Department. (various issues). *Statistical Abstract for British India*, Calcutta: Superintendent Government Printing, India.

Jain, P. C. (1989). 'Emigration and Settlement of Indians Abroad', *Sociological Bulletin*, 38(1), 155–168.

Kamalakanthan, A. and Laurenceson, J. (2005). 'How Important Is Foreign Capital to Income Growth in China and India?', East Asia Economic Research Group discussion paper 4, University of Queensland.

Khadria, B. (1999). *The Migration of Knowledge Workers: Second-Generation Effects of India's Brain Drain*, New Delhi: Sage Publications.

(2013). 'India, Migration 1940s to Present', in Ness, I. (ed.), *The Encyclopedia of Global Human Migration*, 5 vols, Hoboken: Wiley-Blackwell.

Kindersley, R. (1933). 'British Overseas Investments in 1931', *Economic Journal*, 187–204.

Kochhar, K., Kumar, U., Rajan, R., Subramanian, A., and Tokatlidis, I. (2006). 'India's Pattern of Development: What Happened, What Follows?', *Journal of Monetary Economics*, 53(5), 981–1019.

Kohli, A. (2006). 'Politics of Economic Growth in India, 1980–2005, Part 1: 1980s', *Economic and Political Weekly*, 1 April, 1251–1259.

Kotwal, A., Ramaswami, B., and Wadhwa, W. (2011). 'Economic Liberalization and Indian Economic Growth', *Journal of Economic Literature*, 49, 1152–1199.

Kumar, D. (1983). 'The Fiscal System', in Kumar, D. and Desai, M. (eds.), *The Cambridge Economic History of India, Vol. II*, Delhi: Cambridge University Press, 905–944.

Kumar, D. and Desai, M. (eds.) (1983). *The Cambridge Economic History of India, Vol. II*, Delhi: Cambridge University Press.

Lucas, R. E. (1990). 'Why Doesn't Capital Flow from Rich to Poor Countries?', *American Economic Review*, 80(22), 91–96.

Markovits, C. (2002). *Indian Business and Nationalist Politics 1931–39*, Cambridge University Press.

Morris, M. D. (1983). 'The Growth of Large-Scale Industry to 1947', in Kumar, D. and Desai, M. (eds.), *The Cambridge Economic History of India, Vol. II*, Delhi: Cambridge University Press, 553–676.

Nagaraj, R. (1990). 'Industrial Growth: Further Evidence and Towards an Explanation and Issues', *Economic and Political Weekly*, 25(41), 2312–2332.

Panagariya, A. (2013). 'India and China: Trade and Foreign Investment', in Hope, N. C., Kochar, A., Noll, R., and Srinivasan, T. N. (eds.), *Economic Reform in India: Challenges, Prospects, and Lessons*, Cambridge University Press, 96–138.

Panchamukhi, V. R. (1978). *Trade Policies of India: A Quantitative Analysis*, Delhi: Concept Publishing Company.

Pascali, L. (2017). 'The Wind of Change: Maritime Technology, Trade, and Economic Development', *American Economic Review*, 107(9), 2821–2854.

Persaud, A. (2019). 'Escaping Local Risk by Entering Indentureship: Evidence from Nineteenth-Century Indian Migration', *Journal of Economic History*, 79, 447–476.

Prakash, O. (1976). 'Bullion for Goods: International Trade and the Economy of Early Eighteenth-Century Bengal', *Indian Economic & Social History Review*, 13(2), 159–186.

Ray, I. (2009). 'Identifying the Woes of the Cotton Textile Industry in Bengal: Tales of the Nineteenth Century', *Economic History Review*, 62(4): 857–892.

Rodrik, D. and Subramanian, A. (2005). 'From "Hindu Growth" to Productivity Surge: The Mystery of the Indian Growth Transition', IMF working paper 04/77, International Monetary Fund.

Roy, B. (1996). *An Analysis of Long-Term Growth of National Income and Capital Formation in India (1850–51 to 1950–51)*, Calcutta: Firma KLM Pvt.

(2006). *Economic History of India: 1857–1947*, 2nd ed., Oxford University Press.

(2012). *India in the World Economy: From Antiquity to the Present, Vol. 10*, Cambridge University Press.

Sivasubramonian, S. (2000). *The National Income of India in the Twentieth Century*, New Delhi: Oxford University Press.

(2004). *The Sources of Economic Growth in India, 1950–1 to 1999–2000*, New Delhi: Oxford University Press.

Srinivasan, T. N. and Tendulkar, S. D. (2003). *Reintegrating India with the World Economy*, New York: Columbia University Press.

Stone, I. (1999). *The Global Export of Capital from Great Britain, 1865–1914: A Statistical Survey*, London: Macmillan.

Tomlinson, B. R. (1978). 'Foreign Private Investment in India, 1920–1960', *Modern Asian Studies*, 15(3), 655–677.

(1982). 'The Political Economy of the Raj: The Decline of Colonialism', *Journal of Economic History*, 42(1), 133–137.

Twomey, M. J. (1983). 'Employment in Nineteenth-Century Indian Textiles', *Explorations in Economic History*, 20, 37–57.

Wallack, J. (2003). 'Structural Breaks in Indian Macroeconomic Data', *Economic and Political Weekly*, 38(41), 4312–4315.

Wu, H., Das, D. K., Krishna, K. L., and Das, P. C. (2017). 'How Does the Productivity and Economic Growth Performance of China and India Compare in the Post-Reform Era, 1981–2011?', *International Productivity Monitor*, 33, 91–113.

7

Growth and Globalization Phases in South East Asian Development

GREGG HUFF

Introduction

The late nineteenth century opened a new epoch in South East Asian economic history, when globalization became the dominant historical force affecting the region and midwife to the birth of modern South East Asia. Today, globalization is similarly important for South East Asia – that part of the world stretching from the Philippines in the east to Burma in the west, and at South East Asia's southernmost extension the Indonesian Archipelago. In between are South East Asia's other three principal areas: Thailand, Malaya (now the separate states of Malaysia and Singapore), and Indochina, consisting of Vietnam, Cambodia, and Laos.

Between the late nineteenth and early part of the twenty-first century, South East Asian economic history divides into three main phases. Two are long – the periods from 1870 to 1939 and from 1950 to 2020. A single decade – the 1940s – comprises the third. But those years, which encompass World War II and its immediate aftermath, contributed fundamentally in some South East Asian countries to a basic reordering of responses to global forces, as well as to internal policies, altering the course of society and economic development in the region and disrupting a pre-World War II historical unity.

South East Asia's economic history and development are analysed primarily in terms of two especially intense phases of globalization, and focus on long-term flows in the international economy rather than its short-term fluctuations. A first period of globalization-induced growth dated from the 1870s and lasted until the end of the 1920s. The impact of a second phase of swift globalization started in the late 1960s and was fully evident by 1973. Each globalization phase was made

Thanks go to Andrew Bain, Anne Booth, Richard DuBoff, Hal Hill, Mike Montesano, and Pierre van der Eng, for extensive comments and suggestions which have much improved this chapter and warned me of many errors.

possible by transport and communication revolutions and in each the responses of those in the region were fundamental to South East Asia's transformation.

Although emphasizing the long late nineteenth and late twentieth century globalization phases, attention is also drawn to short-term movements in the world economy. Economic development as part of long-term global change had as its corollary openness to short-term fluctuations. And just as the first gave pattern to South East Asian economic history, so the second punctuated this with booms and slumps. These latter include the 1930s and the Asian financial crisis of 1997 to 2000.

The economic history of the World War II Japanese occupation links pre- and post-war South East Asian economic history and greatly facilitates an understanding of both periods. Japanese military conquest almost certainly hastened the end of colonialism, and during post-war decades shaped the histories of Burma, Indonesia, and Vietnam, although less so the rest of South East Asia.

While the periods on either side of World War II include phases of globalization during which countries in the region generally grew particularly quickly, these growth episodes were otherwise marked by sharp contrasts. Among the most immediately obvious are differences in political status. Before World War II, South East Asia was governed by four colonial powers – Britain (Burma and Malaya); the Netherlands (Indonesia); France (Indochina); and the United States (the Philippines). Thailand, nominally independent, was part of Britain's informal empire and had a British financial advisor. As a consequence of decolonization, six South East Asian countries became eleven. Burma (Myanmar), Thailand, and the Philippines remained geographically as before the war, but after the 1954 Geneva Accords, the former French Indochinese administrative divisions of Vietnam, Cambodia, and Laos divided into separate countries; by 1965, Malaya had split into Malaysia, Singapore, and Brunei (independent in 1984); and East Timor separated from Indonesia and then gained sovereignty in 2002.

Pre- and post-World War II economic contrasts derive chiefly from shifting factor endowments and political independence. Before the war, land abundance and high wages relative to southern China and India drew large immigrant inflows to South East Asia. By the 1970s, however, because population growth through natural increase had progressively pressed on land availability, in large parts of South East Asia labour was abundant and cheap by international standards. Within South East Asian countries, expanding populations and increasingly scarce land fuelled cityward migration, transforming pre-1940 South East Asia from among the world's least urbanized regions to one of numerous large cities and three megalopolises.

Beginning in the late 1960s, cheap labour, foreign direct investment, and integration into global value chains organized by multinational enterprises provided the basis for the South East Asian industrialization model. The model's labour component involved workers who were still at home, but whose labour was embodied in labour-intensive manufactured goods largely produced by foreign multinational corporations and exported to developed countries. Additionally, large amounts of labour began to be exported through emigration. In pre-war South East Asia, abundant natural resources substituted for foreign investment. During the 1950s and 1960s, however, South East Asia started to become, for the first time, the recipient of large foreign capital inflows. Initially, capital went into import-substituting industry, mining, and infrastructure, and then, beginning in the 1970s, came principally through foreign multinationals attracted by cheap, abundant labour and manufacturing for export.

Although trade was an 'engine of growth' in each of South East Asia's pre- and post-war globalization phases, natural resource-intensive products comprised the bulk of exports throughout the first phase, while manufactures became key during the second. Growth both before and after World War II contributed to a dualistic economic structure. In neither globalization period was growth chiefly intensive or self-sustaining through technical progress, rather than extensive depending on ever greater inputs. Nevertheless, in each of the periods, growth fundamentally transformed South East Asia's economies and societies.

Pre-World War II South East Asia

Population

In 1870, approximately 55 million people were spread over South East Asia, an area of 1.7 million square miles. By World War II, the region's population stood at roughly 145 million (see Table 7.1). Population densities and economic growth were markedly uneven across pre-war South East Asia (Figure 7.1). Economic growth was fastest in frontier areas and the cities that grew up to serve them. By contrast, South East Asia also had in Java and northern Indochina, especially the Tonkin Delta, two of the world's most densely populated areas, comparable to the thickly peopled parts of India and China. Although Java contributed to Indonesian export output through both estate

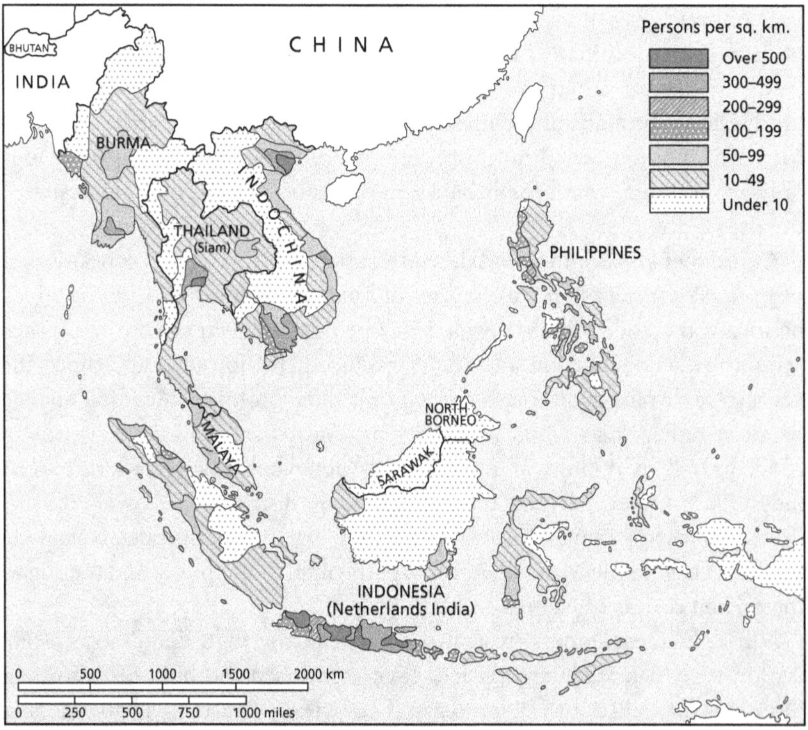

Figure 7.1 South East Asia population density, 1940
Map credit: Redrawn based on a map by Mike Shand, University of Glasgow.
Source: Broek 1944: 180.

and smallholder sectors, it was, like Tonkin, an area where population and food availability were delicately balanced.

Vent-for-Surplus Growth

This first, pre-World War II section of the chapter concentrates on South East Asia's vent-for-surplus regions, where international trade provided the 'vent' or outlet to utilize surplus frontier land, and often surplus labour, in the production of commodities which, unless exported, would not have been worth the effort of producing. Vent-for-surplus trade provided South East Asia's 'engine of growth'. In South East Asia, exports were fundamental to autonomous expenditure and so a major determinant of national income.

Economic growth in pre-war South East Asia, as vent-for-surplus models posit, was predominately extensive, depending on an ever greater use of land and labour inputs to increase exports. For most vent-for-surplus production, agricultural techniques changed little. In the nineteenth century, tin mining needed no more than simple tools and began to change only around 1913, when the exhaustion of easily won deposits necessitated the use of dredges.

Consequent on South East Asia's integration into the world economy after 1870, Nurkse (1959: 18) spoke of a 'lopsided pattern of development', by which he meant the coexistence of well-developed export sectors with traditional economies. Globalization and trade produced this lopsidedness, since the venting of surpluses, although the region's most prominent feature, applied to areas rather than whole countries in South East Asia. Export growth concentrated in regions at first sparsely populated relative to resources: Indonesia's Outer Islands, the rice-growing districts of Lower Burma, Cochinchina, the central plain of Thailand, the tin and rubber belt along the west coast of the Malay Peninsula, parts of the Philippines, and the sugar-specialized islands of Negros and Panay.

Nurkse's 'lopsidedness' was also evident in the high degree of specialization to which trade swiftly led. Rice comprised the bulk of exports in three of the six South East Asian countries – Burma, Thailand, and Indochina. Malaya relied on rubber and tin, and the Philippines on sugar. A variety of tropical products was exported from Indonesia alone, although specialization occurred with increased tin, petroleum, and, especially, rubber production in the Outer Islands. The typical dependence on one or two staple exports in vent-for-surplus trade connects it to the 'staples' theory of Caves (1965) and others, in which just a few commodities drive economic growth.

Western markets were by no means the outlet for all vent-for-surplus production. Specialization in non-food exports, especially in Malaya and Indonesia's Outer Islands, created a large demand for rice imports. South East Asia's rice-specialized countries supplied these, and India and China were important markets for rice from Burma and Indochina, respectively. Integration, both intra-regional and intra-country, led to both Smithian gains through vent-for-surplus utilization of previously idle resources, and Ricardian ones through the realization of comparative advantage. In Burma, for example, Central Burma relied on rice from Lower Burma, and in exchange supplied it with cooking oil, vegetables, gram (bean flour), and other basic foods widely eaten in the south.

Knowles (1928: 138–152) wrote of an 'unlocking of the tropics', while for resource-abundant tropical regions like South East Asia, Myint (1958: 324) chose the metaphor of an 'opening up process'. Throughout South East Asia, this opening up featured a moving frontier and depended heavily – and until 1913, almost entirely – on the response of peasants to an upsurge in global demand for the primary commodities that South East Asia could produce. Late nineteenth- and early twentieth-century South East Asia, as Larkin (1993: 60) remarked of the Philippines, 'shared much in common with the global frontier phenomenon'.

Surplus land existed in all South East Asian countries, and beginning in the latter nineteenth century, previously uncultivated acreage under vent-for-surplus crops increased dramatically (Table 7.1). Across South East Asia from the mid-nineteenth century onwards, 'the huge expansion in cultivation for export', as Brown (1997: 213) observes, was 'achieved almost entirely by bringing into production vast tracts of previously uncultivated land'. To accomplish this, men and women characteristically used only their hands and simple tools. During the twentieth century, the opening of new land was quickest in the Philippines, with increased sugar output, and in Malaya and Indonesia's Outer Islands, where vent-for-surplus opportunities arose with the new staple of rubber. Among the rice-producing countries, much of Burma's expansion occurred in the nineteenth century, while in Thailand most new land was opened in the twentieth century.

Vent-for-surplus models vary. They may involve only unexploited land or other natural resources without alternative domestic use. But Myint's vent-for-surplus model (Myint 1954; Findlay 1970: 70–74), which also features surplus labour, best describes South East Asia. However, not all labour in the new export industries was surplus in the sense of having a zero or near-zero marginal product per person. Some labour was drawn out of handicrafts or other traditional production. Nevertheless, as Ingram (1971: 54) argues for Thailand, the shift of labour from other employment to rice cultivation 'could not have been very great'. Rather, the supply of labour 'received important additions as the existing rice growers gave up leisure' in favour of spending time to cultivate more land. The same was true of rubber smallholders in Indonesia's Outer Islands and Malaya.

When labour was unavailable from the traditional, non-export sectors of South East Asian economies, or was unwilling to be drawn into export production, the densely populated parts of Java and Tonkin and, much more, vast labour reservoirs in India and China supplied workers – an 'unlimited supply of Indians and Chinese willing to travel anywhere to

Table 7.1 South East Asia, population and areas cultivated, 1880–1938

A. Population, 000 persons

	1881	1901	1921	1938
Burma	–	16,071	20,259	25,890
Lower Burma	3,737	5,580	7,047	9,066
Other Burma	–	10,491	13,212	16,824
Indochina	13,679	–	22,597	27,650
Cochinchina	1,679	2,937	3,797	4,620
Other Indochina	12,000	–	18,800	23,030
Thailand	6,200	7,320	9,207	14,464
Malaya	1,710	2,085	3,327	5,004
Indonesia	–	38,204	49,350	60,727
Outer Islands	–	7,851	14,366	19,009
Java and Madura	–	30,353	34,984	41,718
Philippines	6,122	7,635	10,314	16,000

B. Area cultivated, 000 hectares

	1880	1900	1913	1938
Burma (rice)	1,255	3,460	4,181	5,011
Indochina (rice)	522	1,174	2,000	2,200
Thailand (rice)	995	1,293	1,964	3,481
Malaya (rubber)	–	1	435	1,387
Indonesia (rubber)	–	1	110	1,357
Philippines (three main export crops)	–	43	768	1,573

Source: Huff 2003.

work on plantations for a shilling a day' (Lewis 1978b: 15). Export expansion combined with South East Asia's particular geography near India and China as the basis for mass immigration. Between 1881 and 1939, over 15 million Chinese and Indian immigrants came to Burma, Malaya, and Thailand, more than the total population of these three countries in 1881. In the process of Asian globalization, China and India became 'hinterlands' of surplus labour, sending workers to a 'centre' of land-surplus South East Asia, where, in turn, economies were driven by new opportunities for international trade (Table 7.2).

Because of government restrictions, Indonesia, Indochina, and the Philippines received fewer immigrants than Burma, Malaya, and Thailand,

Table 7.2 South East Asia, international factor and commodity flows, 1871–1939

A. Immigration to the United States, Burma, Malaya, and Thailand, 1881–1939, millions of persons, total flow per decade

	1881–1910		1911–29		1930–39	
	Gross	Net	Gross	Net	Gross	Net
United States	5.91	4.10	3.20	2.15	0.70	0.21
Burma	1.45	0.26	3.27	0.50	2.64	0.17
Malaya	1.87	–	2.75	0.78	1.62	−0.07
Thailand	0.34	0.12	0.81	0.27	0.50	0.12
Total South East Asia	3.66	–	6.83	1.55	4.76	0.22
South East Asia as % of United States	61.9	–	213.0	72.1	680.0	104.8

B. South East Asia, merchandise exports, annual averages 1913, US$ millions

	1871–73	1898–1900	1911–13	1925–27	1936–38
Burma	17.58	59.89	119.55	194.44	273.68
Indochina	14.38	31.69	50.73	87.60	129.78
Thailand	4.83	20.34	34.78	81.51	100.83
Malaya	37.09	133.57	196.05	489.07	545.34
Indonesia	62.69	118.92	241.06	490.00	556.80
(Outer Islands)	(9.50)	(35.12)	(102.86)	(256.21)	(368.50)
Philippines	16.11	25.05	48.39	106.41	182.25
South East Asia	**152.68**	**389.46**	**690.56**	**1,449.03**	**1,788.68**

Sources: Huff 2003; Huff and Caggiano 2007.

but nevertheless had sizable Chinese communities, especially in the large cities. In these, apart from Burma, with Rangoon's large Indian presence, Chinese dominated an intermediate level of commerce below large European mercantile houses, banks, and shipping firms. South East Asian societies were characteristically 'plural': indigenous races, Chinese, Indians, and Europeans came in contact with one another in the market place, but mixed little socially, maintaining their own cultures (Furnivall 1948).

Merchandise exports of the six South East Asian countries confirm swift, long-term expansion (Table 7.2). Although separate GDP figures are not available for the Outer Islands, their dynamism is evident from a rapidly growing share of Indonesian exports. In 1874/76, Outer Island exports accounted for 15.2 per cent of the Indonesian total. But thereafter, and during a time when Indonesian real exports grew ninefold, the Outer Island share rose to 42.7 per cent of Indonesia's total in 1911/13, and reached two-thirds by 1936/38. Over the five and a half decades, 1871/73 to 1925/27, South East Asian real exports (including Indonesia as a single entity) grew at an annual average rate of 4.2 per cent, equivalent to a doubling in volume every 16.5 years.

The venting of surpluses encouraged the development of South East Asian transport networks and expanded the size of domestic markets to create further, new sources of growth. Railways, extensive intra-regional shipping, and, by the inter-war years, motorized transport augmented growth, both in their own right and by allowing increasingly larger areas to be drawn into vent-for-surplus production. Trade gains added to growth through widening and deepening markets for locally produced goods and services, and helping to finance infrastructural development and urbanization. In pre-war Indonesia, exports have been shown to account for half of growth (van der Eng 2002) though the percentage was likely higher in most of the region due to its predominately small, quite open economies.

Growth Engines and Convergence

Regional lopsidedness within South East Asian countries and data collection on the basis of colonial (or for Thailand, national) boundaries cause available statistics to mask the speed of economic change. Even so, between 1870 and 1913, GDP per capita figures for countries as a whole indicate significant growth, ranging everywhere in South East Asia from 0.7 per cent to 1.2 per cent per annum (Table 7.3). Despite this, South East Asian incomes, except for Singapore, Indonesia, and the Philippines, already behind Japanese incomes in 1870, were even further adrift by 1913, with GDP per capita of only about half that of Japan (Table 7.3).

Between 1913 and 1929, South East Asia, apart from Thailand, grew swiftly. Malaya's growth, at 3.9 per cent annually, and Singapore's, at 3.3 per cent, were quite rapid. Burma, Indonesia, and the Philippines recorded growth rates at 1.7 per cent, 1.4 per cent, and 2.2 per cent, respectively. Thailand had negative growth partly because rice exports, despite a large increase, did not give rise to important linkages beyond rice milling; little industry existed; urbanization was minimal outside Bangkok; and the country was weakly integrated, due partly to the paucity of roads.

Export-dependent and extremely specialized in just four primary commodities, many of which were already in world oversupply by the late 1920s,

Table 7.3 South East Asia, GDP per capita and relative to US and Japan, 1870–2007

A. GDP per capita

1990 international $	1870	1900	1913	1929	1938	1950	1973	2010
United States	2,445	4,091	5,301	6,899	6,126	9,561	16,689	30,491
Japan	1,011	1,341	1,567	2,302	2,696	1,921	11,434	21,935
Burma	504	699	685	902	740	396	628	3,709
Thailand	608	–	841	793	826	817	1,874	9,372
Malaysia	663	–	900	1,682	1,361	1,559	2,560	10,094
Singapore	864	1,139	1,367	2,335	2,070	2,219	5,977	29,038
Indonesia	517	734	869	1,087	1,057	817	1,544	4,722
Philippines	624	673	988	1,413	1,440	1,070	1,964	3,024
Vietnam	505	–	727	–	–	658	836	3,217

B. South East Asia as a % of leading countries

	1870	1900	1913	1929	1938	1950	1973	2010
Burma								
Ratio to US	20.6	17.1	12.9	13.1	12.1	4.1	3.8	12.2
Ratio to Japan	49.9	52.1	43.7	39.2	27.4	20.6	5.5	16.9
Thailand								
Ratio to US	24.9	–	15.9	11.5	13.5	8.5	11.2	30.7
Ratio to Japan	60.1	–	53.7	34.4	30.6	42.5	16.4	42.7
Malaya/Malaysia								
Ratio to US	27.1	–	17.0	24.4	22.2	16.3	15.3	33.1
Ratio to Japan	65.6	–	57.4	73.1	50.5	81.2	22.4	46.0
Singapore								
Ratio to US	35.3	27.8	25.8	33.8	33.8	23.2	35.8	95.2
Ratio to Japan	85.5	84.9	87.2	101.4	76.8	115.5	52.3	132.4
Indonesia								
Ratio to US	21.1	17.9	16.4	15.8	17.3	8.5	9.3	15.5
Ratio to Japan	51.1	54.7	55.5	47.2	39.2	42.5	13.5	21.5
Philippines								
Ratio to US	25.5	16.5	18.6	20.5	23.5	11.2	11.8	9.9
Ratio to Japan	61.7	50.2	63.1	61.4	53.4	55.7	17.2	13.8
Vietnam								
Ratio to US	20.7	–	13.7	–	–	6.9	5.0	10.6
Ratio to Japan	50.0	–	46.4	–	–	34.3	7.3	14.7

C. Annual average growth

	1870–1913	1870–1950	1913–29	1929–38	1950–73	1973–2010
United States	1.8	1.7	1.6	−1.3	2.4	1.6
Japan	1.0	0.8	2.4	1.8	7.8	1.8
Burma	0.7	−0.3	1.7	−2.2	2.0	4.8
Thailand	0.8	0.4	−0.4	0.4	3.6	4.4
Malaysia	0.7	1.1	3.9	−2.4	2.2	3.7
Singapore	1.1	1.2	3.3	−1.3	4.3	4.3
Indonesia	1.2	0.6	1.4	−0.3	2.8	3.0
Philippines	1.1	0.7	2.2	0.2	2.6	1.2
Vietnam	0.8	0.3	–	–	1.0	3.6

Source: Maddison Project Database, version 2013, incorporating new series for Japan from Fukao et al. 2015.

South East Asia was highly vulnerable to the 1930s world economic collapse. Most countries recorded negative growth (Table 7.3). In Malaya, Burma, and Thailand, large numbers of Chinese and Indian immigrants, no longer with jobs, returned home, often under quite straitened circumstances. Among indigenous South East Asians, the consequences of the slump were worst in Burma, where many cultivators had borrowed against the security of land and lost it through foreclosure by Chettiars and other moneylenders. If cultivators owned their own land, as almost all Malayan, Outer Island, and Thai rubber smallholders did, they could retreat to subsistence cultivation and wait out the storm.

Between the 1870s and the late 1930s, reliance on extensive growth left pre-World War II South East Asian per capita incomes trailing ever further behind the United States, the world leader. Only Malaya, until 1929, threatened to match Japanese per capita income and close the gap on the United States. For other countries, convergence to United States per capita income looked progressively less likely. By 1938, per capita incomes for South East Asian countries were, at best, no more than approximately one-fifth of United States' income, and typically less (Table 7.3).

For trade to become a genuine 'engine of growth', it must give rise to considerable technical change and, as Crafts (1973) emphasizes, create secondary or induced-income effects. If the latter are realized on a substantial scale, the ratio of exports to national income is likely to fall rather than rise, as it appears to have done in South East Asia. Certainly, the region's failure fully to accomplish the first or 'easy' stage of import-substituting industrialization, discussed below, and a lack of technical change in most agriculture mark South East Asia as falling short of Kuznets' modern economic growth.

Foreign Investment

In South East Asian vent-for-surplus growth, natural resources, in combination with cheap labour, were transformed into exports with relatively little foreign investment (Huff 2007). Until World War I, almost all exports originated from Asian miners and small farmers, and this changed only somewhat during the interwar years, mainly as a result of European capital invested to develop rubber estates, and after about 1910 to mine tin and produce petroleum. In contrast to vent-for-surplus countries in the New World, South East Asian per capita exports dwarfed foreign investment. Taking the ratio of per capita exports to per capita foreign investment as a measure, in 1911/13 this export–investment ratio averaged 3.0 in the New World, compared to 14.7 in South East Asia. By 1925/27 the difference in ratios, 3.5 for the New World and 16.7 in South East Asia, were almost unchanged (Table 7.4). Contrary to the stages theory of the balance of payments, South East Asia emerged, even during the early decades of its growth, as a net capital exporter (Huff 2003: 326–327).

Table 7.4 South East Asia and New World exports and foreign investment, 1871–1938

A. Exports per capita (annual averages)

	1871/73	1900/1902	1911/13	1925/27	1936/38
Canada	230	641	605	1,116	831
Argentina	260	621	851	666	431
Australia	891	1,098	1,249	1,005	1,084
South Africa	–	377	699	449	554
Indochina	–	37	46	51	41
Outer Islands (Indonesia)	35	79	146	176	118
Malaya	471	1,071	1,064	1,319	868
Philippines	27	61	79	101	87
Thailand	12	50	61	88	54
Burma	44	107	144	157	120

B. Foreign investment per capita

	1900	1913	1930	1938
Canada	226	385	377	359
Argentina	290	266	140	104
Australia	308	275	300	229
South Africa	157	202	–	145
Indochina	–	9	8	11
Indonesia (Java and Outer Islands)	7	12	16	18
Malaya	–	58	61	50
Philippines	–	10	14	13
Thailand	–	6	5	5

Source: Twomey 2000.

Industrialization and Financial Development

It has been argued that from about the 1860s onwards, a process of deindustrialization accompanied South East Asia's increasing integration into the global economy (Williamson 2011: 70–71). In reality, globalization transformed manufacturing in South East Asia: it destroyed much traditional and cottage industry, but led to the emergence of a new industrial sector, accurately described as manufacturing. Traditional 'manufacturing' employment dropped sharply, but balanced against this was the emergence, by the interwar years, of a base of modern manufacturing consisting of commodity processing and the production of some consumer goods and manufactured materials. Findlay and O'Rourke's (2007: 417) conclusion for Burma that it is difficult to take seriously an argument of twentieth-century deindustrialization also applies to other South East Asian countries: 'never having had a large industrial sector to begin with, the negative deindustrialization effects of primary export growth must have been minimal ... booming exports must have had a positive effect on balance'.

On the eve of World War II, a large share of manufacturing consisted of primary commodity processing. Although technical improvements, such as the standardization of rubber qualities, added to growth, and some processing industries, notably tin smelting in Malaya, were technically advanced, the base of South East Asian manufacturing remained narrow. Throughout South East Asia, a high proportion of manufactures, even basic consumer goods, came as imports. No country could even come close to passing Lewis' (1978a: 219–222) test of successful first-stage import substitution: self-sufficiency in textiles. There were few modern textile plants and traditional manufacture supplied only a fraction of needs. In 1940, village home industry met about one-seventh of Indonesia's textile requirements, a quarter of demand in Burma, and about one-third in Thailand (Indonesia 1947: 123; Hlaing 1964: 105–6; Ingram 1971: 119–120).

While the post-1900 colonial powers generally ensured that the supply of currency met local needs, metropolitan banks geared to the needs of merchant exporters dominated the financial system, with agricultural credit often provided through informal networks. There was therefore little financial development to help promote manufacturing or other industrial growth (Huff 2003).

Urbanization

Because in 1940 South East Asia remained overwhelmingly agricultural and had limited industrialization, urbanization was low, Malaya apart. In the 1930s, 80 per cent or more of those in the region lived outside cities of 10,000 or more. The main cities – all around half a million by 1940 – that emerged during the late nineteenth century were ports, serving as 'gateways' that linked frontier South East Asia to the global economy (Huff 2012). South East Asia's 'gateway' cities included Singapore, Rangoon, Bangkok, Jakarta and Surabaya, Saigon, and Manila. These cities handled the region's staple exports and functioned as commercial centres for this trade and a return supply of manufactured goods, mainly from the West.

Education and Living Standards

In pre-war South East Asia, educational provision widened continuously, but with the exception of the Philippines, where the Americans were committed to an education agenda, still in the 1930s, at most about half of South East Asians had a primary education. There were no universities in Malaya, the richest South East Asian country, until the establishment of the University of Malaya in 1949. When high-quality further education existed, as with the University of Rangoon, it extended to only a tiny minority of the population. Restricted access to education told against the development of human capital, and in countries of high immigration this was further prejudiced by the arrival of the great majority of migrants as young adults (mostly men) without schooling. Relatively few South East Asians were technically trained and were insufficient in number to form the backbone of technologically driven economies.

Generally rising per capita incomes point to improved living standards, despite downwards pressure on real wages due to large inwards migration from the desperately poor areas of India and South China. Although South East Asian living standards remained low, even in vent-for-surplus areas, they were well above subsistence levels, although close to these levels for many people in densely populated northern Vietnam and Java. Probably the greatest improvement in living standards was reflected in the rise throughout South East Asia of a middle class of professionals, civil servants, and well-off merchants and traders, many of the latter Chinese or Indian. By the interwar years, the larger cities, if not the countryside, had a modern infrastructure of gas, electricity, public transport, courts, and government buildings, little of which had existed in 1870.

World War II and Japanese Occupation

By May 1942, the Japanese military controlled virtually all of South East Asia. Japanese occupation swept aside colonial rule by Britain, the Netherlands, and the United States. Although Thailand was occupied by the Japanese, its pre-war government remained in place as the Kingdom's nominal ruler. In Indochina, a pro-Vichy French colonial regime accepted Japanese occupation and was left to administer Indochina until a Japanese coup on 9 March 1945.

Within a year of occupation, Japan began to inflict on South East Asia one of the great macroeconomic crises in modern history. Except in Thailand, available data show plunges in real per capita South East Asian GDP of around 50 per cent during the Japanese occupation and indicate the intensification of a macroeconomic crisis, which, as early as 1944, had pushed incomes in the region back to late nineteenth-century levels (Table 7.5). For the Philippines, Sicat (2015) calculates a drop in 1940 GDP of 50 per cent by 1943 and 70 per cent by 1945. The GDP fall in Malaya is likely to have been similar because of the extreme openness of its economy and dependence on rubber and tin exports, both of which ceased almost entirely. In Burma, the 1946–47 volume of output was 60 per cent of that in 1938–39 (Burma 1951: 2). Thailand apart, in World War II South East Asia, 'Economic life receded from modernity', and countries retreated 'toward an isolation and autarky that harked back to precolonial times' (Bastin and Benda 1968: 127).

Table 7.5 South East Asia and Japan, GDP per capita, 1870–1980 (1990 international $)

	Burma	Malaya	Thailand	Singapore	Indonesia	Indochina	Philippines	Japan
1870	504	663	608	682	608	505	624	737
1913	685	939	841	1,367	869	727	988	1,387
1938	**740**	**1,452**	**826**	**2,070**	**1,057**	**831**	**1,440**	**2,449**
1939	–	1,708	826	2,379	1,038	886	1,508	2,816
1940	–	–	841	–	1,104	803	1,507	2,874
1941	–	–	846	–	1,158	763	–	2,873
1942	–	–	743	–	925	698	–	2,818
1943	–	–	812	–	738	659	–	2,822
1944	–	–	759	–	579	515	–	2,659
1945	–	–	682	–	512	407	–	1,346
1946	–	–	716	–	527	473	646	1,444
1947	–	–	775	–	602	498	875	1,541
1948	–	–	**838**	–	694	512	993	1,725
1949	–	–	826	–	758	562	1,025	1,800
1950	396	**1,665**	836	**2,219**	784	658	1,070	1,921
1956	490	1,505	930	2,333	955	764	1,410	**2,948**
1957	510	1,455	910	2,318	977	775	**1,442**	3,136
1959	555	1,467	992	2,186	987	792	1,501	3,554
1960	564	1,530	1,078	2,310	1,015	799	1,476	3,986
1962	606	1,637	1,149	2,520	1,025	**885**	1,537	4,777
1970	642	2,079	1,694	4,439	**1,231**	735	1,764	9,714
1978	**756**	3,271	2,422	7,752	1,740	806	2,262	12,585
1980	828	3,657	2,554	9,058	1,898	757	2,376	13,428

Note: Data in bold signify 1938 levels of GDP per capita and the earliest date after 1945 when countries first reached a level of GDP per capita comparable to 1938.
Sources: van der Eng 1991; 1992; 1994a; 1994b; Maddison Project Database, version 2013; Vietnam national income: Jean-Pascal Bassino, pers. comm., 6 Feb. 2011; Malaya: Del Tufo 1949.

Declining output in South East Asia was caused by the loss of access to global markets and supplies from them; by the Japanese imposition of South East Asian country, or even intra-country, autarky; and by Japan's attempt to refashion South East Asia's economies to fit into a Greater East Asia Co-Prosperity Sphere, in which Japan would become the economic centre of a largely self-sufficient East and South East Asia. Foreign trade, transport, and public services all plummeted. Japan sent almost no goods to South East Asia. As the region's pre-war stock of imported cloth, manufactures, soap, cigarettes, and medicines dwindled, or even disappeared, the nature of existing development became starkly apparent – narrow commodity specialization, lack of industrialization and extreme dependence on imported goods. South East Asians fashioned substitutes for many basic, now unavailable, goods, including textiles, but with little success because of the lack of a pre-war industrial base, low human capital, few skilled workers, and reliance on imported components. Black markets, along with prostitution and corruption, flourished and became a way of life. Exploitative Japanese policies that required South East Asia to finance its own occupation, mainly through printing money, led to rocketing inflation, or in some countries hyperinflation. South East Asians lived in fear of draconian military rule and the Japanese use of torture. About 20,000 South East Asians became, as comfort women, sex slaves (Huff 2020).

Falls in the availability of food were particularly acute in areas specialized in non-food exports. Most South East Asians who survived occupation ended it malnourished to a greater or lesser degree. War and the need to be able to tap external sources to ensure food security left South East Asia's densely populated areas of northern Vietnam and Java in a perilous position. During 1944 and 1945, famine accounted for a million premature deaths in Vietnam and 2.4 million in Java (Huff 2019).

Overall, a conservative estimate of premature South East Asian deaths is 4.44 million, or 3 per cent of the region's 1941 population of 145 million people (Table 7.6). The vast majority of deaths were civilian, caused by economic conditions and forced labour. Most notorious among the latter were workers on the Siam–Burma railway, and Javanese *romusha* taken by the Japanese for work in Indonesia and elsewhere in South East Asia.

During the 1950s, the per capita GDP of several South East Asian countries languished below pre-World War II levels. Malaya, Singapore, and Thailand were the only countries in which, by 1950, per capita GDP again matched that of 1938. The Philippines first recovered to a 1938 level in 1957, and Vietnam reached this mark in 1962, but soon slid backwards with the escalation of the

Table 7.6 South East Asia, premature civilian deaths due to Japanese occupation, 1941–45 (million persons)

Vietnam famine	1.000
Java famine	2.400
Java *romusha*	0.200
Singapore *sook ching*	0.023
Japanese railways	0.191
Burma Indian exodus	0.030
Philippines	0.500
Others	0.100
Total	4.444

Source: Huff 2020, p. 382.

Second Indochina War. Recovery to the level of 1938 was not recorded until 1970 in Indonesia and 1978 in Burma (Table 7.5).

The August 1945 Japanese surrender and the aftermath of war and occupation set in motion changes that fundamentally shaped much of South East Asian history for two decades or more. Political independence probably came sooner than it otherwise would have, and arguably the region was more politically unstable than it would have been in the absence of war. Every country except Thailand had civil war or revolution. As Lee Kuan Yew (1998: 85) remarked of a relatively less troubled area than much of South East Asia, 'there was no return to the old peaceful, stable, free-and-easy Singapore'. Burma, Indonesia, and Vietnam underwent protracted upheavals. Japanese-trained armies in Burma and Indonesia created the military as a powerful new group. Vietnam's 1944–45 famine was fundamental to the rise of the Viet Minh and Ho Chi Minh (Huff 2019; 2020). Along with Ho, Sukarno in Indonesia, Ne Win in Burma, and Sihanouk in Cambodia were all World War II creations.

Physical destruction was great in the Philippines and Burma, but more important, even in these countries, as elsewhere in South East Asia, was the severe post-war damage to societal infrastructure. The effects of this unfolded gradually, shortages increased, and corruption became rampant. Japanese occupation in Malaya was summed up as 'four years of psychological and physical deterioration' (Cheeseman 1947: 3).

South East Asia since 1950

Divisions in Early Post-War South East Asia

World War II and the Japanese occupation ended seven decades of continuity in South East Asian economic history during which globalization had been the dominant force. By the 1950s, South East Asia had divided into two groups. One, consisting of Thailand, Malaya (including Singapore), and the Philippines, remained part of what Benda (1967: 69–74) calls the Atlantic system, and this group continued its pre-war orientation towards world markets. In these countries, nationalism was moderate and the economy and industrialization remained substantially dependent on private enterprise. The other group, comprising Burma, Indonesia, and North Vietnam (Vietnam after the 1975 reunification of the North and South), turned away from the global economy. Strong nationalisms found expression in socialism, state direction, anti-Westernism, and anti-globalization. The split corresponds to the categorization of South East Asia, suggested by Myint (1965), into outwards- and inwards-looking countries.

Outwards-looking Thailand (despite a succession of military governments), Malaya, and the Philippines had two important historical features in common. One was relatively benign experiences of colonialism, the other distinctly muted post-war nationalisms. In Indonesia, Vietnam, and Burma, pre-war antipathy to colonial rule had been considerable, and after the war nationalism was intense. War and occupation fundamentally shaped all three countries after 1945, through giving rise to a new social group: the military. As well as creating a military elite, the Japanese interregnum had the effect of widening and deepening nationalism, which grew from the preserve of the urban intelligentsia into a potent, countrywide force (Benda 1958: 200). In Vietnam and Indonesia, the combination of wartime experiences and extended, violent independence struggles embedded radical politics.

While in outward-looking South East Asia the Western superstructure created during the colonial era continued to function, for decades after World War II the military-dominated governments in Burma, Indonesia, and Vietnam pushed politics towards forms of socialism or communism. In the three South East Asian countries, the military's moral authority and legitimacy came from being 'born and tested in revolution and anticolonial war'; power was assured largely by an absence of other organized, disciplined, and trained groups to contest military dominance (Bastin and Benda 1968: 180, 195). Colonial Burma, Indonesia, and Vietnam had all lacked a significant indigenous economic or government presence that in the post-war world could have countered the army, facilitating the emergence of dominant, self-perpetuating military oligarchies (Huff 2011: 58–61). Post-war military elites did not have experience or skills in administration or economics, which, together with inwards-looking economic policies, contributed to decades of low or negative growth, high inflation, and falling per capita incomes.

Indonesia began again to turn outwards in 1966 after the economically disastrous Sukarno years. Vietnam started to do so after 1986 with *Doi Moi* (renovation), and then more strongly in the early 1990s. A boost followed in 1994, when the United States lifted its economic embargo. Cambodia went through the horrific years of internecine killing, from 1975 to 1979, which also brought the almost total evacuation of Phnom Penh and the complete breakdown of civil government. But by the 1990s, Cambodia, like Laos, was looking increasingly to the global economy. Burma (Myanmar) might be turning outwards, but to date not decisively.

Second Globalization Phase and South East Asian Industrialization Model

Growth in South East Asia has, in the first instance, always depended heavily on demand from the advanced countries. The phase of globalization under way by the later 1960s created new export opportunities for South East Asian goods. Moreover, these were, compared to the globalization of the 1870s up to 1929, enhanced opportunities. With labour surpluses long exhausted in the United States and western Europe, multinational enterprises began to search for sources of cheap (low-wage, but efficient) labour to produce manufactures for developed country markets. That gave South East Asian countries the opportunity to utilize what, with continuous post-World War II population growth (Table 7.7), had become their principal factor endowment of abundant labour, and, at the same time, to shift workers out of low-productivity agriculture and services and into manufacturing. While agriculture, the source of most pre-World War II exports, grows at most by 3 per cent per year, industry can grow by 8–10 per cent or more annually. These are rates of 'catch-up' growth. Beginning with Singapore in 1966, followed by Malaysia and then Thailand in the 1980s, nearly all South East Asian countries turned away from relying almost solely on import substitution for industrialization and took the opportunity for extremely rapid growth offered by manufacturing for export to global markets. The result, Myanmar apart, was radical economic transformation throughout South East Asia. Starting in the 1970s, the growth that rippled through South East Asia enabled most of its governments to answer 'yes' to the fundamental

Table 7.7 South East Asia, population, 1960–2016 (000 persons)

	Myanmar	Thailand	Malaysia	Singapore	Indonesia	Cambodia	Laos	Vietnam	Philippines
1960	20,986.0	27,397.2	8,157.1	1,646.4	87,792.5	5,722.4	2,121.0	34,743.0	26,273.0
1980	33,369.7	47,385.3	13,798.1	2,413.9	147,490.4	6,692.1	3,258.1	53,700.0	47,397.1
2000	46,095.5	62,958.0	23,185.6	4,027.9	211,540.4	12,152.4	5,329.3	77,630.9	77,991.6
2016	52,885.2	68,863.5	31,187.3	5,607.3	261,115.5	15,762.4	6,758.4	92,701.1	103,320.2

Source: World Bank 2017.

economic question: Did countries grow fast enough to change the structure of the economy and improve levels of living for most people?

The South East Asian industrialization model was largely responsible for rapid growth everywhere in the region except Myanmar and, to some extent, Indonesia, due to its natural resource exports and government hesitancy to look to global production networks (Hill 2018: 479). The model has three main components additional to manufacturing for export. One is an early, and often continuing, reliance on labour-intensive processes; a second, low-cost labour; and a third, dependence on multinationals, as foreign direct investors, to organize production as part of global value chains and then oversee the export of final output mainly to developed country markets. Since 1990, the stock of direct foreign investment, both as a share of GDP and per capita, has increased enormously (Table 7.8). In South East Asia, foreign investment and exports

Table 7.8 South East Asia, stock of inwards foreign direct investment, 1990–2016

A. FDI stock US$ millions

	1990	1997	2007	2016
Myanmar	285	2,673	7,207	23,465
Thailand	8,242	13,333	94,679	191,142
Malaysia	10,318	42,351	75,763	122,030
Singapore	30,468	74,768	420,877	1,123,262
Indonesia	8,732	31,600	79,927	249,859
Cambodia	38	956	3,063	18,166
Vietnam	243	10,358	31,825	115,391
Philippines	3,268	9,499	20,463	64,507

B. FDI/GDP %

	1990	1997	2007	2016
Myanmar	–	–	35.7	34.8
Thailand	9.7	8.9	36.0	47.0
Malaysia	23.4	42.3	39.1	41.2
Singapore	84.3	74.6	233.8	378.2
Indonesia	8.2	14.6	18.5	26.8
Cambodia	–	27.8	35.5	90.8
Vietnam	3.8	38.6	41.1	57.0
Philippines	7.4	11.5	13.7	21.2

Source: World Bank 2017.

Table 7.9 South East Asia, China, and Japan, wages, 2010–2014

A. Average monthly wages, 2014 US$

Thailand	408
Malaysia	682
Singapore	3,731
Indonesia	165
Cambodia	121
Laos	119
Vietnam	212
Philippines	216
Japan	3,111
China	685

B. Average monthly wages in garments, textiles, and footwear, US$

Thailand 2013	227
Indonesia 2014	122
Cambodia 2012	96
Laos 2010	102
Vietnam 2013	182
Philippines 2013	208
China 2013	491

Source: International Labour Organization 2016a: 4; 2016b: 2.

have been strong complements, not substitutes. For South East Asia, an attachment to multinationals could be likened, as Lee Kuan Yew observed of Singaporean growth, to hitching a ride on an escalator.

In most of South East Asia, wages remain far lower than in developed countries, and well below those in China, if perhaps less so for competitiveness when measured as unit labour costs (Table 7.9). Crucially, foreign investment-driven growth has hinged not just on cheap South East Asian labour, but also on sharply falling transport costs, reductions of trade barriers and advances in production technology permitting ever finer divisions of labour. Manufacturing in South East Asia typically necessitates plugging into global value chains. These comprise either the fabrication of components or component assembly into final products, the latter likely incorporating components sourced from other South East Asian or Asian locations with suitably low-cost labour. Although the break-up of production into geographically separate stages means that components come from multiple suppliers, the clustering of many of these nearby or in neighbouring South East Asian countries limits transport costs. Import content tends to be high and value added low, both for component production and assembly operations. For South East Asian countries, a main benefit, certainly at first, of becoming part of a multinational organized global division of labour was employment creation.

Early export-led industrialization in Singapore, where in 1975 manufacturing total hourly compensation (total employer) costs were a fraction of those of the United States, and output per hour probably higher, involved mainly electrical and electronic products, notably integrated circuits, although beginning in 1982 these were eclipsed by disk drives. Between 1986 and 1996, Singapore accounted for half of world disk drive production. In the early 1970s, Malaysia and the Philippines began to copy Singapore's outwards-looking export model, also largely with electronics products, and by the 1990s Thailand and Indonesia had followed suit (Rasiah 2009a: 124–125). Vietnamese manufacturing for export, aided by a US–Vietnam bilateral trade agreement, at first relied substantially on garments and footwear, but now consists mainly of simple electronics and mobile phone assembly. Industrialization in Cambodia began to take off in the late 1990s, and in Laos after 2000. Both countries depend heavily on the so-called CMT (cut, make, and trim) trade in garments, and often not on multinationals, but international buyers sourcing goods for developed country firms. China is a large foreign investor in garment production in both countries, but the United States and European Union are the chief markets (Rasiah 2009b; International Labour Organization 2016a). Myanmar embarked on the assembly of imported fabrics as garments for a time during the mid-1990s and again after 2012. While this has no doubt raised growth, most informed observers point to the unreliability of Myanmar statistics; this chapter consequently reports but does not discuss the figures (Mieno 2013: 106).

A high proportion of South East Asian exports are classified as machinery in Standard International Trade Classification category SITC 7, which encompasses machinery, transport equipment, and electronics and electronic products. All these, as the fragmentation theory outlines, have strong growth potential, due to high-income elasticities of demand and can also be divided into many specialized manufacturing processes and several locations, according to varying labour intensity of production and wage costs. Scope for countries to move from unskilled activities to more skilled and capital-intensive ones enables factor endowments to evolve and comparative advantage to shift towards higher value-added production. In South East Asia, only Singapore has continuously moved up global value chains. That and the Republic's impressive expansion as a provider of financial and other high value-added services helps to account for high per capita incomes.

Although strongly influenced by the Singapore model, other South East Asian countries have not copied it to become developmental states in which the government directs the accumulation of physical and human capital with the objective of climbing the ladder of comparative advantage (Felipe 2018). In much of export-oriented industrialization, notably electronics, the middle-income countries of Malaysia and Thailand retain large, low value-added, substantially assembly industries, heavily reliant on inflows of low-wage migrant workers from elsewhere in South East Asia (Rasiah 2009a: 125–126, 132; Lim 2014: 207). Extensive growth of this sort, of course, has some production linkages, helps to support a growing middle class, and expands the services sector in productive ways. Over the last thirty years in South East Asia, however, services value added has typically accounted for no more than 6–8 per cent of GDP growth (World Bank 2017).

Industrialization in Thailand, in automobiles as well as electronics, illustrates the advantage of integrating into a global value chain and contrasts sharply with Malaysia's approach in making the Proton car of aiming to produce an entire automobile through import substitution. The strategy failed badly. By contrast, Thailand, forced to turn outwards by the 1997 financial crisis, became part of largely Japanese-organized supply and assembly chains, is now the world's largest manufacturer of light pickup trucks and a major exporter of them – the 'Detroit of the East' (Ammar 2011; Warr and Kohpaiboon 2017).

Just as in the pre-1930s period, the progressive response of governments and businesses in South East Asia to the opportunities of globalization that began in the mid-1960s sharply increased exports and was fundamental to GDP growth. Between 1964/66 and 2006/08, exports of goods and services as a percentage of GDP at least doubled in all countries, and in Thailand, Indonesia, and Cambodia rose even more. Subsequently, except in Vietnam's rapidly emerging export economy, the share of exports in GDP declined somewhat, due to the discouragement to globalization of the 2008 financial crisis (Table 7.10).

A remarkable change in export composition lay behind export-led growth. As late as 1974/76, South East Asia, Singapore apart, still exported chiefly primary commodities. By 1995/97, however, with the exceptions of Indonesia (a major oil exporter) and Vietnam (also with large energy exports), manufactures accounted for more than two-thirds to four-fifths of merchandise exports. Most exports went to high-income countries, although Singapore slightly blurs the picture as a high-income recipient of exports from elsewhere in the region and also as an exporter to the rest of (low-income) South East Asia (Table 7.10).

In the little more than two decades between 1972/74 and 1995/97, manufacturing for export and the expanding domestic markets it helped to promote changed the structure of South East Asia's economies from predominately agricultural to industrial. In 1995/97, industry contributed from about one-third to more than two-fifths of GDP everywhere in South East Asia, except Cambodia and Laos, the region's late industrializers. However, by 2006/08, in these two countries, industry, defined as manufacturing, construction, and utilities, made up one-third of GDP (Table 7.11).

The rapid adoption everywhere, except Myanmar, of the South East Asian industrial model was accompanied by high growth rates, typically 5–6 per cent as decade-long annual averages, and because growth tended to be episodic, often in spurts above these rates. Between 1970 and 2010, real GDP per capita increased at least fivefold in almost all of South East Asia. Growth was much slower in the Philippines. A perennial South East Asian laggard, it was held back by an overemphasis on import substitution and rent-seeking politicians (Perkins 2013: 7, 151; Table 7.12).

After increasingly losing touch with United States incomes between 1870 and 1950, and from 1950 to 1973 generally making only slight progress under predominantly import substitution regimes and due to accelerated population increase, South East Asia is now significantly 'catching up'. Even so, the gap remains large, except for Singapore. Tellingly, in 2010, Indonesia, the Philippines, and Vietnam were much further behind the United States (and more so Japan) than in 1870 (Tables 7.3, 7.12).

Development Assessment

Despite recent impressive growth and structural change, South East Asia, with Singapore again the exception, remains partially economically developed at best. Megacities notwithstanding, in all South East Asian countries except Malaysia, about half to two-thirds of populations live in rural areas (Table 7.13). Industrial wages are too near the 'subsistence level' and modern

Table 7.10 South East Asia and US, exports and export composition and direction, 1960–2014/16

A. South East Asia exports of goods and services as % GDP

	Myanmar	Thailand	Malaysia	Singapore	Indonesia	Cambodia	Laos	Vietnam	Philippines	United States
1960	–	16.1	64.5	162.9	11.5	13.9	–	–	11.9	5.0
1964/66	–	17.3	44.3	122.9	10.1	11.4	–	–	19.3	5.0
1974/76	–	20.1	48.8	145.4	24.6	–	–	–	21.8	8.1
1984/86	–	23.6	55.3	152.6	22.9	–	3.5	6.6	24.8	7.2
1995/97	–	42.9	93.0	175.7	26.7	30.1	23.3	38.9	41.9	10.8
2006/08	0.1	69.7	106.0	225.4	30.1	66.5	35.6	69.5	42.3	11.6
2014/16	19.1	69.1	70.6	181.2	21.3	61.8	32.0	89.9	28.4	13.1

B. Manufactures as % merchandise exports

	Myanmar	Thailand	Malaysia	Singapore	Indonesia	Cambodia	Laos	Vietnam	Philippines	United States
1960	0.9	2.1	–	26.2	0.3	1.6	9.4	–	4.6	62.9
1964/66	0.5	2.1	5.2	29.8	0.0	0.6	4.4	–	5.8	62.0
1974/76	4.4	15.0	15.1	42.0	1.1	–	1.4	–	12.2	65.6
1984/86	–	38.4	30.3	53.6	14.1	–	–	–	27.4	69.7
1995/97	–	72.0	75.7	83.9	48.1	–	–	44.1	70.6	78.7
2006/08	–	76.3	74.7	81.4	47.4	97.4	–	51.4	88.6	79.8
2014/15	–	77.0	64.4	74.1	42.8	91.8	–	38.1	82.0	63.1

C. Merchandise exports to high-income countries as % total merchandise exports

	Myanmar	Thailand	Malaysia	Singapore	Indonesia	Cambodia	Laos	Vietnam	Philippines	United States
1960	28.1	81.6	–	57.8	86.7	80.6	–	74.4	95.2	66.3
1964/66	32.2	69.3	–	–	77.8	58.8	–	–	98.2	67.1
1974/76	45.8	78.8	85.2	62.0	95.7	–	–	–	93.1	67.8
1984/86	45.8	77.5	83.8	61.1	94.3	48.2	–	48.5	89.3	72.9
1995/97	48.5	78.5	82.8	61.5	82.6	43.2	13.4	72.8	88.5	71.5
2006/08	17.6	64.4	70.9	49.6	69.3	94.7	21.5	72.1	77.4	65.6
2014/15	14.9	55.0	62.5	46.2	58.9	79.7	10.4	70.2	76.1	59.4

Source: World Bank 2017.

Table 7.11 South East Asia, sectoral distribution of GDP, 1960–2014/16

	1960	1972/74	1984/86	1995/97	2006/08	2014/16
Myanmar						
Agriculture	–	–	–	–	42.5	27.6
Industry	–	–	–	–	20.8	32.8
Services	–	–	–	–	36.7	39.6
Thailand						
Agriculture	36.4	26.9	16.3	9.1	9.6	9.0
Industry	18.5	26.7	32.3	37.2	39.5	36.4
Services	45.0	46.5	51.4	53.7	50.9	54.6
Malaysia						
Agriculture	43.7	30.9	20.3	11.9	9.5	8.7
Industry	24.7	36.4	39.2	43.2	43.7	36.4
Services	31.6	32.7	40.5	44.9	46.7	54.9
Singapore						
Agriculture	3.9	2.1	0.9	0.2	0.0	0.0
Industry	21.2	34.8	35.7	33.6	29.5	26.0
Services	74.9	63.1	63.3	66.2	70.4	74.0
Indonesia						
Agriculture	–	–	–	16.6	13.7	13.4
Industry	–	–	–	43.2	47.3	40.4
Services	–	–	–	40.2	39.0	43.1
Cambodia						
Agriculture	–	–	–	48.0	33.2	28.7
Industry	–	–	–	16.0	26.3	29.7
Services	–	–	–	36.0	40.5	41.6
Laos						
Agriculture				53.9	35.4	19.6
Industry				20.5	27.7	31.7
Services				25.6	36.9	48.7
Vietnam						
Agriculture	–	–	–	–	–	18.9
Industry	–	–	–	–	–	36.7
Services	–	–	–	–	–	44.4
Philippines						
Agriculture	26.9	30.2	24.4	20.4	12.7	10.4
Industry	31.3	35.2	35.9	32.1	33.1	31.0
Services	41.8	34.6	39.7	47.5	54.2	58.6

Note: For 2014/2016 for Indonesia, the sectoral distribution does not add up to 100.0 in the source.
Source: World Bank 2017.

Table 7.12 South East Asia, per capita GDP and relative to US, 1970–2010

A. Per capita GDP (1990 international $)

	1970	1990	1997	2007	2010
United States	15,030	23,201	26,074	31,655	30,491
Myanmar	642	786	1,046	2,843	3,709
Thailand	1,694	4,633	6,559	8,835	9,372
Malaysia	2,079	5,131	7,955	9,590	10,094
Singapore	4,439	14,220	20,231	26,783	29,038
Indonesia	1,231	2,514	3,684	4,156	4,722
Cambodia	647	881	1,093	2,281	2,450
Laos	748	929	1,105	1,594	–
Vietnam	735	1,025	1,588	2,785	3,217
Philippines	1,764	2,197	2,331	2,829	3,024

B. Annual average growth %

	1970–2010	1990–2010	1990–97	1997–2007	2007–10
United States	1.8	1.4	1.7	1.9	−1.2
Myanmar	4.4	7.8	4.1	10.0	8.9
Thailand	4.3	3.5	5.0	3.0	2.0
Malaysia	4.0	3.4	6.3	1.9	1.7
Singapore	4.7	3.6	5.0	2.8	2.7
Indonesia	3.4	3.2	5.5	1.2	4.3
Cambodia	3.3	5.1	–	7.4	2.4
Laos	2.0	3.2	2.5	3.7	–
Vietnam	3.7	5.7	6.3	5.6	4.8
Philippines	1.3	1.6	0.8	1.9	2.2

C. South East Asia as a % US

	1970	1990	1997	2007	2010
Myanmar	4.3	3.4	4.0	9.0	12.2
Thailand	11.3	20.0	25.2	27.9	30.7
Malaysia	13.8	22.1	30.5	30.3	33.1
Singapore	29.5	61.3	77.6	84.6	95.2
Indonesia	8.2	10.8	14.1	13.1	15.5
Cambodia	4.3	3.8	4.2	7.2	8.0
Laos	5.0	4.0	4.2	5.0	–
Vietnam	4.9	4.4	6.1	8.8	10.5
Philippines	11.7	9.5	8.9	8.9	9.9

Source: Maddison Project Database, version 2013.

sector jobs too few to draw this labour from the countryside, as occurs in industrial revolutions. Pre-war South East Asia had 'lopsided' or dual economies, and even though manufacturing became the region's growth engine, a dualistic structure persists. In addition to still large rural populations with underemployment, many South East Asian migrants to cities, hoping for modern sector jobs, have joined a bloated informal economy and become slum dwellers. They comprise between a quarter to around half of urban populations in almost all South East Asian countries.

A search for jobs, a world closely linked by communications innovations, and large country per capita income differentials within South East Asia have combined to divide the region, once a large net recipient of immigrants, into migrant-sending and receiving countries (Table 7.14). By 2007, emigration from South East Asia had reached 5 million, a volume that has made migrant remittances a significant contributor to GDP in a number of countries. Remittances as a percentage of GDP in 2016 were 8.9 per cent in the Philippines and 6 per cent in Vietnam (Coxhead 2018: 182; Tigno 2018: 143). Most South East Asian migrants left the region, often for work in construction or domestic service in the Middle East, but roughly a million went to South East Asia's three migrant-receiving countries of Singapore, Malaysia, and Thailand. Migrant inflows, especially to the latter two countries, to supply low-wage, unskilled industrial workers, discourage economic transition. The effect, as the Rybczynski theorem warns, is to perpetuate labour-intensive industries by augmenting endowments of abundant labour, the reverse of the theorem's hopeful message of a transition towards development by harnessing dynamic comparative advantage through policies that expand supplies of capital and qualified manpower.

Conclusion

During the last 150 years, South East Asia became, first, a collection of resource-dependent export economies, and then, beginning in the 1970s, a region in which growth depended chiefly on exporting manufactures. Despite this shift, the pre-1930 and post-1970 expansionary phases have a crucial similarity: economic growth in each was almost wholly extensive. Both before the 1930s and beginning in the 1970s, South East Asian countries grew chiefly through marshalling greater inputs rather than through intensive growth, which, achieved by technical progress, raises output through the more efficient use of a given bundle of inputs. In the first vent-for-surplus expansionary period, resources came chiefly through cultivating more land

Table 7.13 South East Asia, rural population as % of total population, 1960–2014/16

	Myanmar	Thailand	Malaysia	Indonesia	Cambodia	Laos	Vietnam	Philippines
1960	80.8	80.3	73.4	85.4	89.7	92.1	85.3	69.7
1964/66	79.0	79.8	70.1	84.2	89.2	91.7	83.6	68.4
1974/76	76.1	76.2	62.3	80.7	87.2	88.9	81.2	64.5
1984/86	75.9	71.9	54.1	73.9	86.1	86.2	80.4	57.0
1995/97	74.2	69.6	43.0	62.8	82.3	81.8	77.4	51.8
2006/08	70.1	59.9	31.6	52.5	80.6	70.3	71.5	53.9
2014/16	65.9	49.6	25.3	46.3	79.3	61.4	66.4	55.6

Source: World Bank 2017.

Table 7.14 South East Asia, migrant sending and receiving countries, 1962–2012 (net migrants 000)

	Migrant sending countries							Migrant receiving countries			
	Myanmar	Indonesia	Cambodia	Laos	Vietnam	Philippines	Total migrant sending	Singapore	Malaysia	Thailand	Total migrant receiving
1962	–	−107.5	–	0.08	–	0.4	−107.0	0.4	−48.9	–	−48.5
1972	–	−90.4	−125.0	0.05	–	−237.7	−453.1	5.9	−131.5	402.6	277.0
1977	–	−202.7	−85.0	−198.80	−813.1	−313.6	−1,613.2	14.3	−7.0	287.2	294.5
1992	−700.0	−381.8	409.4	−60.60	−394.2	−504.9	−1,632.1	248.9	298.8	−607.5	−59.8
2002	−1,247.7	−851.3	−35.2	−148.10	−672.3	−1,097.4	−4,052.0	435.6	645.5	373.7	1,454.8
2012	−474.3	−835.0	−150.0	−177.50	−200.0	−650.0	−2,486.8	337.9	781.7	167.3	1,286.9

Notes: Data are net migrant flows. Negative numbers indicate net outflows.
Source: World Bank 2017.

and mobilizing more labour to farm it. That mode of growth created overwhelmingly agrarian, largely unurbanized economies and required little capital.

By contrast, post-1970 growth utilized now abundant South East Asian labour and depended heavily on the movement of labour out of low-productivity to higher-productivity activities and on factor accumulation, the latter realized partly due to foreign direct investment by multinationals manufacturing for export. Between 1980 and 2016, through migration (as the birth rate is far below replacement levels), Singapore's population more than doubled, and by 2016 the per capita stock of foreign direct investment stood at US$200,322. The Republic, however, continues to show low total factor productivity growth, the usual measure of technical progress that fuels intensive growth. Similarly, elsewhere in South East Asia, a transition to growth driven by total factor productivity, and therefore self-sustaining, has yet to occur (Tran 2013: 129–130; Perkins et al. 2018: 19).

Singapore is a South East Asian exception in having a large, globally integrated services sector and essentially no agriculture. Elsewhere in South East Asia, agricultural diversification and the Green Revolution in rice production, which has helped to resolve concerns over food supply, have been important advances. Even so, post-1970 growth in the region, like its pre-1930 counterpart, has the 'lopsided' configuration of dual economies. Notwithstanding remarkable structural change, making industry a greater contributor to GDP than agriculture, the latter still accounts for the larger share of employment. Urbanization has been rapid, and includes three cities of over 10 million, but in all countries except Singapore and Malaysia, rural dwellers comprise from almost half to four-fifths of populations (Table 7.13).

South East Asian countries now seem to be moving towards closing an income gap with the United States, albeit slowly and from large disparities. But large amounts of labour in low-productivity agriculture and informal urban services reveal the incompleteness of the globalization-dependent South East Asian development model. So, too, do an extreme reliance on female labour in South East Asian garment factories and large migrant outflows from a number of countries, as well as the hosting of some of these migrants by Malaysia, Thailand, and Singapore to obtain additional workers to help keep factor input-driven growth on track. Even Singapore, despite concerted efforts to raise total factor productivity growth, has so far had little success.

References

Ammar, S. (2011). 'Thailand after 1997', *Asian Economic Policy Review*, 6, 68–85.

Bastin, J. and Benda, H. J. (1968). *A History of Modern Southeast Asia*, Englewood Cliffs: Prentice Hall.

Benda, H. J. (1958). *The Crescent and the Rising Sun: Indonesian Islam under Japanese Occupation 1942–1945*, The Hague: Van Hoeve.

(1967). 'The Japanese Interregnum in Southeast Asia', in Goodman, G. K. (ed.), *Imperial Japan: A Reassessment*, New York: East Asian Institute, Columbia University, 65–79.

Broek, J. O. M. (1944). 'Diversity and Unity in Southeast Asia', *Geographical Review*, 34(2), 175–195.

Brown, I. (1997). *Economic Change in South-East Asia c.1830–1980*, Kuala Lumpur: Oxford University Press.

Burma. (1951). *The National Income of Burma*, Rangoon: Ministry of National Planning.

Caves, R. E. (1965). '"Vent for Surplus" Models of Trade and Growth', in Baldwin, R. E. et al. (eds.), *Trade, Growth and the Balance of Payments*, Chicago: Rand McNally, 95–115.

Cheeseman, H. R. (1947). *Annual Report on Education in the Malayan Union, 1946*, Kuala Lumpur: Malayan Union Government Press.

Coxhead, I. (2018). 'Vietnam in 2017: Flying Fast into Turbulence', *Asian Survey*, 58(1), 149–157.

Crafts, N. F. R. (1973). 'Trade as a Handmaiden of Growth: An Alternative View', *Economic Journal*, 83, 875–883.

Del Tufo, M. V. (1949). *Malaya: A Report on the 1947 Census of Population*, London: Crown Agents for the Colonies.

Felipe, J. (2018). *Asia's Industrial Transformation: The Role of Manufacturing and Global Value Chains, Part II*, Manila: Asian Development Bank working paper 550.

Findlay, R. (1970). *Trade and Specialization*, Harmondsworth: Penguin.

Findlay, R. and O'Rourke, K. H. (2007). *Power and Plenty: Trade, War, and the World Economy in the Second Millennium*, Princeton University Press.

Fukao, K., Bassino, J.-P., Makino, T., Paprzycki, R., Settsu, T., Takashima, M., and Tokui, J. (2015). *Regional Inequality and Industrial Structure in Japan: 1874–2008*, Tokyo: Maruzen Publishing.

Furnivall, J. S. (1948). *Colonial Policy and Practice: A Comparative Study of Burma and Netherlands India*, Cambridge University Press.

Hill, H. (2018). 'Asia's Third Giant: A Survey of the Indonesian Economy', *Economic Record*, 41(307), 469–499.

Hlaing, U. A. (1964). 'Trends of Economic Growth and Income Distribution in Burma, 1870–1940', *Journal of the Burma Research Society*, 47, 89–148.

Huff, G. (2003). 'Monetization and Financial Development in Southeast Asia before the Second World War', *Economic History Review*, 56(2), 300–345.

(2007). 'Globalization, Natural Resources and Foreign Investment: A View from the Resource Rich Tropics', *Oxford Economic Papers*, 59(5), 127–155.

(2011). 'Finance and Long-Term Development Issues in Southeast Asia', *Asian-Pacific Economic Literature*, 25(1), 56–78.

(2012). 'Export-Led Growth, Gateway Cities and Urban Systems Development in Pre-World War II Southeast Asia', *Journal of Development Studies*, 48(10), 1431–1452.

(2019). 'Causes and Consequences of the Great Vietnam Famine, 1944–1945', *Economic History Review*, 72(1), 286–316.

(2020). *World War II and Southeast Asia: Economy and Society under Japanese Occupation*, Cambridge University Press.

Huff, G. and Caggiano, G. (2007). 'Globalization, Immigration and Lewisian Elastic Labor in Pre-World War II Southeast Asia', *Journal of Economic History*, 67(1), 33–68.

Indonesia [Department of Economic Affairs, Batavia]. (1947). 'The economic condition of Indonesia in mid-1947', *Economic Review of Indonesia*, 1(8), 117–130.

Ingram, J. C. (1971). *Economic Change in Thailand, 1850–1970*, Stanford University Press.

International Labour Organization. (2016a). 'Wages and Productivity in the Garment Sector in Asia and the Pacific and the Arab States', research note, Bangkok: ILO.

(2016b). 'Wages, Productivity and Labour Share in China', research note, Bangkok: ILO Regional Office for Asia and the Pacific.

Knowles, L. C. A. (1928). *The Economic Development of the British Overseas Empire*, London: George Routledge & Sons.

Larkin, J. A. (1993). *Sugar and the Origins of Modern Philippine Society*, Berkeley: University of California Press.

Lee, K. Y. (1998). *The Singapore Story*, Singapore: Times Editions.

Lewis, W. A. (1978a). *Growth and Fluctuations, 1870–1913*, London: Allen & Unwin.

(1978b). *Evolution of the International Economic Order*, Princeton University Press.

Lim, L. Y. C. (2014). 'Singapore's Success: After the Miracle', in Looney, R. E. (ed.), *Handbook of Emerging Economies*, London: Routledge, 203–226.

Maddison Project Database, version 2013. Bolt, J. and van Zanden, J. L. (2014). 'The Maddison Project: Collaborative Research on Historical National Accounts', *Economic History Review*, 67(3), 627–651.

Mieno, F. (2013). 'Toward Myanmar's New Stage of Development: Transition from Military Rule to Market', *Asian Economic Policy Review*, 8, 94–117.

Myint, H. (1954). 'The Gains from International Trade and the Backward Countries', *Review of Economic Studies*, 22(2), 129–142.

(1958). 'The "Classical" Theory of International Trade and the Underdeveloped Countries', *Economic Journal*, 68, 317–337.

(1965). 'The Inward and Outward-Looking Countries of Southeast Asia', *Malayan Economic Review*, 12(1), 1–13.

Nurkse, R. (1959). *Patterns of Trade and Development*, Stockholm: Almqvist and Wicksell.

Perkins, D. (2013). *East Asian Development*, Cambridge, MA: Harvard University Press.

Perkins, D., Rasiah, R., and Thye Woo, W. (2018). 'Explaining Malaysia's Past Growth and Future Prospects', JCI working paper 2, Jeffrey Cheah Institute on Southeast Asia.

Rasiah, R. (2009a). 'Expansion and Slowdown in Southeast Asia Electronics Manufacturing', *Journal of the Asia Pacific Economy*, 14(2), 123–137.

(2009b). 'Garment Manufacturing in Cambodia and Laos', *Journal of the Asia Pacific Economy*, 14(2), 150–161.

Sicat, G. P. (2015). 'The Philippine Economy during the Japanese Occupation, 1941–1945', in Boldorf, M. and Okazaki, T. (eds.), *Economies under Occupation: The Hegemony of Nazi Germany and Imperial Japan in World War II*, London: Routledge, 191–204.

Tigno, J. V. (2018). 'The Philippines in 2017: Popularity Breeds Corruption', *Asian Survey*, 58 (1), 142–148.

Tran, V. T. (2013). 'Vietnamese Economy at the Crossroads: New *Doi Moi* for Sustained Growth', *Asian Economic Policy Review*, 8, 122–143.

Twomey, M. J. (2000). *A Century of Foreign Investment in the Third World*, London: Routledge.

van der Eng, P. (1991). Indonesian National Income, unpublished data made available by the author.

(1992). 'The Real Domestic Product of Indonesia, 1880–1989', *Explorations in Economic History*, 29(3), 343–373.

(1994a). Thailand Estimates of GDP Based on Sompop's Work, unpublished data made available by the author.

(1994b). Historical Estimates of GDP in Malaysia/West Malaysia, 1910–1960, unpublished data made available by the author.

(2002). 'Indonesia's Growth Performance in the Twentieth Century', in Maddison, A., Prasada Rao, D. S., and Shepherd, W. F. (eds.), *The Asian Economies in the Twentieth Century*, Cheltenham: Edward Elgar Publishing, 143–179.

Warr, P. and Kohpaiboon, A. (2017). 'Thailand's Automotive Manufacturing Corridor', working paper 519, Manila: Asian Development Bank.

Williamson, J. G. (2011). *Trade and Poverty: When the Third World Fell Behind*, Cambridge, MA: MIT Press.

World Bank. (2017). *World Development Indicators, 2017*, Washington, DC: World Bank.

8

The Middle East

Decline and Resurgence in West Asia

MOHAMED SALEH

The modern economic history of the Middle East and North Africa (MENA) region has been the subject of a voluminous body of scholarship. Pioneering economic historians of the region all provided invaluable narratives of MENA history (e.g. Issawi 1982; Owen et al. 1998; Owen 2002; Kuran 2012). The objective of this chapter is first to provide the reader with an overview of the economic growth of the MENA region between 1870 and 2010. It will then analyse the underlying sources of growth (geography versus institutions) and the proximate sources of growth (labour, physical capital, and technology). In this regard, the chapter's main contribution lies in putting together major empirical facts about the MENA region at the country-level on the long-term trends of key variables in economic development. These variables include GDP per capita, democracy, population, fertility, mortality, migration, labour force participation, human capital, physical capital, and technology.

The chapter includes four groups of countries within the definition of the MENA region: (1) the Levant (Iraq, Israel, Jordan, Lebanon, Palestine, and Syria); (2) the Arab peninsula (Bahrain, Kuwait, Oman, Qatar, Saudi Arabia, United Arab Emirates, and Yemen); (3) Egypt, Iran, and Turkey; and (4) North Africa (Algeria, Libya, Morocco, and Tunisia). The chapter does *not* include other African and Asian countries with significant Muslim populations, such as Sudan, Mauritania, Pakistan, Afghanistan, and Indonesia.

A puzzling fact that emerges about the economic performance of the MENA region is that it lagged behind the rest of the world (with the exception of sub-Saharan Africa) in the second half of the twentieth century, with respect to democracy, fertility decline, and female labour force participation. The discussion of the role of geography and institutions highlights how geography – in particular, the abundance of natural resources – largely

The author gratefully acknowledges the excellent research assistance by Mennatallah El-Ayadi, and the financial support of the ANR-Labex IAST.

shaped the path of economic development in the region. It is also correlated with the emergence and persistence of undemocratic political institutions and coercive labour institutions. This is the case for the Arab states of the Persian Gulf, Libya, Algeria, Iran, and Iraq (Group A). By contrast, MENA countries that were less rich in natural resources (Group B) witnessed more diverse political development paths, although their political upheavals resulted more often in dictatorships. Their lesser reliance on natural resources made tertiarization more pronounced, though.

MENA Economic History since 1870: An Overview

Europe's Rising Influence and MENA's Deindustrialization, 1870–1914

The economic history of MENA since 1870 has largely been shaped by the rising European influence in the region. The region's increasing contact with Europe via trade, Europeans' settlement in the region, and European capital inflows into the primary sector and the related trade sector, was associated with the 'deindustrialization' of the MENA region throughout the nineteenth century. MENA's traditional manufacturing sector lost competitiveness to more advanced and industrialized European manufacturing.

Trade with Europe grew rapidly during the nineteenth century. Starting from the 1850s, the economies of many MENA countries became centred around the export of primary commodities (cash crops), such as cotton in Egypt, Turkey, and Iran, silk and fruits in the Levant, tobacco in Turkey and the Levant, and sugar in Egypt.

The expansion of the cultivation of cash crops was facilitated by the availability of uncultivated land. But faced with local labour scarcity, there was a surge in slave imports from Sudan, and in the coercion of local labour by large landholders. Expansion of the cultivation and export of cash crops was also made possible by the increase in European capital inflows, and the rise of the banking sector. This period also witnessed the emergence of private property rights on land. MENA countries started to formalize land titles and codify land tenure rights. This process was correlated with the expansion of cash crops.

Europeans started to settle in the region to benefit from trade. North Africa, Egypt, and Palestine received an influx of European immigrants.

The section on MENA Economic History since 1870 draws on Issawi (1982) and Owen (2002).

Under the capitulation agreements between European states and the Ottoman Empire, Europeans residing in the region held extraterritorial rights and were thus subject to their own consulates in the case of conflicts with local Ottoman subjects. Iran held similar agreements with Russia and other European powers under the Qajar dynasty (1794–1925). Although these agreements were initially reciprocal, the shift in the balance of power towards Europe meant that it was European settlers in the MENA region who benefited from the capitulations the most.

It was not only European nationals who benefited from the capitulation agreements though, as European consulates started to sell the protégé status that granted access to European consular courts to Ottoman subjects. This was first directed at local subjects working in European consulates, but then extended to other groups, especially non-Muslim minorities. It has been suggested that the economic superiority of local non-Muslim minorities that has been observed throughout the nineteenth and the twentieth centuries was a consequence of the capitulations and the access to the European legal systems that came with the protégé status. But this narrative needs to be revised. First, while urban non-Muslim minorities (Armenians, Greeks, Levantine Christians, and Jews) may have benefited from the capitulations because they were traders and moneychangers, Coptic Christians of Egypt, the largest non-Muslim population in the region, did not, because they were artisans and bureaucrats. Second, the narrative often blurs the line between local non-Muslims and European immigrants who happened to belong to the same religious affiliation. In doing so, it tends to emphasize the 'foreignness' of local non-Muslims. For example, European Christians and Jews are put in the same group as local Christians and Jews. This mixes up ethnic divisions with religious affiliation.

Along with trade and migration, the transportation sector grew. Large-scale transport projects were carried out in MENA, including, most notably, the Suez Canal that was opened in 1869. Steamships started to navigate the eastern Mediterranean. The first railway line in the region was opened in the 1850s, connecting Cairo and Alexandria in Egypt. The railway network expanded thereafter in the entire region. Telegraphs started to penetrate the region as well.

The result of the growth of trade in cash crops and of transport was a secular decline of the manufacturing sector. Egypt's attempt at state industrialization in textiles under Muhammad Ali Pasha, its autonomous Ottoman viceroy in 1805–48, failed and most of Egypt's state textile manufactories closed down by 1868. In other MENA countries, the share of artisans declined. The deindustrialization was, at least partially, a consequence of the Anglo-Ottoman 1838 Treaty that reduced tariffs imposed by the Ottoman Empire.

Faced by the rising influence of European powers, the Ottoman Empire attempted to increase its capacity to levy taxes and to conscript a modern army via implementing a series of military and fiscal reforms during the nineteenth century in what is known as *Tanzimat*. However, the increased Ottoman public debt led to its default in 1875. Egypt followed course in 1876. European powers gradually captured Ottoman provinces: Algeria in 1830, Tunisia in 1881, and Egypt in 1882. Morocco, which was not part of the Ottoman Empire, was divided between French and Spanish states in 1912. The Levant remained part of the Ottoman Empire until the aftermath of World War I. Iran remained independent throughout the period under the Qajar dynasty.

The Collapse of the Ottoman Empire and the Interwar Period, 1914–45

The fall of the Ottoman Empire in the aftermath of World War I led to the formation of British and French mandates over the Levant: Iraq, Jordan, and Palestine became British mandates, whereas Syria and Lebanon fell under the French mandate. The interwar period also witnessed the formation of modern nation-states, with many MENA countries gaining their full or partial independence. Egypt gained partial independence from Britain in 1922, following a popular revolt in 1919, while Britain continued to hold de facto power in Egypt, especially over the Suez Canal. Iraq gained its independence in 1932. The modern Turkish state was founded in 1923. An Iranian coup in 1921 brought the Qajar dynasty to an end and resulted in the establishment of the rule of the Bahlavi dynasty in 1925. Saudi Arabia was founded in 1933.

The new independent states attempted to impose national control over the economic realm. The capitulations were abolished in Turkey in 1923, in Iraq in 1922, in Iran in 1928, and in Egypt in 1937. The Mandates of Syria, Lebanon, Palestine, and Jordan did not allow the capitulations. National central banks started to emerge. States also regained control over their tariff and trade policies by abolishing commercial treaties with the European powers. Governments tried to increase nationals' share in firm ownership, via establishing national banks and providing credit to locals through private banks.

State-Led Development in the Postcolonial Period, 1945–73

The postcolonial period witnessed the rise of military regimes with socialist and nationalist ideologies. State-led development became the norm in the

1950s and 1960s, under the presidential dictatorships of the region, including Egypt, Syria, Algeria, Tunisia, Iraq, and Libya. At the core of their economic agendas was a stated objective of completing the process of national independence. The major pillars of their legitimacy were the provision of free public education to the masses, confiscation of private entrepreneurships, nationalization of banks and private assets, and land redistribution. Guaranteed employment in the government and public sector for university and secondary school graduates became prevalent in most MENA countries, leading to an expansion in white-collar jobs, especially teachers and accountants.

It remains an open question whether the state-led programmes indeed achieved their objectives. While the programmes stripped Europeans of their privileges, leading to their eventual exodus, they often targeted native non-Muslims. The exodus of the region's urban non-Muslim minorities (with the notable exception of Egypt's Copts), started in the aftermath of World War I, but intensified in the aftermath of World War II. And while the beneficiaries of the nationalization and land redistribution programmes were in principle the masses, the programmes more often than not ended up redistributing economic and political power to a new middle class of military and police officers. This new class quickly adopted the habits of the old elite and maintained the exclusive colonial institutions.

The Arab-Israeli conflict, which started during the interwar period with the intensified migration of European Jewry to Palestine, has been an important factor that shaped the economic and political development of the region in the postcolonial era. It has often been used by military dictators to justify the lack of democratization of the region and the persistence of their notorious military regimes. It has also consumed a large portion of the economic resources of the region.

The Shift to the Market Economy, 1973–2010

The 1973 oil crisis enabled the Arab states of the Persian Gulf to increase their economic and political power. Migration from MENA countries to these countries, in addition to Iraq and Libya, increased. Many MENA countries started to liberalize the economy, while keeping their military dictatorships intact. However, the resulting market systems were still dependent on the state and turned into a form of crony capitalism.

The liberalization of MENA economies was correlated with a surge in inequality. Alvaredo et al. (2019) document that the MENA region has one of the highest levels of income inequality in the world today. If we add to this the lack of democratization and the poor condition of human rights in the region, one can only conclude that the postcolonial regimes did not liberate MENA peoples from colonization. Instead, they preserved the coercive institutions, many of which are even precolonial, to maintain their power over the masses.

Economic Performance of the Middle East, 1870–2010

Figure 8.1A shows the long-term trend of real GDP per capita in 1990 international $ between 1870 and 2010. Here, I draw mainly on Pamuk's (2006) estimates and the revised estimates from the Maddison Project Database, version 2013. Data for the pre-1950 period are scarce; only two data points are available for 1870 and 1913. Figure 8.1B depicts the corresponding average growth rates of real GDP per capita calculated over 1870–1913, 1913–50, and over five-year intervals thereafter. Growth rates enable us to appreciate whether MENA countries achieved modern economic growth (MEG), defined as sustaining an average growth of real GDP per capita of 1 per cent per annum for a sufficiently long period of time so as to quadruple the standard of living.

Levant

There are two major facts about the Levant. First, with the exception of Iraq, the Levant is generally less rich in natural resources than the oil-rich countries in the region. Despite this fact, or perhaps because of it, the Levant has generally witnessed a steady growth trajectory, starting from 1950, as its GDP was less sensitive to oil prices. The second fact is that the Levant was at the core of various foreign and civil conflicts: the Arab-Israeli conflict, the Iraq–Iran wars, the First and Second Gulf Wars, and the Lebanese Civil War. These conflicts led to sharp fluctuations in the region's GDP, even within its non-oil-rich countries.

The non-oil-rich but largely stable Israel witnessed the largest increase in its GDP per capita, which quadrupled between 1950 and 2010, reaching almost $20,000 in 2010. Syria's GDP per capita witnessed a steady increase too, albeit with several fluctuations due to political turmoil, reaching $7,500 in 2010 (the second richest country in the Levant after Israel, as of 2010). Similarly, Jordan witnessed an increase in its real GDP per capita since 1950, albeit with fluctuations due to political turmoil,

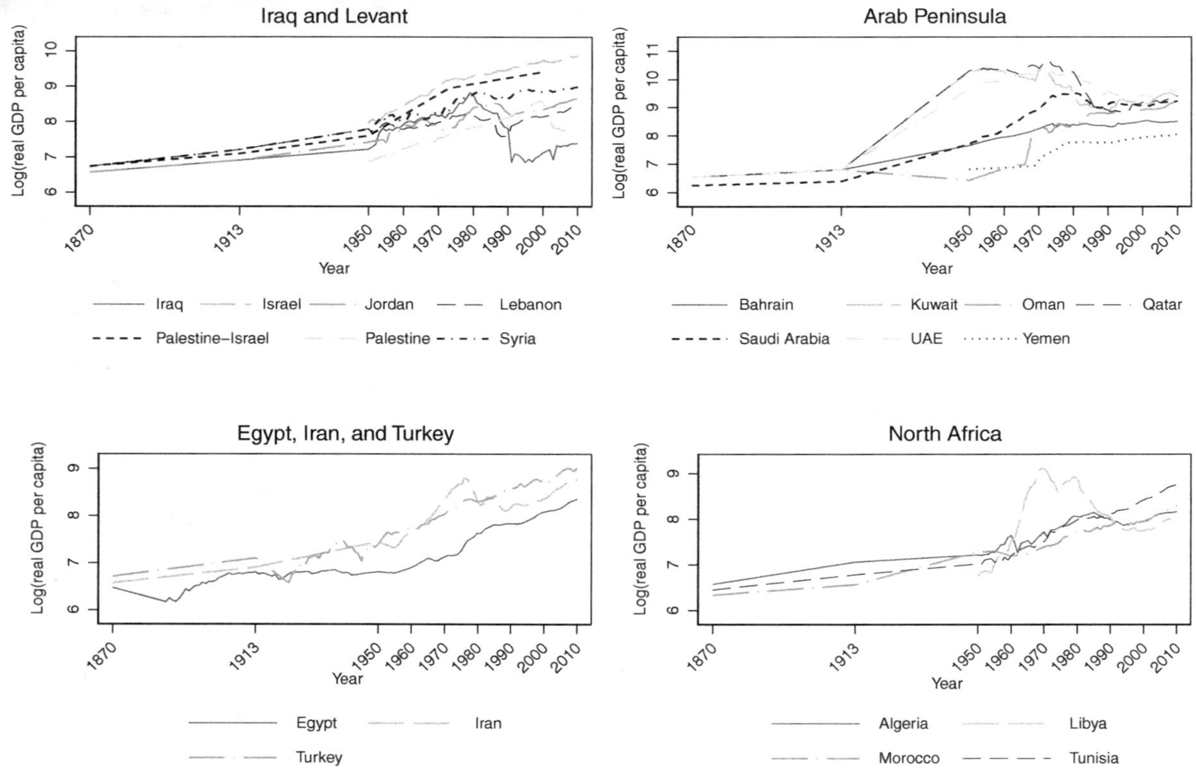

Figure 8.1 Real GDP per capita and its growth rate, 1870–2010. A: Real GDP per capita, 1870–2010. B: Growth rate of real GDP per capita (%), 1870–2010
Notes: Real GDP per capita is calculated in 1990 international $. Growth rates are the average rates over the indicated periods.
Sources: A: Maddison Project Database, version 2013. Real GDP per capita figures in 1870 and 1913 for Bahrain, Kuwait, Oman, Qatar, Saudi Arabia, and UAE, and in 1870, 1913, 1950, 1973, and 2000 for Palestine-Israel: Pamuk 2006. Real GDP per capita figures for Egypt in 1886–1945: Yousef 2002. B. Author's calculations.

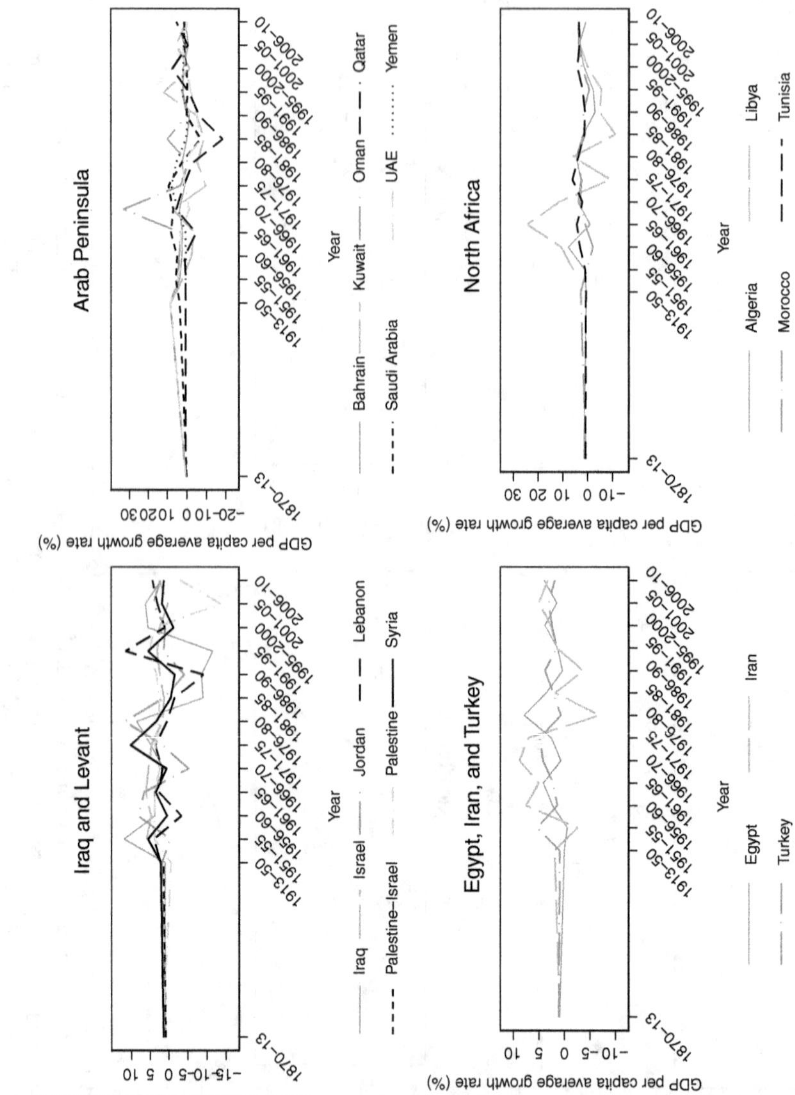

Figure 8.1 (cont.)

reaching ~$5,000 in 2010. Lebanon's GDP per capita increased steadily until 1980, but then declined due to the Lebanese Civil War in 1975–90, before it recovered to reach slightly less than $5,000 in 2010. Palestine's economic performance improved steadily between 1950 and 2000, but it declined in 2000–2010, following the second intifada in 2000–2005. Iraq's GDP per capita increased between 1950 and 1980 (it was the second richest country in the region after Israel in 1980), but then declined steadily due to the Iraq–Iran War in 1980–88 and the Gulf War in 1990–91. The growth rates in panel B of Figure 8.1 show that, within the Levant, only Israel sustained a positive growth rate from 1950 onwards, followed by Palestine (only until 2000). Jordan has maintained a positive growth rate since 1990. Syria, Lebanon, and Iraq all witnessed sharp fluctuations between positive and negative growth rates due to political unrest and, in the case of Iraq, fluctuations in oil prices.

Arab Peninsula

Despite its political stability, the oil-rich Arab peninsula (with the exception of Yemen) witnessed a less stable growth trajectory than the Levant, due to the sensitivity of its economy to international oil prices. United Arab Emirates (UAE), the richest country in this group, with a real GDP per capita of $15,000 in 2010, witnessed impressive growth between 1913 and 1960, a period of stability in 1960–80, followed by a sharp decline in 1980–85 after the end of the 1970s oil crisis, and another period of stable economic performance in 1985–2010. The second and third richest countries, Kuwait and Qatar, exhibited a similar path of economic performance: an increase between 1913 and 1950, fluctuations in 1950–80, a sharp decrease in the early 1980s, and a stable performance since then. With its larger population, Saudi Arabia stood as the fourth richest country in the region in 2010. It also witnessed an increase in its real GDP per capita in 1950–80, followed by a decline. Oman, which relies less on oil than its neighbours, has witnessed a steady rise in its GDP per capita since 1965. The same applies to Bahrain, which exhibited a less impressive growth path. Finally, Yemen, the poorest country in the Arab peninsula, witnessed an increase in its GDP per capita since 1965. In terms of growth, whereas the oil-rich countries in the Arab Peninsula (Kuwait, Qatar, UAE, Saudi Arabia) witnessed sharp fluctuations due to changes in oil prices, other countries in the region (Oman, Bahrain, Yemen), which are less dependent on oil, have mostly maintained positive growth rates since 1950.

Egypt, Turkey, and Iran

Within this group, Iran is a major oil producer. Nevertheless, it is the non-oil-rich Turkey that is the richest country in the group, at $8,000 in 2010, and that witnessed a steadily growing GDP per capita over the period. In comparison, Iran's GDP per capita increased slowly between 1913 and 1950, and rapidly between 1955 and 1975 (due to oil), before it declined sharply in 1975–80, because of the political unrest that accompanied the Iranian Revolution. Its GDP per capita did not recover until after 1990. Compared to Turkey and Iran, Egypt had a less impressive growth trajectory, with a modest increase in 1955–67, the period of state-led development in the postcolonial period, followed by a decline in 1967–75 due to the Arab-Israeli wars in 1967–73. Egypt's GDP per capita did not start to recover until after 1975. In terms of growth, while Egypt and Turkey have witnessed MEG since 1950, the rapid growth of Iran in 1956–75 was reversed after 1975, and its positive growth rates did not occur again until after 1990.

North Africa

Within this group, Algeria and Libya are major producers of oil and natural gas. However, consistent with the pattern that I documented in other regions; it is the non-oil-rich countries (Tunisia and Morocco) that maintained positive growth rates from 1950. Tunisia is the richest country in North Africa, whereas Morocco exhibited steady growth, albeit at a slower rate. By contrast, Algeria's GDP per capita increased steadily until 1985, but then declined due to the Algerian civil war in 1991–2002, and only began to recover in the 2000s. Libya's GDP per capita increased sharply between 1960 and 1980 (albeit with fluctuations), but has declined steadily thereafter.

Summary

To sum up, and as Pamuk (2006) previously documented, although MENA oil-rich countries are still among the richest in the region after Israel, the heyday of their economic performance was reached around 1980, and their incomes declined thereafter due to fluctuations in oil prices. That was certainly the case for the Arab states of the Persian Gulf. It was also the case for Libya, whose GDP per capita fell even below the two non-oil-producing countries in North Africa: Tunisia and Morocco. Political unrest due to foreign and civil wars caused other oil-rich countries in the region (Algeria, Iran, Iraq) to witness frequent swings in their economic performance. Within the non-oil-rich camp, the more politically stable Egypt, Jordan,

Israel, Morocco, Tunisia, Turkey, and Yemen had steadier economic performance paths, with Israel and Turkey standing out as the most economically successful countries in the region. Political turmoil in Lebanon, Palestine, and Syria triggered strong fluctuations in their growth trajectories, though.

Underlying Sources of Growth

Sources of economic growth can be classified into two groups: (a) underlying sources that include geographic and institutional factors, and (b) proximate sources, which are essentially the factors of production (excluding land and natural resources): labour, physical capital, and technology. In this subsection, I discuss the underlying sources of economic growth in the region: Can the variation in economic growth across MENA countries be attributed to the variation in their geographic conditions, or rather to the variation in the quality of their economic and political institutions, such as the rule of law and democracy?

Geography

MENA countries vary widely in their geographic conditions. First, there is wide variation in the availability of water resources and of temperate climate that makes agriculture possible. On the one hand, a few MENA countries are traditionally endowed with fertile cultivable land, either because of the existence of rivers (Iraq and Egypt) or due to rainfall (Turkey, Iran, Syria, Lebanon, Israel, Palestine, Tunisia, Morocco). These countries typically have moderate climates and are mostly in the northern part of the region. On the other hand, Jordan and the Arab peninsula countries are mostly arid, with the exception of Oman and Yemen. Most of the surface area of Egypt, Libya, and Algeria is part of the African Sahara.

Second, MENA countries vary with respect to the abundance of natural resources, such as oil and natural gas. While the Arab countries of the Persian Gulf, Libya, Iran, Iraq, and Algeria, are rich in natural resources, other MENA countries in the region are not as rich.

Third, market access is largely determined by location and the length of the coast line on important international navigation routes. All MENA countries have access to the coast, with the exception of Jordan. The Persian Gulf is perhaps the most important navigable route in the region due to its huge oil reserves, followed by the Red Sea and the Mediterranean Sea that are also important for oil transportation. In these seas, the Strait of Hormuz (UAE, Oman, and Iran), the Suez Canal (Egypt), and the Strait of

Bab-el-Mandeb (Yemen) stand out as the most significant navigation bottlenecks.

Institutions

The quality of political and economic institutions varies across MENA countries. Figure 8.2 plots the long-term evolution of the Polity IV democracy index that ranges from 0 to 10, from the least to the most democratic (Marshall et al. 2016). The figure reveals a well-known fact about the MENA region, namely that with two exceptions, Israel and Turkey, all the other countries in the region are lagging behind the rest of the world with respect to democracy. It also reveals that although this has been a fact since 1950, there were short episodes of democracy in the histories of certain MENA countries (Syria and Egypt) that failed and were replaced by military regimes. In the Levant, Israel had the highest democracy index value in 1950, although it has declined in recent decades. Lebanon's democracy score improved in the 2000s following the civil war. Syria had relatively high democracy scores in the 1940s and 1950s (albeit with interruptions of military rule), but it descended into absolute authoritarianism from the late 1950s. Jordan and Iraq had very low democracy scores throughout their history. Arab states of the Persian Gulf all have absolute monarchies (democracy score = 0). Egypt had a relatively high democracy score during its liberal period in 1922–52, but it descended into absolute military rule from 1952. By contrast, Turkey's democracy score improved throughout the twentieth century, despite episodes of military coups. Iran and North African countries all have very low democracy scores.

Perhaps correlated with authoritarianism, labour rights are generally weak in MENA countries. Disguised forms of slavery are prevalent throughout the region, whether in the agricultural sector or among immigrants in the Arab states of the Persian Gulf. In fact, the region ranks among the worst regions in the world with respect to labour rights.

Despite the poor democratization of MENA countries and their coercive labour institutions, they mostly score better with respect to the rule of law and property rights. UAE has particularly high scores on both indices. Qatar, Jordan, Israel, Tunisia, Morocco, Bahrain, Oman, and Saudi Arabia have relatively high scores as well.

Political stability varies across MENA countries. The Arab-Israeli conflict, which started in the first half of the twentieth century with the increased European Jewish migration to Palestine under the British mandate, resulted in a series of wars in 1948, 1956, 1967, 1973, 1982, 1987, 2000, 2006, and 2009,

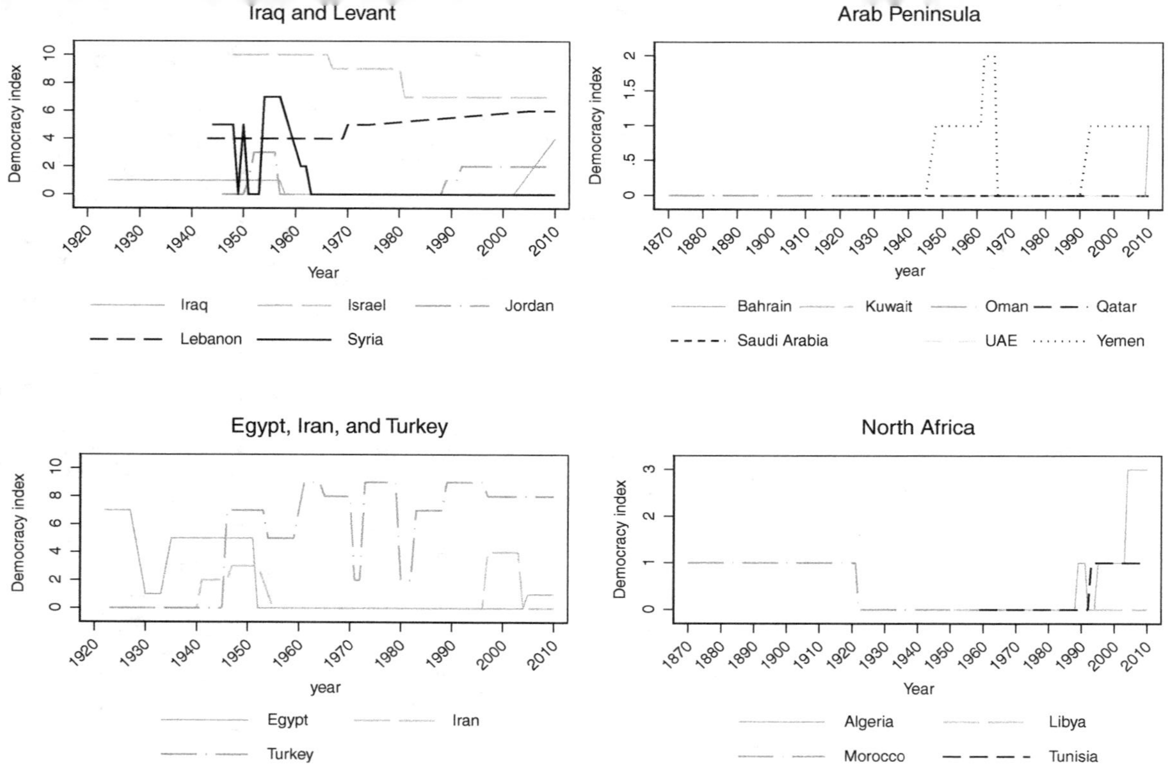

Figure 8.2 Democracy index, 1870–2010

Notes: The democracy indicator is an additive eleven-point scale (0–10). The operational indicator of democracy is derived from codings of the competitiveness of political participation, the openness and competitiveness of executive recruitment, and constraints on the chief executive.

Source: Marshall et al. 2016.

which directly involved Egypt, Syria, Lebanon, and Jordan, besides Israel and Palestine. The Persian Gulf region witnessed a series of wars between Iraq and Iran in 1980–88, and between Iraq and a US-led international coalition in 1990–91. Apart from international wars, Yemen witnessed a devastating civil war in 1962–70, Lebanon in 1975–90, and Algeria in 1991–2002. Popular revolts, military coups, and militant insurgencies by a faction of the population were commonplace throughout the region. The main exceptions here are the Arab states of the Persian Gulf, which were generally politically stable throughout the second half of the twentieth century.

GDP Sectoral Composition

Geography and institutions shape the composition of GDP across the primary, secondary, and tertiary sectors in the MENA region. Figure 8.3A shows the share of the primary sector in GDP, which includes agriculture, hunting, forestry, fishing, and livestock production. In the Levant, Syria had the highest share of the primary sector at around 30 per cent, followed by Palestine, Lebanon, and Jordan, but it declined over time in all four countries. In the Arab Peninsula, in 1960 Oman had the highest share of the primary sector at 80 per cent, although it declined rapidly thereafter due to oil discoveries. Turkey had a relatively high share of agriculture in GDP in 1960 (60 per cent), compared to Egypt and Iran, but again, the share of agriculture declined in the three countries over time. The share of the primary sector persisted at around 20 per cent in North Africa (although the less agricultural Libya had a much lower share).

Figure 8.3B shows the share of the secondary sector in GDP, which includes mining, manufacturing, construction, electricity, water, and gas. One can interpret the mining component of the secondary sector as a proxy for the contribution of oil to GDP, although I am not able to separate mining from the other subsectors in the secondary sector. The other significant subsector in the secondary sector, behind mining, is construction, which is large in many MENA countries. In the Levant, the share of the secondary sector increased in Syria and Jordan, reaching about 35 per cent, but decreased in Lebanon and Palestine to 15 and 25 per cent, respectively. In the Arab Peninsula, the share of the secondary sector is the highest due to its reliance on oil. Iran had a relatively high share of the secondary sector due to oil, but the share declined over time. Egypt and Turkey had a lower but increasing share of the secondary sector. In North Africa, Libya and Algeria had the highest shares of the secondary sector due to oil and natural gas industries.

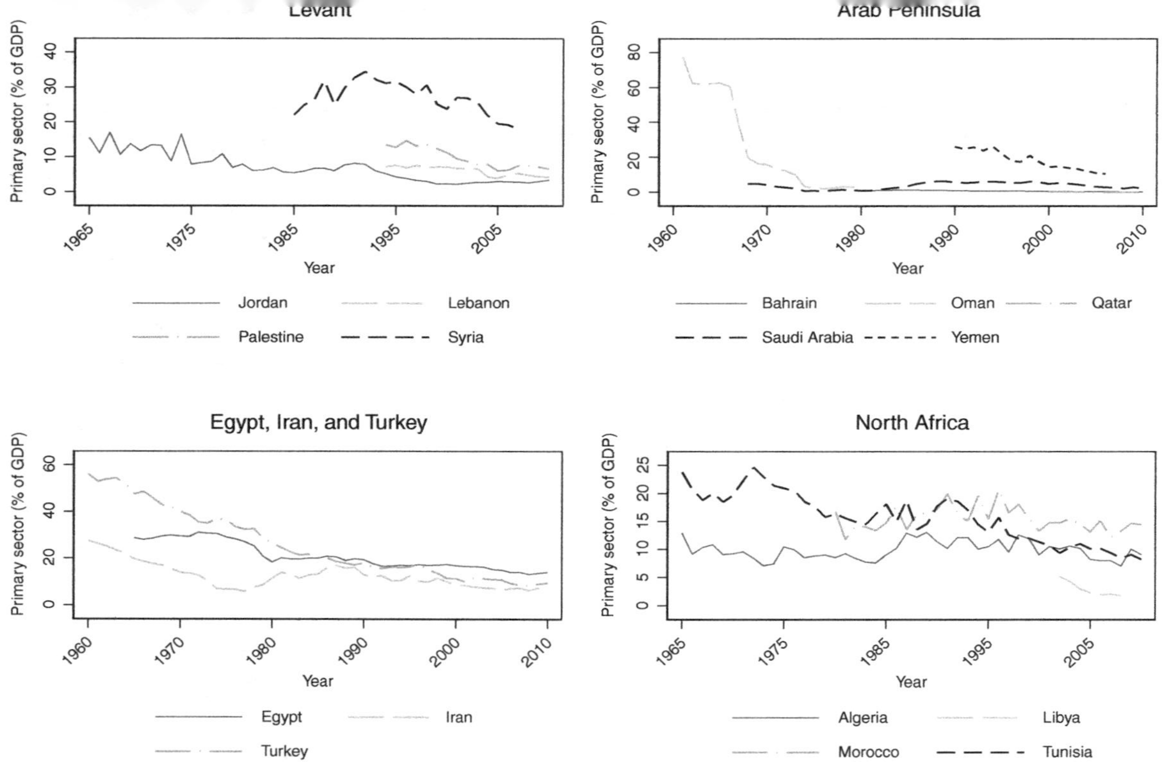

Figure 8.3 Sectoral composition of GDP, 1960–2010. A: Primary sector share of GDP. B: Secondary sector share of GDP. C: Tertiary sector share of GDP
Notes: Primary sector comprises value added in forestry, hunting, and fishing, and cultivation of crops and livestock production. Secondary sector comprises manufacturing, which corresponds to ISIC divisions 15–37, and includes value added in mining, manufacturing (also reported as a separate subgroup), construction, electricity, water, and gas. Tertiary sector comprises services, which correspond to ISIC divisions 50–99, and include value added in wholesale and retail trade (including hotels and restaurants), transport, and government, financial, professional, and personal services, such as education, health care, and real estate services. Also included are imputed bank service charges, import duties, and any statistical discrepancies

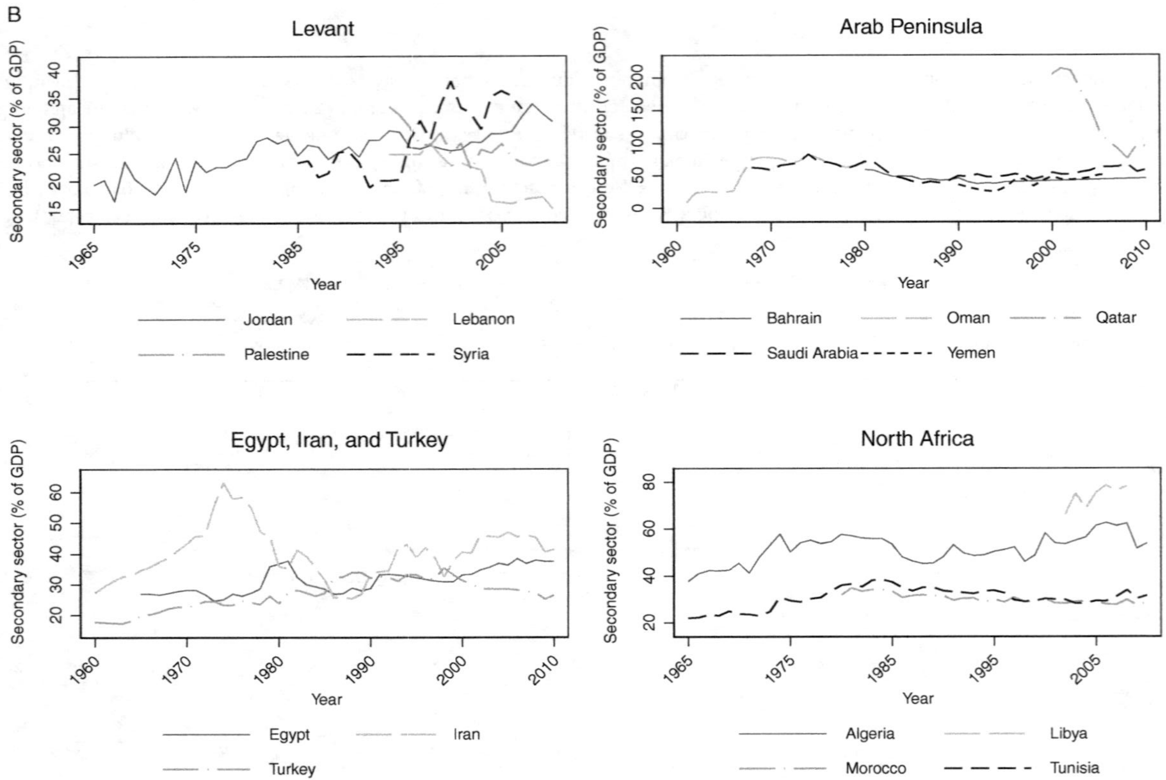

Caption for Figure 8.3 (cont.)

noted by national compilers, as well as discrepancies arising from rescaling. Value added is the net output of a sector after adding up all outputs and subtracting intermediate inputs. It is calculated without making deductions for depreciation of fabricated assets or depletion and degradation of natural resources. The origin of value added is determined by the International Standard Industrial Classification (ISIC), revision 3.
Source: World Bank 2017.

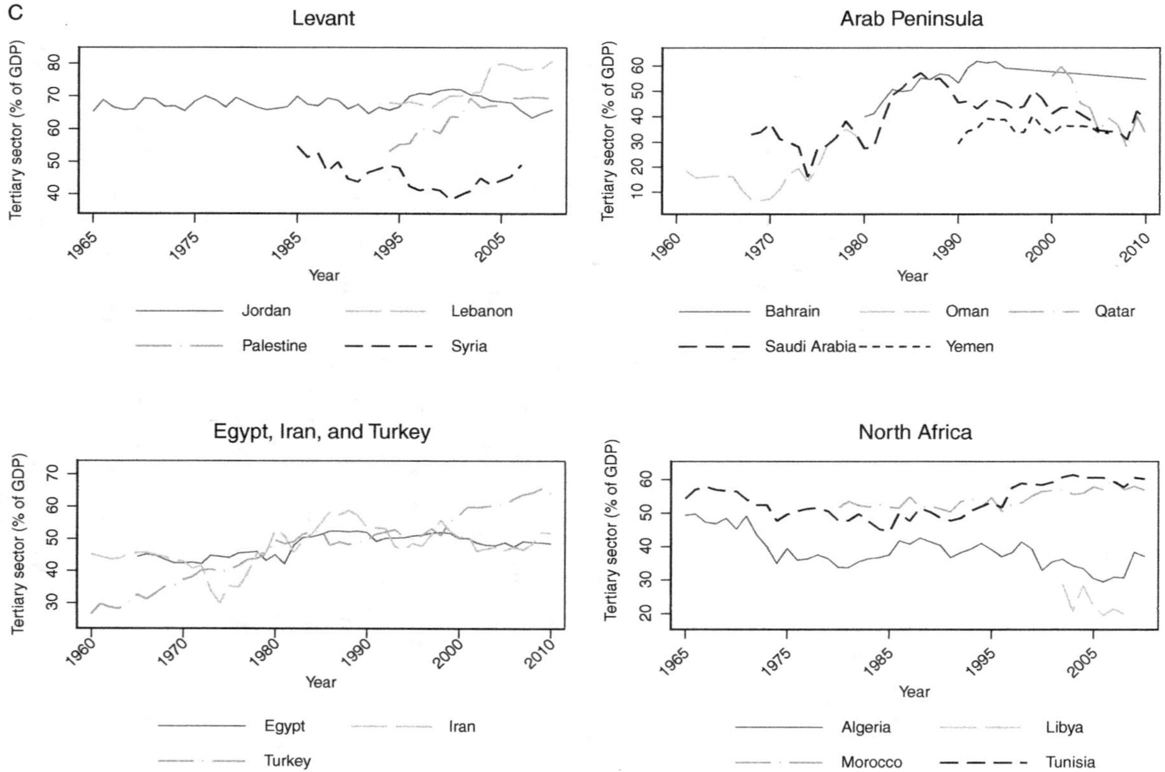

Figure 8.3 (cont.)

Figure 8.3C shows the share of the tertiary sector, which includes services and trade. In the Levant, the share of the tertiary sector is high in Lebanon, Jordan, and Palestine, exceeding 70 per cent of GDP. The share of the tertiary sector in the Arab Peninsula is also sizable, especially in Bahrain, Qatar, and Saudi Arabia. Turkey witnessed a secular increase in the share of the tertiary sector that exceeded 60 per cent by 2010. It also accounts for about 50 per cent of GDP in Egypt and Iran. In North Africa, Tunisia and Morocco have a relatively high share of the tertiary sector, compared to Algeria and Libya, which rely more on oil.

To sum up, while the oil-rich Arab states of the Persian Gulf, Iran, Iraq, Libya, and Algeria have a relatively high share of the secondary sector, the primary sector is significant in Turkey, Syria, Egypt, Morocco, and Tunisia, due to agriculture. 'Tertiarization', or the increase in the share of the tertiary sector, was more pronounced in non-oil-rich countries, such as Jordan, Lebanon, Tunisia, and Morocco. Only Turkey and Israel witnessed successful industrialization.

Summary

One can classify MENA countries into two groups. Group A includes oil-rich countries: Algeria, Iran, Iraq, Libya, and the Arab states of the Persian Gulf (Bahrain, Kuwait, Oman, Qatar, Saudi Arabia, and UAE). Group B includes non-oil-rich countries: Egypt, Israel, Jordan, Lebanon, Morocco, Palestine, Syria, Tunisia, Turkey, and Yemen.

In Group A, the abundance of natural resources has often been blamed for crippling the democratization process of these countries. As the state does not rely on taxation as the main source of its revenue, the masses do not have enough incentive to rebel, thus reducing their bargaining power vis-à-vis the ruling elite, which is a necessary condition to introduce democracy. Furthermore, the richness of the elite due to oil revenues enables it to grant subsidies to the masses to quell rebellion. Consistent with this conjecture, the political systems of all countries in this group are authoritarian: either absolute monarchies (Oman, Qatar, Saudi Arabia, UAE), absolute monarchies with relatively more personal liberties (Bahrain, Kuwait), or presidential dictatorships (Algeria, Iran, Iraq, Libya).

In Group B, the relative scarcity of natural resources and the traditional reliance of most countries in this group on agriculture, imply that social conflict is typically over the control of the coercive power of the (military) state, which enables the confiscation of agricultural land. This social conflict has resulted, more often than not, in military coups, and only exceptionally, in democratic transitions. This pattern has persisted even after the decline of the share of the primary sector. Industrialization succeeded in only two countries in this group: Israel and Turkey. This implied there was no significant capitalist class or 'bourgeoisie' in most countries in Group B. The remaining countries in this group witnessed tertiarization and only limited state industrialization. Private business owners in the tertiary sector continued to rely on the (military) state. In terms of political systems, Group B has more diverse regimes than Group A: two democracies (Israel, Turkey), authoritarian regimes with more personal liberties (Jordan, Lebanon, Morocco), and presidential dictatorships (Egypt, Palestine, Syria, Tunisia, Yemen).

Proximate Sources of Economic Growth

There are two categories of the proximate sources of growth which are impacted by geography and institutions. The first are those that relate to labour, and the second are those that relate to physical capital and technology.

Labour

Economic growth can be partially driven by labour. This can be via an increase in the potential *quantity* of labour, measured by population growth, which is in turn attributable to natural increase (births minus deaths) and/or net immigration. This potential labour force can be employed in production or not, depending on the labour force participation rate and on the employment rate. Besides the increase in the labour force, economic growth can take place due to improvements in the *quality* or productivity of labour, or its stock of human capital, as measured by its educational, occupational, and health attainment. I examine these labour-related drivers of economic growth in the MENA region below.

Population Growth: Natural Increase or Immigration?

Figure 8.4A depicts the long-term trend of population size in MENA. All countries in the region, whether in Group A or Group B, have witnessed rapid population growth since at least 1950. This growth could have been driven by natural growth, the difference between births and deaths, and by (net) immigration. Figures 8.4B and 8.4C depict the crude birth and death rates per 1,000 people since 1950. Most MENA countries had 40–50 births per 1,000 people in 1950–55, which is much higher than the crude death rates (20–30 per 1,000), thus contributing to the rapid population growth starting from

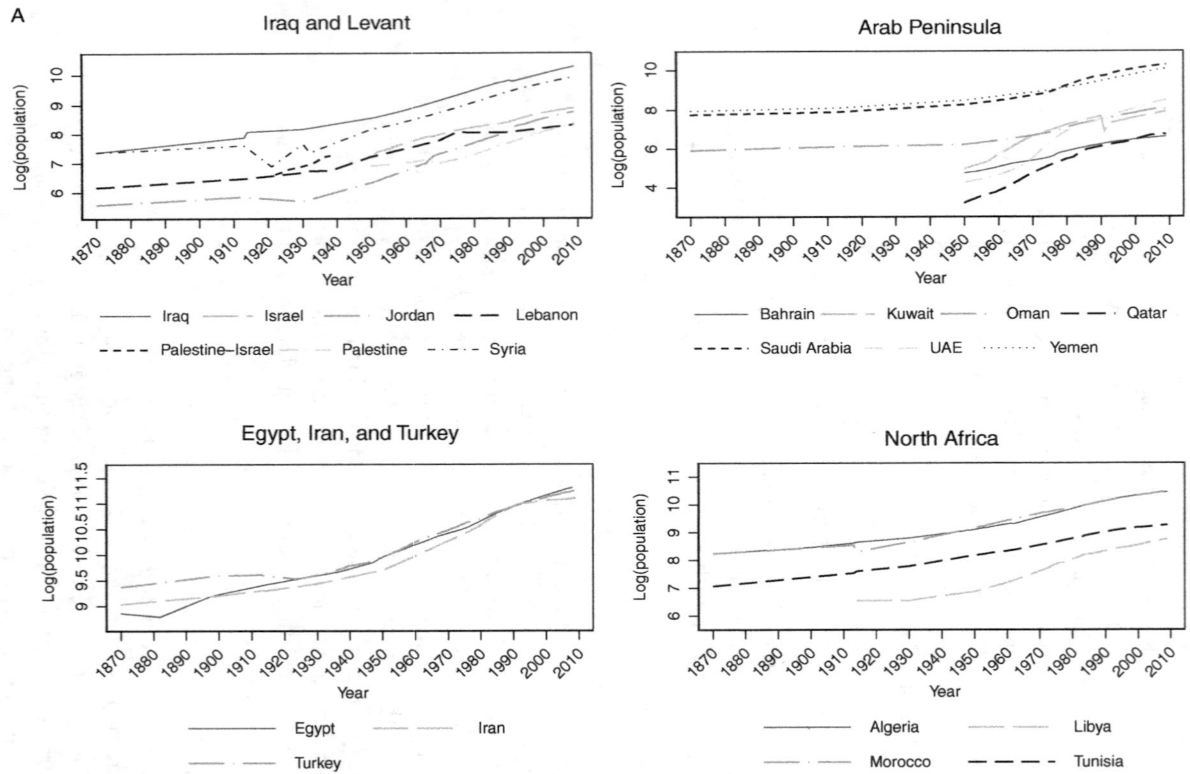

Figure 8.4 Population, births, deaths, and migration, 1870–2010. A: Population, 1870–2010. B: Crude birth rate (per 1,000), 1950–2010. C: Crude death rate (per 1,000), 1950–2010. D: Net migration rate (per 1,000), 1950–2010

Notes: Crude birth/death rate is the number of births/deaths over a given period divided by the person-years lived by the population over that period. It is expressed as an average annual number of births/deaths per 1,000 population.

Sources: Population: Issawi 1982; Hershlag 1997; Maddison Project Database, version 2013. Additional data points for Egypt's population: Egyptian population censuses of 1882, 1897, 1907, 1917, 1927, 1937, 1947. Births, deaths, and migration: United Nations 2015.

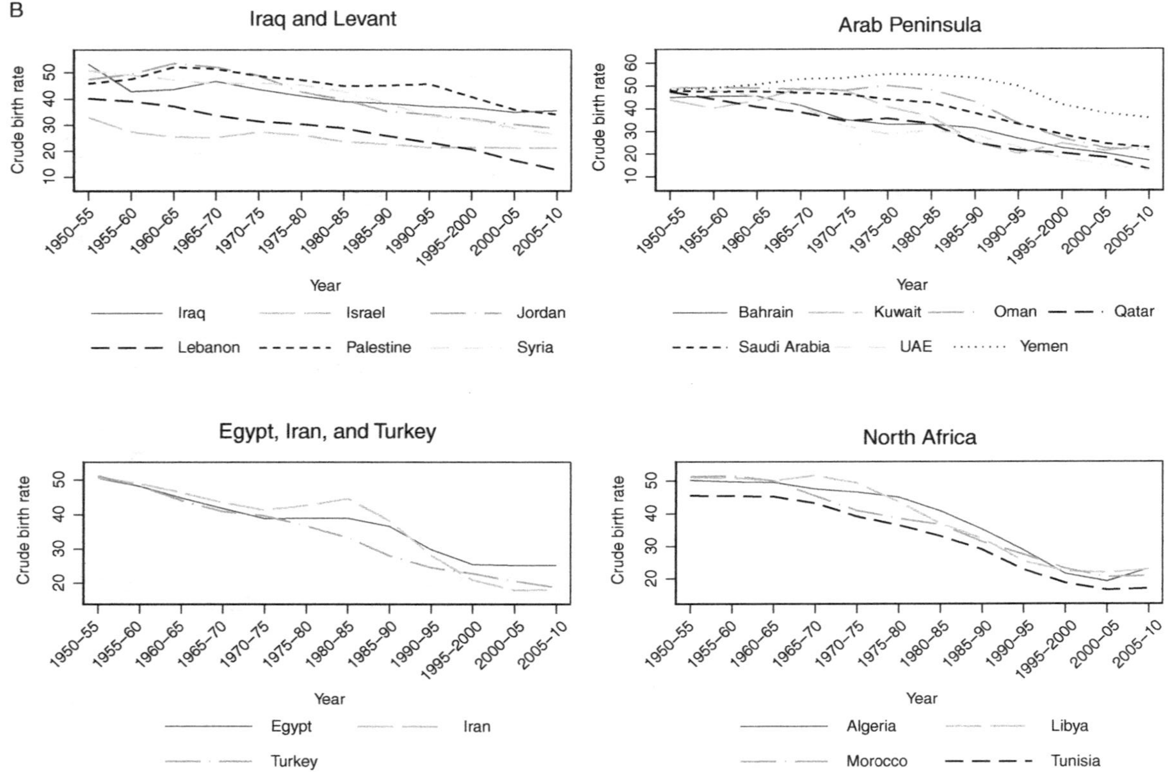

Figure 8.4 (cont.)

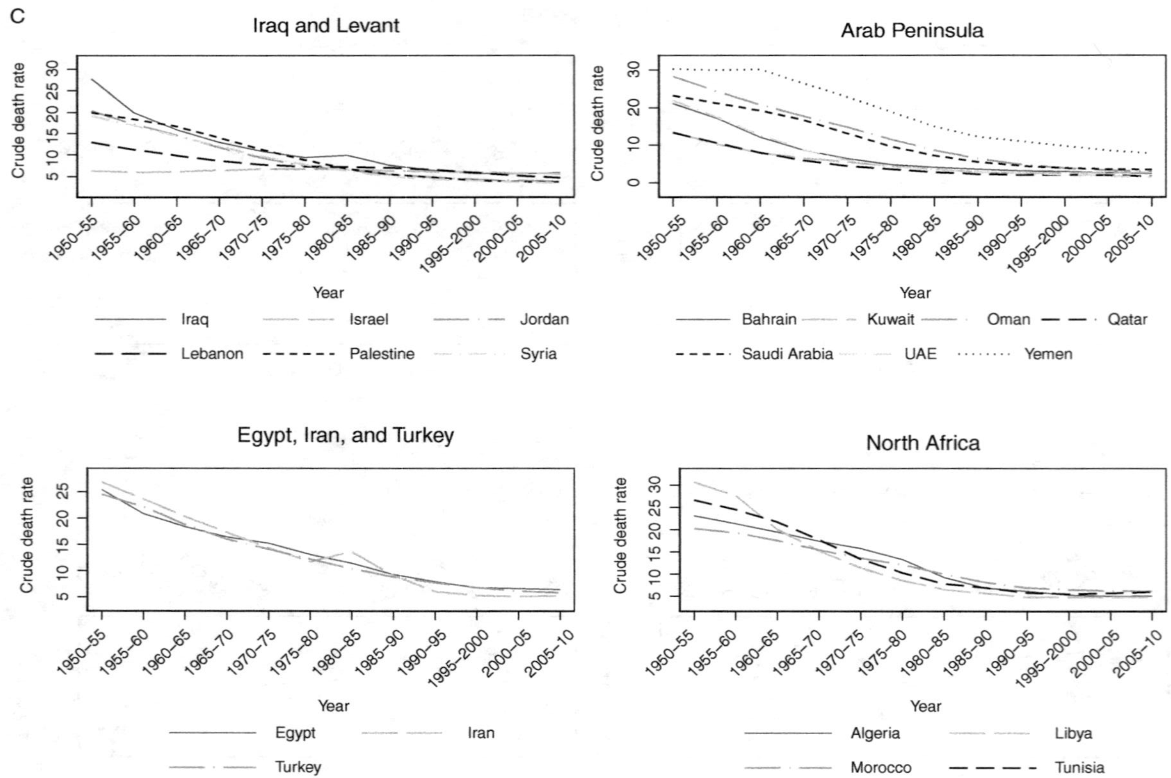

Figure 8.4 (cont.)

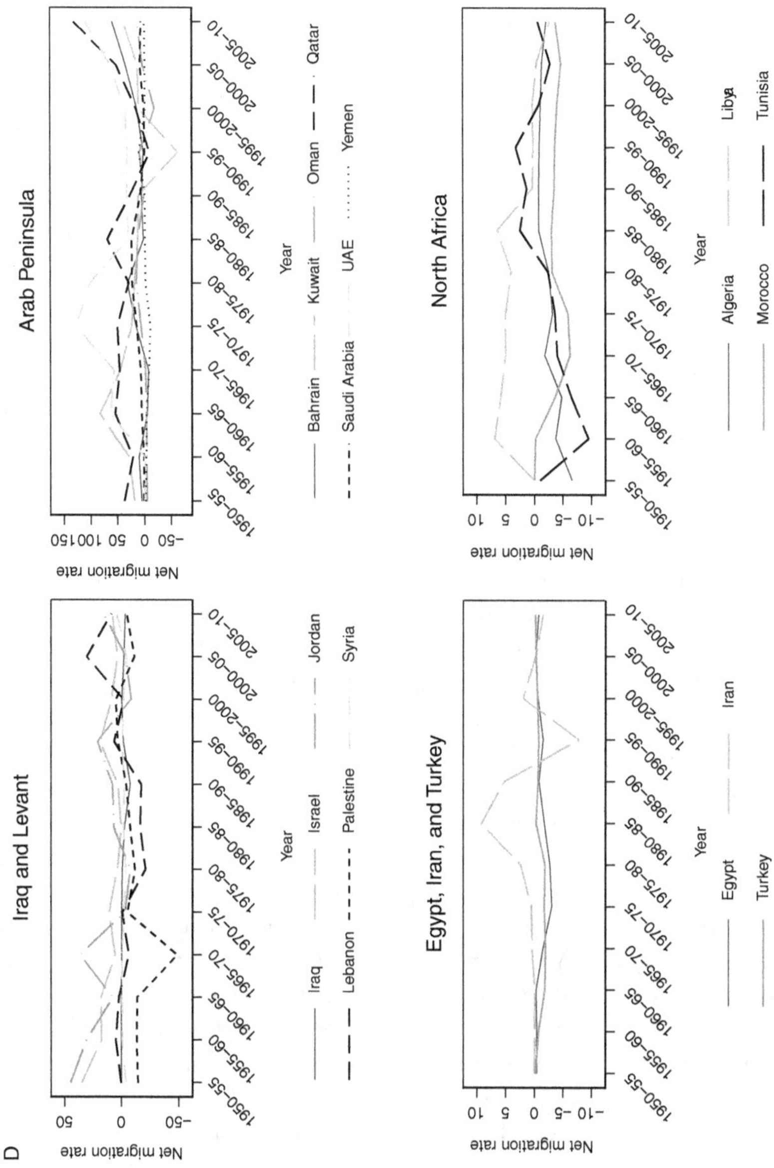

Figure 8.4 (cont.)

the 1950s that we observe in Figure 8.4A. The interesting exceptions here are Israel, where the birth rate was relatively low as of 1950–55, and Lebanon, which had an exceptionally low death rate in 1950–55.[1] This pattern is consistent with the notion that both countries are among the most progressive in the region with respect to health and women's rights. Mortality exhibited a rapid decline in all MENA countries since 1950, reaching a crude death rate below 10 per 1,000 by 2010 (except for Yemen). In the absence of pre-1950 data on crude death rates, it is not possible to date the start of the mortality decline in the MENA region. By contrast, the birth rate started to decline only later, leading to an eventual slowdown in population growth. The lowest birth rates in MENA (slightly more than 10 births per 1,000) in 2005–10 were achieved by Lebanon, UAE, and Qatar. Furthermore, Israel, Bahrain, Kuwait, Oman, Saudi Arabia, Iran, Turkey, Algeria, Libya, Morocco, and Tunisia all reached relatively low birth rates (20–25 births per 1,000) by 2010. However, Iraq, Palestine, Jordan, Syria, and Egypt (all in Group B) still had relatively high birth rates in 2010 (more than 25 births per year).

The decline in birth rates indicates that many countries in the MENA region witnessed a demographic transition – that is, a decline in fertility following the earlier decline in mortality. Examining the total fertility rate (TFR), the number of children ever born per woman (figure not shown) enables me to date the demographic transition. Whereas Lebanon, Iran, UAE, Tunisia, Turkey, Qatar, Bahrain, and Morocco achieved a TFR below 2.5 by 2010, the majority of MENA countries still have relatively high total fertility rates.

Apart from natural population growth, a number of MENA countries witnessed significant emigration and immigration waves that contributed to population growth. Figure 8.4D depicts the net migration rate, the number of immigrants minus the number of emigrants divided by the population. In the Levant, only Israel maintained positive net migration rates in 1950–2010, peaking in 1950–55 and 1990–95, due to continued Jewish immigration to Israel, mostly from Europe. Palestine witnessed consistently negative net migration in 1950–2010, except in 1990–2000, the biggest shock being in 1965–70, due to the 1967 war. Jordan absorbed most of the Palestinian diaspora in 1950–70, especially the two large Palestinian emigration waves in 1948 and 1967. The civil war in Lebanon resulted in a large negative net migration

1 Notably, Oman, Saudi Arabia, and Morocco had relatively low death rates in 1950–55 (~10–15 per 1,000).

shock in 1975–90. Iraq also witnessed negative net migration shocks starting from 1985.

The Arab states of the Persian Gulf in Group A were by far the largest recipients of immigration in the MENA region, which exceeded 10 per cent of the population in UAE and Qatar, although immigration to Saudi Arabia slowed down after 1985. Similarly, Iran witnessed a large positive net migration rate in 1970–90, which, paradoxically, was not reversed during the Iranian Revolution (although it became negative in 1990–95). Libya witnessed large positive net migration rates in 1955–85, but then stopped afterwards.

To sum up, the rapid population growth in MENA countries after 1950 is mostly attributed to natural population increase, except in the Arab states of the Persian Gulf and Libya in Group A, and Jordan and Israel in Group B, which received large immigration waves. Palestine, Lebanon, and Iraq witnessed large emigration shocks due to political instability, but these waves were offset by the high fertility rates in these countries.

Labour Force Participation and Employment

Even if MENA countries witnessed rapid population growth in the second half of the twentieth century, the labour force may not have increased as much due to the non-participation of a significant share of the population in the labour market, especially women. Low rates of female labour participation in the region have been long documented. They are attributable to both (1) the under-enumeration of women's employment in population censuses and household surveys, and (2) institutional and cultural factors that hinder the participation of females in the formal labour market, such as discrimination.

To examine the evolution of labour force participation among males and females, I first employ the World Bank Development Indicators (WDI) for the period 1960–2010. Figure 8.5A shows that the labour force participation rate (LFPR) for males is at least 60 per cent in MENA countries, although there were negative shocks in certain years in Jordan, Egypt, Algeria, and Tunisia. By contrast, females were traditionally much less likely to participate in the labour market in most MENA countries, although they achieved considerable progress in recent years. The paradoxical exception here is Turkey, where the female LFPR was the highest in the MENA region (65 per cent) in 1960, but declined systematically over time. Israel had the second highest female LFPR in 1972 (32 per cent), and improved over time to reach 53 per cent in 2010. However, the largest gains in female LFPR were achieved by the Arab states of the Persian Gulf in Group A: Kuwait, Qatar, UAE, and

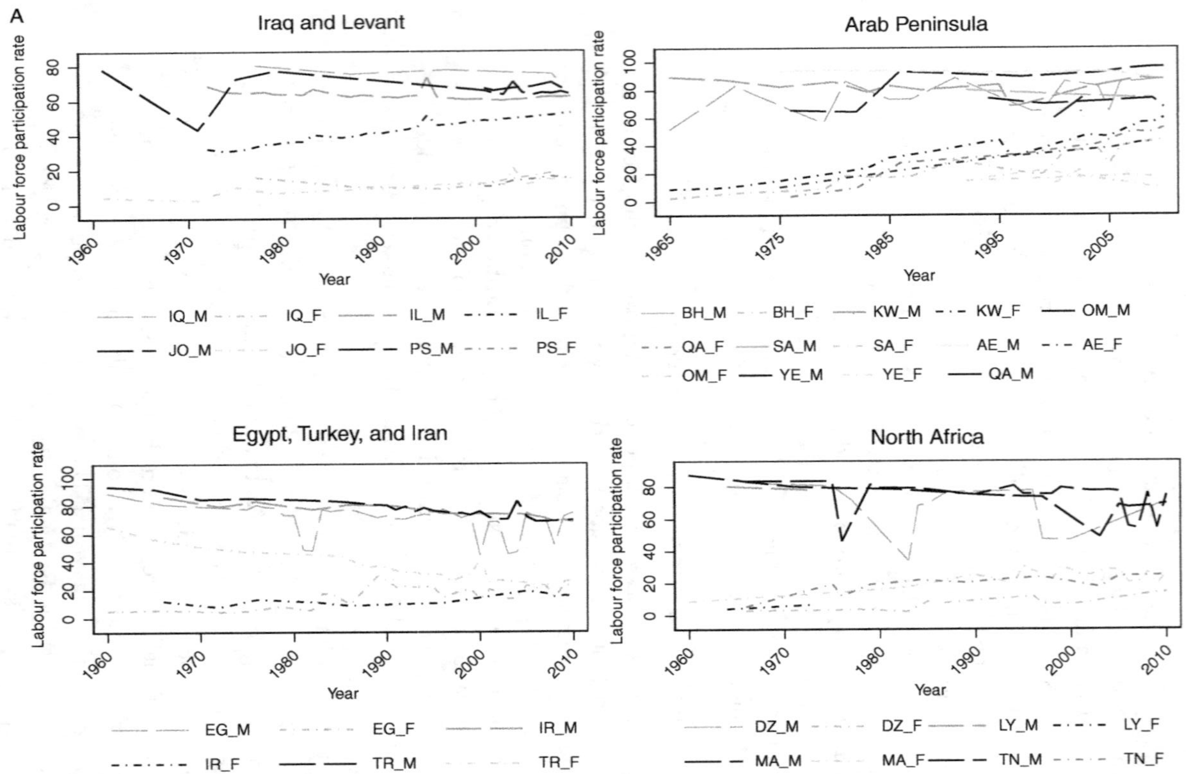

Figure 8.5 Labour force participation rate. A: Labour force participation rate (%), 1960–2010 (ILOSTAT). B: Labour force participation rate (%), by cohort of birth, 1910–70 (IPUMS)

Notes: LFPR is the proportion of the population aged fifteen and older that is economically active (employed + unemployed): all people who supply labour for the production of goods and services. B: Individual-level population census samples of Egypt (1986, 1996, 2006), Iran (2006, 2011), Iraq (1997), Israel (1972, 1983, 1995), Jordan (2004), Morocco (1982, 1994, 2004), Palestine (1972, 2007), and Turkey (1985, 1990, 1994, 2000). Population census samples are pooled for each country and restricted to individuals between thirty and sixty years of age.

Sources: A: World Bank 2017: World Development Indicators; B: Census samples retrieved from Minnesota Population Center 2015.

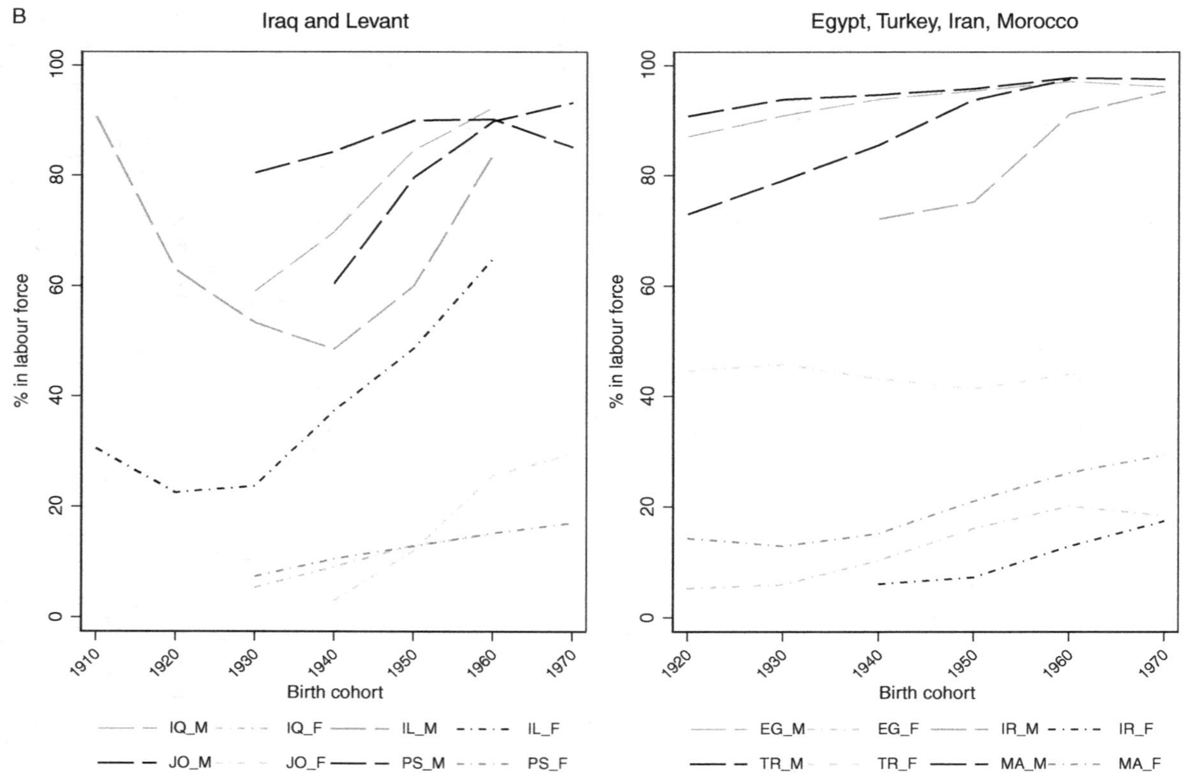

Figure 8.5 (cont.)

Bahrain. Females in Egypt, Tunisia, and Morocco achieved only modest progress.

I augment the analysis of the LFPR by employing the individual-level population census samples that are available on IPUMS-International for Iraq, Israel, Jordan, Palestine, Egypt, Iran, Turkey, and Morocco. I restrict each population census sample to individuals between thirty and sixty years of age (prime working age), in order to isolate secular changes across cohorts from life-cycle changes in labour force participation. I then pool the population census samples for each country and plot the percentage of those who are in the labour force among each of males and females across (decennial) cohorts of birth. Figure 8.5B shows the long-term trend of labour force participation by sex and cohort of birth. While males had close to universal participation in the labour force (at least 80 per cent) in most countries in the sample, female labour force participation was very low. The two exceptions here are Turkey and Israel. The former had a female LFPR around 40 per cent for all cohorts born between 1920 and 1960. The latter had increasing female participation reaching more than 60 per cent for the 1960s cohort. Females in all other countries made little progress, except Jordan. Employment rates (figure not shown) exhibit very similar trends to LFPR, implying that unemployment is not significant within this age group (thirty to sixty years of age).

Human Capital: Educational, Occupational, and Health Outcomes

Did the 'quality' of the labour force, or its stock of human capital, increase in the MENA region? To address this question, I plot in Figure 8.6 the long-term trends of the educational, occupational, and health attainments of labour. Figure 8.6A indicates that the average number of years of schooling has gone up across cohorts of birth in MENA countries, and that female education has converged to that of males, or even exceeded it. Israel has the highest educational attainment in MENA, and female education exceeded that of males by the cohort born in the 1960s. A similar pattern is observed in Jordan, where females also outperformed males in recent cohorts of birth. Palestine presents an interesting case, where females were traditionally better educated than males, and males managed to converge in educational attainment only later on. Iraq witnessed an improvement in male educational attainment up to the 1960s cohort, but then it declined, probably due to the political unrest in the country starting from 1980. Educational attainment of Iraqi females did not converge to that of males. Outside Iraq and the Levant, Iran made the

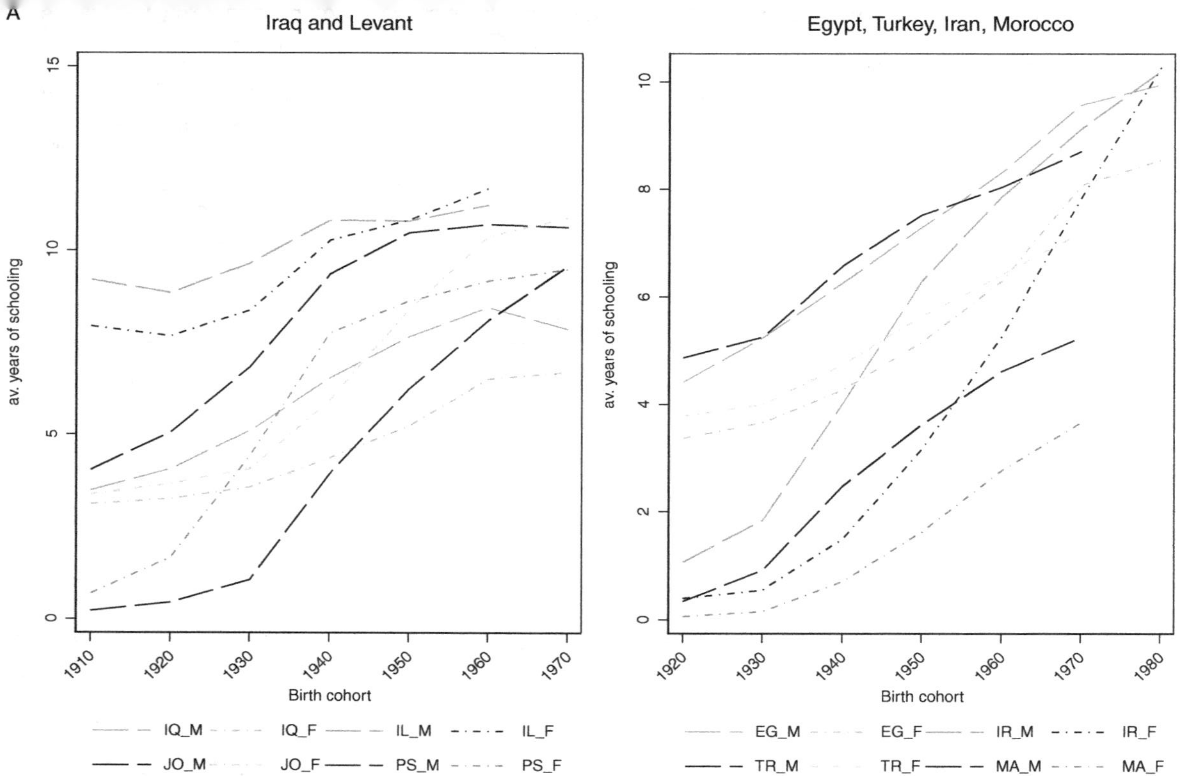

Figure 8.6 Human capital. A: Average years of schooling by cohort of birth, 1910–80. B: Share of white-collar workers (%) by cohort of birth, 1920–70. C: Life expectancy at birth, 1950–2010

Notes: A: The average years of schooling is calculated based on the educational attainment variable: zero years of schooling if no schooling, three years of schooling if less than primary completed, five and six years of schooling if primary (five years) completed and primary (six years) completed, respectively, nine years of schooling if lower secondary general or technical completed, twelve years of schooling if secondary general or technical completed, fourteen years of schooling if some college completed or have post-secondary technical education, and sixteen years of schooling if university completed. B: Occupations are defined according to ISCO88 one-digit classification. White-collar workers are legislators, senior officials,

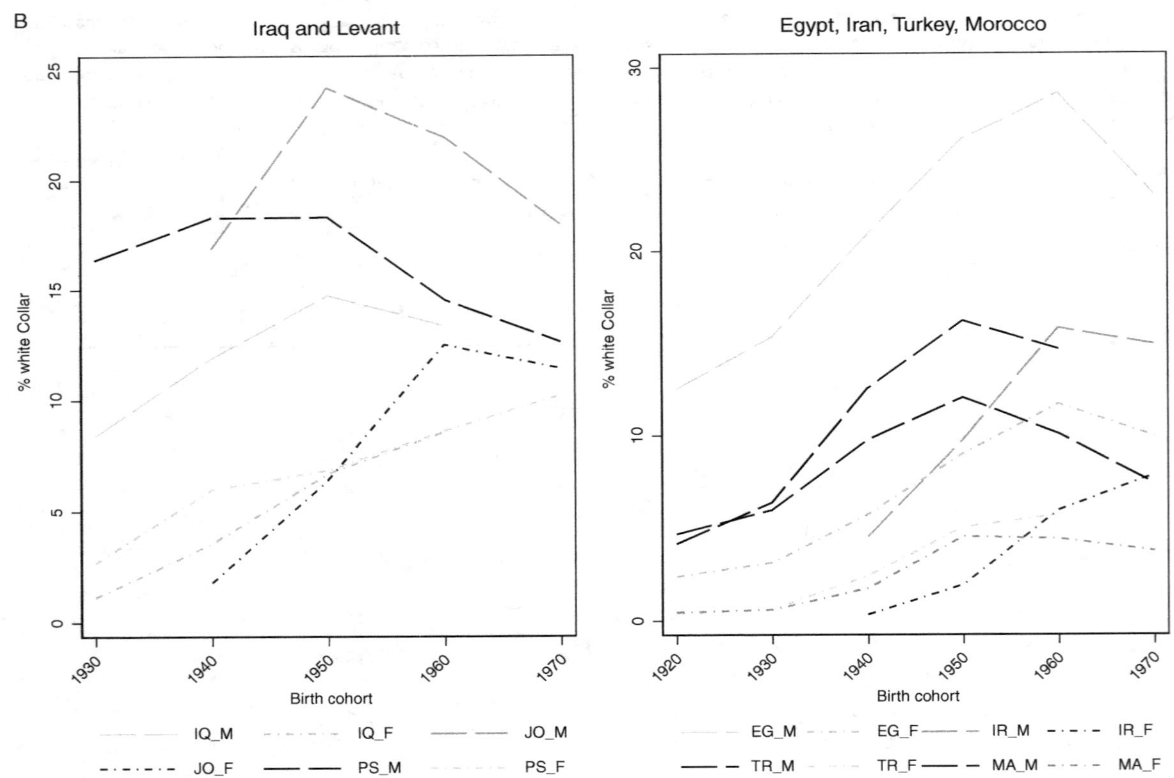

Caption for Figure 8.6 (cont.)

managers, professionals, technicians and associate professionals, and clerks. C: Life expectancy at birth is the average number of years of life expected by a hypothetical cohort of individuals who would be subject during all their lives to the mortality rates of a given period.

A and B: Individual-level population census samples of Palestine (1972, 2007), Iran (2006, 2011), Iraq (1997), Israel (1972, 1983, 1995), Jordan (2004), Morocco (1982, 1994, 2004), Turkey (1985, 1990, 1994, 2000), and Egypt (1986, 1996, 2006). Population census samples are pooled for each country and restricted to individuals between twenty-five and sixty years of age in A and between thirty and sixty in B.

Sources: A and B: Census samples retrieved from Minnesota Population Center 2015; C: United Nations 2015.

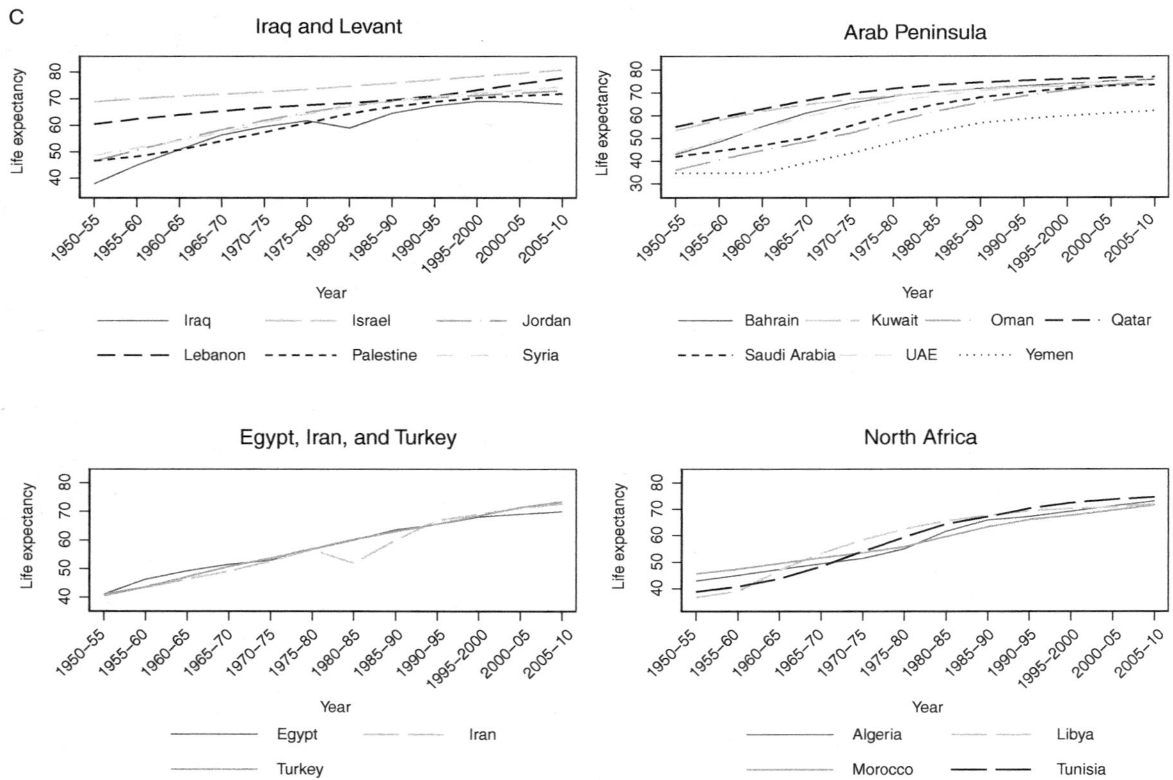

Figure 8.6 (cont.)

most significant improvement in educational attainment for both males and females, achieving complete convergence by the cohort born in the 1980s. Both Turkey's and Egypt's educational attainment increased significantly over time, but the male–female educational gap persisted. Morocco's male and female educational attainment improved over time, but remained lower than other countries in the group, and also did not achieve gender equality in educational attainment.

Figure 8.6B shows the long-term trend of occupational attainment across cohorts measured by the percentage of white-collar workers among employed individuals. An interesting pattern emerges: while the share of white-collar workers increased up to the 1960 cohort, it declined in younger cohorts. Jordan had the highest share of white-collar workers, although it declined among males starting from the cohort born in 1960, and among females starting from the cohort born in 1970. Palestinian females increased their share of white-collar workers, while males witnessed a decline in the share of white-collar workers starting from the 1960 cohort. Similarly, Iraqi males witnessed a decline in the share of white-collar workers starting from the 1960 cohort, although Iraqi females improved their share. Egypt had the highest share of white-collar workers among employed males, reaching 30 per cent in the 1960 cohort, although it started to decline afterwards. Egyptian female occupational attainment improved as well, although it also declined after the 1960 cohort. In Iran, Turkey, and Morocco, male occupational attainment also improved and then declined. Female occupational attainment improved as well, although the male–female occupational gap persisted.

Finally, Figure 8.6C shows the long-term trend of health attainment as measured by life expectancy at birth. All MENA countries witnessed a secular improvement in health conditions, where life expectancy at birth almost doubled in most MENA countries between 1950 and 2010.

To sum up our findings so far, although educational attainment improved in most MENA countries across cohorts, occupational attainment improved up to a certain cohort and then declined. Furthermore, while the gender educational gap disappeared in many countries, the occupational gap (among employed individuals) was more likely to persist. There are two explanations for these findings. First, the secular improvement in occupational attainment up to the 1960 cohort was perhaps driven by the expansion of government size in the postcolonial period. Newly founded bureaucracies, public schools that provided education to the masses, and public hospitals that provided health services, all needed to recruit teachers, physicians, and accountants, hence the improvement in occupational attainment that is observed across cohorts up to the 1960 birth cohort. This process was often formalized by issuing employment guarantees in the government and public sector for secondary school and university graduates. However, the resulting over-employment in government led to a reduction in size after a certain point, hence triggering the decline in occupational attainment. Second, while female educational attainment increased, it was less likely to translate into better labour market outcomes; female labour participation increased but remained modest, and the gender occupational gap persisted. This suggests that female education was aiming at non-labour market outcomes more than labour outcomes, such as finding a better match in the marriage market.

Physical Capital and Technology

Data constraints mean that it is not possible to disentangle the contribution of physical capital in driving economic growth in the MENA region. But to have an idea about its potential contribution, I employ the share of fixed capital formation in GDP as a proxy for changes in physical capital in Figure 8.7A. Gross capital formation consists of 'outlays on additions to the fixed assets of the economy plus net changes in the level of inventories'.[2] Investment in fixed assets and infrastructure in the MENA region was mostly state-led and partially driven by state revenues from natural resources. It often occurred after civil and foreign wars due to reconstruction efforts. In the Levant, the share of gross capital formation in GDP fluctuated between 20 and 40 per cent. It peaked in Israel and Syria in the 1970s, in Jordan in the 1980s, and in Lebanon in the 1990s (in the aftermath of the civil war). In the Arab Peninsula, the share of gross capital formation in GDP has been lower, fluctuating between 10 and 30 per cent. It increased in most Gulf states (Oman, Bahrain, Kuwait, and Saudi Arabia) in the 1970s and 1980s, in the aftermath of the oil crisis, and in Kuwait in the 1990s following the Gulf War. Iran had a systematically higher gross capital formation rate than Egypt and Turkey, although gross capital formation in the latter countries increased in the 1980s. In North Africa, Algeria, Morocco, and Tunisia had gross capital formation

2 According to the World Bank, 'fixed assets include land improvements (fences, ditches, drains, and so on); plant, machinery, and equipment purchases; and the construction of roads, railways, and the like, including schools, offices, hospitals, private residential dwellings, and commercial and industrial buildings. Inventories are stocks of goods held by firms to meet temporary or unexpected fluctuations in production or sales, and work in progress'.

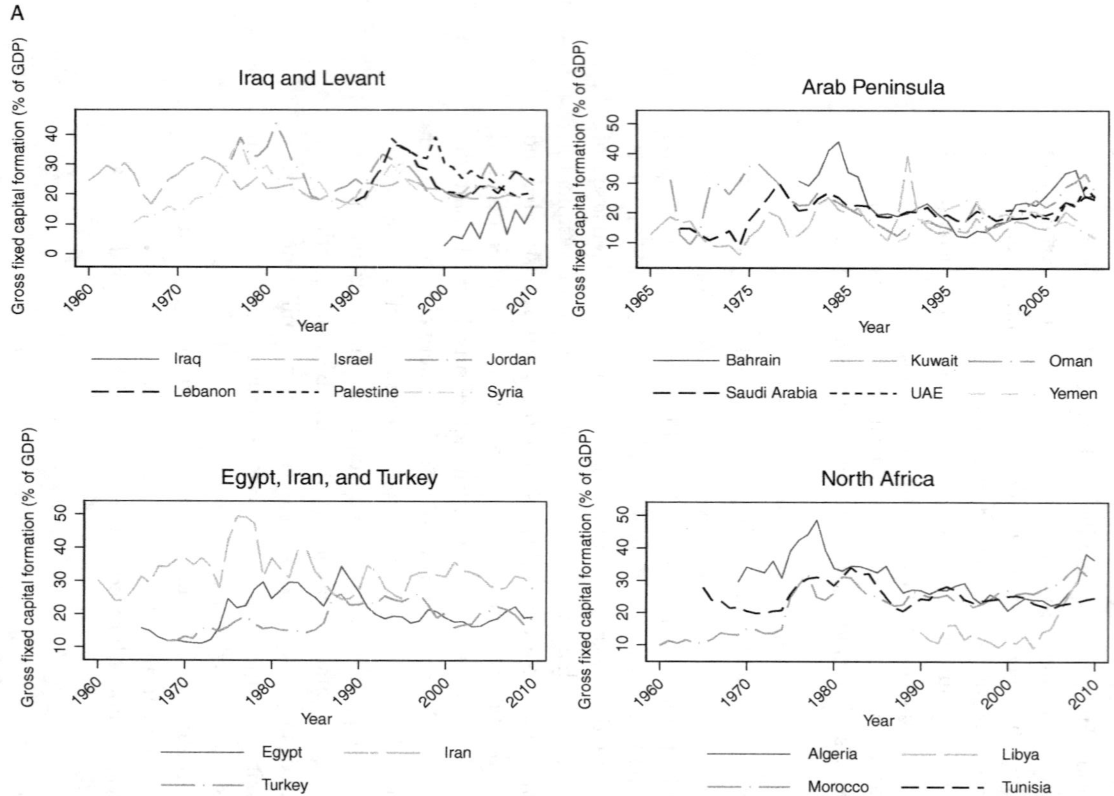

Figure 8.7 Physical capital and technology. A: Gross fixed capital formation, 1960–2010. B: High-technology exports (% of manufactured exports), 1988–2010 Notes: Gross fixed capital formation includes land improvements (fences, ditches, drains, and so on); plant, machinery, and equipment purchases; and the construction of roads, railways, and the like, including schools, offices, hospitals, private residential dwellings, and commercial and industrial buildings. According to the 1993 UN Statistics Division System of National Accounts, net acquisitions of valuables are also considered capital formation. High-technology exports are products with high R&D intensity, such as in aerospace, computers, pharmaceuticals, scientific instruments, and electrical machinery.

Sources: A: World Bank 2020; B: World Bank 2017.

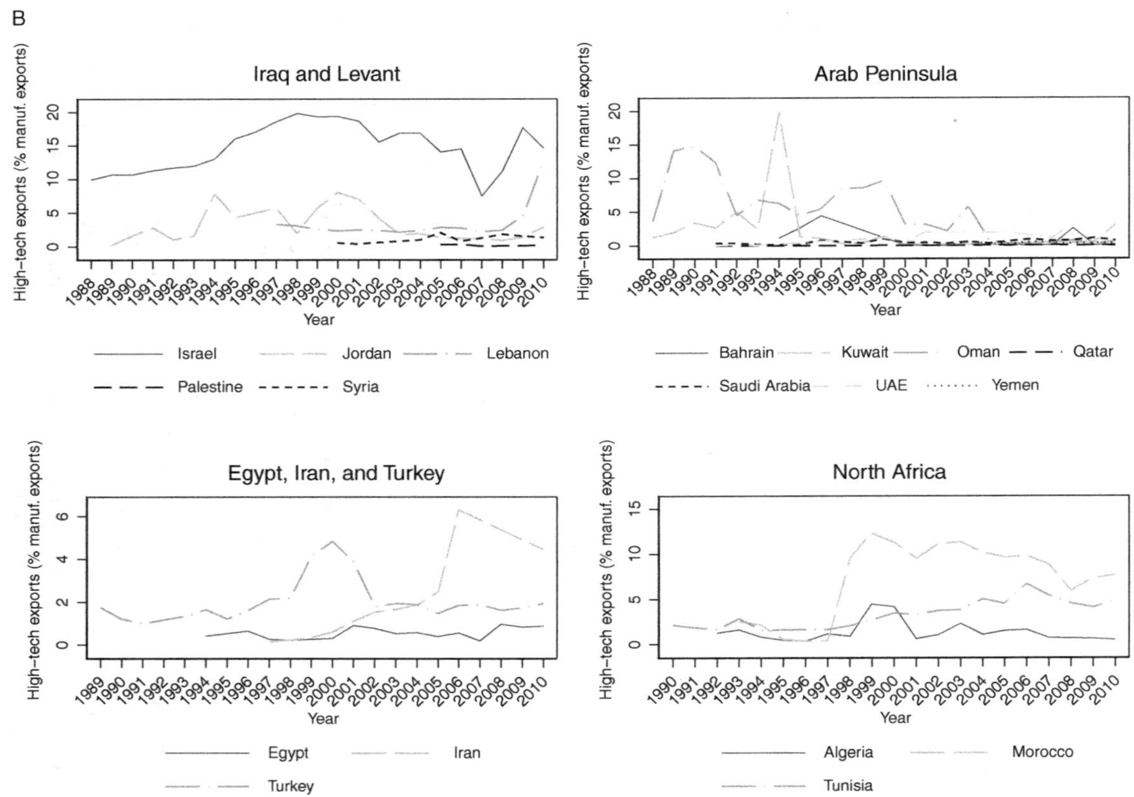

Figure 8.7 (cont.)

rates between 20 and 30 per cent of GDP, whereas oil-rich Libya had very low gross capital formation rates that only increased in the 2000s.

How much did technology contribute to real GDP per capita growth? The share of high-technology exports out of manufactured exports sheds some light on this question. Figure 8.7B plots the long-term trend of this variable over time. In the Levant, only Israel had a relatively high share of high-tech exports, at 15–20 per cent. Lebanon had a high share of high-tech exports in 2009–10. Jordan's share of high-tech exports was about 8 per cent in 2000, but declined afterwards to less than 5 per cent. Both Palestine and Syria had negligible shares of high-tech exports (less than 5 per cent). In the Arab Peninsula, only Oman had a relatively high share of high-tech exports, which reached 15 per cent in 1989, but declined afterwards. Egypt, Iran, and Turkey all had low shares of high-tech exports. In North Africa, only Morocco had a relatively high share of high-tech exports (more than 10 per cent), but it also declined in recent years.

To conclude, physical capital and technical progress played less of a role in driving economic growth in MENA countries. The main exception here is Israel, and to a lesser extent, Oman, Morocco, Jordan, and Lebanon, which all made some progress in this regard.

Conclusion

This chapter highlights some major empirical facts about the pattern and sources of economic growth in the MENA region between 1870 and 2010. Some are probably old facts, while others are new and interesting. Consistent with what we know from Pamuk (2006), oil-rich MENA countries (Arab states of the Persian Gulf, Algeria, Iran, Iraq, Libya) did not exhibit a steady growth trajectory, due to the sensitivity of their economies to oil prices. By contrast, the non-oil-rich countries (Egypt, Israel, Jordan, Lebanon, Morocco, Palestine, Syria, Tunisia, Turkey, Yemen) had more stable growth trajectories, albeit with varying degrees of success. Another major source of economic instability in the region is the political turmoil due to civil and foreign wars, which hit Algeria, Iran, Iraq, Lebanon, Libya, and Palestine. The post-2010 democratic uprisings in the Levant and North Africa, and the consequent devastating civil wars that hit Libya, Syria, and Yemen, certainly added to the economic instability of MENA countries.

While this narrative suggests that geography and, in particular, the abundance of natural resources, largely shaped the growth trajectories of MENA countries, institutions played an important role too, although some may argue that these were themselves an outcome of geography. Oil-rich countries are in general authoritarian because the elites use oil revenues to avoid mass rebellion. Non-oil-rich countries, on the other hand, are more diverse, but the lack of a bourgeoisie, except in Israel and Turkey, arguably hindered democratization in these countries too in the postcolonial period. Tertiarization did not change the power balance between society and the state. The result of all this was the persistence of the coercive political and labour colonial institutions that in some cases were inherited from their Ottoman predecessors in the precolonial period and that continue to serve elite interests.

Geography and institutions affected labour, physical capital, and technical progress, the proximate sources of growth. Population grew rapidly in MENA countries mainly due to natural growth, but migration had its effects, especially in oil-rich countries (immigration) and during episodes of political turmoil (emigration). Human capital increased in terms of educational, occupational, and health attainments, although part of this improvement was mechanical due to the policies of public mass education and guaranteed employment in the government and public sectors, which were adopted by the postcolonial military regimes. Investment in physical capital played a role in economic growth in war-struck countries and in oil-rich countries. Technical progress was minimal in most MENA countries, except in Israel and a few others.

The chapter leaves open a lot to future researchers. The economic history of the MENA region requires a novel narrative that focuses on the living conditions of the local populations and that gives equal voice to all MENA peoples. This narrative should depart from the traditional nationalist-colonial dichotomy. The persistence of MENA's coercive institutions should be documented objectively, regardless of the identity of the ruling elite, whether it is the Ottoman Empire, the colonial administration, or the postcolonial military states, and whether it is foreign or local. This new narrative is possible. It can be built, not only on the colonial sources as has been traditionally the case, but more importantly on the various novel data sources, such as population censuses and cadastral surveys, which are preserved at the local archives of MENA countries, and that were either digitized or await digitization. These underused local archival sources can arguably reshape our understanding of the economic history of the region. Instead of focusing solely on the macro-level and institutional questions, which have inspired the current literature and that continue to inspire scholars today, the novel micro-level large-scale data sources, coupled with rigorous econometric techniques and in-depth historical analysis, can reshape our understanding of these big-picture questions that still occupy MENA scholars.

References

Alvaredo, F., Assouad, L., and Piketty, T. (2019). 'Measuring Inequality in the Middle East 1990–2016: The World's Most Unequal Region?', *Review of Income and Wealth*, 65(4), 685–711.

Hershlag, Z. Y. (1997). *Introduction to the Modern Economic History of the Middle East*, Leiden: Brill Academic Publishing.

Issawi, C. (1982). *An Economic History of the Middle East and North Africa*, New York: Columbia University Press.

Kuran, T. (2012). *The Long Divergence: How Islamic Law Held Back the Middle East*, Princeton University Press.

Maddison Project Database, version 2013. Bolt, J. and van Zanden, J. L. (2014). 'The Maddison Project: Collaborative Research on Historical National Accounts', *Economic History Review*, 67, 627–651.

Marshall, M., Gurr, T., and Jaggers, K. (2016). 'Polity IV Project: Political Regime Characteristics and Transitions, 1800–2013', available online at www.systemicpeace.org/polity/polity4.htm (accessed 29 September 2020).

Minnesota Population Center. (2015). Integrated Public Use Microdata Series, International: Version 6.4 [data set]. Minneapolis: University of Minnesota.

Owen, E. R. J., Owen, R., and Pamuk, Ş. (1998). *A History of Middle East Economies in the Twentieth Century*, Cambridge, MA: Harvard University Press.

Owen, R. (2002). *The Middle East in the World Economy, 1800–1914*, London and New York: I. B. Tauris.

Pamuk, Ş. (2006). 'Estimating Economic Growth in the Middle East since 1820', *Journal of Economic History*, 66(3), 809–828.

United Nations. (2015). *World Population Prospects: The 2015 Revision*, Department of Economic and Social Affairs, Population Division, available online at https://population.un.org/wpp/ (data accessed 20 June 2017).

World Bank. (2017). World Development Indicators, based on International Labour Organization, ILOSTAT database, available online at https://databank.worldbank.org/source/world-development-indicators (data accessed 20 June 2017).

(2020). World Development Indicators (national accounts data and OECD National Accounts data), available online at https://datacatalog.worldbank.org/dataset/world-development-indicators (accessed 29 September 2020).

Yousef, T. M. (2002). 'Egypt's Growth Performance Under Economic Liberalism: A Reassessment with New GDP Estimates, 1886–1945', *Review of Income and Wealth*, 48(4), 561–579.

9

Latin America

Stalled Catching Up

PABLO ASTORGA AND ALFONSO HERRANZ-LONCÁN

Introduction

Latin America made considerable progress in living standards between 1870 and 2010 amid rapid modernization and structural change. The average income in a representative sample of countries, including Argentina, Brazil, Chile, Colombia, Mexico, Uruguay, and Venezuela (LA-7), around 2010 is estimated to be more than 775 per cent higher than in 1870; while the average life expectancy at birth rose from thirty-three years in 1900 to seventy-six years in 2010; and the average literacy rate went from 33 per cent of the population in 1900 to about 95 per cent by the start of this century (MOxLAD). However, despite these remarkable advances, the gap in income per capita between the region and the industrial leaders has widened, increasing, for instance, in the case of the US, from 57 per cent in 1870 to 69 per cent in 2010. The reasons for this are still the subject of heated debate. This chapter assesses the long-term performance of Latin America relative to the developed world in order to identify secular changes in the process of convergence. It also discusses the key transformations in Latin America during the period and developments in the proximate sources of economic growth.

We follow the tradition of economic historians of the region (Thorp 1998; Bértola and Ocampo 2012; Bulmer-Thomas 2013) and adopt a periodization based on three historical epochs: 1870–1929, covering the age of export-led growth to 1914 plus the transition years up to the Great Depression; 1929–79, including state-led industrialization; 1980 onwards, with the debt crisis and the second globalization. This division is also supported by coinciding turning points in the proximate forces of growth and the timing of structural change and the demographic transition (Astorga et al. 2005; 2011).

We are grateful to Leandro Prados de la Escosura for sharing his relative income data set, and to Leticia Arroyo Abad for sharing her wage data for the nineteenth century.

One salient feature of Latin American development is the coincidence in the periodization of the cycles of international integration, the processes of industrialization (capital accumulation) and internal migration (hand in hand with urbanization), and the pace of human capital formation. Broadly speaking, the first period is one dominated by relatively open economies to international trade and factors movements, with export sectors based on primary products and relatively rural populations – growing at moderate rates – with limited educational coverage. The second period is characterized by closed economies embarking on an industrialization effort led by the state, high population growth in increasingly urban societies, and important strides in education coverage. The third period is defined by lower barriers to trade and capital, now in more diversified economies, although many of them still dependent on commodity exports, and largely urban societies experiencing a reduction in population growth rates.

In the next section, we review the record of Latin American catching up – or lagging behind – with the rich economies since 1870. Then, we provide a summary description of developments in the region that underpinned the comparative growth outcome. The final section concludes.

Catching Up Revisited

Diminishing marginal returns to capital and advantages of backwardness are two strong arguments for expecting catching up in GDP per head. In the first case, the more capital per worker is accumulated, the smaller are its returns and the advances in income per capita. Therefore, economies with lower levels of capital per worker have the potential to grow faster than more capital-intensive ones. In the second case, the further away an economy is from the technological frontier, the greater the impact of technical progress made possible from the diffusion of knowledge from the leading economies to the more backward ones. However, income convergence and catching up with the leaders is far from guaranteed, as there are also factors, such as increasing returns to scale, disparities in human capital formation, and barriers to technology transmission, that can support divergence. Differences in institutions are equally likely to result in disparity in prosperity across countries, with the lingering effects of extractive institutions being a major obstacle for economic growth and advances in living standards. As a consequence, throughout history convergence has been the exception rather than the rule (Rodrik 2014).

The commonly used metrics in empirical studies on growth convergence are GDP per capita and GDP per worker (or labour productivity). In the long-run quantitative literature in the region, the former is the focus of attention in Astorga et al. (2005), whereas Prados de la Escosura (2007) considers both metrics. However, there are also good reasons to pay attention to real wages, as they are a better measure of the welfare of ordinary workers, which constitute the vast majority of the population (Bértola et al. 1999; Williamson 1999; Astorga 2017). Comparisons made with these three measures allow for a more nuanced account of convergence. First, by including the impact of the demographic transition, which may explain differences between convergence in GDP per capita versus GDP per worker. And, second, by capturing distributional dynamics, which may result in a different evolution of GDP per worker and real wages. A relatively late demographic transition and high levels of income inequality are two defining features of the process of economic development in Latin America that must be accounted for when explaining the region's convergence record. Moreover, the region's long-term performance has been characterized by excess volatility in GDP, largely associated with recurrent external debt and currency crises. These were at the root of political instability and inflationary episodes, the impact of which also undermined the region's potential for catching up (Bértola and Ocampo 2012).

In order to cover the whole time frame with a consistent group of countries, this section focuses on LA-7, or on LA-6 (which excludes Uruguay). LA-7 accounted regularly for about three-quarters of Latin America's population and GDP during the period. Therefore, when discussing developments over the whole period we rely on the average behaviour of this group as a proxy for the region as a whole.[1]

Historically, Latin Americans have tended to compare their living standards with those of the US. But this comparison is the most demanding, as even western European economies fell behind the US during the second half of the nineteenth century. Also, Southern Europe has been a traditional basis for comparisons with Latin America. In this review of the evidence, we use three yardsticks to assess the region's relative performance: US (the industrial leader after 1900), UK (the industrial leader before 1900) and Spain (the colonial master and a late converging economy). Concentrating on

1 For comparisons with a larger number of Latin American and OECD countries, see Prados de la Escosura 2007. On average, countries not included in LA-7 were poorer than those in the sample. Thus, as shown in Figure 9.1 below, our indicators provide an upper bound of the full regional average.

a selected number of representative countries in both Latin America and the developed world allows us to provide a richer coverage of the metrics of interest in a consistent way over the whole period.

GDP Per Capita

Figure 9.1 (chart on left) presents the relative performance in GDP per capita of LA-7 versus the US. Overall, the ratio fluctuates around a secular divergence trend. It falls from 0.43 in 1870 (an income gap of 57 per cent) to 0.31 (69 per cent) in 2010. The best years for catching up were the last three decades of the nineteenth century and the late 1920s and early 1930s. The latter was a one-off gain, largely reflecting the fact that the Great Depression was felt more strongly in the US. From 1945 onwards, the Latin American coverage can be extended to twenty countries (LA-20). The comparison based on this wider aggregate results in a significantly lower ratio (an average of 0.24 between 1950 and 1982, compared to 0.36 in LA-7), but with a similar trend. The third period was particularly bad for the region's relative performance, despite a recovery in the 2000s driven by a China-led commodity boom.

However, if the comparators are taken from Europe (Figure 9.1, chart on right), the LA-7 performance is cast in a more positive light. Between 1870 and 1929, LA-7 managed to reduce the gap with the UK from a ratio of 0.33 (a 67 per cent gap) to one of 0.48 (52 per cent). Then, they experienced a moderate divergent trend up to *c.*1980, which was followed by two decades with a rapid widening of the income gap, as Latin America was hit by the debt crisis. In the case of Spain, there was a rapid catching up from the 1930s to the 1950s, thanks to high economic growth in LA-7 and war, autarky, and stagnation in Spain. But this episode came to an end in the early 1960s, when Spain started to converge with the more advanced northern European economies.

The LA-7 average in Figure 9.1 ignores important differences in country performance. As shown in Table 9.1, the group's rather disappointing convergence outcome during most of the twentieth century with the US is partly explained by the unfulfilled promise of Argentina and, to a lesser extent, Uruguay. Both were strong candidates for catching up at the turn of the nineteenth century, but started a rapid relative decline after 1940. A contrasting image is given by Venezuela, with a modest record up to the mid-1920s, followed by a sustained catching up driven by oil richness, which came to an end with the debt crisis of the 1980s. The largest dispersion within the group was in the years prior to the outbreak of World War I, as Argentina was pulling away from the group; whereas the highest convergence was

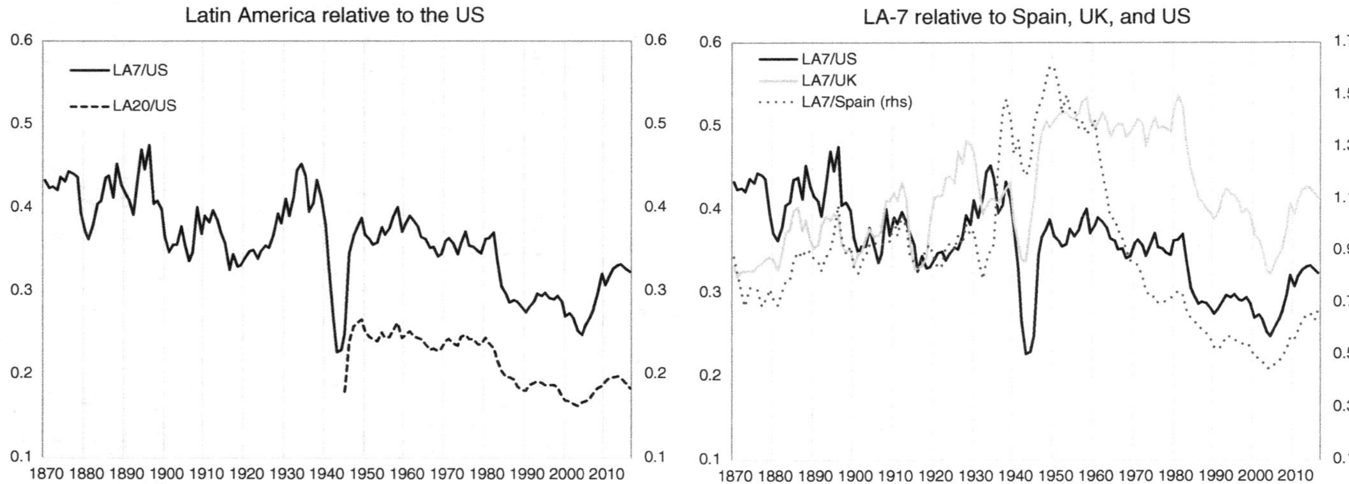

Figure 9.1 Catching up in GDP per capita
Sources: Spain, UK, and US: Maddison Project Database, version 2013; LA-7 and LA-20: MOxLAD (simple averages in both cases).

Table 9.1 GDP per capita relative to the US, by country

	1870	1900	1910	1940	1980	1990	2010
Argentina	0.60	0.74	0.78	0.66	0.44	0.29	0.37
Brazil	0.28	0.14	0.14	0.18	0.26	0.22	0.21
Chile	0.50	0.50	0.54	0.49	0.30	0.28	0.42
Colombia	0.27	0.16	0.16	0.28	0.23	0.21	0.22
Mexico	0.27	0.32	0.33	0.27	0.33	0.26	0.26
Uruguay	0.85	0.52	0.58	0.54	0.35	0.28	0.36
Venezuela	0.23	0.19	0.17	0.49	0.55	0.37	0.32
LA-7	*0.43*	*0.37*	*0.38*	*0.42*	*0.35*	*0.27*	*0.31*
dispersion	*0.56*	*0.46*	*0.52*	*0.36*	*0.32*	*0.21*	*0.27*
South Korea	0.14	n/a	0.09	0.12	0.23	0.38	0.72
Taiwan	0.24	0.16	0.16	0.18	0.28	0.44	0.77

Notes: All ratios are three-year averages. Dispersion is measured by the coefficient of variation.
Sources: LA-7: MOxLAD; South Korea, Taiwan, and US: Maddison Project Database, version 2013.

reached in 1990, at the end of the 'lost decade' – a very effective income leveller across all seven countries.

Table 9.1 also includes information about South Korea and Taiwan, two East Asian economies that also adopted a state-led industrialization model since the 1950s. The LA-7 ratio was well above those in South Korea and Taiwan from 1870 up to *c.*1980, with the relative advantage rising in the 1940s due to sustained growth in Latin America and the impact of World War II in East Asia. The advantage was declining, but still significant up to 1980. But the combination of the Asian 'miracle' and low growth in Latin America erased it, and by 1990, per capita income in South Korea and Taiwan overtook the LA-7 average, being well ahead by 2010 – despite the setback of the 1997 Asian crisis. We expand on the reasons for this change in fortunes in the next section.

GDP Per Worker

Although comparisons based on GDP per capita are the norm, their use hides the potential effects on the convergence process of differences in the timing of the demographic transition. Thus, high population growth can temporarily undermine advances in GDP per capita both by reducing the participation rate (the proportion of the labour force out of the working-age population) and by increasing the dependency ratio (the non-working age as a share of the working-age population). Contrarily, a more mature population with a higher participation rate and a lower dependency ratio is in a better position to benefit from capital accumulation and technology transmission.

As can be seen in Figure 9.2 (chart on the left), there are significant differences in the timing of the demographic transition between the first industrializers and Latin America. The schedules are calculated as the ratio of the economically active population (EAP) to total population, which is a gross measure of the participation rate. In LA-7, after the 1870s and 1880s, when the labour force was growing at a faster rate than the overall population (driven by high migration inflows to Argentina and Uruguay), there was a steady decline in the average participation rate, which was only reversed in the early 1970s as a result of the deceleration in population growth. And by the 1990s the region was collecting a demographic gift that created the conditions for higher levels of income per capita. This demographic pattern in the LA-7 contrasts with that of the UK, a country that had already completed its demographic transition by the turn of the nineteenth century. The US exhibits a secular rise in its participation rate up to the 1990s, with a growing gap relative to LA-7 values – even at times of falling rates, such as 1910–30 and the 1950s. Spain displays a similar profile as LA-7, but did not experience a decline in its participation rate between 1950 and 1970.

During times when the region's participation rate was above that of the comparators, the 'demographic factor' affecting GDP per capita catching up was moving in its favour. But this only occurred between 1870 and 1900 in the comparisons with the US and Spain. For the whole of the twentieth century, the demographic factor was against LA-7, especially between 1950 and 1980. This means that, despite high productivity growth, it was particularly challenging for the region to catch up in per capita terms. To neutralize the effect of differences in participation rates on the catching-up outcome, we show the evolution of the relative performance in GDP per worker in the right-hand chart of Figure 9.2.

Overall, comparisons based on this metric show a more sustained convergence over time than for per capita GDP, although with a final pronounced reversal in both cases. The comparison with the US shows a rising secular trend between 1880 and the end of the 1930s (an increase in the ratio from 0.33 to 0.49), which was interrupted in the first half of the 1940s as the US was embarking on its war effort. Then a more modest second catching-up episode developed from 1950 up to 1980 (a rise in the ratio from 0.44 to 0.49). However, the last two decades brought absolute dispersion and by 2010 the labour productivity gap with the US was larger than in 1870 (0.34 versus 0.36).

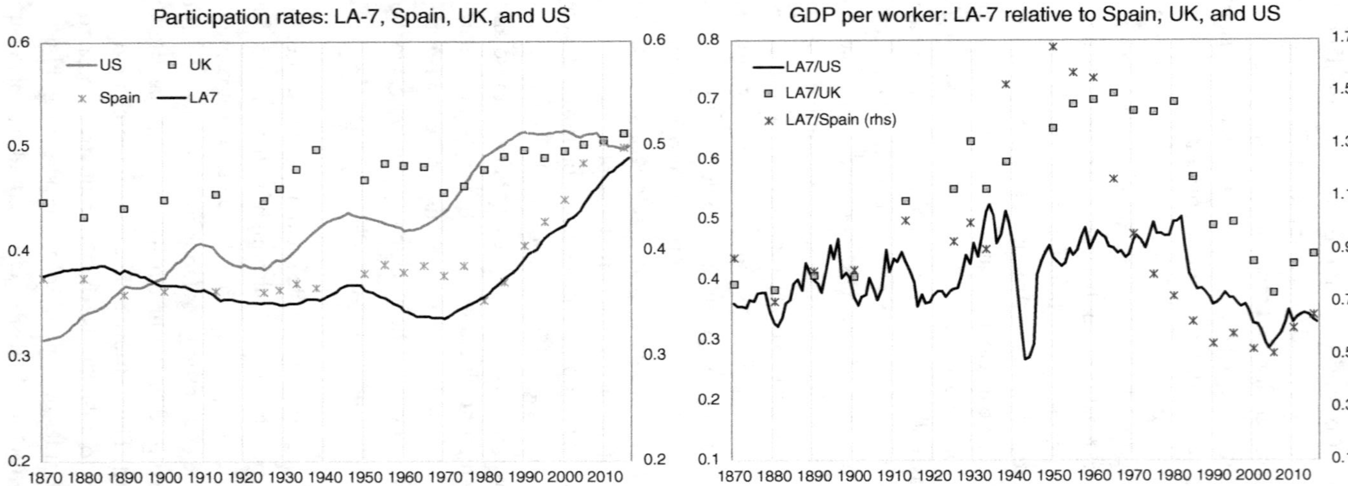

Figure 9.2 Catching up in GDP per worker

Note: Participation rate = EAP divided by population. GDP per worker is calculated as GDP per capita (Figure 9.1) times population/EAP.

Sources: EAP and population: Bértola 2016 for Uruguay; MOxLAD for remaining LA-7; Prados de la Escosura 2007 for UK and Spain up to 2000; US Census Bureau 1975 for US to 1970; official sources thereafter.

All relative growth gains were lost. The comparison with the UK shows a broadly uninterrupted process of catching up until 1970. During the 1960s, LA-7 had managed to close the gap in GDP per worker to 30 per cent. But, again, the last period saw the region lagging behind rapidly.

Real Wages

The use of real wages allows us to explore the role played by income distribution in comparative growth performance. GDP per head includes the remuneration of all factors of production (profits, rents, and wages) and it may not reflect well the median income level in the presence of a skewed distribution (with property income concentrated in the top deciles of the distribution). Figure 9.3 (chart on the left) depicts LA-7's unskilled wages relative to the UK and the US. Also, it includes the LA-6 average wage (we do not have equivalent wage series for Uruguay) relative to the US.

The comparison based on this evidence offers a contrasting view that challenges conventional wisdom based on the previous two metrics. The ratios relative to the US show a secular process of lagging behind in real wages from 1870 to about 1960, which was only interrupted by a modest catching up during the 1960s and 1970s. This is despite sustained growth in real wages in Latin America, particularly between 1920 and 1980 (a 240 per cent increase in the average wage in LA-6; Astorga 2017). This means that catching-up episodes in GDP per head during the twentieth century were likely to have been driven by a better comparative performance of non-wage incomes. The comparison made with unskilled wages in the UK shows a more favourable picture during the first four decades of the twentieth century, when the relative advances in GDP per worker were accompanied by a closing of the gap in unskilled wages. However, overall, those experiencing any catching up in income in the region relative to their counterparts in the industrial leaders were most likely to have belonged to the upper deciles of the distribution.

Figure 9.3 (chart on the right) shows available estimates of the income share of the top decile of the population. It clearly highlights a crucial difference between the distribution dynamics in LA-6 (also true, in all probability, for the region as a whole) and the industrial leaders: the absence in the former of the 'Great Levelling' (Lindert and Williamson 2016) experienced by the latter between the end of World War II and the end of the 1970s. Whilst in the US and the UK (as in other north European countries) there were significant policy efforts to rebalance the distribution of income, in LA-6

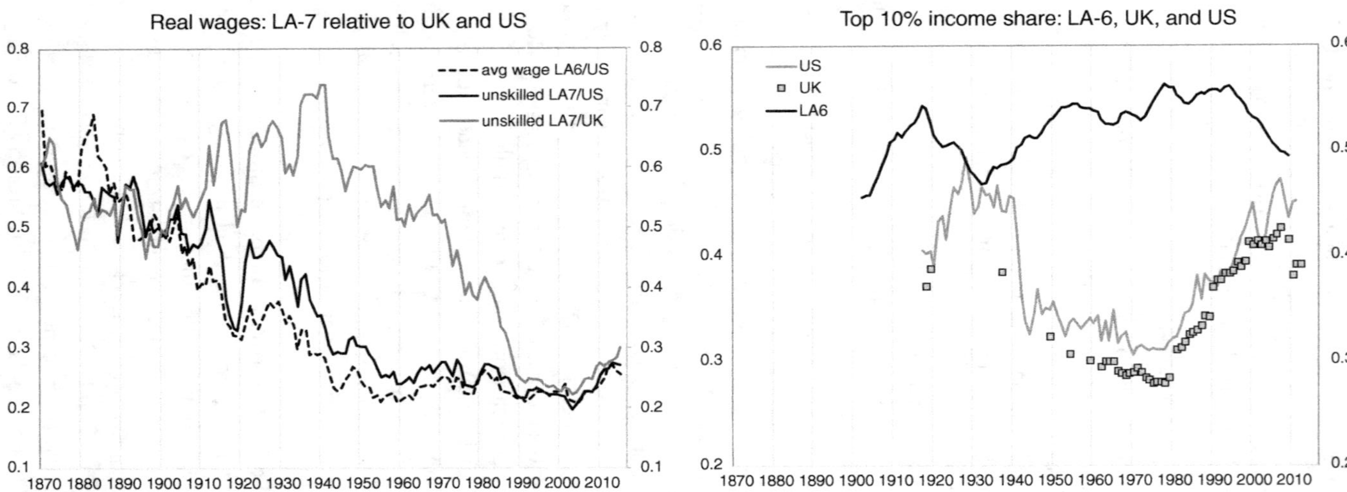

Figure 9.3 Catching up in real wages

Sources: LA-6's real wages, 1870–1900: Arroyo and Astorga 2017; 1900–2011: Astorga 2017; completed to 2015: ECLAC; Uruguay, 1870–2015: Bértola et al. 1999; completed with official sources. For the US, we use 'production workers' hourly compensation' for the average wage, and 'cost of unskilled labour' for the unskilled wage, both from Officer and Williamson 2017. UK's unskilled wage, 1870–1988: Williamson 1995; retailing weekly earnings from the Office of National Statistics thereafter. Top 10 per cent income shares, for US and UK: World Inequality Database; for LA-6: Astorga 2019.

centrifugal forces dominated, resulting in rising inequality and a high concentration of income at the top.[2]

As we will see in the following section, high income inequality in the region is, to a large extent, a reflection of the concentration of assets (e.g. land), the late arrival of democratic – more inclusive – institutions, significant delays in the introduction of mass education (and a more skilful workforce), and, more generally, the provision of public goods. The main reason for the region's poor schooling record was the failure to supply tax support (Lindert 2010) – a clear example of one key area in which the necessary policies were not adopted to create the conditions for convergence.

The Stages of Latin America's Economic Development

The Age of Export-Led Growth

In the second half of the nineteenth century, after decades of widespread economic stagnation and political turmoil, Latin America started to grow, thanks to the pull of the international economy (Kuntz-Ficker 2017). As shown in the previous section, average growth was high enough to allow a moderate convergence with some of the industrial leaders, such as the UK. The region became well integrated within the global economy, mainly as a provider of a very diverse range of primary products: temperate agrarian commodities such as grain, wool, and meat; products of tropical agriculture, including coffee, sugar, and tobacco; or minerals (copper, tin, nitrates, and precious metals). Transport cost reductions and economic growth in the industrial world translated into a boom in international demand for Latin American commodities. Between 1870 and 1929, total and per capita exports grew at a yearly rate of 4.2 per cent and 2.4 per cent respectively in the region (Bértola and Ocampo 2012: 86).

The increase in commodity production and exports was possible thanks to factor accumulation. The region received massive flows of foreign capital and labour, which allowed the exploitation of its natural resources and the expansion of the land frontier. Foreign capital arrived mainly from European countries (especially from the UK), although US investment gradually took off and would become the main source of foreign capital since

2 Although the methods and data used to estimate the top 10 per cent shares are different in each case (wage and overall income data in the LA-6 and fiscal data in the US and the UK), the picture they show is clear enough to support the point.

Table 9.2 Population growth (yearly rate, %)

	1870–1913	1913–29	1929–50	1950–80	1980–2010
Argentina	3.4	2.6	1.9	1.7	1.2
Brazil	2.1	2.1	2.3	2.7	1.7
Chile	1.3	1.3	1.8	2.0	1.4
Colombia	1.8	2.6	1.9	2.7	1.8
Mexico	1.1	0.8	2.5	3.1	1.6
Uruguay	2.9	2.3	1.2	0.9	0.5
Venezuela	1.3	0.8	2.1	3.7	2.2
Latin America	*1.7*	*1.8*	*2.2*	*2.7*	*1.7*

Source: Bértola and Ocampo 2012.

World War I. Foreign capital was an essential channel of technology transfer and allowed infrastructure expansion (especially railways) throughout the period. Capital was accompanied by mass migration from Europe and Asia, particularly in Argentina, Brazil, Cuba, and Uruguay. As a consequence, population grew at a yearly rate of 1.7 per cent (Table 9.2). The railway fostered the expansion of the frontier and made resource extraction possible in the inner areas of each country, while the accumulation of foreign labour helped to compensate the region's relative labour scarcity.

Although capital and labour accumulation largely explain the growth in aggregate exports and output, the capital–labour ratio hardly increased during this period. The pace of technical change was also extremely slow, as shown by the available estimates of total factor productivity (TFP), which grew at 0.13 per cent per year in LA-6 between 1900 and 1936 (Astorga et al. 2011). Thus, labour productivity increases were mainly based on the exploitation of additional reserves of natural resources.

Beyond the average rates of economic growth there was a substantial diversity of national experiences (Table 9.3). The highest levels of exports per capita during the period were reached by Argentina, Uruguay, Chile, Cuba, Costa Rica, and Dominican Republic.[3] With the exception of Chile, these countries were also those that, together with Brazil, had the highest immigration rates. And they were also (with the exception of Dominican Republic) the main recipients of foreign capital, and the countries in which investment per capita was highest (Bértola and Ocampo 2012). The economic dynamism of the Southern Cone and Cuba is confirmed by other indicators, such as

3 Venezuela would join this group in the 1920s, thanks to the take-off of oil exports.

Table 9.3 GDP per capita levels, by country (PPP, 1990 $)

	1870	1900	1910	1940	1980	1990	2010
Argentina	1,468	2,875	3,988	4,342	8,367	6,432	11,820
Brazil	694	557	710	1,154	5,178	4,920	6,762
Chile	1,238	2,065	2,788	3,231	5,638	6,377	13,133
Colombia	676	683	779	1,868	4,244	4,826	6,982
Mexico	651	1,319	1,635	1,788	6,164	6,085	7,832
Uruguay	2,106	2,143	3,029	3,536	6,629	6,465	11,706
Venezuela	570	821	827	3,081	10,213	8,313	9,434
LA-7	*1,058*	*1,495*	*1,965*	*2,714*	*6,633*	*6,203*	*9,667*

Note: LA-7: simple average.
Source: MOxLAD.

energy consumption (Rubio et al. 2010) and railway construction (e.g. Bignon et al. 2015), and appears in stark contrast with sluggish growth in most economies specialized in mining or tropical agriculture. Export-led growth was not only diverse across countries, but also very unstable over time. High dependence on foreign capital inflows made Latin American countries very sensitive to international financial crises. Booms and busts alternated in the region, with major sudden stops affecting most countries in 1873, 1890, 1914, and 1929. Crises often led to defaults and the abandonment of the Gold or Silver Standard.

Despite the specialization in commodity exports, manufacturing industry, encouraged by the needs of commodity processing and increasing consumer demand, expanded in some countries, especially in the Southern Cone, Brazil, and Mexico, where it accounted for 13–20 per cent of GDP by 1929 (Table 9.4). Kuntz-Ficker (2017) has highlighted the positive impact of export-led growth on some economies' industrialization, thanks to income growth, protectionism, and the forward linkages of certain export activities. Gómez Galvarriato and Williamson (2008) have described the industrialization experience of these countries as impressive, compared with the rest of the poor periphery at the time.

As a result of sustained economic growth, urban wages tended to increase almost everywhere in the region. However, they fell behind wages in the industrial economies and grew substantially less than GDP per capita (Williamson 1999; Frankema 2009a). Thus, the first globalization was a period of inequality increase, as is shown also by the rise of top income shares (Figure 9.3). Growing inequality was consistent with movements in factor prices associated with globalization and, more specifically, with the

Table 9.4 Industrial share of GDP (%)

	c.1929	1950	1980
Argentina	20	24	28
Brazil	13	22	30
Chile	13	26	22
Colombia	6	16	22
Mexico	12	17	24
Uruguay	16	19	22
Venezuela	11	12	18
Latin America	10	20	27

Source: Bértola and Ocampo 2012.

increase in the ratio between land rents and wages that took place in migrant recipient countries (Williamson 1999; Arroyo and Astorga 2017).

Moreover, in Latin America, the disequalizing effects of a rising rent–wage ratio were compounded by very high inequality in landownership (Frankema 2009a), which was probably the highest among world regions. Unequal land distribution, largely a legacy of the colonial and postcolonial past, worsened in many countries due to the expropriation of peasants' smallholdings by governments and large landowners. High wealth inequality was the outcome of the gradual consolidation, after the post-independence struggles, of an extractive institutional setting based on a very high concentration of power among the elites. The interests of elites and foreign investors colluded, allowing economic dynamism in a context of generalized political exclusion (Coatsworth 2008). Meanwhile, the region lagged behind in social and labour policies. Tax systems remained undeveloped thanks to the rents coming from a booming external trade, and fiscal resources were mainly spent on the military and infrastructure (railway subsidies). The consolidation of very high inequality rates by the eve of World War I set strict limits on the extent to which the average worker could benefit from economic growth. As is shown below, it also probably constrained the region's growth and convergence prospects during the rest of the twentieth century.

State-Led Industrialization

The period of export-led growth came to an end with the Crash of 1929. Difficulties had started before, when World War I seriously hindered European imports of Latin American commodities. Then, demand from the US became the main engine of Latin American growth during the

1920s, until it gradually collapsed during the Great Depression. The dramatic reduction of world demand was accompanied by the almost total interruption of foreign capital inflows. The consequence was a generalized balance of payments crisis in the region, which brought Latin American real imports down by 62 per cent between 1929 and 1932 (Bértola and Ocampo 2012). The gradual recovery of the US and some European economies gave some relief to the region after 1932, but balance of payment problems returned in 1937, spreading across all Latin American countries a full awareness that the previous growth model was exhausted. The 1930s crisis marked the transition to a completely different growth model, usually known as state-led industrialization, which lasted until a new shared external debt crisis hit the region around 1980. This was the period in which Latin American economic growth was at its highest, and systematically higher than the world average (Table 9.3).

In LA-7, labour productivity grew at a yearly rate of 2.3 per cent between 1937 and 1977, and growth was much less volatile than in the previous period. In contrast to the decades of export-led growth, in this period productivity growth was mainly the result of capital accumulation and technological change. The capital–labour ratio increased very quickly, especially between 1950 and 1980, thanks to high and stable investment rates. Non-residential capital stock grew at unprecedented rates between 1946 and 1981 in the main economies of the region (Table 9.5), and Latin American investment ratios were comparable to those in the fast-growing East Asian economies during the same period (21 per cent in LA-6 versus 22 per cent in East Asia; see Astorga et al. 2011).

Human capital stock also increased substantially thanks to public investment in health and education and rapid urbanization. According to Astorga et al. (2005), the greatest improvement in literacy rates and life expectancy in

Table 9.5 Non-residential capital stock yearly growth rates in several countries (%)

	1900–1920	1930–45	1946–81	1982–2008	1900–2008
Argentina	2.5	1.7	4.9	1.0	3.1
Brazil	3.1	1.7	7.1	2.3	4.6
Chile	2.8	0.4	3.7	7.1	3.3
Mexico	2.4	3.8	6.7	3.3	5.1

Source: Tafunell and Ducoing 2016.

LA-6 took place between 1940 and 1980. Progress in primary enrolment rates was also substantial, and full enrolment was reached in the largest economies by 1980, although those advances were hindered by the relatively poor quality of education systems in many countries (Frankema 2009b). TFP dynamism was also remarkable; its yearly growth rate in LA-6 was 1 per cent between 1937 and 1977, and it was largely associated with embodied technical change, with imports of foreign physical capital growing at high rates at least since 1945.

Given the importance of the agrarian sector, a large share of labour productivity growth took place in agriculture. Agricultural productivity grew steadily thanks to labour shedding, the spread of irrigation and the Green Revolution (Astorga et al. 2011). But labour productivity growth was also partly the result of structural change, since industry and modern services increased their importance within GDP in almost all Latin American economies, at the expense of the primary sector. The industrial GDP share increased nearly everywhere (see Table 9.4), although the highest percentages were reached in the largest economies, and only Argentina, Mexico, and, especially, Brazil managed to develop a really diversified industry. Industrialization was accompanied by the diffusion of modern services and high rates of urbanization; urban population in the region grew at 4.4 per cent yearly between 1950 and 1970, which was an unprecedented rate in world history. Only in the small economies (with the exception of Costa Rica) did commodity exports remain as the main engine of growth.

To a great extent, human development and structural change were associated with a new policy model, which entailed a much more active role of the government in the economy. The earliest policy changes were largely reactive, since the collapse of the international economy forced the countries in the region into devaluation, multiple exchange rates, increasing protection, and exchange controls. All these established an early set of incentives to import substitution and industrialization, which gradually developed into a much more complex structure of policy instruments, including, among others, development banks, nationalization of key industries and utilities, infrastructure, and attraction of foreign direct investment. Protection of domestic markets reduced the region's exposure to external shocks and GDP growth volatility, and, together with increasing urbanization, was the basis for high private investment, aimed at meeting an increasing domestic demand for consumption of industrial goods. Investment rates were also supported by the significant expansion of public capital formation in infrastructure and human capital-related services (health and education).

As highlighted by Bértola and Ocampo (2012), this policy setting was not just about import substitution and industrialization. Policies oriented to the modernization of agriculture were very important everywhere and help to explain the substantial productivity increases in the sector and the rural-urban exodus. In addition, most countries developed efforts to promote exports, although with moderate success. This included the earliest attempts at regional economic integration: the Central American Common Market and the Latin American Free Trade Association (ALALC), both established in 1960, and the Andean Pact, founded in 1969. In a period in which most of the developing world was applying inward-oriented state-led industrialization programmes, economic policy in Latin America may be characterized as being more, and not less, market oriented than in other developing regions.

Productivity increases translated into very high rates of income per capita growth, especially since 1945, although, as in previous decades, with significant differences among countries. It was actually in those countries that grew faster before 1914, such as the Southern Cone and Cuba, where economic growth was slowest in this period. By contrast, in a number of large economies whose previous performance had been rather disappointing, such as Brazil, Mexico, Colombia, Peru, and Venezuela, growth rates were very high in these decades, and they managed to catch up with the former leading economies.

Fast economic growth translated into a rapid decrease in mortality rates, which was joined by a decline in birth rates only with a substantial lag. In fact, fertility rates increased substantially between World War II and the 1960s or 1970s in most countries (Reher and Requena 2014). The result was one of the highest population growth rates in history, amounting to 2.7 per cent yearly between 1950 and 1980 (Table 9.2). Unlike the previous period, this was mostly natural growth, since migration inflows were very low, with the exception of Venezuela. As a consequence of the demographic transition, the age structure of the population changed substantially, dependency ratios increased, and female activity rates remained low. Population therefore grew much faster than the workforce throughout the region, putting a check on convergence in per capita GDP and standards of living.

Improvements in average welfare were also constrained by the high inequality levels inherited from the past. There were some equalizing forces during the period, such as the end of the previous sustained tendency to increasing rent–wage ratios, or the decline in rural underemployment associated with massive rural-urban migration. However, these forces were too weak to make a difference, especially because the demographic transition generated labour surpluses, which prevented increases in unskilled wages, while prevailing educational shortages drove up skilled wages. Moreover, the region remained largely unaffected by the policy changes that reduced inequality in industrialized countries. Governments tried to reform tax systems to make them both more progressive and efficient, but those attempts generally failed, largely due to persistent resistance by vested interests. Most countries also developed labour compacts, including wage regulation and welfare policies. However, those new benefits mainly covered high-income workers and the urban middle classes, leaving aside most of the population working in an expanding informal sector, and giving rise to segmented or truncated welfare states, where redistribution took place only among the better-off (Ferreira and Robalino 2011). Similarly, widespread agrarian reforms were expected to bring some redistribution to the rural areas, but except for Cuba and, to a lesser extent, Mexico and Bolivia, they only affected relatively small minorities of landowners.

Only in Cuba did the revolution bring with it a radical social levelling, while in the Southern Cone, where the expansion of the labour movement and welfare policies were more developed and formal employment more extended, there was a moderate reduction in inequality. For other countries, the available inequality indicators, including the ratio between unskilled wages and per capita GDP, the labour income share, top incomes, or earning inequality stagnated or worsened between 1940 and 1980 (Frankema 2009a; Arroyo and Astorga 2017). The region therefore did not participate in the global trend of inequality levelling during the central decades of the twentieth century, and this had a significant negative impact on average welfare.

The Debt Crisis of the 1980s and the Second Globalization

The limits of the model of state-led growth were reached in the 1970s. Despite widespread industrialization and technology adoption, the region's ability to close the gap with the developed countries and to transition towards industrial exports was limited by insufficient technology and educational policies, particularly when compared with the East Asian fast-growing countries. In that context, several tensions and imbalances jeopardized the persistence of economic growth. The difficulties in expanding exports, together with booming investment and international credit facilities, generated during the 1970s considerable external deficits that were financed with foreign capital. In parallel, governments' growing involvement in the economy and society boosted public spending and provoked large public deficits and increasing inflation rates.

The final outcome of those imbalances was a growing dependence of Latin American economies and governments on external finance, and a high vulnerability to movements in the international credit markets. Under these circumstances, the end of state-led industrialization was associated with a cycle of foreign capital inflows, which started in some countries in the 1960s, spread to the whole region in the 1970s and collapsed in the 1980s. Between 1973 and 1981, Latin America would absorb more than 50 per cent of all debt flows received by the developing world, and would also be the region with the largest share of FDI.

The collapse of the system arrived with the sudden increase of US interest rates in 1980, which provoked an abrupt rise in the region's debt burden (largely contracted at floating interest rates) and was accompanied by a reduction in commodity prices that made the situation even more difficult. Unlike what had happened in the 1930s, no unilateral defaults took place in the 1980s, and insufficient rescue funds and long-lasting negotiations made recovery much slower than fifty years before, despite the initial shock being less serious. The external finance dried up, giving way to a 'lost decade', with significant reductions in the region's GDP per capita. The crisis brought about a substantial setback in the region's industrialization process, and inequality and poverty deteriorated, largely due to the decrease in real wages and formal employment. Growth was only resumed in the early 1990s, although it was interrupted again by the financial shocks of 1997–2001 and – to a lesser extent – by the Great Recession of 2007–08. Those decades of recurrent crises were marked by rapid divergence from the industrial core and also from the rapidly growing East Asian economies. Thus, Korea and Taiwan, which had a similar GDP per capita to the LA-7 in 1980, were four times richer twenty years later.

The debt crisis of the 1980s was not an automatic consequence of the state-led development model, which, in some of the largest countries, had been gradually shifting towards export promotion. However, such pro-export policies had had limited success, largely due to the governments' inability to raise enough fiscal resources to support the necessary infrastructure, R&D, and human capital investment. This represented a crucial difference with the East Asian industrial leaders. Countries like Korea and Taiwan were much more successful in technology adoption, thanks to substantial investment efforts in those areas during state-led industrialization. This raised their competitiveness and allowed a substantial increase in their participation in world exports. In that context, the relative failure of Latin American regional integration initiatives set another limit to export growth and also contrasts with the dynamism of East Asian regional trade.

As had happened half a century before, in Latin America the debt crisis provoked another change in the economic policy model. State-led industrialization was replaced by pro-market reforms. These had three main components: liberalization of markets (e.g. tariff reduction, deregulation of financial systems), reduction in public sector economic activity (involving large-scale privatizations), and macroeconomic stabilization, including a substantial decrease in public spending and inflation control. While these reforms were initially a side effect of the short-term reactions to the crisis, as well as part of the conditionality of International Monetary Fund rescue programmes, they were gradually consolidated in the 1990s to form the new dominant paradigm of economic policy. This new model would remain in place thereafter, despite the introduction of some partial changes (especially since the 2000s).

The new policy model radically transformed the Latin American economies. Macroeconomic stability, with the reduction of fiscal imbalances and inflation, was largely restored in the 1990s, and the region became much more open to trade and foreign capital. Exports were more diversified than a hundred years before, with a gradual reduction in the share of commodities and a moderate increase in medium and high-technology products, at least until the boom in commodity prices of 2003–13. Natural resource-based exports, however, still accounted for more than 50 per cent of all exports until at least 2010.

FDI rose substantially over the period. The destination sectors of foreign investment were often linked to the new export specialization: assembly production (especially in Mexico and Central America), tourism and other services, and natural resource-based products. Nevertheless, the highest boom in FDI, which took place in the 1990s, was mainly associated with the privatization of public companies and the purchase of private firms. The region also participated in international labour flows, but now as a net sender of migrants. Latin American workers moved in huge numbers to the US and, to a lesser extent, to other countries, such as Spain, Canada, or Japan, helping to balance their economies' foreign sector with massive remittances, at least until the Great Recession. Such growing openness to the international economy and widespread liberalization policies had some clearly negative effects, as they increased the vulnerability of the region to financial crises. As a consequence, growth since 1980 has not only been much slower, but also much more volatile than before.

Despite generalized policy reforms, which were partially aimed at restarting productivity dynamism, the evolution of TFP and labour productivity has been rather disappointing since the 1990s, compared with industrial countries' performance. TFP growth in LA-6 was actually negative between 1978 and 2000 (Astorga et al. 2011), and this explains most of the reduction in the rate of labour productivity and GDP per capita growth, compared to the previous period. Even though some sectors (like certain manufactures and modern services) have undertaken substantial productivity increases based on technology acquisition, this has been more than compensated by the expansion of the informal economy. Slow productivity growth is also consistent with the deindustrialization of the region, and with relatively low rates of investment and low capacity to generate new technology. Investment rates did not keep pace with high-growing East Asian economies; for instance, in LA-6 between 1978 and 2000, investment was on average 20 per cent of GDP versus around 30 per cent in East Asia (Astorga et al. 2011). In the largest economies of the region, except for Chile, the rates of growth of non-residential capital stock plummeted in 1981–2008 (Table 9.5).

The disappointing evolution of productivity is consistent with the prevailing deficiencies in the accumulation of human capital and R&D. Educational policies have been relatively inefficient, with the region performing very badly in PISA tests or university rankings (Lindert 2010). Similarly, despite some efforts to develop new technology policies, Latin American rates of investment in R&D, with the partial exception of Brazil, are very low. Actually, public support for R&D investment weakened between the 1980s and 2000s, compared with the previous period (Castellacci and Natera 2016). Differences in R&D with the fast-growing Asian economies, which were already sizeable in 1980, widened significantly thereafter. Moreover, private involvement in R&D, which has been predominant in Korea and Taiwan, has remained very low in Latin America, and patents, which have experienced impressive growth in East Asian economies, have remained stagnant in the region. Since 1980, Latin American inability to undertake a process of structural change towards innovation and more knowledge-intensive production has prevented convergence and condemned the region to remain stuck in a typical middle-income trap.

In this context, poverty and inequality substantially worsened during the lost decade and through the early 2000s, reaching extremely high levels, even in the Southern Cone countries, where they had remained relatively low until the 1970s. In addition to the impact of the crisis and liberalization policies, the military regimes of the 1970s and 1980s contributed to increasing inequality through regressive labour policies and repression of unions, while the delayed impact of the demographic transition on the labour market boosted the supply of unskilled labour. Inequality rates only started to decrease in most countries during the commodity export boom of 2003–13 that supported employment creation and higher wages (particularly of unskilled workers). Also, governments across the region – largely of left-wing orientation – implemented more progressive social spending, adopted educational reforms and favoured pro-labour policies. However, inequality levels have remained comparatively high until the present.

Concluding Remarks

Despite significant advances in living standards, Latin America has not been able to catch up with the advanced economies in GDP per head in the last 150 years or so. It is true that between 1870 and 1980 the region managed to close some of its income gap with the leaders (particularly in GDP per worker), but these relative gains were not sustained, and by the start of the second decade of the twenty-first century the income disparity was wider than in 1870. In recent years, Chile has been the region's most dynamic economy, but even here, GDP per capita today is only around 60 per cent of the US level. And when using real unskilled wages as the comparative metric, the LA-7 outcome is much worse, with a divergent trend that resulted in a widening of the gap relative to the US from about 40 per cent in 1870 to around 80 per cent in 2010. The comparison with the East Asian leading economies, whose GDP per capita levels were below those of Latin America until 1980 – but which have since rapidly converged with the industrial economies – offers further evidence of the region's lacklustre relative performance.

The conditions for catching up were most favourable in the period of state-led industrialization because of the superior record of capital accumulation, advances in mass education, positive TFP and structural change, and relatively low GDP volatility. But convergence in GDP per capita with the US and the UK was stalled during these decades. The causes of this outcome are to be found in a significantly lower growth in TFP compared to the industrial leaders (Wolff 1991) – though with similar growth in labour productivity, poor educational quality, and the timing of the demographic transition. In addition, in contrast to the significant distributional improvement that took place in industrialized countries during those decades, Latin American inequality during the period remained relatively high. But if the comparative performance was modest in the middle period, the early 1980s marked a dismal downturn in the region's living standards. All gains in terms of productivity convergence accumulated over the previous hundred years or so were lost, and the alternation of stagnation with sluggish growth prevented the region from capitalizing on the demographic dividend.

There were also serious shortcomings in the areas of public goods provision (particularly in primary and secondary education), the model of integration with the international economy, and the adoption of technology. These areas clearly stand out in the comparison with East Asia in the closing decades of the last century. The failure to supply tax support for human capital formation and to address income and group-based inequalities meant that the necessary policies to foster productivity and create the conditions for catching up were not adopted. Latin America's international integration was largely based on the export of natural resources and a broad exposure to international financial markets – which tended to have a pro-cyclical effect. This has exacerbated macroeconomic volatility and has undermined investment and technological upgrading into sectors that could have favoured growth and convergence.

Although the reasons for the absence of catching up are complex and diverse, excess volatility, poor productivity, and high inequality remain essential to explaining why the region has been unable to follow the East Asian path of convergence with the developed countries through advances in human capital, R&D, and infrastructure investment. To improve future prospects in standards of living and catching up, the region will need to adopt a development model that delivers sustained and inclusive economic growth. Key elements of this model are a higher rate of investment, a proactive industrial policy (including technology policies), as well as a more diversified export sector and greater intra-regional integration. On the social front, it should include radical fiscal reform and greater redistribution efforts in order to finance a better quality of education and inclusive social services.

References

Arroyo, L. and Astorga, P. (2017). 'Latin American Earnings Inequality in the Long Run', *Cliometrica*, 11, 349–374.

Astorga, P. (2017). 'Real Wages and Skill Premiums in Latin America, 1900–2011', *Revista de Historia Económica – Journal of Iberian and Latin American Economic History*, 35, 319–353.

(2019). The Tails and the Middle: Secular Trends in Income Shares in Latin America. Unpublished research paper.

Astorga, P., Bérges, A. R., and FitzGerald, E. V. K. (2005). 'The Standard of Living in Latin America During the Twentieth Century', *Economic History Review*, 58, 765–796.

(2011). 'Productivity Growth in Latin America During the Twentieth Century', *Review of Income and Wealth*, 57, 203–223.

Bértola, L. (2016). 'El PIB per cápita de Uruguay 1870–2015: una reconstrucción', working paper 48, Economic and Social History Programme, Faculty of Social Sciences, Universidad de la República, Uruguay.

Bértola, L. and Ocampo, J. A. (2012). *The Economic Development of Latin America since Independence*, Oxford University Press.

Bértola, L., Calicchio, L., Camou, M., and Porcile, G. (1999). 'Southern Cone Real Wages Compared: A Purchasing Power Parity Approach to Convergent and Divergent Trends, 1870–1996', working paper 44, Faculty of Social Sciences, Universidad de la República, Uruguay.

Bignon, V., Esteves, R., and Herranz-Loncán, A. (2015). 'Big Push or Big Grab? Railways, Government Activism and Export Growth in Latin America, 1865–1913', *Economic History Review*, 68, 1277–1305.

Bulmer-Thomas, V. (2013). *The Economic History of Latin America since Independence*, Oxford University Press.

Castellacci, F. and Natera, J. M. (2016). 'Innovation, Absorptive Capacity and Growth Heterogeneity: Development Paths in Latin America 1970–2010', *Structural Change and Economic Dynamics*, 37, 27–42.

Coatsworth, J. H. (2008). 'Inequality, Institutions and Economic Growth in Latin America', *Journal of Latin American Studies*, 40, 545–569.

Economic Commission for Latin America and the Caribbean (ECLAC). (2018). CEPALSTAT | Databases and Statistical Publications (data accessed May 2017–May 2018).

Ferreira, F. H. G. and Robalino, D. A. (2011). 'Social Protection in Latin America: Achievements and Limitations', in Ocampo, J. A. and Ros, J. (eds.), *The Oxford Handbook of Latin American Economics*, Oxford University Press, 836–862.

Frankema, E. (2009a). *Has Latin America Always Been Unequal? A Comparative Study of Asset and Income Inequality in the Long Twentieth Century*, Boston, MA: Brill.

(2009b). 'The Expansion of Mass Education in Twentieth-Century Latin America: A Global Comparative Perspective', *Revista de Historia Económica – Journal of Iberian and Latin American Economic History*, 27, 359–396.

Gómez Galvarriato, A. and Williamson, J. G. (2008). 'Was It Prices, Productivity or Policy? The Timing and Pace of Latin American Industrialisation after 1870', NBER working paper 13990, National Bureau of Economic Research.

Kuntz-Ficker, S. (ed.) (2017). *The First Export Era Revisited. Reassessing its Contribution to Latin American Economies*, Cham: Palgrave Macmillan.

Lindert, P. (2010). 'The Unequal Lag in Latin American Schooling since 1900: Follow the Money', *Revista de Historia Económica – Journal of Iberian and Latin American Economic History*, 28, 375–405.

Lindert, P. and Williamson, J. G. (2016). *Unequal Gains: American Growth and Inequality since 1774*, Princeton University Press.

Maddison Project Database, version 2013. Bolt, J. and van Zanden, J. L. (2014). 'The Maddison Project: Collaborative Research on Historical National Accounts', *Economic History Review*, 67, 627–651.

Montevideo–Oxford Latin American Economic History Database (MOxLAD). Latin American Centre, University of Oxford, and Universidad de la República, Uruguay.

Office of National Statistics. (2018). Labour market database (data accessed May 2018).

Officer, L. H. and Williamson, S. H. (2017). Annual Wages in the United States, 1774–Present, MeasuringWorth, available online at www.measuringworth.com/datasets/uswage (data accessed 2017).

Prados de la Escosura, L. (2007). 'When Did Latin America Fall Behind?', in Edwards, S., Esquivel, G., and Márquez, G. (eds.), *The Decline of Latin American Economies: Growth, Institutions, and Crises*, University of Chicago Press, 15–57.

Reher, D. and Requena, M. (2014). 'Was There a Mid-Twentieth-Century Fertility Boom in Latin America?', *Revista de Historia Económica – Journal of Iberian and Latin American Economic History*, 32, 319–350.

Rodrik, D. (2014). 'The Past, Present, and Future of Economic Growth', *Challenge*, 57, 5–39.

Rubio, M., Yáñez, C., Folchi, M., and Carreras, A. (2010). 'Energy as an Indicator of Modernisation in Latin America, 1890–1925', *Economic History Review*, 63, 769–804.

Tafunell, X. and Ducoing, C. (2016). 'Non-Residential Capital Stock in Latin America, 1875–2008: New Estimates and International Comparisons', *Australian Economic History Review*, 56, 46–69.

Thorp, R. (1998). *Progress, Poverty and Exclusion: An Economic History of Latin America in the Twentieth Century*, Washington, DC: Inter-American Development Bank.

US Census Bureau. (1975). *Historical Statistics of the United States: Colonial Times to 1970*, Washington, DC: US Census Bureau.

Williamson, J. G. (1995). 'The Evolution of Global Labor Markets since 1830: Background Evidence and Hypotheses', *Explorations in Economic History*, 32, 141–196.

(1999). 'Real Wage Inequality and Globalisation in Latin America before 1940', *Revista de Historia Económica*, 17, 101–142.

Wolff, E. (1991). 'Capital Formation and Productivity Convergence over the Long Term', *American Economic Review*, 81, 565–579.

World Inequality Database. https://wid.world/data/ (accessed 29 September 2020).

10

African Economic Development
Growth, Reversals, and Deep Transitions

EWOUT FRANKEMA

Introduction

Africa, and in particular sub-Saharan Africa – the focus area of this chapter – is the poorest region of the world at present.[1] Average GDP per capita levels, as well as the percentage share of the population living in extreme poverty, both show that the region lags significantly behind other world regions. In 2015, 41 per cent of Africans below the Sahara lived on less than $1.90 a day, and a staggering 84.5 per cent of Africans lived on less than $5.50 (2011 PPP; World Bank 2020b). There are more stylized facts underpinning the picture of low economic and social development: Africa features the highest share of the labour force employed in agriculture, the lowest share employed in manufacturing, and the highest share of primary commodities in total exports. Child mortality and illiteracy rates, even though they have fallen dramatically since 1950, rank among the highest in the world (World Bank 2020b). Africa also experiences unprecedented high rates of population growth, which raises the challenge to create jobs for growing masses of underemployed youth that flock together in cities. Moreover, a majority of African states still depend on structural development assistance, which is offered through direct support of state finances, as well as an array of subsidized public services provided by foreign NGOs (AfDB/OECD/UNDP 2014).[2]

Throughout the long twentieth century, African societies have been exposed to a great deal of political instability, not infrequently erupting into violent conflict. There were wars at the onset of colonization in the late nineteenth century; African troops were deployed during World Wars

1 Throughout this chapter, 'Africa' will refer to sub-Saharan Africa, excluding North Africa and South Africa, which I will only mention in passing.

2 For the twenty-seven low-income African countries, the official development assistance share of GDP averaged 13 per cent in 2000–2005, and 9 per cent in 2013–14 (AfDB/OECD/UNDP 2014: 49).

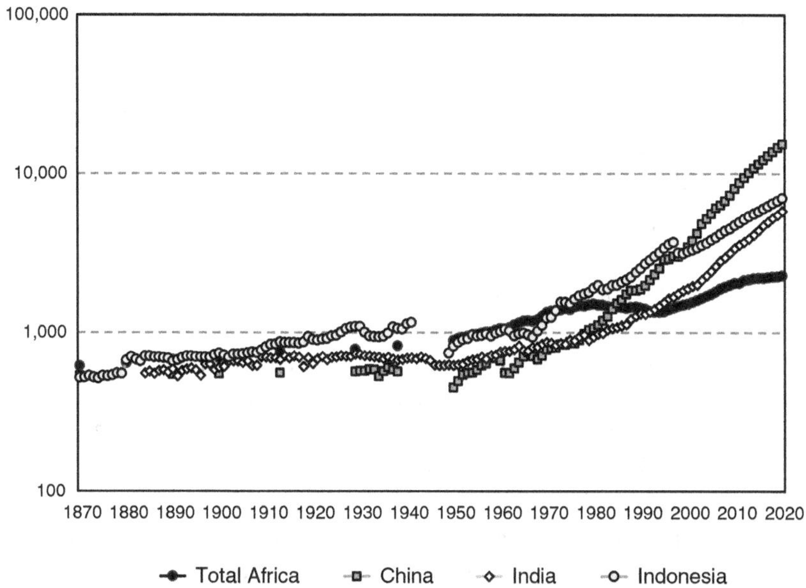

Figure 10.1 GDP per capita in Africa, China, India, and Indonesia, 1870–2020 (constant 1990 US$, log-scale)
Sources: 1950–2010: Maddison Project Database, version 2013; Africa pre-1950: backward extrapolations using Prados de la Escosura 2012: 23, table 10.3; 2010–20: forward extrapolations using International Monetary Fund 2020 (real per capita GDP growth).

I and II; independence wars were fought between the 1950s and 1970s; and during the postcolonial era, many newborn African countries experienced protracted civil warfare (Nugent 2012). A number of African states may qualify as a 'failed' state, or, in the terminology of North et al. (2009), as a fragile or basic 'limited access order'. Even though there has been an upsurge in more optimistic accounts of African economic and political development since the start of the twenty-first century (Bates et al. 2007; Radelet 2010; Young 2012), the general academic sentiment leans towards outright pessimism, or cautious forms of optimism at best (Lipton 2013; Rodrik 2014; Frankema and van Waijenburg 2018).

Figure 10.1 sharpens the main questions addressed in this chapter. This graph presents GDP per capita from 1870 to 2010 for Africa and three major Asian economies: China, India, and Indonesia. It shows that right after World War II, African countries were not the rock-bottom subsistence economies claimed by some scholars (Bloom et al. 1998: 207; Allen 2011: 91). GDP levels around US$900–1,000 per capita in the 1950s were substantially higher than the world's bottom range of US$300–400 per capita. This conclusion is also supported by studies documenting trends in real wages and human stature, or in reconstructed social tables (Moradi 2009; Frankema and van Waijenburg 2012; Bolt and Hillbom 2016). In fact, Africa only became the 'poorest' region of the world in the final quarter of the twentieth century, when other parts of the 'global periphery', and especially Asia, experienced accelerated growth, while Africa plunged into a long depression. Indeed, African economic development has been characterized by successive phases of growth and contraction, a pattern of cycles that has existed for a long time (Jerven 2010; Broadberry and Gardner 2019).

Will this pattern of recurrent growth and contraction transform into a more sustained growth path during the twenty-first century, with upward bending curves like those seen for India, China, and Indonesia? Or will growth reversals continue to hold the region back instead? While the future outlook is not central to this chapter, the insights into the comparative nature of African growth justify deeper historical reflections on the nature and drivers of long-term African development as a counterweight to ahistorical conceptions of 'structural impediments' to African growth (Austin 2008a; Frankema and van Waijenburg 2012). This requires an account that combines a view on the structural weaknesses of African economies, with a view on the deeper transitions that have taken place, and which continue to gradually, and sometimes radically, change their foundations. This chapter seeks to confront both aspects of African economic development since the start of the colonial era up to the present.

Growth, Reversals, and External Trade

Before we take a closer look at the major cycles of growth, we should point out that, historically, African poverty is rooted in a combination of low agricultural productivity and large, albeit diverse, geographic barriers to economic and political integration. Extreme variety in rainfall levels, from deserts to rainforests, as well as erratic year-to-year rainfall, poor quality soils, a lack of navigable river systems and a high incidence of tropical diseases affecting humans, domesticated animals, and crops alike, created a comparatively harsh environment for human reproduction (Iliffe 2007: 1–16). Even though environmentally conditioned specialization created many opportunities for economic exchange, cultivation and herding practices were so diverse that fragmentation often prevailed over integration. Africa did not harbour the environmental conditions for a state like China, nor for the trade intensity that characterized the Mediterranean basin in ancient times, let alone early modern north-western Europe (Frankema 2014). To be sure, this is no reason for geographic 'determinism', but it is important to consider Africa's biogeographic make-up to understand long-term economic volatility *and* to appreciate the profundity of the transitions Africa has experienced during the long twentieth century.

The nineteenth-century 'commercial transition' was a prelude to these transitions. It set the stage for colonial occupation and profound long-term changes of African labour, land and capital markets (more on this below). Slave exports were substituted by increasing volumes of commodity exports (see Manning in Volume I, Chapter 10 of this book).[3] Without this transition, colonial rule would probably have been infeasible (Hopkins 1973; Frankema et al. 2018). Trade revenues provided the basis for colonial state expansion, and the more trade there was to tax, the larger the investment capacity of colonial governments (Frankema and van Waijenburg 2014). Throughout the colonial and postcolonial period, African export industries attracted the lion's share of foreign capital investment. Commodity export growth occurred in the context of overwhelmingly rural economies. Domestic consumer demand was constrained by low population densities, scarce concentrations of people in urban centres and large overland transportation barriers. The surpluses that were generated via growing labour specialization in export production thus weighed heavily in the region's income growth and placed African economies on a more *capitalist* footing (Warren 1980; Sender and Smith 1986; Austin 2005).

Colonial administrators, missionaries, merchants, and settlers largely agreed that 'commercialization' and 'civilization' were two sides of the same coin, as commercialization offered an alternative to internal slave trades and incentivized 'natives' to produce for the market.[4] Yet production for export markets occurred on African as well as foreign initiative, and it allowed colonial as well as African elites to reallocate significant parts of Africa's land and labour resources. Export growth also stimulated a broader process of technological change, since some of the revenues were reinvested into land improvements or imports of technology-intensive manufactures and capital goods for the diffusion of electrification, mechanized transportation, and long-distance communication. The explosive growth of African

3 The British decision to abandon the slave trade in 1807 did not initiate the so-called 'legitimate commerce', but it certainly stimulated its growth (Law 1995).

4 After the imposition of colonial rule, internal slavery was gradually phased out, but replaced by several forms of forced labour (Klein 1998; van Waijenburg 2018).

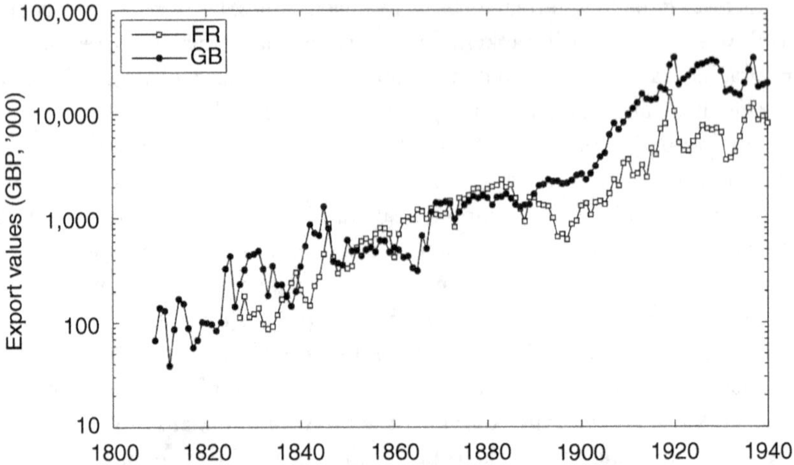

Figure 10.2 Total value of commodity exports from British and French West Africa, 1808–1940 (GBP x 1,000, log-scale)
Sources: African Commodity Trade Database, version 1.3 (Frankema et al. 2018: 243).

populations and cities from the 1940s onwards redirected parts of these capital flows into industries catering to domestic consumer markets.

Figure 10.2 shows the export values for British and French West Africa from 1808 to 1940. It shows a prolonged export boom that tapers off during the scramble for West Africa in the 1880s and 1890s. Figure 10.3 shows that West Africa's export boom was driven by a sharp rise in terms of trade, which stimulated production of palm oil, groundnuts, and gum Arabic, the three main export commodities in the nineteenth century. After the mid-1880s, the relative prices of African exports started to decline. Resistance against colonial encroachment and outright warfare led to major disruptions in ocean-bound trade, especially in the areas that came under French control. After 1900, when most regions were 'pacified' according to euphemistic 'colonial' vocabulary, export growth picked up again. A similar pattern occurred in East and Central Africa, where ivory dominated exports up to 1900, and slave exports continued up to at least the 1870s (Sheriff 1987), to be largely replaced by the export of mineral and tropical agricultural products, such as copper, diamonds, cotton, coffee, tobacco, tea, and sisal.

During the interwar years, trade was more volatile and the overall terms of trade decreased dramatically. Some products, such as rubber and palm oil,

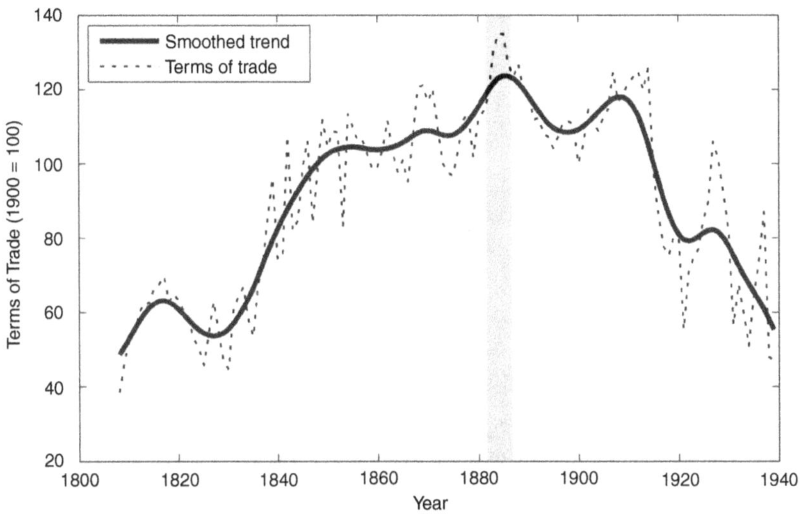

Figure 10.3 Net barter terms of trade, West Africa, 1808–1939 (1900 = 100)
Note: Smoothed trend derived using Hodrick-Prescott filter, with a smoothing factor set to 100.
Sources: African Commodity Trade Database, version 1.3 (Frankema et al. 2018: 247).

experienced fierce competition from Asian producers, whereas other commodity exports, such as cotton and copper, kept rising and recovered quickly from the depression of the early 1930s.[5] Despite the long-term decline in the terms of trade, colonial governments were pressing for specialization in a narrow set of primary export commodities, so that falling prices were compensated by rapidly growing production volumes (see Table 10.1 for West Africa). Colonial administrations funnelled major parts of local government revenues and metropolitan loans into the development of infrastructure (ports, railways, roads, electricity), which lowered transportation costs and stimulated the 'cash-crop revolution' (Tosh 1980) and the growth of mining enclaves.

Prados de la Escosura (2012) has used African trade data to draw conjectures of real per capita output growth for the period 1870 to 1950. He first estimated GDP growth by assuming zero growth in the domestic sectors of the economy, so that the observed growth in the purchasing power of exports, combined with the relative size of the export sector, determines the growth rate (dual approach).

5 For details, see African Commodity Trade Database, www.aehnetwork.org/data-research/african-commodity-trade-database.

Table 10.1 Decomposition of export growth in British and French West Africa, 1853–1929

	Annual average growth (%)			Contribution (%)		
	Purchasing power of export (1)	Import price (2)	Export price (3)	Export volume (4)	Price (5)	Volume (6)
British West Africa (£)						
1853–85	**4.65**	−0.68	0.83	3.14	32	68
1885–1929	**5.49**	1.32	0.46	6.36	−16.00	116.00
French West Africa (fr.)						
1853–85	**4.96**	−1.06	1.67	2.23	55.00	45.00
1885–1929	**1.98**	4.43	3.38	3.03	−53.00	153.00

Source: Frankema et al. 2018: 249, table 10.3.

Table 10.2 Conjectures of GDP per capita growth in Africa, 1870–1950

	Dual approach		Econometric approach	
	Sub-Saharan Africa	Africa	Sub-Saharan Africa	Africa
1870–1900	0.4	0.5	0.3	0.4
1900–1950	0.8	0.7	0.6	0.5
1900–13	1.6	1.4	0.7	0.8
1913–29	0.3	0.3	0.1	0.2
1929–38	0.9	0.9	0.8	0.6
1938–50	0.9	0.6	0.9	0.6

Source: Prados de la Escosura 2012: 22, table 10.2.

Subsequently, he used the econometric association between observed GDP per capita and income terms of trade per capita for the 1950–90 era to infer growth estimates for the period 1870–1938 (econometric approach). His results, shown in Table 10.2, suggest a positive rate of income growth throughout the period, with a particularly strong performance in 1900–1913, a modest rate of growth in 1913–29, and a high growth rate during 1929–38. Notwithstanding the limitations of this estimation method, it appears that African output per capita grew for eight decades in a row. In a study on British Africa, Broadberry and Gardner (2019) show considerable cross-colony variation in growth, but they also point out that the most prolonged economic setback of the region occurred after 1970, and not in the full century before.

It would be wrong, though, to infer that broad segments of the African population benefited from economic growth in the half century between 1870 and 1920, as much of it was 'coerced growth'. Real wages rose in British West Africa and, perhaps to a lesser extent, in the more dynamic parts of French West Africa as well, but in British East Africa real wages stayed close to subsistence level (Bowden et al. 2008; Frankema and van Waijenburg 2012; de Haas 2017a). Moreover, the mobilization and commodification of scarce African labour involved high degrees of suppression. Forced labour, sometimes extracted at gunpoint, was needed for human porterage, for mining, for railway construction, and to run large-scale cultivation schemes. But these investments were not geared to cushion the impact of crises caused by rainfall shocks, famine, disease epidemics, let alone the effects of protracted colonial wars and large-scale mobilization during World War I (Reid 2009: chapter 11). Venereal disease and excessive violence used by the militia of European concession companies contributed to a dramatic population collapse in Central Africa (Vansina 2010). The rinderpest of the 1890s caused great hardship among pastoral groups in East Africa (Kjekshus 1996). Indeed, the early decades of colonial rule were extremely turbulent and mostly unsafe.

This phase of 'coerced growth' started to change, slowly, during the interwar years. Changing conceptions of 'civilization', 'development', and '*mise en valeur*' in European metropoles heralded different approaches to the problem of labour scarcity and a growing call to abolish the harshest forms of forced labour (Okia 2012; van Waijenburg 2018). African practices of soft resistance, violent protest, and emerging 'civil' movements forced colonial governments to reconsider policies of land alienation and forced labour recruitment. The growing influence of educated African elites, missionaries, war veterans, and international organizations such as the International Labour Organization also added to shifting power relations and policy frames with regard to the African labour question, which played out more intensively in the decades leading up to independence (Cooper 1996).

A second terms of trade boom began with the recovery of African commodity export prices in the second half of the 1930s, which continued in the immediate post-war years up to the mid-1970s. During World War II, international trade declined, but the prices of several strategic commodities, such as copper, rubber, and uranium, boomed. In the 1970s, price trends diverged again. The oil crisis caused large windfall gains in oil-producing countries such as Nigeria, Gabon, and Angola, but prices of most tropical cash-crops and minerals collapsed. In the 1980s, when oil prices also came down, the terms of trade declined in virtually all African countries, and this

Table 10.3 Direction of African exports, 1960–2013 (%)

	Africa*	Asia**	Western Europe	Eastern Europe & (former) USSR	North America	Latin America & Caribbean	Other
1960	7	6	69	6	8	1	3
1990	7	7	61	3	19	1	2
2000	10	18	48	0	19	3	2
2013	14	30	40	0	9	4	3

Notes: * Africa incl. North Africa, excl. South Africa. **Asia excl. the Pacific.
Sources: 1960: United Nations, *Yearbook of International Trade Statistics* 1968, table B; 1990: *Yearbook of International Trade Statistics* 1995, table B; 2000 and 2013: *Yearbook of International Trade Statistics* 2014, table D.

setback lasted until the mid-1990s, when a new cycle of commodity price rises set in, which levelled off around 2015.

Although the dominant pattern of specialization was in primary, resource-intensive, or land-extensive commodities, there were major shifts in the direction and composition of trade, two of which are worth highlighting. First, in the export mix, the relative share of tropical cash crops, such as palm oil, rubber, sugar, cotton, coffee, tea, tobacco, and cocoa, declined with the surge of highly valuable mineral resources such as gold, diamonds, copper, tin, and, above all, crude oil. A large part of Africa's trade boom in the two decades between 1995 and 2015 was driven by favourable oil prices. Since the first oil exports in the late 1950s by Angola and Nigeria, the number of African oil exporters has grown steadily.[6] In most of these countries, the oil revenues drive a large part of income growth and directly impact public revenue. Figure 10.4 shows the growth of per capita exports in the non-oil countries, showing that non-oil export growth up to 2010 barely sufficed to make up for the ground lost in the period 1974–2001. Only if we add oil to the mix has the peak of the early 1970s been surpassed.

The second major shift occurred in the *direction* of trade. For about a full century, African exports had been oriented mainly towards European markets, still absorbing some two-thirds of African exports in 1960. Throughout the colonial era, recorded intra-African trade remained low, probably under 10 per cent of the total. This colonial legacy is now dissolving. Table 10.3 shows that during the first three decades after independence (1960–90) the

6 There are currently nine African countries with significant proven oil reserves: Nigeria, Angola, Gabon, Republic of the Congo, Equatorial Guinea, Cameroon, Sudan, Chad, and Mauritania. Ghana has joined this list in recent years.

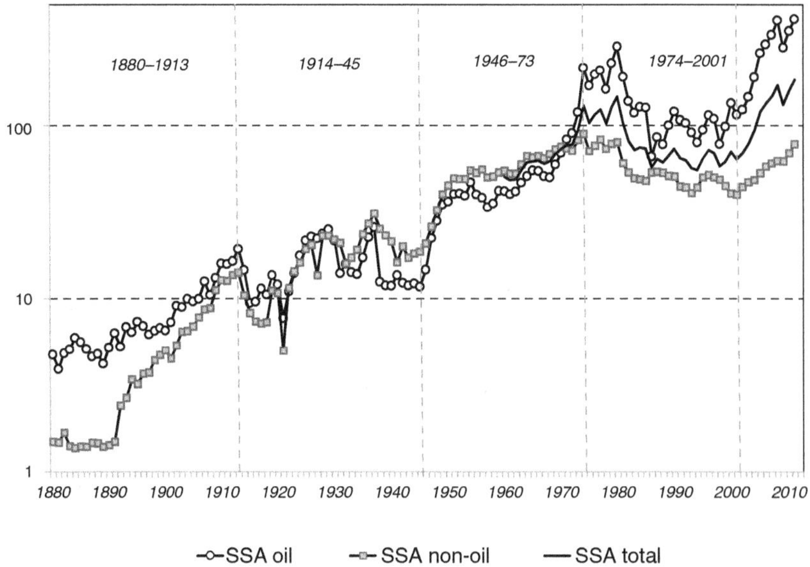

Figure 10.4 Index series of per capita merchandise exports in sub-Saharan Africa, oil and non-oil exporting countries, 1880–2010 (SSA TOTAL 1980 = 100, log-scale)
Note: The oil exporters include Angola, Chad, Republic of the Congo, Equatorial Guinea, Gabon, Mauritania, Nigeria, and Sudan. South Africa is excluded from all series.
Sources: for 1880–1939: author's own calculations, based on the African Commodity Trade Database (Frankema et al. 2018); for 1940–59: Mitchell 2007: table E1; for 1960–2010: *Africa Development Indicators* (World Bank 2020a); population data from Frankema and Jerven 2014.

direction of trade remained largely unchanged, with a growing share for North America at the expense of Europe, and stable but tiny shares for other regions. After 1990 the tables started to shift. Asia, led by China, expanded its share from a meagre 7 per cent in 1990, to 30 per cent in 2013. The share of intra-African trade also doubled, from 7 per cent in 1990, to 14 per cent in 2013. This figure is probably underestimated in the official statistics, as parts of it remain unobserved due to widespread smuggling activities.[7]

The revival of African-Asian trade signals a return to deeper historical trade connections in the Indian Ocean basin, where, amongst other things, Indian cloth was traded for African gold, ivory, and slaves for centuries before the imposition of colonial rule. The declining dependency on Western markets has given African exports a more solid foothold than they had in the early

7 The expanding share of exports to Asia is not exclusively driven by China. India and several South East Asian economies have also enlarged their stake.

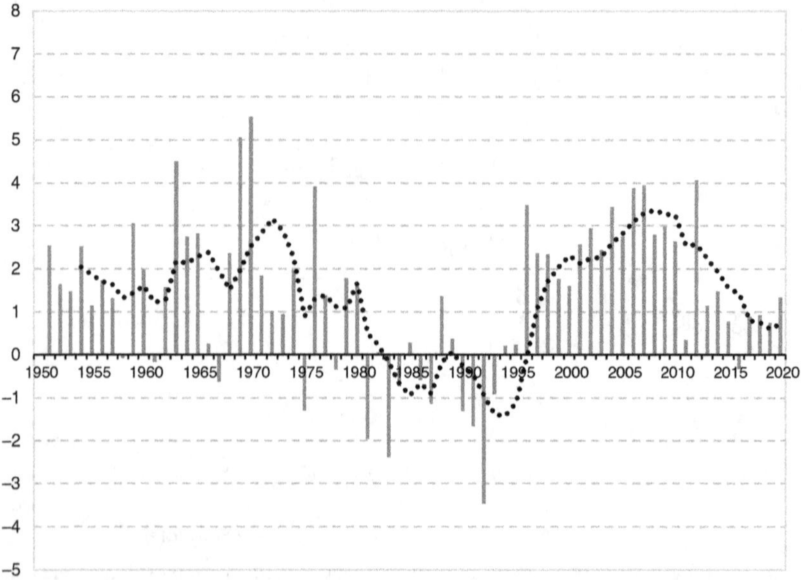

Figure 10.5 Average annual GDP per capita growth in sub-Saharan Africa, 1950–2020 (%)
Note: The growth estimate of 2020 was made before the outbreak of COVID-19.
Sources: 1950–2009: Maddison Project Database, version 2013; 2010–20: International Monetary Fund 2020.

postcolonial era. An important sign of this development is that the deep financial crisis and growth slowdown in Europe and the US of the post-2008 years has not dragged Africa into a new phase of prolonged stagnation, as the crises of the 1930s and the 1970s did.

But growth has remained very volatile. Figure 10.5 shows that the secular trends in trade were closely correlated with the trends in GDP growth. In the two decades between 1995 and 2014, a number of African economies were ranked among the fastest-growing in the world, with annual growth rates of 5–10 per cent being no exception. The aggregate average annual GDP growth rates for sub-Saharan Africa (including South Africa) have been estimated at about 5 per cent since 1995, resulting in a per capita rate of growth slightly over 2 per cent (International Monetary Fund 2012). As demographic growth eroded a major part of total GDP growth, post-1995 per capita growth rates were far from exceptional, and basically meant a return to levels that were observed in the 1950s and 1960s. Part of this growth spurt was a recovery from a long period of stagnation, in which quite a few countries hit rock-bottom in the years 1985–95, thus starting off from very low levels.[8] Yet in the second half of the 2010s, when world commodity markets – especially the oil markets after 2014 – cooled down, growth rates fell back to very modest rates, to be further depressed by the 2020 COVID-19 pandemic.[9]

One of the pre-conditions for the post-1995 growth recovery was the containment of the debt crisis that unfolded during the 1980s and which curtailed long-term investments. The regional average debt burden peaked at 130 per cent of GDP in 1994 and declined to manageable proportions of around 25 per cent in 2006.[10] Debt rescheduling programmes, which were part of broader structural adjustment programmes (SAPs), came along with a stricter application of economic policy orthodoxy, such as money supply controls, inflation targets, exchange rate adjustments, and more shock-proof fiscal policies. SAPs were also combined with political decentralization programmes designed to raise the accountability of African governments. Increased macroeconomic stability and accountability, in turn, have improved the investment climate for African and foreign entrepreneurs. This improved investment climate is illustrated by a doubling of capital investment rates, from a mere 11 per cent in 2000 to 23 per cent in 2012 (International Monetary Fund 2020: 7). But since 2012 African state debt has been growing rapidly again, leading to renewed concerns that history will repeat itself, even though debt ownership has changed to China as well.

Varieties of Capitalism under Colonial Rule

As indicated above, there was no blueprint model for the governance of colonial economies. In some colonies, such as the Gold Coast (Ghana), Nigeria, and Senegal, African farmers and merchants took advantage of existing commercial relations to boost production of cocoa, palm oil, and groundnuts. Elsewhere, commercialization and commodification were enforced by agents of European imperialism, often through co-opted African elites. In other cases, such as the Ugandan cotton sector, external stimulus was soon overtaken by

8 Although the reliability of current and historical GDP estimates has been contested (Jerven 2013), there are no indications that aggregate regional growth rates have been systematically biased to either over- or underestimate growth in particular periods of time. There is also complementary evidence from other economic indicators (e.g. current accounts, state budgets, consumption surveys, investment records) suggesting that the post-1995 growth revival was more than a statistical fantasy.

9 At the time of writing, the magnitude of this shock remained unclear.

10 This figure relates to sub-Saharan Africa excluding South Africa (*Africa Development Indicators*, World Bank 2020a).

African initiative (de Haas 2017b: chapter 5). Plantation owners and mining companies often competed for scarce supplies of (migrant) wage labour and lobbied intensively for measures to avoid paying market-clearing wages. Apart from regulating forced recruitment by colonial agents or private recruitment companies, colonial governments developed other strategies to commodify African labour, such as pass laws, land alienation, the establishment of native reserves, or restrictions on African tenancy, the levying of head, hut, or poll taxes, and racial discrimination in education (Arrighi 1973).

To account for the differences in colonial governance Amin (1972: 504) divided colonial Africa into *trade economies*, *labour reserves*, and areas ruled by *concession-owning companies*. In this threefold typology, the trade economies include the coastal colonies of West Africa, Cameroon, Uganda, Sudan, and Chad (see Figure 10.6). In these areas, African farmers produced the bulk of

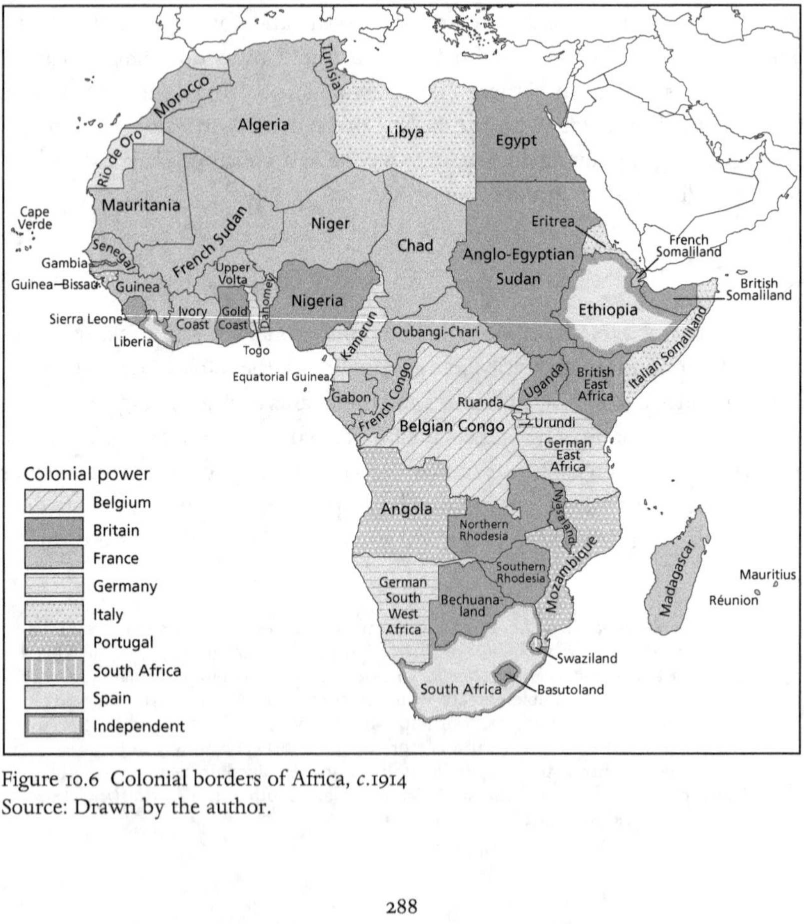

Figure 10.6 Colonial borders of Africa, *c*.1914
Source: Drawn by the author.

agricultural export commodities, while European export companies focused on domestic transportation, shipment, and control of the buyer's market. In some of these colonies, such as Uganda and the Gold Coast, foreign landownership was even prohibited. Colonial governments tended to be less repressive towards local labour and focused most of their interventions on tapping off revenues from trade, via custom duties or, from the 1940s onwards, via marketing boards (Meredith 1986).

In Amin's typology, the Africa of labour reserves included East Africa (Tanzania, Rwanda, Burundi, Kenya, and Uganda), as well as Portuguese Africa (Angola and Mozambique) and Southern Africa (South Africa, Zambia, Zimbabwe, Botswana, and Lesotho). In these areas, colonial institutions were largely geared towards mobilizing African labour for European enterprises engaged in trade, cash-crop cultivation, mining or infrastructural development. Central Africa, including the Belgian Congo and French Equatorial Africa (French Congo, Gabon, and the Central African Republic; but not Chad) made up the Africa of the concession companies. In these areas, chartered companies were granted administrative control over African land, labour, and mineral resources, and often also obtained the right to tax and use force to maintain order.

Although this classification shows that colonial approaches to capitalist production were diverse, it has clear limits for understanding historical change. Chartered companies were granted full administrative powers during the early phase of colonial rule, but almost all of these charters were revoked as companies collapsed under the weight of unsustainable debt. Concession companies obtained charters for selective territories and avoided part of the military costs to subjugate local populations and develop infrastructural connections, but their 'rights' were reduced by expanding colonial administrations during the interwar years (Austen 1987: 123–125). In the 1920s, the British South Africa Company, established by Cecil Rhodes, gave up much of its territorial rights in Southern Africa, and the Portuguese government refused to prolong the concessions of companies active in Mozambique. Concession companies were dismantled or forced to focus on their production activities, while the collection of taxes, the mobilization of labour, and local policing was taken over by the colonial state.[11]

11 Another distinction that has been popularized in the economics literature – between settler and non-settler colonies – is equally problematic (Easterly and Levine 2016). Based on the share of (white) settlers in the total population, only South Africa would qualify as a real settler colony. A more subtle classification scheme focuses on the degree of control exercised by foreign settlers over production factors (land, labour, and capital) and commercially exploitable natural resources (Frankema et al. 2016).

It is probably true that in the trade economies a larger share of African people stood to benefit from export growth and related capital investment, while in mining-dominated colonies (e.g. South Africa, Northern Rhodesia, the Belgian Congo) labour scarcity further curtailed human freedoms. But in the mining regions policy regimes changed too, and sometimes dramatically. For example, workers who were forcibly recruited for the dangerous work in the Katangese copper mines in the 1910s must have been amazed by the material living standards enjoyed by the 'stabilized' workers of the Union Minière in the 1950s, who were probably among the best-paid African manual labourers in sub-Saharan Africa (Juif and Frankema 2018).

South Africa stood apart in many respects. The country emerged out of frontier confrontations between indigenous groups, including the Zulu, Xhosa, Khoisan, Tswana, and Basotho, and settler communities of British, French, and Dutch origin who flowed into the Cape colony from the mid-seventeenth century, supported by the absence of malaria and its strategic location on ocean trade routes. The colony developed in the eighteenth century, amongst other factors, through exports of wine, wool, and other livestock products, and the exploitation of slave labour (Fourie and van Zanden 2013). Yet the mineral discoveries of 1867 (diamonds) and 1886 (gold) changed the game entirely. They further poisoned the already tense political relations between groups of white settlers (the Boer wars, 1880–81 and 1899–1902), as well as between Africans, Europeans, and those of mixed descent. It raised the stakes of white settler elites to control African labour and land. In 1909, South Africa was the first African colony to obtain nominal independence, but it went hand in hand with increasing oppression of African peoples. The Natives Land Act of 1913 restricted the ownership of land by blacks, and in 1948 the elected National Party formalized racial segregation under the infamous apartheid system. The exploitation of its exceptional mineral wealth made South Africa much richer than any other sub-Saharan African country in aggregate, but the inequalities inherent in apartheid jeopardized long-term growth and created a legacy of deep social divisions (Feinstein 2005).

Decolonization, Crises, and Structural Adjustment

Gradually increasing welfare investments were motivated by a growing realization that the legitimacy of colonial rule ultimately depended on delivering upon the 'development' promise. Despite the disruptions caused by World War II, the effects of colonial policy reforms on African living standards became more tangible during the late 1940s and 1950s. More than 80 per cent of the railways that were built during the twentieth century were in place on the eve of World War II (Mitchell 2007: table F1). Larger shares of government budgets were being allocated to education and health care. Economic development programmes also received more funding through imperial loans and grants-in-aid. Governments increasingly took over responsibility for primary and secondary education from Christian missionaries. Universities were established and school enrolments shot up (Frankema 2012). The clearest marker of progress was the acceleration of population growth across the region. Improved access to new medicines (e.g. penicillin) and the extension of health care facilities had significant effects on maternal health and child care (Doyle 2013). Child mortality rates fell, life expectancies lengthened.

Urbanization created new jobs and reconfigured social relations. The number of manufacturing enterprises rose, in particular those producing lighter consumer goods for domestic markets (food and beverages, cigarettes, cotton textiles, footwear, furniture, soap), but also some export-processing of cash crops (cotton ginning, oil-seed crushing), ore smelting, saw-milling, and cement production (Austin et al. 2017). Table 10.4 shows shares of manufacturing in GDP of selected African countries on the eve of independence. These shares varied from 3 per cent in Tanzania to 14 per cent in the Belgian Congo, and 16 per cent in Zimbabwe. In South Africa, manufacturing even comprised 20 per cent of a much larger GDP, but in most other countries – not listed here – shares below 5 per cent were common (Kilby 1975: 472).

The considerable variety of manufacturing development reflected differences in local opportunities as well as economic governance. Colonies with a sizeable mining sector (South Africa, Zimbabwe, Northern Rhodesia, Belgian Congo) demanded manufactured products (food, drinks, clothing, housing, utensils) for increasing urban work forces. Processing industries (e.g. copper refining), construction industries (e.g. cement, steel), and energy provisions were also required to keep the mines going, while growing urban populations with increasing spending capacity deepened the market for consumer manufactures.

The adoption of import substitution industrialization (ISI) policies offered some stimulus to African manufacturing as well. While the French sought to pursue autarky on an imperial scale (Boone 1992), the British feared that overseas competition for British firms would harm the recovery of post-war

Table 10.4 Manufacturing output of selected African countries, 1960 (in 1964 US$)

	Manufacturing/GDP (%)	Population (millions)	GDP ($ millions)	Per capita income ($)	Manufacturing output ($ millions)
S. Rhodesia (Zimbabwe)	16.0	3.6	751	206	120.2
Belgian Congo (DRC)	14.0	14.1	910	58	127.4
Senegal	9.5	3.1	678	218	64.4
Kenya	9.5	8.1	641	79	60.9
Uganda	6.5	6.7	583	87	37.9
Ghana	6.3	6.8	1,503	222	94.7
Cameroon	6.0	4.7	511	109	30.6
Ethiopia	6.0	20.7	1,021	49	61.3
N. Rhodesia (Zambia)	5.5	3.2	511	155	28.1
Ivory Coast	5.3	3.2	584	181	31.0
Sudan	4.8	11.8	909	77	43.6
Nigeria	4.5	40.0	3,500	88	157.5
Angola	4.3	4.8	726	151	31.2
Tanganyika	3.0	9.6	671	67	20.1

Sources: Kilby 1975: 472, table 112; see also Austin et al. 2017: 353.

British industries (Butler 1997). ISI policies were more fully embraced after independence, not only by 'socialist' governments, such as Ghana under Nkrumah (1951–66) and Tanzania under Nyerere (1961–85), but also by 'capitalist' governments, such as Ivory Coast under Houphouët-Boigny (1960–93) and Kenya under Kenyatta (1964–78). Most of these governments also pursued the late colonial habit of five-year development plans to promote key sectors of the economy (Austen 1987: 224–259).

In South Africa and Zimbabwe (Southern Rhodesia), which were granted political autonomy in 1910 and 1923 respectively, ISI policies were adopted earlier and more wholeheartedly. Lobbying groups from various ranks of the settler population used their influence in parliament to rally for policies making unskilled African labour artificially cheap and protecting domestic industries against Western and Japanese imports. In the Belgian Congo, post-war FDI in manufacturing boomed as Belgian firms and settlers sought to diversify their activities (Buelens and Cassimon 2013: 237–241). In contrast, Salazar's dictatorship in Portugal (from 1926 onwards) restricted the influence

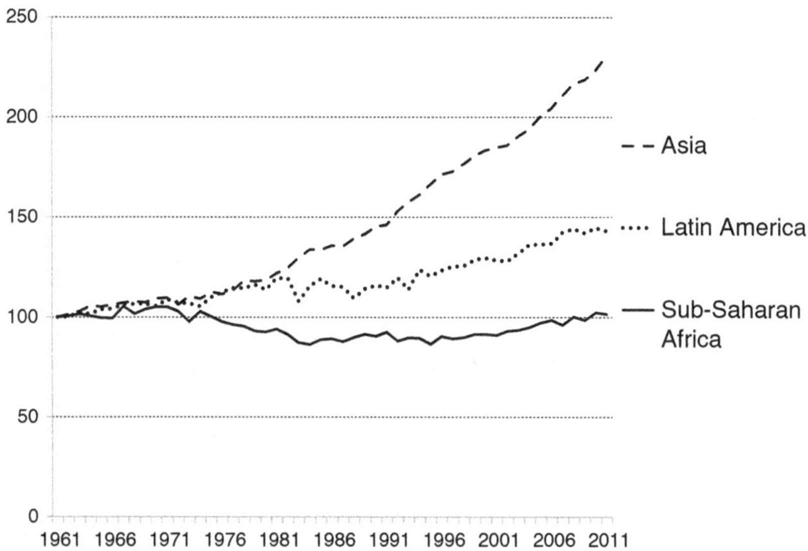

Figure 10.7 Per capita food production in Asia, Latin America, and sub-Saharan Africa, 1961–2011
Sources: Graph from Frankema 2014: 2; data from FAOSTAT 2013.

of Portuguese settlers on their governments and sought to continue the production of raw materials, such as cotton for Portuguese textile firms, thus limiting the former's ability to lobby successfully for local manufacturing enterprises (Clarence-Smith 1989: 177–178). Indeed, by 1960 manufacturing constituted only 4 per cent of GDP in Angola, and 14 and 16 per cent in the Belgian Congo and Zimbabwe, respectively.

That said, food crop agriculture remained the largest sector in terms of output and employment in the majority of African economies. Even though farming systems varied enormously from place to place, the aggregate picture in Figure 10.7 depicts a structural, broadly shared weakness: a lack of productivity growth. After 1970, population growth rates even started to outpace growth in food production, so that only in recent years was per capita production of food just back to 1960 levels. This lack of productivity growth partly explains why the modest upsurge in manufacturing growth came to a halt after the 1970s. Continued rural poverty eroded both domestic consumer demand and domestic savings (Austin et al. 2017). The 'Green Revolution' of the 1940s to 1970s, which lifted considerable parts of the world's 'poor periphery' out of extreme poverty, largely bypassed sub-Saharan Africa. High-yielding varieties of wheat and rice did not suit

African ecologies well, although improved maize varieties did. Markets were insufficiently integrated, food storage remained a critical weakness, fertilizers were hard to come by, and a pronounced 'urban bias' in early postcolonial economic policy, or disastrous collectivization programmes, did not help solve these problems (Lipton 1977; Otsuka et al. 2009).

In the early 1950s, few would have guessed that independence would come within a decade. Only Portugal held on to its colonies until 1975, at the cost of prolonged wars of independence, which eventually undermined Portuguese state finances. The years before and after 1960 were characterized by heightened nationalist sentiment and grand visions of African unity (pan-Africanism). But the spirit evaporated quickly, and in some countries almost immediately. Within two decades the region plunged into a deep economic and political crisis, just at the time that many Asian countries started to experience the welfare gains from agricultural and industrial productivity growth.

In Nyerere's Tanzania, for instance, high ideals of African socialism, cast in the concept of *ujamaa*, resulted in disastrous initiatives of villagization and collectivization. In other places, the artificial and externally secured colonial 'peace' fell apart for lesser aspirations. In many countries, tendencies of political instability were aggravated by the debt crisis of the 1980s to 1990s, which sentenced the region to a long period of economic stagnation, and in several places, such as the Congo, Zambia, Sierra Leone, and Somalia, full-scale economic collapse (Bates 2008; Young 2012). Ethiopia and Liberia, the two countries below the Sahara that had largely escaped colonial domination, did not fare much better. On the contrary, the devastating Ethiopian famine of 1983–85 showed that structural economic weaknesses were not just a colonial legacy, but could also occur in a consolidated state built upon centuries of sedentary plough-based agriculture.

During the colonial era, most African economies had access to metropolitan capital markets, which supplied colonial states with relatively cheap loans that were backed by the metropolitan treasury. In the post-independence era, this dependency shifted. Former French West African states held on to the CFA franc and avoided the hyperinflation that plagued former British West African countries, such as Nigeria and Ghana, but their exports suffered from chronic currency overvaluation (van de Walle 1991). Poorly managed and overambitious development schemes (often part of Five-Year Plans) were financed with increasing (trade) tax revenues at first, but when the export boom came to a full stop in the 1970s, government borrowing became more important to maintain expansionary fiscal policies. These loans were supplied eagerly by global capital markets, glutted by superfluous oil dollars. The influx of large amounts of oil dollars at negative interest rates tempted African leaders, often with short-term political time horizons, to take on uncontrollable levels of debt. When local currencies depreciated and interest rates shot up in the 1980s, this burden became unbearable (Parfitt and Riley 2013).

The SAPs imposed by the IMF and World Bank consisted of severe cutbacks in public expenditure, trade liberalization, and privatization, and, later, also included debt-rescheduling negotiations. These SAPs cut short the government subsidies that underpinned most of the social and economic development programmes, and hit the rural sector particularly hard. The urban bias in policy directives compounded agricultural neglect, led to the deterioration of important public services, and enhanced the invasion of (Western) NGOs filling the gaps left by local and central government bodies.

The political and economic crises were far from uniform, but they did share some commonalities. First, the colonial inheritance of 'states without nations': ethnic, linguistic, cultural, and/or religious divisions played a role in virtually all violent conflicts, and most of these were fought within the confines of colonial territorial borders. Second, in most conflicts, control over valuable resources, and especially the revenues from the export sector, played a role. Resource monopolies and rent extraction facilitated politics based on patrimonialism, clientelism, and corruption, in many respects comparable to the ways in which colonial governments had taken control over wealth and people (Mamdani 1996; Bayart 2009). Third, up to the 1990s, Cold War politics often crept into local African conflict in some way or another. Incumbent regimes as well as opposition groups faced the question of international alliance in their demand for weapons and financial aid. Fighting groups paying lip service to Western capitalism, Soviet-style socialism, or religious fundamentalism were often able to find support somewhere. This international context prolonged local conflicts and raised the chances of new disruptions of fragile political equilibria (Nugent 2012).

Deep Transitions: Changing Economic Geographies

Underneath the patterns of growth and contraction discussed above, there were a number of deep transitions that continued more or less unabated. Africa's booming population is probably the most fundamental of these deep

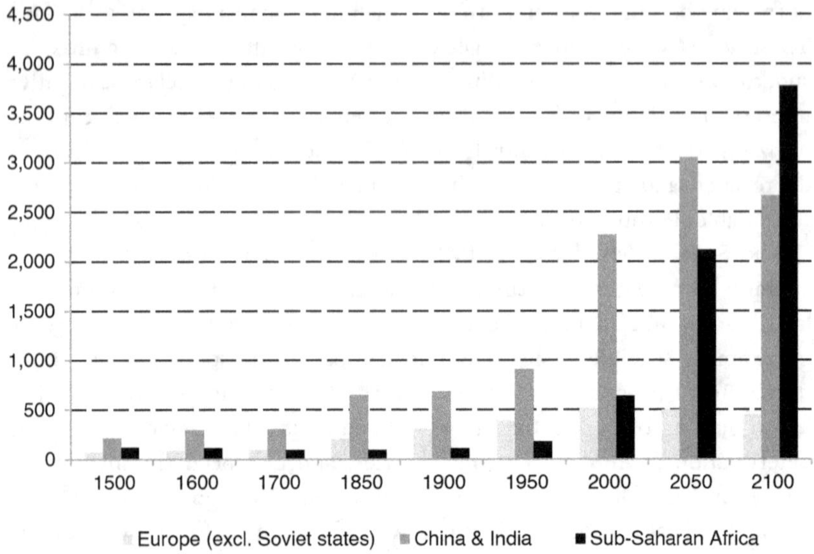

Figure 10.8 Historical and projected population trends in sub-Saharan Africa, Europe, and Asia, 1500–2100 (millions)
Sources: Population estimates, Europe and Asia 1500–1950: Maddison 2010; African estimates 1500–1950: based on Manning 2010; Frankema and Jerven 2014; all figures for 1950–2100: United Nations 2019, medium-fertility scenarios.

transitions. Population growth rates exceeding 3 per cent for decades in a row were historically unprecedented, and even though fertility rates came down in most places after 1980, they remain far above the net replacement threshold. According to the United Nations mid-range population projections, shown in Figure 10.8, sub-Saharan Africa is the only region in the world where substantial demographic growth will continue beyond 2050. With an estimated 4 billion people in 2100, the region may experience a thirty-fold natural increase of population in just two centuries. If these projections hold, Africa will be home to almost 40 per cent of the world's population in 2100 and include five of the ten most populous countries in the world (i.e. Nigeria, Congo, Tanzania, Ethiopia, Niger).

It is uncertain when (natural) population growth started to accelerate, but it certainly varied from region to region. Doyle (2013) has shown that even within relatively confined areas (e.g. the East African great lakes area), the take-off may easily have differed by some two to three decades. For the continent as a whole, the acceleration of demographic growth became visible in the 1940s, but future work on African historical demography may push the dates back somewhat further. Populations in North and South Africa, where disease climates were milder and where access to medicine and health care was more advanced, recorded significant growth already before 1900 (Manning 2010; Frankema and Jerven 2014).

From an economic point of view, there are at least two major implications of the population boom that deserve further exploration. First, the transition from a historically low-populated region (around 5 persons per km^2 in 1950) into one of the most densely populated continents of the world (around 150 persons per km^2 in 2100) is changing relative factor proportions of labour and land fundamentally. The demographic boom is closing the door to the land-extensive agricultural growth trajectory which has dominated African development since the decline of the slave trades, and which continued during the cash-crop revolution of the colonial era (Tosh 1980). Arable land is increasingly becoming a scarce production factor, while the supply of both unskilled and skilled/educated labour has increased steeply.

Second, the demographic boom partly initiated and partly reinvigorated an increasing concentration of scattered rural populations. Demographic growth is thus driving one of the most fundamental (and probably irreversible) changes in the topography of African economies: urbanization. This development has been facilitated by the spread of transportation, information, and communication technology, which provides the necessary infrastructure for large-scale urban food supplies. Whereas Africa has historically always depended on domestic produce for its subsistence, a growing number of countries became net food importers during the final quarter of the twentieth century.

Urbanization also led to profound changes in social and gender relations, and in access to education, information, and knowledge. The changes are particularly visible in the urban service sector, since demand for transportation, communication services, finance, catering, water, and energy has expanded so vastly. The main part of the associated service activities is conducted in the informal sector, where enormous reserves of underemployed youth engage in petty trade, street vending, food processing, handicraft workshops, motorbike drives, small-scale business services, prostitution, and a range of other informal and/or illegal activities. Informal employment shares in African economies typically range from 70 to over 90 per cent of total employment (International Labour Organization 2018: 14). This also means that city and state administrations operate on very thin tax bases. Urban dwellers tend to have a range of 'jobs' to make a living and rely on extensive social networks for credit and insurance. Links between family members living in cities and the countryside are vital for spreading the risk of both economic environments.

Deep Transitions: Institutional Development and Factor Markets

The high shares of informal sector employment show that the institutions required to facilitate broad-based labour productivity growth and provide a minimum basis of social security remain underdeveloped. This type of paralysis is often understood as a problem of rigid 'extractive' institutions inherited from the colonial or precolonial past, acting as structural barriers to growth (Acemoglu et al. 2001; Nunn 2008). However, such popular conceptions of institutional persistence are rather misleading. African societies have undergone tremendous institutional changes during the twentieth century, which have given rise to new institutional complexes embedded in political economic structures that are very different from those prevailing in previous centuries, which is not the same as arguing that they are necessarily better at promoting growth. These institutional complexes have been shaped by the intertwinement of institutions imposed by colonial regimes and the older customary institutions that have survived and adapted to colonial rule. In this process, institutions governing factor markets and the allocation of communal resources were not only reconfigured, they also created new sources for conflict and rent-seeking. A brief sketch of some major transitions in the four principal factor markets – labour, land, and physical and human capital – can give the reader some idea of the depth of these changes.

The transition in African labour markets entailed a shift away from labour coercion through systems of slavery, forced and (debt) bonded labour, towards commodified labour and self-employment, the latter increasingly concentrated in urban informal sectors. Slavery and forced labour are generally regarded as institutional responses to chronic labour scarcity in settings where most African farmers had few incentives to abandon subsistence agriculture. This situation dissolved during the twentieth century in more and more places (Iliffe 2007; Austin 2008b). Coerced labour is now largely shaped by the opposing force: vast supplies of skilled and semi-skilled workers who have little opportunity to resort to subsistence farming. This situation provides ample opportunities for local 'strongmen' to extract labour services. Institutions to protect workers from outright exploitation, such as minimum wage schemes, employment protection, disability insurance, or anti-harassment and anti-child labour legislation, are largely ineffective in informal sector arrangements. In other words, while precolonial and colonial governments officially sanctioned the coercion of labour, postcolonial societies increasingly moved to labour arrangements outside the reach of the state.

In land markets, the transition involved moving from one of myriad systems of communal landownership, often arranged at a village level, based on hereditary claims and enforced through customary law, towards a system of individual property rights, with a special role for large-scale land appropriation by colonial and postcolonial states, which extract(ed) revenue from the lease or sale of alienated land. As a result, African land markets are paralysed by many overlapping claims and legal opacity. Malfunctioning cadastres and growing political stakes in control over land have given rise to intensive land conflicts, especially over high-valued land in or near expanding cities, or between agriculturalists and pastoralists. Overlapping claims to land are by no means a recent phenomenon, but the intensity of land conflict has been aggravated by population growth and increasing (colonial) state intervention in local land markets with corrupting effects (Boone 2014). Indeed, whereas labour became the abundant factor, land has become scarcer, and in both cases the institutions governing factor allocation have changed profoundly.

Markets for capital have seen major expansion during the twentieth century, even though access to financial services from banks or insurance companies remains complicated for the majority of poor African households, who dispose of little savings and other forms of collateral. Capital markets have long been dominated by foreign suppliers. Domestic savings rates have fallen back below 20 per cent of GDP in the past two decades, instead of climbing to rates of 30 per cent, as has been common in many Asian industrializers (World Bank 2020b). Yet government borrowing and FDI has partly diversified from the metropole to other global suppliers, with a particular role for Chinese credit and investments. Nigeria and South Africa, the two largest economic engines south of the Sahara have also expanded their share of FDI in the region, but much of the FDI inflow continues to be very volatile, responding to both world commodity price fluctuations and frequent ruptures in political stability.

Finally, a major transition has occurred in the market for human capital. Although Africa's performance compares unfavourably to other world regions, the education revolution has had a deep impact on social relations and economic capabilities. Literacy and numeracy rates have risen throughout the twentieth century, and have made a large set of basic skills much cheaper than they were at the start of the twentieth century (Frankema and van Waijenburg 2019). New information and communication technologies have given an impulse to knowledge-intensive activities, and it is hard to see how such developments will fail to stimulate labour specialization in the future. That said, most African societies continue to cope with large inequalities in access to education, and social exclusion of the poorest who cannot afford school fees, let alone the fees of private schools and universities offering higher quality education. Unequal access to schooling remains one of the key factors sustaining inequality in African societies, and it is destined to be one of the major political issues of the twenty-first century.

Conclusion

African per capita income levels have fallen significantly behind other world regions during the long twentieth century, but especially after 1973. Despite this appearance of relative stagnation, African economies underwent profound transitions. This chapter has contrasted persistent patterns of recurrent growth and contraction and specialization in primary commodity production, to deeper changes in African economic geographies and institutions governing factor markets. Will Africa embark on a path of sustained economic growth in the twenty-first century?

Pessimists point out that continued dependence on primary commodity exports, weak institutional environments, and frightening rates of population growth will continue to hold the region back. They point out that the ranks of underemployed youth in African cities without a perspective of betterment are swelling every year, and that this continues to undermine prospects of long-term political stability. They also point out that increasing scarcity of vital resources, such as drinking water, rainforests, and pastures, alongside decreasing biodiversity and insecure change of climates, are threatening the region more than ever.

Optimists point out that many historical constraints to growth have been dissolved during the long twentieth century: labour and capital have become less scarce, transportation barriers have been lifted, African labour is no longer tied up in low-productive agriculture, domestic consumer demand is increasing, and life expectancy, literacy rates, and access to electricity, the internet, and clean drinking water have all improved, while rates of extreme poverty continue to fall. They may even argue that Africa's population boom lays the foundation for domestic growth and investment, and a reduction of the external dependencies that have characterized much of the twentieth century.

No matter what the future will bring, it is clear that African economic development will take place in a rapidly changing global economic and political context. By 2050, Asia and Africa together will hold over 80 per cent of the world population (United Nations 2019). The income gap between both regions is growing and may well give rise to a new 'great' divergence. Will Asia's economic renaissance offer new opportunities to Africa, or does it close the windows instead? Will plans to create the world's largest free trade zone in Africa materialize? What happens to intra-African migration if economic inequality across countries rises? These are some of the big issues that will shape the future of new generations of Africans. Their growing weight will have a growing impact on the development of the world economy in the twenty-first century.

References

Acemoglu, D., Johnson, S., and Robinson, J. A. (2001). 'The Colonial Origins of Comparative Development: An Empirical Investigation', *American Economic Review*, 91(5), 1369–1401.

AfDB / OECD / UNDP. (2014). *African Economic Outlook 2014: Global Value Chains and Africa's Industrialisation*, Paris: OECD Publishing.

Allen, R. C. (2011). *Global Economic History: A Very Short Introduction*, Oxford University Press.

Amin, S. (1972). 'Underdevelopment and Dependence in Black Africa: Origins and Contemporary Forms', *Journal of Modern African Studies*, 10(4), 503–524.

Arrighi, G. (1973). 'Labor Supplies in Historical Perspective: A Study of the Proletarianization of the African Peasantry in Rhodesia', in Arrighi, G. and Saul, J. S. (eds.), *Essays on the Political Economy of Africa*, New York: Monthly Review Press, 180–234.

Austen, R. A. (1987). *African Economic History: Internal Development and External Dependency*, London: James Curry / Heinemann.

Austin, G. (2005). *Labour, Land and Capital in Ghana: From Slavery to Free Labour in Asante, 1807–1956*, Rochester Studies in African History and the Diaspora, New York: University of Rochester Press.

(2008a). 'The "Reversal of Fortune" Thesis and the Compression of History: Perspectives from African and Comparative Economic History', *Journal of International Development*, 20, 996–1027.

(2008b). 'Resources, Techniques, and Strategies South of the Sahara: Revising the Factor Endowments Perspective on African Economic Development History', *Economic History Review*, 61(3), 587–624.

Austin, G., Frankema, E., and Jerven, M. (2017). 'Patterns of Manufacturing Growth in Sub-Saharan Africa: From Colonization to the Present', in O'Rourke, K. and Williamson, J. G. (eds.), *The Spread of Modern Industry to the Periphery since 1871*, Oxford University Press, 345–373.

Bates, R. H. (2008). *When Things Fell Apart: State Failure in Late-Century Africa*, New York: Cambridge University Press.

Bates, R. H., Coatsworth, J. H., and Williamson, J. G. (2007). 'Lost Decades: Postindependence Performance in Latin America and Africa,' *Journal of Economic History*, 67(4), 917–943.

Bayart, J.-F. (2009). *The State in Africa: The Politics of the Belly*, 2nd ed., Cambridge: Polity Press.

Bloom, D., Sachs, J., Collier, P., and Udry, C. (1998). 'Geography, Demography, and Economic Growth in Africa', *Brookings Papers on Economic Activity*, 2, 207–295.

Bolt, J. and Hillbom, E. (2016). 'Long-Term Trends in Economic Inequality: Lessons from Colonial Botswana, 1921–74', *Economic History Review*, 69(4), 1255–1284.

Boone, C. (1992). *Merchant Capital and the Roots of State Power in Senegal, 1930–1985*, Cambridge University Press.

(2014). *Property and Political Order in Africa: Land Rights and the Structure of Politics*, New York: Cambridge University Press.

Bowden, S., Chiripanhura, B., and Mosley, P. (2008). 'Measuring and Explaining Poverty in Six African Countries: A Long-Period Approach', *Journal of International Development*, 20(8), 1049–1079.

Broadberry, S. and Gardner, L. (2019). 'Economic Growth in Sub-Saharan Africa, 1885–2008', LSE Economic History working paper 296.

Buelens, F. and Cassimon, D. (2013). 'The Industrialization of the Belgian Congo', in Frankema, E. and Buelens, F. (eds.), *Colonial Exploitation and Economic Development: The Belgian Congo and the Netherlands Indies Compared*, London: Routledge, 229–250.

Butler, L. J. (1997). *Industrialisation and the British Colonial State: West Africa, 1939–1951*, London: Frank Cass.

Clarence-Smith, W. G. (1989). 'The Effects of the Great Depression on Industrialisation in Equatorial and Central Africa', in Brown, I. (ed.), *The Economies of Africa and Asia in the Inter-War Depression*, London and New York: Routledge, 170–202.

Cooper, F. (1996). *Decolonization and African Society: The Labor Question in French and British Africa*, Cambridge University Press.

de Haas, M. (2017a). 'Measuring Rural Welfare in Colonial Africa: Did Uganda's Smallholders Thrive?', *Economic History Review*, 70(2), 605–631.

(2017b). 'Rural Livelihoods and Agricultural Commercialization in Colonial Uganda: Conjunctures of External Influences and Local Realities', PhD thesis, Wageningen University.

Doyle, S. (2013). *Before HIV: Sexuality, Fertility, and Mortality in East Africa, 1900–1980*, Oxford University Press.

Easterly, W. and Levine, R. (2016). 'The European Origins of Economic Development', *Journal of Economic Growth*, 21(3), 225–257.

FAOSTAT. (2013). Food and Agriculture Data, available online at http://faostat.fao.org/site/291/default.aspx (data accessed March–May 2013), Rome: Food and Agriculture Organization.

Feinstein, C. H. (2005). *An Economic History of South Africa: Conquest, Discrimination and Development*, Cambridge University Press.

Fourie, J. and van Zanden, J. L. (2013). 'GDP in the Dutch Cape Colony: The National Accounts of a Slave-Based Society', *South African Journal of Economics*, 81(4): 467–490.

Frankema, E. (2012). 'The Origins of Formal Education in Sub-Saharan Africa: Was British Rule More Benign?', *European Review of Economic History*, 16(4), 335–355.

(2014). 'Africa and the Green Revolution: A Global Historical Perspective', *NJAS – Wageningen Journal of Life Sciences*, 70–71, 17–24.

Frankema, E. and Jerven, M. (2014). 'Writing History Backwards or Sideways: Towards a Consensus on African Population, 1850–2010', *Economic History Review*, 67(4), 907–931.

Frankema, E. and van Waijenburg, M. (2012). 'Structural Impediments to African Growth? New Evidence from Real Wages in British Africa, 1880–1965', *Journal of Economic History*, 72(4), 895–926.

(2014). 'Metropolitan Blueprints of Colonial Taxation? Lessons from Fiscal Capacity Building in British and French Africa, c.1880–1940', *Journal of African History*, 55(3), 371–400.

(2018). 'Africa Rising? A Historical Perspective', *African Affairs*, 117(469), 543–568.

(2019). 'The Great Convergence: Skill Accumulation and Mass Education in Africa and Asia, 1870–2010', CEPR Discussion Paper 14150, Centre for Economic Policy Research.

Frankema, E., Green, E., and Hillbom, E. (2016). 'Endogenous Processes of Colonial Settlement: The Success and Failure of European Settler Farming in Sub-Saharan Africa', *Revista de Historia Económica*, 34(2), 237–265.

Frankema, E., Williamson, J. G., and Woltjer, P. J. (2018). 'An Economic Rationale for the West African Scramble? The Commercial Transition and the Commodity Price Boom of 1835–1885', *Journal of Economic History*, 78(1), 231–267.

Hopkins, A. G. (1973). *An Economic History of West Africa*, London: Longman.

Iliffe, J. (2007). *Africans: The History of a Continent*, 2nd ed., New York: Cambridge University Press.

International Labour Organization. (2018). *Women and Men in the Informal Economy: A Statistical Picture*, 3rd ed., Geneva: International Labour Office.

International Monetary Fund. (2012). *Regional Economic Outlook. Sub-Saharan Africa: Sustaining Growth Amidst Global Uncertainty*, Washington, DC: IMF.

(2020). *World Economic Outlook, October 2020*, Washington, DC: IMF. www.imf.org/external/datamapper/datasets/WEO/1 (accessed 4 November 2020).

Jerven, M. (2010). 'African Growth Recurring: An Economic History Perspective on African Growth Episodes, 1690–2010', *Economic History of Developing Regions*, 25(2), 127–154.

(2013). *Poor Numbers: How We Are Misled by African Development Statistics and What to Do about It*, Ithaca: Cornell University Press.

Juif, D. and Frankema, E. (2018). 'From Coercion to Compensation: Institutional Responses to Labour Scarcity in the Central African Copperbelt', *Journal of Institutional Economics*, 14(2), 313–343.

Kilby, P. (1975). 'Manufacturing in Colonial Africa', in Duignan, P. and Gann, L. H. (eds.), *Colonialism in Africa, 1870–1960*, Cambridge University Press, 475–520.

Kjekshus, H. (1996). *Ecology Control and Economic Development in East African History: The Case of Tanganyika, 1850–1950*, London: J. Currey.

Klein, M. A. (1998). *Slavery and Colonial Rule in French West Africa*, Cambridge and New York: Cambridge University Press.

Law, R. (ed.) (1995). *From Slave Trade to Legitimate Commerce: The Commercial Transition in Nineteenth-Century West Africa*, Cambridge University Press.

Lipton, M. (1977). *Why Poor People Stay Poor: A Study of Urban Bias in World Development*, London: Temple Smith.

(2013). 'Income from Work: The Food-Population-Resource Crisis in "The Short Africa"', *British Academy Review* 22, 34–38.

Maddison, A. (2010). Historical Statistics on World Population, GDP and Per Capita GDP, 1–2008 AD, available online at www.ggdc.net/maddison/ (accessed 29 September 2020).

Mamdani, M. (1996). *Citizen and Subject: Contemporary Africa and the Legacy of Late Colonialism*, Princeton University Press.

Manning, P. (2010). 'African Population: Projections, 1851–1961', in Ittmann, K., Cordell, D. D., and Maddox, G. H. (eds.), *The Demographics of Empire: The Colonial Order and the Creation of Knowledge*, Athens: Ohio University Press, 245–275.

Meredith, D. (1986). 'State-Controlled Marketing and Economic Development: The Case of West African Produce during the Second World War', *Economic History Review*, 39 (1), 77–91.

Mitchell, B. R. (2007). *International Historical Statistics: Africa, Asia and Oceania, 1750–2005*, 5th ed., Basingstoke: Palgrave Macmillan.

Moradi, A. (2009). 'Towards an Objective Account of Nutrition and Health in Colonial Kenya: A Study of Stature in African Army Recruits and Civilians, 1880–1980', *Journal of Economic History*, 96(3), 720–755.

North, D. C., Wallis, J. J., and Weingast, B. R. (2009). *Violence and Social Orders: A Conceptual Framework for Interpreting Recorded Human History*, Cambridge University Press.

Nugent, P. (2012). *Africa since Independence*, 2nd ed., New York: Palgrave Macmillan.

Nunn, N. (2008). 'The Long-Term Effects of Africa's Slave Trades', *Quarterly Journal of Economics*, 123(1), 139–176.

Okia, O. (2012). *Communal Labor in Colonial Kenya Legitimizing Coercion, 1912–1930*, New York: Palgrave Macmillan.

Otsuka, K., Estudillo, J. P., and Sawada, Y. (eds.) (2009). *Rural Poverty and Income Dynamics in Asia and Africa*, London and New York: Routledge.

Parfitt, T. W. and Riley, S. P. (2013). *The African Debt Crisis*, London: Routledge.

Prados de la Escosura, L. (2012). 'Output Per Head in Pre-Independence Africa: Quantitative Conjectures', *Economic History of Developing Regions*, 27(2), 1–36.

Radelet, S. C. (2010). *Emerging Africa: How Seventeen Countries Are Leading the Way*, Baltimore: Center for Global Development.

Reid, R. J. (2009). *A History of Modern Africa: 1800 to the Present*, Oxford: Wiley-Blackwell.

Rodrik, D. (2014). 'An African Growth Miracle?', CEPR Discussion Paper 10005, Centre for Economic Policy Research.

Sender, J. and Smith, S. (1986). *The Development of Capitalism in Africa*, London: Methuen.

Sheriff, A. (1987). *Slaves, Spices and Ivory in Zanzibar: Integration of an East African Commercial Empire into the World Economy, 1770–1873*, London: James Currey.

Tosh, J. (1980). 'The Cash-Crop Revolution in Tropical Africa: An Agricultural Reappraisal', *African Affairs*, 79(314), 79–94.

United Nations. (2019). World Population Prospects 2019, available online at https://population.un.org/wpp/ (accessed 29 September 2020), Population Division, United Nations.

(various issues). *Yearbook of International Trade Statistics*, New York: United Nations.

van Waijenburg, M. (2018). 'Financing the African Colonial State: The Revenue Imperative and Forced Labour', *Journal of Economic History*, 78(1), 40–80.

van de Walle, N. (1991). 'The Decline of the Franc Zone: Monetary Politics in Francophone Africa', *African Affairs*, 90(360), 383–405.

Vansina, J. (2010). *Being Colonized: The Kuba Experience in Rural Congo, 1880–1960*, Madison: University of Wisconsin Press.

Warren, B. (1980). *Imperialism: Pioneer of Capitalism*, London: New Left Books.

World Bank (2020a). *Africa Development Indicators*, Washington, DC: World Bank.

(2020b). *World Development Indicators*, available online at http://data.worldbank.org/data-catalog/world-development-indicators, Washington, DC: World Bank.

Young, C. (2012). *The Postcolonial State in Africa Fifty Years of Independence, 1960–2010*, Madison: University of Wisconsin Press.

11

Australia
Prosperity, Relative Decline, and Reorientation

GARY B. MAGEE

In the diaries of Australians who had served in World War I, it is not uncommon to come across references to the poor physical fitness of the British Tommies alongside whom they had fought. Many Australians expressed genuine surprise at how much bigger, stronger, and often better educated they were than the working-class soldiers of industrial Britain they had encountered (Holbrook 2014). Recent research on the heights of recruits into the Australian Imperial Force during World War I provides empirical support for these observations. It found that soldiers born in Australia in the latter decades of the nineteenth century were taller by a statistically significant measure than those who had been born in Britain: 1.3 centimetres taller than soldiers born in England or Scotland, and as much as 2.1 centimetres larger, on average, than those from Wales (Cranfield and Inwood 2015). At the beginning of the twentieth century, the imposing physical stature of Australians, the vast majority of whom were themselves originally of British stock, was attributed to the comparatively high quality of life they had enjoyed during their formative years in the Antipodes: a striking visualization, one might say, of the successes of Australian economic development.

In this chapter, we consider the Australian economy that had given rise to such physically fit individuals. What underpinned that economy's apparent successes and, crucially, was Australia able to maintain these advantages across the twentieth century into the twenty-first? In order to answer such questions, this chapter first outlines the key contours of Australian economic history between 1870 and 2010, and then places the nation's economic development over this period into a comparative perspective. Overall, the story it tells is a positive one. Despite undergoing relative economic decline and a fundamental reorientation in the direction of its trade over this period, Australia emerged into the twenty-first century with its status as one of the world's most prosperous and advanced societies intact. While numerous challenges remain unresolved and, indeed, threatening to its customary way of life, Australia's experience to date provides a clear-cut example of a society where an abundance of natural resources has proved a blessing rather than a curse.

Population

When the First Fleet arrived in Botany Bay on 24 January 1788, those aboard found a land that was far from unpopulated. The most recent research estimates that between 750,000 and 800,000 Aborigines called Australia home at that point in time (Mulvaney 2002). By 1820, there were 33,543 Europeans (Butlin et al. 2015) residing in the colony, which implies, according to Maddison's (2010) estimates of total Australian population for that year of 334,000, an Aboriginal population of approximately 300,000. This sharp fall in their numbers, however, was only the beginning of a history of population decline wrought by disease and dispossession that steadily reduced indigenous Australians to a very small percentage of the total population (Smith 1980; Hunter 2015). In 1870, approximately a century after the foundation of European Australia, the total population of the country had grown to around 1.8 million, of whom only about 7.1 per cent were indigenous peoples. By the time of federation in 1901, their numbers had fallen even further, to 100,000 or 2.6 per cent of the 3.8 million who resided in Australia (Altman and Biddle 2015).

Thus, by 1871, Australia in terms of population was overwhelmingly of European origin, especially British: 95.2 per cent of the foreign-born population and 97.8 per cent of the total population of Australia were born in what might be called primarily European societies. Of these, the British, accounting for 87.9 per cent of all foreign-born people in Australia and 40.9 per cent of the total population, were by far the most important source of immigrants (Price 1987).

Australia's population has grown steadily in size over time, at an average rate of 1.8 per cent between 1870 and 2008. Figure 11.1 and Table 11.1 outline the course of Australian population history. There was rapid expansion from the 1870s to the early 1890s, with the average annual rate of growth reaching its peak in the 1880s, at 3.6 per cent. From the mid-1890s through to the end of World War II, the rate of growth was somewhat slower, especially during the 1930s and 1940s. More rapid immigration-fuelled population growth, in excess of 2 per cent per annum, reappeared in the 1950s and 1960s, only to return to

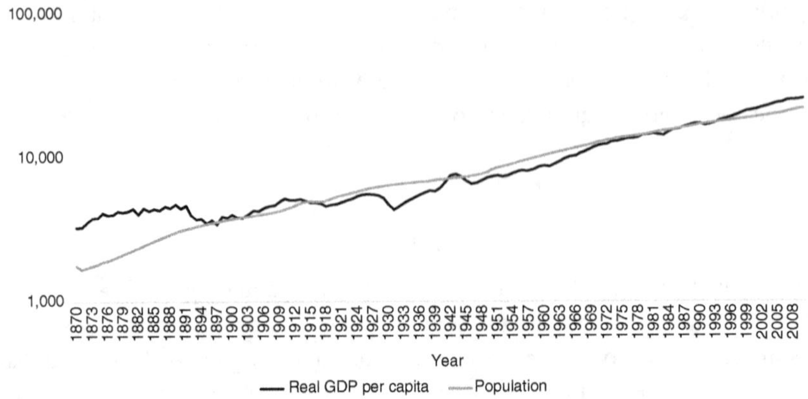

Figure 11.1 Population and real GDP per capita, 1870–2010 (1990 international $)
Note: Logarithmic scale used.
Source: Maddison 2010; Maddison Project Database, version 2013.

lower and declining, yet still positive, growth rates thereafter. By the last decade of the twentieth century, population expansion had retreated to around 1.2 per cent per annum, a rate that was lower than that experienced in any other decade in the period covered (other than the 1930s). According to the 2011 Census, there were 21.5 million people residing in Australia in that year, 669,881, or 3.1 per cent of whom were Aborigines or Torres Strait Islanders. The UK still remained the biggest source of migrants in the community (20.8 per cent), followed by New Zealand (9.1 per cent), China (6.0 per cent), India (5.6 per cent), and Italy (3.5 per cent). British-born individuals now, however, constituted just 5 per cent of the total population, a smaller proportion of the population than at any other time in Australia's history since European settlement (Australian Bureau of Statistics 2011; 2012; 2013).

Growth

For most of its history, Australia's expanding population has enjoyed a high and improving level of income. Between 1870 and 2009, real GDP per capita grew on average at 1.6 per cent a year. Yet there has been considerable fluctuation around this trend. The periods of most rapid growth were experienced in the 1870s and the 1960s. By contrast, the period between 1890 and 1939 was characterized by great volatility, as two major depressions between 1890 and 1897 and 1930 and 1933, and World War I impacted heavily on the Australian economy, leading to bouts of negative growth and high levels of unemployment.

Table 11.1 An overview of Australian economic development, 1870–2009

	Population (average rate of growth)	Real GDP (average rate of growth)	Real GDP per capita (average rate of growth)	Real wages (average rate of growth)	Unemployment rate (average)	Agriculture (average share of GDP)	Mining (average share of GDP)	Manufacturing (average share of GDP)	Tertiary sector (average share of GDP)	Infant deaths per 1,000 live births (average)	Trade as a proportion of GDP (average share of exports + imports out of GDP)	Relative rate of assistance to manufacturing (average rate)	Current account balance as a share of GDP (average)	Net migration's contribution to population growth (average share)	Income share of top 1 per cent (average)
	(1)	(2)	(3)	(4)	(5)	(6)	(7)	(8)	(9)	(10)	(11)	(12)	(13)	(14)	(15)
1870–79	2.0	5.3	3.3	2.3	5.8	26.9	7.9	9.5	55.7	120	33.3	–	−3.4	30.9	–
1880–89	3.6	5.0	1.4	0.9	4.5	23.8	4.4	11.0	60.8	123	28.3	–	−7.5	41.5	–
1890–99	2.0	0.2	−1.8	0.9	11.1	23.3	7.4	11.8	57.5	111	29.1	–	−3.6	6.6	–
1900–1909	1.5	4.2	2.7	0.5	5.9	24.9	9.2	11.7	54.2	90	29.4	19.0	0.7	−2.3	–
1910–19	2.0	1.5	−0.5	0.0	3.7	26.0	5.2	13.1	55.7	68	28.0	18.6	−2.1	17.5	–
1920–29	2.1	3.3	1.2	3.0	5.3	23.2	2.3	14.2	60.3	57	27.8	21.9	−3.4	29.7	11.4
1930–39	0.9	2.1	1.2	0.3	13.1	22.7	2.5	16.6	58.2	41	22.1	46.7	−1.5	4.1	10.2
1940–49	1.3	3.6	2.3	1.7	2.8	–	–	–	–	31	20.1	43.9	0.3	13.7	10.2
1950–59	2.5	4.3	1.8	2.5	1.9	18.8	2.0	27.1	52.1	22	29.0	20.4	−1.8	40.0	8.6
1960–69	2.0	5.1	3.1	2.4	1.9	10.8	2.0	26.4	60.8	19	21.8	10.4	−2.6	39.2	6.8
1970–79	1.5	3.7	2.2	2.6	3.2	6.0	3.8	21.9	68.3	15	21.4	10.7	−1.7	32.2	5.4
1980–89	1.5	3.4	1.9	0.3	7.6	4.5	5.8	17.4	72.3	10	24.9	7.9	−3.9	43.1	5.5
1990–99	1.2	3.6	2.4	1.4	8.8	3.6	4.9	14.2	77.3	6	27.6	2.8	−4.0	36.9	7.2
2000–2009	1.2	3.0	1.8	0.3	5.6	3.1	6.5	11.4	79.0	5	32.2	2.7	−4.6	53.4	8.8
1870–2009	1.8	3.4	1.6	1.4	5.8	16.8	4.9	15.9	62.4	51	26.8	19.2	−2.8	27.4	8.2

Sources: Columns (1)–(3): Maddison 2010; Maddison Project Database, version 2013; columns (4)–(9), (11)–(14): Butlin et al. 2015: 561–580, 589–594; column (10): Mitchell 2013: vol. 1, 223–226; column (12) is derived by calculating the ratio of one plus the average duty paid on dutiable imports to one plus the average rate of assistance on all covered agricultural commodities, subtracting one from the results and multiplying by 100; column (15): Atkinson and Leigh 2007: 251; the figure for the 1920s uses the data for 1921–29; for the 2000s, data for 2000–2003 are used; and for 1870–2009, the data are for the period 1921–2003.

As Table 11.1 highlights, the drivers underlying (and the foci of) the expansion and development of the Australian economy have changed over time. Four distinctive periods of Australian economic history are readily discernible.

Expansion, Depression, and Federation, 1870–1913

In this period, the export-driven growth strategy that, as Meredith's chapter in Volume I (Chapter 11) identified, had begun earlier in the nineteenth century, with wool and then gold, continued to exert its strong and dominant influence over the pattern of Australian economic development (Sinclair 1976; McLean 2013). By 1870, falling transportation costs, both externally as a result of the emergence of faster and cheaper intercontinental shipping, and internally with the development of a denser rail network that increasingly linked farmers to ports, made it easier and commercially more appealing for Australian producers to get their goods to the markets of Europe and Asia (Dyster and Meredith 2012). Moreover, with the advent of viable refrigeration in warehouses and on board ocean-going cargo ships, further, previously untapped elements of Australia's rich natural resource environment – most notably, wheat, frozen meat, and dairy products – were now made available to global consumers. Integral to this growth and diversification of Australia's export-oriented economy was the historically unprecedented volume of British investor- and colonial government-funded construction of key infrastructure, such as rail networks and enlarged, more accessible porting facilities; investments that were, in fact, indispensable for those who wished to export to the other side of the world (Davis and Gallman 2001; Magee and Thompson 2010).

Despite the undoubted importance of agricultural production to the prosperity of the colonies, one would be mistaken to assume that late colonial Australia was just a series of sheep runs, mines, and farms. Often overlooked in accounts of Australian economic history is the fact that by the latter half of the nineteenth century, Australia also had a large service sector and a growing manufacturing base, which together accounted for the majority of economic activity (Butlin 1971). The economic importance and significance of these sectors, especially for productivity, are examined further below. For now, it is worth noting that most Australians in this period and beyond were highly urbanized and cosmopolitan in their experiences and outlook (Frost 1998; 2015). Very few lived on, or made a living directly from, the land.

This export-driven growth strategy certainly paid dividends at first, and Australians enjoyed considerable prosperity through the 1870s and into the 1880s. By the latter decade, however, there were signs that an irrational exuberance founded on the assumption that boom times could continue indefinitely had crept into both investors' and developers' decision-making. This was no more so than in 'Marvellous Melbourne', which experienced a speculative boom of significant proportions (Davison 1978). Rapid economic expansion, based on asset speculation and an unrealistic expectation that further agricultural growth could be obtained through the occupation of new lands, sucked in larger and larger volumes of British capital. In reality, though, the era of such simple expansion onto new and productive lands was drawing to an end. Henceforth, further pastoral and agricultural land could only be made profitable by an ever greater application of technology and capital. When the world price for wool began declining in the latter half of the 1880s, the gaping hiatus between expected and actual returns on many investments became increasingly apparent. It took the London banking crisis of 1890, though, to prick the bubble. The resulting depression was steep, long, and socially damaging (Boehm 1971; McLean 2006). At its peak in 1894, the rate of unemployment rose to 18.7 per cent. The Depression transformed political life in Australia: strengthening the labour movement and giving apparent credence to calls for protectionism, tighter immigration controls, and the regulation of labour markets. The deep social and economic problems of the 1890s, moreover, convinced many that six separate colonial governments working independently of, and indeed often in competition with, each other could not provide solutions to the challenges that confronted them. In 1901, the Commonwealth of Australia came into existence, in large part in the hope that through federation the different Australian colonies, now states, could once again find a path to prosperity. Hampered by the so-called 'Federation Drought' of 1902 and 1903, which approximately halved sheep and cattle numbers, that path proved hard to find. The discovery of gold in Western Australia and an upturn in commodity prices from the mid-1890s certainly aided the process of recovery, but it would not be until 1909, two decades after the commencement of the depression, that the level of real GDP per capita in Australia reached levels attained prior to the onset of depression. And even this was a milestone that was not to be sustained. The arrival of another major drought in 1911 exerted downward pressure once again on Australian living standards. Indeed, when Australia entered World War I, it did so in the midst of a catastrophic failure of its wheat crop and falling income levels.

Relative Economic Decline, 1914–38

World War I was a pivotal moment in Australian history, shaping its sense of national identity and engendering a cultural awakening. Economically, however, it proved nothing less than an utter disaster. Cut off from its export markets in Europe and unable to import machinery, the young nation, lacking a strong manufacturing base of its own that might have risen to fill the void, went into a steep economic decline (Haig-Muir 1995). GDP fell on average by 2.2 per cent per annum over the course of the war, and per capita real income in 1918 was about 11 per cent lower than pre-war levels.

Nor did the end of the war bring much by way of reprieve. Indeed, the interwar period was to prove one of the most tumultuous periods in Australian economic history (Schedvin 1970; Valentine 1987). Epitomizing the economic problems that beset the nation at this time were the growing lines of workers who could not find jobs. Across the 1930s, unemployment, which had begun rising from the mid-1920s, averaged at over 13 per cent and peaked in 1932 at 20 per cent. In large part, the profound economic failures of this period were due to the unpropitious international setting. Shrinking international trade, falling commodity prices, and restrictions on factor flows globally limited Australia's ability to respond in the manner it had traditionally done (viz. through expanding export growth). As a consequence, Australia found itself with a steadily worsening balance of payment deficit and ballooning foreign debt. Worse, this combination of international circumstances encouraged the introduction of protectionism; interventionist industry policy; immigration controls; misguided, if perhaps well-intentioned, rural settlement schemes; and the centralization and regulation of the national labour market. This more interventionist stance, designed to promote stability and provide a platform for recovery (Snooks 1988), instead led Australia, over time, onto a path of a low-productivity import-substituting industrialization, a path which was to send the nation progressively into a relative economic decline that persisted until the final decade of the twentieth century (Broadberry and Irwin 2007).

Return to Boom, 1939–72

The advent of war in 1939 once again provided a profound jolt to the Australian economy. World War II, however, unlike the previous war, galvanized local industry and the economy. The expansion of Australian manufacturing that had occurred over the interwar period provided both a cushion against the disruption to trade wrought by the war, and a base from which Australian industry could grow to supply the many needs of the Allied armed forces active in the Asian and Pacific fields of operations (Mellor 1958). As a result, across the war, the Australian economy grew on average at a rate of 3.5 per cent per annum, with especially rapid growth occurring between 1940 and 1942.

This surge of growth did not end with the war. The immediate post-war years in fact witnessed the return of mass migration and foreign investment to Australian shores, features which had been largely absent since the 1890s. The growth of international trade, rapid technological change, and the freer flow of factors in conjunction with the onset of commodity booms, most notably in minerals, underpinned a return to a sustained period of rapid economic growth and increased prosperity (Maddock 1987). Real GDP per capita grew in excess of 2.5 per cent per annum, and unemployment rarely exceeded 3 per cent. The improving economic climate enabled real annual wage growth of over 2.5 per cent, a rate of growth that had not been experienced since the 1870s. One consequence of this greater sharing of the benefits of the post-war growth was that income inequality steadily fell. Whereas at the outset of World War II over 10 per cent of Australia's income had been taken by the wealthiest 1 per cent of the population, by the 1970s, their share had fallen to around 5.5 per cent.

The high levels of protection first enacted in the interwar period continued to be a major feature of this period as well. The 1950s and 1960s, in fact, were to become the high-water mark of Australian industrialization. The low levels of productivity experienced in much of this new industry, however, posed fundamental problems for its longer-term sustainability.

Reorientation and Renewal, 1973–2010

By the mid-1970s, the golden years of Australia's post-war boom were over. Income growth and wage growth began to decline and unemployment started edging up beyond the historical average rate of 5.8 per cent. Plagued by stagflation, a global economic downturn that cut heavily into demand for coal and minerals, and lumbered by an internationally uncompetitive industrial sector, policymakers in Australia began looking for new directions that might offer new prospects for the economy. Out of this search, a new consensus gradually emerged and took root after the election of the Hawke-Keating government in 1983 (Pagan 1987; Dyster and Meredith 2012). Influenced in part by similar developments elsewhere in the world, this new policy stance, adopted and embraced by all subsequent Australian governments, emphasized trade and financial liberalization and deregulation, deep microeconomic and labour market reform, and a reorientation of Australia's economy towards the needs of the rapidly growing economies of its region, especially Japan, China, and the other newly industrialized countries of Asia (Quiggin 1996; Taylor and Magee 2017).

One of the consequences of this new, more unregulated environment, was the contraction of the Australian manufacturing sector. It was not a completely smooth transition. However, given the political will of the time for change, recessions in the early 1980s and 1990s, during which unemployment rose to around 10 per cent, acted to accelerate rather than stall the reform process. Fortunately, the reformists' agenda soon began paying off. In particular, the strategic turn to Asia that had been taken positioned Australia well to benefit from the renewed mining boom (primarily in bauxite, iron-ore, and aluminium) of the 2000s. As a result, Australia returned to a path of strong growth: growth that once again was propelled by a commodity-based export strategy not unlike that which had been pursued a century earlier. From 1991, a period of uninterrupted and above-average rates of growth and declining unemployment was ushered in. Unlike the previous post-war boom, annual real wage growth, however, was constrained in this boom to well below 1 per cent. The income share of the top 1 per cent of the population began rising as a consequence, and by the early years of the new millennium was sitting once again at levels last experienced in the late 1940s (Atkinson and Leigh 2007).

Openness

A persistent and distinctive feature of Australian economic history has been the nation's openness to the global economy. Throughout its existence the Australian economy has been an export-driven one, in essence exporting agricultural and mining commodities in return for manufactured imports (Dyster and Meredith 2012). Despite severe economic downturns, war, and the utilization of tariffs to protect its growing industrial sector, especially in the middle portion of the twentieth century, trade has always figured largely in Australian society, averaging in value across the whole period at 26.8 per cent of GDP. Liberalization and the minerals boom from the end of the twentieth century has seen that share soar to well in excess of 30 per cent, a degree of international engagement not seen since the 1870s.

Australia's dependence on natural-resource intensive exports, however, has made it particularly vulnerable to commodity price shocks. While an ever present feature of the Australian experience, the impact of this volatility on the nation's overall economic performance, at least compared to other commodity exporting economies in Asia, Africa, and Latin America, has been relatively mild, particularly in the twentieth century. Australian agricultural producers, in particular, have proved very resilient to shocks (Anderson 2017). The comparative stability of Australian state revenues, which has ensured that long-run infrastructure projects continued, irrespective of prevailing commodity prices, as well as the growth of significant domestic manufacturing and service sectors, most markedly after World War II, no doubt have played key roles in moderating the impact of price shocks on the Australian economy (Bhattacharyya and Williamson 2011).

By contrast, commodity price shocks have had a significant impact on income distribution nationally, with the largest beneficiaries being the very richest in Australian society. The scale and direction of these distributional effects have appeared to depend on the specific ownership patterns and concentrations of different renewable and non-renewable resources. A sustained price rise for minerals has thus tended to widen societal inequality in Australia the most, while increasing wool prices typically have operated in the opposite direction (Bhattacharyya and Williamson 2016).

Commodity price shocks have also impacted different parts of the country unequally. Natural resource-based growth in Australia, as elsewhere, has often had a very tight geographical focus. Australia's post-war mining booms, for example, have had far greater effects on Western Australia and Queensland, economies which, as a consequence, have experienced periods of rapid growth followed by precipitous downturns, when mineral prices have begun to slide. Some of the more pernicious effects of such regional inequality, however, have been mitigated by a cycle of migration in and out of affected states aligned to the migrant's economic prospects – a factor especially prevalent in the nineteenth century – and the cross-subsidization between states (through the distribution of tax revenue and government expenditures) implicit in the fiscal federalism of the Commonwealth since 1901. The latter has also ensured that the standard of living in smaller states, such as Tasmania, not blessed with significant mineral deposits or large swathes of arable or pastoral land, has not been allowed to fall too far behind the more populous states of New South Wales and Victoria, states which have normally enjoyed the highest income levels in the country.

Of course, while trade per se has always featured prominently in Australian development, the direction of that trade has varied considerably over time. As Table 11.2 shows, in 1885, three-quarters of all Australian trade was with the UK; by contrast, the main Asian economies together accounted for only 3.1 per cent. At the turn of the century, America and the emerging industrial powers of Europe began to become more important, joined later by Japan, during and after World War I. Nonetheless, in the mid-1930s, just under half of all Australian trade was still with Britain, which was followed in importance by the US and Japan, each of which was responsible for around 10 per cent of Australian trade. Other major Asian nations still accounted for just over 5 per cent.

Following World War II, the importance of Japan in Australian trade continued to grow, and by the 1970s it had become Australia's most important trading partner. This marked the beginning of a much broader drift towards Asia and its emerging markets, especially from the mid-1970s. By 2014–15, China, now responsible for a quarter of all trade, had become Australia's most important trading partner, while the five largest Asian economies combined accounted for 50.5 per cent of Australian trade. The UK, with just 2 per cent of trade, was now just one of many small, though far from insignificant, trading partners.

Underpinning and enabling Australia's reliance on trade has been a willingness and ability to import foreign capital and human capital through migration to support its export sectors and infrastructural development. At most times through its history, Australia has run a current account deficit funded by foreign capital. These inflows were strongest during the boom and the bubble years of the 1870s, 1880s, and early 1890s, in the 1920s, and then again from the 1980s onwards. In the first decade of the twenty-first century, the inflow of foreign capital, on average, amounted to 4.6 per cent of the value of the nation's GDP. This rate of capital inflow was well above the long-term average of 2.8 per cent, indicating a global confidence in the future of the Australian economy not witnessed since the end of the nineteenth century.

Immigration has also played an important role in Australia's economic development, moving very much in tandem with capital inflows and economic conditions. Thus, other than during the first decade of the twentieth century, the war years, and the depression decade of the 1930s, net migration has been a significant driver of population growth. This was especially so during the post-war boom, when the geographical composition of migrants coming to Australia broadened from the British Isles to southern and eastern

Table 11.2 Direction of trade, 1885–2015 (%)

	1885	1895	1905	1915–16	1925–26	1935–36	1945–46	1955–56	1965–66	1975–76	1985–86	1995–96	2005–06	2014–15
China	1.6	0.5	0.5	0.2	0.5	1.2	0.2	0.3	2.3	1.6	2.9	5.1	12.9	27.1
France	2.0	3.9	6.6	1.8	7.4	3.2	2.5	5.1	3.7	1.9	2.2	1.7	2.0	1.1
Germany	1.1	5.0	6.9	0.0	3.3	2.4	0.0	4.5	4.8	4.7	5.4	3.9	3.2	2.7
India	1.2	1.6	4.5	3.5	3.3	1.7	7.3	2.2	1.1	0.7	0.9	1.1	2.7	2.7
Indonesia	0.3	0.6	0.5	1.4	2.8	2.8	0.5	1.9	1.2	1.0	1.1	2.8	2.7	2.1
Japan	0.0	0.3	1.0	4.1	5.1	10.1	0.4	6.7	13.2	26.6	26.0	17.7	15.1	12.3
New Zealand	3.8	3.3	4.1	4.2	2.6	2.8	2.8	3.1	3.8	3.9	4.4	6.0	4.4	3.1
South Korea	0.0	0.0	0.0	0.0	0.0	0.0	0.0	0.0	0.1	1.1	2.8	5.8	5.7	6.3
UK	76.0	71.0	52.3	47.5	41.6	46.2	36.0	37.9	21.6	8.4	5.4	5.0	4.3	2.0
USA	5.1	4.2	5.9	21.5	16.8	10.6	20.8	9.5	18.3	14.6	15.6	14.4	10.2	8.6

Source: Department of Foreign Affairs and Trade 2016.

Europe, Vietnam, Malaysia, and China. In 1871, 46.5 per cent of the population had been born overseas. By 1947, that figure had fallen to 9.8 per cent, after which it resumed its growth such that 27 per cent of those living in Australia in 2010 had been born overseas (Butlin et al. 2015).

Productivity

To what extent has Australia's economic development been driven by extensive and intensive factors? Table 11.3 tracks the path of labour productivity in Australia relative to the UK (Broadberry and Irwin 2007). In 1870, labour productivity was significantly higher in Australia in all sectors other than services. Australia's overall labour productivity lead peaked in the 1880s and 1890s at a level around 40 per cent higher than the UK's. It then dipped to near parity during the drought and recovery years of the first decade of the twentieth century, recovering its lead only somewhat by 1910. From the late 1920s, Australia's lead contracted further and sat for the rest of the interwar period between 8 and 15 per cent above levels in the UK.

Decomposing Australia's relative productivity experience by sector sheds light on what was driving these economy-wide trends. The labour productivity dominance of Australia in agriculture and mining was pivotal. At all times, Australian agricultural productivity was at least twice that of the UK. In 1891, it stood at three and half times the UK level, a result that implies that

Table 11.3 Comparative Australia/UK labour productivity, 1871–1948 (UK = 100)

	Agriculture	Mining	Manufacturing and utilities	Construction	Services	GDP
1871	190.0	145.8	149.7	104.2	100.7	117.6
1881	304.5	136.2	169.8	227.8	108.2	144.9
1891	352.0	271.1	157.6	234.3	92.4	141.0
1901	171.0	299.2	124.1	140.2	87.5	107.7
1911	289.1	380.8	120.7	141.8	95.3	121.6
1920	320.1	416.0	99.2	158.6	103.3	126.9
1929	250.7	357.1	100.5	87.8	105.1	116.6
1935	239.9	200.4	70.2	73.2	113.8	108.1
1937	257.7	229.0	68.0	71.5	114.2	108.5
1948	252.5	319.8	70.9	47.1	116.4	115.7

Source: Broadberry and Irwin 2007: 267–268.

labour productivity in the Australian primary sector was among the highest in the world. The source of Australia's productivity lay in its deeper per capita endowment of quality land, relative to the UK and the US, which it was able to use to produce high-value added pastoral and dairy products (Broadberry and Irwin 2007).

Australian mining also consistently operated at high productivity levels, especially after the discovery of Western Australian gold in the 1890s. From the 1920s, the sector's diminishing share of GDP, however, steadily reduced its impact on overall Australian labour productivity.

Mining's place of influence was taken by the growth of the manufacturing sector. In 1871, Australia's small industrial sector was relatively efficient, with labour productivity sitting about 50 per cent above that of Britain. Moreover, the productivity gap grew slightly over the 1880s, seemingly on the back of its increased exploitation of its large per capita natural resource endowments. By the beginning of the twentieth century, depression, a series of droughts, and the introduction of federal tariffs had begun to undermine the roots of Australia's advantages. Heightened protectionism and a policy of import substitution in manufacturing from the 1920s reinforced the downward trend. While this approach certainly engendered an expansion of the industrial sector, it did so in many instances by artificially propping up patently internationally inefficient firms that would not otherwise have survived. By 1937, Australian labour productivity had slid to approximately two-thirds of British productivity. The relatively rich natural endowment that had made labour productivity in Australian manufacturing high in the nineteenth century failed to be translated into the type of high-productivity, resource-intensive industry that was common in the US. One explanation for this failure may have lain in the fact that a larger proportion of Australia's natural resources were tradable, and thus more readily exportable without processing (McLean 2013).

The story of labour productivity in the construction sector mirrored that of manufacturing, though, being a non-tradable, its decline was in all probability due to structural changes and the introduction of arbitration and other labour market interventions in the years after federation rather than protectionism (Broadberry and Irwin 2007). As for the service sector, its level of labour productivity remained broadly similar to British levels throughout.

Table 11.4, which reports Greasley and Madsen's (2017) recent research on the sources of Australian incomes, sheds further light on the relative roles of productivity growth and the fuller exploitation of natural resources in explaining Australian economic growth. In the period between 1842 and

Table 11.4 Total factor productivity growth, 1842–2009

	Real GDP per capita	Real income per labour hour	TFP	TFP (mineral reserves adjusted)
1842–90	1.57	2.54	1.57	0.67
1891–2009	1.30	1.39	0.79	0.65

Notes: The TFP index reported includes produced capital, pastoral and arable land, and labour hours (allowing for changes in participation rates and average hours worked, but not unemployment or labour quality). The TFP (mineral reserves adjusted) index, in addition, allows for variations in mineral reserves.
Source: Greasley and Madsen 2017: 286.

1890, when Australians enjoyed exceptionally high levels of GDP per capita, its rate of labour productivity growth (1.57 per cent) was entirely accounted for by total factor productivity (TFP) gains, even after allowance is made for the expansion onto lower-yielding pastoral and arable lands. When further considerations are made for the impact of the discovery and working of new mineral deposits, TFP growth falls to just 0.67 per cent. In other words, 26.4 per cent of the growth in labour productivity in this period (and 42.7 per cent of the growth of real GDP per capita) was due to productivity growth associated with improved organizational technology and human capital formation. The traditional story of nineteenth-century growth being driven primarily by a favourable resource endowment, thus, has a ring of truth to it, although there was also a far from insignificant place for productivity growth. Indeed, analysis of Australian patenting history and the nation's active engagement in the global market for technology has demonstrated that Australia was already, by this juncture, a technologically vibrant and globally engaged society, whose inventions and innovations, especially in agricultural machinery and mining, were internationally competitive (Magee 1999; 2000).

Across the course of what might be described as Australia's long twentieth century (1891–2009), the sources of Australian growth changed. Labour productivity growth fell to 1.39 per cent on average, while TFP adjusted for new mineral reserves remained steady, at about 0.65 per cent. The gap between the two TFP measures given in Table 11.4 narrowed dramatically, indicating that the agricultural and mining expansion that had played a pivotal role in driving the growth of real GDP per capita in the latter half of the nineteenth century diminished dramatically in the twentieth century. A more limited growth in capital (physical, human, and natural) intensity, rather than any stalling of productivity growth, drove the decline in the rate of real GDP per capita growth to 1.3 per cent. Indeed, across the two periods reported, the share of improvement in real GDP per capita attributable to productivity gains nearly doubled, from 26.4 to 50 per cent.

Australian Development in Comparative Perspective

In this section, we examine Australia's record of economic performance against two of the most advanced economies of the period, the UK and US, as well as three other resource-rich economies: Canada, New Zealand, and Norway. Of the five chosen comparator countries, four are English-speaking countries that share similar institutional and cultural heritages. Only Norway has not had close historical ties with the UK.

As Figure 11.2 demonstrates, in 1870 Australia's real income per capita was among the highest in the world, well in excess of Norwegian and Canadian, 33 per cent larger than American, and between 2 and 5 per cent greater than those found in the UK and New Zealand respectively. In the last decades of the nineteenth century, this exceptionality of Australian income per capita began to diminish. By 1913, it had fallen behind the US and was sitting neck and neck with New Zealand. Its lead over the other comparators, other than the UK, had also started to be reined in. This was a trend that was to continue across the war and interwar years. In 1950, Australia's relatively sluggish

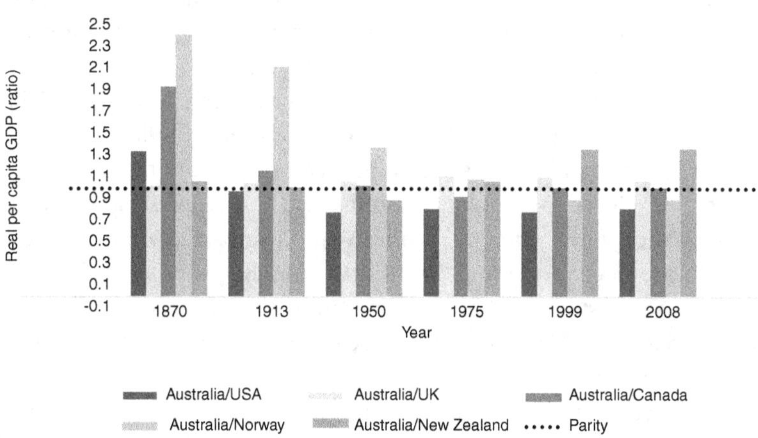

Figure 11.2 Comparative real GDP per capita (1990 international $)
Source: Maddison Project Database, version 2013.

growth performance placed average income there at about three-quarters of American, about 10 per cent behind New Zealand, and roughly on a par with Canada. Moreover, its former massive income per capita lead over Norway in 1870, when Australian income per capita had been just under two and a half times the size of Norwegian, had continued to contract to just 36 per cent. Only relative to the UK had Australian income improved since 1913. Nor did Australia's relative performance markedly improve across the post-war boom. In 1975, its level of income per capita had slid behind Canadian for the first time, while Norwegian income was now less than 10 per cent shy of Australian. Of the comparator nations, only New Zealand and the UK's performance between 1950 and 1975 had been poorer.

Australia's long-run decline in relative income finally showed signs of ending in the 1980s and 1990s. By the end of the twentieth century, the relativities with the UK and US had stabilized, its lead over New Zealand had blown out to 35 per cent, and it now had similar levels of income to Canada. Norway, however, continued its rapid growth and now operated at an average real income level that was 15 per cent above Australia's. In the first decade of the twenty-first century, this renewed burst of relatively strong Australian growth performance continued, with the gap with the US showing signs of narrowing, the opening up of a slight lead over Canada once again, and a stabilization of income levels relative to Norway, the UK, and New Zealand. Taking the long view, however, it is evident that between 1870 and 2008 Australia had improved its income position relative only to New Zealand, and had broadly maintained the status quo only vis-à-vis the UK. While acknowledging the internationally high levels of income enjoyed by Australians throughout, the overall performance of the three other resource-rich countries in our sample – the US, Canada, and Norway – were distinctly better.

But income is not everything: what of the quality of life in Australia? The Human Development Index (HDI) is a measure commonly utilized to gauge broader societal progress (Crafts 2002). It tells a similar story to real income per capita. As Figure 11.3 shows, Australia had the second highest HDI readings in the world prior to World War I, surpassed only by New Zealand. In the interwar period, though, this dominance began to be challenged. By 1950, Australia had been overtaken by the US, while most of the other countries had achieved or come close to achieving parity. This relative decline continued through to the 1990s, when relative gains in the quality of Australian development had begun to reappear. By 1999, it had restored HDI parity with all of our comparator nations other than New Zealand, and by 2010 it had bypassed all other than Norway.

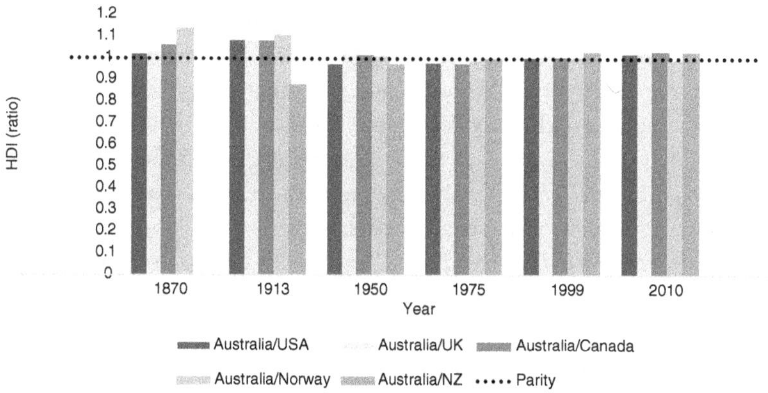

Figure 11.3 Human Development Index
Source: Crafts 1997; 2002; UNDP 2016.

Conclusion

For the large part, modern Australian economic history has been a story of successful development. In spite of the vexing challenges it has faced, Australia has remained a confident, affluent, and resilient society, an achievement that the other chapters in these volumes have shown us should not be taken for granted. Lying at the heart of its success is indubitably the relative abundance of natural resources it has been – and continues to be – able to draw upon. To date, these resources have been a godsend rather than the curse they have proved to be for many other resource-rich nations (Sachs and Warner 2001; Torvik 2009). The secret of Australia's avoidance of the pitfalls that have befallen so many countries similarly blessed appears to lie in the ability of its institutions to adapt successfully in the face of changed circumstances, while remaining supportive of innovative and productive activities (McLean 2013). This flexibility is readily apparent, inter alia, in the decision to federate, in the alacrity with which its producers adopted new technologies and organizations and opened up new markets, and in the reform agenda of the late twentieth century that transformed the Australian economy and reoriented it towards the emerging mass markets to its north.

Australian development, of course, has not been flawless. The current phase of growth has brought with it features not experienced to the same extent during previous spells of growth. Inequality is rapidly on the rise, wage growth is sluggish, the working week is growing longer, and the affordability of housing for everyday Australians has declined dramatically (Huberman and Minns 2007; Butlin et al. 2015). The Australia of the past, the so-called 'working man's paradise', and the distinctive notion of a high quality life for all that it conferred, is under threat to an extent that has never before been witnessed in the nation's history. Moreover, the ongoing plight of indigenous Australians, whose median personal income and life expectancy in 2011 was 62 per cent and 75 per cent of non-indigenous Australians respectively, and who were twice as likely to have never attended school, and more than three times as likely to have been unemployed, further illustrates the appalling gaps in Australian economic development that have yet to be overcome (Altman and Biddle 2015).

Australia's economic history over the last century has also been one of relative economic decline. At the turn of the twentieth century, Australia was amongst the leaders in the world in income and most social indicators of progress. By the mid-twentieth century those leads had been lost. While at first blush such occurrences may be taken as a sign of failure, it is important to remember that progress in Australia has continued apace. It is not so much that Australia has fallen behind; rather, other developed nations have caught up to the quality of life it had helped to pioneer. What was distinctive about the Australian experience is now shared by many others around the world. If our diarists from World War I had been alive today, they no doubt would not only have been amazed by how much stronger, healthier, and better educated their descendants had become, but probably would have realized that these attributes were no longer traits of Australians alone, but ones that were now being enjoyed by an ever larger proportion of the world's population.

References

Altman, J. and Biddle, N. (2015). 'Refiguring Indigenous Economies: A Twenty-First-Century Perspective', in Ville, S. and Withers, G. (eds.), *The Cambridge Economic History of Australia*, Cambridge University Press, 530–554.

Anderson, K. (2017). 'Sectoral Trends and Shocks in Australia's Economic Growth', *Australian Economic History Review*, 57, 2–21.

Atkinson, A. B. and Leigh, A. (2007). 'The Distribution of Top Incomes in Australia', *Economic Record*, 83, 247–261.

Australian Bureau of Statistics. (2011). *Migration, Australia 2011–12*, cat. no. 3412.0, Canberra: ABS.

(2012). *Australian Demographic Statistics*, cat. no. 3101.0, Canberra: ABS.

(2013). *Estimates of Aboriginal and Torres Strait Islander Australians, June 2011*, cat. no. 3238.0.55.001, Canberra: ABS.

Bhattacharyya, S. and Williamson, J. G. (2011). 'Commodity Price Shocks and the Australian Economy since Federation', *Australian Economic History Review*, 51, 150–177.

(2016). 'Distributional Consequences of Commodity Price Shocks: Australia over a Century', *Review of Income and Wealth*, 62, 223–244.

Boehm, E. A. (1971). *Prosperity and Depression in Australia, 1887–1897*, Oxford: Clarendon Press.

Broadberry, S. and Irwin, D. A. (2007). 'Lost Exceptionalism? Comparative Income and Productivity in Australia and the UK, 1861–1948', *Economic Record*, 83, 262–274.

Butlin, M., Dixon, R., and Lloyd, P. J. (2015). 'Statistical Appendix: Selected Data Series, 1800–2010', in Ville, S. and Withers, G. (eds.), *The Cambridge Economic History of Australia*, Cambridge University Press, 555–594.

Butlin, N. G. (1971). *Investment in Australian Economic Development, 1861–1900*, Canberra: ANU Press.

Crafts, N. F. R. (1997). 'The Human Development Index and Changes in Standards of Living: Some Historical Comparisons', *European Review of Economic History*, 1, 299–322.

(2002). 'The Human Development Index, 1870–1999: Some Revised Estimates', *European Review of Economic History*, 6, 395–405.

Cranfield, J. and Inwood, K. (2015). 'A Tale of Two Armies: Comparative Growth in the Mirror of the First World War', *Australian Economic History Review*, 55, 212–233.

Davis, L. E. and Gallman, R. E. (2001). *Evolving Financial Markets and International Capital Flows: Britain, the Americas, and Australia, 1865–1914*, Cambridge University Press.

Davison, G. (1978). *The Rise and Fall of Marvellous Melbourne*, Melbourne University Press.

Department of Foreign Affairs and Trade. (2016). Trade and Investment Statistics, Australia's Direction of Merchandise Trade, Total Trade, available online at www.dfat.gov.au/trade/resources/trade-statistics/Pages/trade-time-series-data (data accessed 11 March 2017).

Dyster, B. and Meredith, D. (2012). *Australia in the Global Economy: Continuity and Change*, 2nd ed., Cambridge University Press.

Frost, L. (1998). 'The Contribution of the Urban Sector to Australian Economic Development before 1914', *Australian Economic History Review*, 38, 42–73.

(2015). 'Urbanisation', in Ville, S. and Withers, G. (eds.), *The Cambridge Economic History of Australia*, Cambridge University Press, 245–263.

Greasley, D. and Madsen, J. B. (2017). 'The Rise and Fall of Exceptional Australian Incomes since 1800', *Australian Economic History Review*, 57, 264–290.

Haig-Muir, M. (1995). 'The Economy at War', in Beaumont, J. (ed.), *Australia's War, 1914–18*, St Leonards: Allen & Unwin, 93–124.

Holbrook, C. (2014). *Anzac: The Unauthorised Biography*, Sydney: University of New South Wales Press.

Huberman, M. and Minns, C. (2007). 'The Times They Are Not Changin': Days and Hours of Work in Old and New Worlds, 1870–2000', *Explorations in Economic History*, 44, 538–567.

Hunter, B. (2015). 'The Aboriginal Legacy', in Ville, S. and Withers, G. (eds.), *The Cambridge Economic History of Australia*, Cambridge University Press, 73–96.

McLean, I. W. (2006). 'Recovery from Depression: Australia in an Argentine Mirror, 1895–1913', *Australian Economic History Review*, 46, 215–241.

(2013). *Why Australia Prospered: The Shifting Sources of Economic Growth*, Princeton University Press.

Maddison, A. (2010). Statistics on World Population, GDP and Per Capita GDP, 1–2008 AD, table 1, available online at www.ggdc.net/MADDISON/oriindex.htm (accessed 29 September 2020), Groningen Growth and Development Centre.

Maddison Project Database, version 2013. Bolt, J. and van Zanden, J. L. (2014). 'The Maddison Project: Collaborative Research on Historical National Accounts', *Economic History Review*, 67, 627–651.

Maddock, R. (1987). 'The Long Boom, 1940–1970', in Maddock, R. and McLean, I. W. (eds.), *The Australian Economy in the Long Run*, Cambridge University Press, 79–105.

Magee, G. B. (1999). 'Technological Development and Foreign Patenting: Evidence from Nineteenth-Century Australia', *Explorations in Economic History*, 36, 344–359.

(2000). *Knowledge Generation, Technological Change and Economic Growth in Colonial Australia*, Melbourne: Australian Scholarly Publishing.

Magee, G. B. and Thompson, A. S. (2010). *Empire and Globalisation: Networks of People, Capital and Goods in the British World, 1850–1914*, Cambridge University Press.

Mellor, D. P. (1958). *The Role of Science and Industry: Australia in the War of 1939–1945, Series 4, Civil, Vol. V*, Canberra: Australian War Memorial.

Mitchell, B. R. (2013). *International Historical Statistics, 1750–2010, Vol. I: Africa, Asia and Oceania*, Basingstoke: Palgrave Macmillan.

Mulvaney, D. J. (2002). 'Difficult to Found an Opinion: 1788 Aboriginal Population Estimate', in Briscoe, G. and Smith, L. (eds.), *The Aboriginal Population Revisited: 70,000 Years to the Present*, Canberra: ANU Press, 1–8.

Pagan, A. (1987). 'The End of the Long Boom', in Maddock, R. and McLean, I. W. (eds.), *The Australian Economy in the Long Run*, Cambridge University Press, 106–130.

Price, C. (1987). 'Immigration and Ethnic Origin', in Vamplew, W. (ed.), *Australians: Historical Statistics*, Broadway: Fairfax, Symes and Weldon Associates, 2–22.

Quiggin, J. (1996). *Great Expectations: Microeconomic Reform in Australia*, St Leonards: Allen & Unwin.

Sachs, J. and Warner, A. (2001). 'The Curse of Natural Resources', *European Economic Review*, 45, 827–838.

Schedvin, C. B. (1970). *Australia and the Great Depression: A Study of Economic Development and Policy in the 1920s and 1930s*, Sydney University Press.

Sinclair, W. A. (1976). *The Process of Economic Development in Australia*, Melbourne: Longman Cheshire.

Smith, L. R. (1980). *The Aboriginal Population of Australia*, Canberra: ANU Press.

Snooks, G. D. (1988). 'Government Unemployment Relief in the 1930s: Aid or Hindrance to Recovery?', in Gregory, R. G. and Butlin, N. G. (eds.), *Recovery from Depression: Australia and the World Economy in the 1930s*, Cambridge University Press, 311–334.

Taylor, J. and Magee, G. (2017). 'In the Aftermath: Consumer Choice and the Deregulation of Australian Retail Banking, 1988–1993', *Australian Economic History Review*, 57, 134–157.

Torvik, R. (2009). 'Why Do Some Resource-Abundant Countries Succeed While Others Do Not?', *Oxford Review of Economic Policy*, 25, 241–256.

UNDP. (2016). Human Development Index trends, 1990–2018, available online at http://hdr.undp.org/en/composite/trends (data accessed 11 March 2017), UNDP Human Development Reports.

Valentine, T. (1987). 'The Depression of the 1930s', in Maddock, R. and McLean, I. W. (eds.), *The Australian Economy in the Long Run*, Cambridge University Press, 61–78.

PART II

*

FACTORS GOVERNING DIFFERENTIAL OUTCOMES IN THE GLOBAL ECONOMY

12

Healthy, Literate, and Smart

The Global Increase in Human Capital

LATIKA CHAUDHARY AND PETER LINDERT

In the past 140 years, the world's population has grown fivefold, even though fertility rates have plummeted. This accelerated growth in world population was caused by a global increase in life expectancy, from thirty years in 1870 to seventy-one years in 2010. At the same time, an increasing number of children have attended schools and acquired some form of formal education across the world. People today live longer, are more literate and numerate, and have more knowledge than people in any other period of world history.

Our chapter tells the story of these impressive gains in human capital. In the first section we document the patterns in life expectancy from 1870 to 2010. The second section identifies the key factors responsible for its increase. Although economic growth and development increased worldwide, income has never been the main driver of life expectancy. Rather, the gains in survival came from public health efforts, medical innovations, and expanding public education. In the third section we turn to education, highlighting the role of public funds in advancing mass education. The fourth section documents the high economic returns to education. More schooling has made individuals and countries more productive. In the fifth section we seek to explain why the whole world is not more educated, given the large economic returns to education. We conclude by contrasting the divergence in income per capita across the world with the relative convergence in human capital.

The Soaring of Life Expectancy

World population quintupled from 1.3 billion in 1870 to 6.9 billion in 2010, as noted in Volume I, Chapter 12 of this book, which discusses demographic transitions, including those after 1870. What led to this increase in world population? Not rising fertility: birth rates and fertility rates declined across the world in the twentieth century. Rather, world population has soared because people are living

Table 12.1 Life expectancy at birth, 1870–2000

	1870	1900	1930	1950	1980	2000
World	38.3	39.9	42.0	49.9	64.0	68.5
Regions						
Advanced Europe	38.9	43.9	57.3	66.6	74.0	78.6
North America	–	–	59.5	68.1	73.9	77.1
Rest of Europe	–	38.4	49.4	58.6	67.6	69.1
Asia	36.6	38.6	32.0	43.4	63.3	69.0
Latin America and Caribbean	–	29.1	36.7	51.9	65.4	72.0
Middle East	–	–	–	41.0	58.4	70.9
Africa	–	–	35.4	38.0	51.3	54.2
Oceania	–	–	64.9	64.1	70.8	75.5
Min	34.4	24.0	25.0	25.3	39.9	40.1
Max	50.9	53.5	64.9	71.6	76.6	81.2
No. Countries	10	35	42	180	180	180

Source: van Zanden et al. 2014. The regional averages are population-weighted based on the data reported by van Zanden et al. 2014.

much longer. A baby born in 1870 could expect to live thirty years. A baby born in 2001 could expect to live sixty-seven years (Riley 2005). Such a remarkable jump in the world's life expectancy had never happened before 1870.

Table 12.1 and Figure 12.1 map the history of life expectancy by region and for select countries.[1] A few caveats are in order before we interpret the patterns. We have few countries in Asia and Africa reporting life expectancy before 1950. In contrast, we have a complete series for Sweden and the United Kingdom back to 1870 and earlier.

Although life expectancy increased in every part of the world, the timing of its take-off, also known as the 'health transition' or 'epidemiological transition', was different between the developed and developing world. People began to live longer in advanced parts of Europe, such as England and Sweden, beginning in the 1870s (Easterlin 1999). The lengthening of life was rapid in the late nineteenth and early twentieth centuries, averaging two to four years per decade in the developed countries. But it slowed down

1 The underlying data on life expectancy come from the OECD's global well-being project (van Zanden et al. 2014). We assign countries to geographic regions based on the United Nations country grouping. The UN country grouping divides Europe into European Union and Rest of Europe. We changed these groups. We grouped Austria, Belgium, Denmark, Finland, France, Germany, Greece, Iceland, Ireland, Italy, Luxembourg, Netherlands, Norway, Portugal, Spain, Sweden, Switzerland, and UK as Advanced Europe. The remaining European countries are under Rest of Europe.

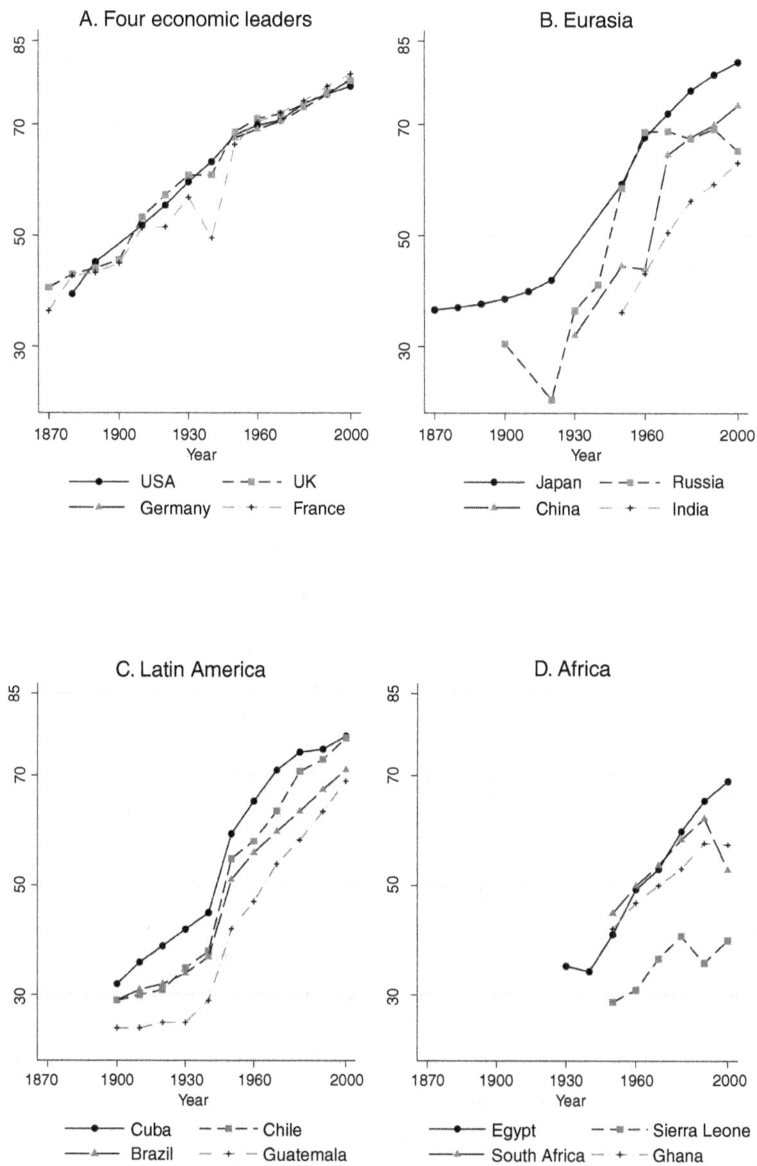

Figure 12.1 Life expectancy, select countries
Source: van Zanden et al. 2014.

between 1950 and 2010, with life expectancy increasing by less than two years per decade. Unlike the developed countries, Asia, Africa, and Latin America saw only modest gains in the early twentieth century. Their transition to higher life expectancy began in the 1940s and 1950s. Asia's record has been particularly impressive, rising from forty-three years of lifespan in 1950 to sixty-nine years in 2000.

For rich countries, the story is one of steady progress, despite setbacks during the 1918 influenza pandemic and the two world wars. Citizens of Nordic countries have always lived longer. The United States was an early leader, but its increase slowed down after 1950. In 2010, a baby born in the United States could expect to live seventy-nine years, lower than in Spain or Italy (eighty-two years) even though US income per capita is 1.7 times as high. That said, the general picture is one of convergence to increasing life expectancy throughout the developed world.

In eastern Europe, life expectancy increased rapidly in the 1950s, but it has remained relatively stagnant since then. Russia's graph shown in Figure 12.1B is representative of the region's other countries. In Russia, alcohol-related mortality among working-age men increased following the collapse of the former Soviet Union and continues to be a problem (Zaridze et al. 2014).

In Asia, we find a more optimistic picture of progress, with a few cracks (Figure 12.1B). Japan has been the clear leader. As early as 1870, life expectancy in Japan, at thirty-seven years, was comparable to more advanced countries. Japan continued to make steady progress over the twentieth century. Today Japan enjoys one of the highest life expectancies in the world, at eighty-three years. South Korea and Singapore have followed Japan, with life expectancy in 2010 exceeding that in the United States.

In China, the Great Leap Forward famine between 1959 and 1961 killed millions. Yet life expectancy began to increase in the mid-1960s, after the reversal of Mao's policies, and China has since experienced a steady pace of health improvements, with a life expectancy of seventy-four years in 2010, just six years short of the average in advanced countries. India, in comparison, has seen less impressive gains, from thirty-six years in 1950 to sixty-four years in 2010. An increase of twenty-eight years is nothing to scoff at, but India's relative performance is disappointing. Her poorer neighbours, Bangladesh, Nepal, and Sri Lanka, all enjoy higher life expectancy (Drèze and Sen 2013). India's less than stellar health performance is similar to her progress in schooling, as we discuss later in the chapter.

Looking at Latin America, we see continuous progress (Figure 12.1C). Here, the patterns are uniform across countries at different levels of development. In 2010, life expectancy in Cuba and Chile was seventy-eight years, even though Cuba's income per capita was only a quarter of Chile's. This calls into question the effect of income in driving life expectancy, a point we return to in the next section.

For Africa, the road to higher life expectancy has been rougher (Figure 12.1D). As a whole, the continent did well in the 1960s and 1970s, keeping pace with global improvements. However, the HIV/AIDS epidemic, beginning in the 1980s, took a heavy toll. The effects of the epidemic have been devastating in countries like South Africa and Botswana. For example, in Botswana life expectancy declined by twelve years, from sixty-two years in 1980, before the epidemic, to forty-eight years in 2009. Countries in North Africa where HIV is less widespread have higher life expectancy. In other parts of Africa, such as Sierra Leone, civil war, poverty, and less education have contributed to poor health. Health outcomes in Africa are more unequal today compared to those in Asia or Latin America. We turn next to identifying the factors correlated with the global soaring of life expectancy.

Why Are People Living Longer Today?

Preventing child deaths from infectious diseases has been the main driver of improvements in life expectancy over the past 140 years. As countries learned to prevent the spread of infectious diseases, mortality rates fell first in developed countries, followed by a fifty-year lag in developing countries.

Although social scientists agree that fewer child deaths from infectious diseases contributed to higher life expectancy, they continue to debate why infant mortality declined. On one side, scholars point to income growth (McKeown 1976). In this view, the increase in income in early nineteenth-century Europe and the United States allowed people to consume more calories. Better nutrition, in turn, helped people fight infectious diseases and live longer.

The historical evidence, however, challenges this explanation. While income per capita and life expectancy are positively correlated, the causal effect of income on health is less clear. Life expectancy began to increase in the advanced countries of Europe around the same time, *c.*1870, even though individual countries were at different points in their development cycle (Easterlin 1999). As Figure 12.2A shows, there was no clear relationship between life expectancy and income per capita in 1870 among the set of countries with data on life expectancy. Norway and Sweden had higher life

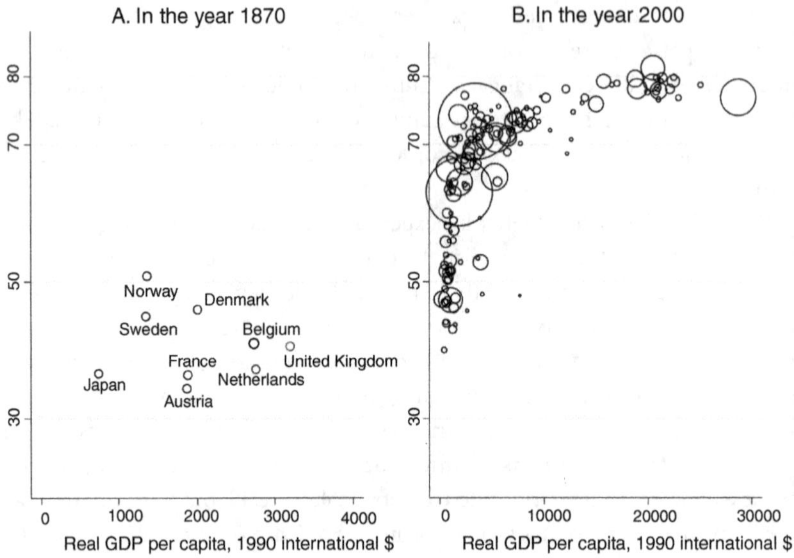

Figure 12.2 Life expectancy and income
Note: Observations in Figure 12.2B are population weighted.
Source: van Zanden et al. 2014.

expectancy than the United Kingdom, even though their income per capita was less than half that of the United Kingdom.

The relationship was even more tenuous for developing countries. Many poor Asian and African countries date the beginning of their health take-off to the 1940s and 1950s, when economic growth was slow. The increase in life expectancy had begun many years before the arrival of sustained income growth in the 1960s.

Scholars on the other side of the debate have pointed to fundamental medical innovations, such as penicillin in the 1940s. One cannot dispute the critical role of antibiotics in fighting infectious diseases, but again, the timing of these innovations does not match the decline in mortality, at least for developed countries. Adult mortality and infant mortality from infectious diseases began to decline in the late nineteenth century, almost fifty years before the advent of mass-produced antibiotics. Mortality fell not because people learned to treat infectious diseases, rather because people learned to control the spread of infectious diseases (Easterlin 1999).

Before the mid-nineteenth century, as western Europe and the United States were urbanizing, poor sanitation and polluted water led to more infectious diseases and higher mortality in cities. Although the move to clean the water supply had roots in the discredited 'miasma theory', it reduced the spread of infectious diseases. An understanding that cholera and typhoid spread through polluted water came next, in the 1850s. Shortly afterwards, scientists discovered that bacterial and viral pathogens caused diseases (i.e. germ theory). Vaccines to prevent infectious diseases arrived in the 1890s. Then, public health campaigns became commonplace in the United Kingdom and United States, where people were taught the importance of washing hands and disinfecting water, among other lifestyle changes to prevent the spread of disease (Deaton 2013). Local governments played a critical role by promoting health campaigns, building sewage facilities, and cleaning the water supply.

Undoubtedly, rich countries had more money to spend on sanitation and infrastructure. Yet politics was important. Since big or small infrastructure projects require local coordination, political coalitions in support of change were key in the United Kingdom and the United States (Deaton 2013). For example, as US women began to vote, local spending on public health increased by 45 per cent. In turn, women pushed for public funding of hygiene campaigns, leading to fewer children dying from infectious diseases (Miller 2008). In neither country was income the primary constraint. Rather, extending the right to vote allowed more people to press for change to improve their health and that of their children.

Medical innovations were key for developing countries. Here, the big fall in infant mortality and the rise in life expectancy began in the 1950s, with the spread of penicillin and sulfa drugs to treat infectious diseases (Deaton 2013). Did higher incomes in developing countries lead to faster adoption of new medical technologies? Again, the answer is unclear. Many successful efforts were top-down programmes run by the World Health Organization and the United Nations International Children's Emergency Fund (UNICEF). Today, the Gates Foundation and other non-profit organizations vaccinate many children in hard-to-reach places. Such global campaigns have had tremendous success even in countries with low incomes, poor infrastructure, and weak governance.

That said, income and development enhance public health efforts. As countries become richer, they have more money to spend on health. This helps to explain the positive, albeit non-linear, cross-sectional relationship between life expectancy and income per capita, the famous 'Preston curve' we see today (Figure 12.2B). But does higher income *cause* better health? Scholars continue to debate this question. Drawing on the historical record, our assessment is that income may play a complementary role, but it is not necessary or sufficient to guarantee better health outcomes on its own.

Aside from income, scholars also point to the fundamental role of education. More educated people have better information on preventing diseases and can undertake the necessary actions to promote better health. By many accounts, the spread of mass education has been the single biggest boon for health worldwide. For example, teenagers living in US states that were early adopters of compulsory schooling laws had more schooling *and* lived longer (Lleras-Muney 2005). In many poor countries, increasing female literacy has led to lower infant mortality because even here educated mothers are more likely to wash their hands, seek prenatal care, and have higher birth weight babies (Deaton 2013).

In fact, the historical data suggest that education has been more strongly correlated with life expectancy than the level of income. Figure 12.3A shows that years of schooling correlated well with survival as early as 1870. The link between health and education remains strong in 2000 (Figure 12.3B) and today. Of course, it is hard to say which came first, better health or more education. Even so, the twentieth century brought global triumphs for health *and* for education.

The Rise of Education

Since 1870, humans have learned to read, write, count, and discover, at a pace much faster than in any earlier era. Economically useful learning has accelerated at work, at school, and away from both work and school. Of these three sources of learning, the easiest to document historically is the rise of schooling. Let us turn next to the growth and inequality in people's years of formal education, before turning to the evidence of how much was actually learned in school and its economic pay-off.

Soaring School Enrolments and Educational Attainment since 1870

Like the gains in life expectancy, the rise of schooling since 1870 has been immense. It far exceeded the entire rise of schooling from antiquity to 1870. Table 12.2 and Figure 12.4 map the history of adults'

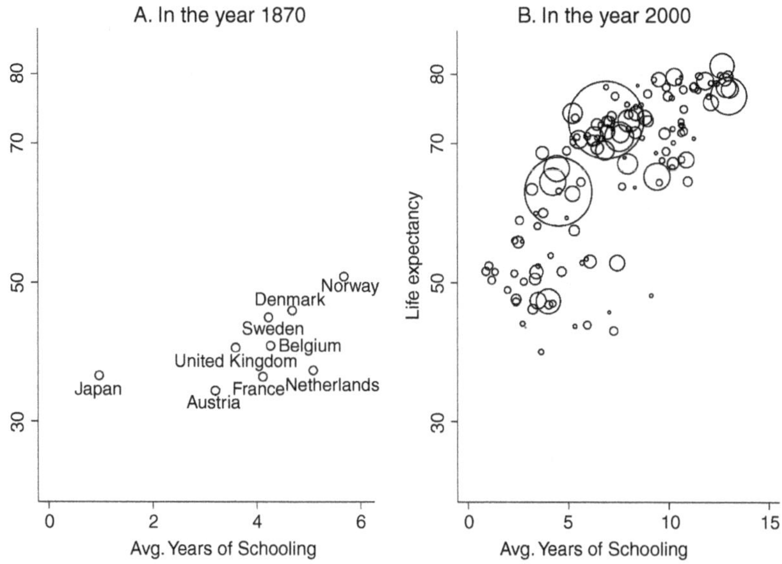

Figure 12.3 Life expectancy and average years of schooling
Note: Observations in Figure 12.3B are population weighted.
Source: van Zanden et al. 2014.

educational attainment, that is, the number of years for which the average person of working age (fifteen to sixty-four years) had been enrolled in school, all the way from 1870 to 2010.[2]

Back in 1870, only one in ten of the world's adults had ever been to school, and even in advanced European countries that share averaged below 35 per cent. In those days, furthermore, a large share of the students who were officially enrolled in school, even in some of the most advanced countries, did not actually attend school for most of the year, so that the number of days, or full-time years, that an adult had been enrolled overstates the number that they actually attended. So actual school attendance back in 1870 was less than Table 12.2's numbers imply. Today, by contrast, the enrolment figures reflect something closer to the number of full-time, or 180-day, years that each adult has been in school.

2 Since adults get their schooling earlier, in childhood, we should think of the figures for 1870 adults, aged fifteen to sixty-four, as referring to school enrolments that took place back in the 1850s, on average; similarly, the educational attainments for 2010 typically were centred in the 1990s. For the details of how the numbers of years attained by adults were calculated from the earlier rates of children's enrolments, see Lee and Lee 2016.

Table 12.2 Educational attainment of the population aged fifteen to sixty-four, 1870–2010

	Any schooling (% of persons, 15–64)			Average years of schooling		
	Total	Female	Male	Total	Female	Male
World (111 data-supplying countries)						
1870	10.0	8.4	11.5	0.5	0.4	0.5
2010	87.1	83.0	91.2	8.4	8.0	8.8
Advanced Europe (18 countries)						
1870	31.0	25.5	36.9	1.5	1.2	1.8
2010	98.7	98.6	98.7	11.6	11.6	11.6
North America (2 countries)						
1870	74.4	72.2	76.6	4.1	4.2	4.1
2010	99.7	99.7	99.7	13.2	13.3	13.1
Rest of Europe (9 countries)						
1870	13.3	10.3	16.4	0.6	0.5	0.8
2010	98.2	97.4	99.1	10.8	10.7	10.9
Asia (18 countries)						
1870	1.1	0.5	1.6	0.0	0.0	0.1
2010	85.1	79.4	90.6	7.7	7.0	8.3
Latin America and Caribbean (25 countries)						
1870	6.3	2.4	10.0	0.2	0.1	0.3
2010	94.4	94.0	94.7	8.7	8.7	8.6
Middle East (6 countries)						
1870	0.0	0.0	0.1	0.0	0.0	0.0
2010	81.2	75.3	86.9	7.9	7.4	8.3
Africa (31 countries)						
1870	0.8	0.1	1.6	0.0	0.0	0.1
2010	69.6	63.7	75.6	6.0	5.4	6.5
Oceania (2 countries)						
1870	51.9	38.7	61.6	2.0	1.6	2.2
2010	99.4	99.4	99.4	11.6	11.7	11.5

Notes: The regional averages were calculated from national rates by weighting according to each country's population aged fifteen to sixty-four. Countries were grouped into regions based on the United Nations grouping.
Source: Lee and Lee 2016.

The rise of schooling has been worldwide. For example, as of 2010, the average working-age adult in Africa had been enrolled in school for six years, which is more than triple the average number of years for adults in advanced countries back in 1870, and even more than the 4.3 years that the average adult had attained in the United States, the world's most schooled nation,

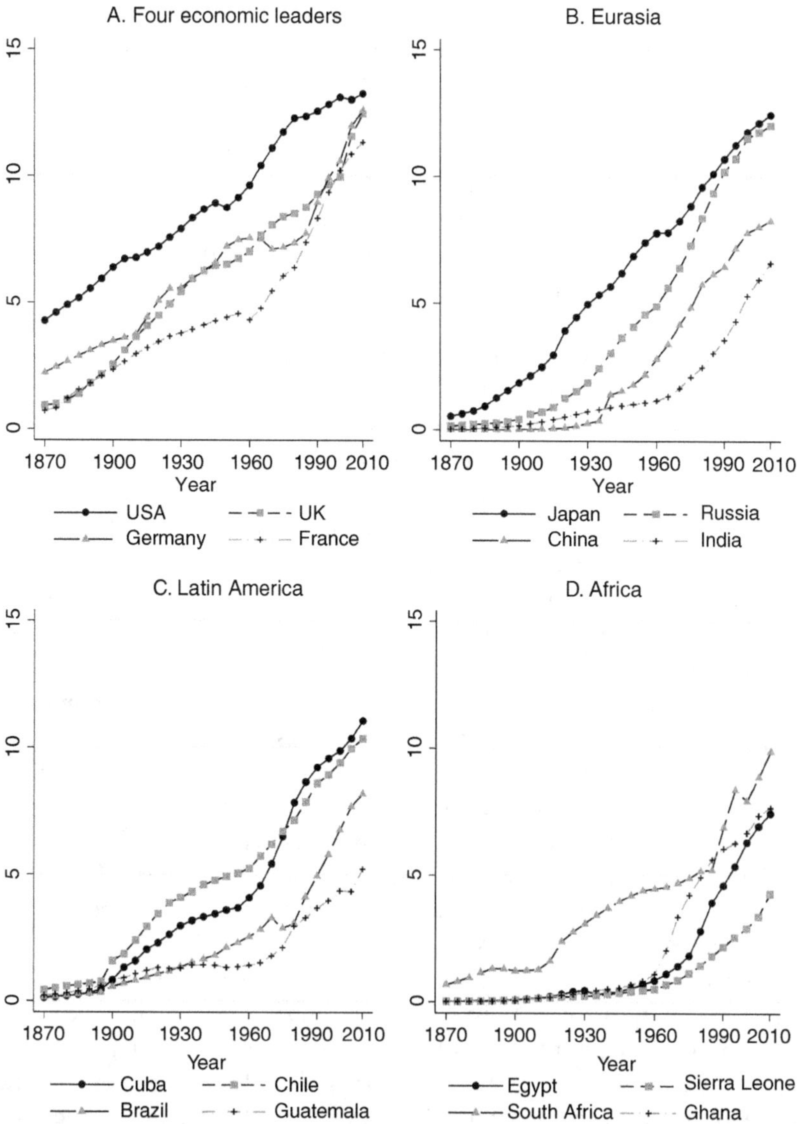

Figure 12.4 Average years of schooling, select countries
Source: Lee and Lee 2016.

back in 1870. Enrolments have risen similarly in South Asia, the other least schooled of the major regions: from 0.03 years per working-age adult in 1870 to 4.0 years in 2010. Both in Africa and in South Asia, the rate has been accelerating, with most of the enrolment gains coming in the post-war period (1950–2010 here) rather than across the previous eighty years. The parallels with life expectancy are unsurprising given the mutually reinforcing relationship between the two.

By our 1870 starting point, the Americans, with the Canadians and Swiss not far behind, had already overtaken Germany as leaders in educational attainment, and have retained that top position ever since. Remember that this leadership refers to the enrolment quantity, and not the quality of the education gained, a point to which we return below. Among the three European countries represented in Figure 12.4A, there were some reversals. Although we often start economic histories of the nineteenth century with Britain and its Industrial Revolution, Germany was in fact ahead of Britain in school enrolments until the early twentieth century. Then, under the Nazis and during the early post-war years (1933–50), a whole generation of German children suffered lower enrolments in secondary and higher education, with the result that German adults' average attainment of total schooling sagged from 1955 to 1975, before catching up again.

Further east, the great Eurasian powers lagged far behind until the 1970s or later. Of the four nations shown in Figure 12.4B, Japan led the others by far before the 1970s. By then, Russia, along with the rest of the Soviet Union and eastern Europe, began to catch up rapidly. China, though it shared the communist emphasis on mass education, has not caught up as rapidly, mainly because of the interruptions to schooling during Chairman Mao's disastrous Great Leap Forward (1958–61) and his Great Proletarian Cultural Revolution (1966–76). On the other hand, China's enrolments have always exceeded those of India.

Within the Latin American and Caribbean region, Brazil, the largest nation, always lagged behind such education leaders as Chile and Argentina, as suggested by Figure 12.4C's contrast between Chile and Brazil.[3] Chile had the region's top enrolments for a century – until Castro's Cuba expanded basic education enough to make Cuba's adult population the region's most schooled from 1975 on. Had great schooling been sufficient for greater average incomes, Cuba would be the region's richest country today. However, Cuba since the 1959 Revolution is peculiar not only in its strong commitment to education and health, but also in its inability to give good income opportunities to its highly

3 Figure 12.4C records a dip in the average schooling of Brazil's adults between 1970 and 1980. This seems to have been produced by a drop in Brazil's enrolment rate for primary school during the 1950s. In that decade, government policy priorities seem to have shifted towards monumental infrastructure construction and away from primary education.

educated populace. A more typical kind of poverty in Latin America is poverty with low education, as illustrated by Figure 12.4C's dreary history of school enrolments in low-income Guatemala. The same low education remains characteristic of much of Central America, except for better-performing Panama and Costa Rica.

Within Africa, South Africa and Botswana are clear leaders, with average schooling around ten years as of 2010. Egypt has not achieved similar gains, despite having a higher income. Figure 12.4D contrasts African countries where progress has been more rapid, as shown for Ghana, and those where schooling has increased very slowly, as in Sierra Leone. At the bottom of the African ladder are countries like Niger, Burkina Faso, and Mali, with some of the lowest levels of education in the world. In fact, average schooling is just one year for this group, even below where the advanced countries were in 1870. But they are in the minority, with the rest of Africa enjoying higher levels of education.

Before we dig deeper into the reasons for the rise in schooling, an unmistakable pattern in the rise of schooling needs emphasis. Public spending has been critical for the expansion of mass education. No country has expanded its primary or secondary education to cover more than half the relevant age group without having taxpayers pay for almost all of it. In fact, even such libertarian champions as Adam Smith, Thomas Jefferson, and Milton Friedman all called for universal primary schooling funded primarily by taxpayers.[4] Public spending is even more critical for education than for health, where technological advances, such as antibiotics, raised life expectancy in developing countries at low cost. By contrast, people today are educated in much the same way as in the past. They sit in classrooms and listen to teachers. In richer places, the schools are housed in nicer buildings and teachers are present for the full school day, but other facets of teaching have changed little.

The Gender Dimension of Educational Ascent

Thus far we have looked at the history of schooling received by everybody, both males and females. Yet societies have treated the two sexes very unequally, in education as in other respects, and greater discrimination has had negative effects on the economic growth of the more discriminating societies. When and where did girls receive the

4 See Lindert 2004: 87–127, 153–154.

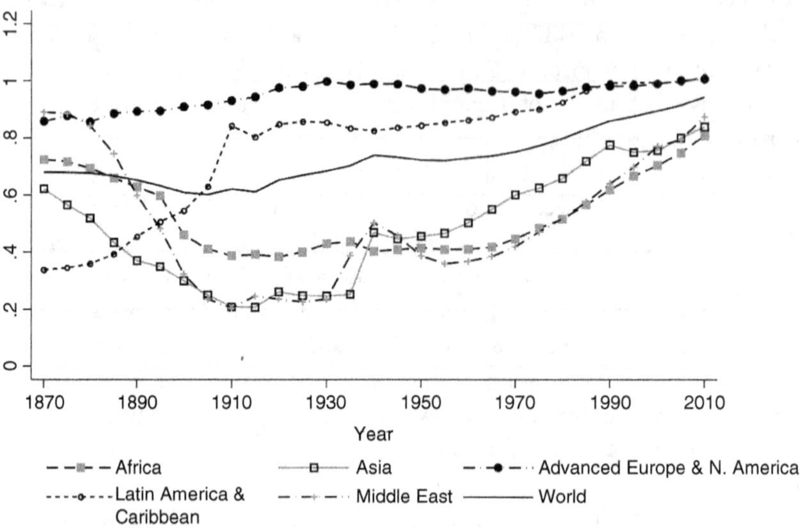

Figure 12.5 Ratio of average years of schooling, female/male
Source: Lee and Lee 2016.

least, or the most, schooling relative to boys? Table 12.2 and Figure 12.5 provide some answers.

There has been an unmistakable march towards gender parity in educational attainment, led by the advanced countries. Even as early as 1870, women were attending school longer in the United States and Canada, 4.2 years compared to 4.1 for men. And, since the 1980s, among the advanced countries as a whole, women have received the majority of university undergraduate degrees. The Middle East and the still-developing countries of Asia are lagging behind the rest of the world by about a century, reaching advanced countries' female/male education ratios of 1910 only around the year 2010. Here, the high female–male ratio for the Middle East in 1870 in Figure 12.5 is deceptive because no one was attending school in those countries in the late nineteenth century.

By contrast, the still developing countries of Latin America and eastern Europe have kept pace with the most economically advanced countries in terms of gender equity in education. Latin America is especially impressive. Even though it began the period with a female–male ratio under 0.4 in 1870, it rapidly expanded female education in the next few decades, with the ratio exceeding 0.8 by 1910. South Asian countries like India continue to struggle with stubborn and persistent gender differences in education. Are economic or cultural factors responsible? Given the long history of such differences over changing economic times, culture is perhaps a bigger part of the South Asian story.

The education of females strongly promotes economic development, in ways that one would miss if one pursued only the direct effects of a female's education on her own wages. While it cannot explain all differences in economic growth, the scholarly literature has developed a consensus that a mother's greater schooling means fewer children and greater investments of time and money into the health and productive powers of each child. For a variety of familiar reasons, mothers have always delivered more inputs into child development than have fathers.[5]

The dependence of children's survival and earning power on their mother's education carries a clear implication for economic history: as emphasized earlier, the regions that gave a greater share of education to females in the past have, partly for this reason, achieved greater cumulative gains in life expectancy and GDP per capita. The pro-growth aspect of gender equity is something that the east Europeans and Latin Americans have got right, and it is something that most of Asia, the Middle East, and Africa have got wrong.

The Achievement of Basic Learning

How are we to compare countries' progress in the quality of what was learned? Here we can look at four kinds of learning that children should possess by the time they mature – (1) literacy, (2) numeracy, (3) abstract problem-solving and IQ, and (4) the mastery of basic materials in mathematics, science, and reading for content. The four indicators of what students have learned have changed over time.

Literacy rates, our first measurable learning skill, is useful for comparing the progress of advanced countries up to about 1930, and for comparing developing countries' progress even today. Learning to read and write is related to the first four years of primary schooling. True, an individual can be taught to read and write without going to school, and many did so in the past. Yet literacy and primary schooling are close correlates.

In today's advanced countries, most of the spread of literacy came before 1870. For the world as a whole, however, adults had not learned to read and

5 See King and Hill 1997: 11–20, for example.

write until the generations of children born after 1870. As of 1870, an estimated 79 per cent of the world's adults were still illiterate. In western Europe and its offshoots in North America and Australasia, the share unable to read and write was much lower, at 37 per cent. In the early twenty-first century, much of the world still lagged behind the literacy that western Europe and its offshoots had achieved back in 1870, unlike what Table 12.2 showed about adults' attainment of school years. Specifically, Africa was still just matching those advanced countries' 1870 adult literacy, and in South Asia, 48 per cent of adults were illiterate as of 2000, even though both regions had much higher school enrolment rates than the advanced countries had had back in 1870. This lag of literacy's progress behind the rise of school enrolments hints that in Africa and (especially) in South Asia, the combination of school systems, parents, and social environments may have had low efficiency in delivering basic literacy.

Numeracy (or quantitative literacy) is another historical clue that, like the ability to read and write, reveals much about human learning in earlier history. Numeracy refers to the human ability to add, subtract, and remember numbers relevant to their lives.

To reveal historical patterns in this ability, economic historians have constructed something like a fingerprint for numeracy. Looking at census records, they have followed the ability of people to state the exact numbers of years of age, both their own ages and those of their family members. This is a reasonable indicator of people's sense of numerical facts. These scholars have used something called 'age heaping' to reveal a lack of attention to numbers. When asked 'How many years old are you?' people in less numerate societies give an answer ending in five or (especially) in zero, much more than they give answers ending in other digits. As a result, in a not so numerate society, the census will reveal suspiciously many people aged thirty or thirty-five, and suspiciously few aged twenty-eight, twenty-nine, thirty-one to thirty-four, thirty-six, or thirty-seven. An index of such age heaping, heaping on the final digits zero and five, measures poor numeracy.

Economic historians now know the historical patterns in numeracy from all over the world. Accurate numeracy, or the lack of that 'age heaping', strongly correlates with modernization and with literacy. So say both detailed micro-studies within a country and the global history of regions' numeracy rates. And as with the rise of literacy, much of the rise of numeracy was achieved before 1870. The world history of numeracy suggests that it correlates with GDP per capita, but the correlation weakens over time. The relationship is interesting, even though we cannot be sure which way the causation runs.[6]

It is unsurprising that literacy and numeracy showed up very early as payoffs from schooling. After all, these were the two modest objectives of one's brief schooling in the nineteenth century, aside from learning religion and discipline.

Various tests for *IQ*, or *abstract problem-solving ability*, have been developed in advanced countries since 1900. Many think such test scores measure innate 'aptitude' and not the hard work one has put into learning the subject matter taught in school. Yet intelligence test scores have always reflected one's acquiring of skills that are taught in school, rather than purely innate abilities.

We know that the various IQ-type tests reflect the learning environment, and not just genetic differences, thanks to work led by James R. Flynn since 1984. In what has become known as the 'Flynn effect', he noticed that average scores rose over the decades on any given IQ test, a result now extended to about thirty countries (Flynn 2012). Flynn further found that when the test was recalibrated so that the average on a new version would be one hundred again, students given both the new test and the old one averaged well above one hundred on the old one, implying even more improvement in IQ. Over the entire period 1900–2012, the average IQ score rose almost thirty points, implying that the average test-taker in 2012 was more capable than 95 per cent of those back in 1900. The typical rate of change – about 2.18 IQ points per decade, or about 7 points per generation – was too fast for genetic change to achieve in a large population. Rather, with the help of formal schooling and the increased stimuli of modern life, human minds are adapting to a more complex world. An important further result is that the rates of improvement continue to be faster in populations that are still undergoing the process of economic development, suggesting a catching up in IQ as a country catches up economically. Similarly, historically less privileged groups within a country have also made faster gains in IQ-type test scores than more privileged groups.

What role has the rise in formal schooling played in the rise of problem-solving ability and other aptitudes covered on such tests? Formal schooling may not be the sole cause of the rise of such abilities. There could be roles for other dimensions of modernization, such as improvements in health. Still,

6 A'Hearn et al. 2009.

scholars seem to agree that formal education deserves some part of the credit.[7]

International *knowledge testing in maths, science and reading*, the last of the four clues about basic learning that we explore here, comes the closest to judging the school learning itself, since these exams test what students learned in school, not their innate ability.

Since 1964, international agencies have developed a few dozen different tests of international student achievement in maths, reading, and/or science. Until the 1990s, these were limited and selective in their international coverage. Starting from the 1990s, however, the international knowledge tests became more uniform in their sampling and their subject-matter coverage. We focus here on the OECD's Programme for International Student Assessment (PISA), which tests fifteen-year-olds on their knowledge of maths and sciences, and on their reading ability. PISA is administered every three years, starting in the year 2000, and covers more than thirty countries. Although PISA tries to sample school districts randomly, some selection biases are likely to remain.

Table 12.3 and Figure 12.6 report results for an average of nine PISA test scores, those for maths, reading, and science for each of the test years 2006, 2009, and 2012. Figure 12.6 also shows the positive correlation between knowledge exam scores and GDP per capita. What is more, GDP per capita is positively correlated not only with PISA scores for fifteen-year-olds, as shown here, but with every other main educational indicator we are presenting in this chapter – with other international test scores, with IQ scores, and with educational attainment.

East Asia, Finland, and Canada consistently rank at the top, above western Europe and three English-speaking offshoots (USA, Australia, and New Zealand), in PISA knowledge scores, just as it does in IQ. The outstanding East Asian performances are illustrated at the top of Figure 12.6. One note of caution is in order, however. It is unclear if the high scores for the mainly Chinese entities reporting PISA scores (Hong Kong, Macao, Taipei, and the new Beijing-Shanghai-Jiangsu-Guangdong combined score) should be applied to the entire Chinese population, since these tests were conducted in cities with high family incomes and privileged access to the best education.

7 Rough international correlations support this hunch: internationally, the national-average IQ scores seem to correlate strongly with the quality of schooling, as reflected in the average scores on the PISA achievement tests in 2006–12 (correlation coefficient = 0.826 for forty-three countries).

Table 12.3 Average PISA achievement scores of fifteen-year-olds, 2006–12, versus real GDP per capita, 2010

	Average income 2010	Average PISA 2006–12		Average income 2010	Average PISA 2006–12
Western Europe & offshoots			*Eastern Europe & former USSR*		
Australia	37,381	517	Albania	7,234	390
Austria	36,474	501	Bulgaria	12,453	430
Belgium	35,050	510	Croatia	17,015	479
Canada	34,223	526	Czech Rep.	23,047	497
Denmark	35,608	500	Estonia	18,574	518
Finland	32,684	542	Hungary	18,654	492
France	31,065	497	Kazakhstan	14,461	407
Germany	33,613	510	Latvia	14,750	488
Greece	25,430	468	Lithuania	16,281	481
Iceland	30,864	493	Montenegro	11,032	406
Ireland	35,704	507	Poland	17,827	507
Israel	24,391	459	Romania	13,139	426
Italy	29,195	481	Russian Fed.	17,187	472
Luxembourg[(a), (b)]	77,728	486	Serbia	9,340	438
Netherlands	37,498	519	Slovakia	20,905	481
New Zealand	26,451	519	Slovenia	24,709	501
Norway	49,991	494			
Portugal	22,886	483	*Middle East and North Africa*		
Spain	28,923	483	Jordan	6,111	401
Sweden	35,003	494	Qatar[(b)]	111,074	361
Switzerland	44,182	516	Tunisia	8,922	389
UK	32,284	501	Turkey	13,775	449
USA	42,047	491			
			East Asia		
Latin America			Hong Kong[(a)]	43,593	547
Argentina	14,085	391	Indonesia	4,373	387
Brazil	9,422	396	Japan	30,583	529
Chile	15,097	435	Korea, Rep.	27,079	542
Colombia	8,293	391	Malaysia	16,576	413
Costa Rica	9,923	427	Singapore[(a)]	58,268	549
Mexico	12,348	415	Taipei[(a)]	32,889	527
Peru	8,632	372	Thailand	9,727	426
Uruguay	12,621	420			

Notes: (a) Leading city only. (b) Beyond the income range of Figure 12.6. PISA scores are taken from the OECD national averages of the maths, reading, and science literacy scores for 2006, 2009, and 2012. In a few cases, a score was unavailable for one of the tests, or for all three tests, in 2006, so that the average refers to fewer tests. The real incomes per capita are the current-price PPP values of gross domestic expenditures per person, from Penn World Table 8.1.

Source: PISA Database, www.oecd.org/pisa/data/; Penn World Table, version 8.1, www.rug.nl/ggdc/productivity/pwt/pwt-releases/pwt8.1?lang=en.

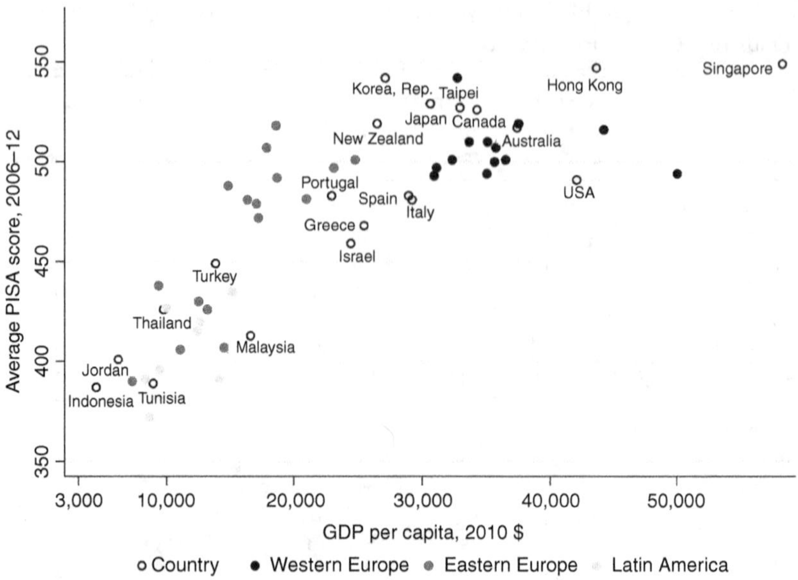

Figure 12.6 Test scores and income
Note: See Table 12.3 above.
Source: PISA Database, www.oecd.org/pisa/data/; Penn World Table, version 8.1, www.rug.nl/ggdc/productivity/pwt/pwt-releases/pwt8.1?lang=en.

There is a curious tendency for countries on the Mediterranean to have lower scores than in north-west Europe, not only in PISA, but also in IQ. Of the countries included in Table 12.3 and Figure 12.6, the lowest average scores of the western Europeans are those for Israel, Greece, Italy, Spain, and (almost Mediterranean) Portugal, with even lower scores for nearby Tunisia and Turkey. In the 2015 PISA tests, these countries were joined in the lower ranks of knowledge scores by their Mediterranean neighbours, Malta and Croatia.

Students in eastern Europe and the former Soviet Union seem to perform as well as those in western Europe, even though their families have lower real incomes on average. This result, so clear in Figure 12.6, seems to reflect the split legacy of the communist era before 1991. On the one hand, the long communist interlude retarded the advance of productivity. On the other, it succeeded in lifting the educational quantities and quality of learning in eastern Europe to the western European level, as we saw when surveying the rise in enrolments in Table 12.2.

As a whole, the United States and Australasia do not perform as well as their counterparts in north-west Europe. The United States has been famously mediocre in its performance on the international tests, even though it has a higher income per capita than those in north-west Europe. In the PISA scores, the United States tends to rank about thirtieth out of about sixty test-taking countries or regions today, and was always near the median position in the expanding PISA community.

Latin America's performance has been particularly troubling ever since the early twentieth century. For most of the twentieth century, the problem was one of lower public spending and low enrolments of the poor (Lindert 2010). Yet since the 1990s, at least, the gains in Latin America's enrolments have not been matched by any gains in student learning, as reflected in test scores.[8]

How Much More Productive Has Schooling Made Us?

Economists use two approaches to estimate the effect of extra years of schooling on output or income: a macro production function approach and a returns approach. Each has its limitations and its insights.

Production Function Approach

Economists have estimated how much real output per person one obtains from inputs of either education or knowledge, along with other inputs, such as labour employment, physical capital, and land. Most of the literature uses just years of schooling as a human capital input, even though an individual's years of schooling fail to capture schooling quality, on-the-job learning, health, and cognitive ability.

The attempt to find production function causality has had to struggle with some familiar problems of extracting a statistical confession from the data. One problem is endogeneity: education and knowledge variables affect overall national product, and they are affected by it. While earlier research suggested a small or insignificant effect of education, recent evidence using better data and techniques (de la Fuente and Doménech 2006) finds that more schooling does make countries richer. Indeed, the effects of actual knowledge, as proxied by test scores, are significant predictors of economic success across countries (Hanushek and Woessmann 2015).

8 Hanushek and Woessmann 2015: 112–128.

Table 12.4 Private returns to another year of schooling, large and positive

	All levels	Primary	Secondary	Tertiary	Male primary	Female primary	Male tertiary	Female tertiary
	2000–2010							
Advanced Europe	8.5	7.6	4.9	10.3	9.5	9.6	9.8	12.1
Africa	13.2	13.3	10.5	22.9	11.2	13.7	22.7	24.5
Asia	9.3	10.0	7.2	16.0	8.7	8.2	15.7	18.8
Rest of Europe	9.0	12.0	5.5	11.5	10.8	11.0	11.9	13.3
Latin American & Caribbean	10.5	9.0	6.6	18.0	9.0	9.6	18.0	18.9
Middle East	4.0	11.2	1.7	4.9	9.9	14.6	5.0	12.4
North America	12.9	1.6	4.7	13.1	3.3	–	12.8	14.4
Oceania	11.2	13.9	7.4	13.5	15.7	10.4	12.6	14.4
World	9.9	10.3	6.9	15.1	9.7	10.5	15.1	16.9

	All levels	Primary	Secondary	Tertiary	All levels	Primary	Secondary	Tertiary
	1990–99				1980–89			
Advanced Europe	6.8	7.4	7.5	9.6	5.7	8.6	7.5	6.5
Africa	5.5	24.2	13.3	11.9	12.5	22.8	20.1	11.0
Asia	10.7	15.1	8.9	10.1	10.3	13.3	9.6	10.3
Rest of Europe	6.2	14.0	4.1	6.5	4.6	3.3	2.3	5.8
Latin American & Caribbean	9.9	15.0	11.4	11.5	14.1	17.9	10.8	12.4
Middle East	–	–	–	–	4.5	2.0	26.0	24.0
North America	10.0	–	–	–	8.9	–	10.0	12.0
Oceania	–	–	12.4	9.5	8.0	12.8	19.4	8.4

Note: Individual countries were assigned to geographic regions based on the United Nations geographical country grouping.
Sources: 2000–2010: Montenegro and Patrinos 2014; 1990–99 and 1980–89: Psacharopoulos and Patrinos 2004.

Rate of Return Approach

To answer the question 'What are the private and social costs and benefits of extra schooling?', the most relevant kind of measure reckons both costs and benefits, and views education as an investment in one's future. That is, how much does an investment in extra education cost, what are its net benefits in terms of higher earnings in the future, and what is the internal rate of return showing how the future benefits stack up against the initial costs?

Although one could estimate a social rate of return, here we focus on private returns to schooling, for which labour economists have constructed estimates for many countries. Table 12.4 summarizes the findings, drawing on work by Psacharopoulos, Patrinos, and Montenegro. Before harvesting the rich suggestions offered by Table 12.4's numbers, a few caveats are in order. These estimates compare the average earnings of different sets of people, with different abilities and attributes, not any one person's economic fortunes with and without school. Yet we believe the simple OLS-based returns in Table 12.4 are reasonably accurate because most causal estimates find larger effects of education on earnings.

Another, more important, pitfall is that the measures of earnings in later life exclude data on people who are self-employed. This is a serious problem, especially in developing countries, where education in fact increases labour force participation. The measures also miss psychic income, the pure non-economic joy (or annoyance?) of having spent the extra time in school.

Four remarkable patterns stand out in Table 12.4's summary of global returns in the 1980s to 2000s. The first pattern is that the private rate of return averages 9.9 per cent a year for each additional year of schooling. Interestingly, the return is stable across time, with past work reporting global returns of 9–13 per cent (Psacharopoulos 1994; Psacharopoulos and Patrinos 2004). While average years of schooling across the world increased from 6.6 years in 1980–85 to almost 12 years in 2011 (Montenegro and Patrinos 2014), the worldwide return to an additional year of education has declined only slightly, from a high of 13.3 per cent in the 1980s to Table 12.4's 9.9 per cent in 2000–2010. Global demand for education is still increasing faster than the global supply of educated labour.

The second pattern is that the private rates of return in the advanced European countries have been lower than those in the still-developing countries. In the 1980s, returns in Africa averaged 12.5 per cent compared to 5.7 per cent in advanced countries of Europe. We continued to observe similar patterns in the 2000s. Development lowers the rates of return.

The third pattern is that returns are higher for women compared to men. This was true in the past and is still true today. For all levels of education together, females' average returns to schooling are 11.4 per cent, compared to 9.1 per cent for men. The difference is visible at every level of education.

The fourth and final pattern is a change in the private returns by education level. Returns to primary education were higher in the past. This is no longer true. In the 2000s, the returns to tertiary education averaged 15.1 per cent, compared to 10.3 per cent to primary education. One potential reason is perhaps the increasing size of the service sector worldwide, which employs more people with tertiary education.

Aside from some differences, the general picture is one of large and positive private returns to education, ranging from 4 to 14 per cent for each additional year of education. Increasing years of schooling lead to higher wages around the world, especially for women, and especially for people in poor countries. Indeed, this was true in the past and is true today.

Why Isn't the Whole World Highly Educated?

As discussed in the previous section and shown in Table 12.4, the returns to schooling are large and positive. Further, rates of return in less developed countries are higher than in developed countries. What explains this striking pattern?[9] It cannot be that less developed economies have greater demands for the services of educated persons. If that were the driving force in the development pattern, then we would expect to see people responding by getting more education in poorer countries – exactly the opposite of what we observe throughout history. The difference between developed and less developed countries' markets for schooling cannot lie on the demand side. Rather, it must be that less developed countries are held back by powerful constraints on the supply of schooling, especially held back in their attainment of *primary* schooling. Why? What is holding them back?

The causes behind the delays in primary education are both very general and very specific to individual countries. To start at the most general level, income is correlated with every aspect of education. Poorer countries have lower enrolment, spend less money on education, and have fewer teachers per student. We immediately face a familiar chicken-and-egg problem: Are

9 Our section title owes a debt to Richard Easterlin's (1981) presidential address to the Economic History Association, 'Why Isn't the Whole World Developed?'. Indeed, despite the breadth of his title, his address in fact focused on the human capital question of why primary school enrolment rates have remained so low for so much of the world.

countries poorer because their adults have received less primary education, or is primary education less common because they are poorer?

Helped by some comparative statistics, scholars have developed a list of primary suspects that have held back primary education in some countries more than in others. We concentrate here on the retarding factors experienced before World War II, ones that are salient even today. Aside from income itself, the following three forces most promoted primary education before World War II: political voice, ethnic homogeneity, and religious unity.

Political voice mattered greatly because primary schooling depended on public tax financing the world over, as we noted earlier. The more inclusive and universal was the right to vote, the more the taxpaying public paid for schools. Where political voice was restricted to wealthy elites or to (non-communist) autocrats, basic education was denied to children who were not elites. Those in power saw mass primary education as a tax burden and as a force that might make docile workers challenge them and seek better-paying jobs elsewhere. In terms of international comparisons, the role of broader voting rights in promoting mass schooling has been described in the history of the Americas, in the history of OECD industrialized countries, and in the larger sweep of all modern history (Lindert 2004; Engerman et al. 2009).

Ethnic homogeneity has also strongly promoted the supply of public primary education. Primary education, like other kinds of public goods, is supplied more generously in a homogeneous population, one where taxpayers are willing to grant that tax-based public expenditures are a benefit to all of 'us'. Conversely, ethnic fractionalization breaks down the political will to fund public goods through government, under the more negative belief that it is wasting 'our' tax money on 'them'. The negative effects of ethnic fractionalization on such government expenditures as public health, public education, and infrastructure have been widely demonstrated statistically.[10] What applies to ethnic divisions also applies to rigid social divisions, as in India (Chaudhary 2009).

The same goes for religious unity. If one organized religion dominates in society, there will be little controversy about whether the government gives out taxpayers' money in subsidies to schools run by that religion. Yet the controversy boils over quickly when different religions either oppose using taxpayer money for secular schools, or try to gain taxpayer support for their own schools.

10 See, for example, Alesina et al. 1999; Lindert 2004: chs. 5, 7, 15–17.

Any answer to the global question posed in the heading of this section must start with higher fractionalization and elite influence in still-developing countries, which makes public funding of education hard.

Conclusion

In spite of the challenges developing countries face today, the global human capital picture is one of impressive gains and hope for future progress. Even in the poorest parts of the world, namely in sub-Saharan Africa and South Asia, people were living longer and spending more time in school in 2010 than people in the rich countries in 1870.

Life expectancies and schooling are not only increasing, but also converging. In 1870, life expectancy in countries at the ninetieth percentile of the distribution was 1.8 times higher than countries on the tenth percentile of the distribution (90/10 ratio). In 2000, the same 90/10 ratio in life expectancy was only 1.5. We see the same picture for education. The 90/10 ratio in average years of schooling was 106 in 1870, yet in 2000 the same ratio was only 4.1. Similarly, for the adults within countries, the numbers of years of schooling have also been converging dramatically since 1870 (Lee and Lee 2016). In contrast, it is well known that income per capita diverged across the world in the same period. The 90/10 ratio for income per capita was 5.3 in 1870, but increased to 27 by 2000.

To borrow a phrase from Lant Pritchett (1997), since 1870 there has been a long-run 'convergence, big time' in human capital, one that contrasts sharply with his 'divergence, big time' in incomes recently.

References

A'Hearn, B., Baten, J., and Crayen, D. (2009). 'Quantifying Quantitative Literacy: Age Heaping and the History of Human Capital', *Journal of Economic History*, 69(3), 783–808.

Alesina, A., Baqir, R., and Easterly, W. (1999). 'Public Goods and Ethnic Divisions', *Quarterly Journal of Economics*, 114(4), 1243–1284.

Chaudhary, L. (2009). 'Determinants of Primary Schooling in British India', *Journal of Economic History*, 69(1), 269–302.

de la Fuente, A. and Doménech, R. (2006). 'Human Capital in Growth Regressions: How Much Difference does Data Quality Make?', *Journal of the European Economic Association*, 4(1), 1–36.

Deaton, A. (2013). *The Great Escape: Health, Wealth, and the Origins of Inequality*, Princeton University Press.

Drèze, J. and Sen, A. (2013). *An Uncertain Glory: India and its Contradictions*, Princeton University Press.

Easterlin, R. A. (1981). 'Why Isn't the Whole World Developed?', *Journal of Economic History*, 41(1), 1–17.

(1999). 'How Beneficent Is the Market? A Look at the Modern History of Mortality', *European Review of Economic History*, 3(3), 257–294.

Engerman, S. L., Mariscal, E. V., and Sokoloff, K. L. (2009). 'The Evolution of Schooling Institutions in the Americas, 1800–1925', in Eltis, D., Lewis, F., and Sokoloff, K. (eds.), *Human Capital and Institutions: A Long Run View*, New York: Cambridge University Press, 93–142.

Flynn, J. R. (2012). *Are We Getting Smarter? Rising IQ in the Twenty-First Century*, Cambridge University Press.

Hanushek, E. A. and Woessmann, L. (2015). *The Knowledge Capital of Nations*, Cambridge, MA: MIT Press.

King, E. M. and Hill, M. A. (1997). 'Women's Education in Developing Countries: An Overview', in King, E. M. and Hill, M. A. (eds.), *Women's Education in Developing Countries: Barriers, Benefits, and Policies*, Baltimore: Johns Hopkins University Press, 1–50.

Lee, J.-W. and Lee, H. (2016). 'Human Capital in the Long Run', *Journal of Development Economics*, 122, 147–169.

Lindert, P. H. (2004). *Growing Public: Social Spending and Economic Growth since the Eighteenth Century*, 2 vols, Cambridge University Press.

(2010). 'The Unequal Lag in Latin American Schooling since 1900: Follow the Money', *Revista de Historia Económica*, 28(2): 375–405.

Lleras-Muney, A. (2005). 'The Relationship between Education and Adult Mortality in the United States', *Review of Economic Studies*, 72(1), 189–221.

McKeown, T. (1976). *The Modern Rise of Population*, New York: Academic Press.

Miller, G. (2008). 'Women's Suffrage, Political Responsiveness, and Child Survival in American History', *Quarterly Journal of Economics*, 123(3), 1287–1327.

Montenegro, C. E. and Patrinos, H. A. (2014). 'Comparable Estimates of Returns to Schooling Around the World', policy research working paper 7020, Education Global Practice Group, World Bank.

Pritchett, L. (1997). 'Divergence, Big Time', *Journal of Economic Perspectives*, 11(3), 3–17.

Psacharopoulos, G. (2004). 'The Returns to Investment in Higher Education: A Global Update', *World Development*, 22: 1325–1343.

Psacharopoulos, G. and Patrinos, H. A. (2004). 'Returns to Investment in Education: A Further Update', *Education Economics*, 12(2), 111–134.

Riley, J. C. (2005). 'Estimates of Regional and Global Life Expectancy, 1800–2001', *Population and Development Review*, 31(3), 537–543.

van Zanden, J. L., Baten, J., Mira d'Hercole, M., Rijpma, A., Smith, C., and Timmer, M. (eds.) (2014). *How Was Life? Global Well-Being since 1820*, Paris: OECD.

Zaridze, D., Lewington, S., Boroda, A., Scélo, G., Karpov, R., Lazarev, A. et al. (2014). 'Alcohol and Mortality in Russia: Prospective Observational Study of 151,000 Adults', *Lancet* 383(9927), 1465–1473.

13

Proximate Sources of Growth

Capital and Technology

RAJABRATA BANERJEE, ROBERT INKLAAR, AND HERMAN DE JONG

Introduction

The post-1870 period has been an era in which a wide range of countries engaged in rapid capital accumulation, through investments in production facilities, machines, and infrastructural outlays – as well as through investment in human capital in the form of schooling. Many innovations and newly developed technologies were incorporated in new capital equipment. Yet despite rapid investments, income differences between rich and poor countries are nowadays larger than at the beginning of the nineteenth century. Many studies have shown that accumulation of physical and human capital accounts for only a small part of cross-country differences in economic growth.

To understand why, we need to consider the relations between capital accumulation, technological change, and productivity growth. Recent research has focused on differences in technology adoption across countries and in the intensity with which technologies are applied. First of all, it takes time before a technology has diffused in an economy to such an extent that it leads to higher incomes. Second, available technologies are not always appropriate for countries given their factor endowments or their institutions (David 1990; Allen 2012; Comin and Mestieri 2016). The introduction of new technologies may thus favour countries differently, depending on their economic and social development (Aghion et al. 2014).

The main aim of this chapter is to examine differences in economic growth around the world since 1870, starting with the initial divergence when the United States and western Europe showed much faster growth than other regions of the world, to the subsequent (selective) convergence when primarily Asian countries managed to start closing the income gap through sustained economic growth. An important tool for this examination is growth accounting, which decomposes growth of GDP per capita into contributions from the accumulation of physical and human capital and from the efficiency with which these types of capital are being used in the economy, defined as total factor productivity (TFP). TFP is determined as a residual, the portion of output growth not explained by growth of capital and labour used in production. So we need to consider a wider set of factors, including technology development and adoption, structural change, globalization, and the nature of technological regimes.

To illustrate this last point and to introduce the periodization that structures the remainder of this chapter, Figure 13.1 charts the skill premium – the ratio of wages of skilled to unskilled workers – in the labour market of the United States, whose economy has set the pace for others to follow during this period. The first period, from 1870 to 1910, can be characterized as one of capital-intensive industrialization, and during this period, skilled workers in the US saw their earnings rise more rapidly than unskilled workers, which

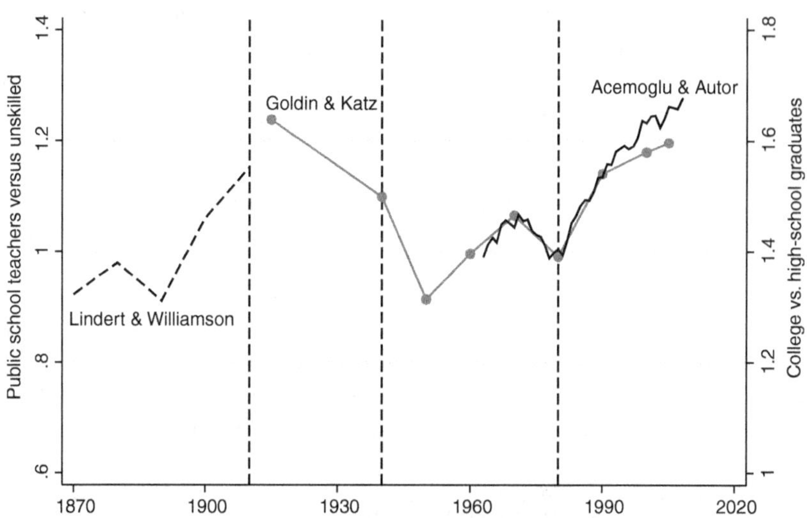

Figure 13.1 The skill premium in the US labour market, 1870–2008
Notes: Figure shows the wage of public school teachers relative to unskilled workers (left axis, Acemoglu and Autor 2011) and the wage of college graduates relative to the wage of high-school graduates (right axis, Goldin and Katz 1997; Lindert and Williamson 2016).
Sources: 1870–1910: Lindert and Williamson 2016: table 7-4; 1915–60: Goldin and Katz 1997: table A8.1; 1963–2008: based on Acemoglu and Autor 2011: figure 1.

can reflect the fact that skilled workers' productivity increases with the introduction of new technologies, while less-skilled workers are displaced by these technologies. The second period, from 1910 to 1940, was the diffusion of the Second Industrial Revolution, with increasing electrification and rising relative demand for less-skilled workers leading to a peak and then a decline in the skill premium. We characterize the period from 1940 to 1980 as one of globalization and convergence. During this period, technological change did not lead to sustained changes in the skill premium. The final period, since 1980, can be characterized by the rapid adoption of information and communication technologies (ICT), the attendant reshaping and fragmentation of global production, and a rapid rise in the skill premium.[1]

Note that this periodization is primarily inspired by technological phases, rather than turning points in growth experience (such as the Great Depression and the 1973 oil crisis) or in geopolitics, such as the two world wars. This is not to deny the importance of such factors, but rather to provide a sharper focus on technological development. Note also that this chapter covers a selection of the regions presented in this volume. To provide a quantitative perspective for this long and diverse period, we rely on data from the Maddison Project Database, version 2013,[2] supplemented with information on physical and human capital, for the period until 1950, and on the Penn World Table, version 9.0 (Feenstra et al. 2015) for growth accounting information for the period since 1950.

Variations in Patterns of Industrial Expansion, 1870–1910

During the 1870–1910 period, many European countries showed a GDP per capita growth of around 0.9 to 1.5 per cent per year, which was typically higher than the 0.9 per cent of the European leader, the United Kingdom, but notably slower than the 1.8 per cent of the United States (see Table 13.1). The UK, as the first industrializer, had realized international economic

1 Other factors, like the slowdown in the rate of growth of educational attainment for American cohorts born after World War II, may have played a role. See e.g. Card and Lemieux 2001.

2 Figures are based on the Maddison Project Database, version 2013, but growth rates of GDP per capita are very similar in the 2018 version of the database (Bolt et al. 2018). Estimates of comparative levels of GDP per capita are a more active area of debate, and, especially for high-income countries, different sides of the debate imply different interpretations of comparative growth in terms of income and productivity convergence. We have therefore omitted such a perspective for the early period and instead point the interested reader to e.g. Bolt et al. 2018.

Table 13.1 Growth of GDP per capita and its sources in Europe and the US, 1870–1910 (%)

	GDP/capita	Human capital	Physical capital	TFP
France	1.2	0.8	1.1	0.3
Germany	1.5	0.5	2.2	0.3
Italy	0.9	0.4	1.5	0.1
Spain	1.1	0.7	1.6	0.1
United Kingdom	0.9	0.9	1.2	−0.1
United States	1.8	0.6	2.2	0.5

Notes: Table shows average annual growth between 1870 and 1910 for GDP per capita, factor inputs per capita, and TFP. TFP is computed assuming an output elasticity of capital of 0.4 and constant returns to scale. Human capital is computed based on average years of schooling and assumed returns to schooling, as in Caselli 2005.
Sources: Maddison Project Database, version 2013; Lee and Lee 2016 for average years of schooling; Gallardo Albarrán 2018 for physical capital.

leadership by applying capital-intensive technologies that made production systems in textiles, and in other manufacturing industries, more productive. Factories with water- and steam-powered machines replaced small-scale workplaces, and the mechanization of the production process led to specialization of labour. Diffusion of steam power was fast in some sectors, like textiles, mining, and metal manufacturing, but these were initially relatively small sectors in the total economy. TFP growth acceleration was therefore slow (see Volume I, Chapter 13 of this book).

The so-called Second Industrial Revolution was driven by further technical advance and the development of communication and transportation networks. The industrial expansion of Germany and Italy, for example, was closely linked with the growth of the railway network, by creating demand for the metal and machinery industry, but also by establishing national markets. Investment banks raised the necessary capital to finance these new networks and industries. This period saw the rise of modern businesses with managerial hierarchies in manufacturing and service industries (Chandler 1990). Larger markets and reliable connections were an incentive to increase manufacturing capacity and to invest in marketing and sales. New business structures characterized by big plants and firms emerged, in particular in science-based manufacturing sectors like metallurgy, (electro)chemicals, and mechanical and electrical engineering.

One of the most remarkable characteristics of this era was the development of a sizable transatlantic income and productivity gap between the US economy and the developed economies of Europe. For example, within manufacturing, US productivity levels were at least twice as high as in the industrialized countries in Europe. Why? First, it has been argued that low relative labour costs and relatively scarce natural resources in Europe discouraged the substitution of machinery for skilled labour. The incentive to economize on fixed capital, in turn, constrained the adoption of labour productivity enhancing technology. If technological innovation proceeds as a cumulative process, the initial choice of technique matters, and it may lead to lock-in of firms and industries in a particular industrial pattern that is likely to change only gradually over time. Second, whereas the US relied on high levels of human capital accumulation through formal education aimed at managerial and researcher skills, Germany and the UK relied on shop-floor workers who were trained under an apprenticeship system (Broadberry 1997). Third, it has been suggested that the – on average – smaller scale of European production negatively affected labour productivity. The technologies of the Second Industrial Revolution involved mass production techniques with high fixed costs but low variable costs. Large establishments obtained labour productivity benefits through economies of scale (Chandler 1990). The US adopted standardization and high-throughput production technology more widely than European countries. Establishment size can be viewed as a proxy for technology according to Hannah (2008), who observed that giant production units (over a thousand workers) were particularly representative for modern industries. Although the size of the European market was not that different from the US, and thus allowed for big production units, European countries had relatively more small establishments than the US. Indeed, 25 per cent of the manufacturing labour productivity gap between Germany and the US in 1909 can be explained by differences in establishment size (Veenstra and de Jong 2016).

Diffusion of the Second Industrial Revolution, 1910–40

Between 1910 and 1940, GDP per capita growth was not much different from the period 1870–1910. Growth rates of physical capital were slightly lower, which, by definition, resulted for some countries in higher TFP growth compared with 1870–1910. Following World War I, the introduction of statutory hours and paid vacations led to rapid reductions in the working week of industrial workers. Not taking these declines in working hours into account means that the TFP growth rates in the table will be too low, though the precise extent is hard to gauge, given that there are no good estimates of economy-wide working hours. That said, all countries in the table saw large declines in the length of the working week, from an average of fifty-nine hours in 1913 to forty-five hours in 1938, so the cross-country comparison of TFP growth is less affected by the omission of working hours in the growth accounts.

The Nature of American Economic Leadership

In the trans-World War I years and the interwar period, American economic leadership expanded further. Most remarkable was a further growth in manufacturing efficiency. The American lead was brought on by capital deepening in the electricity (1910s), manufacturing (1920s), and distribution (1930s) sectors of the economy, which initiated a broad expansion of productivity (TFP) in the 1930s and 1940s (Field 2011). Robert Gordon (2016) has introduced the concept of 'one big wave' to describe an era of unprecedented productivity advance that has been unique in economic history so far.

From the turn of the nineteenth to the twentieth century, the US saw a rapid transformation from steam engines to electricity as the primary source of energy in industry (Figure 13.2). Normally, technological change

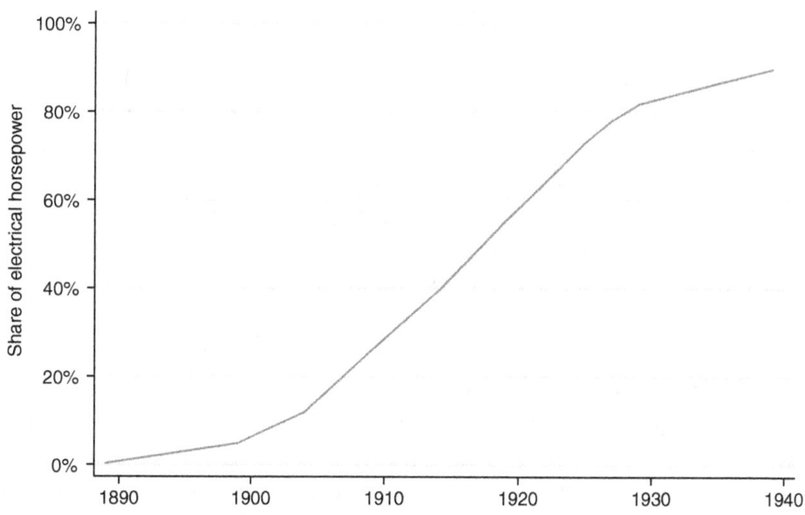

Figure 13.2 Electrification in US manufacturing, 1890–1940
Sources: United States Department of Commerce 1919, 1929, 1939.

(the combined result of invention, adoption, diffusion, and structural change) is a process of incremental innovations and small improvements. 'General-purpose technologies', like steam engines and electricity (and the computer in the post-World War II period), however, have the potential for pervasive use in many applications. The use of electrical power as a source of energy not only reduced the quantity of energy used per machine, it also brought on more efficiency in factory organization. It had the potential to save on other types of capital as well, but it also required learning and it took time to develop complementary inputs. This delay between the introduction of large technical innovations and resulting improvements in productivity – the so-called 'productivity paradox' – is inherent in economic history (David 1990).

Process innovations in manufacturing production were accompanied by efficiency improvements in management, like Taylorism and scientific management, and by the application of new materials and products spilling over to distributive sectors through the motorization of the economy in the 1930s. Nelson and Wright (1992: 1946) see the shift from coal to petroleum as the basic feedstock for chemical plants as a 'Remarkable blend of mass production, advanced science, and American resources'. It was an era of Schumpeterian new combinations. Many of these developments were 'hidden', for the reason that the Great Depression literature has mainly been focused on the explanation of the output not produced, the income not earned, and resources not exploited (Field 2011). Between 1929 and 1941, the American economy witnessed hardly any growth of labour input and capital in the private non-farm economy, whereas output had risen by 33–40 per cent. Implicitly, growth rates of TFP were very high (Inklaar et al. 2011). The low growth of capital suggests disembodied technical change, like better factory layout, standardization, economies of scale, and an increase in investments in R&D. A successful 'national innovation system' had emerged, based on applied knowledge from large firms, research laboratories, and universities. This could not easily be copied by European countries. In Europe, R&D expenditure as a percentage of GDP was much lower than in the US.

Why the European Experience Was Different

Broadberry and Crafts (1992) explained the US/UK productivity gap in manufacturing by looking at higher concentration ratios and lower human capital in British industries, for example. Restrictive practices in Britain may have hampered competition and the necessary adjustment to new technologies. But that leaves us with a puzzle: although labour productivity in manufacturing fell further behind the US, the capital intensity gap between

Table 13.2 Growth of GDP per capita and its sources in Europe and the US, 1910–40 (%)

	GDP/capita	Human capital	Physical capital	TFP
France	1.0	0.5	0.8	0.4
Germany	1.6	0.9	1.2	0.6
Italy	1.0	0.8	1.7	−0.2
Spain	0.3	0.0	0.7	0.0
United Kingdom	1.3	0.9	1.4	0.1
United States	1.2	0.6	0.9	0.5

Notes: Table shows average annual growth between 1910 and 1940 for GDP per capita, factor inputs per capita, and TFP. TFP is computed assuming an output elasticity of capital of 0.4 and constant returns to scale. Human capital is computed based on average years of schooling and assumed returns to schooling, as in Caselli 2005.
Sources: Maddison Project Database, version 2013; Lee and Lee 2016 for average years of schooling; Gallardo Albarrán 2018 for physical capital.

the US and Europe narrowed, indicating that there was no lack of physical capital, as is shown in Table 13.2 (Broadberry 1997).

Data envelopment analysis (DEA) reveals that European manufacturing was below the frontier that was defined by American industries. DEA is different from the Solow growth model that implicitly presupposes that factor inputs are being used to their full potential. In the Solow equation, TFP is a residual, a part of output growth that cannot be explained by the combined movements in measured inputs. Differences in TFP across countries are interpreted as differences in disembodied technology. In contrast, DEA distinguishes between capital accumulation in industries (machine intensity as measured by the horsepower of installed machines per worker), technological change (measured by labour productivity), and relative efficiency change (the residual). The idea is that follower countries need to go through two phases of development to close the gap to the frontier and catch up to the leader. In the first phase, capital accumulation is needed to transform the production process. In the short run this might lead to efficiency loss. In particular in the interwar period, with rapid technological change, learning processes might have generated many inefficiencies.

There are many examples of capital deepening in the UK – for example, in the motor vehicle industry and through the installation of automatic machinery in many manufacturing industries. Best-practice plants in the UK were close to US plants in terms of capital intensities and productivity. But the difference in total manufacturing productivity levels was caused by a much higher proportion of plants employing outmoded methods in the UK compared with the US. And for Germany, Timmer et al. (2016) found that old, less-dynamic industries, like textiles and metals production, were operating at much lower capital intensities than in the US, thus showing a different technological path. Capital intensities in innovative industries, such as machinery, electrical engineering, and chemicals were closer to the US industries. In these industries, lower labour productivity can be mainly explained by the inefficiency with which techniques were used, rather than differences in applied techniques. New machinery involved extensive transformation of the production process and routines had to be adapted to new production methods.

A different way to measure innovation activity and the nature of technological change is by looking at patent data and the patent system. Cantwell (1991) studied patent data and found that early in the twentieth century, US and German firms took a path of innovation that was more suited to the needs of mass production and mechanization, which characterized a new technological system in which the opportunities were greatest. Germany developed an efficient national innovation system in the period spanning the two world wars. Ristuccia and Tooze (2013) have pointed out that capital deepening in the German machine tool industry during the 1930s was an important foundation for the country's post-World War II growth miracle.

Industrialization Outside the Western Core

Countries outside the western core that were trying to catch up to the world's technology frontier deployed various development strategies. Examples mentioned here are the Stalinist industrialization policy in Soviet Russia, labour-intensive industrialization in Japan and East Asia, and the policy of import substitution in various Latin American countries. Russian industrialization accelerated with the introduction of the First Five-Year Plan in 1928, which prioritized state-led accumulation of physical capital, like structures and machinery, and complementary investments in human capital (Allen 2003: 94–96). Forced collectivization of agriculture sped up the transfer of labour from the countryside to the factories in the cities. Potentially, a planned reallocation of labour from the primary to the secondary sector may lead to a rise in output per head because productivity levels in manufacturing are higher than in agriculture. After 1933, TFP indeed rose rapidly, and it continued well into the post-World War II period (Allen 2003: 195). This development model was copied by the socialist economies of Czechoslovakia, Hungary,

Poland, and Yugoslavia. But the planning system suffered from price controls, inefficiencies, and soft budget constraints. The 1970s marked the end of the labour surplus economy, to which the Soviet leadership had no answer.

East Asian industrialization was labour intensive. Countries adapted Western technology and organizations, but these were suited to the local factor conditions. Labour, rather than capital or land, was utilized as a major source of competitive advantage because it was relatively more abundant. Manufacturing industries absorbed and utilized labour more fully, for example, through night-shift systems, such as in the rural weaving centres and small urban machine shops in pre-World War II Japan. This strategy was also adopted in Korea and China (Austin and Sugihara 2013). Recent research however, points also at the importance of human capital in this process (Saito 2013: 95). Skill formation became an important ingredient of the post-World War II success of Japanese manufacturing. Characteristic of Japan's national innovation system was the promotion of tacit knowledge and the accumulation of firm-specific skills, based on industry-wide uniformity of technology. In the Japanese patent system, firms could quickly acquire the research results of their competitors, leading to efficient technology spillovers. In the post-World War II period, industrialization became much more capital intensive.

Latin American industrialization since 1870 was able to develop with capital and labour from Europe, leading to an increase in commodity production and higher exports (Kuntz-Ficker 2017). But export-led growth ended by 1929, when human capital formation was weak and capital remained mobile (Lewis 2013: 254). For this reason, the state had to play a central role in industrialization. Latin American industrial policies were supported by increased productivity growth and embodied technological change between 1937 and 1970. But state-led industrialization growth ended by the 1970s, and compared to East Asia, the region could not close the gap with the developed countries (see Astorga and Herranz-Loncán, Chapter 9 of this volume). Protectionism and import-substituting industrialization, in principle, could have continued to boost economic growth by fostering structural change, but with rising inequality and educational shortages, institutional reforms failed to maintain productive dynamism. The allocation of the labour surplus from agriculture to manufacturing had a positive effect on aggregate productivity growth. But within manufacturing, such a structural change effect was hardly visible. Growth was primarily driven by traditional industries with a low technology intensity, and TFP growth was therefore limited.

One important factor in these narratives of growth and its proximate sources is the role of structural transformation. Figure 13.3 illustrates the typical pattern of structural transformation, where low-income economies are dominated by their agricultural sectors – most commonly in the form of subsistence farming – employing close to all people. As countries develop, agriculture invariably shrinks and the industrial and services sectors grow. To understand the process of industrialization, understanding why structural change occurs, and why not, is important. When drawing lessons from historical episodes of structural change to better understand the development prospects of lower-income countries today, it is important to realize that modern industrial sectors employ fewer people than they did in the past, thanks to labour-saving technological change. Rodrik (2016) refers to this process as premature deindustrialization and it poses a notable challenge for development today. It may explain why cross-country convergence in

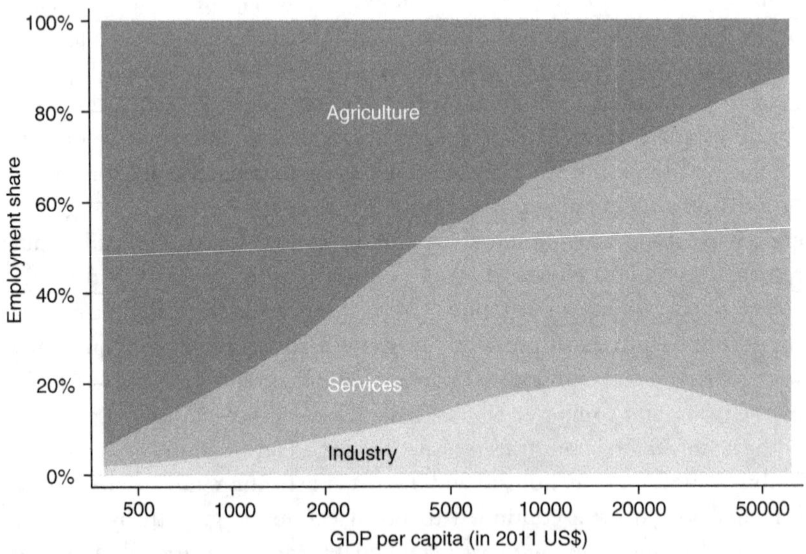

Figure 13.3 Economic development and structural transformation
Notes: The figure shows a non-parametric trend of each sector's employment share against GDP per capita, based on the LOWESS function in Stata (bandwidth = 0.8). Industry covers mining and manufacturing; services cover all industries of the economy except agriculture and industry.
Sources: GGDC 10-sector database on sectoral employment (Timmer et al. 2015); Penn World Table version 9.0 (Feenstra et al. 2015) on GDP per capita.

manufacturing productivity does not necessarily lead to convergence in GDP per capita.

Globalization and Convergence, 1940–80

The Rise of East Asia

The post-World War II period is characterized by a rapid increase in globalization, with higher levels of international trade activity and income convergence among most developed countries. Remarkably, this period of globalization shares similarities with the late nineteenth century, with a trade boom and income convergence among rich countries. However, what makes this second globalization period different is the emergence of the developing world, in particular the East Asian economies. While many countries in the developing regions continued to struggle to industrialize and liberalize their trade and financial sectors, early signs of the impact of globalization were seen in eight newly industrializing countries (NICs): Hong Kong, Singapore, Taiwan, Malaysia, South Korea, Indonesia, Japan, and Thailand.

These countries experienced significant growth differences among themselves during this period as they moved along distinct phases of economic development. One is a difference in degree: all NICs grew more rapidly than the US, like Taiwan and Singapore, but Indonesia's growth advantage was quite modest, at 3 per cent. Another is a difference in timing, with Japan starting to grow rapidly soon after World War II, and starting to slow down already around 1970. While Japanese economic growth virtually came to a standstill during the 1980s, many East Asian countries, such as South Korea, Hong Kong, Singapore, and Malaysia, continued to grow until Asia was hit by a massive financial crisis in 1997 (Hayashi and Prescott 2002).

The East Asian countries grew faster than the US in this twenty-year period, with GDP per capita growing at 5.8 per cent on average (see Table 13.3). Growth in capital intensity was also significantly higher than in the US. South Korea and Taiwan displayed extraordinary growth in their capital stock, with an increase of around 9 per cent per annum. By implementing labour-saving technological change, the overall living standard improved significantly in this region.

The growth in output was predominantly driven by reallocation of labour to the manufacturing sector and capital deepening, and less by total factor

Table 13.3 Growth of GDP per capita and its sources in East Asia, 1960–80 (%)

	GDP/ capita	Human capital	Physical capital	Labour quantity	TFP
Hong Kong	6.1	1.6	5.4	0.4	2.4
Indonesia	3.0	2.0	1.9	0.6	1.2
Japan	6.1	0.4	9.5	−0.4	2.1
Malaysia	5.1	2.5	4.4	0.7	2.1
Korea	6.1	3.6	9.3	1.5	0.7
Singapore	7.0	2.5	7.3	1.8	1.6
Taiwan	6.8	1.9	8.6	0.9	1.9
Thailand	5.8	0.8	6.0	0.4	2.2
East Asia average	5.8	1.9	7.0	0.7	1.7
United States	2.6	1.5	3.0	0.4	0.6

Notes: Table shows average annual growth between 1960 and 1980 for GDP per capita, factor inputs per capita, and TFP. TFP is computed assuming an output elasticity of capital of 0.4 and constant returns to scale. Labour quantity reflects changes in hours worked per capita.
Sources: Penn World Table, version 9.0 (Feenstra et al. 2015).

productivity (Young 1995). Compared to the exceptional growth rates of GDP per capita and physical capital, TFP growth rates are less remarkable (Collins et al. 1996). The average annual TFP growth of these countries was 1.7 per cent, which still compares favourably to the 0.6 per cent in the United States. But we have to keep in mind that all these countries came from much lower levels of development than the US. Many factors contributed to the high growth of the East Asian economies, such as rapid increase in domestic investment, human capital deepening, exports and outward-oriented government policies, and technology transfer.

Technology transfer from developed to developing economies through licensing played an important role in many East Asian economies, in particular South Korea, Japan, and Thailand (Mowery and Oxley 1995). Japan's manufacturing industries recovered quickly after World War II. Japan restored its technological development by importing new machineries and equipment from overseas and by hiring highly skilled consultants from abroad (Odagiri and Goto 1999). These policies were particularly important to bridge the technological gap in chemicals and metal products, and in electrical and mechanical engineering. Inward technology transfer intensified through further expansion of a national innovation system, which developed into a network of public and private companies that performed R&D and

Table 13.4 Investment and exports shares in East Asia, 1960–80 (% of GDP)

Countries	Gross investment share		Merchandise exports share	
	1960	1980	1960	1980
Hong Kong	0.20	0.24	0.44	0.64
Singapore	0.50	0.46	3.01	1.39
South Korea	0.12	0.37	0.02	0.26
Taiwan	0.17	0.31	0.07	0.36
Malaysia	0.20	0.32	0.60	0.36
Indonesia	0.05	0.16	0.37	0.23
Thailand	0.17	0.20	0.10	0.10
Japan	0.26	0.37	0.06	0.13
East Asia average	0.21	0.30	0.58	0.44
United States	0.25	0.25	0.05	0.09

Sources: Penn World Table, version 9.0 (Feenstra et al. 2015).

supported commercial innovations suited to the domestic economy (Freeman 1987).

Export and trade policies were important too. Hong Kong, South Korea, and Taiwan had exceptional growth rates in exports as compared to other East Asian countries. The exports share as a percentage of GDP of Hong Kong, South Korea, and Taiwan increased from 0.44, 0.02, and 0.07, respectively, to 0.64, 0.26, and 0.36, respectively between 1960 and 1980 (see Table 13.4). A key factor that initiated high export growth was the substantial expansion of GATT and UNCTAD memberships of developing countries. More favourable and differential treatment on tariff concessions was provided to the developing countries under the GATT agreement in order to achieve a substantial increase in their foreign exchange earnings, exports diversification, and trade volumes. At the same time, innovations in the shipping industry and upgraded facilities in South East Asian ports revolutionized world trade (Sien 2003).

The NICs were successful in avoiding inflation and keeping the real interest rate high. This was complemented by a strong bank-based financial system, favourable tax policies that encouraged private investment, and increased access to government credit. High growth rates in exports were thus complemented by high investment rates. Government policies encouraged investment in export-oriented industries. Programmes were introduced to encourage private investment in technology transfer, on-the-job education, and training and better infrastructure (Stiglitz 1996). Except Singapore, all other countries experienced an increase in their investment shares in the economy. While the investment share in the US remained at 0.25 in the period 1960–80, the share of NICs increased from 0.21 in 1960 to 0.30 in 1980. The investment shares more than doubled in Taiwan and tripled in South Korea between 1960 and 1980 (see Table 13.4). Last but not least, an important factor leading to the East Asian miracle was the presence of favourable initial conditions preceding the take-off in the 1960s. By the 1960s, universal primary schooling was already in place in these countries, except for Indonesia, and secondary enrolment rates were also high for Japan, South Korea, and Taiwan.

The rise of East Asia in the mid-twentieth century is a remarkable phenomenon in its own nature. Balanced government intervention and industrial policies targeted towards overall improvement of the institutional structure and development requirements of society were probably key to the successes of these countries (Rodrik 2008). These include open government policies, greater incentives for investments in physical and human capital, free and unregulated markets, openness in trade and capital flows, better institutional quality, and low inequality. All these factors contributed towards this remarkable performance.

While the East Asian countries displayed extraordinary growth during this period, the Latin American countries experienced a reversal of fortune. The average per capita GDP of the Latin American economies was 30 per cent of the US in 1950, but it dropped to 23 per cent in 2001. Between 1960 and 1980, the average per capita growth rate of the Latin American countries was only 2.3 per cent. Growth rates of capital intensity and labour productivity were also lower, signs of less rapid capital accumulation and less favourable initial conditions than in the East Asian countries. In contrast to East Asian investments, which were financed by domestic savings, Latin American investments depended heavily on international borrowing. In the absence of political stability, government savings were low and net external borrowing skyrocketed. The region initially attracted foreign capital flows; however, instead of an increase in export capacity, with unfavourable economic conditions, growth rates gradually slowed down in the 1980s, resulting in a crisis (Alesina and Rodrik 1994).

Western Europe and the United States

The period until 1980 saw remarkable growth in several East Asian countries, by any standard, but in the Western world, too, growth rates were

Table 13.5 Growth of GDP per capita and its sources in Europe and the US, 1940–80 (%)

	GDP/ capita	Human capital	Physical capital	Labour quantity	TFP
France	3.5	0.5	3.9	−0.8	3.0
Germany	2.7	0.9	4.7	−0.6	0.9
Italy	3.7	0.8	4.2	−0.4	1.8
Spain	3.8	0.5	4.5	−0.8	2.3
United Kingdom	1.6	0.6	2.4	−0.4	0.6
United States	2.5	0.7	2.8	0.0	1.0

Notes: Table shows average annual growth between 1940 and 1980 for GDP per capita, factor inputs per capita, and TFP. TFP is computed assuming an output elasticity of capital of 0.4 and constant returns to scale. Human capital is computed based on average years of schooling and assumed returns to schooling, as in Caselli 2005. Labour quantity refers to changes in total hours worked per capita and covers only to the period 1950–80.
Sources: Penn World Table, version 9.0 (Feenstra et al. 2015); Maddison Project Database, version 2013; Lee and Lee 2016 for average years of schooling; Gallardo Albarrán 2018 for physical capital.

higher than before or since, as shown in Table 13.5. These figures were drawn primarily from the Penn World Table, supplemented by estimates of GDP per capita from the Maddison Project Database and information on physical (Gallardo Albarrán 2018) and human capital (Lee and Lee 2016). Precise growth numbers can vary from source to source, but this period is commonly viewed as the Golden Age of growth (Crafts and Toniolo 1996; Gordon 2016).

As Table 13.5 shows, growth in GDP per capita exceeded 2.5 per cent per year everywhere, except in the United Kingdom, supported by rapid accumulation of physical and human capital, but also by rapid TFP growth. These strong income improvements enabled broad-based declines in hours worked per capita, increasing leisure time. This was also a period during which inequality within most Western countries remained stable or declined (see Figure 13.1), which implies that welfare improvements have been even more impressive than improvements in GDP per capita.

Figure 13.4 illustrates that for the western European countries, convergence to the United States was an important aspect of their rapid growth

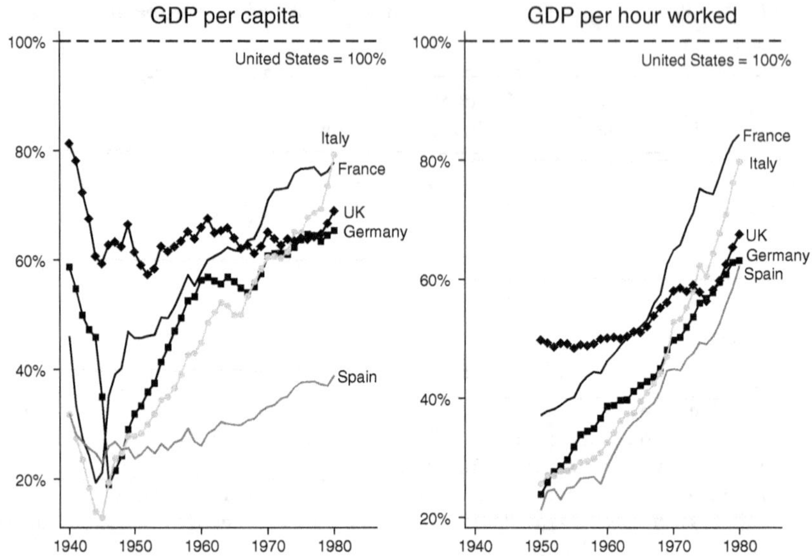

Figure 13.4 GDP per capita and per hour worked in western Europe, 1940–80 (United States = 100%)

Notes: These figures rely on GDP data expressed in comparative levels, the *CGDPo* variable in Penn World Table and *CGDPpc* in the Maddison Project Database.

Sources: Penn World Table, version 9.0 (Feenstra et al. 2015), extended using Maddison Project Database, version 2018 (Bolt et al. 2018) before 1950.

rate. As the GDP per capita figure – with data since 1940 – shows, this picture of convergence is partly a recovery from a substantial relative decline around World War II. However, in particular on the basis of GDP per hour worked, it is clear that the five large European countries were much closer to the level of the United States by 1980 than at the start of the period. Only the UK stands out with a rather high relative level of GDP per capita and GDP per hour worked at the start of the period, and a position in the middle of the European countries at the end. Crafts (2018) has labelled this the 'post-war British productivity failure', blaming weak competition, which exacerbated corporate governance and industrial relations problems. For the other European countries, though, more rapid investment in – primarily – physical capital and higher TFP growth were the main factors that enabled the convergence of labour productivity and income levels close to those in the US.

Information Technology-Enabled Inequality, 1980 Onwards

Productivity and Inequality: The IT Revolution in the Western World

While the 1940–80 period was one of rapid growth in productivity (and living standards), the period since 1980 has seen a much more modest pace of change in western Europe and the United States. As Table 13.6 shows, GDP per capita growth rates were in the 1–2 per cent per annum range, with much more modest growth from increases in physical capital and TFP as important factors in accounting for the growth slowdown relative to the earlier period.

At the same time, it was during this period that information and communication technologies (ICT) started to become ever more important. The pace of technological progress was set by Moore's law, by which chip (and hence computer) performance doubled every two years or faster. Like electricity before it, ICT is a general-purpose technology that can be utilized across all industries in the economy and, as a result, ICT assets have become much more widely used in this period (Table 13.7).

The impact of ICT has certainly been substantial: productivity growth in the sector producing ICT goods and services has been high in most countries, increasing aggregate growth, in particular, in countries such as the United

Table 13.6 Growth of GDP per capita and its sources in Europe and the US, 1980–2014 (%)

	GDP/ capita	Human capital	Physical capital	Labour quantity	TFP
France	1.3	0.6	2.0	−0.6	0.6
Germany	1.6	0.4	2.0	−0.5	1.0
Italy	1.0	0.9	2.1	−0.1	−0.4
Spain	1.6	0.8	3.0	0.0	0.0
United Kingdom	1.9	0.7	1.5	0.0	0.9
United States	1.7	0.3	1.5	0.0	0.9

Notes: Table shows average annual growth between 1980 and 2014 for GDP per capita, factor inputs per capita, and TFP. TFP is computed assuming an output elasticity of capital of 0.4 and constant returns to scale. Human capital is computed based on average years of schooling and assumed returns to schooling, as in Caselli 2005. Labour quantity refers to changes in total hours worked per capita.
Source: Penn World Table, version 9.0, www.rug.nl/ggdc/productivity/pwt/pwt-releases/pwt9.0?lang=en (Feenstra et al. 2015).

Table 13.7 Share of ICT capital income in GDP in Europe and the US, 1980 and 2016 (%)

	1980	2016
France	1.7	3.9
Germany	2.5	2.0
Italy	1.6	2.5
Spain	2.1	3.3
United Kingdom	1.8	2.9
United States	2.0	3.7

Source: The Conference Board *Total Economy Database™ Growth Accounting and Total Factor Productivity, 1950–2016.*

States. Furthermore, the increased investment in ICT assets increases the amount of ICT capital per hour worked, contributing substantially to labour productivity growth, again, with the United States as one of the leading countries. Finally, there is every indication that some of the more intensive ICT-using services industries – notably wholesale and retail trade, again, notably in the United States – managed to improve their TFP growth. These changes were concentrated in the 1995–2004 period, during which the United States experienced higher labour productivity and TFP growth than before or since (Timmer et al. 2010). Evidence suggests that the productivity gains from ICT are not unlike those of earlier technological breakthroughs, like steam and electricity, yet the broader tide of productivity growth has not turned.

Beyond its impact on productivity, ICT has also had a notable impact on inequality. ICT, like earlier technologies, has made it possible to automate tasks that had previously been performed by workers. In particular, tasks that are routine (or repetitive) have proven amenable to automation: in earlier phases, mostly routine manual tasks (e.g. harvesting of grain) have been automated, while ICT has enabled routine cognitive tasks (e.g. archiving or bookkeeping) to be automated. Conversely, ICT has improved the productivity of those in non-routine cognitive jobs, who can rely on ever more capable computers and software for routine tasks. As a result, those in high-skilled (high-educated) jobs have gained in terms of employment opportunities and wages, while those in the middle of the skill distribution have lost out (Autor 2015).

Continued Globalization and the Rise of China and India

Foreign direct investment (FDI) is critical for technological diffusion and import of new technologies, such as ICT. However, technological diffusion is successful only when the domestic economy has adequate absorptive capabilities, such as human capital formation. Access to better technology, for example via increased foreign capital flows, has to be accompanied by domestic capacity building to successfully absorb new technology (Lee 2001; Banerjee and Roy 2014). By 1995, most of the East Asian countries attained universal primary education and the average education attainment in East Asia was 6.4 years, which was substantially higher than other developing regions. With increased human capital deepening, financial deregulation, high domestic savings, and low government borrowings, the East Asian economies experienced an upsurge in net FDI from US$10.2 billion in 1990 to US$38.1 billion in 1993 and US$61.1 billion in 1996 (Lee 2001). This contributed to high GDP growth rates in the East and South Asian economies during the early 1990s. Since domestic saving was primarily sourced from households, household and government sectors were actually net non-borrowers. In contrast, most of the foreign borrowing through FDI and other capital flows landed in the private sector in the second half of the 1990s. Consequently, higher foreign debt, combined with a fixed exchange rate system, caused inflationary pressure in the region and triggered the Asian financial crisis in 1997.

Since 1980, Europe, America, and Japan experienced slower growth rates. In contrast, the highly populous economies of China and India started to grow at unprecedented rates. Whilst almost 60 per cent of world population was under severe poverty in 1960, this share has fallen to less than 5 per cent in 2010, due to high income growth in China and India alone. China and India share many similar demographic features and have a mutual geographical border, but they are very different in terms of their institutional settings and current economic policies. Although the improvements in growth performance in both countries are often explained in terms of wide-ranging reforms undertaken during the 1980s and 1990s, there are debates regarding the timing of the implementation of these reforms and their effects on long-run growth (Bardhan 2012). Table 13.8 shows growth of GDP per capita and productivity of these two countries, East Asia, and the US. Since the 1980s, as the reforms took place and the economies became more open, growth rates have risen in every decade. High growth rates of TFP and capital intensity are proof of increasing technological progress and capital deepening. Between 1980 and

Table 13.8 Growth of GDP per capita and its sources in China, India, East Asia, and the US, 1980–2014 (%)

%	GDP/ capita	Human capital	Physical capital	Labour quantity	TFP
China	6.5	1.1	8.8	0.1	2.3
India	4.4	1.4	4.0	0.6	1.3
East Asia	3.9	1.4	4.9	0.5	0.6
United States	1.7	0.3	1.5	0.0	0.9

Notes: The countries in the 'East Asia' group are Hong Kong, Indonesia, Japan, Malaysia, Korea, Singapore, Taiwan, and Thailand. Table shows average annual growth between 1980 and 2014 for GDP per capita, factor inputs per capita, and TFP. TFP is computed assuming an output elasticity of capital of 0.4 and constant returns to scale. Human capital is computed based on average years of schooling and assumed returns to schooling, as in Caselli 2005. Labour quantity reflects changes in hours worked per capita.
Source: Penn World Table, version 9.0 (Feenstra et al. 2015).

2014, average TFP and capital growth rates were 2.3 and 8.8 per cent, respectively, for China, and 1.3 and 4.0 per cent, respectively, for India. These rates, particularly for China, are much higher than in the East Asian countries and the US. Comparing China and India, we observe that factor intensities, growth rates in TFP, capital intensity, and labour productivity are consistently higher in the former since 1980 (see Table 13.8). With higher investment rates, China experienced higher GDP per capita growth than India and most other East Asian countries during this period (Felipe et al. 2008).

Some recent studies cast serious doubts on the high growth rates of China, suggesting that the official GDP estimates are substantially overestimated. For instance, while the official average GDP growth rate between 1980 and 2012 is 10 per cent, an estimate by Angus Maddison and Harry Wu is three percentage points lower for the same period. Based on the new estimates, TFP growth is also substantially smaller than earlier estimates by Bosworth and Collins (2008). Using the Maddison-Wu estimates and the China Industrial Productivity Database, Wu (2016) shows that China only achieved a TFP growth rate of 0.83 per cent per annum in the years between 1980 and 2012. This is a much lower figure than the official rate of 2.3 per cent in Table 13.8.

Growth accounting by Bosworth and Collins (2008) suggests very different sources of growth patterns in these two economies, with merchandise export-led growth driving China's economic performance, and service sector-led growth for India. Their innovative absorptive capabilities, but not cutting-edge domestic innovations, were complemented by high capital deepening that facilitated development of high-quality products and services for global markets (Altenburg et al. 2008). For India, both domestic technology capability building and foreign technology spillovers remained important sources of its growth process from the 1950s (Banerjee and Roy 2014). Being a more homogeneous society, and having cultural similarities with neighbouring Asian countries and a centralized decision-making process, China had the opportunity to undertake reforms at a much faster pace than India and achieved higher growth rates. Felipe et al. (2008) argue that, in fact, China and India are on very different growth paths, where the challenge for India is to increase its investment rate and capital accumulation, and China needs to rethink whether investment should remain the primary driver of growth.

Despite high growth rates, misallocation of resources is a concern for both India and China (Hsieh and Klenow 2009). The growth in GDP per capita in both countries is driven more by growth in capital accumulation than by growth in TFP and human capital (see Table 13.8). Consequently, if more resources are reallocated towards technological progress and human capital formation – for example, universal primary education and higher secondary and tertiary education – high growth may be sustained in the long run. In particular, higher levels of human capital will contribute to a better absorption of ICT technologies, which is crucial for further development of manufacturing and services within these economies (Lee 2001). Although China had some progress with radical reforms in the education system in the 1980s and 1990s, more work is needed to realize a higher return to education in the long run.

Concluding Remarks

In this chapter, we have outlined how the development, diffusion and adoption of new technologies have shaped economic growth over the past 150 years. One of our important arguments has been that major technological phases are distinct from periods of global war or major changes in growth patterns, which have usually been employed to distinguish relevant periods. Before 1940, large-scale industrialization and new technologies originated in the United States, leading to rapid growth there, and then diffusing to western European countries. After 1940, countries in western Europe largely caught up to American productivity levels, and the countries in East Asia represent a subsequent frontier of technology adoption and growth. The combination of technology diffusion and export-led growth in Japan, Korea, Taiwan, and, more recently, China and India has enabled tremendous growth in living standards. These changes in cross-country income-level inequality have also had their within-country counterparts. As we have highlighted, the more recent period of IT-enabled growth primarily benefited high-skilled workers in Europe and the US, while low- and middle-skilled workers were squeezed by competition from machines and workers in low-wage countries.

For the follower economies, the challenges are in escaping poverty and inequality, and at the same time to maintain a high growth rate. These economies suffer from structural and institutional problems that require more immediate attention (Bardhan 2012). In a heterogeneous society with high inequality, such as in India, it is very difficult to take collective actions and implement reforms, particularly in the interests of the poorer sections of society. Conversely, in a more homogeneous society, such as in China, it is much easier to make a uniform decision, but the actions of a centralized government could be too rigid at times. Nevertheless, in the more recent period, the export-oriented strategies received greater attention as compared to improvements in the quality of human capital, domestic innovations, and consumption-led growth.

References

Acemoglu, D. and Autor, D. (2011). 'Skills, Tasks and Technologies: Implications for Employment and Earnings', in Ashenfelter, O. and Card, D. (eds.), *Handbook of Labor Economics, Vol. 4b*, Amsterdam: Elsevier, 1044–1171.

Aghion, P., Akcigit, U., and Howitt, P. (2014). 'What Do We Learn from Schumpeterian Growth Theory?', in Aghion, P. and Durlauf, S. N. (eds.), *Handbook of Economic Growth, Vol. 2*, Amsterdam: North Holland, 515–563.

Alesina, A. and Rodrik, D. (1994). 'Distributive Politics and Economic Growth', *Quarterly Journal of Economics*, 109, 465–490.

Allen, R. C. (2003). *Farm to Factory: A Reinterpretation of the Soviet Industrial Revolution*, Princeton University Press.

(2012). 'Technology and the Great Divergence: Global Economic Development since 1820', *Explorations in Economic History*, 49, 1–16.

Altenburg, T., Schmitz, H., and Stamm, A. (2008). 'Breakthrough? China's and India's Transition from Production to Innovation', *World Development*, 36, 325–344.

Austin, G. and Sugihara, K. (eds.) (2013). *Labour-Intensive Industrialization in Global History*, London: Routledge.

Autor, D. (2015). 'Why Are There Still So Many Jobs? The History and Future of Workplace Automation', *Journal of Economic Perspectives*, 29, 3–30.

Banerjee, R. and Roy, S. S. (2014). 'Human Capital, Technological Progress and Trade: What Explains India's Long-Run Growth?', *Journal of Asian Economics*, 30, 15–31.

Bardhan, P. (2012). *Awakening Giants, Feet of Clay: Assessing the Economic Rise of China and India*, Princeton University Press.

Bolt, J., Inklaar, R., de Jong, H., and van Zanden, J. L. (2018). 'Rebasing "Maddison": New Income Comparisons and the Shape of Long-Run Economic Development', GGDC Research Memorandum, Vol. GD-174, Groningen Growth and Development Centre.

Bosworth, B. and Collins, S. M. (2008). 'Accounting for Growth: Comparing China and India', *Journal of Economic Perspectives*, 22, 45–66.

Broadberry, S. N. (1997). *The Productivity Race: British Manufacturing in International Perspective, 1850–1990*, Cambridge University Press.

Broadberry, S. N. and Crafts, N. F. R. (1992). 'Britain's Productivity Gap in the 1930s: Some Neglected Factors', *Journal of Economic History*, 52, 531–558.

Cantwell, J. A. (1991). 'Historical Trends in International Patterns of Technological Innovation', in Foreman-Peck, J. (ed.), *New Perspectives on the Late Victorian Economy*, Cambridge University Press, 37–72.

Card, T. and Lemieux, Th. (2001). 'Can Falling Supply Explain the Rising Return to College for Younger Men? A Cohort-Based Analysis', *Quarterly Journal of Economics*, 116, 705–746.

Caselli, F. (2005). 'Accounting for Cross-Country Income Differences', in Aghion, P. and Durlauf, S. N. (eds.), *Handbook of Economic Growth*, Amsterdam: North Holland, 679–741.

Chandler, A. (1990). *Scale and Scope: The Dynamics of Industrial Capitalism*, Cambridge, MA: Belknap Press.

Collins, S. M., Bosworth, P. P., and Rodrik, D. (1996). 'Economic Growth in East Asia: Accumulation Versus Assimilation', *Brookings Papers on Economic Activity*, 2, 135–203.

Comin, D. and Mestieri, M. (2016). 'If Technology Has Arrived Everywhere, Why Has Income Diverged?', *American Economic Journal: Macroeconomics*, 10, 137–178.

Crafts, N. F. R. (2018). *Forging Ahead, Falling Behind and Fighting Back: British Economic Growth from the Industrial Revolution to the Financial Crisis*, Cambridge University Press.

Crafts, N. and Toniolo, G. (eds.) (1996). *Economic Growth in Europe since 1945*, Cambridge University Press.

David, P. A. (1990). 'The Dynamo and the Computer: An Historical Perspective on the Modern Productivity Paradox', *Economic History of Technology*, 2, 355–361.

Feenstra, R. C., Inklaar, R., and Timmer, M. P. (2015). 'The Next Generation of the Penn World Table', *American Economic Review*, 105, 3150–3182.

Felipe, J., Laviña, E., and Fan, E. X. (2008). 'The Diverging Patterns of Profitability, Investment and Growth of China and India during 1980–2003', *World Development*, 36, 741–774.

Field, A. (2011). *A Great Leap Forward: 1930s Depression and US Economic Growth*, Yale University Press.

Freeman, C. (1987). *Technology Policy and Economic Performance: Lessons from Japan*, London: Frances Pinter.

Gallardo Albarrán, D. (2018). *Health, Well-Being and Inequality over the Long Run*, University of Groningen.

Goldin, C. and Katz, L. F. (1997). 'Why the United States Led in Education: Lessons from Secondary School Expansion', NBER working paper 6144, National Bureau of Economic Research.

Gordon, R. J. (2016). *The Rise and Fall of American Growth: The US Standard of Living since the Civil War*, Princeton University Press.

Hannah, L. (2008). 'Logistics, Market Size, and Giant Plants in the Early Twentieth Century: A Global View', *Journal of Economic History*, 68, 46–78.

Hayashi, F. and Prescott, E. C. (2002). 'The 1990s in Japan: A Lost Decade', *Review of Economic Dynamics*, 5, 206–235.

Hsieh, C. T. and Klenow, P. J. (2009). 'Misallocation and Manufacturing TFP in China and India', *Quarterly Journal of Economics*, 124, 1403–1448.

Inklaar, R., de Jong, H., and Gouma, R. (2011). 'Did Technology Shocks Drive the Great Depression? Explaining Cyclical Productivity Movements in US Manufacturing, 1919–1939', *Journal of Economic History*, 71, 827–858.

Kuntz-Ficker, S. (2017). *The First Export Era Revisited: Reassessing its Contribution to Latin American Economies*, Cham: Palgrave Macmillan.

Lee, J. W. (2001). 'Education for Technology Readiness: Prospects for Developing Countries', *Journal of Human Development*, 2, 115–151.

Lee, J. W. and Lee, H. (2016). 'Human Capital in the Long Run', *Journal of Development Economics*, 122: 147–169.

Lewis, C. M. (2013). '"Colonial" Industry and "Modern" Manufacturing: Opportunities for Labour-Intensive Growth in Latin America, *c.*1800–1940', in Austin, G. and Sugihara, K. (eds.), *Labour-Intensive Industrialization in Global History*, London: Routledge, 231–262.

Lindert, P. H. and Williamson, J. G. (2016). *Unequal Gains: American Growth and Inequality since 1700*, Princeton University Press.

Maddison Project Database, version 2013. Bolt, J., and van Zanden, J. L. (2014). 'The Maddison Project: Collaborative Research on Historical National Accounts', *Economic History Review*, 67, 627–651.

Mowery, D. C. and Oxley, J. E. (1995). 'Inward Technology Transfer and Competitiveness: The Role of National Innovation Systems', *Cambridge Journal of Economics*, 19, 67–93.

Nelson, R. R. and Wright, G. (1992). 'The Rise and Fall of American Technological Leadership: The Post-War Era in Historical Perspective', *Journal of Economic Literature*, 30, 1931–1964.

Odagiri, H. and Goto, A. (1999). *Technology and Industrial Development in Japan*, Oxford University Press.

Ristuccia, C. A. and Tooze, A. (2013). 'Machine Tools Production and Mass Production in the Armaments Boom: Germany and the United States, 1929–44', *Economic History Review*, 66, 953–974.

Rodrik, D. (2008). *One Economics, Many Recipes: Globalization, Institutions, and Economic Growth*, Princeton University Press.

(2016). 'Premature Deindustrialization', *Journal of Economic Growth*, 21, 1–33.

Saito, O. (2013). 'Proto-Industrialization and Labour-Intensive Industrialization: Reflections on Smithian Growth and the Role of Skill Intensity', in Austin, G. and

Sugihara, K. (eds.), *Labour-Intensive Industrialization in Global History*, London: Routledge, 85–106.

Sien, C. L. (ed.) (2003). *Southeast Asia Transformed: A Geography of Change*, Singapore: Institute of Southeast Asian Studies.

Stiglitz, J. E. (1996). 'Some Lessons from the East Asian Miracle', *World Bank Research Observer*, 11(2), 151–177.

Timmer, M. P., Inklaar, R., O'Mahony, M., and van Ark, B. (2010). *Economic Growth in Europe: A Comparative Industry Perspective*, Cambridge University Press.

Timmer, M. P., de Vries, G. J., and de Vries, K. (2015). 'Patterns of Structural Change in Developing Countries', in Weiss, J. and Tribe, M. (eds.), *Routledge Handbook of Industry and Development*, London: Routledge, 65–83.

Timmer, M. P., Veenstra, J., and Woltjer, P. J. (2016). 'The Yankees of Europe? A New View on Technology and Productivity in German Manufacturing in the Early Twentieth Century', *Journal of Economic History*, 76, 874–908.

United States Department of Commerce. (various issues). *Biennial Census of Manufactures*, Washington, DC: Government Publishing Office.

Veenstra, J. and de Jong, H. (2016). 'A Tale of Two Tails: Establishment Size and Labour Productivity in United States and German Manufacturing at the Start of the Twentieth Century', *Australian Economic History Review*, 56, 198–220.

Wu, H. X. (2016). 'Sustainability of China's Growth Model: A Productivity Perspective', *China & World Economy*, 24(5), 42–70.

Young, A. (1995). 'The Tyranny of Numbers: Confronting the Statistical Realities of the East Asian Growth Experience', *Quarterly Journal of Economics*, 110, 641–680.

14

Underlying Sources of Growth
First and Second Nature Geography

PAUL CARUANA-GALIZIA, TOSHIHIRO OKUBO, AND NIKOLAUS WOLF

Introduction

Long-run economic growth, measured as growing real income per capita, is driven by improved efficiency in the use of available resources. Modern economic theory assumes that real income per person is a meaningful summary statistic for well-being and that consuming more of a good and a greater variety of goods increases well-being. We will follow this approach here and focus on the role of geography on the process of long-run growth. A simple way to conceptualize economic growth is to analyse how efficiently factors of production (labour, capital, and natural resources) were combined to produce output. To explain variation in efficiency, several authors have suggested distinguishing between proximate causes for growth and fundamental causes (such as institutions and geography). The key difference is the extent to which these factors can be changed, for example, by some political intervention. While it is – in principle – possible to improve technology and education rather quickly, it is much harder to change the institutional framework of a society or even the geographical environment of a country.

Cronon (1992) suggested distinguishing between 'first nature' and 'second nature' geography. First nature geography refers to physical geography, such as climate or the availability of natural resources, while second nature geography refers to geography shaped by human activity, such as the location of human settlements, political boundaries, and infrastructure. Like institutions, second nature geography can be changed, but these changes will be costly, slow, and rare. An important feature of second nature is that it allows for path-dependency. With increasing returns in production and costly trade, small initial differences in economic development can accumulate over time and be a fundamental cause of growth (Krugman 1991a). The main variable of interest in these models is the accessibility of markets (i.e. market potential). Intuitively, a location with good access to a large market can attract more economic activity, which, in turn, would lead to a larger market – a positive feedback.

Baldwin (2006; 2016) argued that the interplay between institutions and geographical characteristics has changed fundamentally over the last 200 years. He suggested distinguishing between a 'first unbundling' and a 'second unbundling'. The first unbundling occurred during the Industrial Revolution, when the development of railways, telegraphs, and telephones made it possible to concentrate production in some locations and transport goods to distant markets all over the world. Thereby, regions could start to specialize in some specific industries and transport goods to other regions. The pattern of specialization would be determined by factor endowments and regional variation in factor productivity. More recently, the development of IT and lower costs of telecommunication, together with further reduction in transport costs, made it possible to split tasks within production across regions, the 'second unbundling'. Tasks and organizations inside a firm can be split and diversified geographically. For example, headquarters can be separated from production sites and located in urban areas, while routine tasks in production could be offshored to low-wage countries. Our interest in this chapter is mainly the period during and after the first unbundling until the beginning of the second unbundling.

We briefly document stylized facts about first and second nature geography in the long run. We review the debate on geography versus institutions and some of its main findings for long-run growth based on global data. This is complemented with case studies on Japan, 1890–1940, and European regions over the entire twentieth century, which allow us to focus more on the role of geography, given that institutional and cultural differences *within* countries will be more limited than *across* countries. We will then use a simple framework to analyse the factors for long-run growth and present evidence for a balanced panel of countries, covering all parts of the world over the period 1910–2015. We conclude with a brief discussion of geography and growth in the light of Baldwin's distinction between the first and the second 'unbundlings'.

Some Stylized Facts and Literature on First Nature and Second Nature Geography and Growth

First Nature and Economic Growth

There is a sizeable literature on the role of geographical factors on economic development and we can only provide a very selective survey of this. Among the key first nature geographical characteristics that have been discussed in the literature on twentieth-century development is the quality of agricultural land, natural resources (notably oil, gas, and coal), climate and disease environment (such as malaria), and access to waterways (sea, lakes, or rivers).

Let us start with the simple observation that a sufficient provision of food is a necessary precondition for economic development. Food can be produced locally or traded against other goods and services. Hence, in the absence of trade, a region with better conditions for food production should feature a larger population per area. Ramankutty et al. (2002) construct an index of agricultural land suitability, based on relationships between croplands, climate conditions, and soil characteristics. Their index shows the probability that given climate and soil, a certain grid cell on the global map will be cultivated. Ashraf and Galor (2011) document a positive correlation between such an index (aggregated up to countries) and population density as estimated around 1500. Hence, regions with better land suitability experienced extensive growth in the form of population growth. Ashraf and Galor (2011) also show that this did not typically translate into higher standards of living or intensive growth, in line with the idea of a 'Malthusian trap'. Note, however, that their estimates of historical population density and living standards are crude and that the index by Ramankutty et al. (2002) is based on modern data. Figure 14.1 shows the huge variation in agricultural land suitability across the globe around 2000. The map shows the fraction of grid cell suitable for agriculture as defined in Ramankutty et al. (2002). Parts of Europe and North America, the regions around the Black Sea, north-eastern China, but also some regions in eastern Africa and South America show high suitability for agriculture.

The correlation between an index of land suitability and current economic development is typically very weak. For a sample of fifty states, 1870–2010, we find a pairwise Pearson correlation between the index and population density of 0.36 (1900) and 0.45 (2010), but with GDP per capita of only 0.18 (1900), which further weakens to −0.03 (1950) and 0.03 (2010), each with high standard errors. Beyond data issues, a likely reason for this is trade. If regions with a comparative advantage in agriculture specialize in this sector, this can hamper the development of other sectors and limit their long-run growth prospects (Matsuyama 1992; Redding 1999). But suitable land does not imply a comparative advantage in agriculture. We will return to this issue below in the context of mineral resources. Another reason for weak correlations is that the direct effect of first nature geography on intensive growth is often dominated by second nature geography and institutions. For example, land

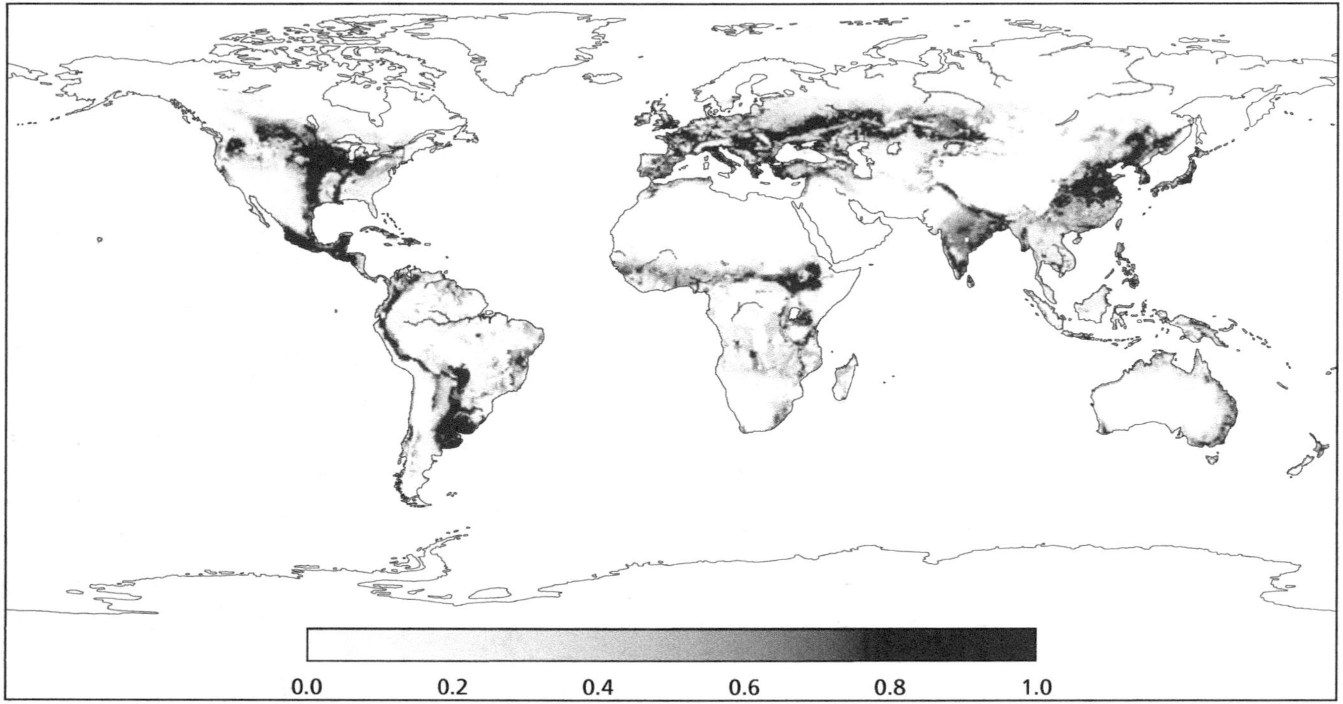

Figure 14.1 Suitability for agriculture
Source: Redrawn based on data from the Center for Sustainability and the Global Environment, Nelson Institute, University of Wisconsin-Madison.

productivity was (weakly) correlated with levels of GDP per capita in 1900. But it is unlikely that this reflects evidence for first nature geography as a fundamental cause for growth. Rather, better institutions and technology, including irrigation systems and chemical fertilizers, increase yields per crop, and higher income levels incentivize peasants to switch production to higher-yielding products, such as vegetables, dairy, or meat. Kopsidis and Wolf (2012) show for nineteenth-century Prussia that countries with better access to urban markets have higher grain yields and, more generally, produce agricultural products with higher yields, after controlling for land suitability. Engerman and Sokoloff (1994; 2002) argued for a more complex interplay between land suitability, institutions, and growth. To explain the very different development path between South and North America, they suggested that variation in the suitability of land for different types of agriculture led to wealth inequality and affected long-run growth via the choice of institutions.

Natural resources have long been considered to be a major determinant of growth. Figure 14.2 shows that natural resources such as gas and crude oil are unevenly distributed across the world, with concentration of proven resources in both high- and low-income countries (for example, Canada, the USA, Norway, and Saudi Arabia in the first case, but also Venezuela and Nigeria in the second).

Undoubtedly, the availability of water power and coal had a positive effect on the spread and growth of industry in nineteenth-century Europe (Crafts and Wolf 2014; Fernihough and O'Rourke forthcoming). Instead, for more recent periods, many authors have argued that an abundance in natural resources can be harmful for economic growth, with Sachs and Warner (1995) coining the term, a 'natural resource curse'. Sachs and Warner (1995) found for a cross-section of countries that a higher ratio of commodity exports to GDP in 1970 was associated with slower average growth over the next twenty years. The ensuing literature was based on panel data and attempted to explain the paradoxical result either in terms of a 'Dutch disease' (e.g. Gylfason et al. 1999) or via some interaction with institutional change. For example, a discovery of natural resources can subsequently weaken institutions and thus hamper growth (Ross 2001; Leite and Weidmann 2002; Sarr et al. 2011). In this vein, resource discoveries can lead to institutional lock-in and prevent a modernization of both the economy and society at large (Acemoglu et al. 2001; 2002). However, these studies assume that knowledge and availability of natural resources are exogenously given and time-invariant. While this is less of an issue for other first nature characteristics, natural resources such as coal, oil, or gas require search efforts

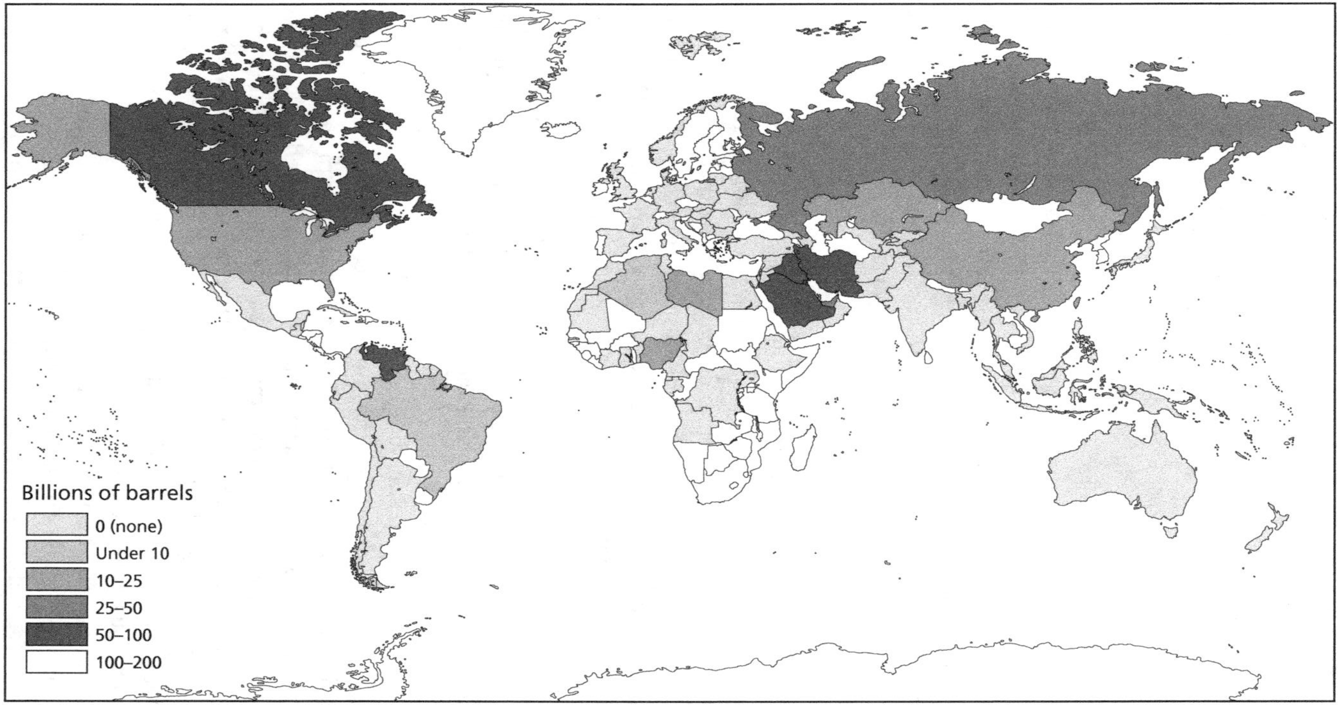

Figure 14.2 World crude oil reserves
Source: Redrawn based on a map from the Energy Information Administration 2017.

and large-scale investment to be exploited. Therefore, most previous studies on the 'resource curse' did not reveal much about the causal effect of natural resources on growth due to a lack of time variation. Haber and Menaldo (2011) show for a large panel of countries going back to 1800 that changes in resource reliance (notably on oil) were not systematically associated with a rise in political authoritarianism. Similarly, Smith (2015) uses variation over time in the discovery of natural resources to estimate their treatment effect on growth in GDP per capita. He finds that discoveries have a positive effect on growth for non-OECD countries, in line with the historical literature on the role of energy for industrialization. However, he also finds that countries with resource discoveries often failed to diversify their economies and showed less tendency towards democratic regime change than elsewhere. Overall, this suggests that an abundance of natural resources has ambiguous effects on long-run development. Similar to the evidence on land suitability, what matters most seems to be the interplay between first nature geography and other fundamentals, such as institutions.

Next, we consider the role of climate and disease environment for economic development. A long-standing argument from Jones (1981) is that Europe had better prospects for economic development than other parts of the world, due to beneficial climatic conditions, in particular the Gulf Stream, and a lower probability of natural disasters such as earthquakes. Diamond (1997) extended the argument to include a broader range of environmental factors and to argue against a decisive role for genetic differences on long-run development. Along these lines, Malaney and Sachs (2002) stressed the negative role of location in the tropical zones for economic development, notably due to the high risk of malaria and related diseases. Figure 14.3 shows the predicted all-age incidence rate (clinical cases per 1,000 population per annum) of malaria (Plasmodium falciparum) for the year 2017.

Malaney and Sachs (2002) argue that the disease environment has not only an indirect, but also a strong and lasting *direct* effect on growth, in contrast to Engerman and Sokoloff (1994), Acemoglu et al. (2001), Easterly and Levine (2003), or Rodrik et al. (2004). Similarly, McCarthy et al. (2000) show that there is a two-sided relationship between malaria and growth, as economic development also fosters health care and hence methods to fight diseases. After taking this into account, they find a significant negative causal effect running from malaria to growth.

To conclude our discussion of the direct role of first nature geography on development, we consider access to waterways via the sea, lakes, or rivers. A main characteristic of the nineteenth century was the transport revolution

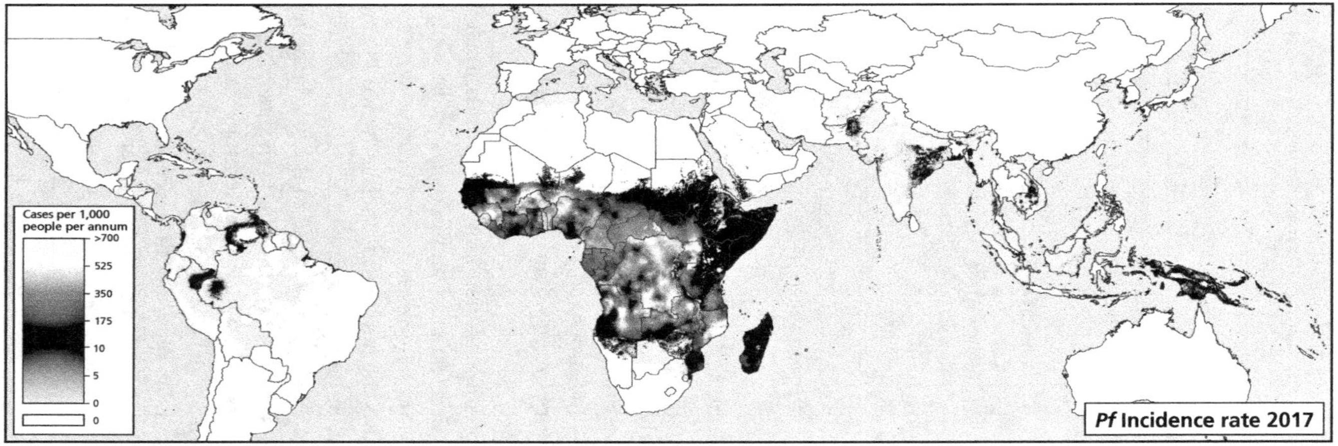

Figure 14.3 Global distribution of malaria risk, 2017
Source: Redrawn based on a map from https://malariaatlas.org. Creative Commons Attribution 3.0 Unported Licence.

Table 14.1 Ten largest cities and distance to sea, 1900, 1950, and 2010

1900		1950		2010	
Name	Sea distance	Name	Sea distance	Name	Sea distance
London	61.4	New York	0.0	Tokyo	0.0
New York	0.0	London	61.4	Delhi	848.3
Paris	134.8	Tokyo	0.0	São Paulo	51.9
Berlin	141.9	Paris	134.8	Mumbai	0.0
Chicago	1139.2	Shanghai	0.0	Mexico City	279.7
Vienna	415.2	Moscow	600.8	New York	0.0
Tokyo	0.0	Buenos Aires	0.0	Shanghai	0.0
St Petersburg	0.0	Chicago	1139.2	Calcutta	124.0
Manchester	50.7	Ruhr	164.0	Dhaka	202.7
Philadelphia	82.5	Calcutta	124.0	Karachi	0.0

Sources: Chandler 1987; Modelski 2003; UN Department of Economic and Social Affairs 2016.

that helped to reduce the costs of transportation of goods and people over both water and land. A growing body of evidence suggests that good natural transportation and early improvements (canals) contributed to the economic development of Great Britain in the late eighteenth and early nineteenth centuries (Bogart 2014). In Europe, port cities and cities located on large rivers grew systematically more strongly than others over the long run, as shown in Bosker and Burigh (2017).

And access to water still matters today. While most trade between adjacent countries takes place on road and railways, most long-distance trade takes place via waterways (Hummels 2007). Location close to the sea is still beneficial. Table 14.1 lists the ten largest cities in the world and their respective distance to the sea, in 1900, 1950, and 2010.

Most of these megacities are very close to the sea; indeed, some of them developed around ports and large river deltas in the first place, such as Tokyo, Shanghai, and New York. Chicago is an interesting case to which we will return below. But more generally, population density in coastal zones (100 km from the sea) was, in 1990, about three times higher than average population density (Small and Nicholls 2003), and a growing share of the world population lives in the low-elevation coastal zone (LECZ), driven by large coastward migration (Neumann et al. 2015). At the other extreme are landlocked countries, which suffer from their location. Nearly half of all low-income countries of today are landlocked, while only three of the thirty-five high-income economies are landlocked (Arvis et al. 2012). As shown in Radelet and Sachs (1998) and MacKellar et al. (2000), landlocked countries trade significantly less and have lower growth rates than countries with direct access to the sea.[1]

Second Nature and Economic Growth

Let us reconsider the case of Chicago. In *Nature's Metropolis: Chicago and the Great West*, William Cronon (1992) argued that 'second nature' made Chicago a central place for agriculture, industry, and trade, especially the construction of railroads and the concentration of trade and population itself (Krugman 1991a). The most remarkable fact about the rise of Chicago to one of the biggest global agglomerations in the first half of the twentieth century is the *absence* of obvious beneficial first nature characteristics. Instead, Cronon (1992) suggested that Chicago grew due to a change in second nature, triggered by improved infrastructure. If local economic activity benefits from internal scale effects or exerts positive effects on neighbouring activity ('spillovers'), then a decline in trade costs can lead to the emergence of large and self-reinforcing economic concentrations (Krugman 1991a; 1991b). A large literature has documented that the decline in trade costs during the nineteenth century, due to the construction of railroads and the replacement of sailing vessels by steamers, had a causal effect on the concentration of economic activity (measured, for example, in terms of urbanization). Moreover, a somewhat smaller literature has shown that such a reallocation of activity between locations was indeed a cause for rising labour productivity and a rise in GDP per capita.

We will first briefly review the evidence on declining trade costs between 1870 and 2010, before we describe changes in population density and concentration, and finally discuss some implications for economic growth. Jacks et al. (2008) use a theoretically founded gravity model to estimate an index of trade costs for the US, France, and the UK and eighteen of their trade partners, 1870–2000, based on bilateral trade, total trade, and output data. Their results suggest that a decline in both transport costs and tariffs contributed to the decline in trade costs over time. Trade costs declined dramatically between 1870 and 1913, increased during the interwar years, and then started

1 Note, however, that this evidence suffers from omitted variable bias, because the status of being landlocked is time-invariant.

to fall again after 1945, in line with a narrative of a first globalization, a globalization backlash, and a second globalization.

After 1945, the world experienced a bloc-wise reintegration around the USA and the USSR, with China, India, and other East Asian economies integrating from the mid-1980s onwards. According to Baier and Bergstrand (2001), reintegration in the OECD countries was mainly driven by trade liberalization, notably tariff reductions. Fouquin and Hugot (2016) show how institutional factors mattered for the long-run change in trade costs by estimating a tariff equivalent of average border effects. The effect of borders declined over the nineteenth century, increased sharply after 1914, and declined again only in the late 1970s. Moreover, Fouquin and Hugot show how economic integration became increasingly regionalized, such that the elasticity of trade flows with respect to geographical distance actually increased after 1945. Economic integration between European countries, for example, proceeded much faster than global integration. Moreover, Bernhofen et al. (2016) estimate that for a large sample of 157 countries, the effect of containerization on trade integration dwarfs the effect of trade liberalization. Related, Yi (2003) has shown how vertical specialization and a fragmentation of value chains can account for some of the second globalization. Hence, there is agreement that trade costs declined dramatically between 1870 and 1913, increased until 1945, and then declined again. But the driving factors behind this decline are still debated, in particular for the second globalization.

Several studies explored how the change in trade costs affected the geographic location of economic activity and economic growth. Redding and Venables (2004) show that a useful summary statistic for second nature geography is access to markets. A simple metric was already suggested by US geographer Harris (1954), in the form of market potential, measured as the sum of distance-weighted GDP of all regions in the neighbourhood. Jacks and Novy (2018) discuss how market potential can be derived theoretically as a function of world GDP, domestic GDP, domestic trade, and domestic trade costs only, which simplifies the analysis of long-run developments considerably. A general problem with this line of thinking is that market access involves an element of reverse causation, where a larger local market will benefit from better market access to neighbouring markets and vice versa. If we want to understand how market access matters for economic growth, we need to take such reverse causation seriously. We will address this issue further below, using instrumental variables.

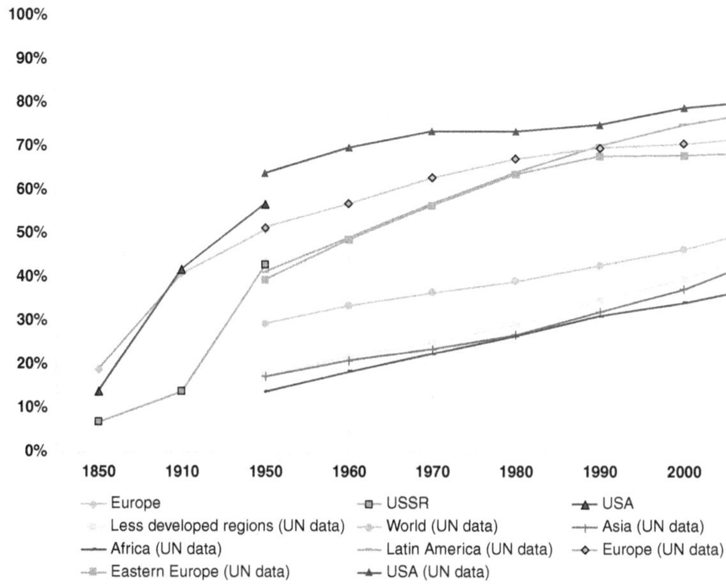

Figure 14.4 Global urbanization rate, 1870–2010
Sources: 1850–1950: Bairoch 1988 (urbanization rate is percentage of population living in locations with more than 5,000 inhabitants); 1950–2010: UN Department of Economic and Social Affairs 2016 (urbanization rate is percentage of population at mid-year residing in urban areas).

Hornung (2015) shows how the construction of railroads affected the population growth of cities for the case of Prussia, 1840–71. He finds that cities that gained access to the railway network grew substantially faster than comparable cities without such access. He also shows that this population growth is associated with a spatial concentration of industrial production, fostered by in-migration from villages and other cities. On a global scale, we observe a rapid increase in urbanization rates – the share of people living in cities – accompanied by both a growing number of cities and growing average city sizes. Figure 14.4 shows the development of urbanization rates, 1870–2010.

Not only has the number of cities grown, but also their average and maximum size. The largest cities (metropolitan areas) in 2010 reach above 30 million (Tokyo and Shanghai), comparable to the total population in 1870 of countries like France (38 million), Germany (39 million), the UK (31 million), or the USA (40 million).

This remarkable spatial concentration of population, which started during the late nineteenth century was directly related to a concentration of industrial production and employment, as suggested by Baldwin's 'first unbundling'. Crafts and Venables (2003) compiled data to document the enormous concentration of global industrial production in the decades after 1870. Between 1880 and 1950, Europe and North America accounted for roughly two-thirds of global industrial production, but below 20 per cent of world population. A similar picture emerges from the share of countries in global manufacturing trade, where, first the UK, and then increasingly, from 1880 onwards, other European countries and the USA gain a dominating position. After 1950, Western dominance in industrial production declines, mostly due to the industrialization of economies in East, South East, and South Asia. Instead, Europe, North America, and Japan maintain a very strong concentration in some service sectors, for example in finance.

We can summarize the role of second nature using market access, as suggested by Jacks and Novy (2018), for a global sample of fifty countries. Globally, market access improved by an average annualized growth rate of 5.8 per cent (with a range between 7.7 per cent [China] and 3.9 per cent [Zambia]). Behind this change is a combination of declining barriers to trade – which, in turn, interact with first nature characteristics, such as access to the sea, as well as institutional change – and a growing size of markets. But does improved market access indeed cause economic growth in terms of GDP per capita, or does it merely reflect the effect of other factors, such as institutional change? Put differently, is market access a proximate or a fundamental cause of growth?

Given the complexity of possible interaction between institutions, first nature geography, and second nature geography, most studies have focused on specific countries, to limit institutional variation and problems with data quality. Ciccone and Hall (1996) estimate for US counties in 1988 the effect of increases in employment density on labour productivity, using instrumental variables. They find that more than half of the variance in output per worker can be explained by variation in the density of economic activity. In related work, Ciccone (2002) finds very similar effects of density on labour productivity for France, Germany, Italy, Spain, and the UK. Redding and Sturm (2008) tested the role of market access in the context of German division, an arguably exogenous change in access to markets. They show that cities close to the internal border between West and East Germany had similar population growth before 1945, but fell back thereafter compared to West German cities

Table 14.2 Correlation between market access, railway density, and GDP per capita, fifty countries, 1910, 1950, and 2010

	LN (GDP/capita)	LN (market access)
1910		
LN (GDP/capita)	1.00	–
LN (market access)	0.42 (0.01)	1.00
LN (railway density)	0.63 (0.00)	0.89 (0.00)
1950		
LN (GDP/capita)	1.00	–
LN (market access)	0.48 (0.00)	1.00
LN (railway density)	0.47 (0.00)	0.84 (0.00)
2010		
LN (GDP/capita)	1.00	–
LN (market access)	0.67 (0.00)	1.00
LN (railway density)	0.35 (0.02)	0.59 (0.00)

Note: p-values in parentheses. LN is the natural logarithm.

further away from that border. Ahlfeldt et al. (2015) look at an even smaller scale and analyse the effect of division and unification of Berlin on the location of economic activity across several thousand housing blocs within the city, for the period 1936–2006. They find that the local concentration of population and employment has a very large positive effect on activity in the neighbourhood, but also that this effect is extremely localized. For example, the employment effect declines after one minute of travel time to 69 per cent, and after two minutes to below 50 per cent.

Consider now, for a global set of countries since 1910, the correlation between market access, as estimated by Jacks and Novy (2018), the density of railways as a proxy for infrastructure quality, and GDP per capita. Table 14.2 gives the results.

The correlations suggest a strong systematic relationship between GDP per capita and the two measures of second nature geography across our global sample and over time. But beyond the specific case studies mentioned earlier, it remains questionable to what extent second nature actually causes economic growth. Is there a direct role for second nature or does it affect growth only indirectly, especially via the effect of institutions? In the next section we consider two cases, for which we have rather good data.

Case Studies: Geography and Growth in Japan and Europe

Japan, 1890–1940

Japan today is a highly centralized state, organized into forty-seven prefectures, which have remained unaltered since 1890. Tokyo (with the largest population and the capital) and Osaka (with the second largest population) are the 'bipolar core prefectures' of the Japanese economy. They are surrounded by Kanagawa with the largest port (Yokohama), Hyogo with the second largest port (Kobe), and Kyoto, which had been the capital city for a long time in Japan before the Meiji Restoration.

In the 1850s, Japan's trade suddenly opened to foreign countries due to US and European political pressure, after 250 years of autarky (Bernhofen and Brown 2005). Tariffs were controlled by foreign countries until 1911. After Japan regained its autonomy over trade policy, tariffs increased in the 1920s and hiked with the Great Depression, while Japan's trade was shifted away from the US and Europe towards Asia (Okubo 2008). The 1890s also witnessed a rapid improvement of infrastructure. The basic railway network was almost completed in the 1890s (Minami 1965), which promoted interregional transportation and the mobility of labour and capital. Japan's Industrial Revolution occurred in the 1920s, when the industrial structure of the country drastically changed, from light industry and labour-intensive sectors to heavy industry and capital-intensive sectors. An important factor was the 'electric revolution' and the diffusion of electric motors since 1900 (Minami 1976). The total horsepower of electric motors exceeded that of steam engines already in the late 1910s, while in the late 1920s the share of electric motors in the total motive power of manufacturing accounted for more than 80 per cent.

The main question of our case study on Japan is in relation to the interplay between industrial development and geographic concentration. Yuan et al. (2009) investigated the prefectural industrial structure in the pre-war period of Japan. They calculate regional value added from 1890 to 1940 and describe income and industrial development across Japanese prefectures. As they have shown, Kyoto, Osaka, and Nara were the early industrial core in 1874. During the Meiji Restoration, Osaka largely developed heavy industries, such as armament industries and shipbuilding, and had the highest manufacturing output in Japan in 1890. On the other hand, Tokyo largely developed an industrial cluster until 1909 and created the known bipolar urban system with Osaka. In the 1920s and 1930s, Aichi, Hyogo, and Kanagawa developed industrial agglomerations of heavy industries. We also note that the Japanese economy after 1940 was under military control, which affected industrial location choices and output.

Our evidence is based on Japan's manufacturing census (Ministry of Commerce and Manufacturing of Japan), which covers all manufacturing firms in Japan and includes the number of employees and total output by prefecture and sector. With this we constructed time-consistent data for eight sectors (textile, food and beverage, metal products, machineries, chemical, pottery and stone products, lumber and wood products, and printing) for the years 1920–40.[2] We complement this with data on factor endowments and institutional quality, taken from the *Imperial Japan Statistical Yearbook*; the population data are taken from the *Population Census*, which is conducted every fifth year (Statistics Bureau of Japan).

Consider economic concentration in terms of population, manufacturing output, and manufacturing employment. A prominent hypothesis about second nature geography is the home market effect, where manufacturing becomes increasingly concentrated in large markets, caused by an interaction of trade costs and increasing returns to scale (Helpman and Krugman 1985). Alternatively, manufacturing might locate in the neighbourhood of energy resources, such as water power or coal. With the rapid improvement of transport infrastructure in Japan and the rise of manufacturing, Japan is an interesting case to study this.

We measure concentration by Gini indices, applied here to manufacturing employment, output, and population at the level of prefectures (Figure 14.5). The index in population is much lower than in manufacturing, but increases substantially over time, as people move to Tokyo and Osaka. Moreover, the fact that the index in manufacturing output is always above that of employment indicates that some manufacturing sectors enjoy scale economies. While it is not conclusive, this evidence is in line with a 'home market effect', where manufacturing activity is more than proportional to concentration of population. After World War II, the Gini index of employment and output jumps up and continues to increase.

2 The survey covers all manufacturing plants with more than five employees. However, the survey after 1939 (until 1942) covers all plants without any thresholds. We note that all available data are aggregate by sector and prefecture, which makes it difficult to construct time-consistent data. According to Yuan et al. (2009), a few prefectures have many small-scale plants which were not covered by the Census. The percentage of small plants account for around 20 per cent in total output in the Yamanashi, Nara, Oita, and Kagoshima prefectures. In the post-war period, the survey covers all plants from 1956 to 1980.

Figure 14.5 Gini indices of population, output, and employment, Japan, 1920–1960s

Next, we want to explore the relationship between second nature and economic growth more directly. We approximate GDP with value added at prefectural level for several specific years (1890, 1909, 1925, 1935, and 1940) from Yuan et al. (2009), and calculate a prefecture's market potential as the sum of value added of all neighbouring prefectures weighted by distance. First, we plot GDP per capita and market potential (MP) at prefectural level. Overall, all panels of Figure 14.6 show positive correlations between them. In 1890 and 1909, the core prefectures (Tokyo: 13, Osaka: 27, Hyogo: 28, Kyoto: 26, and Kanagawa: 14) take larger values than any other prefectures and show positive correlations between GDP per capita and MP. On the other hand, evidence on some other prefectures is less clear. Hokkaido (1) and Okinawa

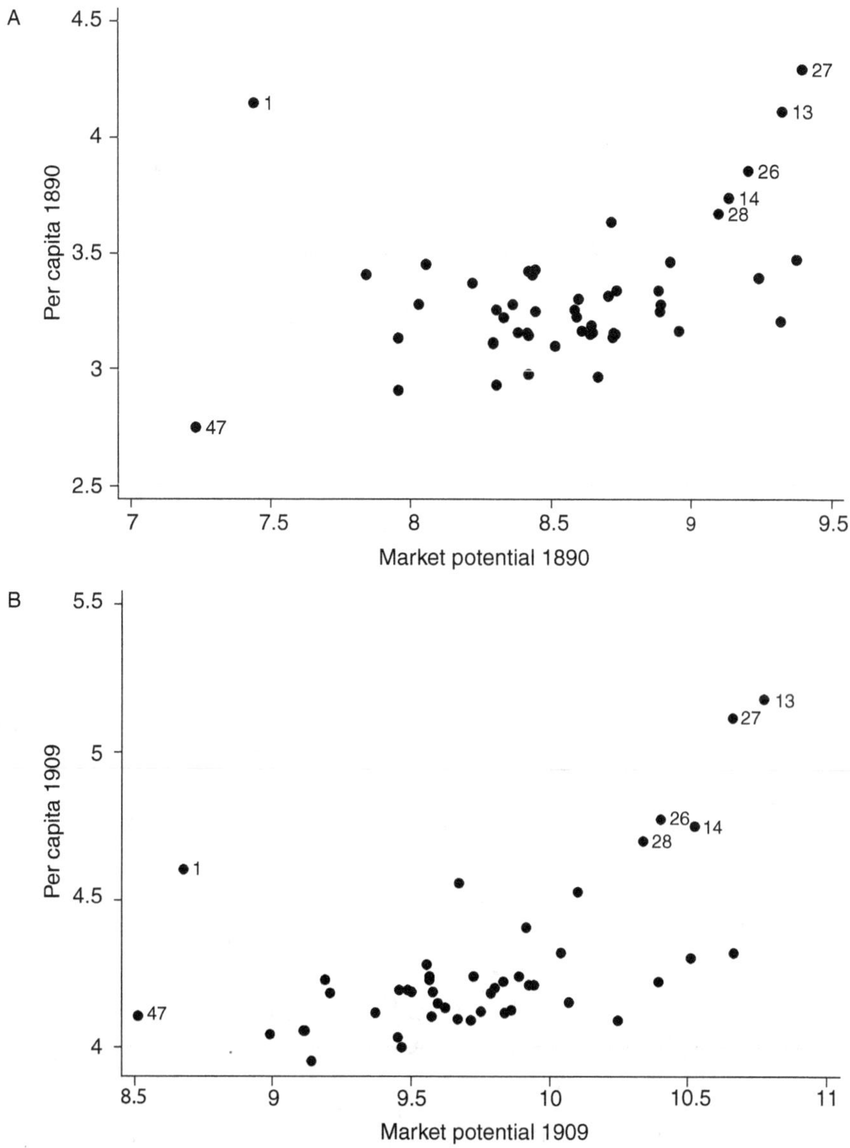

Figure 14.6 Market potential and GDP per capita, Japan, 1890–1940

(47) seem to be outliers. Hokkaido was a newly developed region after the Meiji Restoration. The government cultivated fields and artificially developed agriculture, mining, and manufacturing. In terms of the first nature, we

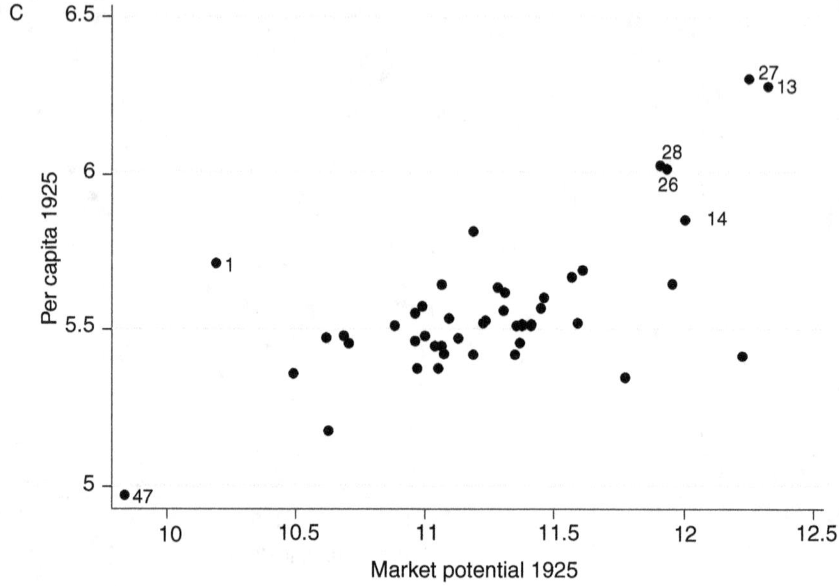

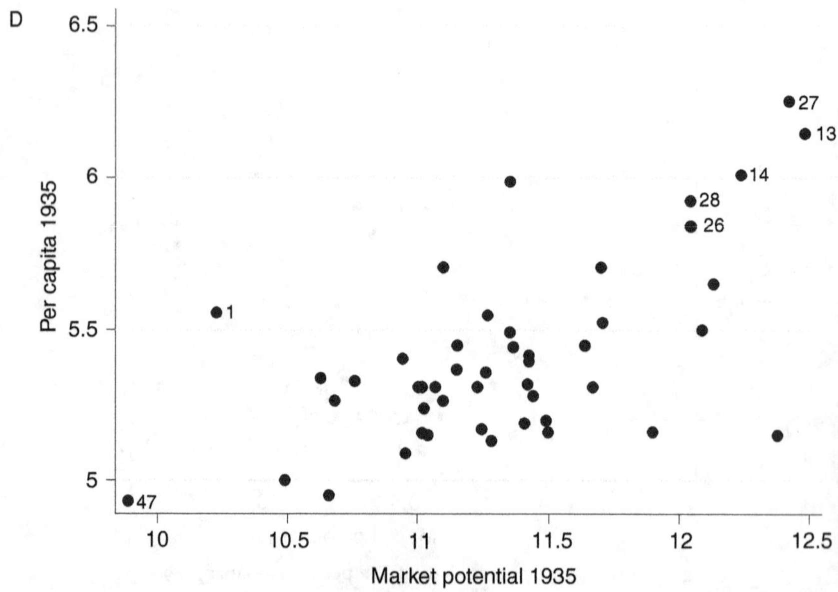

Figure 14.6 (cont.)

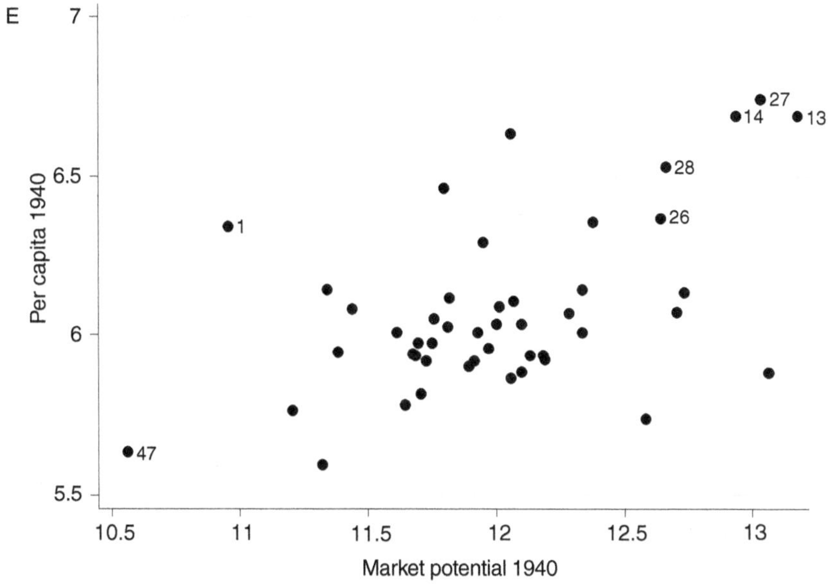

Figure 14.6 (cont.)

mentioned the importance of distance to the sea. However, this does not seem to matter much for our case of Japan. There are eight landlocked prefectures, but they do not show particularly low development nor are they outliers, maybe due to a well-developed internal transport network.[3] Together, the evidence for all years 1890–1940 shows strong positive correlations between market potential and GDP per capita.

But do these positive correlations between market potential and GDP still hold after taking into account that prefectures differ in terms of 'institutions' and 'first nature', such as resource endowments? We focus on the year 1925 and distinguish between market potential measured by GDP (MP1925) and market potential measured by manufacturing output (MPmanu1925). The second set of variables reflects primary resource endowments, here (Industrial crop), intermediate input ratio of primary sectors (Intermediate), mineral wealth (number of minerals produced by each prefecture num_mine), and total output of minerals (mining).[4] The third set of variables approximates institutions and social variables

3 Landlocked prefectures are Tochigi (9), Gunma (10), Saitama (11), Yamanashi (19), Nagano (20), Gifu (21), Shiga (25), and Nara (29).

4 Industrial crops in our study are tea, tobacco, cotton, mulberry, rapeseed, and hemp. The intermediate input ratio of primary sectors in each sector is calculated from an IO table in 1935 by Nishikawa and Koshihara (1981). Primary sectors are defined as

Table 14.3 Correlation between GDP and market potential (OLS)

	coefficient	(t-stat)	coefficient	(t-stat)
MP1925	0.253865	(2.39)		
MPmanu1925			0.182203	(2.18)
Industrial crop	−0.03696	(−1.13)	−0.02469	(−0.77)
Intermediate	−0.3329	(−1.16)	−0.29728	(−0.96)
num_mine	0.092745	(1.54)	0.080358	(1.29)
mining	−0.00166	(−0.18)	−0.00344	(−0.35)
doc_cap_1000	0.501412	(3.16)	0.537276	(3.2)
birth_ratio	4.583411	(0.39)	4.500132	(0.37)
self_farm_ratio	0.095171	(0.24)	−0.0134	(−0.03)
conflict	0.020155	(0.85)	0.013192	(0.47)
_cons	2.467815	(2.01)	2.131424	(1.48)
Obs.	47		47	
R-sq	0.632		0.619	

Note: Dependent Variable: GDP.
Source: See text.

using medical doctors per 1,000 persons (doc_cap_1000) and the birth ratio (birth_ratio). Finally, we control for the number of conflicts between farmers and landowners (conflict), and the ratio of small farmers (self-farm ratio). These are measures of expropriation and protection of property rights, widely used in the literature to reflect social capability.

Table 14.3 reports the results of simple OLS regressions. In all estimations, MP has always a positive and significant effect (indicated by a high t-statistic). Beyond this, only doctors per capita is significantly positive, while we cannot detect any significant relation between GDP and mineral resources, acreage of industrial crops, intermediate ratio of mineral sectors, birth rates, or political characteristics.

We note that market potential is correlated with GDP by construction, so that, again, these results are merely indicative. But the results suggest that it was second nature rather than first nature that explains variation in economic development in Japan during the 1920s and 1940s.

European Regions, 1900–2015

Rosés and Wolf (2019) provide a survey of the economic development of roughly 170 regions in Europe from 1900 until 2010, with a focus on economic

agriculture, mining, and fishery. Since the IO table is at national level, the intermediate input ratio at prefectural level is approximated by a weighted average of prefectural sectoral output.

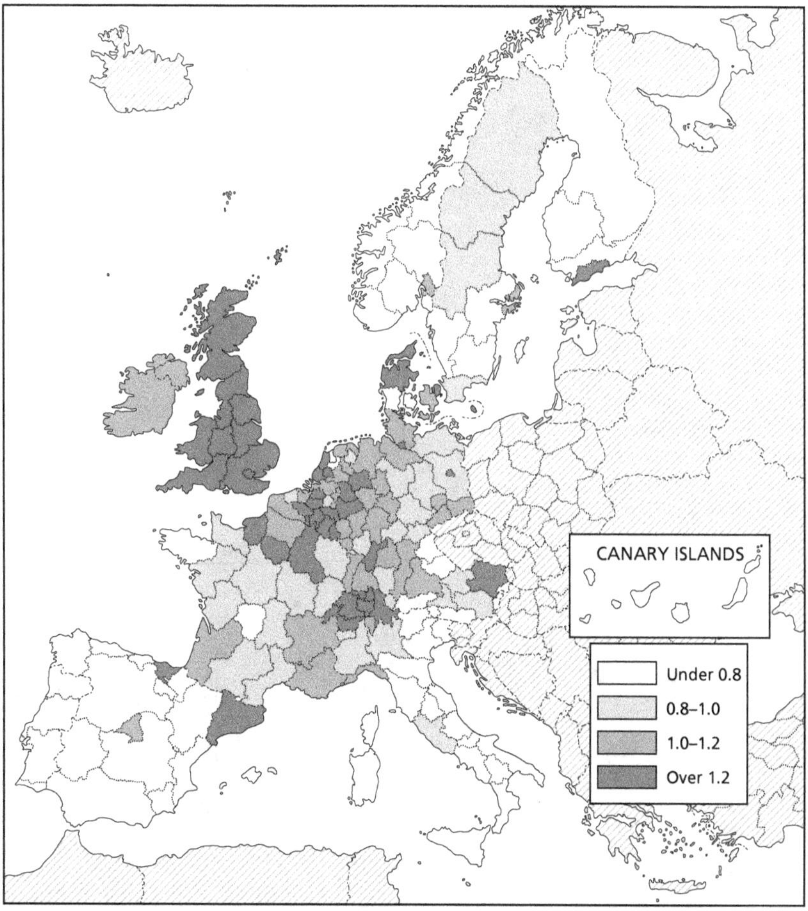

Figure 14.7 GDP per capita across European regions, 1900
Sources: Authors' own, and data from Rosés and Wolf database on regional GDP, v6 2020.

geography. We extend this here until 2015 using the recent version of the Rosés and Wolf database on regional GDP (2020). A convenient starting point is a comparison between Figures 14.7 and 14.8, showing the variation in GDP per capita (in 1990 international $) in 1900 and 2015, respectively.

We see a core–periphery pattern, where the dominant clusters of development in the UK, the Benelux states, Germany, and Northern Italy in 1900 have become less compact, while the strength of capital cities in contrast to their hinterland is now more visible than a century ago.

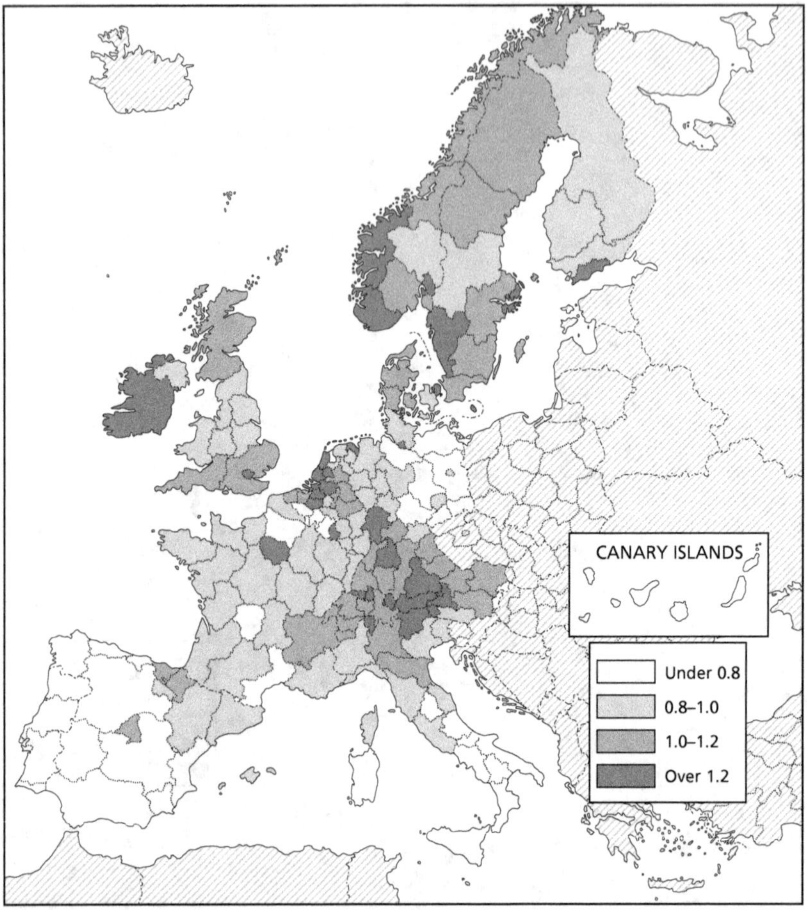

Figure 14.8 GDP per capita across European regions, 2015
Sources: Authors' own, and data from Rosés and Wolf database on regional GDP, v6 2020.

What can explain this change, and what would be the role of first or second nature geography in this? In the following, we will briefly document structural change – that is, changes in employment between the three main sectors, agriculture, industry, and services. Next, we describe how the concentration of activity in terms of regional GDP and population developed over time, before we summarize the evidence based on a simple regression framework.

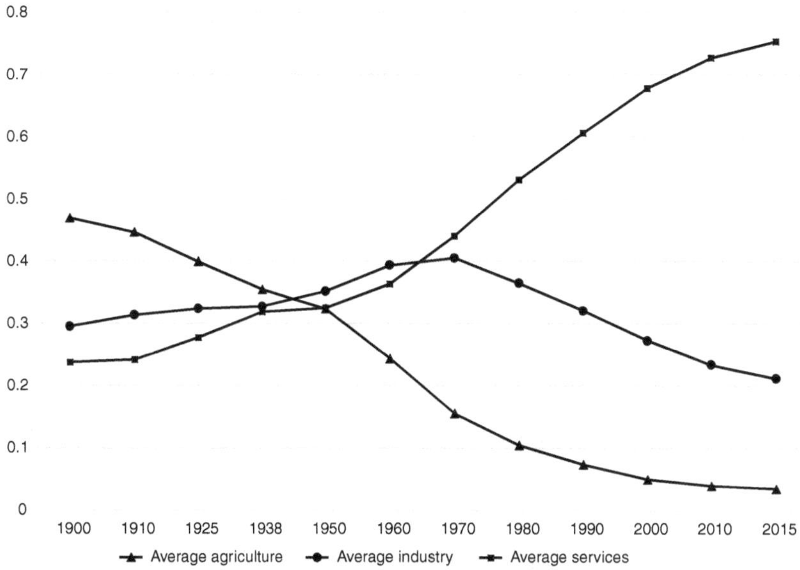

Figure 14.9 Employment shares in agriculture, industry, and services (average across 173 regions), 1900–2015
Sources: Authors' own, and data from Rosés and Wolf database on regional GDP, v6 2020.

Around 1900, about 45 per cent of total employment was still in agriculture, followed by industry (30 per cent) and services (15 per cent). These averages mask large variation, as some regions are still nearly entirely characterized by agriculture, such as Galicia in Spain or Nord-Norge in Norway, while other regions are strongly industrialized (like Hainaut in Belgium) or have transformed into a service economy (like London, with about 68 per cent of employment in services). Over time, many people left agriculture to find employment in industry and services. As shown in Figure 14.9, industrial employment in (western) Europe reaches its peak between 1960 and 1970, before it starts to decline. From the 1980s onwards, most employment is in services.

While in 1900 many regions were still rather similar in their employment structure, there was a marked specialization: agriculture continued to be the dominant sector only in a small number of regions, while a growing number of regions specialized in industry. By 2015, service employment is the dominant feature in most regions, obviously with a strong concentration of some service activities, notably financial services in large urban centres. A way to

Figure 14.10 Share of capital regions in GDP of all European regions, 1900–2015
Sources: Authors' own, and data from Rosés and Wolf database on regional GDP, v6 2020.

capture these changes is the location quotient, which measures the specialization of a region in a given sector, normalized by the share of that sector in total employment. The coefficient of variation over this measure summarizes the changes in employment structures across regions and over time. In 1900, this measure was around 0.43 for agriculture, 0.44 for industry, and 0.44 for services. In contrast, in 2015, the coefficient of variation for agriculture had increased to 0.8, for industry it had declined to 0.26, and for services to 0.1. Both industry and services were spreading to all parts of Europe, and services became the overall dominant sector after 1960. In contrast, only a few regions maintained substantial shares in agriculture. Within the service sector, we observe that specific types of services, such as financial services, are concentrated in a few metropolitan regions and contribute to regional divergence from about 1980.

Figure 14.10 shows the share of capital regions in total European GDP over time. We see that this share was increasing until 1938, before it started a slow decline, in line with the often documented convergence across European countries and regions after 1945. From 1980 onwards, however, we find that capital regions are, on average, expanding more rapidly than other parts of

Figure 14.11 Gini indices for population and GDP, European regions, 1900–2015
Sources: Authors' own, and data from Rosés and Wolf database on regional GDP, v6 2020.

Europe, driven by the concentration of high value-added services in metropolitan areas.

As for our case study on Japan, we again employ the Gini coefficient as our measure of inequality. Following Krugman (1991a), we constructed a locational Gini index, based on the share of each region in total population, respectively, total GDP. This coefficient is bounded between zero (all regions have equal shares) and one (all activity is concentrated in one region).

Clearly, the concentration of economic activity as measured by regional GDP has declined over time, again in line with findings on convergence and related to the spread of industry and services in the first half of the twentieth century. If anything, this tendency became stronger after 1945, probably fostered by institutional convergence due to European integration. However, around 1980 we find a reversal of this trend and increasing concentration, this time in terms of both GDP and population. If we inspect Figures 14.7 and 14.8 above again, some regions are doing much better in attracting people and business than others, and these tend to be capital regions. Instead, other formerly rich regions have fallen behind and are losing business and people.

Rosés and Wolf (2019) test three hypotheses about European economic growth, based on previous work by Solow (1956), Barro and Sala-i-Martin (1995), and Temin (2002). First, initially poor regions should grow more rapidly because investment in capital would have a higher return the lower the capital stock per worker. Related to this, we would expect the regions that suffered heavy destruction of physical capital during the two world wars to show higher growth afterwards. Second, regions with beneficial institutions should grow faster, which would include the status of a capital region within a state, but also early access to the European market. Finally, we would expect that first nature characteristics and second nature summarized by access to markets matter for regional growth performance. Rosés and Wolf (2019) find strong evidence in favour of all three hypotheses. Reconstruction growth mattered after both wars, albeit with a lot of variation over time. Convergence was particularly rapid after 1945, but stagnated after 1980. This was accompanied by beneficial effects of European integration, where the status of a capital region, but also accession to the European Community, seemed to foster economic growth. Access to the eurozone was less clearly associated with beneficial effects. After all these factors have been taken into account, geographical characteristics are still found to have a lot of explanatory power, but their role was changing over time. Good access to coal was beneficial during the first half of the twentieth century, but became detrimental afterwards. Related, good soil quality seemed to be a burden rather than a blessing in a long-run perspective. An explanation for both phenomena can be that regions would specialize according to their comparative advantage. Regions with good soil and abundant mineral resources seem to be in danger of being locked into backward and less productive economic activities. This would include regions such as Wales, or regions in northern France or in Wallonia, which excelled as early centres of heavy industry, but failed to diversify their economy during the 'second unbundling': their industry now faces low-cost competition from other parts of the world, while the high value-added service activities concentrate in urban agglomerations. This latter aspect is underpinned by strong evidence for market access. In a long-run perspective stretching from 1900 to 2010, regions with better market access were growing substantially faster than others, after controlling for their institutional and first geography environment. The dramatic change in employment structure from industry to services since 1960 apparently did not weaken this, quite the opposite.

Synopsis: Institutions Versus First Nature and Second Nature Geography

The evidence so far has suggested that geography in a broad sense has a substantial causal effect on economic development, especially second nature geography measured as market access or market potential. Nonetheless, first nature geography, in the form of disease environment, natural resources and access to water, and institutions, is also likely to have a causal effect on growth. Rodrik et al. (2004) attempt to show which factors explain the huge variation in GDP per capita in a large cross-section of seventy-nine countries around 1995. They include variables to capture institutional quality, first nature and second nature geography, and find that institutions dominate all other factors. However, in their conclusion they warn that their results should be treated with caution, notably due to the difficulty in measuring the relevant variables and due to our ignorance about the underlying mechanisms. Another main problem is that Rodrik et al. (2004) consider only trade openness, but not market access. Hence, they approximated changes in trade costs but ignored the (changing) size of accessible neighbours. Redding and Venables (2004) refine their exercise in two important ways. First, they use a measure of market access that is derived from theory. Second, they suggest using geographical distance to main centres of economic activity (New York, Rotterdam, and Tokyo) as an instrument to deal with the problem of reverse causation. With this, they find evidence (for a slightly larger set of 101 countries and the year 1994) that three variables capture most of the variation in GDP per capita in the sample – market access, the risk of expropriation, and the prevalence of malaria. We take this as an inspiration to analyse the dynamics of economic growth in a panel of fifty countries, for the period 1910–2010.

There are several challenges to such an exercise. First, the first nature variables, such as risk of malaria or landlocked status, are either time-invariant or their time-variation is very hard to capture for any longer time horizon. Therefore, our results on these factors need to be interpreted with caution and we refer to recent work in this area, such as Smith (2015). Second, market access, as in Redding and Venables (2004), requires measures of bilateral trade for all countries in the sample and over time. These data do not (yet) exist. But we follow Jacks and Novy (2018) and their suggestion to derive a theoretically founded measure of market access based on country GDP, world GDP, domestic trade, and domestic trade costs. We gratefully acknowledge that they shared their data on market access with us. We use distance to New York,

Brussels, and Tokyo with time interactions as instruments to deal with reverse causation. Third, we capture institutional quality with a time-varying measure of executive constraints, which has been widely used in the political science literature. Clearly, this is also subject to issues of reverse causation because richer countries are more likely to develop such constraints (Acemoglu et al. 2001). Nevertheless, if the challenge is to focus on the role of geography as in our chapter, this way of controlling for institutional quality should tend to overestimate their role and, if anything, limits the effect we can find for geographical factors. Table 14.4 shows our findings.

The main result is that second nature geography, as captured by market access (the variable, ln MP), has a very strong and causal effect on economic growth, not only in a cross-section, but also in a panel (Jacks and Novy 2018). To read the table, note that the statistical significance is indicated by the p-value, which depends on the estimated standard errors (the latter are shown in parentheses). We highlight the significant estimates for market access in bold font. Once we allow for general time effects (column 2) we find that market access has a strong effect on levels of GDP per capita. To account for possible reverse causation, all estimates shown here are instrumented with their distance to core markets. Our results hold after controlling directly for the main variables suggested in the literature, notably institutional quality (captured by 'Executive constraints') and first nature variables (captured by 'Petroleum', etc.). These latter do have some effect, but second nature seems to dominate that, reversing the finding from Rodrik et al. (2004). Once we also allow for unobserved country effects (columns 3–5), we have to drop all time-invariant variables, but find an even stronger role for market access. Finally, if we split our sample into the years 1910–49 and 1950–2010, we find that market access matters much more for the recent period, while the effects of institutional quality for growth seem to weaken. Related to this, the coefficient on railway density also turns positive once we allow for unobserved country effects. We are well aware of the shortcomings of such a regression approach. Still, it suggests that variation in market access is one deep cause for variation of GDP per capita around the world.

Conclusion: The Changing Role of Geography

How does geography matter for long-run economic growth? We surveyed the large recent literature on the topic and argued that there is compelling evidence in favour of an effect of geography via several channels. We

Table 14.4 GDP per capita and market potential – instrumental variable estimates (balanced year* distances to Tokyo, New York, and Brussels, second stages)

Variables	(1)	(2)	(3)	(4)	(5)
			ln GDP per capita		
LN market potential	−0.023100	**0.106000*****	**0.659000*****	−0.118000	**0.371000*****
	(0.045100)	(0.029800)	(0.102000)	(0.146000)	(0.118000)
Executive constraints	0.151000***	0.070900***	−0.002060	0.022200***	0.008860*
	(0.014900)	(0.008740)	(0.004360)	(0.006980)	(0.005340)
Petroleum	0.002550	0.005680***			
	(0.003180)	(0.001230)			
Malaria stability	−0.540000***	−0.564000***			
	(0.038700)	(0.019700)			
Landlocked	0.791000***	0.682000***			
	(0.083600)	(0.034600)			
LN railway density	−0.124000***	−0.077200***	0.033300***	0.196000***	0.021000***
	(0.012600)	(0.006350)	(0.002930)	(0.071600)	(0.003640)
Agricultural suitability	−0.001680	−0.005820***			
	(0.001370)	(0.000856)			
Constant	7.662000***	6.323000***			
	(0.400000)	(0.325000)			

Table 14.4 (cont.)

Variables	(1)	(2)	(3)	(4)	(5)
Observations	1,332	1,332	1,332	485	847
R-squared	0.292000	0.744000	0.938000	0.717000	0.912000
Number of countries	14	14	14	14	14
Country FE	N	N	Y	Y	Y
Year FE	N	Y	Y	Y	Y
Period	All	All	All	<1950	>=1950

Notes: Estimation based on a balanced data set. LN is the natural logarithm; FE stands for fixed effects. Robust standard errors are shown in parentheses. Levels of statistical significance are indicated with *, where *** $p<0.01$, ** $p<0.05$, * $p<0.1$.
Sources: See text.

distinguished between first nature and second nature geography: the former stands for all elements of physical geography, such as climate or the availability of natural resources, and the latter for man-made features of geography, such as the location of settlements, political boundaries, or infrastructure. These factors, in turn, can affect economic development directly or indirectly, via institutions. There is broad empirical support for all of these channels, but we attempted to provide more specific evidence from two case studies, on Japanese prefectures during the country's rapid industrialization period, 1890–1940, and on Europe, covering 173 regions over the period 1900–2015. Both case studies suggest that second nature geography is essential. For Japan, we showed that the prefectures with best market access experienced the most rapid industrialization. For Europe, we showed again that market access is important, but also that there are substantial changes over time. While European regions converged until about 1980, because backward parts of the continent experienced structural change away from agriculture towards industry and services, this trend was reversed. In the last decades, metropolitan regions around the capital cities grew faster, while others, including many of the former industrial regions, started to fall behind. On a global level, this is mirrored in an increasing role for market access. This evidence ties into the idea of the two 'unbundlings' of production since 1800 (Baldwin 2006; 2016). Once transport costs were low enough to make it profitable to trade even bulky goods over long distances, regions specialized along their comparative advantage (e.g. due to resource endowments). The place of production was separated from the place of consumption. More recently, however, we see a new, second unbundling, facilitated by even lower costs of transportation and improved communication. Now the production process itself is split into parts, where, for example, labour-intensive production takes place in countries and regions with low wages, while rich metropolitan regions specialize in services, such as research, finance, or marketing. Old industrial agglomerations in Europe started to fall behind in the 1980s, while capital regions experienced above-average growth. It looks as if such a fragmentation of value chains is becoming more important, and that it proceeds faster within a common institutional framework, such as regional trade agreements (Johnson and Noguera 2017). While this opens new opportunities for both rich and poor countries to become part of such global production networks, this is likely to strengthen the role for market access and benefits from economic density within countries for the time being.

References

Acemoglu, D., Johnson, S., and Robinson, J. A. (2001). 'The Colonial Origins of Comparative Development: An Empirical Investigation', *American Economic Review*, 91(5), 1369–1401.

(2002). 'Reversal of Fortune: Geography and Institutions in the Making of the Modern World Income Distribution', *Quarterly Journal of Economics*, 117(4), 1231–1294.

Ahlfeldt, G. M., Redding, S. J., Sturm, D. M., and Wolf, N. (2015). 'The Economics of Density: Evidence from the Berlin Wall', *Econometrica*, 83(6), 2127–2189.

Arvis, J. F., Mustra, M. A., Ojala, L., Shepherd, B., and Saslavsky, D. (2012). *Connecting to Compete 2012: Trade Logistics in the Global Economy*, Washington, DC: World Bank.

Ashraf, Q. and Galor, O. (2011). 'Dynamics and Stagnation in the Malthusian Epoch', *American Economic Review*, 101(5), 2003–2041.

Baier, S. L. and Bergstrand, J. H. (2001). 'The Growth of World Trade: Tariffs, Transport Costs, and Income Similarity', *Journal of International Economics*, 53(1), 1–27.

Bairoch, P. (1988). *Cities and Economic Development: From the Dawn of History to the Present* (trans. Christopher Braider), University of Chicago Press.

Baldwin, R. (2006). 'Globalisation: The Great Unbundling(s)', *Economic Council of Finland*, 20(3), 5–47.

(2016). *The Great Convergence*, Boston, MA: Harvard University Press.

Barro, R. and Sala-i-Martin, X. (1995). *Technological Diffusion, Convergence and Growth*, New Haven: Yale University, Economic Growth Center.

Bernhofen, D. M. and Brown, J. C. (2005). 'An Empirical Assessment of the Comparative Advantage Gains from Trade: Evidence from Japan', *American Economic Review*, 95(1), 208–225.

Bernhofen, D. M., El-Sahli, Z., and Kneller, R. (2016). 'Estimating the Effects of the Container Revolution on World Trade', *Journal of International Economics*, 98, 36–50.

Bogart, D. (2014). 'The Transport Revolution in Industrialising Britain', in Floud, R., Humphries, J., and Johnson, P. (eds.), *The Cambridge Economic History of Modern Britain, Vol. 1: 1700–1870*, Cambridge University Press, 368–391.

Bosker, M. and Burigh, E. (2017). 'City Seeds: Geography and the Origins of the European City System', *Journal of Urban Economics* 98(C), 139–157.

Chandler, T. (1987). *Four Thousand Years of Urban Growth: An Historical Census*. Lewiston: St David's University Press.

Ciccone, A. (2002). 'Agglomeration Effects in Europe', *European Economic Review*, 46(2), 213–227.

Ciccone, A. and Hall, R. E. (1996). 'Productivity and the Density of Economic Activity', *American Economic Review*, 86(1), 54–70.

Crafts, N. and Venables, A. (2003). 'Globalization in History: A Geographical Perspective', in Bordo, M. D., Taylor, A. M., and Williamson, J. G. (eds.), *Globalization in Historical Perspective*, University of Chicago Press, 323–370.

Crafts, N. and Wolf, N. (2014). 'The Location of the UK Cotton Textiles Industry in 1838: A Quantitative Analysis', *Journal of Economic History*, 74(4), 1103–1139.

Cronon, W. (1992). *Nature's Metropolis: Chicago and the Great West*, New York: W. W. Norton.

Diamond, J. (1997). *Guns, Germs, and Steel: The Fates of Human Societies*. New York: W. W. Norton.

Easterly, W. and Levine, R. (2003). 'Tropics, Germs, and Crops: How Endowments Influence Economic Development', *Journal of Monetary Economics*, 50(1), 3–39.

Engerman, S. L. and Sokoloff, K. L. (1994). 'Factor Endowments: Institutions, and Differential Paths of Growth among New World Economies: A View from Economic Historians of the United States', NBER historical working paper 0066, National Bureau of Economic Research.

(2002). 'Factor Endowments, Inequality, and Paths of Development among New World Economics', NBER working paper 9259, National Bureau of Economic Research.

Fernihough, A. and O'Rourke, K. H. (forthcoming). 'Coal and the European Industrial Revolution', *Economic Journal*, available online early at: https://academic.oup.com/ej/advance-article/doi/10.1093/ej/ueaa117/5955447 (accessed 8 March 2021).

Fouquin, M. and Hugot, J. (2016). 'Two Centuries of Bilateral Trade and Gravity Data: 1827–2014', working paper 015129, Universidad Javeriana-Bogotá.

Gylfason, T., Herbertsson, T. T., and Zoega, G. (1999). 'A Mixed Blessing: Natural Resources and Economic Growth', *Macroeconomic Dynamics*, 3(2), 204–225.

Haber, S. and Menaldo, V. (2011). 'Do Natural Resources Fuel Authoritarianism? A Reappraisal of the Resource Curse', *American Political Science Review*, 105(1), 1–26.

Harris, C. D. (1954). 'The Market as a Factor in the Localization of Industry in the United States', *Annals of the Association of American Geographers*, 44(4), 315–348.

Helpman, E. and Krugman, P. R. (1985). *Market Structure and Foreign Trade: Increasing Returns, Imperfect Competition, and the International Economy*, Cambridge, MA: MIT Press.

Hornung, E. (2015). 'Railroads and Growth in Prussia', *Journal of the European Economic Association*, 13(4), 699–736.

Hummels, D. (2007). 'Transportation Costs and International Trade in the Second Era of Globalization', *Journal of Economic Perspectives*, 21(3), 131–154.

Jacks, D. S. and Novy, D. (2018). 'Market Potential and Global Growth over the Long Twentieth Century', *Journal of International Economics*, 114, 221–237.

Jacks, D. S., Meissner, C. M., and Novy, D. (2008). 'Trade Costs, 1870–2000', *American Economic Review*, 98(2), 529–534.

Johnson, R. C. and Noguera, G. (2017). 'A Portrait of Trade in Value-Added over Four Decades', *Review of Economics and Statistics*, 99(5), 896–911.

Jones, E. (1981). *The European Miracle: Environments, Economies and Geopolitics in the History of Europe and Asia*, Cambridge University Press.

Kopsidis, M. and Wolf, N. (2012). 'Agricultural Productivity across Prussia during the Industrial Revolution: A Thünen Perspective', *Journal of Economic History*, 72(3), 634–670.

Krugman, P. R. (1991a). *Geography and Trade*, Cambridge, MA: MIT Press.

(1991b). 'Increasing Returns and Economic Geography', *Journal of Political Economy*, 99 (3), 483–499.

Leite, C. and Weidmann, J. (2002). 'Does Mother Nature Corrupt? Natural Resources, Corruption, and Economic Growth', in Abed, G. T. and Gupta, S. (eds.), *Governance,*

Corruption, and Economic Performance, Washington, DC: International Monetary Fund, 159–196.

McCarthy, D., Wolf, H., and Wu, Y. (2000). 'The Growth Costs of Malaria', NBER working paper 7541, National Bureau of Economic Research.

MacKellar, L., Woergoetter, A., and Woerz, J. (2000). *Economic Development Problems of Landlocked Countries*, Vienna: Institute for Advanced Studies.

Malaney, P. and Sachs, J. (2002). 'The Economic and Social Burden of Malaria', *Nature*, 415 (6872), 680–685.

Matsuyama, K. (1992). 'Agricultural Productivity, Comparative Advantage, and Economic Growth', *Journal of Economic Theory*, 58(2), 317–334.

Minami, R. (1965). *Tetsudo to Denryoku* [Railways and Electric Power, vol. 12 of Estimates of Long-Term Economic Statistics of Japan since 1868, ed. Okawa, K., Hinohara, M., and Umemura, M.], Tokyo: Toyo Keizai Shinposha.

(1976). 'Insatsugyou ni okeru Douryoku to Gijutsu Kakushin' [Motor and Technological Innovation in Printing Industry], *Keizai Kenkyu*, 27(1), 28–35.

Modelski, G. (2003). *World Cities: −3000 to 2000*. Washington, DC: Faros 2000.

Neumann, B., Vafeidis, A. T., Zimmermann, J., and Nicholls, R. J. (2015). 'Future Coastal Population Growth and Exposure to Sea-Level Rise and Coastal Flooding: A Global Assessment', *PLOS ONE*, 10(3), e0118571.

Nishikawa, S. and Koshihara, H. (1981). '1935 nen no Tounyu Sanshutsu Hyo' [IO Table of year 1935], in Nakamura, T. (ed.), *Senzen no Nihon Keizai* [Japanese Economy before WWII], Tokyo: Yamakawa Shoten.

Okubo, T. (2008). 'Shake Hands or Shake Apart? International Relationship of Japan with Global Blocs', *Économie internationale*, 1(113), 35–64.

Radelet, S. and Sachs, J. D. (1998). 'Shipping Costs, Manufactured Exports, and Economic Growth', presented at the Annual Meeting of the American Economics Association, Chicago, 3–5 January.

Ramankutty, N., Foley, J. A., Norman, J., and McSweeney, K. (2002). 'The Global Distribution of Cultivable Lands: Current Patterns and Sensitivity to Possible Climate Change', *Global Ecology and Biogeography*, 11(5), 377–392.

Redding, S. (1999). 'Dynamic Comparative Advantage and the Welfare Effects of Trade', *Oxford Economic Papers*, 51(1), 15–39.

Redding, S. J. and Sturm, D. M. (2008). 'The Costs of Remoteness: Evidence from German Division and Reunification', *American Economic Review*, 98(5), 1766–1797.

Redding, S. and Venables, A. J. (2004). 'Economic Geography and International Inequality', *Journal of International Economics*, 62(1), 53–82.

Rodrik, D., Subramanian, A., and Trebbi, F. (2004). 'Institutions Rule: The Primacy of Institutions over Geography and Integration in Economic Development', *Journal of Economic Growth*, 9(2), 131–165.

Rosés, J. R. and Wolf, N. (eds.) (2019). *The Economic Development of Europe's Regions: A Quantitative History since 1900*, New York: Routledge.

Rosés and Wolf database on regional GDP, v6. (2020). Available online at http://nikolauswolf.eu (accessed 29 September 2020).

Ross, M. L. (2001). 'Does Oil Hinder Democracy?', *World Politics*, 53(3), 325–361.

Sachs, J. D. and Warner, A. M. (1995). 'Natural Resource Abundance and Economic Growth', NBER working paper 5398, National Bureau of Economic Research.

Sarr, M., Bulte, E., Meissner, C., and Swanson, T. (2011). 'On the Looting of Nations', *Public Choice*, 148(3–4), 353–380.

Small, C. and Nicholls, R. J. (2003). 'A Global Analysis of Human Settlement in Coastal Zones', *Journal of Coastal Research*, 19, 584–599.

Smith, B. (2015). 'The Resource Curse Exorcised: Evidence from a Panel of Countries', *Journal of Development Economics*, 116, 57–73.

Solow, R. M. (1956). 'A Contribution to the Theory of Economic Growth', *Quarterly Journal of Economics*, 70(1), 65–94.

Statistics Bureau of Japan. (various years). *Imperial Japan Statistical Yearbook*. Tokyo: Ministry of Internal Affairs and Communications.

(various years). *Population Census*. Tokyo: Ministry of Internal Affairs and Communications.

Temin, P. (2002). 'The Golden Age of European Growth Reconsidered', *European Review of Economic History*, 6(1), 3–22.

UN Department of Economic and Social Affairs. (2016). *United Nations Demographic Yearbook 2014*. New York: United Nations.

US Energy Information Administration. (2017). *International Energy Outlook 2017*. Washington, DC: US Energy Information Administration.

Yi, K. M. (2003). 'Can Vertical Specialization Explain the Growth of World Trade?', *Journal of Political Economy*, 111(1), 52–102.

Yuan, T, Settsu, T., Bassino, J.-P., and Fukao, K. (2009). 'Senzen ki Nihon no Kennai Souseisan to Sangyou Kouzou' [Prefectural GDP and Industrial Structure in Interwar Japan], *Keizai Kenkyu*, 60(2), 163–189.

15

Underlying Sources of Growth

Institutions and the State

JAMES FOREMAN-PECK AND LESLIE HANNAH

Two characteristics differentiate today's rich countries from many poor and middle-income ones. One is that the rich are all market economies in which production is largely undertaken by privately owned joint stock companies (henceforth, capitalist corporations). The other is that most of the wealthy are representative democracies (oil-rich economies being exceptions).[1] However, capitalist democracies have widely differing commitments to tax redistribution, levels of state ownership, health and welfare policies, and the balance between protecting established property rights and interventions to remedy the system's perceived failings. Autocrats have also promoted economic growth – President Xi of China follows a long tradition – and have sometimes succeeded over a lower range of GDP per head. However, economic growth eventually seems to expand demands for participation: in the later twentieth century, military dictatorships in Taiwan, South Korea, and Spain liberalized, and communist autocrats in eastern Europe conceded free elections.

While democracy, capitalism, and wealth are correlated, the possibility and nature of causation among the three is much debated. Major themes in Western literature – pioneered by Nobel-prizewinning economic historian Douglass North, and enriched by many others[2] – are when these correlations emerged and how they are structurally related. We follow this 'new institutional economics' approach here. Wealth-maximizing political institutions are hypothesized to be inclusively representative, sometimes leading towards full democracy, combined with respect for minorities. Arguably political *and*

1 In 2018, no country that was an autocracy (Polity IV definition, see note 9, below) had an income per head of more than $15,000 if it was not heavily dependent on fossil fuel exports. Countries that were autocratically ruled and did not have the option to export fossil fuels were poor (Roser 2018).

2 For instance, North and Thomas 1973; Haber et al. 2008; Acemoglu and Robinson 2012; Lamoreaux and Wallis 2017; Alston et al. 2018.

economic 'open access' – representative political institutions and ready access to incorporation or similar enterprise forms – are mutually reinforcing and conducive to high living standards, broadly shared (North et al. 2009).

Institutions are the patterns of interaction that govern and constrain the relationships of individuals – the 'rules of the game'. Relevant rules include written laws, formal social conventions, informal norms of behaviour, and shared beliefs about the world. This variety ensures that institutions are often difficult to define precisely. The institutional form of some states includes the rule of law, in others, the rule of arbitrary terror. Institutions are often hard to create and highly persistent. Institutional economics attempts to understand why and under what conditions they emerge.

Institutions facilitating transitions from limited to open access must allow the circulation of elites. Elites may be elected, but in a low-income, feudal society such as contemporary Pakistan, at best, they can still be a 'selectorate'. New people must be allowed access to power, changing the social structure, but without too much collateral damage to society. Peaceful transitions, therefore, may entail outgoing elites being permitted to hold on to their wealth, so they abandon power without violence. The condition of peaceful circulation, in turn, needs acceptance of a rule of law for elites that offers them a form of legal protection. A second condition is that there must be substantial numbers of independent, perpetually lived organizations, such as corporations; these can undertake more economic activities than finite life organizations. Political control of the military is an essential third condition. The failure of the military coups in 1981 and 1982 marked the success of the Spanish transition to open political and economic access. Control is essential to reduce threats of violence and trade disruption, and cutting the risk of expropriation by the military increases the benefits of markets. When economies and societies satisfy these three conditions and become wealthier, open-access transition and sustained economic growth are more likely to occur (North et al. 2009).

The 'Washington consensus' – or the 'Manchester school' as similarly free market, liberal[3] ideas were known in the nineteenth century – never goes uncontested (Stiglitz 2003).[4] It is concretely expressed in the World Bank's detailed policy prescriptions and 'Doing Business' index (www.worldbank.org). The 'good' institutions it recommends include democracy,

3 We use the term 'liberal' in its original European – or modern 'neoliberal' – sense to mean anti-authoritarian supporters of individual freedom, free markets, and a limited state, not in the modern American English sense (broadly the opposite).

4 Before 1914, the Manchester school was similarly contested by Marxists, American institutionalists, German *Kathedersozialisten*, British Fabian socialists and many others.

an independent judiciary, uncorrupted and efficient bureaucrats, secure property rights, a politically independent central bank, easy and cheap business registration, transparent and market-oriented corporate governance, and a responsive legal system (with common law systems judged to perform well on this dimension).

A frequent problem in understanding their role today is that institutions have often existed for decades. They have sometimes evolved with minimal formal deliberation (the unwritten British 'constitution') rather than being consciously constructed (the American Constitution, though that, too, evolved). It is sometimes difficult to identify origins, causes, and effects separately from those of related institutions, or cultural background, with which they interact. For example, Haber et al. (2008) contend that correlations between favourable economic outcomes and Anglo-American common law systems are not causal: both the outcomes and common law judgments are triggered by third factors, representative political institutions and tolerably equal economic access.

Some institutions – such as patents, education, and demographic norms – are discussed in other chapters. We pay special attention here to the development of business incorporation and its relation to evolving representative government. The capitalist corporate form – and some state-owned substitutes – came to dominate enterprise in almost all post-agrarian societies by the end of the twentieth century, and political institutions played a key role in this development. North et al. (2009) maintain that under the 'natural state' (a coalition of elites), economic growth can take place, but will eventually be choked off as the basis of elite power comes under threat. The transition to sustained economic growth requires the transformation of both political and economic institutions, so that they can become mutually supporting. Traditional – feudal, monarchical, established religion, class- or caste-bound – societies usually restrained political and economic open access. Sometimes the move to more representative government occurred because incumbent elites made mistakes that weakened their hold on power (Treisman 2017). For those outside the elite, the overthrow of such systems in the name of 'modernity' often seemed a prerequisite for growth and development. In that limited sense, American and French revolutionaries overthrowing monarchy and aristocracy, Lenin's execution of the tsar and attacks on the bourgeoisie, and Maoist revolutionaries undermining Confucianism and the Manchukuo dynasty were all on the same page. All also seriously risked oversimplifying (sometimes murderously) the problematic transition to modernity.

We set the scene with a survey of economic and political institutions in 1870 and the concentration of wealth in western Europe and North America. We go on to consider the experience and institutional features of the first non-Western modernizer after 1870, Japan. The third section summarizes the non-market institutions and state development from 1917 of the communist alternative states. This is followed by a brief account of the key characteristics of the hybrid state-driven capitalist economies that begin to appear after 1945. In each section we rely heavily, but not uncritically, on the North et al. (2009) framework to interpret the relationships between economic development and political and economic institutions.

Economic and Political Institutions in 1870

In 1870, political economists – as institutional economists were then called – had strong views on the characteristics of desirable institutions and were confident they were the cause, not merely the happy result, of prosperity. They used Christianity and 'civilization' as synonyms: 'Christendom' meant the developed world (Mulhall 1881). Many historians agreed with the leading sociologist, Max Weber, that the Protestant religion especially had promoted capitalist prosperity (Weber 1930).[5] Most Islamic countries have experienced difficulties in growing rich (except on oil) and generally have had autocratic governments (Kuran 2011). Yet economic growth, at the time of writing, is more widely shared by non-Protestant countries, and *rich* countries have become more agnostic. Religious institutions as causes of national economic growth are accordingly less prominent in today's institutional economics than they were in the past.

One obvious feature of the world of 1870 was how distant the bulk of humanity was from the North et al. (2009) ideal of 'open access' or 'inclusive' institutions. Living standards were already high in much of western Europe, north America, and Australasia, where governments fostered widespread (if imperfectly democratic) participation in both dispersed capitalist corporations and representative political assemblies. It was still a matter of heated debate whether some institutions – like limited liability, patents, or democracy – were aids to, or barriers to, economic progress. Not until the early twentieth century did three rich countries – Finland, Australia, and New Zealand – introduce a franchise close to that considered democratic today (including women).

5 For a broader discussion of the interactions between culture (generally learned informally from parents, civil society, or churches) and institutions (which are more deliberate – and often political – creations), see Alesina and Giuliano 2015.

Some, like France and Switzerland, did not do so until after World War II. One near approach to a more generous definition of democracy – universal adult *male* franchise – in the French Second Republic only demonstrated its dangers: it had led, in 1852, to the endorsement of the autocratic Napoleon III. In the richest countries, statesmen either judged a wider franchise undesirable or, accepting it was inevitable, fretted about ensuring broader commitment to the existing polity and social hierarchy. They pressed for wider education, modest social protections, or for restricting radicals, labour unions, and (within empires) native independence movements.

Most of the world's population lived under absolute hereditary rulers, subject to few formal restraints (Russia, China, Japan, Brazil, the Ottomans) or direct rule by a controlling power (British India, French Indochina, American Alaska). In the developed world, most states (including the UK, Germany, Italy) were monarchies, though with some representative government and serious restraints on the arbitrary exercise of regal power. Only in America (north and south) did republics predominate. Nation states were the basic institutional framework for political and economic development: their governments were the authors of legislation and incubators of formal institutions. People, capital, goods, and ideas moved across national borders, but they travelled more easily within those borders, especially borders that enclosed linguistic or culturally homogeneous communities. Newspapers, political activities, social interactions, education systems, transport improvements, and laws increasingly reinforced national links. Mill (1861) argued that representative government 'was next to impossible in a country made up of different nationalities'. The Habsburg monarchy, though opting not to merge its 9 million German-speakers into the new German confederation of 1870–71, did separate the government of its constituent Austrian and Hungarian kingdoms. Mill's point was important, as nation states consolidated, but also raised as many questions as it answered: were the Irish British? Were Poles and Alsatians German? Were Muslims or Buddhists Indian? Could one really create a nation out of US polyglot immigrants when the north disagreed with the south on as fundamental an issue as slavery?

The number of sovereigns had declined as states consolidated and major sovereigns annexed weaker ones, and their number was to decline further, notably with the European 'scramble for Africa', to fifty-four by 1914.[6] European empires, which had administered a third of the world's land surface

6 War-induced break-ups were to increase that to seventy-six by 1949, and later decolonizations resulted in today's level of around 200 nation states (Gancia et al. 2016: 1).

in 1800, controlled over 84 per cent by 1914 (Fieldhouse 1973). Rich nation states (excluding their empires) in 1870 were about equal in size: populations were 40 million (USA), 39 million (Germany), 38 million (France), and 31 million (UK). Many more people lived in recognizably poorer countries with autocratic governments (Russia with 83 million, the Indian subcontinent with 300 million, and China with 358 million together accounted for 58 per cent of the world's population).

International institutions – European empires apart – were almost non-existent. Bodies such as the International Commission on the Danube worked well for riparian states; the International Office of Telegraphy was set up 1869 and the International Bureau of Weights and Measures in 1870. The Hague Tribunal (another forerunner of today's United Nations for resolving international disputes) had to wait until 1899. Nonetheless, international trade (the increasingly protectionist US excepted) was relatively free, facilitated by tariff reduction agreements and acceptance of the 'most favoured nation' clause. Communications were improving: the French opened the Suez Canal (speeding up communication between Europe and Asia) in 1869, and in the same year, the US completed North America's first transcontinental railway, both expanding trade opportunities. The Victorian 'worldwide web' was almost complete, with a working cable across the Atlantic by 1866, India and Singapore connected by 1870, and Australia and major cities on Asia's Pacific coastline following in 1871 (Foreman-Peck 1995). These achievements left sub-Saharan Africa as the only major region not then linked to rapid telegraphic communication.

The connection that North et al. (2009) hypothesized between open access in the political and the economic spheres might be expected to show up earliest and most clearly in the US, a self-consciously new and different country. The many constituent states were experimenting with open access both politically and economically, by extending the franchise and general incorporation laws. The number of corporations per capita in the US was already high by European standards by the middle decades of the nineteenth century (Hannah 2014). However, there was considerable variation between US states in allowing incorporation with limited liability by simple registration and political open access. Few believed that opening access to organizations of all kinds could both spark sustained economic growth and enhance the workings of democratic politics (Lamoreaux and Wallis 2017).

A more mixed pattern can be seen globally. China, Japan, many uncolonized Asian and African states, the Russian and Ottoman Empires, and much of south-eastern Europe lacked general incorporation statutes in 1870 and for several more decades. On the other hand, most rich countries with some form of representative government had a general incorporation statute then or soon after: for example, France in 1867 and Germany in 1871. It is difficult to discern a clear or deliberate link between moves to open access politically and economically. Britain had relatively easy access to a variety of company forms, even before its registration statutes of 1844 and 1855, already offering individual charters liberally for turnpikes, banks, canals, and railways. It had a long tradition of parliamentary government, but extended the democratic franchise only slowly in four major steps between the reforms of 1832 and full adult suffrage in 1929. British colonies, even those autocratically ruled rather than self-governing, had open access to limited liability (based on the British legislation, with local variants) decades before they approached representative government. India's incorporation statute dates from 1857, while its first taste of national elections (with a franchise as restricted as early nineteenth-century Britain's) was as late as 1920.

Germany soon regretted the liberality of its 1871 corporate registration statute: regulatory oversight was tightened in 1884 and 1896, and there remained considerable suspicion of limited liability and stock exchange speculation. In 1910, Germany still had one of the lowest levels of corporations per capita in the rich world. By contrast, Norway had no incorporation statute until 1910, but its government did not outlaw free contracts for corporate forms; Norwegians actually contracted extensively and competently, achieving the highest levels of corporations per head in Europe *before* they had a general incorporation statute. The tsar insisted on corporations being individually chartered in Russia proper until his abdication in 1917. Yet within the Russian Empire, the Grand Duchy of Finland, despite limits on its representative institutions, had long allowed incorporation liberally by registration (Foreman-Peck and Hannah 2015; Hannah 2015).

Corporations served many purposes. One clearly related to economic growth was the provision of capital by many small shareholders. This gave a wider range of citizens a stake in business profits through stock exchange investments, while permitting the achievement of economies of scale and integration or network benefits by large, listed businesses (Williamson 1981). There was no stock exchange in 1870 in the whole of East Asia, nor in much of Latin America and Africa, but there were £6.8 billion of securities on the main European stock exchanges and £0.6 billion on the New York Stock Exchange. On both sides of the Atlantic, government securities dominated, the main exceptions being railways raising the unprecedentedly large and lumpy development funds that this new technology required. In 1870, the largest railway corporations were in France, Britain, and India; US railways were smaller, but rapidly catching up. Most of the world's population had yet to see a railway: 93 per cent of 1870 railway mileage was in Europe and North America, with most of the remainder in India (Woytinsky and Woytinsky 1955). Railways were also a proxy indicator of the global application of steam power: 70 per cent was then used on railways, the rest in steamships or as a power source in modern factories.

Many countries without railways were determined to catch up with this symbol of modernity. The insecure Habsburg and Russian emperors had once feared railways for spreading revolution, but increasingly understood their military and economic value and offered state guarantees and investments. The Qing in Peking resisted incursions of this Western business and technology, but soon Chinese modernizers were seeing that as grounds not for national self-congratulation, but for plotting the revolutionary overthrow of the Qing dynasty. Some countries that lagged in permitting open access to incorporation for railways made alternative arrangements. Gerschenkron (1962) argued that both governments and banks could be effective institutional substitutes for securities markets in funding development. This is echoed by modern economists, conscious that banks and state guidance have played a similar role in later successful growth spurts in Japan, South Korea, and elsewhere (Levine 1997). Prussian mutual savings banks funded early railways, and with the 1880s nationalizations of private lines, state railways became dominant in Germany. The French government planned the development of its rail system and, from 1859, guaranteed returns for investors to accelerate development. Even state-owned railways often relied on stock markets to raise capital. Later scholarship has emphasized that relations among securities markets, banks, and the state were more complex than Gerschenkron allowed, and not solely driven by backwardness (Forsyth and Verdier 2003). It is now more common to emphasize that banks and securities markets can be complements as much as substitutes: within a broad range, the balance between the two is arguably inconsequential (Fohlin 2016; though cf. Carlin and Mayer 2003).

Indian railway development required state aid, and the self-governing colonists in Australasia and Canada also favoured nationalized or state-aided railways. Britain itself was the only major country which provided little but open-access charter rights in support of railways, relying entirely on private enterprise, with only modest regulation. Even in the US, most investment in canals and more than a quarter of rail investment had been state-supported before the civil war, and the federal government still subsidized transcontinental railroads. Nonetheless, de Tocqueville considered US citizens (relative to the French) unusually adept at forming associations (and that was correct for small corporations). From the 1870s, the US moved more decisively towards private enterprise, with budget surpluses repaying government debts and 'crowding in' investments in private railroad bonds and equities. The US then tolerated high rates of railroad bankruptcies, firmly resetting America's path towards private capitalism. One French commentator noted that the US had less capital than 'sterile' France, but used it more effectively for business because of its move to open-access institutions (Coquelin 1864: 287).

Japan

The underdeveloped economy of 1870 that most successfully modernized over the next century was Japan. Marx (1867) believed that 'the industrially more developed country presents to the less developed country a picture of the latter's future', a view (unusually) shared by Japanese elite reformers. Among those who had travelled to San Francisco with Japan's 1859 mission, Yukichi Fukuzawa had been impressed by Americans' equality, freedom from government controls and cultural superstitions, generosity to foreigners, and coaches drawn by horses (not men), but was less impressed by Americans' propensity to keep on dirty shoes indoors and their overt republicanism (Fukuzawa 1948). He wanted to preserve but modernize an enlightened monarchy.

Elite opinion-formers like Fukuzawa wanted to change their country, but also to protect it from the European and American colonialism that was encroaching on independent Asian nations. They believed that by copying Western technology and institutions Japan could, and should, match the West's wealth and military power. The Japanese are sometimes pictured as having wisely chosen foreign institutional models: the British navy and Post Office, the Prussian army, the Belgian central bank, German civil law. In fact, the process of deciding what to copy and the question of how to adapt them to Japanese needs was far from simple. Was the Belgian central bank really the world's best? Was it sensible to copy the British peerage and House of Lords? Acemoglu and Robinson (2012) note that the Japanese drive for modernization was comparable with what happened in Britain and Germany, where the non-industrial elites maintained their political power despite the process of industrialization. The strategy was to industrialize while also reducing the chances of counter-revolution by ensuring the cooperation of most of the existing power centres and developing central government military power. Berkowitz et al. (2003) stress the importance of receptivity for the success of transplanted legal systems; German civil law attracted the Japanese elite because it was more certain and top-down than common law. Japan first adopted an American-style banking system, but soon found continental European models more congenial. In 1899, Japan adopted a version of German corporate law, but developed it more liberally than Germany, as an open-access institution (Hannah and Kasuya 2016).

Political choices were also complex and changing. The Meiji Constitution was initially autocratic, but flexed to more democratically elected and representative cabinets in the 1920s. In the 1930s, it fell to autocratic military control. State business initiatives were also flexible. After the pioneering government-run Tokyo–Yokohama line, railways were mainly developed by the private sector. The state then lacked the fiscal capacity to undertake large investments, but nationalized many railways in 1906. Industrial pilot plants – initially government-owned – were gradually privatized, as capitalist groups developed a capacity to finance and manage them.

This complexity has led some historians to claim Japan as a triumphant example of capitalist markets; others to extol its state-led planning. In fact, Japan was a complex and diverse economy, with both governments and markets at different times driving development with varying success. The Japanese elite selectively copied and modified Western institutions to promote economic development. However, restoring political open access to complement economic open access on the North et al. (2009) model was the work of post-1945 US occupiers, enforcing elite acceptance of more democratic norms.

Communist Alternatives

In Russia, Kerensky's reformist government supplanted the autocratic tsar in 1917 and immediately replaced the restrictive corporation law with economic open access. However, after Lenin's October Revolution, the Bolsheviks made more radical attempts to change institutions and drive industrialization faster. They aimed comprehensively to overthrow old elites and change the distribution of power. While Japan embraced trade with the West and social stability at home, the USSR pursued a quite different course. The Bolsheviks suppressed much trade with capitalist nations in favour of self-sufficiency,

Table 15.1 Features of capitalist and USSR economic systems

Feature	Peacetime capitalist	USSR peacetime command
Decision-making structure	Decentralized	Centralized
Mechanisms for information and coordination	Primarily market, but with state regulation	Compulsory plans, restricted labour and retail markets
Property rights	Primarily private ownership	State ownership of all productive assets
Incentives and corporate governance (CG)	Material (cash) and moral (social trust, civil norms); CG based on equity markets	Material (cash privileges), moral (communist ideology), coercion; CG based on state

Sources: Adapted from Gregory and Stuart 1995: 27; Davis 1999.

repudiated the foreign debts the tsar had incurred to finance industrialization and wars, and brutally enforced a more 'socialist' society.

Rejection of the apparently successful global capitalist and quasi-democratic order was supposedly a pathway to the final goal of egalitarian communism. This objective generated enthusiasm both inside and outside the new Soviet Union, but 'democratic centralism' (a Soviet euphemism for dictatorship) was less admired. Key characteristics, summarized in Table 15.1, were top-down autocratic central planning, the expropriation by the Soviet state of most private property (though some small private enterprises were permitted under the New Economic Policy in 1921–28), the elimination of multi-party electoral choice and a ban on emigration. The pervasive secret police maintained party orthodoxy, assisted by murder or effective enslavement of dissenters in the Gulag: autocracy on a scale no nineteenth-century autocrat had considered. The civil war the Bolsheviks provoked and won, and its aftermath, were disastrous.

Despite this setback, by the later 1930s, Stalin's Soviet Union had achieved GDP per capita levels similar to those that uninterrupted tsarist growth rates would have attained. It was again near to the output levels of the poorer European powers. It had overtaken a capitalist eastern Europe divided by the post-1918 peace agreements into inefficiently small and protectionist nations. Stalin's Five-Year Plans forced a shift of labour and, especially, capital, in a 'big push' of heavy industrialization, focused on military and capital goods. The aims of the planning system were primarily security and military superiority. The pay-off came with the Soviet Union defeat of Nazi Germany by 1945. Among the costs in the 1930s were the oppression of kulaks (the most enterprising peasants) and forced collectivization of agriculture that triggered a famine, killing millions; a further million were murdered in Stalin's purges of 1937–38. In eastern Europe after 1945, the regime also suppressed democracy (or nationalist autocracy) in countries occupied by Soviet armed forces.

The USSR's impressive post-1945 capacity to maintain growth and successfully develop technologies such as nuclear weapons and the 1957 Sputnik satellite caused some to expect the Soviet bloc to overtake the West. By the 1970s, however, the absence of market signals and the incentive problems of the centrally planned economy were obviously slowing economic growth. Yet the system was resistant to reform efforts, even as more attention was given to supplying consumer goods. More adventurous reformers in eastern Europe were suppressed by the Soviet military. Resources devoted to the military continued to be a high, but – even to the planners themselves – opaque proportion of GDP. A modest estimate is that in 1980, one-fifth of Soviet GDP was allocated for military purposes.

Production was decentralized in separate organizations. These were typically much larger than capitalist corporations (even in industries with only modest scale economies) and had little planning autonomy (Pryor 1973). Poor innovative capacity in such bureaucracies (notably in services and information technology) and increasing stagnation frustrated managers and bureaucrats as well as consumers. The Soviet Union failed to develop the computer technology that might have increased the effectiveness of the planning system, and Western computers remained on the Cold War embargo list of NATO powers and Japan. The 'fixer', fraud, and corruption became essential means of achieving enterprise plan targets. Soviet bloc economies of eastern Europe were generally less dominated by the state, the extreme case being Yugoslavia, which decentralized to worker-managed firms, 'guided' by the Communist Party. Nonetheless, these economies appear to have converged on higher US living standards at a slower rate than non-communist economies with comparable (initial) productivities.

Recognizing the repeated failure of economic reform in the face of vested interests, President Gorbachev concluded that political reform must come first. He permitted private business ownership from 1988 and, soon after, the collapse of the political monopoly of European communist autocracies, symbolized by the breaches of the Berlin Wall in 1989. In the centrally planned economies, the overdeveloped branches of industry typically had low productivity and their products were uncompetitive in world markets. In consequence, one of the main tasks of transition from a command to a market economy was the reallocation of resources within manufacturing to competitive sectors, and from industry to services.

This required gradualism, yet the Western neoliberal doctrine prevailing in the 1990s favoured a programme of rapidly introduced, comprehensive reforms that included price liberalization, mass privatization, foreign trade liberalization, and currency convertibility (Blanchard et al. 1994). In retrospect, one of the most critical omissions from this doctrine was the role of institutions in coordinating the activity of market economies. Consequently, despite democratic elections and capitalist markets, the new Russian core struggled with poor performance under 'crony capitalism'. There was rather more impressive catch-up in parts of eastern Europe. Open-access political and economic orders were more successfully implemented, enabling some post-communist states to join the European Union. In other offshoots of the former Soviet Union, notably the central Asian republics and Belarus, autocrats remained in power. Russian interventions and their own crony capitalist developments rendered democracy in Ukraine and Georgia precarious, and economic performances generally worse than Russia's. When strong parliamentary systems were adopted, they countered the adverse effects of inherited autocratic institutions on economic evolution. Yet the adoption of open-access democracy was apparently more difficult than adopting capitalism, thanks to history and ethnicity (Djankov and Hauck 2016).

Chinese communists extended their rule over China by 1949. Mao's People's Republic was one of the world's poorest countries: earlier development had been weak outside foreign enclaves like Shanghai. After the formation of a republic in 1912, warlordism, civil war, the Japanese invasion of 1937, and corruption weakened areas controlled by Chinese capitalists and communists alike. In 1949, the expectation of life at birth was only forty years, and China's GDP per head was only 70 per cent of India's, about one-fifth of the world average, and 15 per cent of the USSR's (Maddison 2001). Under Mao, the newly unified country was increasingly resistant to foreign influences. Life expectancy improved slightly, but otherwise there was no catching up with the living standards of the rest of the world or the Soviets.[7]

Initially, the new regime showed familiar Stalinist features. Mao eliminated many landlords, rich peasants, and 'counter-revolutionaries'. His 'Great Leap Forward' (1958–62) collectivized agriculture and attempted to stimulate

7 In 1973, its GDP per head was still only 21 per cent of the world average and had fallen slightly to 14 per cent of the USSR's (Maddison 2001). Modernizing countries in that era generally grew faster than more advanced countries.

rural industrialization. This policy resulted in perhaps tens of millions of deaths (the precise figures are unknown) through famine, taking national output backwards, not forwards. Then, in the 'Cultural Revolution' (1966–76), the Red Guards murdered intellectuals and political dissidents, while others were forced out of cities into manual labour, destroying expertise and compromising output. By the time Mao died in 1976, Chinese living standards had fallen even further behind those of the USSR, though the communist party remained firmly in political control.

Mao's communist successors were markedly more successful in catching up with the Soviets, achieving higher living standards by careful management of the transition to capitalist markets. They extensively re-engaged with the international system of trading, expanding Western technology adoption and multinationals' inward investments well above 1949 levels. By contrast, relaxations of restrictions on private property, on currency, and on capital controls were gradual and selective, ensuring that the Communist Party's political and economic controls were maintained. Popular support for the policy revisions came from the relief of survivors escaping the horrors of Maoism, and the embrace by the young of a more consumerist and educated, if increasingly inegalitarian, society.

Paradoxically, Mao's disastrous policies, by devolving more responsibility to local cadres rather than central planners, laid some of the groundwork for China's transition. Cadres were encouraged to compete economically against other provinces. China's choices were also driven by its limited resources: it could not subsidize cronies and buy popularity with oil revenues as much as better-endowed Russia did. Moreover, China's vast expanse, in 1973 encompassing 22.5 per cent of world population, compared with the USSR's 6.4 per cent, made greater devolution of control a natural response (Lardy 1975). Explicit policy choices to foster open access to capitalist organizations and markets were, however, critical innovations, intensified under the leadership of Deng Xiaoping in 1978–89 and his successors. A transition from collective agriculture back to family farming under the 'household responsibility system' was especially helpful (Harrison 2014). The reform process deepened with the expansion of locally owned 'township and village enterprises', and in the 1990s with sweeping privatization of state-owned industry, though the communist elite retained considerable control over capital allocation and governance. State-owned enterprises were reduced from producing four-fifths of output in the 1980s to one-fifth today, but still dominate sectors from transport to power. By 2016, China's GDP per capita at PPP of $15,399 nearly equalled the increased world average of $16,318. Much of the gap with Russia ($26,490)[8] had been reduced and China was well ahead of India ($6,616). However, it was still far behind countries of Chinese culture that had escaped Maoism: Taiwan ($48,111), Hong Kong ($58,322), and Singapore ($87,855).

In a North et al. (2009) society, the two forms of 'open access' – economic and political – go hand in hand. Despite some lags and reversals, they are mutually reinforcing in the richest societies. Communist China has become the foremost modern example of promoting economic growth through encouraging reasonably open access to economic institutions, while maintaining closed access politically. According to North et al. (2009), at some future point it will open up politically or economic growth will cease. An alternative view is that the efficiency of authoritarian rule has been transformed by the internet revolution, and its economic success will continue to offer legitimacy to a political regime able to benefit from capitalist markets and competitive quasi-open-access corporate organizations.

State-Driven Development of Capitalist Markets

China is not the only exponent of state-driven development under one-party rule. Many capitalist countries and nations liberated from colonial empires in the decades following 1945 succumbed to their own authoritarian strongmen. These people severely restricted capitalist 'open access' economic institutions, through expropriations, nationalizations, tariffs, licensing, and controls. But as Figure 15.1 shows, the big drop in the population under autocracy is the end of Qing dynasty in China in 1911, and the arrival of Sun Yat Sen's pseudo-democratic republic. The sudden fall in the population in colonies in the late 1940s and the rise in the spread of democracies is driven by the independence of India and Pakistan. With the collapse of the Soviet empire, 1989 was a critical year for the ending of autocratic communist regimes.

The largest capitalist developing nation was India. The Indian subcontinent was less disadvantaged by war than nominally independent China, but its colonial government was increasingly perceived as illegitimate, both within India and by the Left in Britain. Britain's Labour government in 1947 conceded independence, under which the separation of Muslim Pakistan

8 In terms of life expectancy (which, by the second decade of the twenty-first century, was over seventy), China has done better than Russia, where life expectancy at birth peaked at sixty-five in the 1960s and has since declined.

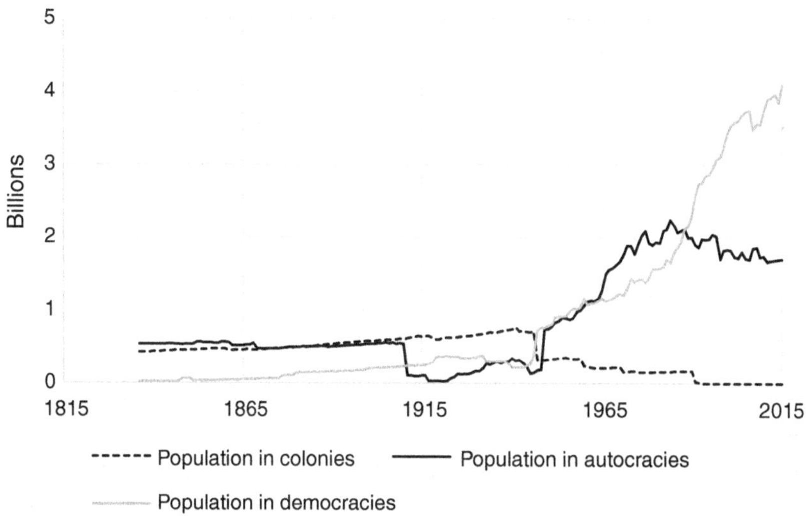

Figure 15.1 World population under democratic and autocratic rule
Sources and notes: Calculated from Roser 2018. Regimes are the Polity IV categories.[9]

from the secular Indian republic created a refugee crisis and millions of deaths. India's economic growth then accelerated under favourable global macroeconomic conditions. Its representative parliamentary institutions, restricted to a narrow franchise under the British (only 12 per cent of Indians could vote in 1937), expanded to a broad democracy. The Congress Party accepted changes of government through electoral defeat, from an early stage in the provinces, and nationally in the late 1970s: no small achievement given the early records of other third world offshoots of the British Empire (Pakistan, Bangladesh, Burma, and almost all African ex-colonies). However, under Jawaharlal Nehru (prime minister 1947–64, and an admirer of Russian industrialization) and his daughter, Indira Gandhi (prime minister 1966–77 and 1980–84), India experienced poor growth rates in GDP per

9 The Polity score captures a 'regime authority spectrum' on a 21-point scale, ranging from −10 (hereditary monarchy) to +10 (consolidated democracy). Polity scores can also be converted into regime categories in a tripartite categorization of 'autocracies' (−10 to −6), 'anocracies' (−5 to +5), and 'democracies' (+6 to +10). The democracy indicator is derived from assessments of the competitiveness of political participation, the openness and competitiveness of executive recruitment, and constraints on the chief executive. Autocracies are defined as authorities that sharply restrict or suppress competitive political participation. Their chief executives are chosen in a regularized process of selection within the political elite, and once in office they exercise power with few institutional constraints (Marshall et al. 2017).

head, even compared to Mao's China, and its acceleration in recent decades has also been less impressive than China's.

Was Indian experience a failure of capitalism? There was certainly much more market activity and private capital among Indian peasants and small businesses than in China. But, as in many ex-colonies, liberation from European rule was taken to mean liberation from free trade, laissez-faire, and open-access policies. These were blamed for backwardness, not celebrated as a means for overcoming it. The Congress Party pursued broadly socialist policies of extending nationalization to banks, insurance companies, and other industries. They protected favoured local producers by tariffs and licensing, also backtracking on openness to modern machinery imports (Roy 2018). The number of joint-stock companies had been steadily expanding under colonial 'open access' policies, in absolute and per capita terms, powered by an exuberantly capitalist native bourgeoisie in major coastal cities. Then, for nearly three decades after independence, extant companies per million people declined and reached a post-war low, even in absolute terms, in 1962.

Only with the relaxation of this 'Licence Raj' did economic 'open access' flourish. The number of corporations per million people expanded from 54 in 1970 – a lower level than under British rule or than the capitalist international norm – to 83 in 1980, 241 in 1990, 538 in 2000, and 707 in 2010 (www.mca.gov.in). Even so, public sector employment accounted for 71 per cent of the total in the 'organized' sector in 1991, and 69 per cent in 2000 (Tomlinson 2013). With liberalization, Indian growth rates increased substantially. From an annual average of 1.25 per cent over the years 1960–80, per capita GDP growth reached 3.68 per cent in 1980–2004, and was even higher over the following decade.[10] However, relative to China, India's poor infrastructure investment, limits on global integration, and perhaps greater personal freedoms (notably for bearing children and voting) held back economic growth. Moreover, the continuation of some aspects of the Licence Raj limited the growth of larger factories: factories employing more than 200, at the time of writing, now account for only one-tenth of the manufacturing workforce, compared with over half in China (Joshi 2017). Political and bureaucratic corruption – violation of law by public officials for private gain – also ranked India behind China (respectively 87th and 78th out of the 178 countries) in Transparency International's Corruption Perceptions Index

10 Calculated from https://data.worldbank.org/indicator/NY.GDP.PCAP.KD?locations=IN (accessed 29 September 2020).

in 2010. Corruption reduces the efficiency of both the public sector and private enterprise. One estimate of the 'underground economy' of India in the late 2000s was that it accounted for 50 per cent of the official GDP and there were many illicit capital outflows. Soon to become the most populous country in the world, India has more 'open access', both politically and economically, than most developing countries. But the jury is still out on whether it will be able successfully to close the present gap with China, Russia, or, more distantly, with the West.

More autocratically capitalist economies than India experienced rapid economic growth and the transition to 'open access' politics after 1960. The Korean military dictator, President Park Chung-Hee, threw the country's leading businessmen in jail when he came to power in 1961 (Rodrik 1997). They were released only after Park extracted promises from them that they would each undertake specific industrial investments. Given how the Korean economy prospered, these businessmen may well have been better-off for these forced investments. The critical change (as in China) was not a transformation in the structure of power, but the absorption of new ideas by those in power. Reform happened not when vested interests were defeated, but when different strategies were used to pursue those interests, or when interests themselves were redefined.

This may explain why sometimes autocracy produces better economic results than democracy. Authoritarian regimes can impose 'open access' or liberal economic policies, being freer than those who are subject to democratic control to introduce unpopular policies that produce short-term pains and long-term gains. Good autocracy is a 'selectorate' where incumbents can be changed if they do not work well (Besley and Kudumatsu 1998). Britain in the eighteenth century and China today might be so classified, but African dictatorships and North Korea are at the other end of the spectrum. East Asian selectorates after 1945 might include Indonesia, Singapore, South Korea, Taiwan, and Thailand. Poland and Romania performed tolerably under communism (until the 1980s), and Spain under Franco or Chile under Pinochet also experienced rapid economic growth. These regimes show that market competition can be promoted while maintaining autocratic control, though, most of them, unlike China, have become democratic since becoming wealthier.

Extractive African institutions were poor at providing public goods, but adept at siphoning off state revenues for elites, and post-independence autocracies were little better (or even worse) than some colonial governments (Acemoglu and Robinson 2012). From the 1980s, more pro-market structural adjustments were introduced. The erratic economic performance

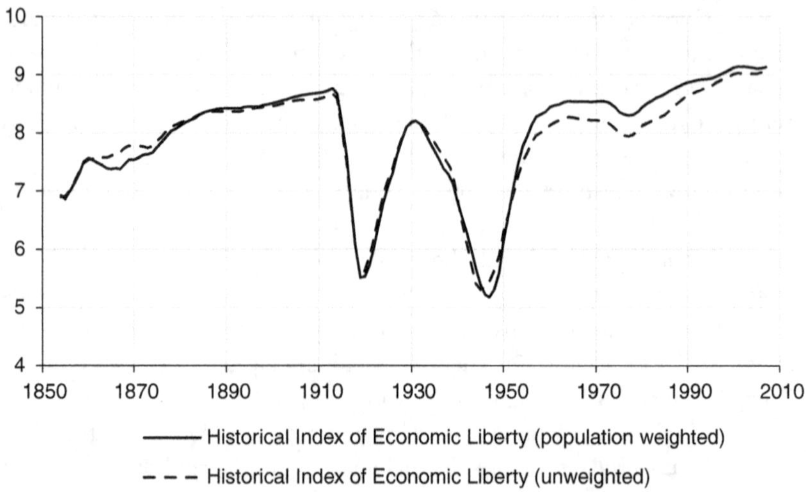

Figure 15.2 Indices of economic liberty in OECD countries, 1870–2007
Sources: Prados de la Escosura 2016, with updated data set at https://espacioinvestiga.org/hiel-eng/?lang=en (accessed 29 September 2020).

of modern Latin America is often attributed to the institutions embedded under the Spanish and Portuguese empires. Governments with limited fiscal capacity failed to deliver public goods and to distribute the costs and benefits of independence equitably (Irigoin 2016). By increasing indirect taxes, debt, and money creation, elite governments transferred fiscal burdens to non-elite constituents or to future generations. Taxpayers favoured a low and regressive taxation. However, Costa Rica shows that persistent effects of poor imperial institutions were not inevitable. From 1890, the country maintained the highest Polity IV democracy score, and is a low crime area with a GDP per head triple that of neighbouring Nicaragua (https://data.worldbank.org/indicator/NY.GDP.PCAP.PP.CD).

Progress towards liberal 'open access' economic policies was undone with trade restrictions and increased government interventions in the 1930s that intensified during World War II, as shown by Figure 15.2. But after 1945 there was a slow reversal, so that the 1913 level was recovered in the 1990s. The indices of Figure 15.2 define economic liberty as where privately owned property is securely protected, contracts are enforced, prices stable, barriers to trade small, and resources are mainly allocated through the market.[11]

11 This definition of liberty might be too negative, excluding positive enablers such as welfare, health, and education spending, which arguably empower the poor more than

These composite, five-year moving average indices show similar trends to an alternative indicator of changes in financial institutions (Rajan and Zingales 2003). An indicator of the number of corporations shows more consistent upward movement, with the notable exceptions of Nazi Germany and communist regimes (Hannah 2015), and, as noted above, post-independence India.

Why were open-access, or inclusive institutions, not more widely adopted? The answer of North et al. (2009) is that elite power would or could have been threatened. Many nineteenth-century elites did not want these institutions at all: in Afghanistan, Thailand, and Ethiopia, they did not believe that aping successful Western economies was good for their societies, fearing a loss of national identity, as well as power. After World War II, the success of capitalism induced more emulators, both democratic and autocratic.

Conclusion

By 2000, the most dramatic institutional changes still being digested were in those countries that had made a transition from one political party controlling a centralized, state-owned, planned economy to a market economy[12] with an open-access democratic political system. India's recent history broadly fits this transition, and the end of European communism is also a striking example. Early on, the principal strategic transition options were the 'big bang' and 'gradualism'. Those in favour of gradualist transition urged caution because they recognized the difficulties of creating new institutions and anchoring new patterns of behaviour, while 'big bang' advocates judged that the forces of reaction would lack the time to build up their resistance. Poland was one of the effective states establishing new institutions quickly, while Russia proved to be among the least successful. In Russia, macroeconomic stabilization was jeopardized by failures to collect taxes; industrial restructuring was hamstrung by inadequate legal safeguards for private property; competition policy was blocked by regulatory capture; and development of adequate social safety nets was stillborn. Eventually, Vladimir Putin, a former KGB officer with a populist flair, reasserted the importance of state institutions (or their crony capitalist heirs), while ceasing to respect some democratic norms.

do negative freedoms. This is considered in Prados de la Escosura's (2015) human development index for a wider range of countries.

12 Predominantly privately owned, decentralized, and governed by market mechanisms.

Linear development, or convergence towards open-access societies, cannot be taken for granted; rather, oscillation between limited access and open societies in response to major shocks, such as those of the 1930s, has been the norm. More recently, Venezuela slid from a high level of democracy on the Polity IV measure in the 1970s and 1980s, to almost the lowest level of 'open access' by 2009.[13]

Institutions are usually deeply rooted and highly persistent. But numerous influential human agents have been willing to try to change them, as historical examples from Fukuzawa through Lenin, Hitler, Roosevelt, and Mao to Deng and Thatcher indicate, sometimes with disastrous, sometimes with favourable, consequences. The net result of these and other human agents working against the power of established institutions – good and bad – is that the world is richer and more people have access to open economic and political orders than ever before. Yet many remain without such access and, even in the rich world, there are broader discontents with the inegalitarian or environmental features of the present economic and political order.

Schumpeter (1942) was wrong about the demise of capitalism and democracy. So was Francis Fukuyama (1992), when he prematurely announced the 'End of History', the universalization of liberal democracy as the final form of human government. He underrated the political reaction of groups suffering from globalization (Rodrik 1997; Djankov and Hauck 2016). Liberal democracy is not admired by the Islamic Republic of Iran, the Chinese Communist Party, or the 'Bolivarian' Venezuelan revolution, but their alternatives have so far had limited appeal. The prosperity and freedom open-access orders offer remain the most attractive option for those changing country today, whether refugees (who often have good reason to distrust autocrats) or economic migrants. With German reunification in 1990, barriers between the communist East and the capitalist West were completely dismantled: capital moved east and people moved west, but people won hands down, because it is easier for people to prosper with good institutions. Re-establishing institutions throughout eastern Europe to make capital and democracy prosper was a slower and more difficult, uncertain process: such is the power of institutional conditioning. History suggests that the existence of workably attractive capitalist democracies is unlikely to prevent nationalist, revolutionary, and populist leaders continuing to fashion alternatives, whether by force or by democratic debate.

13 Germany fell from an index number of 6 to 0 between 1932 and 1933; and Venezuela, more recently, declined from 9 to 1. See footnote 9 above for Polity IV ratings.

References

Acemoglu, D. and Robinson, J. R. (2012). *Why Nations Fail: The Origins of Power, Prosperity and Poverty*, New York: Crown.

Alesina, A. and Giuliano, P. (2015). 'Culture and Institutions', *Journal of Economic Literature*, 53, 898–944.

Alston, E., Alston, L. J., Mueller, B., and Nonnenmacher, T. N. (2018). *Institutional and Organizational Analysis: Concepts and Applications*, New York: Cambridge University Press.

Berkowitz, D., Pistor, K., and Richard, J.-F. (2003). 'Economic Development, Legality, and the Transplant Effect', *European Economic Review*, 47, 165–195.

Besley, T. and Kudamatsu, M. (1998). 'Making Autocracy Work', in Helpman, E. (ed.), *Institutions and Economic Performance*, Cambridge, MA: Harvard University Press, 452–510.

Blanchard, O., Froot, K., and Sachs, J. (1994). *The Transition in Eastern Europe*, University of Chicago Press.

Carlin, W. and Mayer, C. (2003). 'Finance, Investment, and Growth', *Journal of Financial Economics*, 69, 191–226.

Coquelin, C. (1864). 'Capital', in Coquelin, C. and Guillaumin, G.-U. (eds.), *Dictionnaire d'Economie Politique, Vol. 1*, Paris: Guillaumin, 273–288.

Davis, C. M. (1999). 'Russia: A Comparative Economic Systems Interpretation', in Foreman-Peck, J. and Federico, G. (eds.), *European Industrial Policy*, Oxford University Press, 319–397.

Djankov, S. and Hauck, O. (2016). 'The Divergent Postcommunist Paths to Democracy and Economic Freedom', Peterson Institute for International Economics working paper 16–10.

Fieldhouse, D. K. (1973). *Economics and Empire, 1830–1914*, Ithaca: Cornell University Press.

Fohlin, C. (2016). 'Financial Systems', in Diebolt, C. and Haupert, M. (eds.), *Handbook of Cliometrics*, Berlin: Springer, 393–430.

Foreman-Peck, J. (1995). *A History of the World Economy since 1850*, New York: Harvester Wheatsheaf, 2nd ed.

Foreman-Peck, J. and Hannah, L. (2015). 'The Diffusion and Impact of the Corporation in 1910', *Economic History Review*, 68, 962–984.

Forsyth, D. J. and Verdier, D. (eds.) (2003). *The Origins of National Financial Systems: Alexander Gerschenkron Reconsidered*, London: Routledge.

Fukuyama, F. (1992). *The End of History and the Last Man*, London: Hamish Hamilton.

Fukuzawa, Y. (1948). *The Autobiography* (trans. E. Kiyooka), Tokyo: Hokuseido Press (original serialized in a Japanese newspaper, 1898–99).

Gancia, G. A., Ponzetto, G. A. M., and Ventura, J. (2016). 'Globalization and Political Structure', CEPR Discussion Paper 11159 (revision issued Sept. 2018), Centre for Economic Policy Research.

Gerschenkron, A. (1962). *Economic Backwardness in Historical Perspective*, Boston, MA: Harvard University Press.

Gregory, P. R. and Stuart, R. C. (1995). *Comparative Economic Systems*, 5th ed., Boston, MA: Houghton Mifflin.

Haber, S., North, D. C., and Weingast, B. R. (2008). *Political Institutions and Financial Development*, Stanford University Press.

Hannah, L. (2014). 'Corporations in the US and Europe 1790–1860', *Business History*, 56, 865–899.

(2015). 'A Global Corporate Census: Publicly Traded and Close Companies in 1910', *Economic History Review*, 68, 548–573.

Hannah, L. and Kasuya, M. (2016). 'Twentieth-Century Enterprise Forms: Japan in Comparative Perspective', *Enterprise and Society*, 17, 80–115.

Harrison, M. (2014). 'Communism and Economic Modernization', in Smith, S. A. (ed.), *The Oxford Handbook of the History of Communism*, Oxford University Press, 387–406.

Irigoin, A. (2016). 'Representation without Taxation, Taxation without Consent: The Legacy of Spanish Colonialism in America', *Revista de Historia Económica*, 34, 169–208.

Joshi, V. (2017). *India's Long Road: The Search for Prosperity*, Oxford University Press.

Kuran, T. (2011). *The Long Divergence: How Islamic Law Held Back the Middle East*, Princeton University Press.

Lamoreaux, N. R. and Wallis, J. J. (eds.) (2017). *Organizations, Civil Society, and the Roots of Development*, Chicago: National Bureau of Economic Research/University of Chicago Press.

Lardy, N. R. (1975). 'Economic Planning in the People's Republic of China: Central-Provincial Fiscal Relations', in US Congress, Joint Economic Committee, *China: A Reassessment of the Economy*, Washington, DC: Government Printing Office, 94–115.

Levine, R. (1997). 'Financial Development and Economic Growth: Views and Agenda', *Journal of Economic Literature*, 35, 688–726.

Maddison, A. (2001). *The World Economy: A Millennial Perspective*, Paris: Organisation for Economic Co-operation and Development.

Marshall, M. G., Gurr, T. R., and Jaggers, K. (2017). *Political Regime Characteristics and Transitions, 1800–2017: Dataset Users' Manual*, Vienna, VA: Center for Systemic Peace.

Marx, K. (1867). *Das Kapital*, Hamburg: Meissner.

Mill, J. S. (1861). *Considerations on Representative Government*, London: Parker, Son and Bourn.

Mulhall, M. G. (1881). *Balance Sheet of the World for Ten Years, 1870–1880*, London: Stanford.

North, D. C. and Thomas, R. P. (1973). *The Rise of the Western World: A New Economic History*, Cambridge University Press.

North, D. C., Wallis, J. J., and Weingast, B. R. (2009). *Violence and Social Orders: A Conceptual Framework for Interpreting Recorded Human History*, New York: Cambridge University Press.

Prados de la Escosura, L. (2015). 'World Human Development: 1870–2007', *Review of Income and Wealth*, 61, 220–247.

(2016). 'Economic Freedom in the Long Run: Evidence from OECD Countries (1850–2007)', *Economic History Review*, 69, 435–468.

Pryor, F. L. (1973). *Property and Industrial Organization in Communist and Capitalist Nations*, Bloomington: Indiana University Press.

Rajan, R. G. and Zingales, L. (2003). 'The Great Reversals: The Politics of Financial Development in the Twentieth Century', *Journal of Financial Economics*, 69, 5–50.

Rodrik, D. (1997). *Has Globalization Gone Too Far?*, Washington, DC: Institute of International Economics.

Roser, M. (2018). 'Democracy', published online at OurWorldInData.org, retrieved from https://ourworldindata.org/democracy (accessed 29 September 2020).
Roy, T. (2018). *A Business History of India*, Cambridge University Press.
Schumpeter, J. A. (1942). *Capitalism, Socialism and Democracy*, New York: Harper.
Stiglitz, J. E. (2003). *Globalization and its Discontents*, London: Penguin.
Tomlinson, B. R. (2013). *The Economy of Modern India from 1860 to the Twenty-First Century*, Cambridge University Press.
Treisman, D. (2017). 'Democracy by Mistake', NBER working paper 23944, National Bureau of Economic Research.
Weber, M. (1930). *The Protestant Ethic and the Spirit of Capitalism* (trans. T. Parsons), London: Allen & Unwin (originally published in German, 1904).
Williamson, O. (1981). 'The Modern Corporation: Origins, Evolution, Attributes', *Journal of Economic Literature*, 19, 1537–1568.
Woytinsky, W. S. and Woytinsky, E. S. (1955). *World Commerce and Governments*, New York: Twentieth Century Fund.

16

Living Standards, Inequality, and Human Development

LEANDRO PRADOS DE LA ESCOSURA AND MYUNG SOO CHA

During the last 150 years, technological development improved living standards, shifted the composition of output, drove globalization, and also changed relative factor returns and hence income distribution. These changes occurred in parallel with the improvement in well-being, which depended on health, education, political and civil liberties, the environment, leisure, and security, as well as the consumption of goods and services.

How much have living standards improved, and how equally have the fruits of economic growth been distributed among different income groups since 1870? How did different regions of the world perform in terms of raising income and improving welfare? Did high-income countries (western Europe, its offshoots, and Japan), referred to as 'the West' hereafter, do better vis-à-vis the developing countries, 'the Rest' hereafter?

In this chapter, we focus on three issues. First, we look at the average improvement in material welfare, as captured by per capita GDP and consumption. Then we discuss the extent to which the less affluent members of different countries benefited from economic growth and how income inequality affected welfare. Lastly, we look beyond GDP to examine human development, which includes achievements in education and health.

GDP and Consumption

Per capita GDP is one of the most commonly used measures of living standards. Comparing per capita GDP of different countries converted into a common currency unit (say, the US dollar) using market exchange rates usually provides misleading pictures of inter-country income gaps, because

We have benefited from comments and suggestions by the editors and participants in preparatory conferences at Oxford and Tokyo. Branko Milanovic kindly provided his latest estimates on global inequality.

the procedure does not take into account international differences in price levels.

Correcting for cross-country price gaps, known as purchasing power parity (PPP) adjustment, is no straightforward undertaking, because it involves the painstaking collection of price information for a large number of goods and services in different countries. The comparative assessment of growth performance is an even more daunting task because it requires estimating cross-country price gaps in more than one year. For this reason, to construct a panel data set showing how per capita GDP in different countries evolved over time, Angus Maddison (2006) resorted to a shortcut, which was to project backwards and forwards the PPP-adjusted per capita output for 1990 (expressed as 1990 international $ hereafter), using growth rates derived from historical per capita GDP series for individual countries.

This procedure is based on the assumption that the relative prices prevailing within the basket of goods and services used to construct the PPP for 1990 are applicable to non-benchmark years, which may be harmless for short periods, but introduces serious distortions over a century and a half.[1] Despite the biases caused by shifts in relative prices over time, Maddison's database has been used in numerous studies exploring the causes of economic development and growth. The following paragraphs outline the growth performance of different regions in the past 150 years, as suggested by the Maddison Project Database, 2013 version.

In 2015, the world average per capita income was nearly ten times higher than in 1870. Over the past 150 years, per capita output grew at widely different rates in different parts of the world, as indicated by the thirty-fold increase in Japan, the fifteen-fold increase in the European offshoots and China, and the threefold increase in sub-Saharan Africa. Between 1870 and 2015, per capita output grew fivefold in North Africa, eightfold in India and eastern Europe, and twelve-fold in Russia. Per capita output growth in Latin America, the rest of Asia outside China and Japan, and western Europe roughly matched the world average (Table 16.1).

The average world per capita output grew faster in some periods than in others, with per capita output growth falling below the growth trend rate during 1870–2015 (1.6 per cent) during the first half of the twentieth century, in the wake of the world wars and the Depression (0.9 per cent), rising above the trend growth rate in 'the Golden Age of Capitalism' (1950–70) (2.9 per cent),

1 See the discussion in Prados de la Escosura (2000). For an illustration of the index number problem, see Fukao et al.'s (2006) comparison of Japan, Korea, and Taiwan in the early twentieth century.

Table 16.1 Real GDP per head: levels (1990 international $) and annual growth rates (% per annum), world regions, 1870–2015

	Western offshoots	Western Europe	Eastern Europe	Russia	Latin America	North Africa	Sub-Saharan Africa	Japan	China	India	Rest of Asia	World
Real GDP per head (1990 international $)												
1870	2,126	1,970	1,033	762	800	740	558	737	505	533	636	853
1913	5,142	3,435	1,847	1,422	1,507	1,021	674	1,387	464	673	921	1,491
1929	6,551	3,995	2,116	1,386	1,921	1,101	687	2,026	473	728	1,142	1,743
1950	9,456	4,272	2,300	2,841	2,452	1,133	825	1,921	376	619	924	2,099
1970	14,613	9,646	4,696	5,575	3,935	1,803	1,233	9,714	776	868	1,781	3,736
1990	22,353	15,464	5,903	7,779	5,086	2,705	1,129	18,789	1,448	1,309	3,251	5,060
2015	31,840	20,728	8,746	9,222	7,630	4,289	1,779	22,791	7,582	4,332	6,480	8,301
Real GDP per head (annual % growth)												
1870–1913	2.1	1.3	1.4	1.5	1.5	0.8	0.4	1.5	−0.2	0.5	0.9	1.3
1913–50	1.6	0.6	0.6	1.9	1.3	0.3	0.5	0.9	−0.6	−0.2	0.0	0.9
1950–70	2.2	4.1	3.6	3.4	2.4	2.3	2.0	8.1	3.6	1.7	3.3	2.9
1970–90	2.1	2.4	1.1	1.7	1.3	2.0	−0.4	3.3	3.1	2.1	3.0	1.5
1990–2015	1.4	1.2	1.6	0.7	1.6	1.8	1.8	0.8	6.6	4.8	2.8	2.0
1870–2015	1.9	1.6	1.5	1.7	1.6	1.2	0.8	2.4	1.9	1.4	1.6	1.6

Source: Maddison Project Database, 2013 version.

Table 16.2 Real per capita consumption and GDP growth (%)

	1870–2006		1913–2006		1950–2006	
	GDP	Consumption	GDP	Consumption	GDP	Consumption
Latin America	–	–	1.8	1.7	1.8	1.6
Western offshoots	2.0	1.8	1.9	1.7	1.9	2.0
Europe	1.8	1.6	2.1	1.9	2.8	2.6
Asia	–	–	3.2	2.5	3.5	2.9
South Africa	–	–	–	–	1.2	1.4

Source: Barro and Ursúa 2008.

and then converging to the trend growth rate in the last half-century (1.8 per cent during 1970–2015).

Furthermore, the pattern of comparative growth differed depending on period. During the first wave of globalization (1870–1913), the US thrived, China suffered stagnation, and India and sub-Saharan Africa achieved sluggish growth, with Europe (including Russia) and Latin America growing at rates close to the world average. During the first half of the twentieth century, the Soviet Union achieved a remarkable advance, and the European offshoots made respectable progress, which was followed not far behind by Latin America's performance. The average income growth in Europe, Africa, and Asia (China in particular) was below the world average, with the exception of Japan, where income grew in the first half of the twentieth century at a rate close to the world average. In the Golden Age (1950–70), both western Europe and Japan far outperformed the rest of the world, and socialist eastern Europe, China, and the rest of Asia (less India) also did better than the world average. Although world income growth slowed down considerably after 1970, Asia, and particularly India and China, forged ahead, while sub-Saharan Africa and Russia fell behind.

How did these gains in average incomes translate into improvements in living conditions? Although a straightforward way of answering this question is to look at consumption, unfortunately, the available evidence on per capita consumption mostly refers to present-day developed countries. Robert Barro and José Ursúa's (2008) data set allows one to compare trends in real per capita GDP and private consumption across world regions. As Table 16.2 shows, private consumption per person improved less rapidly than per capita income. The difference reflects the faster growth of other demand components of GDP, capital formation and public consumption, in particular.

However, per capita consumption likely increased more rapidly than the Barro and Ursúa data set suggests, because more and more of the goods and services that used to be privately supplied (education, health, and so on) came to be provided by the government. As an increasing number of countries made the transition to democracy, fiscal redistribution took place in the form of tax-based social transfers, which included assistance for poor families, unemployment compensation, public non-contributory pensions, housing subsidies, and public health expenditures (Lindert 2004).

Although an international and historical database on private and public consumption is unavailable, we may draw on the systematic variations in the composition of aggregate demand associated with rising levels of per capita income to infer how private and public consumption evolved over time. Panel A of Table 16.3 shows that as per capita income rose from 1990 international $1,000 to $12,000 in European countries during the late nineteenth and twentieth centuries, the share of private and government consumption in GDP trended in opposite directions, with the share of private consumption shrinking by 27 percentage points of GDP (from 87.7 per cent to 60.4 per cent) and the share of public consumption expanding by 11 percentage points (from 5.8 per cent to 16.7 per cent).[2] As a result, the share of total consumption (including both private and public) shrank only by 16, rather than 27, percentage points, from 93.5 per cent to 77.1 per cent of GDP. Meanwhile, capital formation raised its share significantly (from 8.3 per cent to 23.0 per cent), suggesting the presence of powerful incentives to sacrifice present-day consumption in order to achieve higher levels in the future.

Panel B of Table 16.3 compares the composition of aggregate demand in pre-World War I Europe and the developing world during the Golden Age, which were estimated, respectively, by Prados de la Escosura (2007) and Hollis Chenery and Moshe Syrquin (1975). Within the 1990 international $1,000–4,000 income range, which corresponds to average world income between the late nineteenth and mid-twentieth centuries, overall consumption, including both private and public consumption, accounted for a larger part of the aggregate output in pre-1914 Europe than in the post-1950 developing world, because the smaller share of public consumption was more than offset by the smaller share of investment in pre-1914 Europe.

2 Public consumption includes national defence expenditure, which does not necessarily increase welfare.

Table 16.3 Patterns of development

A. Modern Europe

Panel A. Modern Europe	1000	2000	3000	4000	6000	8000	10000	12000
Demand (% GDP)								
Private consumption	87.7	80.1	75.7	72.5	68	64.9	62.4	60.4
Government consumption	5.8	8.8	10.6	11.9	13.7	14.9	15.9	16.7
Total consumption	93.5	88.9	86.3	84.4	81.7	79.8	78.3	77.1
Investment	8.3	12.4	14.8	16.5	18.9	20.6	21.9	23.0

B. Pre-1914 Europe and Golden Age

Private consumption (% GDP)				
Modern Europe (1850–1990)	87.7	80.1	75.7	72.5
Pre-World War I Europe	84.7	82.0	80.5	79.4
Developing countries (1950–70)	66.7	64.5	62.5	61.7
Public consumption (% GDP)				
Modern Europe (1850–1990)	5.8	8.8	10.6	11.9
Pre-World War I Europe	6.2	6.9	7.3	7.6
Developing countries (1950–70)	13.5	13.8	14.4	14.8
Total consumption (% GDP)				
Modern Europe (1850–1990)	93.5	88.9	86.3	84.4
Pre-World War I Europe	90.9	88.9	87.8	87.0
Developing countries (1950–70)	80.2	78.3	76.9	76.5
Investment (% GDP)				
Modern Europe (1850–1990)	8.3	12.4	14.8	16.5
Pre-World War I Europe	8.8	11.1	12.4	13.3
Developing countries (1950–70)	19.0	21.0	22.6	23.3

Sources: Prados de la Escosura 2007; Chenery and Syrquin 1975.

In short, over the course of the past 150 years, per capita real output growth translated into less than proportional improvements in per capita private and public consumption, and the gap between per capita output growth and per capita private consumption growth widened over time.

Finally, the composition of consumer expenditure shifted dramatically as a result of technological progress, a more assertive role of government, and higher average income. In the United States, for example, between 1869 and 2013, the share of perishable goods (including food, beverages, tobacco, printed material, and fuel) in consumer expenditure declined from one-half to one-tenth, while the share of services jumped from one-quarter to two-thirds. Moreover, in 2013, spending on categories that did not exist in 1869 (recreation, motor vehicles, appliances, communication, education) represented more than half of all consumer expenditure (Gordon 2016: 38–39).

Living Standards at the Bottom

Referring to averages, per capita consumption or output is mute about the welfare of those at the bottom of the income distribution. How did the lower income groups fare as different countries of the world were successively engulfed by the waves of industrialization and globalization?

Real wages of unskilled workers – that is, nominal wages divided by a consumer price index (CPI) – are the standard measure of the living standards enjoyed by the poor. Real wage indices typically do not tell how well-off workers are, but whether their living standards have improved or deteriorated. Welfare ratios, derived by dividing 'average annual earnings . . . by the cost of a poverty line consumption bundle for a family' (Allen 2001: 425), provide information on the levels as well as the changes in workers' material well-being. Specifically, welfare ratios exceeding 1 indicate income levels allowing consumption above the poverty line, and those below 1 unsustainably low living standards.[3] Hence, one can compare welfare ratios across different places as well as over time.

Welfare ratios can be calculated using a relatively limited amount of information, which includes nominal wage rates and prices of goods comprising a consumption basket required for subsistence. To derive historical welfare ratios in Europe, Robert Allen (2001: 245) supposed that an adult worked 250 days per year to support a family of two adults and two children, an assumption that became standard in subsequent studies estimating welfare ratios in the rest of the world. Welfare ratios are usually calculated using nominal wages observed in urban areas, where unskilled workers may have worked as many as 250 days per year. In the countryside, however, a typical work year was likely to have been considerably shorter, and significant nominal urban-rural wage gaps existed, especially outside Europe and its offshoots (Heldring and Robinson 2012). All this implies that the welfare ratios derived following Allen's (2001) procedure are likely to overestimate workers' living standards.

3 Allen et al. (2011) refined Allen's metric distinguishing between 'barebones' and 'respectability' baskets, with the cost of the barebones basket defining an absolute poverty line.

Table 16.4 reproduces and summarizes the welfare ratios estimated for different countries between the mid-nineteenth and mid-twentieth centuries. Welfare ratios more than doubled from about 2 to nearly 6 in the Netherlands (Amsterdam) and Germany (Leipzig) from 1870 to 1913, while in Britain (London) the ratio, already as high as 4 in 1870, achieved a twofold increase (Allen et al. 2011). In Austria-Hungary, between the mid-nineteenth century and the eve of World War I, welfare ratios improved in the western regions (present-day Austria and Czechia), but remained stagnant in the eastern regions (including present-day Slovakia, Hungary, Croatia, Slovenia, and Romania) (Cvrcek 2013).

Meanwhile, in the Americas, welfare ratios rose from below 2 in the mid-nineteenth century to above 5 in the early twentieth century in the United States (Philadelphia) (Allen 2014), while in Mexico (Mexico City), the welfare ratio increased moderately from the 1870s to 1930, despite the setback during the revolutionary 1910s (Challú and Gómez-Galvarriato 2015).

In Asia, including Japan (Kyoto/Tokyo), China (Beijing, Canton, Suzhou/Shanghai), India (Bengal), and Turkey (Istanbul), welfare ratios, remaining above the subsistence level, tended to rise during 1870–1913 (Allen 2007; Allen et al. 2011; Caruana-Galizia 2015). In Istanbul, welfare ratios increased by 60 per cent between the 1860s and the eve of World War I, but stagnated around the subsistence level in Egypt.[4]

In the early twentieth century, welfare ratios exceeded unity in East Asia, as shown by the evidence gathered on main cities in China (Beijing), Taiwan (Taipei), Korea (Seoul), and, especially, Manchuria (Dalian) (Cha 2015). Between 1900 and 1938, welfare ratios grew only in Japan, stagnating in Korea and Taiwan, and declining in China and Manchuria (Cha 2015). On the eve of World War II, welfare ratios in Japanese cities were above 2, with those in Taiwan and Manchurian cities staying not far behind, but the stagnant welfare ratio of unskilled workers in Korean cities did not differ significantly from the level of subsistence.

Turning to sub-Saharan Africa, welfare ratios exceeded subsistence levels in Natal and the Cape Colony for both white and black workers, while in Natal, native workers were below the subsistence level until the 1880s (de Zwart 2011). White labourers enjoyed improvement in living standards over time, while real wages of black workers stagnated, which resulted in widening income differentials across racial lines. The living standards of natives also improved over

4 Özmucur and Pamuk (2002); Allen (2014). In Istanbul, the welfare ratio rose by 15 per cent between the 1820s and 1914, because most of the 60 per cent represented a recovery after the early nineteenth century decline (Özmucur and Pamuk 2002).

Table 16.4 Welfare ratios: a global view

	1850s	1860s	1870s	1880s	1890s	1900s	1910–13	1910s	1920s	1930s	1940s	1950s	1960–65
EUROPE													
Amsterdam	2.4	2.1	2.2	2.8	3.5	4.7	5.5						
London	4.5	4.8	5.3	6.4	7.6	7.4	8.1						
Leipzig	2.3	2.6	2.4	3.3	4.5	4.4	5.8						
Milan	0.8	1.0	1.1	1.3	1.6	1.3	1.9						
LATIN AMERICA													
Mexico City	2.1	1.9	2.5	2.6	2.1	2.5	2.4	1.9	2.9				
ASIA													
China								1.3	1.2				
Japan								1.5	2.2	2.3			
Korea								1.3	1.5	1.4			
Taiwan								1.6	1.9	1.7			
Calcutta/Bengal				1.3	1.8	1.4	1.5						
Istanbul	3.4	2.9		3.0	3.4	3.9	3.9	4.4					
Cyprus				2.9	2.5	2.0	1.7						
AFRICA													
South Africa													
Cape Colony													
European	3.8	3.7	4.3	4.4	4.4	5.8	5.4						
Black	2.5	2.4	2.8	2.4	2.1	2.8							
Nyasaland						0.5	0.7	0.7	0.7	1.2	1.0	1.3	1.4

West Africa										
Gold Coast	1.9	2.2	2.4	2.4	2.4	2.6	3.4	3.1	4.1	5.1
Sierra Leone	1.5	1.8	1.9	1.9	1.4	1.2	1.8	1.6	2.4	3.1
Nigeria	2.1	2.8	3.0	2.6	2.3	1.9	2.2	1.9	2.0	2.3
The Gambia	2.5	2.7	2.8			1.6	2.4	2.0	2.6	4.3
East Africa										
Tanganyika						2.0	1.4	1.1	1.6	2.7
Kenya			1.3	1.3	1.2	1.0	1.1	1.3	1.7	2.2
Mauritius	1.4	2.1	2.2	1.9	1.8	3.3	3.4	2.5	3.7	4.5
Uganda			1.1	0.7	1.0	1.6	1.6	0.9	1.1	

Sources: Allen et al. 2011; de Zwart 2011; Frankema and van Waijenburg 2012; Caruana-Galizia 2015; Cha 2015; Challú and Gómez-Galvarriato 2015.

time to reach the subsistence level by the end of the nineteenth century. White workers enjoyed similar levels of welfare ratio to those prevailing in western Europe, and black labourers fared better than Asian workers.

Ewout Frankema and Marlous van Waijenburg (2012) studied living standards in nine countries in British Africa from 1880 to the early 1960s.[5] Their results suggest that unskilled urban workers enjoyed a level of consumption well above the subsistence level already during 1880–1914, except in Nyasaland (present-day Malawi). It is worth noting that welfare ratios were significantly higher in West than in East Africa. In the interwar period, long-term improvement took place across the board, although more slowly in East than in West Africa. Lastly, Dácil Juif and Ewout Frankema (2018) show remarkable improvements occurring in Katanga (Congo) and Northern Rhodesia (Zambia), where miners moved from around subsistence in the early 1920s to welfare ratios of 7–8 by the late 1950s, but these levels were exceptionally high among African workers.

To sum up, welfare ratios increased in most places from the late nineteenth to the early twentieth centuries, and around 1913, unskilled workers' living standards were often above the 'poverty line' (Table 16.4).

While existing welfare ratio estimates typically refer to the pre-World War II era, standard real wage indices exist for unskilled workers during the post-1945 period. Figure 16.1 plots the annual growth rate of unskilled real wages (Y-axis) against per capita output growth (X-axis) in twenty-six countries in the Americas, Australasia, and Europe. Real wage growth typically refers to the period 1870–1988 for the West, and 1900–2000 for the Rest. On average, real wages grew by 1.4 per cent per year, with growth taking place more rapidly in East Asia than in Latin America. Per capita output growth achieved by the twenty-six countries is positively correlated with unskilled real wage growth. Except for Britain, Denmark, Ireland, and Sweden, the data points lie below the 45 degrees line (broken line) from the origin, suggesting that lower income groups benefited less from the economic growth occurring in the past century and a half than did higher income groups. The differential growth in unskilled real wages and per capita output is also indicated by the slope of the regression line (dotted line), showing that a 1 percentage point increase in per capita output growth was associated with a 0.59 percentage point increase in unskilled real wages.

From 1870 to 2000, the number of hours worked per employee fell from over 3,000 to roughly 1,500 in Europe, and from slightly less than 3,000 to 1,800 in

5 The welfare ratios for sub-Saharan Africa have been computed by assuming 312 working days per year, rather than the standard 250 days. As Juif and Frankema (2018) point out, 312 working days refer to regular workers, while temporary migrants usually worked below 200 days per year.

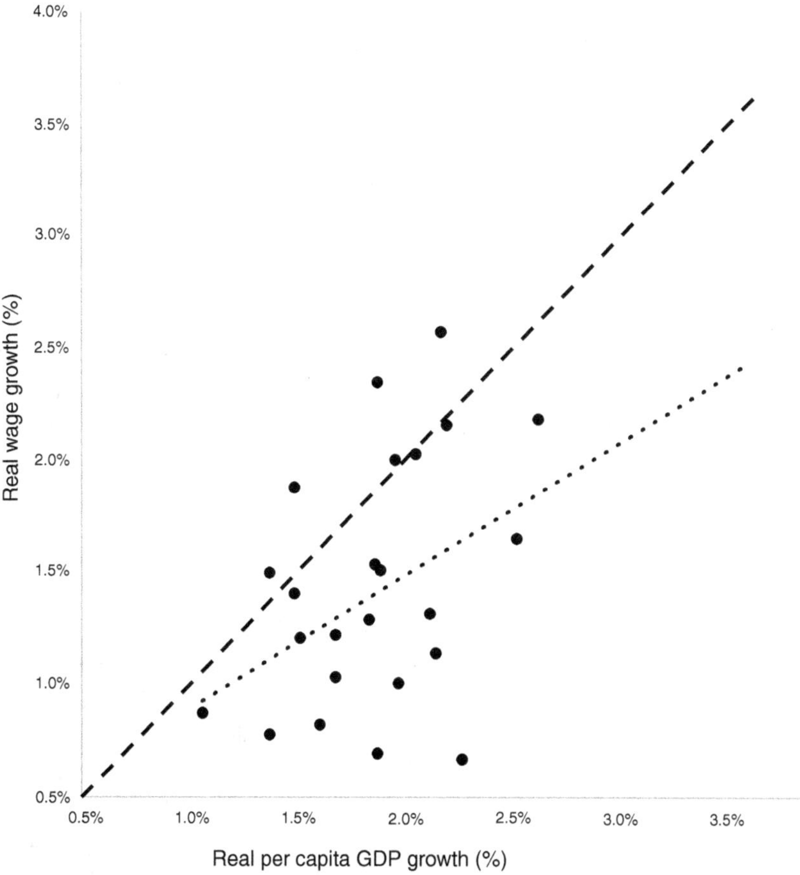

Figure 16.1 Per capita GDP and real wage growth (%)
Notes: The dashed line is the 45 degrees line indicating equal growth of real wages and real per capita GDP. The dotted line is the line of best fit showing the association between the growth of real wages and real GDP per capita.
Sources: Bank of Japan 1966; Ohkawa 1968; Japan Statistical Association 1987/1988; Williamson 1995; Mizoguchi 2008; Maddison Project Database, 2013 version; Cha 2014; Makino and Minami 2015; Astorga 2017.

North America and Oceania (Huberman and Minns 2007). In East Asia, working hours declined from 3,200 in 1930 to 2,000 in 2015 in Japan, from 3,225 to 2,216 in Taiwan during 1950–2001, and from 2,470 to 2,267 in South Korea during 1963–2015.[6] Working hours contracted in Latin America as well. In 1950, the

6 The sources for Japan, Korea, and Taiwan, respectively, are from Japan Statistical Association (1987/1988), and Mizoguchi 2008.

number of working hours was about 2,000 in Argentina and Brazil, 2,400 in Mexico, and 2,700 in Chile, which fell to 1,700 in Argentina and Brazil, and 2,000 and 2,200 in Chile and Mexico, respectively, by 2015 (Conference Board 2018). Since some of the real wage growth rates in Figure 16.1 are based on hourly or daily wage rates, but others refer to wage earnings per month or year, the reduction in working hours implies that the gap between per capita output and annual wage earnings growth would have been wider than suggested by the slope of the regression line in Figure 16.1.

Different trends in real wages and real incomes per head are anything but puzzling, as they refer to different types of income: while per capita GDP is based on the returns to all factors of production (including physical and human capital, natural resources, and raw labour), unskilled wages represent the rewards for raw labour. Thus, the gap between per capita output and unskilled real wage growth, as seen in Figure 16.1, suggests changes occurring in the distribution of income over the past century.

Inequality

While the Gini coefficient represents one of the best-known and most comprehensive measures of income inequality, it has been computed for only a limited number of countries and usually for a relatively recent period. Hence, we begin by presenting the somewhat more abundantly available evidence on the concentration of income at the top of the distribution, to compare income inequality across countries and to track changes in income inequality over time.

Pioneered by Simon Kuznets (1953), the estimation of top income shares has been carried out in an increasingly refined way, for an increasingly large number of countries, by Tony Atkinson and Thomas Piketty, and their collaborators, over the last two decades. Income tax returns data are essential for the calculation, which means that long-run estimates of top income shares are available typically for OECD countries. Available estimates, typically beginning from 1913 and presented as Figure 16.2, suggest: 1) a drop in income concentration in the early twentieth century, a development known as the Great Levelling, which was not reversed after World War II; and 2) the resurgence of income inequality after 1980, particularly in Anglo-Saxon countries (Figure 16.2A).

Figure 16.3 presents the Gini coefficients for seven rich countries from the late nineteenth to the early twenty-first century. They convey the impression of income inequality first rising and then falling, which confirms the hypothesis known as the Kuznets curve. Studies on income inequality in the

Figure 16.2 Top 1 per cent share in total before tax income in OECD and in the Rest. A: Anglo-Saxon countries. B: Other OECD countries. C: The Rest

Sources: World Inequality Database (WID), http://wid.world/es/series/ (accessed 29 September 2020).

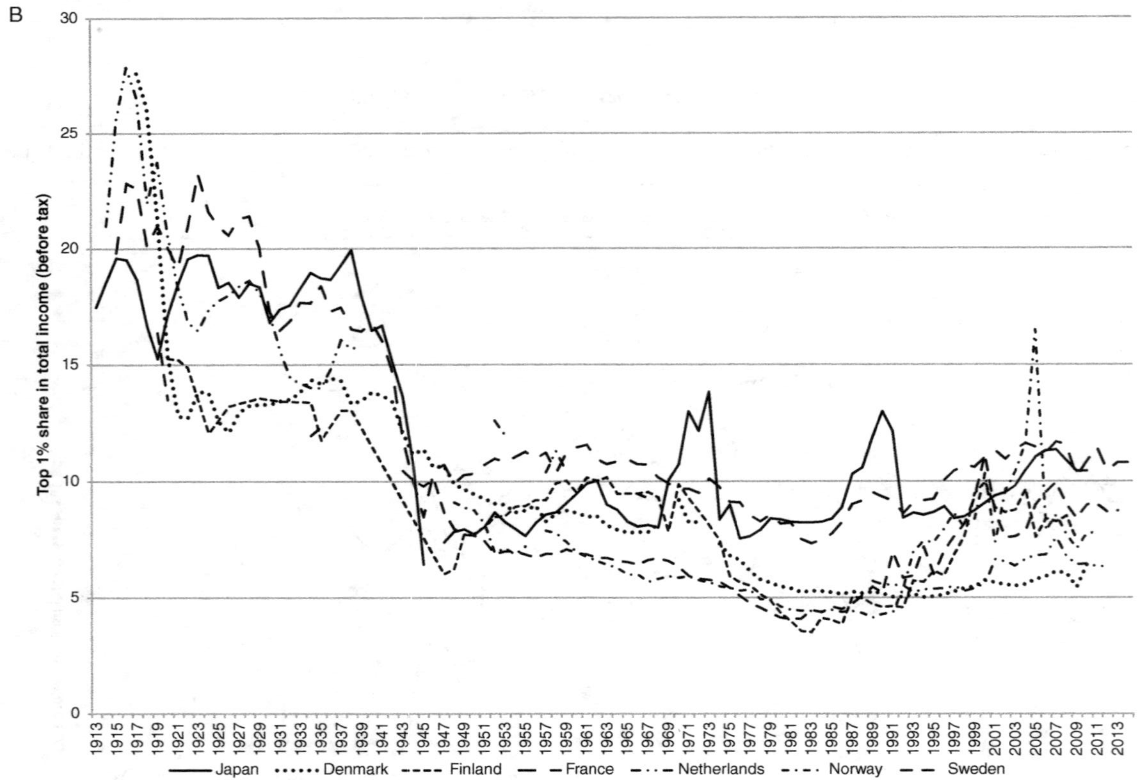

Figure 16.2 (cont.)

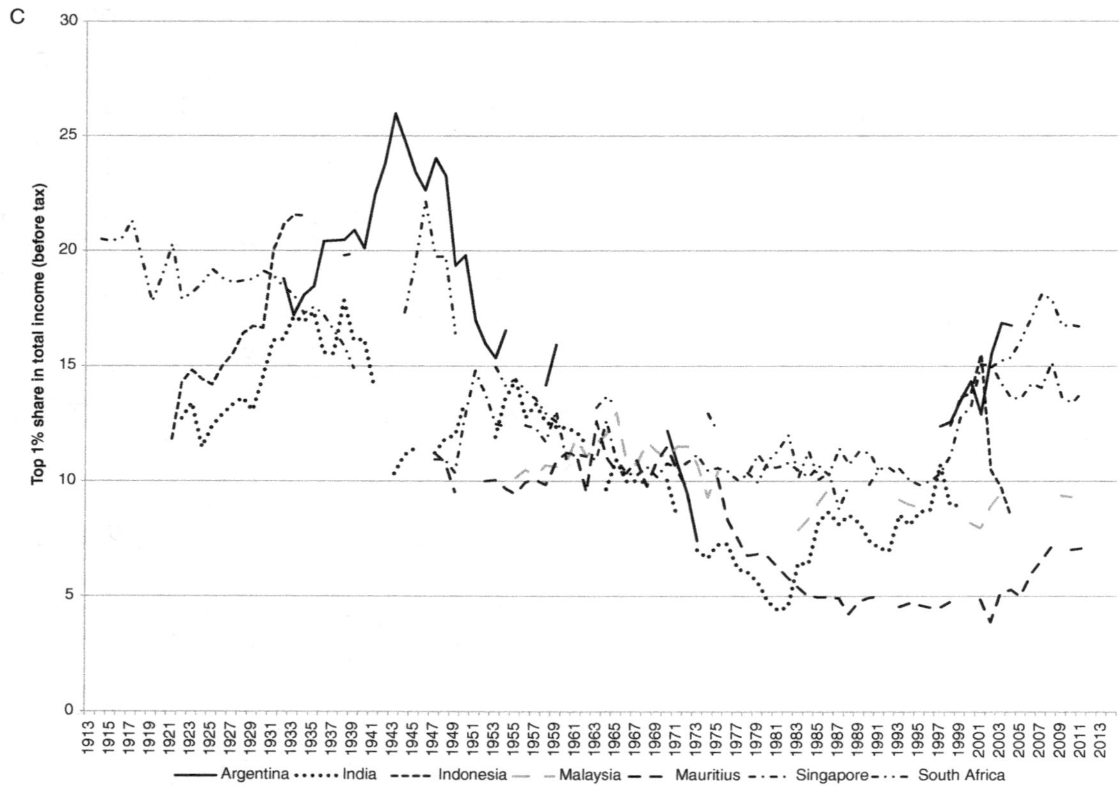

Figure 16.2 (cont.)

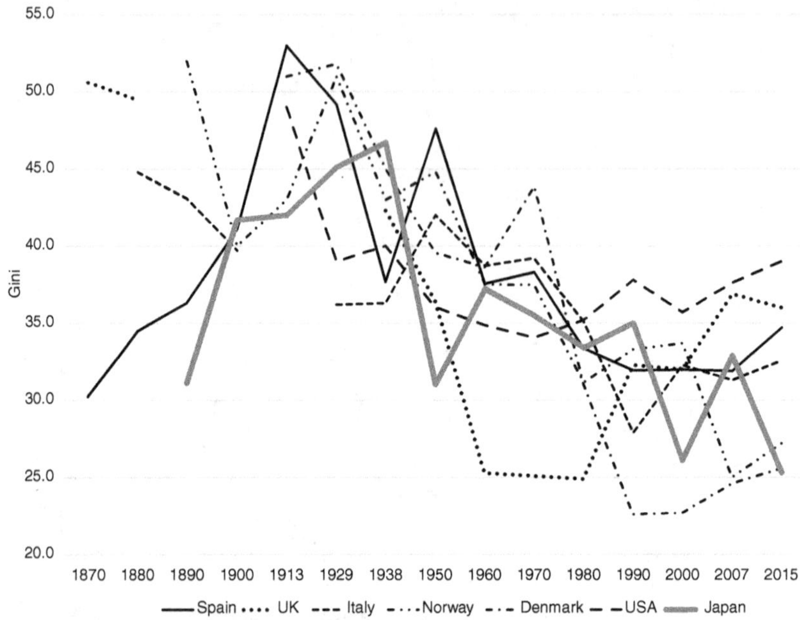

Figure 16.3 Income inequality in OECD countries, 1870–2015 (Gini)
Sources: Prados de la Escosura 2008; OECD 2019.

Kuznetsian tradition explain inequality in terms of economic forces, such as the supply of and demand for skilled labour. Kuznets (1955) posited an inverted U-shape association between income inequality and the level of per capita income, the so-called Kuznets curve. Kuznets (1955) explained the non-linear relationship in terms of widening and then narrowing of the skill premium, which depends on the supply of and demand for skills.

As Branko Milanovic (2016) observed, the two separate measures of income inequality are broadly consistent with each other in the sense that the falling top income share in the early twentieth century corresponded with the downswing in the Gini coefficient, and that indications are found of the Gini rising in recent decades.

Nevertheless, it should be noted that the two measures look at different parts of the distribution. The Gini focuses on the middle (mode) and excludes the very top and bottom of the distribution, while the top income share is mute about the middle and the bottom of the distribution. In addition, the two measures are affected in different degrees by tax evasion and by the fact that only a very small fraction of the population was subjected to income taxation in many countries prior to the mid-twentieth century. It makes sense, therefore, that the trends seen in Figures 16.2 and 16.3 do not match perfectly.

The recent rise in income inequality, particularly in high-income countries, has been accounted for by skill-biased technological change expanding the demand for skilled workers and widening the earning gap between skilled and unskilled workers (Goldin and Katz 2008; Kaplan and Rauh 2013). This development was reinforced by globalization lowering the price of capital goods and thereby encouraging the substitution of capital goods for unskilled labour (Milanovic 2016).

Studies focusing on top income shares, however, tend to highlight politics as the driver of income inequality. In this interpretation, the decline of income concentration between 1913 and 1950 is accounted for by a fall in top capital incomes due to wealth destruction, inflation, bankruptcy, and policies to finance war debts. Additionally, progressive income and estate taxation, which was introduced to a great extent under the communist threat and under the pressure coming from trade unions and left-wing parties, not only prevented the inequality contraction from being reversed, but also speeded up the decline in top income shares in the post-World War II era. In the last decades of the twentieth century, when the Soviet threat was over, economic liberalization caused the concentration of income at the top of the distribution by favouring property and high salary income earners.[7]

Is the post-1980 increase in inequality primarily due to politics and rent-seeking? Or is it due to supply and demand interaction between technology and education? Do higher incomes of the top 1 per cent reflect market imperfections or higher productivity? As the comparison of Figures 16.2A and 16.2B shows, the top income shares rose irrespective of whether or not a country underwent the political and policy shocks as highlighted by the political explanation, which suggests that technological progress and globalization should be an essential part of any account of the recent rise in income inequality.

The long-run evidence on interpersonal income inequality, mostly for Europe and its offshoots, tends to suggest that the level of income inequality today is roughly comparable to that in the mid-nineteenth century, even though some world regions (Latin America, sub-Saharan Africa) have not experienced the

7 The proponents of the political explanation emphasize tax cuts, deregulation, liberalization of capital markets, and privatization as the main causes of rising inequality in the US and the UK since the 1980s (Alvaredo et al. 2013). Furthermore, new executive remuneration policies raised political pressure for cutting top taxes (Atkinson et al. 2011).

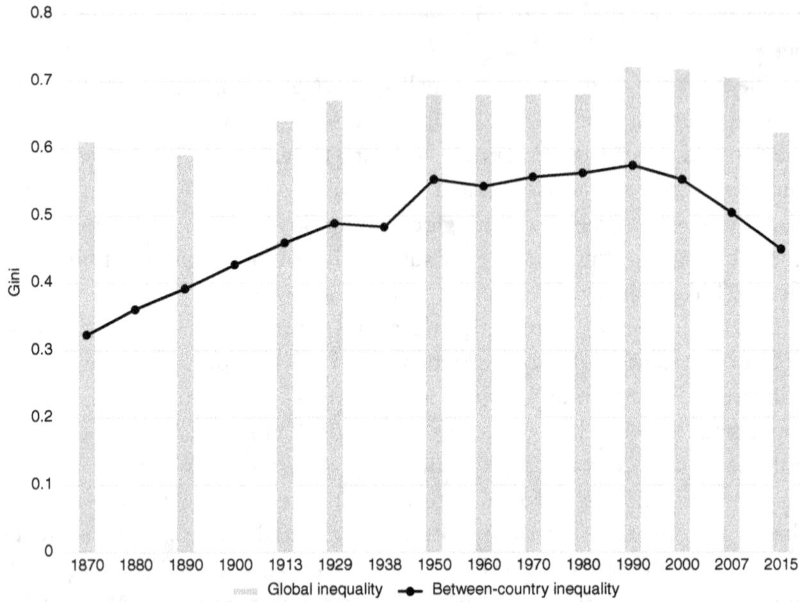

Figure 16.4 Global and between-countries income inequality, 1870–2015 (Gini)
Note: Although van Zanden et al. 2014 also provide global inequality estimates derived from per capita GDP at 1990 international $, we have chosen their estimates with per capita GDP at 2005 international $ to keep consistency with Lakner and Milanovic 2016 estimates.
Sources: Between-countries inequality (1990 international $): Prados de la Escosura 2018; global inequality (PPP 2005 $): van Zanden et al. 2014 (pre-1990) and Lakner and Milanovic 2016 (post-1990).

sharp decline in within-country inequality that we find in the West. If within-country inequality typically remained trendless over the long run (Ravallion 2018), it follows that global income equality, which is the sum of within- and between-country inequality, would have followed the trend in between-country inequality. Using 1990 international $ per capita GDP, Prados de la Escosura (2018) calculated between-country inequality (that is, population-weighted income dispersion among countries in the world), which tended to rise from 1870 to 1990 and then fell. These trends are consistent with the estimates of global income inequality, which first rose from the early nineteenth century to the mid-twentieth century, then stabilized during the second half of the century (van Zanden et al. 2014), and finally declined slightly from 1990 (Lakner and Milanovic 2016). Figure 16.4 confirms that global and between-country inequalities exhibit a common trend, and that the latter has been the main driver of global dispersion of world citizens' incomes over the last century and a half.

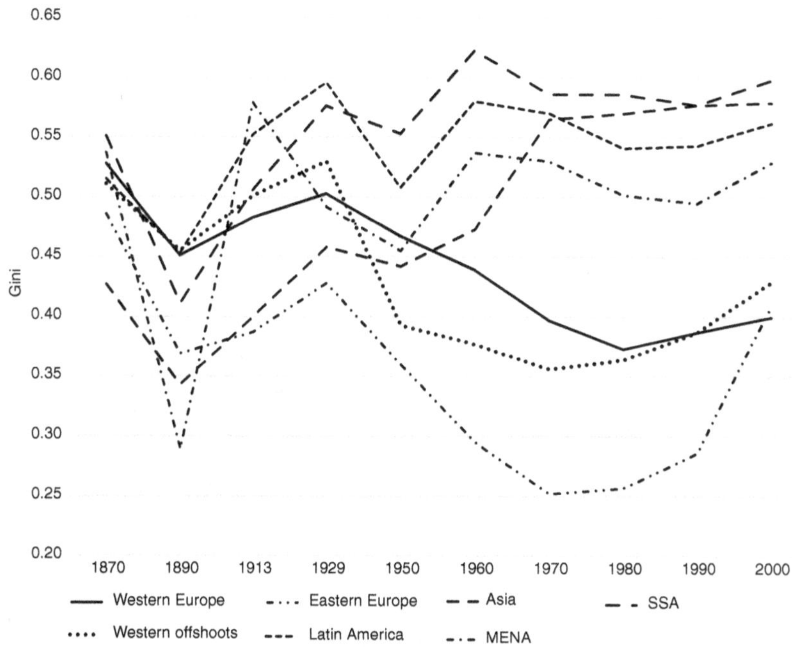

Figure 16.5 Income inequality in world regions, 1870–2000 (1990 international $) (Gini)
Note: MENA: Middle East and North Africa; SSA: sub-Saharan Africa.
Source: van Zanden et al. 2014.

As van Zanden et al. (2014) show, income inequality trended in different ways in different world regions. Figure 16.5 shows that income inequality peaked in 1929 in all regions (no data are available for the 1930s and 1940s). World regions parted ways in the subsequent decades. In Europe and its offshoots, inequality declined to a trough in 1970 (1980 for western Europe) and increased from around 1980, especially in eastern Europe. In the rest of the world, after a contraction during the Depression and World War II, inequality surged in the 1950s, reaching a plateau that stabilized in the second half of the century. Peaking in 1970, inequality subsequently stabilized in Asia.

Branko Milanovic's inequality extraction ratio (IER) is an alternative measure of income inequality. The IER measures the distance from a country's inequality to the inequality possibility frontier, namely, 'the maximum Gini that is achievable at a given level of mean income provided that all population but an infinitesimally small elite live at the subsistence minimum' (Milanovic 2011: 501). That is, the IER compares the actual level of

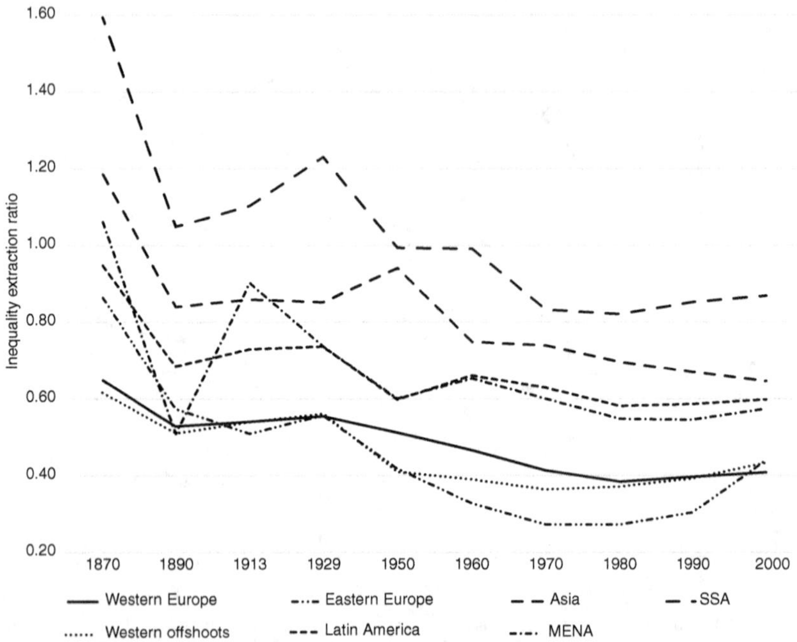

Figure 16.6 Inequality extraction ratio in world regions (1990 international $)

Notes: IER compares the actual level of inequality to the maximum potential inequality. IER = G/G*, where G and G* are observed and maximum feasible Gini. And G* (μ) = (α − 1) / α, where α is the ratio between the mean income (μ) and the subsistence minimum(s) set equal to 1990 international $300. MENA: Middle East and North Africa; SSA: sub-Saharan Africa.

Sources: Observed Gini: van Zanden et al. 2014: maximum potential Gini, G*: derived using data in Maddison Project Database, 2013 version.

inequality to the maximum potential inequality that can be endured without the population starving to death.

Figure 16.6 shows a declining trend in the IER because rising income levels increased the maximum potential inequality. During 1890–1929, the IER rose in different parts of the world, as a joint result of sluggish growth and rising income inequality. These two developments also accounted for the surging IER in eastern Europe and sub-Saharan Africa, and the more moderate rise in Latin America at the end of the twentieth century. In the Western offshoots and western Europe, the IER increased since 1990, which reflected primarily the rise in inequality. Finally, while the Gini rose in Asia and remained largely stable in Latin America during the second half of the twentieth century, the

IER fell in both regions, and more rapidly in Asia than in Latin America, because living standards improved more rapidly in Asia.

According to Figure 16.6, the IER exceeded unity in sub-Saharan Africa in 1870 and 1929 (and not far away from 0.9 until 1960), and also in Asia in 1870. The implication is that the income inequality prevailing in these societies was not sustainable given the low income levels. However, the Asian and African IERs may not be too accurate, because inequality estimates are overestimated or per capita income underestimated, or both.

The IER can be seen as showing the impact of income inequality on welfare. Although sub-Saharan Africa and Latin America had similar Gini coefficients (0.55–0.60) during the second half of the twentieth century, they differed significantly in terms of the IER, around 0.8 in sub-Saharan Africa and 0.6 in Latin America. Vis-à-vis the state of perfectly equal distribution of incomes, the comparable Ginis in the two regions would have resulted in a substantially larger reduction in welfare in Africa than in Latin America, because the similar income inequality would have reduced consumption of poorer families having higher marginal utility to a greater extent in Africa than in Latin America.

There are reasons to believe that the IER depends on the political regime, which defines the ability of the elite to extract surplus from producers. In eastern Europe, after falling to 0.25 in the 1970s, the IER jumped to 0.4 with the demise of socialism. Meanwhile, in regions under democratic rule, including western Europe and the European offshoots, although inequality rebounded after 1980, IERs in 2000 were not much different than in 1980, which was about 0.4, revealing the West's economic progress and relatively low inequality. Finally, the declining trends in the IER across different regions may reflect political regimes becoming less oppressive, with elites losing power to extract as democratic transitions take place.

Well-Being Beyond GDP

So far, trends in well-being have been discussed entirely in terms of material welfare. The concept of human development, defined as 'a process of enlarging people's choices', provides a multidimensional measure of well-being. The United Nations Human Development Index (HDI) has three dimensions: a healthy life, access to knowledge, and all other aspects of well-being,

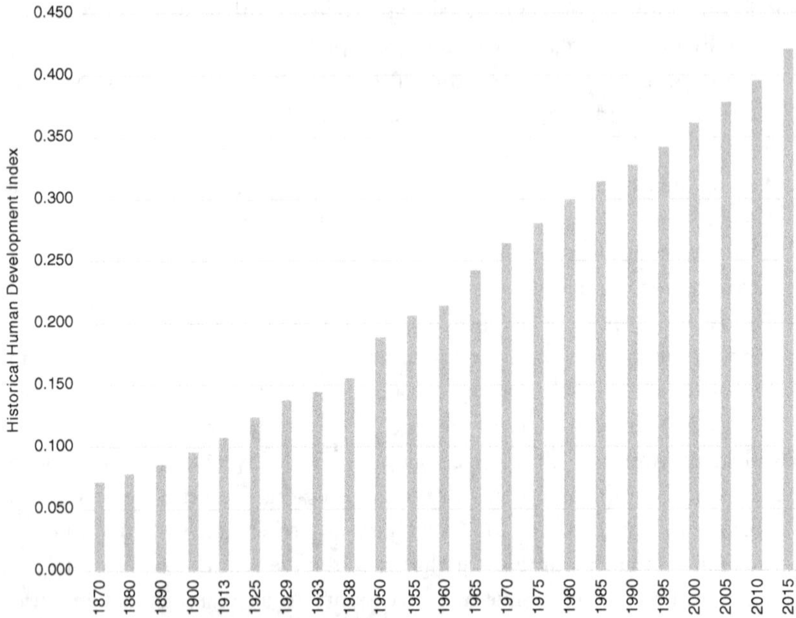

Figure 16.7 World human development, 1870–2015
Source: Prados de la Escosura 2015 (updated).

which are proxied, respectively, by life expectancy at birth, years of schooling, and per capita income. Per capita income enters the index at a declining rate (log-transformed), since its power to expand capabilities declines as its level rises (Anand and Sen 2000). These are combined into a synthetic measure using a geometric average (UNDP 2010). Since each of the three dimensions is considered indispensable, they are assigned equal weights.

The Historical Index of Human Development (HIHD) improves on the UNDP HDI, allowing for the fact that in social dimensions (life expectancy and schooling) quality improvements are associated with increases in quantity, so an increase in a quantity indicator of the same magnitude represents a greater achievement the higher the level at which they take place (Prados de la Escosura 2015).

World human development as measured by HIHD shows a long-run upward trend, increasing sixfold between 1870 and 2015, at a pace of 1.2 per cent per year (Figure 16.7). Three main phases can be distinguished: first, steady and moderate progress up to 1913; second, acceleration during the period 1913–70 (except for World War II); and third, deceleration from 1980.

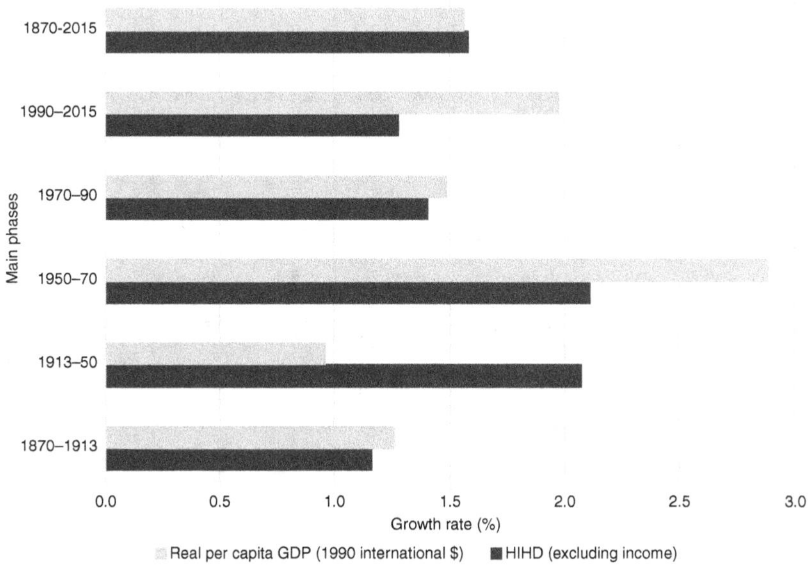

Figure 16.8 World human development (HIHD*) and GDP per head growth, 1870–2015 (%)
Note: * HIHD excluding the income dimension.
Source: Prados de la Escosura 2015 (updated).

Although human development (excluding the income dimension) and real per capita GDP followed similar growth trends over the long run, they grew at different rates in the shorter run (Figure 16.8). Specifically, during the globalization backlash, occurring between 1914 and 1950, clear discrepancies emerged. Although real per capita GDP stagnated or declined as world commodity and factor markets disintegrated, the spread of health and education around the world was not interrupted.

The absolute gap in the level of HIHD widened between OECD countries and the Rest from 1870. However, in relative terms, the Rest has been catching up with the West since the late 1920s, which was more rapid in pre- than in post-1970 decades. However, by 2007 the human development level in the Rest represented only half that of the West (Figure 16.9).

A sustained progress in life expectancy at birth and education occurred in different world regions in the past century and a half. It was the advance in these social dimensions that caused world human development to improve over time, with life expectancy being the driving force before the 1950s and education taking the lead thereafter.

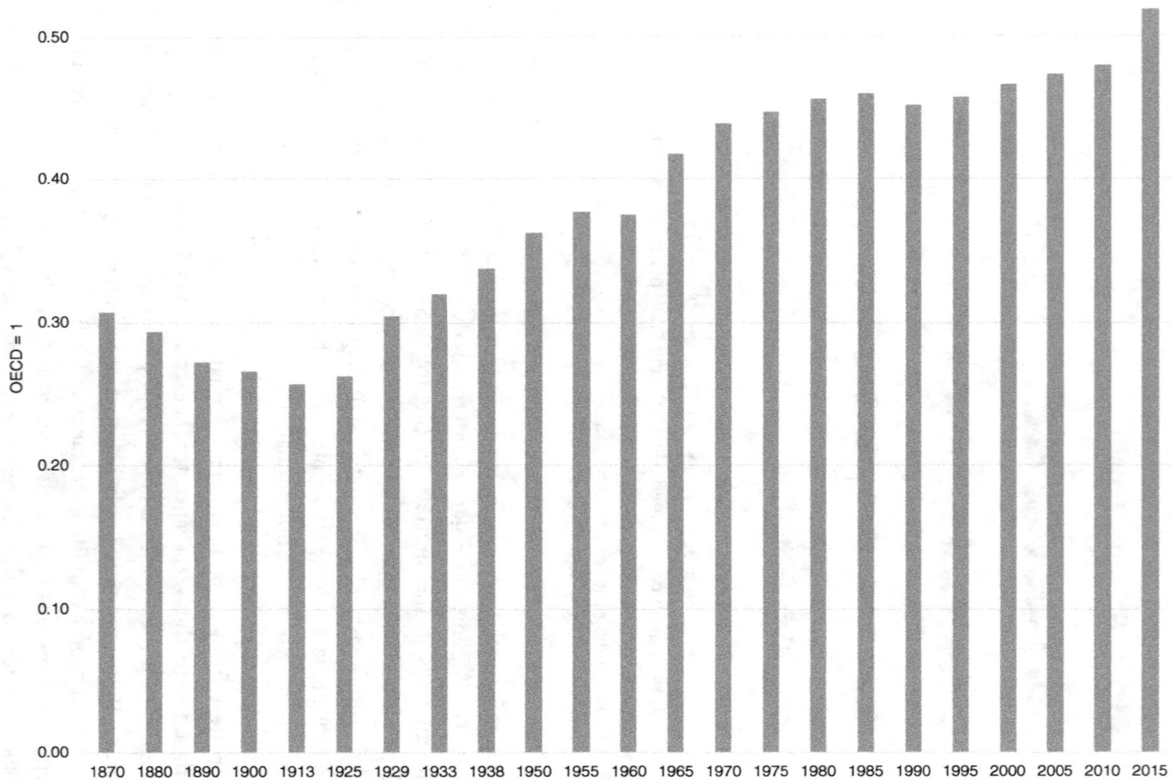

Figure 16.9 Relative human development in the Rest, 1870–2015 (OECD = 1)
Source: Prados de la Escosura 2015 (updated).

Advances in medical knowledge have been responsible for the sustained increase in life expectancy since the late nineteenth century (Riley 2005; Cutler et al. 2006). Technological advances resulted in two distinct health transitions occurring in sequence. The first health transition was driven by the diffusion of the germ theory of disease since the 1880s (Preston 1975), which led to the introduction of new vaccines (since the 1890s) and drugs to cure infectious diseases (sulpha drugs since the late 1930s, and antibiotics since the 1950s) (Easterlin 1999; Jayachandran et al. 2010). The result was a reduction in mortality for all age groups, but especially for infants and children. The second health transition refers to mortality falling among the elderly as a result of better treatment of respiratory and cardiovascular disease, combined with better health and nutrition in their early years (Eggleston and Fuchs 2012; Deaton 2013). It was the second transition that has accounted for the sustained gains in life expectancy at birth and healthy life years in the late twentieth and early twenty-first centuries. Health improvements have resulted not only in a longer life, but also in longer and healthy life years (Mathers et al. 2001). In the West, improvements in life expectancy associated with the second health transition have driven human development advances since 1870. In the Rest, the role of life expectancy in human development advance was crucial during 1913–70, when infectious diseases gave way to chronic diseases under the first health transition. But life expectancy gains have slowed down in the Rest since the late twentieth century, as the demographic and first health transitions came to an end.

Conclusions

How have economic growth, industrialization, and globalization affected the well-being of different income groups in different parts of the world over the last one and a half centuries? Here there are some of the answers we suggested in this chapter:

- Consumption per person has grown over time, but more slowly than GDP per capita, because the share of private consumption declined, although this was partly offset by the rising share of public consumption, often with a redistributive aim.
- Available estimates of top income shares and Gini coefficients suggest that within-country income inequality fell from the early to the late twentieth century, but rose in recent decades.

- Although living standards improved in different parts of the world, the gap between the West and the Rest, and between-country inequality more generally, widened over time until the 1990s, when the trend reversed.
- Income inequality among world inhabitants followed a similar trend, increasing up to 1990 and finally declining in the twenty-first century.
- Substantial long-run gains in human development have taken place in the world without being slowed down during 1914–50, a period of economic stagnation and globalization backlash.

References

Allen, R. C. (2001). 'The Great Divergence in European Wages and Prices from the Middle Ages to the First World War', *Explorations in Economic History*, 38(4), 411–447.

(2007). 'India in the Great Divergence', in Hatton, T. J., O'Rourke, K. O., and Taylor, A. M. (eds.), *The New Comparative Economic History: Essays in Honor of Jeffrey G. Williamson*, Cambridge, MA: MIT Press, 9–32.

(2013). 'Poverty Lines in History, Theory, and Current International Practice', Discussion Paper 685, University of Oxford, Department of Economics.

(2014). 'American Exceptionalism as a Problem in Global History', *Journal of Economic History*, 74(2), 309–350.

Allen, R. C., Bassino, J.-P., Ma, D., Moll-Murata, C., and van Zanden, J. L. (2011). 'Wages, Prices, and Living Standards in China, 1739–1925: In Comparison with Europe, Japan, and India', *Economic History Review*, 64(S1), 8–38.

Alvaredo, F., Atkinson, A. B., Piketty, T., and Saez, E. (2013). 'The Top 1 Percent in International and Historical Perspective', *Journal of Economic Perspectives*, 27(3), 3–20.

Anand, S. and Sen, A. K. (2000). 'The Income Component of the Human Development Index', *Journal of Human Development*, 1, 83–106.

Astorga, P. (2017). 'Real Wages and Skill Premiums in Latin America, 1900–2011', *Revista de Historia Económica/Journal of Iberian and Latin American Economic History*, 35(3), 319–353.

Atkinson, A. B., Piketty, T., and Saez, E. (2011). 'Top Incomes in the Long Run of History', *Journal of Economic Literature*, 49(1), 3–71.

Bank of Japan. (1966). *Meiji ikō honpō chuyō keizai tōkei*, Tokyo: Bank of Japan.

Barro, R. J. and Ursúa, J. F. (2008). 'Macroeconomic Crises since 1870', *Brookings Papers on Economic Activity*, spring, 255–335.

Caruana-Galizia, P. (2015). 'Strategic Colonies and Economic Development: Real Wage in Cyprus, Gibraltar, and Malta, 1836–1913', *Economic History Review*, 68(4), 1250–1276.

Cha, M. S. (2014). *Kiawa kijŏgŭi kiwŏn*, Seoul: Haenam.

Cha, M. S. (2015). 'Unskilled Wage Gaps within the Japanese Empire', *Economic History Review*, 68(1), 23–47.

Challú, A. and Gómez-Galvarriato, A. (2015). 'Mexico's Real Wages in the Age of the Great Divergence, 1730–1930', *Revista de Historia Económica/Journal of Iberian and Latin American Economic History*, 33(1), 83–122.

Chenery, H. B. and Syrquin, M. (1975). *Patterns of Development, 1950–1970*, Oxford University Press.

Conference Board. (2018). 'Total Economy Database, Output, Labor and Labor Productivity, 1950–2018', www.conference-board.org/data/economydatabase/index.cfm?id=27762 (accessed 29 September 2020).

Cutler, D., Deaton, A., and Lleras-Muney, A. (2006). 'The Determinants of Mortality', *Journal of Economic Perspectives*, 20(1), 97–120.

Cvrcek, T. (2013). 'Wages, Prices, and Living Standards in the Habsburg Empire, 1827–1910', *Journal of Economic History*, 73(1), 1–37.

Deaton, A. (2013). *The Great Escape: Health, Wealth and the Origins of Inequality*, Princeton University Press.

de Zwart, P. (2011). 'South African Living Standards in Global Perspective, 1835–1910', *Economic History of Developing Regions*, 26(1), 49–74.

Easterlin, R. A. (1999). 'How Beneficent is the Market? A Look at the Modern History of Mortality', *European Review of Economic History*, 3, 257–294.

Eggleston, K. N. and Fuchs, V. (2012). 'The New Demographic Transition: Most Gains in Life Expectancy Now Realized Late in Life', *Journal of Economic Perspectives*, 26(1), 137–156.

Frankema, E. and van Waijenburg, M. (2012). 'Structural Impediments to African Growth? New Evidence from Real Wages in British Africa, 1880–1965', *Journal of Economic History*, 72(4), 895–926.

Fukao, K., Ma, D., and Yuan, T. (2006). 'International Comparison in Historical Perspective: Reconstructing the 1934–1936 Benchmark Purchasing Power Parity for Japan, Korea, and Taiwan', *Explorations in Economic History*, 43, 280–308.

Goldin, C. and Katz, L. F. (2008). *The Race between Education and Technology*, Cambridge, MA: Harvard University Press.

Gordon, R. J. (2016). *The Rise and Fall of American Growth: The US Standard of Living since the Civil War*, Princeton University Press.

Heldring, L. and Robinson, J. A. (2012). 'Colonialism and Economic Development in Africa', NBER working paper 18566, National Bureau of Economic Research.

Huberman, M. and Minns, C. (2007). 'The Times They Are Not Changin': Days and Hours of Work in Old and New Worlds, 1870–2000', *Explorations in Economic History*, 44(4), 538–537.

Japan Statistical Association. (1987/1988). *Nippon chōki tōkei sōran*, Tokyo: Japan Statistical Association.

Jayachandran, S., Lleras-Muney, A., and Smith, K. V. (2010). 'Modern Medicine and the Twentieth-Century Decline in Mortality: Evidence on the Impact of Sulfa Drugs', *American Economic Journal: Applied Economics*, 2(1), 118–146.

Juif, D. and Frankema, E. (2018). 'From Coercion to Compensation: Institutional Responses to Labour Scarcity in the Central African Copperbelt', *Journal of Institutional Economics*, 14(2), 313–343.

Kaplan, S. N. and Rauh, J. (2013). 'It's the Market: The Broad-Based Rise in the Return to Top Talent', *Journal of Economic Perspectives*, 27(3), 35–56.

Kuznets, S. (1953). *Shares of Upper Income Groups in Income and Savings*, Cambridge, MA: National Bureau of Economic Research.

(1955). 'Economic Growth and Income Inequality', *American Economic Review*, 45 (1), 1–28.

Lakner, C. and Milanovic, B. (2016). 'Global Income Distribution: From the Fall of the Berlin Wall to the Great Recession', *World Bank Economic Review*, 30(2), 203–232.

Lindert, P. H. (2004). *Growing Public: Social Spending and Economic Growth since the Eighteenth Century*, Cambridge University Press.

Maddison, A. (2006). *The World Economy*, Paris: OECD Development Centre.

Maddison Project Database, 2013 version. Bolt, J. and van Zanden, J. L. (2014). 'The Maddison Project: Collaborative Research on Historical National Accounts', *Economic History Review*, 67, 627–651.

Makino, F. and Minami, R. (2015). *Chūgoku*, Tokyo: Toyokiezaishimposha.

Mathers, C. D., Sadana, R., Salomon, J. A., Murray, C. J. L., and Lopez, A. D. (2001). 'Healthy Life Expectancy in 191 Countries', *Lancet*, 357, 1685–1691.

Milanovic, B. (2011). 'A Short History of Global Inequality: The Past Two Centuries', *Explorations in Economic History*, 48(4), 494–506.

(2016). *Global Inequality: A New Approach for the Age of Globalization*, Cambridge, MA: Belknap Press.

Mizoguchi, T. (2008). *Taiwan*, Tokyo: Toyokiezaishimposha.

OECD. (2019). Income Distribution Database, available online at https://stats.oecd.org/Index.aspx?DataSetCode=IDD (accessed 15 February 2019).

Ohkawa, K. (1967). *Bukka, Chōki keizai tōkei, Vol. 8*, Tokyo: Toyokeizaishimposha.

Özmucur, S. and Pamuk, S. (2002). 'Real Wages and Standards of Living in the Ottoman Empire, 1489–1914', *Journal of Economic History*, 62(2), 293–321.

Prados de la Escosura, L. (2000). 'International Comparisons of Real Product, 1820–1990: An Alternative Data Set', *Explorations in Economic History*, 37(1), 1–41.

(2007). 'European Patterns of Development in Historical Perspective', *Scandinavian Economic History Review*, 55(3), 187–221.

(2008). 'Inequality, Poverty, and the Kuznets Curve in Spain, 1850–2000', *European Review of Economic History*, 12(3), 287–324.

(2015). 'World Human Development: 1870–2007', *Review of Income and Wealth*, 61(2), 220–247.

(2018). 'Well-Being Inequality in the Long Run', CEPR Discussion Paper 12920, Centre for Economic Policy Research.

Preston, S. H. (1975). 'Mortality and Level of Development', *Population Studies*, 29, 231–248.

Ravallion, M. (2018). 'Inequality and Globalization: A Review Essay', *Journal of Economic Literature*, 56(2), 620–642.

Riley, J. C. (2005). *Poverty and Life Expectancy: The Jamaica Paradox*, New York: Cambridge University Press.

United Nations Development Programme (UNDP). (2010). *Human Development Report*, New York: Oxford University Press.

van Zanden, J. L., Baten, J., Foldvári, P., and van Leeuwen, B. (2014). 'The Changing Shape of Global Inequality, 1820–2000: Exploring a New Dataset', *Review of Income and Wealth*, 60(2), 279–297.

Williamson, J. G. (1995). 'The Evolution of Global Labor Markets Since 1830: Background Evidence and Hypotheses', *Explorations in Economic History*, 32(2), 141–196.

17
Trade and Immigration

DAVID S. JACKS AND JOHN P. TANG

Introduction

Trade and immigration have reappeared as major policy issues in the present day and for good reason. The past century and a half has witnessed a dramatic rise, fall, and resurgence of globalization, as measured in the movement of goods and labour. In this chapter, we describe long-run trends in merchandise trade and immigration, as well as attempt to characterize the relationship between the two. Although there are a number of limitations on available data – particularly for immigration – and thus on our ability to be truly global in our outlook, this chapter is one of the first to take a very long-run perspective on these two phenomena while capturing the bulk of recorded trade and immigration patterns.

We observe that these two forces moved largely in parallel in the decades leading up to World War I, collapsed during the interwar period, and then rebounded but with much more pronounced growth in trade. There was also a large redistribution in the regional sources of goods and people, shifting from the former industrialized core countries (Europe) to those in the former periphery (Asia), as well as significant variation in these flows within regions over time and changes in the composition of merchandise trade towards manufactured goods dating from 1950.

The second part of our chapter examines the relationship between these two phenomena with a long-panel analysis of Canada and the US, which together received the bulk of both goods and immigrants for most of this period. We find that their bilateral exports are positively correlated with inward migration from those trade partners, suggesting complementarity based on factors of production. However, a more rigorous regression analysis using a triple differences framework in combination with changes in US immigration policy in the interwar period indicates the opposite, and this result is consistent with long-standing economic theory (Mundell 1957).

While this result may be due to unaccounted-for changes in immigration policy and/or the specific decades covered, it does suggest the need for more empirically rigorous work. These results and the historical patterns of the trade in goods and immigration are explained in greater detail below.

Global Trends in Immigration and Trade

This section provides the reader with an overview of developments in immigration and trade over the period from 1870 to 2010. Apart from the evidence at the global level, the various subsections consider immigration and trade at different levels of granularity, allowing us to identify the moving parts which are sometimes obscured in national aggregates. Thus, we consider, in turn, immigration flows into six settler economies for the full period, immigrant stocks in the United States for the full period, and immigrant stocks in twenty-one advanced economies from 1960 to 2010. Likewise, we consider regional shares in world exports, country shares in regional exports, and the share of manufactured goods in merchandise exports, all over the full period from 1870 to 2010.

Immigration Flows and Stocks

Determinants of migration are varied, but can generally be characterized as either push or pull factors and often work in conjunction. Push factors, meaning conditions that incentivize migrants to leave their home country, can include domestic structural change, low relative wages, civil instability, and policy changes. Pull factors that induce migrants to arrive in particular destination countries can range from higher wages and network effects to institutional similarity, imperial preferences, and transportation costs. But before we begin, we should clarify what constitutes immigration for the purposes of this chapter. Most succinctly, immigration is not synonymous with migration. What we have in mind here is the voluntary movement of individuals across national borders for purposes of permanent relocation. Thus, we *exclude* from consideration large migration streams associated with:

- changing borders (e.g. individuals born in British India but finding themselves resident in one of its subsequent partitioned states, either voluntarily or not);
- displacement due to domestic conflict, famine, natural disaster, and/or interstate conflict (e.g. various waves of refugees, starting from World War II);

- immigration flows which proved to be temporary in nature (as evidenced by return migration) and to not dramatically affect the demographic profile of destination countries (e.g. the significant out-migration from China in the nineteenth century); and
- within-border movements of individuals through frontier expansion (e.g. the United States or Han settlement in Manchuria in the nineteenth century).

Although there is a significant historical literature which speaks to these issues, we abstract away from them for the purposes of this chapter due to our desire to address developments with available data (cf. McKeown 2004; Moses 2012). That being said, the broad trajectory of immigration's rise, fall, and resurgence sketched here corresponds largely with the trajectory of the forms of migration enumerated in the four excluded migration types above.

Even in this case, our task is complicated by the fact that much of the data we possess on immigration flows and stocks conflate the movement of individuals across international borders for purposes of permanent versus temporary relocation. With these caveats in mind, we next consider the accumulated evidence of immigration in the form of flows and stocks, with emphasis on areas of comparatively recent settlement and into advanced economies, respectively.

Immigrant Flows into Six Settler Economies, 1870–2010

Given the inconsistency and unavailability of comprehensive migration records for many countries, we focus on a subset of countries that received the vast majority of recorded migrants during the past century and a half.[1] This follows work by Madsen and Andric (2017), who compiled records of immigrant flows into the six primary settler economies of the nineteenth century. These countries are Argentina, Australia, Brazil, Canada, New Zealand, and the United States, and they were relatively attractive destinations in the sense of push and pull factors. The purposes of Madsen and Andric (2017) lie in assessing the connection between immigrant flows and the subsequent trajectories of unemployment in these destination countries. Our concern lies chiefly with documenting the size and composition of these

1 Notably, this precludes discussion of important immigration flows such as the large Chinese and Indian diasporas that emerged in Asia, eastern Africa, and the eastern Pacific during this period. Data unavailability similarly affects other countries that were developing at the time and lacked the resources or interest in tracking flows or stocks of inward or outward migration.

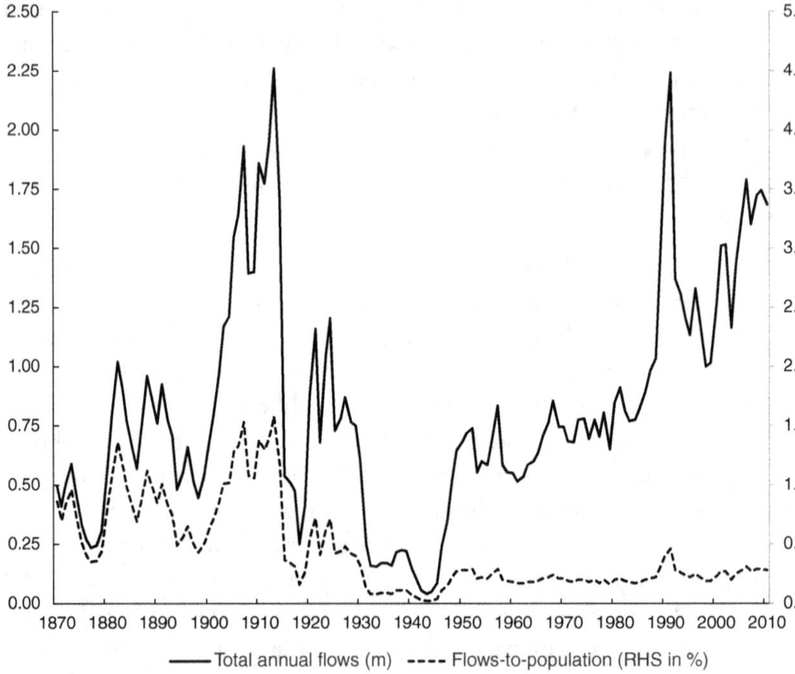

Figure 17.1 Immigration flows into settler economies, 1870–2010
Sources: DEMIG 2015; Madsen and Andric 2017.

flows, which were both considerable and heterogeneous over time, and migrants' countries of origin.

Figure 17.1 starts with Madsen and Andric (2017) as a baseline and supplements it with the figures for bilateral immigrant flows reported in the DEMIG TOTAL database (DEMIG 2015). The first series for total annual flows of immigrants (in millions) highlights the growth in immigrant flows from 1870 and the role of 1913 as the high-water mark, with 2,261,644 individuals landing in these six destination countries in that year. As mentioned earlier, the sources of this marked rise in the late nineteenth century are typically thought to be found in the combination of large gaps in economic and political opportunity between source and destination countries, liberal immigration policies in destination countries, low passenger transportation costs, and, in some instances, the relationship between metropoles and their colonies (Hatton and Williamson 1998; Magee and Thompson 2010).

These developments proved to be relatively short-lived, as immigrant flows ground to a near halt due to the world wars and restrictive policy reforms in destination countries, especially in the United States starting in the 1920s. Unsurprisingly, 1943 marked the nadir, with a mere 41,247 individuals landing. From then, there was nowhere to go but up: the immediate post-World War II period gave rise to a significant burst in immigrant flows, followed by a gradual rise up to the 1980s, which also seem to be an inflection point in the series. Only starting in 1988 do flows consistently exceed 1 million individuals per year. With nearly 1.5 million individuals entering these settler economies in an average year in the period from 1900 to 1914, we are witnessing flows nearly reattaining the heights of the 1900s.

Some caution is warranted in pushing this observation too far: the population base of the six destination countries considered here increased dramatically between the 1900s and the 2000s (specifically, by a factor of 4.5 between 1910 and 2010). Thus, the second series in Figure 17.1 depicts these immigrant flows as a percentage of the combined population of the destination countries. Over the entire period from 1870 to 1910, this percentage averaged 0.89, with a significant uptick to over 1.25 per cent in the decade before World War I, and with significant country-level variation: for instance, Brazil averaged 0.45 per cent throughout the period, while New Zealand averaged 3.37 per cent in the same (remarkably, with 11.98 per cent for the single year of 1874). This ratio collapsed in the period bookended by the world wars for the reasons outlined already. The equivalent average for the period 1915–50 was a mere 0.25 per cent, and an equivalent low of 0.02 per cent was separately registered in both 1943 and 1944. From 1950, there has been a remarkable consistency in the ratio of flows to resident population, with an average figure of 0.23 per cent during 1950–2010. In terms of shares, we are presently experiencing nowhere near the same rates as prevailed in the age of mass immigration in general, and the 1900s in particular.

Turning to the issue of composition, Figure 17.2 depicts the shares of immigrant flows into settler economies over the same period, 1870–2010. In large part, this is a story of the receding and then burgeoning role of the United States in absorbing immigrant flows.

There is relative stability in the share for the US from 1870 to 1914, with the country absorbing 61.60 per cent of all immigrant flows.[2] Restrictions in the form of the Literacy Act of 1917, the Emergency Quota Act of 1921, and – most importantly – the Immigrant Restriction Act of 1924 significantly cut into this American share, so that by 1933 it reached an all-time low of 14.72 per cent. At

2 This stability is even more marked if we consider northern America as a unit of analysis: Canada and the US absorb fully 72.30 per cent of all immigrant flows in this period.

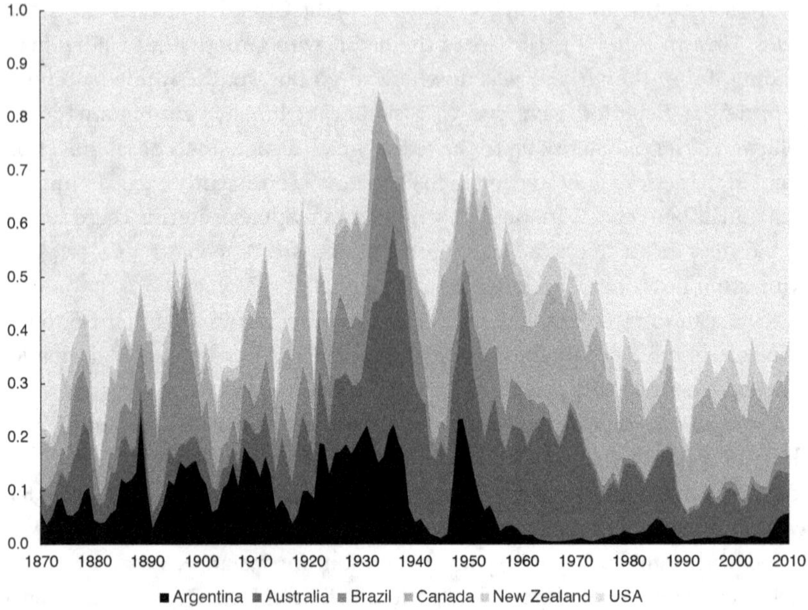

Figure 17.2 Shares of immigrant flows by destination country, 1870–2010
Sources: DEMIG 2015; Madsen and Andric 2017.

the same time, there were only 7 years out of 141 in which the US was not the single largest destination of immigrant flows. This is the period 1932–38, which was not exactly known for being a time of economic resilience for the US. From then on, the US continuously increased its share until roughly 1980. In the subsequent 30 years, the US alone absorbed 68.16 per cent of all immigrant flows. Other significant developments in this regard can be seen in the virtual collapse in immigrant flows to South America and, in particular, to Argentina from 1940. Whereas Argentina and Brazil respectively absorbed 11.98 and 8.38 per cent of all immigrant flows from 1870 to 1940, they respectively absorbed only 2.87 and 2.31 per cent of all immigrant flows from 1940 to 2010. In contrast, Australia, Canada, and New Zealand picked up most of the slack, absorbing 21.61 and 33.93 per cent across 1870–1940 and 1940–2010, respectively.

Again, caution may be warranted in interpreting some of these figures, particularly for the period of mass immigration before World War I. Underlying Madsen and Andric (2017) is the work of Ferenczi and Willcox (1929), which relied upon compilations by the US Bureau of Immigration of manifests of all passengers taken aboard in foreign ports provided by shipping companies, as required by the Passenger Act of 1819.

However, there are many sources of measurement error and leakage, all the way down to the reporting of passengers by individual ships, and all the way up to the State Department's treatment of aggregated data, as revisited by Bandiera et al. (2013). In their work, they find that immigrant flows into the US in 1900–1910 and 1910–20 may have respectively been 20 and 170 per cent higher than reported by Ferenczi and Willcox (1929). Thus, the quality of data is uncertain for years outside the range of their consideration, and for outside of the US, which presumably relied on similar primary sources.

One way forward may be to consider stocks of the foreign-born in census data for which there are no known problems. This approach is not entirely unproblematic for it likely lumps permanent and temporary immigrants together. More importantly, there is surprisingly little consistent evidence across countries on the stock of the foreign-born, except for the US from 1870 to 2010, and for twenty-one advanced economies from 1960 to 2010.

Immigrant Stocks in the United States, 1870–2010

Recognizing possible limitations on immigrant flow data, we first consider immigrant stocks in the US over this period as illustrative of developments further afield. Here, the key word is illustrative, as we cannot presuppose that the US is representative of trends in world immigration. At the same time, the US alone was home to 30.31 per cent of the world's more than 140 million immigrants enumerated in 2010 by the OECD (Dumont et al. 2010).

Bearing this in mind, Figure 17.3 depicts the evolution of the stock of foreign-born in the US from 1870 to 2010. As Figures 17.1 and 17.2 suggest, there was a significant rise in the number of US residents born abroad in the period from 1870 to 1910, from 5.57 to 13.52 million. This rate of increase declined significantly between 1910 and 1930, with the latter date apparently representing the peak of pre-World War II immigrant stocks.[3] What follows is a slow decline into 1970, when there is a sharp reversal in the series, which continues until the end of the period and which coincides with significant changes in US immigration law, namely the Immigration and Nationality Act of 1965.

More dramatically, Figure 17.3 also depicts the ratio of foreign-born to total population. Between 1870 and 1910, there was relative stasis in the foreign-born register, averaging 14.15 per cent of the total population. Thus, the significant increase in the number of US residents born abroad was almost exactly matched

3 We say 'apparent' as this stock is more likely to have actually peaked in 1920 than in 1930, as depicted in Figure 17.3. This stems from the fact that the combined number of self-reported Austrians and Germans fell by 895,057 – or 28.35 per cent – between 1910 and 1920 (Jacks 2005).

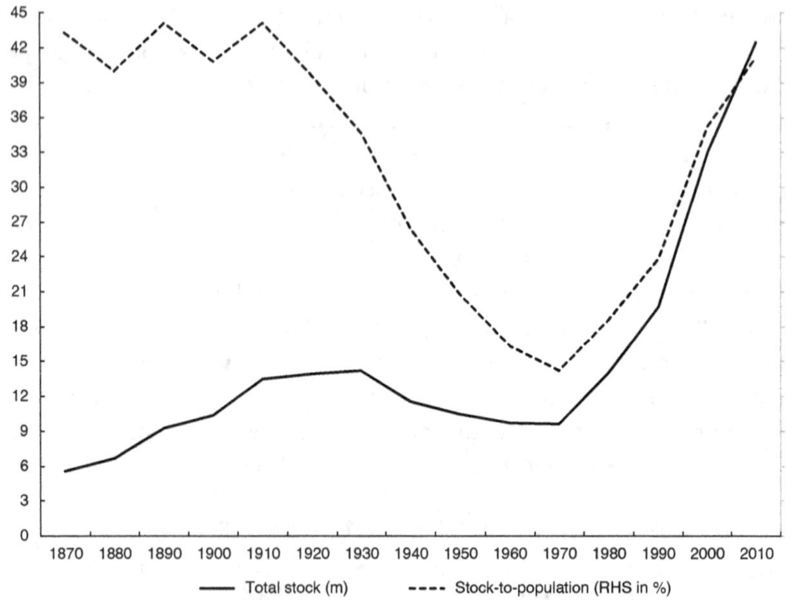

Figure 17.3 Stock of foreign-born in the US, 1870–2010
Source: Abramitzky and Boustan 2017.

by proportionate increases in the native-born stock. From 1910, this ratio steadily declined, as immigration flows slowed and then ground to a near halt in the 1930s and 1940s. Given the lag between immigrant flows and stocks, it is not surprising that this ratio bottomed out at 4.73 per cent in 1970. In that year, immigrant stocks in the US began to rise again and at a rate greatly exceeding the proportional increase in native-born stock. Consequently, in 2010, this ratio stood at 13.72 per cent, suggesting that – at least in the US – the process of immigration has nearly made up for the ground lost in the previous century.

Figure 17.4 decomposes this series of total immigrant stocks into six regions of origin: Africa, Asia, Europe, North America, Oceania, and South America. Perhaps the single most striking change over this period has been the rapid erosion of the share of European origin migrants, starting from 1960. In 1870, this share stood at 88.81 per cent. Although generally declining, it still stood at 74.98 per cent in 1960, but by 2010, it stood at a relatively paltry 14.20 per cent.[4] Although there has been some gain from 1960 in those of

4 The literature traditionally emphasizes the changing composition within this category of Europe – from a wide predominance from northern and western Europe towards those of southern and eastern Europe (Abramitzky and Boustan 2017). That is, in 1870

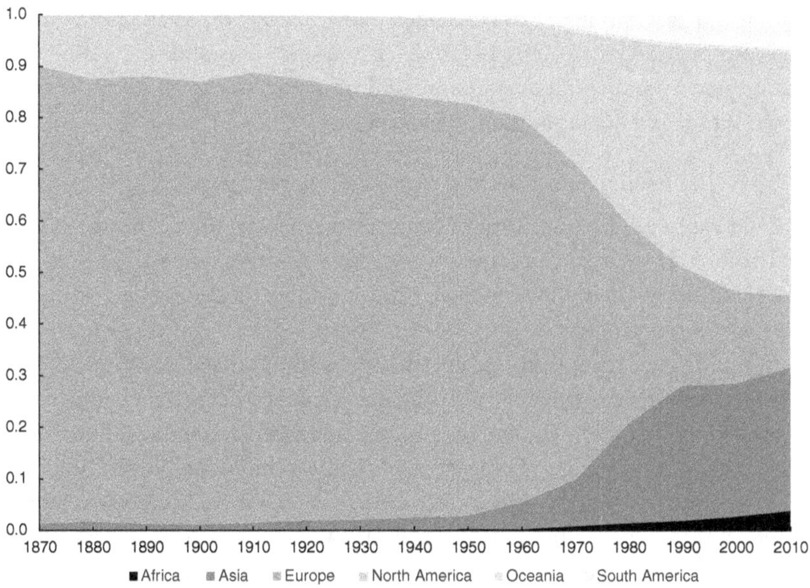

Figure 17.4 Shares of US foreign-born by region of origin, 1870–2010
Source: Abramitzky and Boustan 2017.

African and South American origin, those of Asian and other North American origin have been the standouts.

Asia began with 1.16 per cent in 1870, grinding upwards to 5.07 per cent in 1960. From there, a veritable explosion occurred, particularly up to 1990, so that its share stood at 27.80 per cent in 2010. Likewise, the share of North America began at 9.85 per cent in 1870, increased up to 18.30 per cent in 1960, and settled at 46.90 per cent in 2010. Critically, we define North America to include Canada, the Caribbean, Central America, and Mexico. This catch-all term masks significant changes within the designation of North America. Those born in Canada were 90.09 per cent of all immigrant stocks from North America in 1870, 53.77 per cent in 1960, and 4.69 per cent in 2010. The equivalent figures for Mexico were 7.75 per cent, 32.51 per cent, and 60.13 per cent. Thus, apart from the rapid rise in the share of Mexico, there has been a significant increase for the Caribbean and for Central America as well. The Immigration and Nationality Act of 1965 – which broke the link between immigration flow

the former regions represented 87.04 per cent of all immigrant stocks, while the latter regions represented 1.69 per cent. By 1930, the respective figures were 41.19 per cent and 41.67 per cent. This near parity has been maintained from that point forward.

quotas and past immigrant stocks, ended the virtual ban on Asian immigration, and also provided for extensive family reunification – is almost certainly the key to understanding the changes in US immigrant stocks (in terms of both composition and count) in the last half-century.

Immigrant Stocks in Advanced Economies, 1960–2010

Having explored the trajectory of immigrant stocks in the US between 1870 and 2010, it is then an open question of how representative the prevailing patterns for the US are for the developed world's experience with immigration *writ large*. Unfortunately, and somewhat surprisingly, there are scant long-run historical data on immigrant stocks in advanced economies. This changed from 1960 – a year already flagged as marking a critical turning point for the United States – for the twenty-one advanced economies depicted in Figure 17.5. Admittedly, these are exclusively nations in North America, Oceania, South America, and western Europe, so we are thereby excluding from consideration immigrant stocks in Africa, Asia, and eastern Europe. Yet, again, our sample is home to 67.62 per cent of the world's more than 140 million immigrants enumerated in 2010 (Dumont et al. 2010).

Using these data, Figure 17.6 depicts immigrant stocks in these advanced economies from 1960 to 2010. The total stock in millions does not have a clear inflection point in 1970, as it does for the US. Rather, there is relatively constant growth, with the figures nearly doubling, from 33.04 million in 1960 to 60.74 million in 1990. Thereafter, an additional 34.61 million immigrants were added up to 2010. This pattern mirrors the immigrant stock-to-total population ratio as it rose from 5.34 to 9.63 per cent in 1960 and 2010, respectively. Thus, the near tripling of immigrant stocks over this period outstripped the proportional increase in population from 618.38 million to 990.47 million.

Figure 17.7 shows the shares of immigrant stocks by destination, plotted for Europe, North America, Oceania, and South America. Generally speaking, there is relative constancy across destinations: Europe began and ended with values of 39.96 and 45.16 per cent; North America with values of 42.45 and 46.38 per cent; and Oceania with values of 6.16 and 6.40 per cent, respectively. All of these gains came at a cost to a single region, South America, which saw its share of foreign-born plummet from 12.43 to 2.73 per cent over these fifty years. This view is corroborated by the shares of immigration flows depicted in Figure 17.2: after the 1940s and, in particular, the 1960s, Argentina and Brazil registered few fresh arrivals.[5]

5 This is not simply a story of relative decline either: from 1870 to 1940, there were 10,982,062 cumulative immigrant arrivals in Argentina and Brazil; and from 1940 to 2010, there were only 3,243,599.

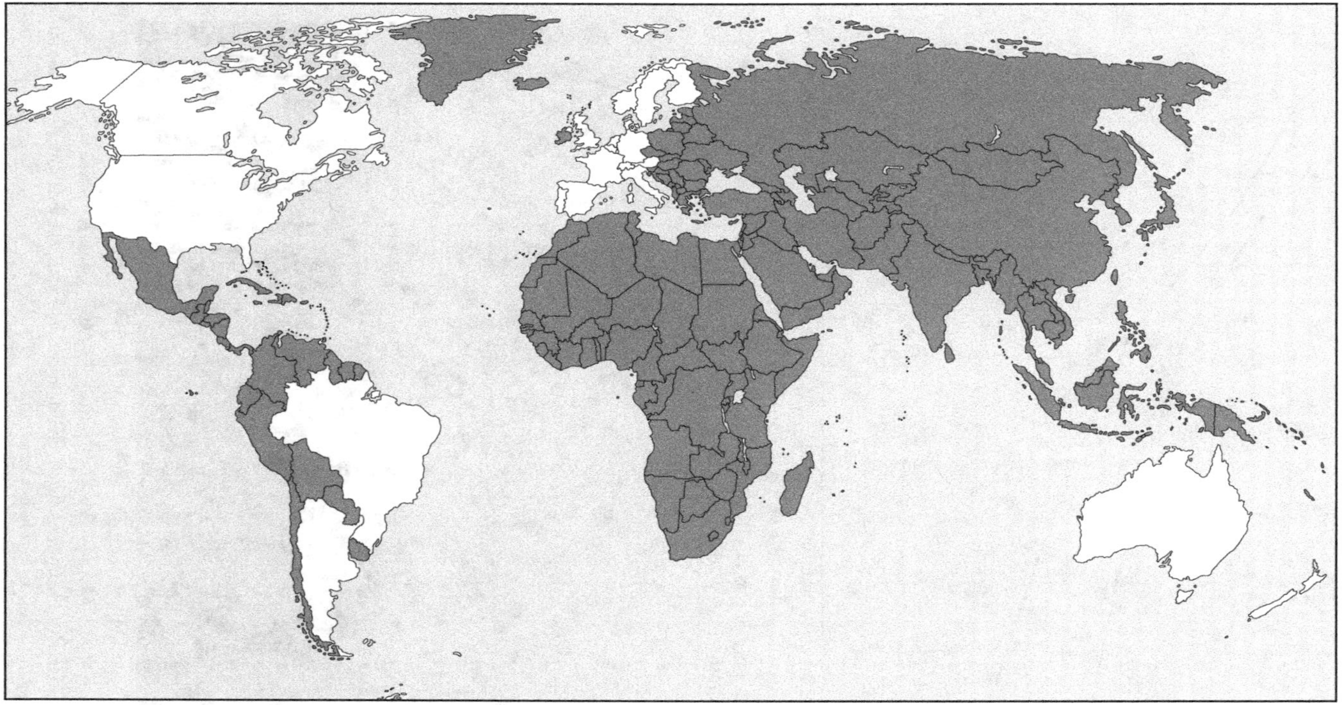

Figure 17.5 Sample countries for immigrant stocks (n = 21), 1960–2010

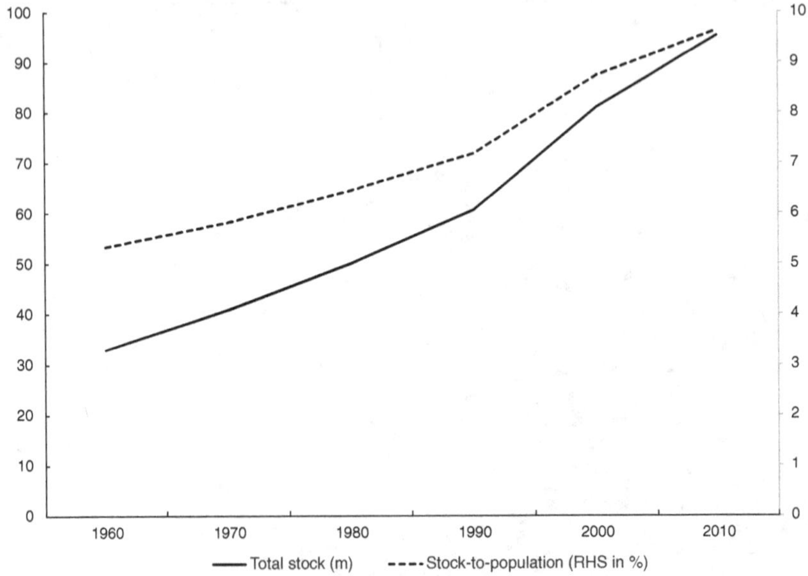

Figure 17.6 Immigrant stocks in advanced economies, 1960–2010
Sources: Dumont et al. 2010; Ozden et al. 2011.

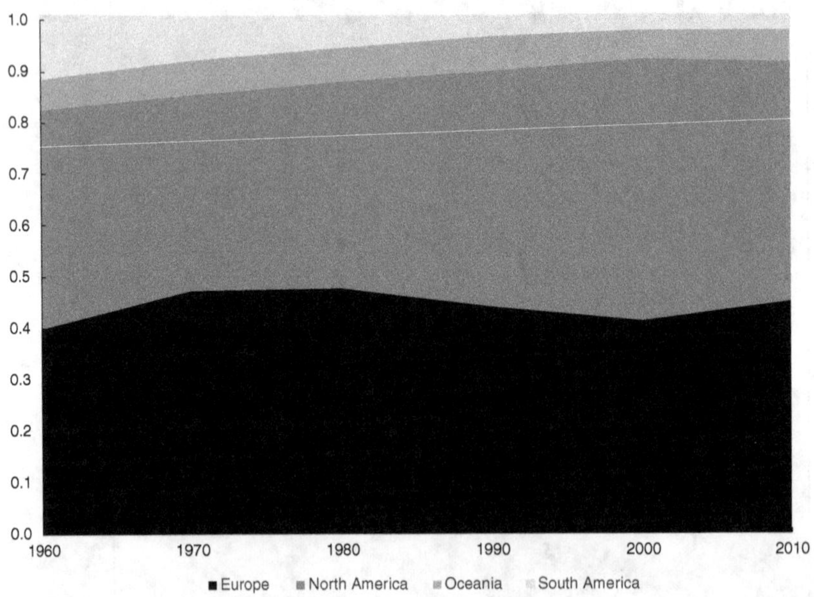

Figure 17.7 Shares of immigrant stocks in advanced economies by destination, 1960–2010
Sources: Dumont et al. 2010; Ozden et al. 2011.

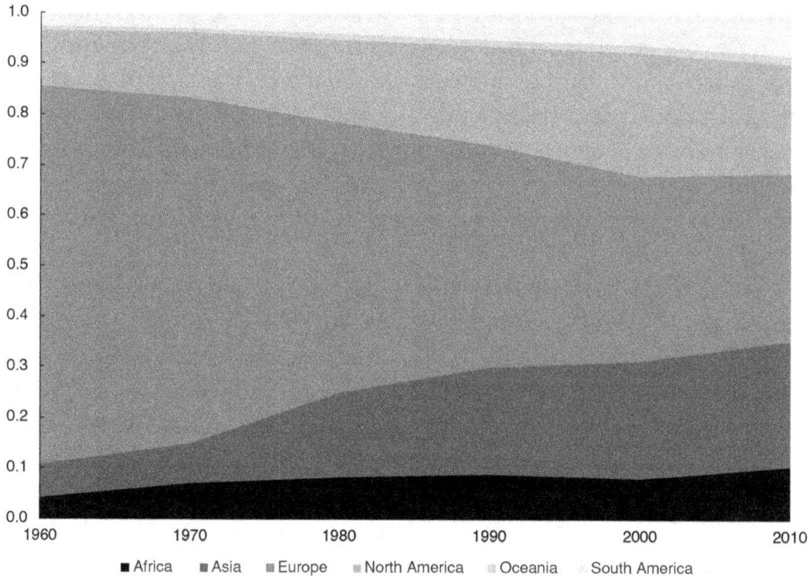

Figure 17.8 Shares of immigrant stocks in advanced economies by origin, 1960–2010
Sources: Dumont et al. 2010; Ozden et al. 2011.

Figure 17.8 decomposes this series of total immigrant stocks into six macro-regions of origin. It repeats many of the patterns established in Figure 17.4 for the US: relative constancy of the share for Oceania (+0.79 pp over the period), gradual increases in the African and South American shares (+6.18 pp and +5.64 pp, respectively), and rapid increases in the Asian and North American shares (+18.31 pp and +10.71 pp, respectively), with the latter being driven primarily by Mexican immigration to the US. All of these increases occurred when the share of individuals born in Europe and living abroad was in rapid decline (−41.64 pp). Thus, apart from some idiosyncrasies – primarily the change in region of origin from Europe to North America – the US experience does not look substantively different vis-à-vis the level of these twenty-one advanced economies. Given the even larger role which the US played in absorbing immigrant flows historically, this suggests that the patterns outlined in Figures 17.3 and 17.4 for the period 1870–1960 are consistent with immigration trajectories at the global level.

Trade Flows

As with migration, the literature identifies trade determinants with relative factor endowments and prices, transport costs, trade policies and agreements, currency arrangements, institutional factors, and firm productivity.[6] To outline major developments in world trade flows, we rely on two previous data collection efforts: one between 1870 and 2000 (Jacks et al. 2011) and one from 1910 to 2010 (Jacks and Novy 2018). We then add new data for a select number of countries to account for differences in the two samples, using the sources cited in these two papers. Overall, we have an annual data set on aggregate merchandise exports for fifty-two countries over the period 1870–2010.

Figure 17.9 summarizes the sample graphically, with uncoloured countries those in our sample. On average, they represent 86 per cent of world GDP in the period 1870–2010 (Maddison Project Database, 2013 version). Thus, somewhat in contrast to the previous figures for immigration, we are confident that the figures presented for world exports represent the underlying population. Finally, we abstract away from international trade in services, which, although fairly negligible in 1870, climbed from 9 per cent to 20 per cent of the value of all international trade from 1970 to 2010 (cf. World Trade Organization 2010; Loungani et al. 2017). This choice is largely predicated by the fact that systematic evidence on the trade in services is hard to come by even for the 1990s and 2000s, much less for earlier periods (Francois and Hoekman 2010).

Global Trends

Figure 17.10 plots aggregate merchandise exports for our fifty-two countries and shows the substantial variation in the growth of international trade over this period. From 1900 to 1910, trend growth in global exports was 3.25 per cent per year relative to trend growth in global GDP of 2.06 per cent. The sources of this trade boom are fairly easy to locate: burgeoning incomes and declining trade costs (on average, 33 per cent lower in 1913 than in 1870) due to maritime and overland transport revolutions; commercial policy liberalization; and the development and improvement of transaction technologies (e.g. the classical Gold Standard) (Jacks et al. 2011).[7]

That said, there was considerable heterogeneity over the 141 years. For example, while tariff levels were relatively unimportant to growth before World War I, they rose during the interwar period (e.g. the 1930 Smoot-Hawley Tariff in the United States), as economies sought to limit the domestic

6 For a more general theoretical discussion of these determinants, see Keller et al. in Volume I, Chapter 17 of this book.

7 This is also discussed in greater detail in Chapter 14 of this volume above, by Paul Caruana-Galizia et al.

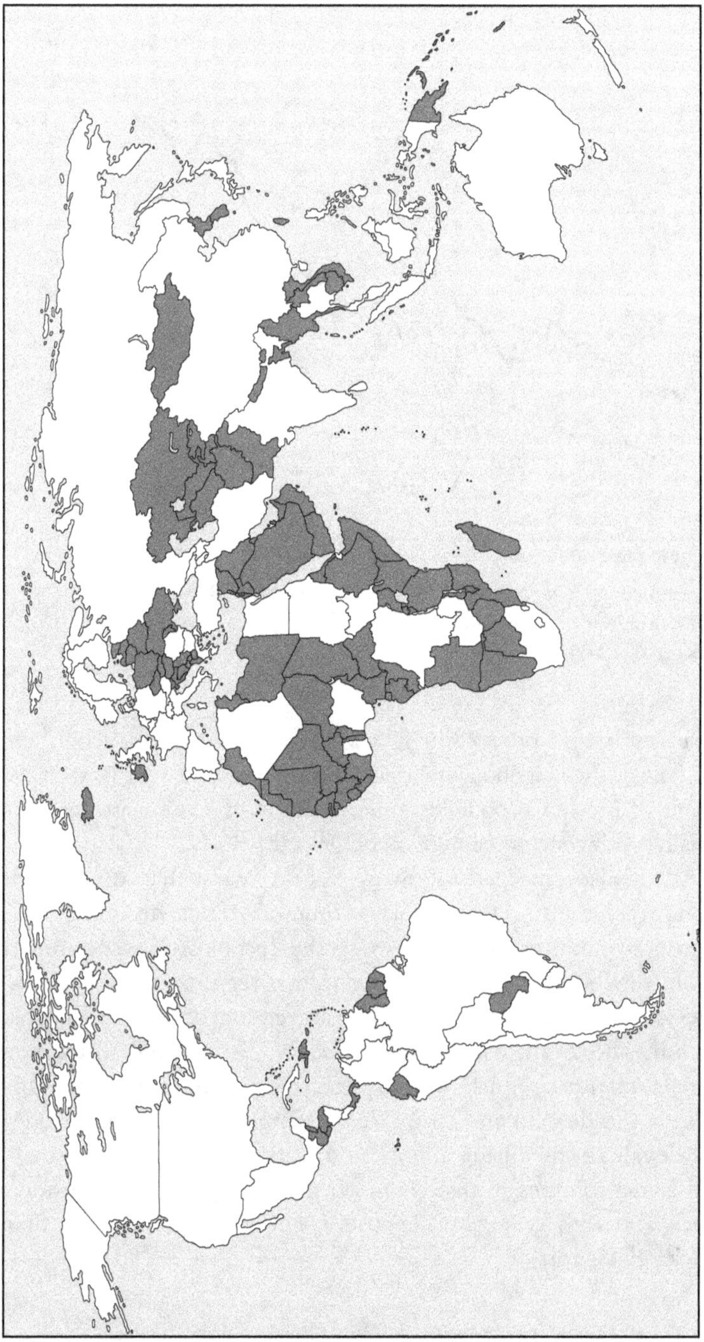

Figure 17.9 Sample countries for world exports (n = 52), 1870–2010

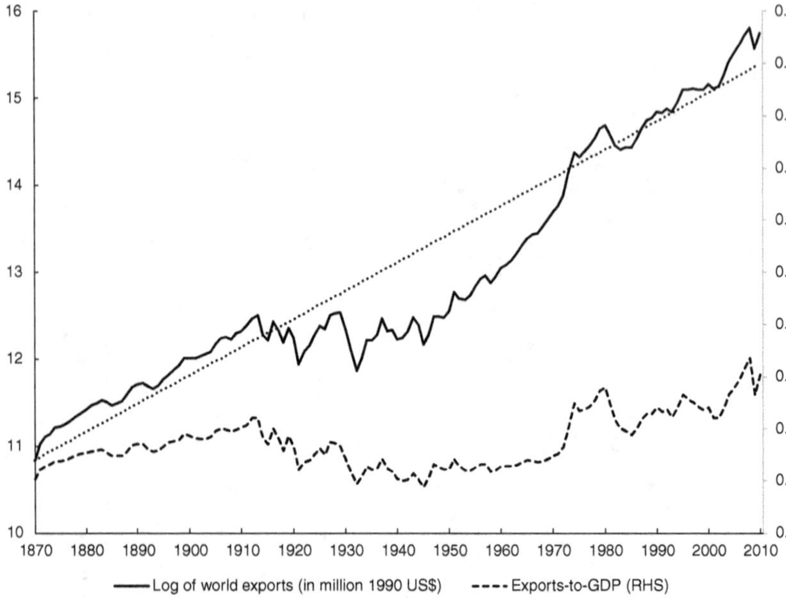

Figure 17.10 World exports, 1870–2010
Sources: Jacks et al. 2011; Jacks and Novy 2018.

impact of excess world production following wartime reconstruction and engaged in beggar-thy-neighbour policies. Only after World War II, with the establishment of Bretton Woods institutions, did tariff levels start declining internationally, with concomitant effects on growth.

Other factors also emerged following World War I that affected the global economy. Despite cessation of wartime hostilities, declining trade costs confronted countervailing forces in the form of transport sector cartelization, new state formation and borders, regional trade and currency blocs (e.g. sterling and yen), the resurrection of a hobbled Gold Standard, but, above all, a lingering sense of discord and distrust in international relations. Thus, a sharp recovery into 1929 was fully reversed with the descent into the Great Depression and the currency crises and devaluations during this period, setting a seesaw pattern in which real trade volumes in 1950 were no greater than they were forty years earlier, and with average trade costs 13 per cent higher in 1939 than in 1921 (Jacks et al. 2011).[8]

8 See also Chapter 18 of this volume below, by Barry Eichengreen and Rui Pedro Esteves.

The period 1950–2000, however, witnessed a distinct resurgence in global trade. This was primarily a function of changes in commercial policy and openness, the creation of institutions like the General Agreement on Tariffs and Trade (GATT) to facilitate international exchange, and a limited but distinct role for change in transport sector technology (i.e. trade costs averaged 16 per cent lower in 2000 than in 1950). This process continued throughout the early 2000s, but accelerated largely due to the rise of China and its return to world markets following its WTO ascension. While regional trade blocs also grew in prominence and economic size following the war (e.g. European Common Market, British Commonwealth, North and South American free trade areas), these largely complemented the policies established under the broader GATT and WTO frameworks. Finally, Figure 17.10 shows the prevailing trend for the period 1870–1913. Thus, over the course of the twentieth century, World War I introduced a long period of disruption in the pace of globalization which recovered only in the 1970s, and then was consistently surpassed in the 1990s.[9]

9 It is also instructive to consider aggregate exports normalized by the sum of GDPs for the sample countries to capture the relative degree of openness over time. This exports-to-GDP ratio indicates that the high-water mark of 1913 was reattained only in 1974. The subsequent thirty-five years then bore witness to some fits and starts, but demonstrated an otherwise upward trend so that the ratio attained an all-time high of 0.168 in 2008. These figures are only illustrative, as two issues remain and cannot be corrected for, given the current state of data. First, aggregate exports figures are in gross terms, whereas GDP figures are in value-added terms, suggesting it would be inaccurate to think of this ratio as capturing how much of GDP is traded in a given year. Furthermore, there have been large changes in how much value added is traded over time: the rise of vertically integrated production processes across international borders (i.e. global supply chains) could act to 'inflate' the value of the openness ratio relative to a world in which only final capital and consumption goods are shipped over international borders (Johnson and Noguera 2017).

Second, in the period 1870–2010, there has been a remarkable change in the composition of final output in all of the sample countries, as the service sector began to rise significantly from the nineteenth century. For example, the service sector comprised roughly 25 per cent of US output in 1870, whereas in 2010 the equivalent figure was 80 per cent. In light of this, the degree to which *tradable goods* are actually traded will necessarily differ from the degree to which *all goods* are actually traded (notwithstanding the measurement of gross versus value-added figures). As an example of how this distinction matters, Feenstra (1998) documents that, for the US, the ratio of merchandise trade to merchandise value added rose from 13.2 to 35.8 per cent between 1913 and 1990, whereas the openness ratio of the US only rose from 0.0668 to 0.0678 over the same period. Thus, secular changes in the composition of domestic output towards services could then act to 'deflate' the value of the openness ratio relative to a world in which the share of non-tradable goods remained constant. Recent work suggests that the ratio of world exports to world GDP would be roughly 25 percentage points higher in 2015 if expenditure patterns had remained unchanged from 1970 (Lewis et al. 2018).

On balance, these two forces would serve to cancel each other out, but it remains unclear a priori which force would predominate in this instance.

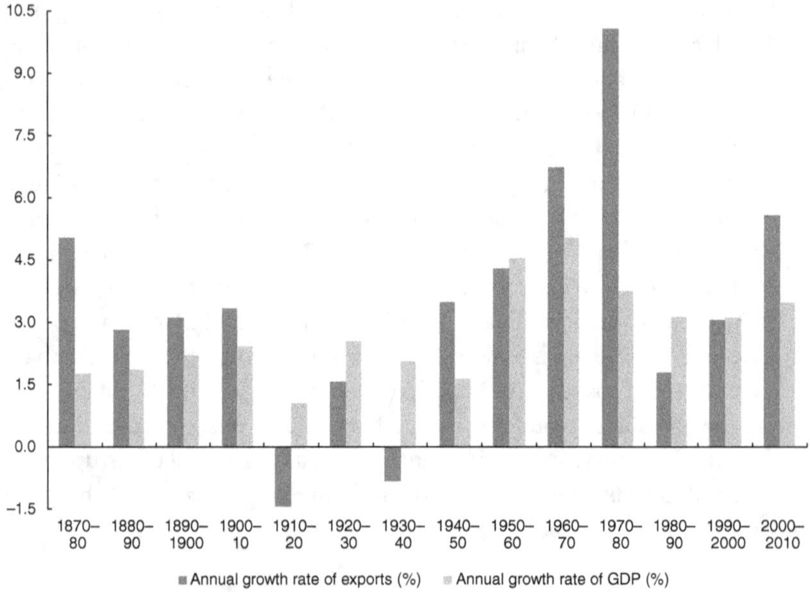

Figure 17.11 Growth of world exports versus world output by decade, 1870–2010
Sources: Jacks et al. 2011; Jacks and Novy 2018.

Finally, Figure 17.11 plots world export and world output growth rates by decade for this period. Thus, we can identify subperiods in which the globalization of trade surged and waned. This approach may also minimize some of the concerns highlighted earlier, since deep changes in the structure of production and trade are less worrisome at the horizon of a decade as opposed to a century. With this mind, there are particular decades where trade growth significantly exceeded output growth: 1870–80, 1940–50, 1970–80, and 2000–2010. Likewise, there are particular decades when output growth significantly exceeded trade growth: 1910–20, 1920–30, 1930–40, and 1980–90.

Changes in Regional and Country Shares

Important changes in the composition of these aggregate export flows can be explored both in terms of regional shares of global exports and in terms of country shares of regional exports. Naturally, this approach brings perspective on the relative economic fortunes of various parts of the world over these 141 years. Figure 17.12 decomposes world exports into shares by region. The decline of the European share stands out, since apart from the time of the

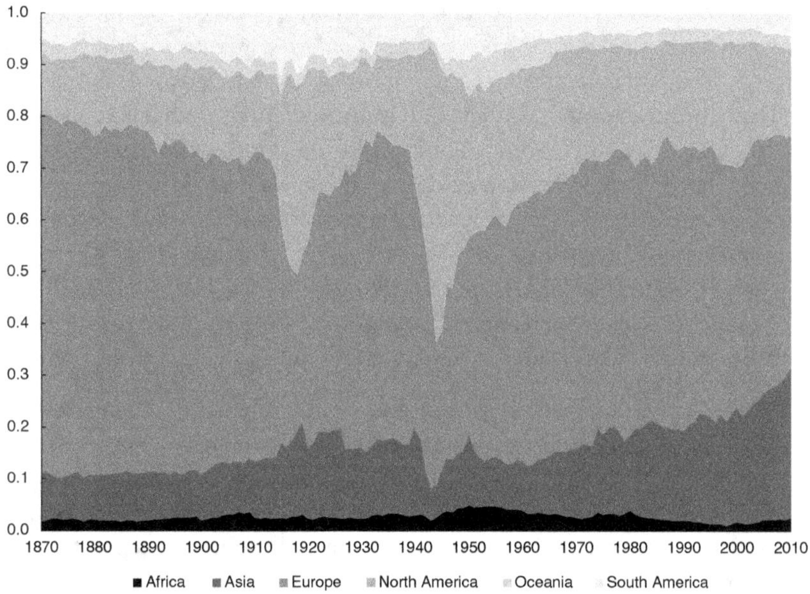

Figure 17.12 World export shares by region, 1870–2010
Sources: Jacks et al. 2011; Jacks and Novy 2018.

world wars, total European exports have been the largest for any particular region for every year from 1870.[10] There is an obvious and pronounced downward trend beginning in 1870, with the European share dropping from 69.90 per cent in 1870 to 57.73 per cent by 1913. Apart from the shocks of the world wars, the other largest movement occurred from 1945 to 1990 (or from 27.19 to 55.48 per cent, respectively) which clearly represents the integrative effort of the EEC, ECU, and EU. Interestingly, this share stalled in the 1990s and resumed its downward trend, with Europe accounting for 44.44 per cent of world exports in 2010.

The other important macro-regions in this regard are Asia and North America. Asia began in 1870 with a 9.03 per cent share, experienced significant growth until 1919 with a 17.72 per cent share, and returned nearly to its 1870 level in 1960 with a 9.47 per cent share. From there, it has experienced nearly uninterrupted growth, hurtling to a 29.29 per cent share in 2010. North America began in 1870 with an 11.55 per cent share and ended in 2010 with

10 Here, we have simply added exports of all European countries to arrive at European exports, and likewise for all other regions. Thus, this figure necessarily includes trade within regions – for example, intra-European trade.

a 17.06 per cent share, but experienced tremendous peaks corresponding with 1917 and 1944, representing 37.68 per cent and 55.86 per cent of the world's exports. The remaining three regions of Africa, Oceania, and South America collectively began with a 9.51 per cent share and ended with a 9.21 per cent share of world exports. Some churning also occurred within this group of regions, but the most noticeable development was the decline in exports from South America, which peaked in 1915 at 12.55 per cent, recovered somewhat in the immediate post-World War II period, and then went into a state of near terminal decline, ending in 2010 with a 4.18 per cent share.

A focus on shares within regions may give a sense of the relative economic fortunes of particular countries. The six panels of Figure 17.13 demonstrate:

(1) the relative stability of Algeria and South Africa in African exports (collectively, 41.70 per cent and 46.02 per cent in 1870 and 2010); the dramatic rise in the Nigerian share from 1970 as it emerged as a petro-state; and the dramatic decline in the Rest of Africa category, which reflects the decline of Egypt as a dominant source of exports (e.g. 53.07 per cent of all African exports in 1870 and 9.43 per cent in 2010);

(2) the decline in Indian predominance in Asian exports from a maximum of 60.28 per cent in 1871 to a minimum of 3.28 per cent in 1986; the corresponding rise of Japan from a share of 3.60 per cent in 1870 to a maximum of 68.42 per cent in 1986 (with significant variation in between, primarily associated with World War II); and the recent massive surge in the Chinese share, which had previously peaked in 1922 at 22.2 per cent, languished during much of the twentieth century, and experienced nearly uninterrupted growth from 1978, attaining a 46.47 per cent share in 2010;

(3) the constancy of the French share of European exports – the disastrous interwar period notwithstanding – with an average value of 12.35 per cent; a reversal of fortune in northern Europe, with Germany and the UK beginning the period with respective shares of 17.21 and 28.08 per cent and ending the period with respective shares of 24.68 per cent and 7.86 per cent; and appreciable growth in the Rest of Europe category, from 38.99 to 57.53 per cent over this period;

(4) the overwhelming share of the US in North American exports with a minimum value of 60.72 per cent in 2005; share increases by both Canada and Mexico, with Canada's run-up primarily being achieved by 1970, and Mexico's rise starting in the wake of NAFTA in the 1990s; and export collapse from the Caribbean and Central America, from 11.01 to 0.79 per cent between 1870 and 2010;

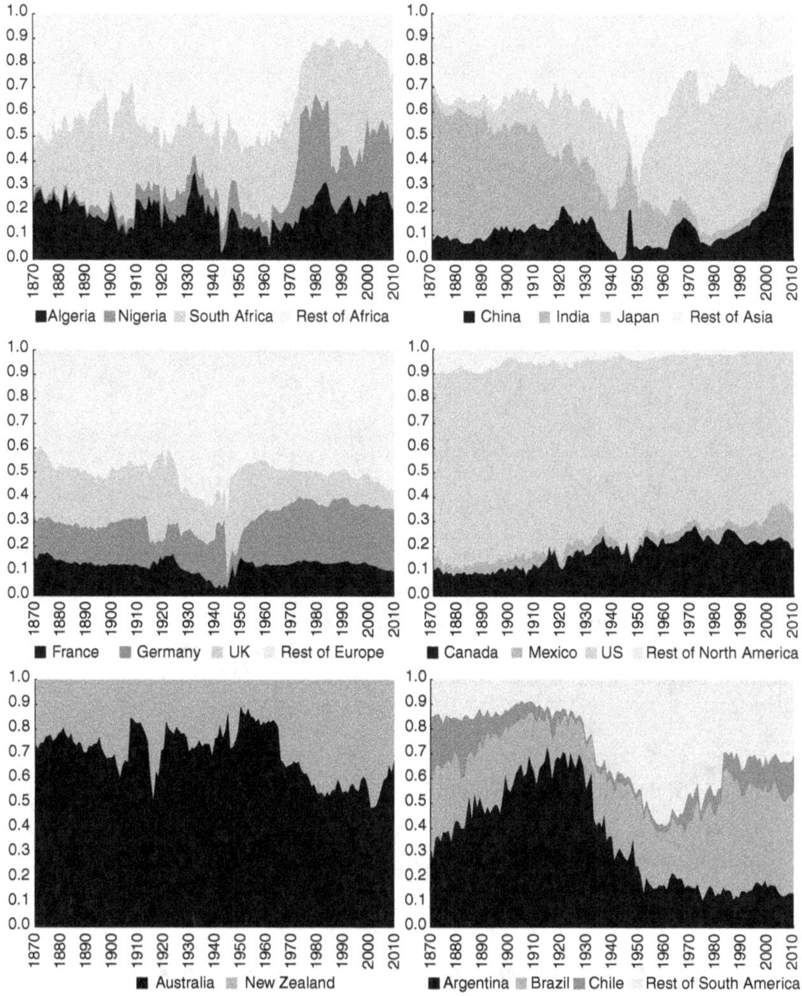

Figure 17.13 Regional export shares by countries within regions, 1870–2010
Sources: Jacks et al. 2011; Jacks and Novy 2018.

(5) the dominance of Australia in Oceania, coupled with a still strong performance by New Zealand throughout, given the fact that the Australian economy was, on average, five times larger than New Zealand during this period; and
(6) early leadership of Argentina in South American exports, reaching a peak of 73.20 per cent in 1915, with a rough maintenance of this figure until

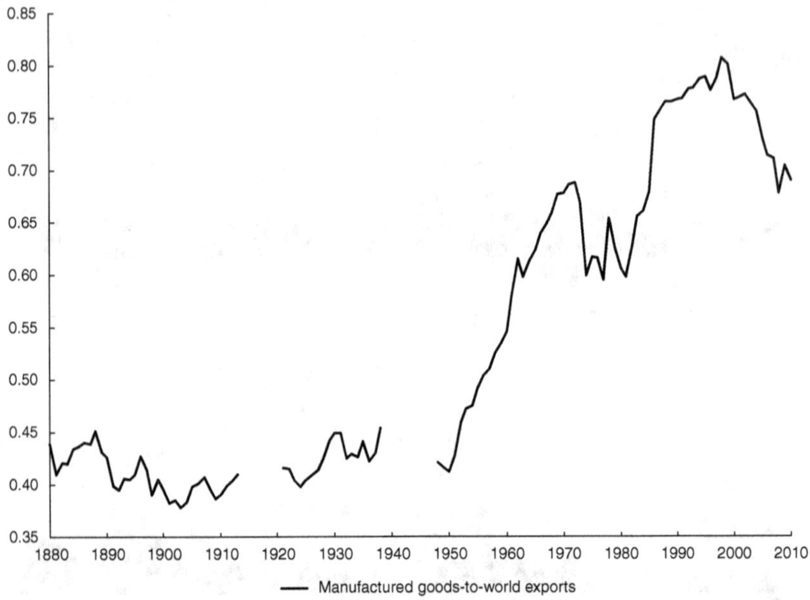

Figure 17.14 Share of manufactured goods in world exports, 1880–2010
Sources: League of Nations 1945; Lewis 1952; United Nations 1962; United Nations Statistical Division 2003; World Trade Organization 2010; Jacks et al. 2011; Jacks and Novy 2018.

1929, after which its share entered terminal decline, bottoming out at 11.34 per cent in 1975; and later dominance of Brazil, starting in 1945, when its share first exceeded that of Argentina and was maintained into 2010 with a share of 41.72 per cent.

Changes in the Composition of Trade over Time

There is some limited evidence in the historical record regarding the composition of trade in terms of constituent commodity flows as opposed to destination and origin countries. However, to our knowledge, no one until now has produced consistent evidence on even the simplest of commodity classifications – manufactured goods versus primary products. Figure 17.14 draws on various sources to chart the share of manufactured goods in world exports from 1880, the earliest date for which such tabulations have been made at a global scale. Remarkably, the share of manufactured goods was stable in the sub-period of 1880–1950, averaging in export value share 41.49 per cent, with an estimated linear trend growth rate of 0.01 per cent.

This constancy is congruent with an influential line of thought that sees trading relationships in this period, but especially before World War I, as one between industrial core countries and peripheral, often dependent, primary economies (cf. O'Rourke and Williamson 1999; Findlay and O'Rourke 2007). This 'Great Specialization' largely reflected differences in factor endowments and comparative advantage across countries. What is surprising is that the share remained stable even during a period of time in which former peripheral nations like Canada, Japan, and the United States industrialized. While there is evidence that intra-regional trade flows changed in composition – for example, the growing share of Japanese manufactured exports (Meissner and Tang 2018) – primary production and its trade continued to increase on both the extensive and intensive margins of an ever-changing periphery and survived the two world wars intact.

Figure 17.14 identifies 1950 as being a turning point in this series. The trade in manufactures share rose from 41.22 per cent in that year to a local maximum of 68.82 per cent in 1972. Apart from setbacks associated with commodity (e.g. oil) price shocks in the 1970s, this share continued to rise in value, cresting at 80.67 per cent in 1998.[11] This departure from the long-standing composition of trade in 1950 may stem from the rise of intra-industry trade, which refers to the degree to which firms compete with one another in the global marketplace within and not across industrial classifications (Grubel and Lloyd 1975). We also note that the primal forces behind the rise of intra-industry trade itself coincide with the establishment of the GATT in 1948 that targeted tariff reductions on industrial products, and with the golden age of Western growth from 1945 to 1973, affecting income per capita and population growth.

Another important change in the structure of production and trade which began in the early 1970s, but only saw its full articulation in the 1990s and 2000s, was the process of vertical specialization, which likely pushed the manufactured share to even greater heights. At its heart, vertical specialization relates to how multinational firms – which now dominate international trade – specialize in particular stages of a good's production and develop global supply chains where the parts of final goods may be traded many times over international borders (cf. Feenstra 1998; Hummels et al. 2001; Yi 2003; Johnson and Noguera 2017). Thus, the degree to which vertical specialization takes root will mechanically increase the manufactured share even if the level

11 Not coincidentally, 1998 marked the beginning of another massive run-up in real commodity prices throughout the 2000s (Jacks 2013).

of trade in finished goods remains constant, which it did not in the late twentieth century.

The Relationship between Immigration and Trade

Having described the contours of immigration and trade over these 141 years, we next address the relationship between the two. Economic theory suggests that the two phenomena are inversely related: as trade increases, returns to the factors of production – particularly, labour – become equalized between trade partners and reduce the incentives for migration (Mundell 1957). This result is derived from the Heckscher-Ohlin-Vanek model of trade, where countries differ in factor endowments and, thus, factor mobility is motivated solely by the differences in factor prices. Thus, trade and immigration act as substitutes.[12]

Complications arise, however, when factors are not completely mobile, firms are monopolistically competitive, and/or specific factors exacerbate differences within and between countries (Venables 1999). For example, trade and migration costs impede factor price equalization, and the same industries across countries may vary in which factor is used intensively. Apart from trade based on factor endowments, increased trade may correspond with more immigration or a combination of immigration responses (that is, an inverse U-shaped relationship) that depends on the composition of endowments, technologies, and trade and immigration costs.

While there is a large body of empirical research examining the impact of immigration on receiving countries, particularly on wages, few modern studies place immigration in an open economy context linked to trade flows or across multiple countries (Kohli 1999). The historical evidence is also mixed: the first wave of globalization at the turn of the twentieth century was marked by both growing trade and immigration, in contrast to the post-World War II era strongly favouring the movement of goods. Thus, how well the data correspond with different models may depend on the period being studied. For instance, endogenous frontier models, which apply to settler economies like Argentina and the US in the nineteenth century, are

12 A separate, but related issue, is the role of capital mobility, which may compound or mitigate the effects from either trade or immigration (see Markusen 1983). Chapter 18 of this volume below, by Barry Eichengreen and Rui Pedro Esteves, provides the historical context of capital market integration.

Table 17.1 Pairwise correlations between trade and migration, 1870–2000

	Northern America	Canada	United States
All years			
Gross bilateral export and migrant shares	0.299***	−0.033	0.374***
Gross bilateral import and migrant shares	0.011	−0.101	−0.008
Observations	429	167	262
1870–1910			
Gross bilateral export and migrant shares	0.375***	−0.051	0.422***
Gross bilateral import and migrant shares	−0.027	−0.082	−0.116
Observations	155	60	95
1910–50			
Gross bilateral export and migrant shares	0.158*	0.015	0.177*
Gross bilateral import and migrant shares	−0.077	−0.115	−0.110
Observations	150	59	91
1950–2000			
Gross bilateral export and migrant shares	0.103	−0.093	0.207**
Gross bilateral import and migrant shares	0.102	−0.234**	0.175*
Observations	186	72	114

Significance: *** 1 per cent, ** 5 per cent, * 10 per cent. Northern America comprises the two-country panel of Canada and the United States and each of their bilateral trade and migrant flows by trade partner. Unidentified countries are omitted. The years used in the correlation analysis are every decade between 1870 and 2000 or as indicated.

Sources: Gross bilateral export and import shares calculated from Jacks et al. 2011; Jacks and Novy 2018; immigration shares calculated using gross inflows as a share of total population from Madsen and Andric 2017.

more likely to predict complementarity between trade and factor mobility and not substitution.

We noted earlier that the challenges in tracking immigration over time make a comprehensive analysis of the link between trade and immigration infeasible. We partially address these concerns by using bilateral trade and immigrant flows for each major trade and migration partner of Canada and the United States between 1870 and 2000, measured decennially – that is, we match gross export and import shares of Canada and the US with immigrant inflows from the same country. In Table 17.1, bilateral export shares are positively and significantly correlated with migrant shares over the entire period, particularly for the United States (0.37). The coefficients for the US are positive in each sub-period, particularly during the first wave of globalization before World War I (0.42). In contrast, import shares are generally not statistically significant, with only the sub-period following World War II positive and weakly significant for the US and negative and significant for Canada.

One should be careful, however, in assessing the complementarity or substitutability of trade and immigration using raw correlations in the data. Other forces could drive their co-movement and establishing the true relationship between the two variables is difficult without exogenous variation in either trade or immigration. One potential way forward is to exploit changes in immigration policy in the United States in the early twentieth century. In particular, the introduction of immigration quotas in the 1920s induced large changes in the growth rates and subsequent stocks of immigrants, differentiated by origin country. These origin country migration changes could then conceivably be related to bilateral trade pattern changes in a more causal fashion. Thus, the trade of countries 'treated' with quotas that were binding can be compared with those unaffected in a standard gravity model.[13]

With respect to our specification of the gravity model, one of the strongest conclusions to have emerged from the extensive related literature is that precise inference relies upon a proper treatment of so-called multilateral resistance (Anderson and van Wincoop 2003) – that is, an unobserved average trade barrier effect may potentially bias any estimates of the effects of changes in bilateral trade costs. Put differently, there may have been either countervailing or reinforcing changes in the bilateral trade costs separating other countries from one another that accompanied any potential reduction in the supply of immigrants to the United States.

This perspective requires the inclusion of time-varying exporter and importer effects in the gravity model. Consequently, we combine Canadian bilateral trade data with the equivalent from the United States from 1920 and 1940, allowing for (an admittedly scant) seventeen precise country matches. Here, we augment a standard difference-in-differences linear regression specification to allow for any differential growth in Canadian versus US trade with quota-affected countries. The resulting triple-differences specification pools observations on Canadian and US bilateral trade in two periods

13 The full implementation of the quota system in 1924 was associated with a drop in European immigration to the US from 4.5 million during 1910–14 to less than 800,000 during 1925–29 (Ager and Hansen 2017). Some countries were more affected than others due to the fact that quotas were assigned on the basis of the foreign-born population in 1890 and not 1920. Consequently, Belgium, Greece, India, Italy, Japan, Russia, and Turkey are in our sample and were determined to have binding immigration quotas on the basis of data from 1890.

(1920 and 1940) and includes indicator variables for bilateral pairs involving a quota-affected country, bilateral pairs involving the United States, and bilateral pairs in 1940 along with a full set of interaction terms. The coefficient of interest is that for the full interaction of *Quota-USA-time*, which indicates the degree to which the United States' bilateral trade with quota-affected countries changed at a differential rate to that of Canadian bilateral trade with the same.

It should be emphasized that this specification controls for all country-specific, but time-variant unobserved variables, in particular GDP. As such, it is a fairly exacting specification to test for the relationship between trade and immigration. The results, reported in Table 17.2, show that the coefficient associated with *Quota-USA-time* for both exports and imports is positive, suggesting that for at least the interwar period, trade and immigration may have been substitutes. However, this evidence is more suggestive than definitive given changes in Canadian immigration policy over the same period when World War II disrupted trade, and there is evidence for complementarity between trade and immigration emerging from recent studies using even sharper discontinuities in policy, such as Parsons and Vézina (2016). Nevertheless, our results provide historical and empirical evidence in favour of factor-embodied substitution in line with economic theory.

Conclusion

Concern and backlash towards trade and immigration in recent years may reflect the return of trade flows and immigration stocks to heights not seen since the 1900s. Two world wars and a global depression notwithstanding, countries are more interconnected than ever before, even if the composition and sources of those goods and people have changed over time.

In this chapter, we described the patterns of both trade in goods and immigration between 1870 and 2010, noting some of the differences and similarities in the two periods of globalization bookending these years. While our analysis is limited by data availability and the results remain suggestive, we capture the bulk of recorded trade and migration, document their evolving patterns, and are among the first to consider the relationship between the two in the long-run. Our evidence suggesting substitutability between the two, in turn, may inform policy discussions that neglect to account for knock-on effects when considering each phenomenon in isolation. There still exist substantial gaps in our understanding, such as coverage

Table 17.2 Gravity model for bilateral trade of Canada and the US with partner countries

	(1) Dependent variable: NA exports	(2) Dependent variable: NA imports
Quota fixed effect	−1.2096	−1.1805
standard error	0.5036	0.4370
p-value	0.02	0.01
USA fixed effect	2.3075	2.3213
standard error	0.2668	0.4595
p-value	0.00	0.00
Quota–USA interaction	0.5398	1.2688
standard error	0.5377	0.4774
p-value	0.32	0.01
Time fixed effect	1.5877	1.4072
standard error	0.0875	0.1271
p-value	0.00	0.00
Quota–time interaction	−3.8223	−0.6545
standard error	0.5740	0.3570
p-value	0.00	0.07
USA–time interaction	−1.3752	−1.4942
standard error	0.0942	0.1406
p-value	0.00	0.00
Quota–USA–time interaction	1.5045	0.6567
standard error	0.6063	0.3826
p-value	0.01	0.09
	n = 68	n = 68

Notes: Results in column (1) are generated from a single regression pooling exports from 1920 and 1940. Results in column (2) are generated from a single regression pooling imports from 1920 and 1940. Poisson pseudo-maximum-likelihood (PPML) used for all regressions. Exporter and importer fixed effects have been suppressed, while standard errors are clustered on countries. Belgium, Greece, India, Italy, Japan, Russia, and Turkey are in the sample and were determined to have binding immigration quotas.
Source: Bilateral trade data drawn from Jacks and Novy 2018.

of undocumented immigration, trade in services, and some developing regions. Nor do we engage in normative discussions about the welfare gains or losses from both forces. Whether these two features of globalization continue uninterrupted in the future naturally remains to be seen.

References

Abramitzky, R. and Boustan, L. (2017). 'Immigration in American History', *Journal of Economic Literature*, 55(4), 1311–1345.

Ager, P. and Hansen, C. W. (2017). 'Closing Heaven's Door: Evidence from the 1920s US Immigration Quota Acts', available online at https://ssrn.com/abstract=3059439 (accessed 29 September 2020), SSRN.

Anderson, J. E. and van Wincoop, E. (2003). 'Gravity with Gravitas: A Solution to the Border Puzzle', *American Economic Review*, 93(1), 170–192.

Bandiera, O., Rasul, I., and Viarengo, M. (2013). 'The Making of Modern America: Migratory Flows in the Age of Mass Migration', *Journal of Development Economics*, 102(1), 23–47.

DEMIG. (2015). *DEMIG TOTAL, version 1.5*, International Migration Institute, University of Oxford.

Dumont, J.-C., Spielvogel, G., and Widmaier, S. (2010). 'International Migrants in Developed, Emerging and Developing Countries: An Extended Profile', OECD Social, Employment and Migration Working Papers 114, Paris: OECD Publishing.

Feenstra, R. (1998). 'Integration of Trade and Disintegration of Production in the Global Economy', *Journal of Economic Perspectives*, 12(4), 31–50.

Ferenczi, I. and Willcox, W. F. (1929). *International Migrations, Vol. I: Statistics*, New York: Gordon and Breach Science Publishers.

Findlay, R. and O'Rourke, K. (2007). *Power and Plenty: Trade, War, and the World Economy in the Second Millennium*, Princeton University Press.

Francois, J. and Hoekman, B. (2010). 'Services and Trade Policy', *Journal of Economic Literature*, 48(3), 642–692.

Grubel, H. G. and Lloyd, P. J. (1975). *Intra-Industry Trade: The Theory and Measurement of International Trade in Differentiated Products*, London: Macmillan.

Hatton, T. and Williamson, J. G. (1998). *The Age of Mass Migration*, Oxford University Press.

Hummels, D., Ishii, J., and Yi, K.-M. (2001). 'The Nature and Growth of Vertical Specialization in World Trade', *Journal of International Trade*, 54(1), 75–96.

Jacks, D. (2005). 'Immigrant Stocks and Trade Flows, 1870–1913', *Journal of European Economic History*, 34(3), 625–649.

Jacks, D. (2013). 'From Boom to Bust: A Typology of Real Commodity Prices in the Long Run', NBER working paper 18874, National Bureau of Economic Research.

Jacks, D. and Novy, D. (2018). 'Market Potential and Global Growth over the Long Twentieth Century', *Journal of International Economics*, 114, 221–237.

Jacks, D., Meissner, C. M., and Novy, D. (2011). 'Trade Booms, Trade Busts, and Trade Costs', *Journal of International Economics*, 83(2), 185–201.

Johnson, R. C. and Noguera, G. (2017). 'A Portrait of Trade in Value Added over Four Decades', *Review of Economics and Statistics*, 99(5), 896–911.

Kohli, U. (1999). 'Trade and Migration: A Production-Theory Approach', in Faini, R., de Melo, J., and Zimmermann, K. (eds.), *Migration: The Controversies and the Evidence*, Cambridge University Press.

League of Nations. (1945). *Industrialization and Foreign Trade*, Geneva: League of Nations.

Lewis, L. T., Monarch, R., Sposi, M. J., and Zhang, J. (2018). 'Structural Change and Global Trade', Federal Reserve Bank of Dallas Globalization and Monetary Policy Institute working paper 333.

Lewis, W. A. (1952). 'World Production, Prices and Trade, 1870–1960', *Manchester School*, 20 (2), 105–138.

Loungani, P., Mishra, S., Papageorgiou, C., and Wang, K. (2017). 'World Trade in Services: Evidence from A New Dataset', IMF working paper 17/77, International Monetary Fund.

McKeown, A. (2004). 'Global Migration, 1846–1970', *Journal of World History*, 15(2), 155–189.

Maddison Project Database, 2013 version. Bolt, J. and van Zanden, J. L. (2014). 'The Maddison Project: Collaborative Research on Historical National Accounts', *Economic History Review*, 67(3), 627–651.

Madsen, J. B. and Andric, S. (2017). 'The Immigration–Unemployment Nexus: Do Education and Protestantism Matter?', *Oxford Economic Papers*, 69(1), 165–188.

Magee, G. and Thompson, A. (2010). *Empire and Globalisation: Networks of People, Goods and Capital in the British World, c.1850–1914*, Cambridge University Press.

Markusen, J. (1983). 'Factor Movements and Commodity Trade as Complements', *Journal of International Economics*, 14(3–4), 341–356.

Meissner, C. M. and Tang, J. (2018). 'Upstart Industrialization and Exports: Evidence from Japan 1880–1910', *Journal of Economic History*, 78(4), 1068–1102.

Moses, A. (2012). 'Emigration and Political Development: Exploring the National and International Nexus', *Migration and Development*, 1(1), 123–137.

Mundell, R. (1957). 'International Trade and Factor Mobility', *American Economic Review*, 47 (3), 321–335.

O'Rourke, K. and Williamson, J. (1999). *Globalization and History: The Evolution of a Nineteenth-Century Atlantic Economy*, Cambridge, MA: MIT Press.

Ozden, C., Parsons, C., Schiff, M., and Walmsley, T. (2011). 'Where on Earth is Everybody? The Evolution of Global Bilateral Migration 1960–2000', *World Bank Economic Review*, 25(1), 12–56.

Parsons, C. and Vézina, P.-L. (2016). 'Migrant Networks and Trade: The Vietnamese Boat People as a Natural Experiment', IZA Discussion Paper 10112, Institute of Labor Economics.

United Nations. (1962). *International Trade Statistics 1900–1960*, New York: United Nations.

United Nations Statistical Division. (2003). United Nations Commodity Statistics Trade Database (UN COMTRADE), New York: United Nations.

Venables, A. (1999). 'Trade Liberalisation and Factor Mobility: An Overview', in Faini, R., de Melo, J., and Zimmermann, K. (eds.), *Migration: The Controversies and the Evidence*, Cambridge University Press.

World Trade Organization. (2010). *International Trade Statistics 2010*, Geneva: World Trade Organization.

Yi, K.-M. (2003). 'Can Vertical Specialization Explain the Growth of World Trade', *Journal of Political Economy*, 111(1), 52–102.

18
International Finance

BARRY EICHENGREEN AND RUI PEDRO ESTEVES

Introduction

'International finance' is a deceptively simple term. 'Finance', of course, refers to the management, creation, and study of money, banking, credit, investments, assets, and liabilities.[1] It follows that any study of finance, much less one spanning a century and a half, will have to cover a lot of ground. The qualifier 'international' would seem, at first glance, to require less nuance and helpfully restrict the investigation to financial transactions across borders. But this observation begs the question of whose borders exactly. Early in the period that we consider, a considerable volume of cross-border finance flowed from the metropolitan financial centres to colonial dependencies and was not, therefore, international in the strict sense of the word – although these flows raise many of the same analytical issues as financial transactions between sovereign nations.

We grapple with these puzzles in what follows. We start by characterizing capital flows in the long run, organizing our discussion in the next section around six facts relating to the volume and volatility of capital flows over a century and a half, measured in both net and gross terms. We also introduce evidence of an association between financial crises and large capital flows.

We then connect up the discussion with exchange rates and monetary policies. The organizing framework for this section is the 'trilemma', the idea that countries cannot simultaneously attain the three desiderata of free international capital mobility, exchange rate stability, and monetary autonomy. We describe where countries situated themselves relative to the trilemma over time and consider the political economy of their choices.

Finally, we study the connections between international finance and economic and financial stability. Whereas historians argue that pegged exchange rates and open capital accounts are engines of instability, theorists and others

1 This according to Investopedia: www.investopedia.com/terms/f/finance.asp (accessed 29 September 2020).

have been known to counter that these policies have been successfully reconciled with economic and financial stability under suitable institutional and political circumstances. In an effort to adjudicate this dispute, we present consistent measures of growth and debt crises over the century and a half covered in this chapter and discuss how their incidence is related to those institutional and political circumstances and, more generally, to the nature of the international monetary and financial regime.

Six Facts about Capital Flows

Figure 18.1 and Table 18.1 present data on a century and a half of international capital flows. We split the timeline into four familiar periods: pre-World War I, the interwar years, the Bretton Woods period, and the period of financial liberalization since the early 1970s. To the best of our knowledge, we are the first to compile a continuous series for de facto capital market integration over this arc of history.[2] Because capital flows are a bilateral phenomenon, we are forced to choose one side of the equation to normalize the flows. We adopt the viewpoint of the main recipients of foreign capital in history – that is, emerging and developing nations. All figures are normalized by the GDP of net recipients, and we exclude from the figures the main capital exporting nations.

Net flows have long been used in the empirical literature on financial crises and current account reversals (Feldstein and Horioka 1980; Jones and Obstfeld 2001). They are also a natural counterpart to the predictions of growth theory for international factor flows. Risk- or productivity-adjusted differentials in rates of return on capital should lead to capital flowing from capital-rich nations to capital-poor countries, these theories suggest, fuelling economic growth in the latter (Lucas 1990).

The preferred measure of net capital flows is the financial account of the balance of payments. Unfortunately, a consistent data set on financial accounts (provided by the IMF) is available only from 1970. For earlier periods, researchers must therefore use as proxies other components of the balance of payments. The mirror image of the current account is frequently utilized, motivated by the balance of payments identity.[3] It is generally a good proxy, aside from specific

2 We stand on the shoulders of giants, of course. For previous empirical reconstructions of long-term capital flows, see Jones and Obstfeld 2001; Obstfeld and Taylor 2004. A different literature takes the dual approach of quantifying financial integration by the covariance of the returns of domestic assets and a measure of global returns. For recent attempts along these lines, see Quinn and Voth 2008; Bekaert and Mehl 2017.

3 *Current Account + Financial Account + Capital Account* should theoretically add up to zero, save for errors and omissions.

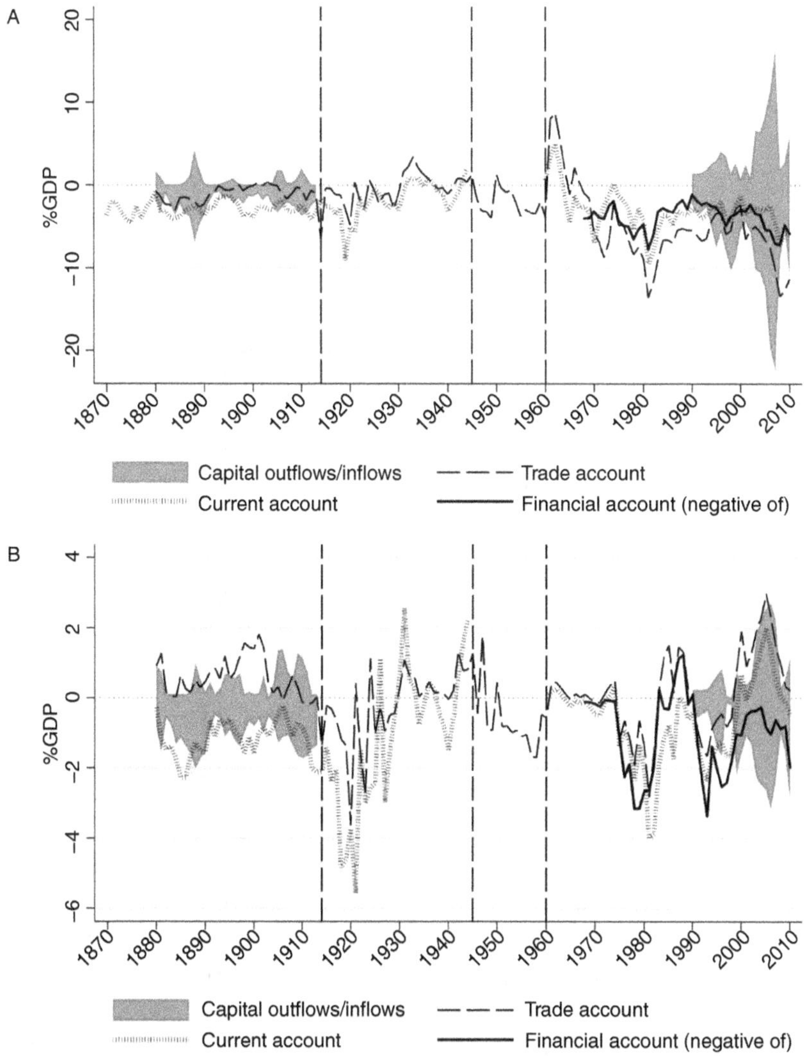

Figure 18.1 Capital flows, 1870–2010. A: Unweighted averages. B: Weighted averages (by GDP)

periods of large official interventions in the balance of payments. Intra-government loans, official development assistance, and the accumulation of large foreign exchange reserves by emerging nations since the 1990s are examples of such exceptions.

Table 18.1 Summary statistics of capital flows, 1870–2010

	1870–1913				1914–45		1960–79			1980–2010				
	Net flows		Gross flows		Net flows		Net flows			Net flows			Gross flows	
	TA	CA	Inflows	Outflows	TA	CA	TA	CA	FA	TA	CA	FA	Inflows‡	Outflows‡
Average†	−0.89	−2.66	3.75	2.43	0.22	−1.55	−6.22	−2.88	−7.02	−3.94	−3.53	9.41	5.03	−7.02
Median	−0.08	−1.92	2.95	1.05	0.07	−0.56	−4.25	−3.17	−4.00	−3.32	−2.84	6.64	2.88	−4.00
CV	−5.53	−1.47	1.36	1.66	23.55	−3.67	−2.06	−2.49	−2.45	−2.56	−2.54	1.08	1.55	−2.45
Correlations														
TA	1				1		1			1				
CA	0.40***	1			0.52***	1	0.53***	1		0.64***	1			
FA							0.40***	0.64***	1	0.43***	0.74***	1		

Notes: All variables in percentage of individual countries' GDP. TA = trade account; CA = current account; FA = financial account; † unweighted; ‡ 1990–2010; *** significant at 1 per cent.
Sources: See text.

A more imperfect proxy is the trade account. The accuracy of this proxy depends not only on the capital account being small, but also on net income from abroad being unimportant. The latter condition is frequently assumed but may not be warranted – for example, in periods or countries that pay or receive large labour income transfers (emigrant remittances) or capital returns. Nevertheless, in the absence of a coordinated reconstruction of the historical balance of payments, researchers regularly resort to this proxy.

A different perspective comes from the predictions of macro-finance, which emphasize the incentive to diversify and pool risk through cross-border capital flows. Gross flows are the empirical counterpart of these models, pointing up the problem that small net capital flows may disguise large cross-country gross flows. Moreover, the literature on capital-flow bonanzas and sudden stops emphasizes how not only flows, but also large cross-country gross positions may spread financial instability, particularly during periods of global crisis (Forbes and Warnock 2012; Cavallo et al. 2015).

For the purposes of this chapter we assembled a historical data set on gross capital flows into and out of emerging and developing nations. This combines data on international capital exports prior to World War I with the data made available by the IMF since 1990. Although these data straddle only half of our period, they cover the two phases of intense financial globalization.

Figure 18.1 is divided into two panels that plot the same yearly averages of each of the series. Panel A plots the series as unweighted averages of individual country values, whereas panel B weighs each country's data by its share in total GDP. The values in Table 18.1 are unweighted. Unweighted averages are more representative of the significance of capital flows to individual nations, whereas their weighted equivalents are a better representation of aggregate flows. The contrast is obvious, for instance, by comparing the sign of the trade and capital accounts in the last two decades. In panel A, the average emerging economy ran a trade deficit, whereas in panel B, the GDP-weighted trade balance was positive most of time, owing to large net exports from China and other South East Asian nations.

From these series, we can extract six stylized facts about capital flows in the long run.

1. International capital flows were more economically significant in the pre-1914 world and since the breakdown of the Bretton Woods system. This is especially evident when we weigh flows by the size of each nation's GDP

(Figure 18.1B), reflecting the fact that unweighted averages (Figure 18.1A) are more sensitive to outliers.[4]

2. Before the late 1970s, the only instance when (weighted) average capital inflows, as measured by the current account, exceeded 2 per cent of GDP was immediately after World War I. Apart from this period of post-war readjustment and recovery, emerging nations' net inflows consistently remained below 2 per cent of GDP. In contrast, the median current account in the last five decades increased to 3 per cent of GDP.
3. This rise in the size of flows has been accompanied by an increase in their volatility. The coefficient of variation of the current account reached a maximum in the interwar years. It has been about 70 per cent larger since the 1970s than it was in the pre-1914 period.
4. Trade accounts are poor proxies for net capital flows. Even though the correlation between trade and current accounts is positive and significant throughout, the current account is a better proxy for the financial account in the period for which we have information on the latter. Nevertheless, the correlation between the three variables appears to have increased during the Bretton Woods period and until the late 1990s.
5. Net measures disguise much larger gross capital flows in the two periods for which we have data. The scale of the cross-border flows in recent times is also roughly twice of the gross flows in the earlier period.
6. Systemic crises are associated with large gross flows in both directions. Spikes in capital inflows and outflows are as evident around the Baring crisis of 1890 and the 1907 crisis, as around the 1998 East Asian crisis and the more recent global financial crisis of 2007–09.

Facts 1 and 2 are consistent with accounts of the two eras of financial globalization, interrupted by the autarkic interregnum of the interwar period and the relative closure of the financial account during the Bretton Woods years (Eichengreen 1996). Within this consensus, there are authors who offer a stylized view of a U-shaped evolution of financial integration, bookended by similar levels of financial integration pre-1914 and post-1980 (Obstfeld and Taylor 2004).

This view is supported by a measure of de jure capital openness compiled by Quinn (2003), which is reproduced in Figure 18.2. According to this measure, capital market openness has not yet fully recovered the level

4 We excluded from Figure 18.1 and Table 18.1 the largest 1 per cent and the smallest 1 per cent of countries by GDP, but there are still some outliers by scale of capital flows in particular periods.

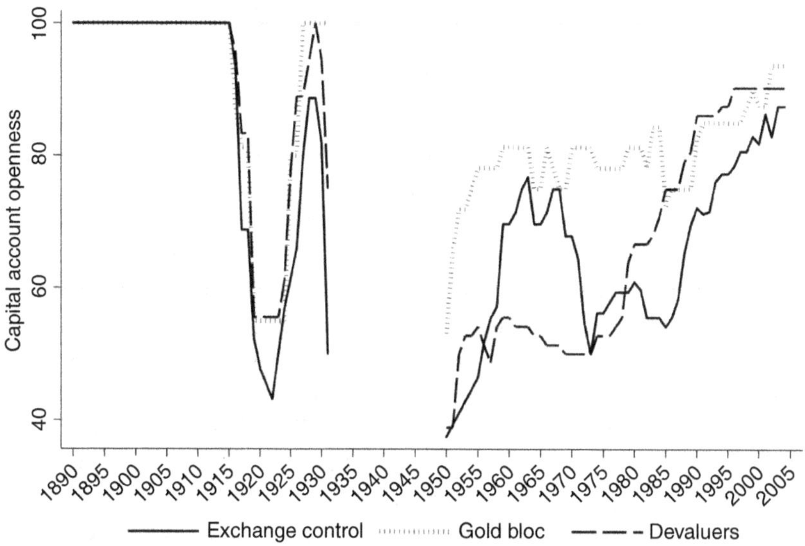

Figure 18.2 *De jure* financial account openness, 1890–2004
Note: Average values by group of nations, normalized for 100 = total openness.
Source: Quinn 2003.

reached before 1914. Other authors disagree, arguing that capital market integration is greater today than before World War I (Bordo et al. 1999; Mauro et al. 2002; Quinn and Voth 2008).

The data here are more consistent with the view that financial integration today has overtaken its historical counterpart and had exceeded it already in the 1970s. Rather than a U, financial globalization appears to have followed a 'swoosh' pattern (Bekaert and Mehl 2017). But more than just the scale of capital flows changed over the century and a half covered in this chapter. Their composition and the financial architecture conveying them changed as well.

A standard classification distinguishes private capital flows by investment motive. Portfolio flows reflect diversification motives. If, however, investors send their money abroad to acquire a controlling interest in foreign businesses, the flow is classified as foreign direct investment (FDI).[5]

5 This can be accomplished by setting up new production facilities abroad ('greenfield' FDI) or acquiring existing companies ('brownfield' FDI). The distinction between portfolio flows and FDI is not obvious to the historian or statistician. International organizations classify a firm as 'foreign-owned' if a non-national investor holds at least 10 per cent of its equity (Organisation for Economic Co-operation and Development

Portfolio investment dominated prior to World War I, as the investments in emerging markets were securitized by the main European stock markets and widely distributed to the public of retail investors (Edelstein 1982; Eichengreen 2003). A large fraction of this portfolio was composed of foreign government bonds, followed by investments in infrastructure (railways) and extractive sectors (Feis 1930; Woodruff 1966; Fishlow 1985).[6]

This composition started to change in the interwar years, as multinational companies (MNC) became a major vehicle for US and European FDI (Wilkins 1991).[7] Capital controls and domestic financial regulation in the Bretton Woods period reinforced this tendency, when MNCs directly acquired assets in foreign nations as a way of avoiding new regulatory barriers (Desai et al. 2004). At the same time, the market for sovereign bonds of developing nations was replaced by direct lending by commercial banks in the US and Europe (Eichengreen 2003). The rise of a new market for emerging markets bonds and equity in the 1990s then changed the structure of capital flows once more. Even though the new pattern is similar to that of the pre-1914 era, the greater importance of FDI and MNCs are still distinctive features.[8] They have substantive implications, since FDI is generally thought to have a greater positive impact on the growth of recipient nations and is less associated with financial volatility.[9]

Fact 3 is consistent with the temporal incidence of financial crises. The frequency of crises since the collapse of Bretton Woods is more than double that in the classic Gold Standard era (Bordo et al. 2001). But it is also much higher in the interwar years, as expected, and even the Bretton Woods era recorded more frequent crises than the classical Gold Standard era.[10]

The correlation between trade and current accounts (fact 4) also varies over time. It is much tighter in the post-World War II period than before 1914, especially when we use the GDP-weighted averages of the two net measures

2008). Outside of this classification there are still other forms of private flows, such as bank deposits, corporate and bank loans, and trade credit.

6 This ordering of sectors is related to nineteenth-century information asymmetries. In a world without easy access to reliable information, European investors preferred to apply their money in better-documented industries, such as railways and governments (Eichengreen 2003).

7 Simultaneously, the US became the main market for securitizing investment in emerging countries, at least until the Great Depression (Kindleberger 1973).

8 According to the IMF, FDI has averaged well over half of capital inflows to emerging economies during the last two decades (International Monetary Fund 2014).

9 On this topic see, among many, Alfaro et al. 2004; Eichengreen 2003.

10 We will return in the section on financial crises to the association between capital flow volatility and crises.

(Figure 18.1B). In contrast, the correlation is negative in the last decade of the nineteenth century and the first two decades of the twentieth.[11]

To understand the implications, it is useful to return to the balance of payments identity. If we assume that official interventions registered in the capital account were negligible, then we can approximate the financial account with the current account:[12]

−Financial Account = Current Account = Trade Account + Net Income from Abroad

This expression implies that a negative correlation between current and trade accounts, as observed in the late nineteenth century, is only consistent with large income flows. It has long been known that the core European nations in the nineteenth century ran weak or even negative trade balances that were financed by large invisible receipts and income from investment abroad (White 1933; Cairncross 1953). Emerging markets, for their part, were able to run large current account deficits, funded by capital exports from the European core and later the United States. But they had to pay their creditors via trade surpluses.

One possible explanation is that the rate of return on European investment in emerging nations was relatively high in the late nineteenth century, higher than the growth rate in capital exporting nations.[13] Emerging countries were only able to repay foreign investors by generating foreign exchange through large trade surpluses, while capital exporters could easily fund their trade deficits with this income stream.[14] Conversely, the positive correlation between trade and current accounts after World War II would imply lower rates of return on foreign investment. This is consistent with a situation of capital over-accumulation, where the return on foreign investment is below the domestic growth rate. This 'global savings glut' was highlighted by Bernanke (2005) for the recent period and could have contributed to the historically low yields on the eve of the 2007–09 financial crisis.

11 The correlations are −0.38*** in the 1890s, −0.62*** in the 1900s, and −0.56*** in the early 1910s (before the war).

12 This is probably not a bad approximation for the pre-1914 period, when emerging nations did not typically accumulate significant gold or foreign exchange reserves.

13 This condition is referred to as 'dynamic efficiency'. It implies that foreign investment is more attractive than domestic investment, such that capital exports are an efficient application of the nation's capital. See Eugeni 2016 for details.

14 This despite the international downward convergence of yields between 1890 and 1914 noted by Mauro et al. 2002. An older literature on 'Victorian decline' blamed the inefficient export of capital from the UK for the stagnation of the UK economy in the late nineteenth to early twentieth centuries (Cain and Hopkins 1980; Temin 1987).

This interpretation of the relation between the trade and capital accounts raises some interesting questions about the nature of capital flows in different periods. For instance, was the tight correlation between the trade balance and the current account in the Bretton Woods period driven by low perceived returns on foreign investment because of closed capital accounts? Why was the same correlation so high in the 1980s and 1990s, a period of increasing capital flows and high global returns?

Any attempt to answer these questions must cope with the fact that official capital transactions may confound or exaggerate the correlation between the trade and current accounts. The accumulation of large foreign exchange reserves by emerging economies is part of the explanation for the high correlation observed over the last two decades.

Despite the larger size of bilateral gross flows in the recent period (fact 5), the median capital outflow from emerging nations before World War I was still substantial, in the order of 1 per cent of GDP (Table 18.1). This period has frequently been characterized as one of 'development finance', when capital flowed from capital-rich mature economies to capital-poor emerging nations (Fishlow 1985; Clemens and Williamson 2004; Schularick and Steger 2010). That this was not entirely the case, as shown by these outflows, again points to the need for further investigation. That investigation could start by attempting to determine what fraction of these capital outflows from emerging markets may reflect measurement error. First, the database of gross flows prior to 1914 was built from the perspective of the capital exporters, such that we only have indirect information on capital inflows to emerging nations.[15] Therefore, the capital outflow figures were derived from the balance of payments identity: *Gross outflows* = *Gross inflows* – *Current Account* – *Capital Account*, assuming, again, that transactions on capital account averaged zero. Nevertheless, any official interventions in the capital account will be recorded incorrectly as private capital flows.[16]

Subject to this caveat, fact 6 suggests that our estimates of gross capital flows behave as expected, especially in periods of generalized financial instability. If we equate the severity of a crisis to the scale of combined gross inflows and outflows, the Baring crisis of 1890 and the 1907 US stock

15 See Stone 1999 and Esteves 2007 on the methodology used to compute gross capital flows.

16 Measurement error in other components of the balance of payments will also result in biased estimates of gross capital flows when using the balance of payments identity above. For instance, in the absence of reliable sources on tourism, transportation, and financial and legal services, 'invisible payments' to the rest of the world may be incorrectly classified as gross capital outflows.

market crash are the most dramatic such events before 1914. The scale of these two crises is comparable to the retrenchment at the time of the 1998 East Asian crisis, but it is dwarfed by the 2007–08 subprime crisis, when inflows and outflows were twice as large. It would be interesting to compare this episode with the 1929 crash, but gross flows have not been reconstructed for this period. These spikes in capital flows have been investigated by Forbes and Warnock (2012), who distinguish between 'surges' and 'stops' of foreign capital inflows and the 'flight' and 'retrenchment' of domestic capital outflows. The authors show how foreign stops and domestic flights react more to global factors – particularly uncertainty and risk appetite – than to local shocks.

When one looks more closely, it emerges that the timing of the peaks in the two gross flows series is not necessarily coincident. In the historical crises, the peaks happened between one and two years prior to the actual financial panic, with a shorter gap for the two recent crises. During the crisis, capital flows tail off dramatically. This time pattern is broadly consistent with the sudden stop view of financial crises in emerging nations (Bordo et al. 2010).

Trilemmas in History

The trends documented in Table 18.1 and Figure 18.1 illustrate the ebb and flow of financial globalization but say nothing about the causes of those fluctuations or the policy choices adopted by countries with respect to financial openness and capital-flow management. While most countries did not avoid the large cycles depicted in Figure 18.1, this does not mean that they necessarily embraced financial integration to the same extent.

As a first step in disaggregation, Figure 18.2 plots a measure of *de jure* financial openness for three groups of countries, as classified by a League of Nations study of exchange rate policies in the 1930s. So-called 'gold bloc' countries persisted in pegging their currencies to gold and maintaining an open financial account for longer than others; 'devaluers' were first to drop their pegs and allow their currencies to depreciate; while 'exchange control' countries kept their pegs, but only by imposing strict capital controls. This ordering is reflected in the average values of the indices of capital openness for the three groups of countries. A striking aspect of Figure 18.2 is the remarkably high persistence in attitudes towards capital controls among these groups of countries. The previous members of the gold bloc were the first to liberalize after World War II, and mostly persisted on that track subsequently, while the exchange control countries reverted to stricter capital account restrictions after the collapse of the Bretton Woods system in 1971.

We organize our discussion of countries' behaviour around the concept of the macroeconomic 'trilemma'. According to this concept, policymakers in open economies are constrained to choose only two out of three desirable, but conflicting, objectives: exchange rate stability, monetary autonomy, and financial openness. Recognition that macro policy and financial openness might be at loggerheads is not new.[17] Early contributions developed similar ideas to explain why the nineteenth-century network of international finance was not successfully reconstructed after World War I (Keynes 1919; Feis 1930). A subsequent literature then described how the lessons drawn from the global financial crisis of the 1930s shaped and informed the institutional framework devised at the 1944 Bretton Woods Conference (Nurkse 1944; Eichengreen 1996).

Others have also sought to investigate the trilemma historically. Obstfeld et al. (2004; 2005), for example, showed how monetary policy autonomy was conditioned by exchange rate regimes and financial openness in different periods. Although their results are consistent with the trilemma broadly defined, they found a surprisingly high degree of monetary autonomy, including for countries on a peg and with an open financial account.[18] Other authors focusing on the recent period have attributed this departure from a binding trilemma to the large foreign exchange reserves of emerging nations, especially since the late 1990s (Aizenman et al. 2013; Blanchard et al. 2015). By accumulating reserves, countries are able to sterilize capital inflows or, when needed, insulate the current account and domestic financial conditions from capital outflows. Whether this explanation is pertinent to earlier historical periods is an open question (to which we return below).

In this section, we extend existing trilemma indices back to the 1890s and test a number of possible drivers of countries' revealed preferences over time. Figure 18.3 summarizes the averages of the three indices by period and type of economy (advanced versus emerging/developing).[19]

17 On the intellectual history of the open-economy trilemma, see Irwin 2011.

18 They also found that capital controls per se did not allow for much autonomy, perhaps because of 'fear of floating' on the part of emerging markets (Calvo and Reinhart 2002).

19 From 1987 on, we defined as advanced all economies above the threshold for high-income economies as classified by the World Bank. We extended this income threshold back to World War II by deflating it by the US GDP deflator. Prior to World War II we used our own discretion, building on the qualitative literature, in classifying nations as advanced.

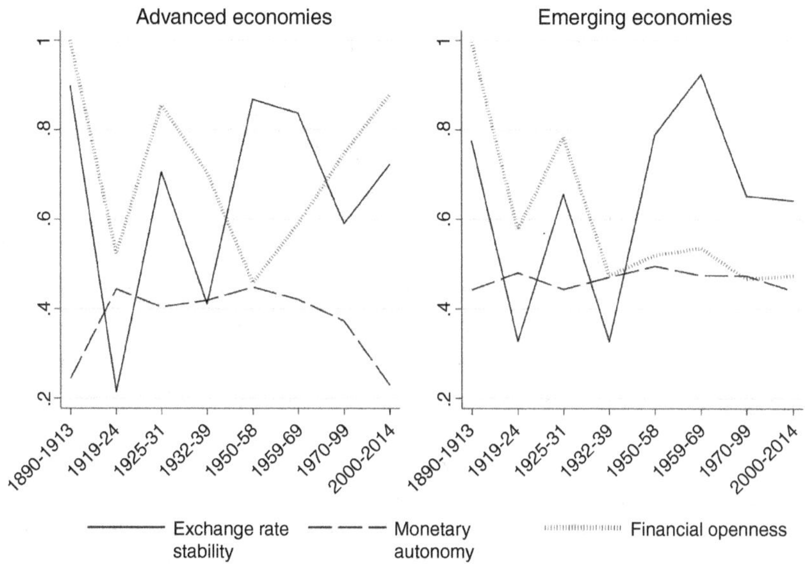

Figure 18.3 The trilemma indices, 1890–2014
Note: War years excluded.
Source: See text.

Each index is normalized to run between zero (no attainment of the policy objective in question) and one (full attainment).[20] We distinguish eight periods: the classical Gold Standard (pre-1914), the early 1920s float, the interwar Gold Exchange Standard (1925–31), the Great Depression years (after 1931), the early post-war period (prior to the removal of controls on current account transactions at the end of 1958), the heyday of the Bretton Woods system (to the end of the 1960s), the three decades following its demise, and the new millennium.

The broad trends are well known, from the clear preference for open capital accounts and exchange rate stability during the two periods under gold, to lower financial openness during Bretton Woods, and the more recent recovery of openness at the expense of monetary independence. In particular, the twenty-first century inaugurated a period when, despite less frequent pegs, exchange rate stability and monetary independence returned to the levels last seen under the interwar Gold Exchange Standard.[21] Consistent with Obstfeld et al. (2004),

20 For a description of the methodology used in constructing these indices, see Aizenman et al. 2013.

21 Rey (2015) refers to this as the macroeconomic dilemma, given her view that floating exchange rates are not an effective protection of monetary autonomy with open financial accounts.

the monetary autonomy index displays less variation over time and across type of economy. If foreign exchange reserves have indeed been accumulated as a substitute for capital controls, then these seem to have been used to protect a degree of monetary autonomy, at least in emerging economies.[22] In general, advanced countries had a greater preference for exchange rate stability and financial openness than emerging and developing economies, except in the periods following the breakup of the two main international fixed exchange rate regimes (the classical Gold Standard and the Bretton Woods system).[23]

Because averages may obscure a substantial degree of underlying variation across periods and countries, we used country data to estimate a model of the determinants of trilemma choices. Since the three trilemma indices are bounded between 0 and 1, we have to transform, first, the left-hand side variables to give them full support, which we do by running pseudo-logit models.[24] On the right-hand side, we include six explanatory variables, as well as dummies for the eight periods in Figure 18.3. The left-hand side in this regression is then similar to a log odds ratio, and we can recover the marginal effects of each of the explanatory variables x on the actual trilemma indices.[25]

Table 18.2 lists these marginal effects for a large sample of between 35 and over 170 countries and territories between 1890 and 2014.[26]

In the first three columns, we list the estimates of the model for emerging and developing economies. The results for advanced countries are then in the last three columns. Since all regressions include period effects, the estimates represent the impact of the explanatory variables on individual nations' choices over and above the common trends apparent in Figure 18.3.

Consistent with the predictions of standard open-economy macroeconomic models, large, advanced nations (as measured by real GDP) are less likely to adopt a peg and better able to sustain a relatively high degree of monetary autonomy. This would be the situation of countries issuing reserve

22 We cannot test this hypothesis for lack of historical data on reserve accumulation. Moreover, part of this stability may be illusory, since the three indices were constructed separately, whereas the trilemma assumes that there is a binding constraint connecting them ('pick two out of three').

23 The advanced country preference for stable exchange rates is driven by euro area membership in the most recent period, when we follow Aizenman et al. (2013) in coding these countries as possessing fixed rates.

24 Because the logistic function has a cumulative density function of $F(x_{it}) = \frac{1}{1+e^{\alpha+\beta' x_{it}}}$ where x is a particular vector of covariates, we can invert the function and get a linear regression: $\ln\left(\frac{F(x_{it})}{1-F(x_{it})}\right) = \alpha + \beta' x_{it} + \tau_t + \epsilon_{it}$, where τ_t are period dummies.

25 The formula for the marginal effects is simply $\frac{\partial F(x)}{\partial x} = \beta F(x)[1 - F(x)]$.

26 The country coverage changes because of the increasing number of nations and territories reporting data over time.

Table 18.2 Determinants of trilemma choices

Variables	(1) Exchange rate stability	(2) Monetary autonomy	(3) Financial openness	(4) Exchange rate stability	(5) Monetary autonomy	(6) Financial openness
GDP	−0.003	−0.055***	−0.029***	−0.093***	0.043***	0.005
	(0.012)	(0.009)	(0.006)	(0.010)	(0.012)	(0.007)
GDP per capita	0.006***	−0.003**	0.017***	0.002	−0.005**	0.010***
	(0.002)	(0.002)	(0.002)	(0.001)	(0.002)	(0.001)
Trade openness	0.013	−0.115***	0.025***	−0.007	0.014	0.035***
	(0.011)	(0.017)	(0.005)	(0.009)	(0.010)	(0.009)
Colony	0.147***	−0.015	0.019			
	(0.040)	(0.031)	(0.012)			
Democracy	−0.004***	0.005***	0.006***	−0.004**	−0.002	−0.005*
	(0.001)	(0.001)	(0.001)	(0.002)	(0.002)	(0.003)
Polity2	−0.002***	0.002***	0.004***	−0.002**	−0.000	−0.003*
	(0.001)	(0.001)	(0.001)	(0.001)	(0.002)	(0.002)
Period effects	Yes	Yes	Yes	Yes	Yes	Yes
Observations	3,792	1,814	2,840	1,355	1,092	1,344
R-squared	0.128	0.076	0.163	0.342	0.210	0.322

Note: estimates of marginal effects with robust standard errors in parentheses. Periods defined as in Figure 18.3, excluding war years (1914–19 and 1940–49). *** $p<0.01$, ** $p<0.05$, * $p<0.1$

currencies, such as Great Britain before World War I or the United States more recently, whose size and economic clout allowed them to act, effectively, as price-setters in international capital markets (a situation referred to as 'exorbitant privilege', as in Eichengreen 2011).

Conversely, large developing countries tend to be financially less open, yet despite this, possess less monetary autonomy. If we compare countries by their standards of living (GDP per capita) instead of their size, it appears that richer nations in both groups gravitate towards the Gold Standard combination of exchange rate stability and financial openness, while forsaking monetary autonomy. The results suggest further that trade and financial openness are complementary – countries that depend more on trade have a tendency to open the capital account. They are also consistent with the idea that trade openness, because it encourages countries to open the capital account, limits monetary independence, although this pattern comes through strongly only for emerging economies.[27]

Colonial status shows up as a significant determinant of exchange rate stability, not surprisingly, since colonies tended to peg to their colonizer.[28] Interestingly, there is no correlation of colonial status with capital account openness or monetary autonomy, although some historical literature suggests that there should be an association.

Finally, we test the effect of democracy on the trilemma by considering two indices from the POLITY IV project (Marshall et al. 2016). The first is a measure of institutionalized democracy, while the second is the difference between that measure of democracy and an index of autocratic or authoritarian regimes. These measures are denoted 'Democracy' and 'Polity2', respectively. In both cases, larger values correspond to more democratic polities.

The results are that more democratic regimes prefer financial openness and monetary autonomy to pegging their currencies. This is consistent with the conclusions of earlier studies (e.g. Eichengreen 1996). The pattern is evident in the interwar period, when the rise of universal suffrage was partly responsible, in this view, for the difficulty in returning to the Gold Standard, since the newly empowered working classes refused to sacrifice domestic economic conditions to the target of a fixed peg and pressured their governments to exercise their monetary autonomy. Given the opposition to capital controls of financial interests (which also have a voice in democratic political systems), the trilemma was then resolved by floating the exchange rate, either as a conscious policy choice or due to a crisis. A similar association between democracy and floating exchange rates is evident in the post-war period, where the explanation is plausibly similar (see e.g. Leblang 1999).

Future researchers could extend these results in a number of directions. One extension would consider the interaction between political regimes, economic structure and party politics or ideology, related literature having shown that different political parties (right wing versus left wing) tend to support pegs in certain circumstances and floating exchange rates in others (Berdiev et al. 2012). Another might consider the role of larger systems, from the Gold Standard and the sterling and dollar areas to the European Monetary System and now the euro area.

27 We measure trade openness as the sum of exports and imports over GDP.

28 Some colonial pegs persisted after the end of colonial administration; examples include the CFA franc of the former French West African colonies and some members of the former sterling area.

Finally, our model does not distinguish between policy preferences and the capacity of governments and societies to deliver on those preferences. The negative sign of democracy measures in the model for exchange rate stability (Table 18.2) can be interpreted as an expression of policy preferences, but equally as an indication of the prevalence historically of weak pegs owing to the existence of weak institutions that are obstacles to making credible commitments (Bordo and Flandreau 2003). Likewise, the prevalence of capital controls can be both a policy preference and an indication of the difficulty of making credible commitments to the pursuit of stable monetary, exchange rate, and financial policies. Better measures of the strength of institutions and the capacity of governments and societies to make credible commitments would enable investigators to distinguish between these interpretations.

Crises of International Finance

The history of international finance is all but synonymous with the history of financial crises. The Great Depression, a macroeconomic crisis if ever there was one, and the 1931 financial crisis precipitated the transition from the Gold Exchange Standard to the dirty (managed) float of the 1930s, and from open capital accounts to capital controls. The 1971 run on the dollar was similarly the event precipitating the transition from the Bretton Woods gold–dollar standard to the post-Bretton Woods float. Financial crises are evident throughout international financial history. Not for nothing did Charles Kindleberger entitle the first chapter of his classic *Manias, Panics, and Crashes*, 'Financial Crisis: A Hardy Perennial' (Kindleberger 1978).

To a large extent, the debate over desirable trilemma choices is a debate over the susceptibility of those different regimes to crisis risk. Modern conventional wisdom is that pegged exchange rates, when operated in an environment of open capital accounts and high capital mobility, are dangerously susceptible to speculative attack and collapse. But this modern conventional wisdom is hard to reconcile with the observation that exchange rates were successfully stabilized, often for long periods, under the classical Gold Standard. The IMF's 'new' or 'institutional' view suggests that governments should move cautiously when contemplating the removal of capital controls, since open capital accounts can be associated with serious economic excesses and imbalances, in developing countries in particular (International Monetary Fund 2012). Again, however, this view sits uneasily with the observation that open capital accounts were successfully maintained, in advanced and developing countries alike, prior to 1913. Whether one set of arrangements, or regime, is more crisis-prone than another is, as economists like to say, an empirical question.

Bordo et al. (2001) provide an early summary of the historical evidence. They tabulate and compare the frequency of currency crises, banking crises and twin crises since 1880, contrasting the various international monetary and financial regimes. Currency crises are episodes when there is a forced change in parity, abandonment of a pegged exchange rate, or an international rescue. Banking crises are episodes when one observes either bank runs, widespread bank failures and the suspension of the convertibility of deposits into currency, or else significant banking sector problems resulting in the erosion of most or all banking system collateral or a fiscally underwritten bank restructuring. In twin crises, both types of events occur in the same or immediately adjoining years. The authors follow a constant sample of twenty-one countries over time.[29]

Currency crises, they show, were less frequent under the classical Gold Standard than in the interwar years, the Bretton Woods period, or the post-Bretton Woods float (the frequency of these crises was more than three times as high under each of these subsequent regimes). This finding confirms the truism that there was something special about currency stability under the classical Gold Standard. Eichengreen (1996) emphasizes distinctive aspects of not just the economic, but also the political context. Governments and societies prioritized exchange rate stability relative to other economic policy goals. Stabilizing the exchange rate was seen as the principal means by which the authorities could ensure a relatively stable price level. There was limited awareness of other goals. Unemployment was not conceived as a macroeconomic phenomenon that might be targeted by policy; instead, contemporaries referred to and thought of the unemployed as casual labourers, vagrants, and the destitute. Lacking an agreed definition of unemployment, governments did not gather data on its extent. There was no agreed theory linking central bank policy to unemployment or the trade cycle, as macroeconomic fluctuations were known. The electoral franchise was limited and, in many countries, subject to a property requirement, so even had workers wanted central banks to prioritize and target unemployment, they had limited ability to make their preferences felt.

29 For the recent period they compare an expanded sample of fifty-six countries. Recall the discussion in our introduction of the dilemma of whether to consider a balanced or unbalanced panel.

A qualification is that currency crises were noticeably more frequent in emerging markets, in Latin America for example, than in the industrial core. Although there have been a number of studies of these so-called peripheral economies (see, inter alia, Keynes 1913; Ford 1962; de Cecco 1974; della Paolera and Taylor 2003), there is little agreement on what explains the contrast; there is a tendency to wave one's hands, to say 'weaker institutions', and to move on. A number of these countries had broader electoral franchises, preventing the monetary authorities from prioritizing exchange rate stability above all other goals. They sometimes lacked a central bank to accumulate reserves and manage the capital account. Some were specialized in the production and export of a narrow range of commodities, exposing them to unusually high price level and balance of payments volatility. They were on the receiving end of the substantial capital flows described above, exposing them to the sudden-stop problem.

In addition, emerging markets often had narrower and less developed banking and financial systems. When the direction of capital flows reversed, or even when inflows slowed, liquidity and solvency problems could therefore develop. Investors would flee not just the banking system, but also the country, and the currency could come crashing down. Banking crises and twin crises were more frequent in emerging markets than industrial countries in the 1880–1913 period. But banking crises in the advanced countries were far from unknown, something to which the rich literature on the United States attests (Sprague 1910; Jalil 2015). The frequency of banking crises was not less under the Gold Standard than subsequently. Bordo et al. (2001) estimate banking crisis frequency to have been higher in 1880–1913 than under both Bretton Woods (1945–71) and the post-Bretton Woods float (1973–97). And as twenty-first-century experience reminds us, the banking crisis problem is still with us.

From this point of view, the interwar period stands out. The two decades from 1919 to 1939, and especially the 1930s, saw a higher incidence of crises than in any of these other periods. Crises in these decades were spread evenly between banking crises, currency crises, and twin crises. Economic historians have ascribed the exceptionally unstable nature of this period to changes in economic and political circumstances. Kindleberger (1973) emphasizes the change in the source of capital imports relative to pre-war years, as a less experienced set of New York-based financial institutions replaced the London financial houses as the principal source of international finance. Foreign investment, in his view, became more volatile, less discriminating, and more prone to reversals. Eichengreen (1996) emphasizes changed political

Table 18.3 Crisis frequency

Period	External debt crises	Growth crises
1880–1913	0.097	0.054
1919–39	0.236	0.103
1946–71	0.117	0.027
1972–99	0.188	0.054
2000–2010	0.119	0.021

Sources: See text.

circumstances. The electoral franchise had been broadened, consciousness of unemployment was greater, and central banks now found it more difficult to credibly elevate exchange rate stability above other policy goals. International political tensions associated with the reparations tangle in the 1920s and remilitarization in the 1930s made it more difficult for European countries to agree on the cooperative management of exchange rates and capital flows, especially once an isolationist United States withdrew from the international stage. Just as our analysis of trilemma choices in Table 18.2 highlights the influence of both economic and political factors, this discussion of crises suggests that their incidence cannot be understood by considering either economics or politics in isolation from one another.

In Table 18.3 we extend the historical comparison to growth crises and sovereign debt crises. Growth crises are defined, following Ghosh et al. (2014), as episodes that are in the bottom fifth percentile of growth declines (current year relative to the average of the previous three years). Sovereign debt crises are identified as defaults on interest or principal and/or restructuring, including instances where rescheduled debt is extinguished on terms less favourable than the original obligation. Data on growth rates are from the Maddison Project Database and the IMF's *International Financial Statistics*; data on external debt crises are from the database underlying Reinhart and Rogoff (2009). Here we follow an unbalanced panel of countries, with coverage expanding over time.

For external debt crises, the picture is broadly consistent with what we see for currency crises. Debt defaults were far from unknown under the classical Gold Standard, but they were less frequent than subsequently. In the same way that countries were able to successfully stabilize their exchange rates more frequently than subsequently, they were able to repay what they borrowed – it is not surprising that these two aspects of international financial stability went hand in hand. The interwar period again stands out for the opposite reason: just as there was an exceptionally high instance of banking and currency crises, there was an exceptionally high incidence of debt defaults. The frequency of external debt crises rose between the Bretton Woods years 1946–71 and the remainder of the twentieth century, as capital controls were relaxed and the volume of international capital flows recovered. It then fell back subsequently, creating the hopeful possibility that emerging markets, in particular, would make progress in learning how to manage external debt.

Growth crises look similar, with one prominent exception. Growth crises or collapses were relatively frequent during the classical Gold Standard years – as frequent or more frequent as under Bretton Woods, in the last quarter of the twentieth century, and in the first decade of the twenty-first. The Gold Standard, it would appear, succeeded in reconciling exchange rate stability with high international capital mobility, including a relatively stable record of external debt repayment, but not in delivering a high level of macroeconomic stability. Whether this real-sector volatility reflected the banking crisis problem, whether the exchange rate stability and record of relatively smooth external debt repayment were achieved at the expense of macroeconomic stability, or whether the explanation lies elsewhere is an important question to pursue.

Conclusion

In this chapter, we have provided three perspectives on the last century and a half of international finance. The first perspective, emphasizing international capital flows, shows how international capital mobility and the extent of financial integration trace out a U-shaped pattern over time: high before the Great Depression, low from the 1930s to the 1970s, and then increasingly high again in the years that follow. The second perspective describes the policy trade-offs between capital mobility, exchange rate stability, and monetary autonomy that provide the starting point for understanding these intertemporal changes. The third perspective looks in more depth at the consequences of those choices for economic and financial stability in particular. These three perspectives provide a framework for thinking about the evolution of the international monetary and financial system.

Our three perspectives also point to an agenda for research. Many readers will have already thought of important topics that bear further investigation, focusing perhaps on particular countries, markets, and events. We would point as well to the importance of gathering additional historical data on the operation of the international financial system. Information on gross capital flows, for example, remains spotty. Country coverage of many variables is incomplete. Shaping the future of the international and monetary system in positive directions requires better understanding of its history. But better understanding of its history requires not just developing and testing hypotheses, but also continuing with the hard work of filling in the data gaps.

References

Aizenman, J., Chinn, M., and Ito, H. (2013). 'The "Impossible Trinity" Hypothesis in an Era of Global Imbalances: Measurement and Testing', *Review of International Economics*, 21, 447–458.

Alfaro, L., Chanda, A., Kalemli-Ozcan, S., and Sayek, S. (2004). 'FDI and Economic Growth: The Role of Local Financial Markets', *Journal of International Economics*, 64 (1), 89–112.

Bekaert, G. and Mehl, A. (2017). 'On the Global Financial Market Integration "Swoosh" and the Trilemma', NBER working paper 23124, National Bureau of Economic Research.

Berdiev, A., Kim, Y., and Chang, C.-P. (2012). 'The Political Economy of Exchange Rate Regimes in Developed and Developing Countries', *European Journal of Political Economy*, 28, 38–53.

Bernanke, B. (2005). 'The Global Saving Glut and the US Current Account Deficit', remarks at the Sandridge Lecture, Virginia Association of Economists, Richmond, VA.

Blanchard, O., Adler, G., and de Carvalho, I. (2015). 'Can Foreign Exchange Intervention Stem Exchange Rate Pressures from Global Capital Flow Shocks', NBER working paper 21427, National Bureau of Economic Research.

Bordo, M. and Flandreau, M. (2003). 'Core, Periphery, Exchange Rate Regimes, and Globalization', in Bordo, M., Taylor, A., and Williamson, J. (eds.), *Globalization in Historical Perspective*, University of Chicago Press, 417–472.

Bordo, M., Eichengreen, B. and Irwin, D. A. (1999). 'Is Globalization Today Really Different than Globalization a Hundred Years Ago?', in Collins, S. and Lawrence, R. (eds.), *Brookings Trade Policy Forum*, Washington, DC: Brookings Institution.

Bordo, M., Eichengreen, B., Klingebiel, D., Martinez-Peria, M. S., and Rose, A. (2001). 'Is the Crisis Problem Growing More Severe?', *Economic Policy*, 16(32), 51–82.

Bordo, M., Cavallo, A., and Meissner, C. (2010). 'Sudden Stops: Determinants and Output Effects in the First Era of Globalization, 1880–1913', *Journal of Development Economics*, 91(2), 227–241.

Cain, P. and Hopkins, A. (1980). 'The Political Economy of British Expansion Overseas, 1750–1914', *Economic History Review*, 33(4), 463–490.

Cairncross, A. (1953). *Home and Foreign Investment, 1870–1913: Studies in Capital Accumulation*, Cambridge University Press.

Calvo, G. and Reinhart, C. (2002). 'Fear of Floating', *Quarterly Journal of Economics*, 107(2), 379–408.

Cavallo, E., Pedemonte, M., Powell, A., and Tavella, P. (2015). 'A New Taxonomy of Sudden Stops: Which Sudden Stops Should Countries Be Most Concerned About?', *Journal of International Money and Banking*, 51, 47–70.

Clemens, M. and Williamson, J. (2004). 'Wealth Bias in the First Global Capital Market Boom, 1870–1913', *Economic Journal*, 114, 303–337.

De Cecco, M. (1974). *Money and Empire: The International Gold Standard, 1890–1914*, Oxford: Blackwell.

Della Paolera, G. and Taylor, A. (eds.) (2003). *A New Economic History of Argentina*, New York: Cambridge University Press.

Desai, M., Fritz Foley, C., and Hines, J. R. (2004). 'A Multinational Perspective on Capital Structure Choice and Internal Capital Markets', *Journal of Finance*, 59(6), 2451–2487.

Edelstein, M. (1982). *Overseas Investment in the Age of High Imperialism: The United Kingdom, 1850–1914*, New York: Columbia University Press.

Eichengreen, B. (1996). *Globalizing Capital: A History of the International Monetary System*, Princeton University Press.

(2003). *Capital Flows and Crises*, Cambridge, MA: MIT Press.

(2011). *Exorbitant Privilege: The Rise and Fall of the Dollar*, Oxford University Press.

Esteves, R. (2007). 'Between Imperialism and Capitalism. European Capital Exports before 1914', mimeo.

Eugeni, S. (2016). 'Global Imbalances in the XIX, XX and the XXI Centuries', *Economics Letters*, 14, 69–72.

Feis, H. (1930). *Europe, the World's Banker, 1870–1914*, New Haven: Yale University Press.

Feldstein, M. and Horioka, C. (1980). 'Domestic Saving and International Capital Flows', *Economic Journal*, 90, 314–329.

Fishlow, A. (1985). 'Lessons from the Past: Capital Markets During the Nineteenth Century and the Interwar Period', *International Organization*, 39, 38–93.

Forbes, K. and Warnock, F. (2012). 'Capital Flow Waves, Surges, Stops, Flight and Retrenchment', *Journal of International Economics*, 88, 235–251.

Ford, A. G. (1962). *The Gold Standard, 1880–1914: Britain and Argentina*, Oxford: Clarendon Press.

Ghosh, A., Ostry, J., and Qureshi, M. (2014). 'Exchange Rate Management and Crisis Susceptibility: A Reassessment', IMF working paper 14/11, International Monetary Fund.

International Monetary Fund. (2012). 'The Liberalization and Management of Capital Flows: An Institutional View', International Monetary Fund.

(2014). 'How Do Changes in the Investor Base and Financial Deepening Affect Emerging Market Economies?', in *Global Financial Stability Report, April 2014*, ch. 2, International Monetary Fund.

Irwin, D. (2011). *Trade Policy Disaster: Lessons from the 1930s*, Cambridge, MA: MIT Press.

Jalil, A. (2015). 'A New History of Banking Panics in the United States, 1825–1929: Construction and Implications', *American Economic Journal: Macroeconomics*, 7, 295–330.

Jones, M. and Obstfeld, M. (2001). 'Saving, Investment, and Gold: A Reassessment of Historical Current Account Data', in Calvo, G., Dornbusch, R., and Obstfeld, M. (eds.), *Money, Capital Mobility, and Trade: Essays in Honor of Robert Mundell*, Cambridge, MA: MIT Press, 303–363.

Keynes, J. M. (1913). *Indian Currency and Finance*, London: Macmillan.

(1919). *The Economic Consequences of the Peace*, London: Macmillan.

Kindleberger, C. (1973). *The World in Depression, 1929–1939*, Berkeley: University of California Press.

(1978). *Manias, Panics and Crashes: A History of Financial Crises*, New York: Basic Books.

Leblang, D. (1999). 'Political Institutions and Exchange Rate Commitments in the Developing World', *International Studies Quarterly*, 43, 599–620.

Lucas, R. (1990). 'Why Doesn't Capital Flow from Rich to Poor Countries?', *American Economic Review*, 80(2), 92–96.

Marshall, M., Gurr, T., and Jaggers, K. (2016). *Polity IV Project: Political Regime Characteristics and Transitions, 1800–2015*, Vienna, VA: Center for Systemic Peace.

Mauro, P., Sussman, N., and Yafeh, Y. (2002). 'Emerging Market Spreads: Then Versus Now', *Quarterly Journal of Economics*, 117(2), 695–733.

Nurkse, R. (1944). *International Currency Experience*, Geneva: League of Nations.

Obstfeld, M. and Taylor, A. (2004). *Global Capital Markets: Integration, Crisis, and Growth*, Cambridge University Press.

Obstfeld, M., Shambaugh, J., and Taylor, A. (2004). 'Monetary Sovereignty, Exchange Rates, and Capital Controls: The Trilemma in the Interwar Period', *IMF Staff Papers*, 51, 75–108.

(2005). 'The Trilemma in History: Tradeoffs among Exchange Rates, Monetary Policies, and Capital Mobility', *Review of Economics and Statistics*, 87(3), 423–438.

Organisation for Economic Co-operation and Development. (2008). *OECD Benchmark Definition of Foreign Direct Investment*, 4th ed., Paris: OECD.

Quinn, D. (2003). 'Capital Account Liberalization and Financial Globalization, 1890–1999: A Synoptic View', *International Journal of Finance and Economics*, 8, 189–204.

Quinn, D. and Voth, H.-J. (2008). 'A Century of Global Equity Market Correlations', *American Economic Review Papers and Proceedings*, 98, 535–540.

Reinhart, C. and Rogoff, K. (2009). *This Time Is Different: Eight Centuries of Financial Folly*, Princeton University Press.

Rey, H. (2015). 'Dilemma not Trilemma: The Global Financial Cycle and Monetary Policy Independence', NBER working paper 21162, National Bureau of Economic Research.

Schularick, M. and Steger, T. (2010). 'Financial Integration, Investment, and Economic Growth: Evidence from Two Eras of Financial Globalization', *Review of Economics and Statistics*, 92(4), 756–768.

Sprague, O. (1910). *History of Crises under the National Banking System*, Washington, DC: National Monetary Commission.

Stone, I. (1999).*The Global Export of Capital from Great Britain, 1865–1914: A Statistical Survey*, London: Macmillan.

Temin, P. (1987). 'Capital Exports, 1870–1914: An Alternative Model', *Economic History Review*, 40(3), 453–458.

White, H. (1933). *The French International Accounts*, Cambridge, MA: Harvard University Press.

Wilkins, M. (ed.) (1991). *The Growth of Multinationals*, Aldershot: Elgar.

Woodruff, W. (1966). *Impact of Western Man: A Study of Europe's Role in the World Economy 1750–1960*, London: Macmillan.

19
War and Empire

JARI ELORANTA AND LEIGH GARDNER

An Imperial World and its Demise

By the beginning of the twentieth century, a combination of military and economic advantages allowed a growing number of imperial powers to control much of the world's land area and population. This expansion facilitated the movement of people, goods, and capital, but it came at a cost of considerable violence and disruption for colonized people and also provided the motivation for global conflict. Little more than a half-century later, however, these empires had collapsed, and a new hegemonic order had emerged, dominated by the rivalry between the United States and the Soviet Union and their respective allies.

The new superpowers of this era did not attempt the formal rule of formerly colonized territories on anything like the same scale. Instead, they relied on tools of informal influence developed in the previous era. This did not prevent them from engaging in debilitating arms races, but it shifted some of the costs onto poorer countries where proxy wars were waged. The demise of this order has seen the return of asymmetric warfare and counter-insurgency techniques, and has created new instabilities in the world economy.

How colonial rule shaped the economic and political development of the world has been debated since it was still a going concern. In the twenty-first century, the debate has been revived by a series of influential publications in economics and related fields, which use innovative econometric methods to understand the causal links between different aspects of colonialism and later outcomes.[1] This work has raised important questions, but has also been criticized for compressing decades of historical change and neglecting the role of indigenous actors in shaping colonial institutions.[2] Efforts to address

1 To name just a few examples, see La Porta et al. 1999; Acemoglu et al. 2001; Banerjee and Iyer 2005; Huillery 2009; Wantchekon et al. 2015; Easterly and Levine 2016.
2 Austin 2008; Bayly 2008; Bolt and Gardner 2020.

these points have generated a rapid increase in new quantitative research on Asia, Africa, and Latin America.

The chapter investigates the complex and multiple links between colonialism, war, and economic development. Colonialism was as much a response to the unprecedented expansion in global trade which began during the nineteenth century as it was a cause. As trade expanded, countries competed to gain control over new and growing markets in ever more distant parts of the world. As this competition intensified, informal influence gave way to formal territorial control in much of Asia and Africa. Acquiring and defending these territorial empires increased tension between European powers, and helped to lay the foundations for the two world wars.

While the demands of the war effort increased the importance of colonies to metropolitan states, they also helped to undermine the system of colonial rule. Colonizing countries weakened by the war struggled to cope with pressure from nationalist movements energized by rhetoric about self-determination and resistance to the hardships of economic depression and war. Over the two decades following the end of World War II, most colonies became independent. Cold War dynamics shaped the entry of these new states into the ranks of sovereign governments. While the Cold War era was different from the colonial era in many respects, the chapter considers some parallels between the two. Finally, the chapter concludes by examining how the legacies of this history have shaped the post-Cold War world.

Imperialism and Trade

The renewed expansion of empires in the late nineteenth and early twentieth centuries was closely linked with the rapid growth of international trade, finance, and the Second Industrial Revolution. It was once common to view the connection between these two as a coercive act, in which imperial powers extracted resources from their colonies.[3] However, more recent work on the economic history of colonized regions has altered this perception. First, 'globalization' in the sense of integration of international markets happened earlier in the nineteenth century, before this amplified phase of European territorial acquisition.[4] Figure 19.1 gives data on the exports of different world regions from 1800 to 1938, and shows that a major part of this

3 The phrase 'extractive institutions' has had a resurgence since the publication of Acemoglu et al. 2001.

4 O'Rourke and Williamson (2002) date this approximately from the 1820s. The question of when globalization began remains the subject of debate. See also de Vries 2010.

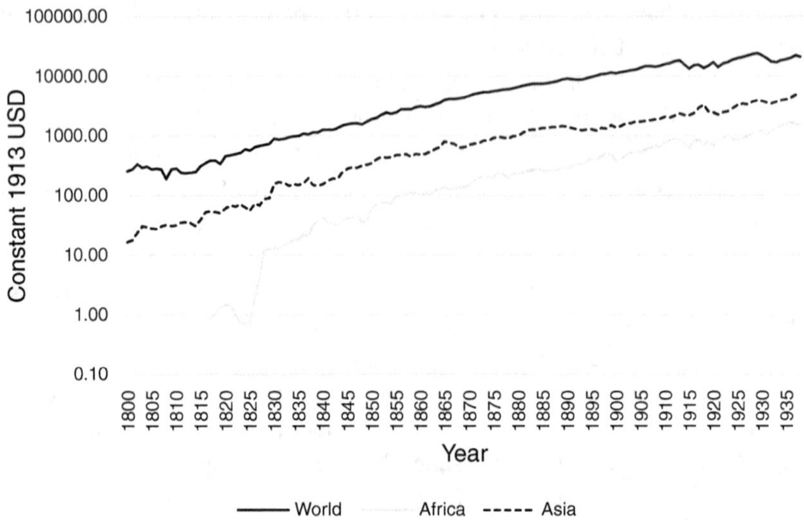

Figure 19.1 Exports, 1800–1938 (constant 1913 $)
Source: Federico and Tena Junguito 2016.

trade expansion occurred prior to formal colonial conquest in the later nineteenth century. Merchants and producers in the colonies were just as alive to the opportunities offered by a changing global economy as those in Europe, and trade between these regions relied on their cooperation (Bayly 2008; Law 2009).

Competition between imperial powers over the proceeds of this trade helps explain why they invested in colonial conquest on such a scale at the end of the century. One interpretation of the 'scramble' for territory in West Africa argues that it was the weaker of the two powers in the region, namely France, which took the initiative in colonial conquest, as colonial produce was more important to France than to Britain (Frankema et al. 2018). The same applies to the Middle East, where the decline of the Islamic sphere made it attractive for the colonial powers (Hopkins 1973; O'Rourke and Williamson 1999).

Once colonial conquest had occurred, however, imperial policies and institutions played an important role in facilitating further growth of export industries. Mitchener and Weidenmier (2008) find that being part of an empire doubled the external trade of colonies relative to countries that were not colonized. They attribute this principally to a combination of imperial trade policies, which helped to promote colonial trade through preferential tariffs and the creation of customs unions, and other factors that helped to reduce transaction costs, including the use of metropolitan currencies like British sterling in colonies and shared administrative languages.

Colonial governments were also proactive in the promotion of export trades, granting generous incentives to metropolitan business and mobilizing capital raised in metropolitan markets to construct infrastructure and reduce transport costs. Figure 19.2 compares the yield on government bonds for colonies and independent countries before 1914. While the bond yields of colonized countries remained only slightly above those of British consols, often used as a benchmark for the lowest possible sovereign risk in this period, the yields of bonds issued by sovereign nations are both higher and more volatile.[5]

Why investors were attracted to colonial securities remains the subject of debate. Ferguson and Schularick (2006) argue that British colonialism guaranteed sound financial management and a common legal framework, which reassured investors that debts would be serviced in time. In contrast, Accominotti et al. (2011) maintain that these better terms reflected the fact that colonies were subsidiary governments to the British government, and

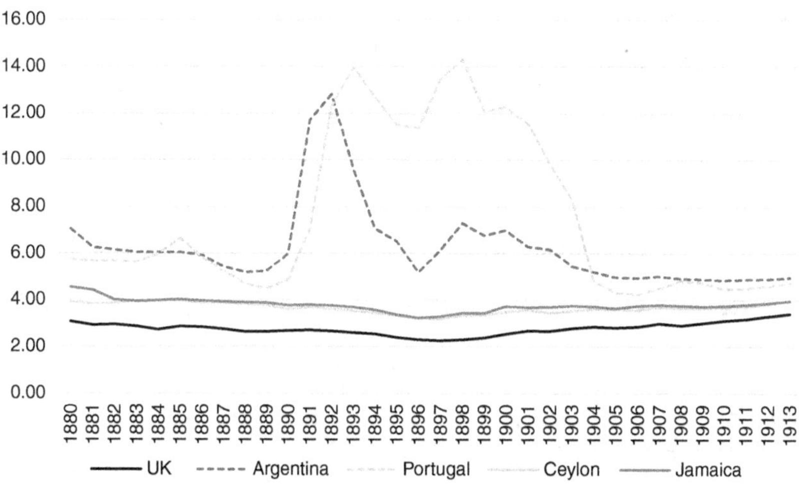

Figure 19.2 Yield on government bonds, 1880–1914
Source: Accominotti et al. 2011.

5 The historiography of the 'empire effect' is particularly dominated by Britain and its colonies, which may not be typical. Less research is available on the ways in which other empires channelled external funds to their colonial territories.

thus their credit reflected that of the imperial power rather than their own fundamentals. Focusing particularly on West Africa, Gardner (2017) argues that this advantage was not necessarily automatic. Instead, imperial institutions took active steps, through market-making and other means, to make marginal colonial bonds more attractive.

For the countries that remained formally independent, access to capital often involved some sacrifice of sovereignty in the form of international financial controls or other concessions to the lending country. Mitchener and Weidenmier (2010) argued that such interventions, collectively labelled 'supersanctions' could also reduce spreads on the bonds of independent countries, though Gardner (2017) finds for independent Liberia that the decrease was not as large as for British colonies in West Africa. Further, such interventions often resulted in political unrest in borrowing countries, and also influenced their strategic alignments during wartime (Tooze and Ivanov 2011; Tuncer 2015).

The primary use of foreign capital by colonial and independent governments alike was the construction of infrastructure, particularly railways, which also made up a large proportion of overall public spending by colonial governments. Booth (2007: 245) finds that across South East Asia by the early twentieth century, public works constituted in the order of 40 per cent of public spending by Dutch, British, and French colonial governments in the region. The same was true in sub-Saharan Africa after the initial period of colonial conquest in the first part of the twentieth century (Frankema 2011; Gardner 2012). Table 19.1 gives a breakdown of public spending patterns in

Table 19.1 Colonial public spending in Asia and Africa in the 1930s (share of total spending)

	Administration	Security	Public works	Social spending	Debt service
Vietnam	25.4	18.2	24.8	3.1	4.5
Netherlands East Indies	38.0	26.0	6.0	12.0	13.0
Federated Malay States	34.0	2.0	20.0	20.0	9.0
Gold Coast	27.0	13.0	37.0	13.0	4.0
Kenya	22.0	13.0	19.0	13.0	33.0

Notes: Asia figures: 1931; Africa figures: 1938.
Sources: Booth 2007: 252; Frankema 2011: 148.

selected colonies in Asia and Africa. Investments in infrastructure, particularly railways, had significant effects on the structure of colonial economies and the ways in which they developed thereafter by reducing transport costs and shaping the second-nature geography of colonies (Chavez et al. 2014; Jedwab et al. 2017; Donaldson 2018; Herranz-Loncán and Fourie 2018).

Infrastructure investments facilitated rapid growth in the export of primary goods, but there was little investment in either state capacity or the human capital of the indigenous population. This left both indigenous producers and colonial governments with limited ability to cope with the economic instabilities of the interwar period, which led to rising unrest. Falling producer prices, accumulated debts and agitation for rent decreases allowed urban elites in India to link a broader campaign for independence to peasant organizations for the first time (Roy 2012: 220–221). Cocoa producers in the Gold Coast held up their supply in a bid to increase prices (Austin 1988). From 1934, there was a wave of strikes by labourers on sugar estates in the Caribbean (Fraser 1996). Colonial governments often responded violently. In Zambia, a strike by copper miners protesting low pay and increased taxation was met with open fire by colonial troops, leaving several mineworkers dead (Gardner 2012: 122–123). These movements formed the building blocks for political parties and other organizations that began to press for outright independence. This was just one way in which colonialism was linked to violence and warfare across the nineteenth and twentieth centuries.

Imperialism and Conflict

Imperial governments managed to shift much of the burden of local expenditures in the colonies to local taxpayers, including policing. However, the defence of empires remained costly for metropolitan states. Davis and Huttenback (1986: ch. 5) argue that defence expenditures represented significant transfers to colonial governments from imperial budgets. While the definition of 'transfer' can rightly be queried – what they were paying for was their own ability to stay in power – it remains the case that local instability placed growing pressure on imperial and colonial budgets alike. At the same time, competition between a growing number of imperial powers was a key contributor to the two global conflagrations of the twentieth century, which had considerable costs for both colonies and colonizers.

Data on defence spending show considerable increases during the period of colonial expansion. Kennedy (1989: 191–192) argues that 'it is probably impossible to disentangle the "British" from the "imperial" element of

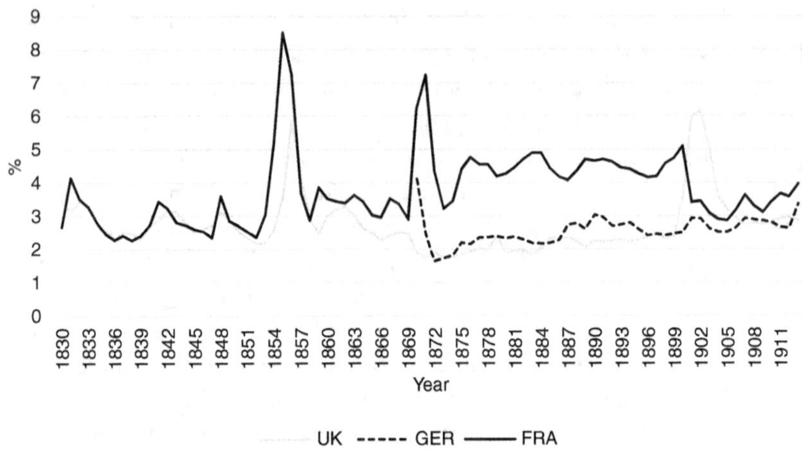

Figure 19.3 Defence expenditures of UK, Germany, and France, 1830–1913 (% of GDP)
Sources: Eloranta 2005; 2007.

defence expenditures'. Regardless, we can discern general patterns based on national spending data, as seen in Figure 19.3. The spending of the three imperial nations differed in the nineteenth century. For example, French defence spending increased until the beginning of the twentieth century before converging to the other two nations. German and British expenditures declined, after some earlier volatility, until the 1870s, when they started to rise again, due to the colonial expansion. This is also reflected in the size of military forces, naval tonnage in particular. The protection of the massive British empire required a substantial naval fleet and, as seen in Figure 19.4, the UK was the clear naval leader before World War I, and leading along with the US until World War II, and the US took a clear lead only afterwards.

The distribution of responsibility for imperial defence expenditures varied between empires, and as yet there has been limited research on the bargaining that took place between colonial and metropolitan governments and the ways it changed over time. The British government managed to outsource at least some of the costs of imperial conquest and defence to colonial taxpayers, most notably in India, causing long-standing tension between the government of India and the imperial government (Leake 2014). Alexopoulou (2018) uses a comparison of Portuguese and British Africa to argue that the former had to bear a larger share of the defence burden because they could not benefit from the same economies of scale as the larger empire.

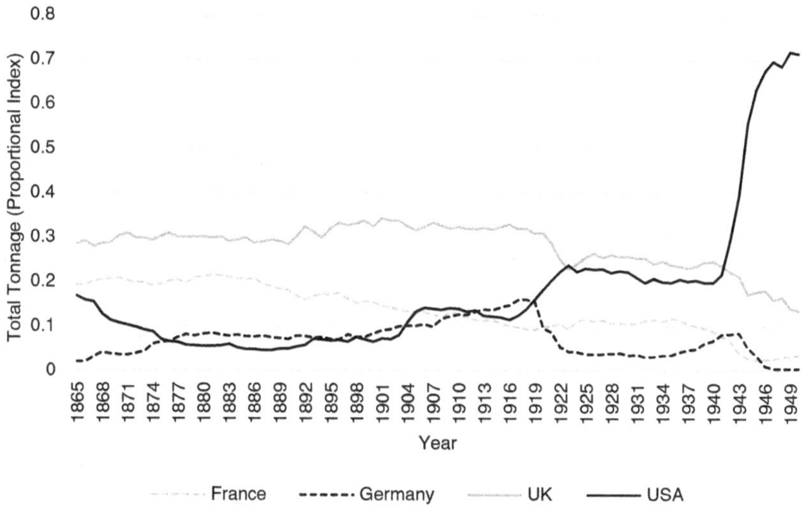

Figure 19.4 Total proportional tonnage of France, Germany, UK, and USA, 1865–1950
Source: Crisher and Souva 2014.

Perhaps more important than the direct defence costs of empire were the indirect implications. Imperialism, and imperial competition were also important contributors to the two world wars. These were not the only causes, by any means. The bigger picture was complicated and included wider military competition between belligerent powers, shifting patterns of alliances and power balances within Europe, and the rise of nationalism (see Eloranta 2007 for further discussion). However, colonial expansion was part of a path towards a massive conflict that few could foresee. Trade routes to the colonies represented vital arteries for the European empires, and the competition for territory across the globe increased tensions among them, particularly as the amount of available territory dwindled.

World War I became one of the first true global total wars in history, and victory was determined by economic resources. The richer, and usually more democratic, countries mobilized more men and materiel for the war, and their war industries proved quite capable of serving the needs of the global war machine. The economic disorganization of Russia, Austria-Hungary, and Germany resulted in major disruptions of supply lines and led to outright subsistence crises. Subsequently, economic protests turned at the final stage of the war into mass movements against existing political regimes (Blum et al. 2014).

Colonies also contributed resources and manpower needed for the war effort, though the scale of their contributions was restricted by both distance and the comparatively low level of development (Broadberry and Harrison 2005). Still, these contributions were often seen in local terms as substantial and often became the subject of disputes and resentment. Over 2.5 million soldiers fighting for Britain came from outside the British Isles, and 1.5 million of those men came from India. India also provided materiel and other support to the tune of £479 million. In return, India was promised reforms and greater autonomy, which, by and large, did not materialize, and thus contributed to the interwar independence movement there (Tai-Yong 2000). The same was true in Africa. Overall, about 440,000 indigenous soldiers, together with 140,000 settlers of European descent and 268,000 indigenous war workers travelled from Africa to Europe between 1914 and 1918 to take part in the war, mainly as part of French forces. High casualty rates and sometimes forced recruitment of these soldiers generated organized resistance, which laid the groundwork for nationalist movements later in the century (Koller 2014).

Overall, World War I represented a huge shock to global trade, politics, and the movement of people, even though the majority of the fighting was focused on the European continent. European nations experienced immense transformations involving extensive state regulation, substitution of market mechanisms by state officials, and the introduction of new military technologies. The role of non-European producers increased during the war and this led to price competition; industrial sectors were reconfigured during wartime, which resulted in displacement effects after the conflict; and the war hastened industrialization outside of Europe, which further eroded the European imperial systems (Findlay and O'Rourke 2007).

The interwar period was one of tremendous instability and institutional failures, like the League of Nations as a disarmament mechanism, in Europe and other regions. The human costs and injuries resulting from the war damaged the European economies even more than the destruction of capital. Another notable feature of the interwar economy was the significant decline in foreign trade, even in the 1920s – this development was mainly caused by national and autarkic commercial policies. This policy shift often had a dramatic effect on the colonized territories, as imperial powers began to see their empires as self-contained units, heightening imperial competition over resources. Moreover, the high defence spending often meant only modest growth in other types of government spending (Lindert 1994; Eloranta et al. 2014).

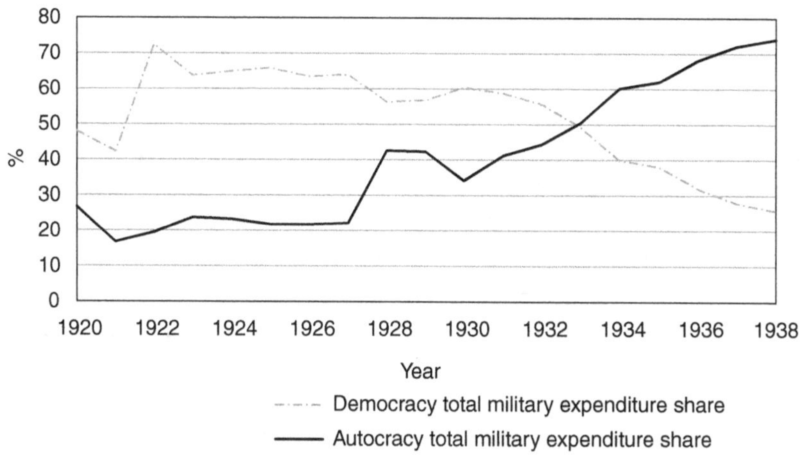

Figure 19.5 Total real military spending shares of the democracies versus the autocracies in the seventeen-country system, 1920–38

Notes: Autocracies included, either for the whole period or partially: Germany (1933–38), Italy (1922–38), Japan (1933–38), Portugal (1926–38), Spain (1936–38), and USSR. Democracies included: Belgium, Denmark, Finland, France, Netherlands, Norway, Portugal (1920–25), Spain (1920–35), Sweden, Switzerland, UK, and USA.

Source: Eloranta 2017 and the sources listed in it.

These wider legacies helped sow the seeds for another conflict, which emerged two decades after the armistice. World War II was the most expansive and costly conflict in human history. As in the case of World War I, its origins were complicated. One of the key features, for certain, was the rise of authoritarian regimes in the 1920s and 1930s, and their quest for greater resources and territory, including existing and new colonies. The arms race that ensued in the 1930s was extensive, and some states like Germany and Japan were already on a war footing by 1938. Japan was in conflict with China by the time hostilities in Europe began. As we can see in Figure 19.5, the military spending share of the autocracies increased substantially in the 1930s, while democracies were much slower to rearm in response. Thus, the Axis powers (initially Germany, Japan, and Italy, as per the Tripartite Pact signed in September 1940) were in a better position to enter World War II. After that, the extreme total war nature of the conflict and the importance of resources, with the United States and the USSR joining the Allies, gave the Allies the edge. Also, the impact of World War II was much more profound for the economies of Axis countries.

In many ways, although separated by a twenty-year 'interwar period', the two wars can be understood as a single historical process to which the European colonial dimension was fundamental; Europe was the theatre of a long 'civil war', fuelled by rising nationalism and the clash of empires. However, World War II began in Asia before spreading across the world, although most of the belligerents realized that the conflict in Europe would be the key battleground (Land and Eloranta 2016). Overall, the conflict led to almost 100 million casualties around the world, and ethnic cleansing and other forms of violence towards civilian populations became widespread tools of suppressing one's enemy. The destruction of capital, again globally, was much more extensive in World War II, since it was a much more mobile war, fought on many continents. Moreover, the bang for the buck in weaponry increased rapidly prior to and during the war, hence the destruction from bombings and ground assaults became devastating.

Colonies again played a vital role in turning the war into a truly global conflict. Colonial troops were needed both in Europe and to protect the colonies, the trade routes, and the vital resources. India provided 2.5 million men for the British war effort. British colonies in Africa served as staging posts for military operations. Allied operations employed large numbers of colonized people in various capacities, boosting the local economies temporarily. Moreover, the colonies provided many crucial strategic materials and metals, as did many of the neutral states like Sweden (Sherwood 2011; Golson 2012). However, World War II also hastened the independence movements in many of the European colonies, as they were again promised freedoms and autonomy that failed to materialize quickly. The next two sections examine the collapse of the European empires and the establishment of a new hegemonic order in their wake.

Collapse and Decolonization

Even the victorious imperial powers emerged from war weakened, both economically and financially. At the same time, political ideas emerging during this period, along with economic hardship in the colonies, helped to empower expanding nationalist movements in many colonies (see e.g. Manela 2007). As Hopkins (2018: 695) puts it, 'aspirations derived from Western liberalism and absorbed by urban elites led to demands for a new deal for the colonial world that the imperial powers could neither accommodate nor eliminate'. Which of these factors played the dominant role in precipitating decolonization remains a subject of debate. Whatever the cause, the transfer of power meant difficult choices for a number of actors, including the leaders of newly independent governments, businesses and producers, and the former colonizers, about what their future relationship should be. International institutions – first the League of Nations, then the United Nations and the post-war international financial institutions – became important players in the debates about decolonization as newly independent countries joined one by one.

While the first transfers of power back to the colonial populations in the twentieth century occurred just after the end of World War II, most colonies experienced a final period of interventionist colonial rule before achieving sovereignty from the late 1950s onward. One reason for this was the perceived importance of colonial territories in overcoming post-war dollar deficits among the European imperial powers (White 2011). This was a key motivation in the return of the Dutch and French governments to South East Asia in an effort to revive links to their colonies (van der Eng 2003). Increasingly ambitious colonial development projects had the same motive, though their success was often limited by both bad planning and limited resources. While not all such initiatives were failures, they were not enough to address the accumulated grievances of the colonial period.

Over the decades following the end of World War II, imperial powers ceded control over their colonies to new governments. This transfer was not always peaceful. In some colonies, the attempts by colonizing countries to retain their colonial possessions resulted in protracted conflict exacerbated by the tensions of the Cold War. Vietnam, Algeria, Mozambique, and Angola stand out as prominent examples. These conflicts sometimes had considerable financial consequences for the colonizers, but even larger economic and human costs for the former colonies. Even where the process of decolonization itself did not involve conflict, internal divisions masked during the fight for independence made political stability difficult to establish after independence was achieved. Richard Rathbone (2008: 13), in a study of Ghanaian independence in 1957, compared images from the celebrations in Accra to wedding photographs: 'large numbers of people who loathe one another can be forced to smile when faced by a camera and the implications of a permanent record'. In some cases, these rifts proved fatal to the post-independence state, resulting in violent and traumatic splits. Even where the state remained whole, however, divisions could create severe disruption. In Nigeria, the Biafran War became one of the major humanitarian crises of the decolonization era (Achebe 2012).

Independent states faced a range of questions connected to the end of their relationships. One was in deciding the extent of future relationships with former colonizers. Colonial rule encompassed political, cultural, and commercial connections between the colonizer and the colonized. Dismantling all of these relationships quickly could be costly. Head et al. (2010) show that, on average, trade between former colonies and their former colonizers declined in the decades following the transfer of power. The decline was particularly stark in countries where decolonization had involved conflict. Some former colonies elected to maintain closer ties than others. Most of what had been French Africa, for example, remained within the colonial currency union even while other African countries officially moved towards at least nominal monetary independence (Schenk 1997; Stasavage 2003).

Another difficulty, greater for Africa than for Asia, was in filling public sector roles abandoned by expatriate officials. Particularly in African colonies, where education had been largely outsourced to missionaries, there was very limited provision of secondary and tertiary education during the colonial period (Frankema 2012). Notoriously, there were only three college graduates in the whole of the Congo when it attained independence in 1960 (Akyeampong 2018: 70). In a comparison of Indonesia and the Congo, for example, Frankema (2013: 169) argues that 'the nationalist leaders who steered Indonesia toward independence had a distinctively better educational background than the Congolese leaders'. A larger indigenous intellectual class also provided a system of 'checks and balances' that was absent in the Congo.

A third issue was in changing the structure of colonial economies, diversifying away from the primary exports prioritized in the colonial period. Post-independence governments approached this in a variety of ways, though in most cases there was extensive state intervention in economic development. While this was true in both Asia and Africa, the outcomes were often very different between the two regions. A number of former colonies in Asia managed to achieve both sustained growth and structural change across this period. In Africa, on the other hand, the gains from economic growth in the first decades of independence were largely erased by a protracted period of crisis from the 1970s, and growth has remained dependent on international demand for primary commodities (Page 1994; Broadberry and Gardner 2016).

For newly independent countries, efforts to address these issues became intertwined with the global geopolitics of the Cold War. Both Western powers and the Soviet Union angled to bring new nations into their sphere of influence. The new governments of many colonies were often sympathetic, at least to some degree, to Soviet economic policies, which suggested an alternative model to the one introduced by the colonizers. During the 1950s and 1960s, while growth was relatively weak in eastern Europe, the economic decline that would set in from the middle of the 1970s was not yet apparent (Harrison 2017: 199–200; Vonyó 2017: 248–249). For newly independent states, capitalism 'smacked of "neo-colonialism" because, by putting them back in the arms of Western expatriate capital, it would seem to subvert the achievement and purpose of political independence'. In response, a number of African governments adopted policies of 'African socialism', which varied in its precise definition, but were an attempt to search for 'an indigenous model of economic development' (Akyeampong 2018: 70). Still, wary of the political climate, many newly independent governments avoided committing to either side by adopting policies of non-alignment with regard to international affairs, particularly following the 1955 Bandung Conference (Hopkins 2018: 698). They also adopted a diverse array of economic policies in the years after independence (see e.g. Nugent 2012: ch. 5). Despite these efforts to avoid great power politics, the 'hot' portion of the Cold War was fought largely through proxy wars in the former colonies. The collapse of territorial empires meant that poorer countries bore a larger share of defence costs than they had under colonial rule. Like the imperial order which preceded it, the new order of great power competition also had implications for conflict outside Europe and North America.

The Cold War and the New Order

The end of World War II led to a reorientation of the global political system, in which the United States assumed a new leadership role in world politics, extending the dominant economic status it had established over fifty years earlier. However, it was not able to mimic its predecessors in establishing territorial control over other states to the same degree (Hopkins 2018: 692). Instead, the world oriented itself around the two rival blocs in the West and East. With the establishment of NATO in 1949, a formidable defence alliance was formed by the capitalist countries. The USSR, also rising to new prominence after the war, established the rival Warsaw Pact in 1955 to counter NATO, which cemented the military competition of the Cold War for decades to come. According to the Composite Index of National Capability, a measure of a country's ability to exercise influence, the Soviet Union actually overtook the United States in 1970 (Harrison 2017: 202). However, military competition with the West proved unsustainable in the long run.

The Cold War confounded any expectation that the loss of the dependent colonies would allow the former imperial powers to decrease their defence spending in the first decades after independence. Both the former colonizers and newly independent states built up their defence establishment during this early period. Rockoff (2012: 265) argues that for the United States 'the Cold War was costlier in financial terms than hot wars in Korea and Vietnam, and indeed, more intensive in terms of total resources used than World War II'. As part of the Cold War competition, defence spending levels rose fast and peaked during the early 1950s – in fact, the spending levels were the highest for centuries, especially relative to economic resources. For example, the American military burden (defence spending as a percentage of GDP) increased above 10 per cent in 1952–54, and the United States retained a high mean value of 6.7 per cent for the post-war period, until the Cold War ended. Great Britain and France incurred similar levels after the Korean War.

Part of this armaments race was due to technological advances that led to increases in the cost per soldier – it has been estimated that technological increases have produced a mean annual increase in real costs of around 5.5 per cent in the post-war period (Ferguson 2002; Eloranta 2003). According to some figures, the Soviets were spending approximately 60–70 per cent of the American level in the 1950s, and the USSR actually spent more on its military establishment than the United States in the 1970s. Nonetheless, the United States maintained a massive advantage over the Soviets in terms of nuclear warheads, and the NATO countries as a whole held an insurmountable lead over the Warsaw Pact members in the 1970s and early 1980s.

Despite this initial ramping up of defence spending, conflicts were largely restricted to regions outside the direct control of the main protagonists. Colonial legacies loomed large in many of the proxy wars of the period, such as the Korean War, the Vietnam War, and Afghanistan. Other conflicts, particularly in Latin America, erupted when domestic political disputes were escalated by external interventions (Reid 2009: ch. 4). On the flip side, indigenous actors would also use links to the superpowers to serve their own interests – according to Christopher Clapham (1996: 139–140), 'for African rulers, the superpowers could therefore be regarded very largely as a resource'. Angola and Mozambique are both good examples, in which rival parties called on military aid from the Soviet Union and the United States.

Some of these conflicts continued to simmer even after world defence spending levels began a slow decline from the 1970s onwards, with the

Reagan years being an exception for the USA. In 1986, the US military burden was 6.5 per cent, whereas in 1999 it was down to 3.0 per cent. The USSR was spending almost as much on its armed forces as the United States until the mid-1980s, and the Soviet military burden was still 12.3 per cent in 1990. Under the Russian Federation, with declining GDP, this level dropped rapidly to 3.2 per cent in 1998. Similarly, other nations downscaled their defence spending in the late 1980s and the 1990s. Part of this reduction was the fact that they no longer were holding on to their colonies, at least not directly (see Figure 19.6). As seen in Figure 19.7, however, the average African defence spending (as a share of GDP) increased rapidly until the late 1990s, and then followed a slightly declining global trend, at least until the 2010s. Central American and Caribbean defence spending stayed at a lower level than most world regions, peaking in the mid-1980s, and declining thereafter.

After 1989: The World under American Hegemony and Beyond

The economic collapse in the Soviet Union from the 1970s gathered speed in the 1980s, culminating in the demise of the Soviet east European sphere of influence in 1989 and the dissolution of the USSR in 1991. This reshaped the political order of the world again. The United States emerged as the world's only real superpower – a role that it embraced sometimes awkwardly. It needed to maintain its presence in many parts of the world, sometimes despite objections from the other players in the international system. It continued to exert influence over the policies of poorer countries, largely through international organizations and foreign aid, as well as a network of military bases around the world. In the twenty-first century, however, American supremacy has also been challenged, by other nations, especially China, and by global processes like the economic globalization and impending climate conditions that require global policy solutions and collaboration via international institutions.

The reduction in defence spending discussed in the previous section was only temporary. Overall, according to the Stockholm International Peace Research Institute (SIPRI) figures, there was a reduction of around one-third in real terms in world defence spending in 1989–96. In the global scheme, world military expenditure was still highly concentrated in the hands of a few countries at the end of the twentieth century, with the fifteen major spenders accounting for 80 per cent of the world total in 1999. The newest defence spending estimates for the early twenty-first century seem to display

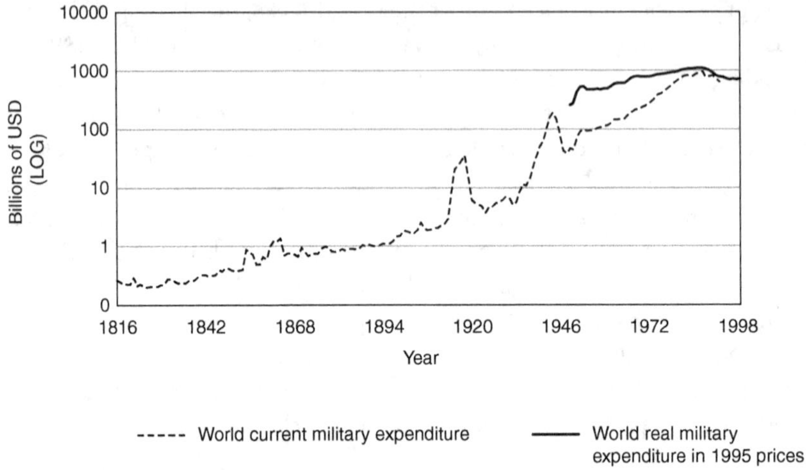

Figure 19.6 World defence spending, 1816–2000
Source: Singer and Small 1993.

a persistent growth trend in world military expenditures once again, due to new threats such as international terrorism and interstate rivalries of the century.

From the perspective of many former colonies, the period since 1989 has often been marked by political instability and sometimes severe civil conflicts (see Figure 19.8). Civil war has become the most common form of warfare since the 1990s, with obvious economic and human costs for affected countries (Abadie and Gardeazabal 2003). The mechanism by which these conflicts can be linked to past events remains the subject of debate. Ethnic divisions and weak government institutions, frequently implicated in many of the civil wars of the 1990s, were often exacerbated by historical contingencies (Alesina and La Ferrara 2005). However, not all countries with high levels of ethnic diversity have experienced large-scale conflicts. Collier and Hoeffler (2004) have argued that access to finance, principally through the export of primary commodities, explains the incidence of civil war better than objective measures of grievance.

Some of the political instability in the developing world can be linked to economic upheaval. The collapse of the Soviet Union seemed to leave the world with a single economic model to follow, thus laying the groundwork for the Washington Consensus, a set of policies which informed development efforts and US-led foreign aid through the 1980s and 1990s (Williamson 2008).

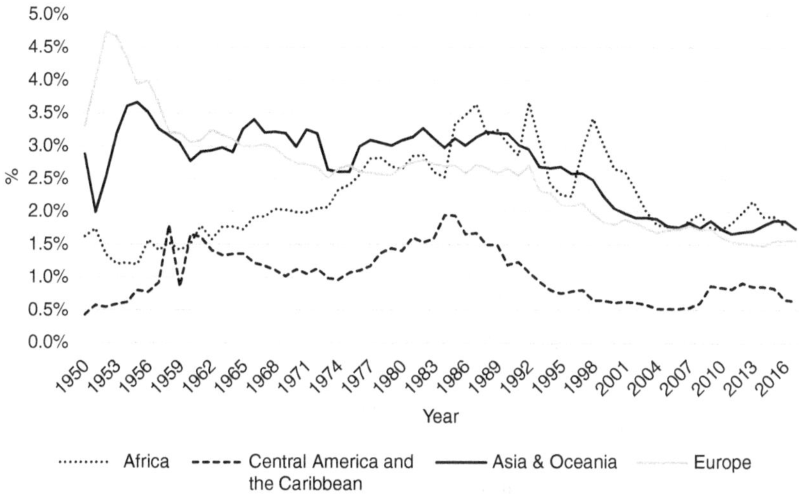

Figure 19.7 Defence spending among regions, 1950–2017 (as % of GDP)
Source: Stockholm International Peace Research Institute, SIPRI Military Expenditure Database, available online at www.sipri.org/databases/milex (accessed 29 September 2020).

Structural adjustment programmes often involved the dramatic scaling back of state intervention in the economy, reforms which frequently met with political opposition.

The nature of warfare shifted in this more recent phase, away from the sort of entrenched great power conflicts and towards the counter-insurgencies of the independence wars. To some degree, this diminished the impact of the technological advances of the post-World War II period, which had increased the bang for the buck globally to make direct great power conflicts, especially nuclear confrontations, very rare. In conflicts in Iraq and Afghanistan, for example, high-tech remote weapons have struggled to eradicate pockets of counter-insurgency, even after initial military domination. At the same time, local political institutions have remained weak, thus extending the duration of the wars beyond that of twentieth-century wars. Ethnic and other divisions in societies touched by these conflicts, often former European colonies, have remained strong, and efforts to build nations from sectarian societies have typically failed in the broadest sense. Twenty-first-century warfare has become asymmetric, between technologically advanced greater powers and poorer societies, yet this gap in capacity has not turned the tide in favour of

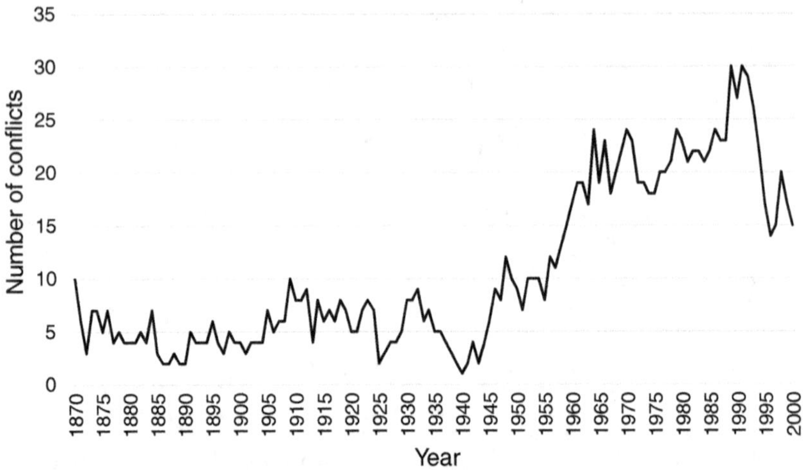

Figure 19.8 Armed internal conflicts, 1870–2010
Source: Clio Infra dataset, available online at www.clio-infra.eu/data/Armedconflicts(Internal)_Compact.xlsx (accessed 29 September 2020).

the larger players. Institutional path dependence appears to be difficult to overcome by military advantages alone.

Conclusion

Imperialism of the nineteenth and twentieth centuries drew the map which still shapes the modern world. Colonization was a continuation of earlier trade links established with Africa and Asia, as technological advances and competition between European powers transformed commercial relationships into territorial conquest. Colonial expansion fuelled the pre-World War I arms race as well as the onset of the war itself. Moreover, the cost of shaping and ruling over these colonies was substantial, and the excessive focus on defence, and absence of infrastructural and other investment, eventually contributed to the local resistance to European rule. The world wars required the Europeans to lean heavily on their colonies, and the colonized peoples expected reciprocity afterwards, only to find that none was forthcoming.

Conflicts and competition, in the form of proxy wars, was the nature of the global power realignment after World War II, with the USA and the Soviet Union vying for supremacy around the globe. The traditional European empires began to splinter in this environment, as they also started to shift their focus on domestic problems, including the build-up of more modern military establishments and extensive social safety nets. The global struggle between capitalist and communist camps thrust the newly established independent states in Africa and Asia into new territory, often leading to violence and political suppression, aided by external interventions. Conflicts peaked during the Cold War in the 1970s and 1980s and then started to wane, as did the Cold War itself. With the end of the Cold War, global tensions and defence spending decreased, at least until the early 2000s. The new wave of globalization that began in the 1970s has resulted in massive increases in wealth and living standards among large Asian countries like China, yet it has had limited impact in most of Africa. Recently there has been a slowdown of globalization and global trade, and world defence spending has started to increase again.

Old colonial ties remain influential in sometimes intangible ways. During the 2014 Ebola epidemic in West Africa, medical aid followed old colonial connections, with Britain, France, and the USA sending disproportionate amounts to countries with which they had historical ties (O'Grady 2014). More broadly, old colonial ties remain influential in determining flows of foreign aid (Alesina and Dollar 2000). The successors to the imperialists of the nineteenth and early twentieth centuries – in their time, the Soviet Union, the United States, and potentially China – have not replicated the creation of territorial empires in the same way. However, there are parallels between the two periods. Smaller, poorer states often find it difficult to avoid entanglements in great power politics, and external interventions intended in part to prevent conflict between global powers frequently lead to civil conflict, with high human and economic costs. Foreign capital remains a tool of influence. Popular discussions of aid by China and other rising economic powers to Africa, for example, often speculate about the political aims of donors (see e.g. Alden 2007; Carmody 2017). The rapid increase in the number of Chinese firms operating in Africa, along with the massive investments and loans that China has provided to various parts of Asia and Africa, has reinforced the notion of economic imperialism being alive and well. Western powers, of course, have attempted to do similar things, although populist and nationalist politicians in these countries have made these efforts more difficult. Imperialism is still a part of the global political and economic system, as are trade and conflicts. Research on the global economic histories of war and colonialism can thus help to shape understandings both past and future.

References

Abadie, A. and Gardeazabal, J. (2003). 'The Economic Costs of Conflict: A Case Study of the Basque Country', *American Economic Review*, 93, 113–132.

Accominotti, O., Flandreau, M., and Rezzik, R. (2011). 'The Spread of Empire: Clio and the Measurement of Colonial Borrowing Costs', *Economic History Review*, 64, 385–407.

Acemoglu, D., Johnson, S., and Robinson, J. A. (2001). 'The Colonial Origins of Comparative Development: An Empirical Investigation', *American Economic Review*, 91, 1369–1401.

Achebe, C. (2012). *There Was a Country: A Personal History of Biafra*, London: Allen Lane.

Akyeampong, E. (2018). 'African Socialism; or, the Search for an Indigenous Model of Economic Development?', *Economic History of Developing Regions*, 33, 69–87.

Alden, C. (2007). *China in Africa*, London: Zed Books.

Alesina, A. and Dollar, D. (2000). 'Who Gives Foreign Aid to Whom and Why?', *Journal of Economic Growth*, 5, 33–63.

Alesina, A. and La Ferrara, E. (2005). 'Ethnic Diversity and Economic Performance', *Journal of Economic Literature*, XLIII, 762–800.

Alexopoulou, K. (2018). 'An Anatomy of Colonial States and Fiscal Regimes in Portuguese Africa: Long-Term Transformations in Angola and Mozambique, 1850–1970', PhD thesis, Wageningen University.

Austin, G. (1988). 'Capitalists and Chiefs in the Cocoa Hold-Ups in South Asante, 1927–1938', *International Journal of African Historical Studies*, 21, 63–95.

(2008). 'The "Reversal of Fortune" Thesis and the Compression of History: Perspectives from African and Comparative Economic History', *Journal of International Development*, 20, 996–1027.

Banerjee, A. and Iyer, L. (2005). 'History, Institutions and Economic Performance: The Legacy of Colonial Land Tenure Systems in India', *American Economic Review*, 95, 1190–1213.

Bayly, C. A. (2008). 'Indigenous and Colonial Origins of Comparative Economic Development: The Case of Colonial India and Africa', World Bank Policy Research Working Paper 4474.

Blum, M., Eloranta, J., and Osinsky, P. (2014). 'Organization of War Economies', in Daniel, U., Gatrell, P., Janz, O., Jones, H., Keene, J., Kramer, A., and Nasson, B. (eds.), *1914–1918-online. International Encyclopedia of the First World War*, Free University of Berlin, available online at https://encyclopedia.1914-1918-online.net/article/organization_of_war_economies (accessed 29 September 2020).

Bolt, J. and Gardner, L. (2020). 'How Africans Shaped British Colonial Institutions: Evidence from Local Taxation', *Journal of Economic History*, 80, 1189–1223.

Booth, A. (2007). 'Night Watchman, Extractive, or Developmental States? Some Evidence from Late Colonial South-East Asia', *Economic History Review*, 60, 241–266.

Broadberry, S. and Gardner, L. A. (2016). 'Economic Development in Africa and Europe: Reciprocal Comparisons', *Revista de Historia Económica*, 34: 11–37.

Broadberry, S. and Harrison, M. (2005). 'The Economics of World War I: An Overview', in Broadberry, S. and Harrison, M. (eds.), *The Economics of World War I*, Cambridge University Press, 3–40.

Carmody, P. (2017). 'The Geopolitics and Economics of BRICS' Resource and Market Access in Southern Africa: Aiding Development or Creating Dependency?', *Journal of Southern African Studies*, 43, 863–877.

Chavez, I., Engerman, S. L., and Robinson, J. A. (2014). 'Reinventing the Wheel: The Economic Benefits of Wheeled Transportation in Early Colonial British West Africa', in Akyeampong, E., Bates, R. H., Nunn, N., and Robinson, J. (eds.), *Africa's Development in Historical Perspective*, Cambridge University Press, 321–365.

Clapham, C. (1996). *Africa and the International System: The Politics of State Survival*, Cambridge University Press.

Collier, P. and Hoeffler, A. (2004). 'Greed and Grievance in Civil War', *Oxford Economic Papers*, 56, 563–595.

Crisher, B. B. and Souva, M. (2014). 'Power at Sea: A Naval Power Dataset, 1865–2011', *International Interactions*, 40(4), 602–629.

Davis, L. E. and Huttenback, R. A. (1986). *Mammon and the Pursuit of Empire: The Political Economy of British Imperialism, 1860–1912*, Cambridge University Press.

de Vries, J. (2010). 'The Limits of Globalization in the Early Modern World', *Economic History Review*, 63(3), 710–733.

Donaldson, D. (2018). 'Railroads of the Raj: Estimating the Impact of Transportation Infrastructure', *American Economic Review*, 108, 899–934.

Easterly, W. and Levine, R. (2016). 'The European Origins of Economic Development', *Journal of Economic Growth*, 21, 225–257.

Eloranta, J. (2003). 'National Defense', in Mokyr, J. (ed.), *The Oxford Encyclopedia of Economic History, Vol. 4*, Oxford University Press, 30–33.

(2005). 'Military Spending Patterns in History', in Whaples, R. (ed.), *EH.Net Encyclopedia*, available online at http://eh.net/encyclopedia/military-spending-patterns-in-history/ (accessed 29 September 2020).

(2007). 'From the Great Illusion to the Great War: Military Spending Behaviour of the Great Powers, 1870–1913', *European Review of Economic History*, 11, 255–283.

(2017). 'Review of How States Pay for Wars by Rosella Cappella Zielinski', *Journal of Military History*, 81, 1176–1178.

Eloranta, J., Andreev, S., and Osinsky, P. (2014). 'Democratization and Central Government Spending, 1870–1938: Emergence of the Leviathan?', in Hanes, C. and Wolcott, S. (eds.), *Research in Economic History*, Emerald Publishing, 1–46.

Federico, G. and Tena Junguito, A. (2016). 'World Trade, 1800–1938: A New Data-Set', EHES Working Paper 93, available online at https://e-archivo.uc3m.es/handle/10016/26605 (accessed 29 September 2020), European Historical Economics Society.

Ferguson, N. (2002). *The Cash Nexus: Money and Power in the Modern World, 1700–2000*, London: Basic Books.

Ferguson, N. and Schularick, M. (2006). 'The Empire Effect: The Determinants of Country Risk in the First Age of Globalization', *Journal of Economic History*, 66, 283–312.

Findlay, R. and O'Rourke, K. H. (2007). *Power and Plenty: Trade, War and the World Economy in the Second Millennium*, Princeton University Press.

Frankema, E. (2011). 'Colonial Taxation and Government Spending in British Africa, 1880–1940: Maximizing Revenue or Minimizing Effort?', *Explorations in Economic History*, 48, 136–149.

(2012). 'The Origins of Formal Education in Sub-Saharan Africa: Was British Rule More Benign?', *European Review of Economic History*, 16, 335–355.

(2013). 'Colonial Education and Post-Colonial Governance in the Congo and Indonesia', in Frankema, E. and Buelens, F. (eds.), *Colonial Exploitation and Economic Development: The Belgian Congo and the Netherlands Indies Compared*, London: Routledge, 153–177.

Frankema, E., Williamson, J., and Woltjer, P. (2018). 'An Economic Rationale for the West African Scramble? The Commercial Transition and the Commodity Price Boom of 1835–1885', *Journal of Economic History*, 78, 231–267.

Fraser, C. (1996). 'The Twilight of Colonial Rule in the British West Indies: Nationalist Assertion vs Imperial Hubris in the 1930s', *Journal of Caribbean History*, 30, 1–25.

Gardner, L. (2012). *Taxing Colonial Africa: The Political Economy of British Imperialism*, Oxford University Press.

(2017). 'Colonialism or Supersanctions: Sovereignty and Debt in West Africa, 1871–1914', *European Review of Economic History*, 21, 236–257.

Golson, E. B. (2012). 'Did Swedish Ball Bearings Keep the Second World War Going? Re-Evaluating Neutral Sweden's Role', *Scandinavian Economic History Review*, 60, 165–182.

Harrison, M. (2017). 'The Soviet Economy, 1917–1991: Its Life and Afterlife', *Independent Review*, 22, 199–206.

Head, K., Mayer, T., and Ries, J. (2010). 'The Erosion of Colonial Trade Linkages after Independence', *Journal of International Economics*, 81, 1–14.

Herranz-Loncán, A. and Fourie, J. (2018). '"For the Public Benefit?" Railways in the British Cape Colony', *European Review of Economic History*, 22, 73–100.

Hopkins, A. G. (1973). *An Economic History of West Africa*, London: Longman.

(2018). *American Empire: A Global History*, Princeton University Press.

Huillery, E. (2009). 'History Matters: The Long-Term Impact of Colonial Public Investments in French West Africa', *American Economic Journal: Applied Economics*, 1, 176–215.

Jedwab, R., Kerby, E., and Moradi, A. (2017). 'History, Path Dependence and Development: Evidence from Colonial Railways, Settlers and Cities in Kenya', *Economic Journal*, 127, 1467–1494.

Kennedy, P. (1989). 'The Costs and Benefits of British Imperialism 1846–1914', *Past and Present*, 125, 186–192.

Koller, C. (2014). 'Colonial Military Participation in Europe (Africa)', in Daniel, U., Gatrell, P., Janz, O., Jones, H., Keene, J., Kramer, A., and Nasson, B. (eds.), *1914–1918-online. International Encyclopedia of the First World War*, Free University of Berlin, available online at https://encyclopedia.1914-1918-online.net/article/colonial_military_participation_in_europe_africa (accessed 29 September 2020).

Land, J. and Eloranta, J. (2016). 'Wartime Economies, 1939–1945: Large and Small European States at War', in Doumanis, N. (ed.), *The Oxford Handbook of European History, 1914–1945*, Oxford University Press, 461–479.

La Porta, R., Lopez-de-Silanes, F., Shleifer, A. and Vishny, R. (1999). 'The Quality of Government', *Journal of Law, Economics and Organization*, 15, 222–279.

Law, R. (2009). 'Introduction', in Law, R. (ed.), *From Slave Trade to 'Legitimate' Commerce: The Commercial Transition in Nineteenth-Century West Africa*, Cambridge University Press, 1–31.

Leake, E. M. (2014). 'British India Versus the British Empire: The Indian Army and an Impasse in Imperial Defence, circa 1919–39', *Modern Asian Studies*, 48, 301–329.

Lindert, P. H. (1994). 'The Rise of Social Spending, 1880–1930', *Explorations in Economic History*, 31(1), 1–37.

Manela, E. (2007). *The Wilsonian Moment: Self-Determination and the International Origins of Anticolonial Nationalism*, Oxford University Press.

Mitchener, K. and Weidenmier, M. D. (2008). 'Trade and Empire', *Economic Journal*, 118, 1805–1834.

(2010). 'Supersanctions and Sovereign Debt Repayment', *Journal of International Money and Finance*, 29, 19–36.

Nugent, P. (2012). *Africa since Independence: A Comparative History*, 2nd ed., Basingstoke: Palgrave Macmillan.

O'Grady, S. (2014). 'Colonial Lines Drawn Again for Ebola Aid', *Foreign Policy*, 22 September.

O'Rourke, K. H. and Williamson, J. G. (1999). *Globalization and History: The Evolution of a Nineteenth-Century Atlantic Economy*, Cambridge, MA: MIT Press.

(2002). 'When Did Globalisation Begin?', *European Review of Economic History*, 6, 23–50.

Page, J. (1994). 'The East Asian Miracle: An Introduction', *World Development*, 22, 615–625.

Rathbone, R. (2008). 'Casing "the Kingdome into Another Mold": Ghana's Troubled Transition to Independence', *Round Table*, 97, 705–718.

Reid, M. (2009). *Forgotten Continent: The Battle for Latin America's Soul*, New Haven: Yale University Press.

Rockoff, H. (2012). *America's Economic Way of War: War and the US Economy from the Spanish-American War to the Persian Gulf War*, Cambridge University Press.

Roy, T. (2012). *India and the World Economy*, Cambridge University Press.

Schenk, C. R. (1997). 'Monetary Institutions in Newly Independent Countries: The Experience of Malaya, Ghana and Nigeria in the 1950s', *Financial History Review*, 4, 181–198.

Sherwood, M. (2011). 'Colonies, Colonials and World War Two', available online at www.bbc.co.uk/history/worldwars/wwtwo/colonies_colonials_01.shtml (accessed 29 September 2020).

Singer, J. D. and Small, M. (1993). *National Material Capabilities Data, 1816–1985*, Ann Arbor: Inter-University Consortium for Political and Social Research.

Stasavage, D. (2003). *The Political Economy of a Common Currency: The CFA Franc Zone since 1945*, Aldershot: Ashgate.

Tai-Yong, T. (2000). 'An Imperial Home-Front: Punjab and the First World War', *Journal of Military History*, 64, 371.

Tooze, A. and Ivanov, M. (2011). 'Disciplining the "Black Sheep of the Balkans": Financial Supervision and Sovereignty in Bulgaria, 1902–38', *Economic History Review*, 64, 30–51.

Tuncer, C. (2015). *Sovereign Debt and International Financial Control: The Middle East and the Balkans, 1870–1914*, Basingstoke: Palgrave Macmillan.

van der Eng, P. (2003). 'Marshall Aid as a Catalyst in the Decolonization of Indonesia, 1947–49', in Le Sueur, J. D (ed.), *The Decolonization Reader*, New York: Routledge, 123–138.

Vonyó, T. (2017). 'War and Socialism: Why Eastern Europe Fell Behind between 1950 and 1989', *Economic History Review*, 70, 248–274.

Wantchekon, L., Klasnja, M., and Novta, N. (2015). 'Education and Human Capital Externalities: Evidence from Colonial Benin', *Quarterly Journal of Economics*, 130, 703–757.

White, N. J. (2011). 'Reconstructing Europe through Rejuvenating Empire: The British, French and Dutch Experiences Compared', *Past and Present*, 210, 211–236.

Williamson, J. (2008). 'A Short History of the Washington Consensus', in Serra, N. and Stiglitz, J. E. (eds.), *The Washington Consensus Reconsidered: Towards a New Global Governance*, Oxford University Press, 14–30.

Index

Index

www.ingramcontent.com/pod-product-compliance
Lightning Source LLC
LaVergne TN
LVHW052210200926
848481LV00001B/68
* 9 7 8 1 3 1 6 6 1 2 2 7 9 *